Property Testing

Arnab Bhattacharyya • Yuichi Yoshida

Property Testing

Problems and Techniques

 Springer

Arnab Bhattacharyya
School of Computing
National University of Singapore
Singapore, Singapore

Yuichi Yoshida
National Institute of Informatics
Chiyoda-ku, Tokyo, Japan

ISBN 978-981-16-8624-5   ISBN 978-981-16-8622-1   (eBook)
https://doi.org/10.1007/978-981-16-8622-1

This Springer imprint is published by the registered company Springer Nature Singapore Pte Ltd.
The registered company address is: 152 Beach Road, #21-01/04 Gateway East, Singapore 189721, Singapore

To Boo, Mamma, Aditi, Shaunak & Sumedh.
To Megumi, Hajime & Satoru.

Preface

Property testing is an emerging area that aims for algorithms that decide whether the input satisfies a predetermined property in sublinear time in the input size, or even in *constant* time, that is, independent of the input size.

Of course, we cannot correctly solve problems in sublinear time without reading the whole input; so, we need several assumptions or compromises. First, we assume that query access to the input is available through which we can get a small part of the input in constant time. Second, we compromise with approximate decisions; that is, we only aim for algorithms that distinguish inputs satisfying the predetermined property from those that are *far* from satisfying it. Such algorithms are called *testers* for the property, and it has been shown in the past few decades that there are sublinear-time testers for many properties on various objects such as strings, graphs, and functions.

The first goal of this book is to introduce important results and techniques in property testing to a broad audience. To design efficient testers and show their correctness, we will make use of a variety of connections to other areas of mathematics and computer science, such as combinatorics, graph theory, matroid theory, computational learning theory, and coding theory. We hope that the reader appreciates how beautifully these connections are employed for the purpose of designing and analyzing property testers.

The second goal of this book is to show characterizations of constant-query testable properties, which have been obtained for (dense) graphs, functions over finite fields, and constraint satisfaction problems (CSPs). One reason for showing such characterizations is their intrinsic value: they themselves are surprising and fundamental results. Another reason is that, through the arguments toward those characterizations, we can get insights into what constant-query testers actually test. For example, the characterizations for graphs and functions over finite fields are derived from general decomposition results, which decompose graphs or functions into the structured part and the pseudorandom part in a suitable sense. Here, we borrow results developed in additive combinatorics. Another characterization is known for testing whether an assignment to a CSP instance is a satisfying assignment. Here, we will make use of an area called universal algebra, which yields a useful language for studying properties of CSPs.

This book consists of three parts. The first part provides an introduction for readers who are inexperienced in the foundation of property testing. The second part studies testing specific properties on strings, graphs, functions, and CSPs. We also cover vectors and matrices over the real. The third part is more advanced and explains general conditions, including full characterizations, under which properties are constant-query testable.

As the area of property testing is very broad, it is impossible to cover all relevant topics in this book. Notably, we decided to omit property testing of probability distributions, as it is a vast area with many techniques independent of other topics. Property testing is also a very active and fast-moving research area, and so we expect some of the results mentioned here will be outdated by the time this book is in your hands[1]. For this reason, we have focused more on broad areas and techniques, sometimes at the cost of not presenting the tightest results known for specific problems.

We attempted to keep the book as self-contained as possible. However, the reader is assumed to be comfortable with basic notions of probability, linear algebra, and algorithms. The first and second parts of the book are intended for first-year graduate students in computer science. It should also be accessible to undergraduate students with an adequate background. The third part can be used by researchers or ambitious graduate students intending to obtain a deeper understanding of property testing.

Arnab Bhattacharyya, Singapore
Yuichi Yoshida, Tokyo, Japan

---

[1] For example, the main question of Chapter 12 got resolved just before the book went out to press!

Acknowledgments

We thank Kazuo Iwama for bringing us the idea of writing a book on property testing. We are grateful to Mio Sugino for patiently supporting us throughout the publishing process. We thank Eric Blais, Irit Dinur, Noah Fleming, Prahladh Harsha, Hiro Ito, Aixi Li, Ilan Newman, Asaf Shapira, Nobutaka Shimizu, Kazuki Watanabe, and Lu Yuxun for carefully reading the draft and providing feedback that helped greatly improve the quality of this book.

Contents

List of Notations

Basics notations

$[n]$	The set $\{1, 2, \ldots, n\}$.
$\mathbb{Z}$	The set of integers.
$\mathbb{Z}_{\geq 0}$	The set of non-negative integers.
$\mathbb{Z}_{>0}$	The set of positive integers.
$\mathbb{R}$	The set of real numbers.
$\mathbb{R}_{\geq 0}$	The set of non-negative real numbers.
$|A|$	The size of a finite set A.
$\binom{[n]}{k}$	The family of k-element subsets of $[n]$, i.e., $\{\{i_1, i_2, \ldots, i_k\} : 1 \leq i_1 < i_2 < \cdots < i_k \leq n\}$.
$d_{\mathrm{H}}(f, g)$	The Hamming distance between two functions f and g on the same (finite) domain D, i.e., $d_{\mathrm{H}}(f, g) := |\{x \in D : f(x) \neq g(x)\}|$.
$\delta_{\mathrm{H}}(f, g)$	The relative Hamming distance between two functions f and g on the same (finite) domain D, i.e., $\delta_{\mathrm{H}}(f, g) = d_{\mathrm{H}}(f, g)/|D|$.
$f(n) = \widetilde{O}(g(n))$	$f(n) = O(g(n) \cdot \log^c n)$ for some $c > 0$.
$f(n) = \widetilde{\Omega}(g(n))$	$f(n) = \Omega(g(n)/\log^c n)$ for some $c > 0$.
$f(n) = \widetilde{\Theta}(g(n))$	$f(n) = \widetilde{O}(g(n))$ and $f(n) = \widetilde{\Omega}(g(n))$.

Notations for probability theory

$\mathbf{E}[X]$	The expectation of a random variable X.
$\mathbf{Var}[X]$	The variance of a random variable X.
$X \sim \mathcal{D}$	A random variable X is sampled according to the distribution $\mathcal{D}$.
$X \sim D$	A random variable X is sampled uniformly at random from the domain D.

$\mathcal{D}(a)$ The probability that a is sampled from the distribution $\mathcal{D}$.

$d_{\mathrm{TV}}(\mathcal{D}, \mathcal{D}')$ The total variation distance between two distributions $\mathcal{D}, \mathcal{D}'$ on the same domain D, that is, $\sup_S |\mathrm{Pr}_{a \sim \mathcal{D}}[a \in S] - \mathrm{Pr}_{a \sim \mathcal{D}'}[a \in S]|$. When D is finite, $d_{\mathrm{TV}}(\mathcal{D}, \mathcal{D}') = \frac{1}{2} \sum_{a \in D} |\mathcal{D}(a) - \mathcal{D}'(a)|$.

$d_{\mathrm{KL}}(\mathcal{D}\|\mathcal{D}')$ The Kullback-Leibler divergence (or KL-divergence) of $\mathcal{D}'$ from $\mathcal{D}$, that is, $d_{\mathrm{KL}}(\mathcal{D}\|\mathcal{D}') = \int_\Omega \mathcal{D}(a) \log \frac{\mathcal{D}(a)}{\mathcal{D}'(a)} \mathrm{d}a$, where Ω is the domain of $\mathcal{D}$ and $\mathcal{D}'$.

Notations for graph theory

$\deg_G(v)$ The degree of a vertex $v \in V$ in a graph $G = (V, E)$.

$G[S]$ The subgraph of a graph $G = (V, E)$ induced by $S \subseteq V$.

$E_G(S, T)$ The set of edges between vertex sets S and T in a graph $G = (V, E)$, i.e., $\{\{u, v\} \in E \mid u \in S, v \in T\}$.

$E_G(S)$ The set of edges within a vertex set S in a graph $G = (V, E)$, i.e., $E \cap \binom{S}{2}$, where $\binom{S}{2} = \{\{u, v\} : u, v \in S, u \neq v\}$.

$d_G(S, T)$ The density between vertex sets S and T in a graph $G = (V, E)$, i.e., $\frac{|E_G(S,T)|}{|S||T|}$.

$d_G(S)$ The density within a vertex set S in a graph $G = (V, E)$, i.e., $\frac{|E_G(S)|}{\binom{|S|}{2}}$.

$\Gamma_G(v)$ The set of neighbors of a vertex v in a graph $G = (V, E)$, i.e., $\{u \in V \setminus \{v\} \mid \{u, v\} \in E\}$.

$\Gamma_G(S)$ The set of neighbors of a vertex set S in a graph $G = (V, E)$, i.e., $\{u \in V \setminus S \mid \{u, v\} \in E \text{ for some } v \in S\}$.

$\deg_G^+(v)$ The out-degree of a vertex $v \in V$ in a digraph $G = (V, E)$, i.e., $\deg_G^+(v) = |\{(v, w) \in E\}|$.

$\deg_G^-(v)$ The in-degree of a vertex $v \in V$ in a digraph $G = (V, E)$, i.e., $\deg_G^-(v) = |\{(u, v) \in E\}|$.

Notations for linear algebra

$\|v\|_p$ for $p \geq 1$ The ℓ_p norm of a vector $v \in \mathbb{R}^n$, that is, $\left(\sum_{i \in [n]} |v_i|^p\right)^{1/p}$.

$\|v\|_0$ The ℓ_0 norm of a vector $v \in \mathbb{R}^n$, that is, the number of non-zero elements in v.

$\|A\|_p$ for $p \geq 1$ The ℓ_p norm of a matrix $A \in \mathbb{R}^{n \times m}$, that is, $\max_{v \in \mathbb{R}^m : v \neq 0} \frac{\|Av\|_p}{\|v\|_p}$.

$\|A\|_F$ The Frobenius norm of a matrix $A \in \mathbb{R}^{n \times m}$, that is, $\sqrt{\sum_{i \in [n], j \in [m]} |A_{ij}|^2}$.

$v|_S$ The $|S|$-dimensional subvector of a vector $v \in \mathbb{R}^n$ such that $(v|_S)_i = v_i$ for $i \in S$, where $S \subseteq [n]$.

$A|_{S \times T}$ The $|S|$ by $|T|$ submatrix of a matrix $A \in \mathbb{R}^{n \times m}$ such that $(A|_{S \times T})_{ij} = A_{ij}$ for $i \in S$ and $j \in T$, where $S \subseteq [n]$ and $T \subseteq [m]$.

Part I

Chapter 1
Introduction

It is most often taken for granted that if an algorithm has to solve a non-trivial computational problem, it must read its input. The goal of *property testing* is to surmount this seeming inevitability. The surprising story this book will tell is that for many natural computational problems, one can design algorithms that read a vanishingly small fraction of the input!

property testing

1.1 A Vignette: Monotonicity Testing

An array A of n numbers is *monotone* if $A[i] \leq A[i+1]$ for all $i \in [n-1]$. The following array is monotone:

monotonicity

| 2 | 8 | 21 | 22 | 100 | 101 | 102 | 200 | 223 | 224 |

while the following is not:

| 2 | 8 | 21 | 22 | 100 | 102 | 101 | 200 | 223 | 224 |

It is intuitively obviously that in order to decide whether an array is monotone or not, we need to look at all the entries in the worst case. As in the example above, an array may be non-monotone due to only one entry which could be anywhere, and so we cannot avoid scanning through the whole array.

On the other hand, the second array pictured above is "almost monotone" because we can make it monotone by editing only one entry. For certain applications, it might be fine for an algorithm to err on such inputs and declare them to be monotone. We are thus led to the following natural problem: distinguish monotone arrays from those that are not "almost monotone."

Formally, for a parameter $\epsilon \in (0, 1)$, we say an array A of length n is ϵ-*far from monotone* if $> \epsilon n$ entries of A need to be edited to make it monotone. A *monotonicity tester* is an algorithm that gets the parameter ϵ and access to an input array A and must successfully distinguish A being monotone versus A being ϵ-far from monotone. Note that when A is non-monotone but not

ϵ-farness

monotonicity tester

ϵ-far from monotone, there is no guarantee on the tester's behavior. So, if $\epsilon > 1/n$, the tester is allowed to err on the non-monotone array shown above.

Amazingly enough, when ϵ is a constant (e.g., 1%), we can design a monotonicity tester that reads $\ll n$ entries of its input!

> **Theorem 1.1.** *For any $\epsilon \in (0,1)$, there is a monotonicity tester that on access to input A queries $O(\epsilon^{-1} \log n)$ entries, outputs* MON *if A is monotone and outputs* NONMON *with probability 99% if A is ϵ-far from monotone.*

The tester is a randomized algorithm, and the probability above is with respect to the randomness of the algorithm[1]. In fact, any tester that makes $\ll n$ queries needs to be randomized (see Problem 1.5).

The first idea for a monotonicity tester that may occur to the reader is to select a random $i \in [n-1]$ and check whether $A[i] \leq A[i+1]$. This does not work even for $\epsilon = 1/2$. Consider the following array:

| 101 | 102 | 200 | 223 | 224 | 2 | 8 | 21 | 22 | 100 |

On the one hand, the array is $1/2$-far from monotone. On the other hand, unless $i = 5$ is selected, which happens with probability $O(1/n)$, the check $A[i] \leq A[i+1]$ will pass, and so, this is not a valid monotonicity tester.

The second idea that may occur to the reader is to select a random pair $(i,j) \in [n]^2$ with $i < j$ and check whether $A[i] \leq A[j]$. This strategy performs badly for the following array:

| 8 | 2 | 22 | 21 | 101 | 100 | 200 | 102 | 224 | 223 |

The array is $1/2$-far from monotone, but unless $j = i+1$ is selected, which happens with probability $O(1/n)$, the check $A[i] \leq A[j]$ will pass.

It turns out that the following algorithm is a monotonicity tester[2] satisfying the guarantees of Theorem 1.1.

Algorithm 1.1 Binary Search-based Tester

Input: An integer n, $\epsilon \in (0,1)$, and query access to an array A of length n.
1: **for** $q := 2\epsilon^{-1}$ times **do**
2:     Sample i from $[n]$ uniformly at random.
3:     Query $A[i]$.
4:     Do a binary search for $A[i]$.
5:     Output NONMON if binary search fails to find i.
6: **end for**
7: Output MON.

---

[1] To be clear, the guarantee of Theorem 1.1 holds for *every* array that is ϵ-far from monotone, not 99% of arrays that are ϵ-far from monotone.

[2] In the pseudocode, we assume that A consists of distinct entries. This is without loss of generality because the tester can pretend that the i'th entry of A is the pair $(i, A[i])$ and compare pairs using lexicographic order.

The reader should pause at this point and convince herself that on arrays of length n similar to the above two counterexample arrays, each iteration of the for-loop in Algorithm 1.1 outputs NonMon with constant probability. We will formally prove correctness later in this chapter (in Section 1.6).

1.2 Why Property Testing?

Traditionally, the gold standard for efficiency of algorithms has been running time that is polynomial in the length of the input. However, with the routine appearance of large datasets in our computing environments, polynomial-time or even linear-time algorithms are too slow, especially when we need to analyze the data interactively. As big data rapidly grows on the web, in finance, and in research domains such as astronomy and biology, it is urgent to design algorithms that run faster than linear time.

Property testing can be a remedy for this situation because it aims for time complexity *sublinear* in the input size, that is, in $o(n)$ time where n is the input size. Of course, there are problems that are tractable in polynomial time but are intractable in sublinear time. For example, as discussed above, $\Omega(n)$ time is necessary to decide whether an array is monotone or not.

The key relaxation that permits sublinear running time is that we require property testing algorithms to only make an *approximate decision*. Here, approximate decision means that we only care about distinguishing objects satisfying a particular property from objects that are *far* from satisfying the property. Intuitively speaking, we say that an object is far from the property if modifying a small fraction, say, 1%, of the object does not make it satisfy the property. Throughout this book, *testing* is a synonym for making such an approximate decision.

sublinear

approximate decision

testing

Besides the scenario mentioned above where the size of the input makes a linear-time algorithm prohibitive, there are several other situations in which the trade-off between sublinear time and approximate decision is appealing:

- **When deciding the property of interest is NP-hard**: For example, think of 3-colorability of a graph, that is, whether we can color vertices by using three colors so that any two adjacent vertices have different colors. It is well known that deciding 3-colorability is NP-complete, and hence it is intractable in general, even when the graph is small. However, under a reasonable query model, we can test 3-colorability in constant (!) time (Section 4.3.3).
- **Pruning before an exact decision**: Even if we want to determine exactly whether the property of interest is satisfied or not, we can use a tester for pruning. If the tester accepts, then the property is satisfied for sure[3].

---

[3] Here, we assume that the tester always accepts objects satisfying the property, as the tester for monotonicity

If the tester rejects, we simply run the exact procedure to decide whether the property is satisfied or not. As the tester runs fast, the overhead of running it is small. The total time complexity will be significantly reduced when the input is far from satisfying the property.

- **When the input itself contains noise**: The input itself may have noise when it is retrieved by experiment or from sensors. In such a case, it is not very important to exactly decide properties of the input. Instead, we may want to use a property tester because it only looks at a small fraction of the input, and hence, its output is robust against small amounts of noise.

These considerations are not merely theoretical. There are several important computational problems in which an approximate decision is required. We briefly discuss two:

- **Polling**[4]: Suppose that two candidates are running for an election. There are n electors each voting for one candidate, and the candidate with more votes will be elected. Of course, all the votes need to be counted to get the final result, but is it possible to get some preliminary result by sampling a small number of votes?

  We can rephrase this question as a property testing problem. Suppose that the n votes are stored in an array $A[1], \ldots, A[n]$. Then, the election of the first candidate can be seen as a property of A, that is, the property is satisfied if the first candidate has more than $n/2$ votes in A. Let P denote this property. Then, A is ϵ-far from P if we must flip more than ϵn votes to elect the first candidate. In other words, the second candidate wins by more than $2\epsilon n$ votes, which means that the second candidate is a clear winner.

  If there is an efficient tester for P, then we can use the result of the tester to report a preliminary result. Specifically, if the tester accepts (resp., rejects) we report that the first (resp., second) candidate will win. Indeed, if the first candidate actually wins, then we report so with high probability, and if the second candidate is a clear winner, then we report that the second candidate will win with high probability.

- **Formal Verification**: The goal of formal verification is to verify the correctness of a software or hardware (often as a black box). For example, electrical circuits used in a spacecraft may err because they are exposed to cosmic rays, and we want to detect the error before it causes a catastrophe. As another example, suppose that there is a software for cellphones that delegates some heavy part (such as image processing) of the computation to a cloud server. Then, we may want to quickly verify that the result sent from the cloud server is correct.

  In typical applications, it is computationally intractable to enumerate all inputs, thereby checking correctness. Hence, if one only has black box access to the algorithm being tested, it is natural to resort to the framework of property testing, where there are often much more efficient algorithms.

---

[4] The same considerations also apply to post-election auditing.

1.3 Formal Framework for Property Testing

We now establish a rigorous framework for designing and analyzing testers. Before delving into the formalisms, let us look at a simple testing problem that we will use as a running example through the rest of the section.

Suppose the property to be tested is whether a string $s \in \{0,1\}^n$ is the all-one string, that is, $s = 1^n$. Obviously, to exactly solve this problem, any algorithm will need to look at all the characters in s, hence requiring $\Omega(n)$ time. To circumvent this issue, we relax the problem by requiring an approximate decision. Say that a string $s \in \{0,1\}^n$ is *ϵ-far from the all-one string* if it contains more than ϵn 0's. We regard ϵ as a constant independent of n.

ϵ-farness

Think of any deterministic algorithm that tries to distinguish the all-one string from strings ϵ-far from the all-one string. In the worst case, even when the input string is ϵ-far, we may end up reading $n - \epsilon n$ 1's before reading the first 0. We can adversarially construct such a string by disassembling the algorithm and putting 1's on the first $n - \epsilon n$ positions it reads. Hence, any deterministic algorithm must read at least $n - \epsilon n$ characters in the worst case even with approximate decision, which results in linear time complexity.

We can remedy this issue by introducing randomness. Consider a randomized algorithm that samples $q := 2\epsilon^{-1}$ characters from the string and accepts if and only if none of the characters is 0. It always accepts the all-one string. The probability that it finds 0 in an ϵ-far string is at least:

$$1 - (1 - \epsilon)^q \geq 1 - \exp(-\epsilon q) = 1 - \exp(-2) \geq \frac{2}{3},$$

where we used $1 - x \leq \exp(-x)$ in the first inequality. This means that we can reject any ϵ-far string with probability at least $2/3$. The time complexity is clearly $2\epsilon^{-1}$, which is independent of the input size (recall that we regard ϵ as a constant independent of the input size).

Let us first fix some conventions regarding how distance to a property is measured and the computational model. Formally, a *property* $\mathcal{P}$ is a family of object sets $\{\mathcal{P}_n\}_{n \in \mathbb{Z}_{>0}}$, where $\mathcal{P}_n$ is a set of objects of size n. We say that an input satisfies $\mathcal{P}$ if it belongs to $\mathcal{P}_n$ where n is the input length.

property

1.3.1 Distance to Properties

For an integer $n \geq 1$ and a set R, the *Hamming distance*[5] between two functions $f, g : [n] \to R$, denoted by $d_{\mathrm{H}}(f, g)$, is defined as:

Hamming distance

$$d_{\mathrm{H}}(f, g) = |\{i \in [n] : f(i) \neq g(i)\}|.$$

---

[5] The term Hamming distance is usually used to denote the distance between strings. Here, we identify the functions f and g with strings of length n over the alphabet R.

relative Hamming
distance

The *relative Hamming distance* $\delta_H(f, g)$ between f and g is defined as $d_H(f, g)/n$.

Suppose each $\mathcal{P}_n$ corresponds to a class of functions from $[n]$ to a set R. For such a property, the *Hamming distance* between $f: [n] \to R$ and $\mathcal{P}$, denoted by $d_H(f, \mathcal{P})$, is defined as:

Hamming distance

$$d_H(f, \mathcal{P}) := \min_{g \in \mathcal{P}_n} d_H(f, g).$$

relative Hamming
distance

The *relative Hamming distance* $\delta_H(f, \mathcal{P})$ between f and $\mathcal{P}$ is defined as $d_H(f, \mathcal{P})/n$.

Most objects we study in this book are represented as functions of the form $f: [n] \to R$, and hence a property $\mathcal{P}$ can be regarded as a family of function sets. Then, for $\epsilon \in (0, 1)$, we say that f is *ϵ-far from* $\mathcal{P}$ if $\delta_H(f, \mathcal{P}) > \epsilon$. For the all-one string case in the previous section, a string $s \in \{0, 1\}^n$ can be regarded as a function $s: [n] \to \{0, 1\}$, and $d_H(s, \mathcal{P})$ coincides with the number of zeros in s. Hence, the definition of ϵ-farness in the previous section corresponds to the definition of ϵ-farness given in terms of δ_H.

ϵ-farness

We note though that we sometimes define ϵ-farness in an ad hoc way when objects cannot be naturally represented by functions. For certain applications, it may be more relevant to use other notions of distance than Hamming distance. In these cases, we will be explicit about what ϵ-farness refers to.

1.3.2 Computational Cost

word RAM model

To measure the running time, we usually adopt the *word RAM model*, in which we can perform operations on $O(\log n)$ bits in constant time. To understand why, consider the tester for the all-ones property. To implement it, we need to be able to perform a query to the input in constant time. This means that we need to be able to specify an index, which requires $O(\log n)$ bits, in constant time, thus necessitating the RAM model.

query complexity

Having said that, in this book, we mainly focus on *query complexity*, which is the number of times the input is accessed. How a query is defined depends on the data representation. As mentioned above, typically input objects will be represented as functions $f: [n] \to R$ for a set R. In this case, a query refers to the evaluation $f(i)$ for some $i \in [n]$. For instance, if a graph on n vertices is represented as an adjacency matrix A, then a query reveals $A(i, j)$, that is, whether vertices i and j are adjacent or not. If the graph is represented as a collection of incidence lists L_i for each vertex i, then a query reveals $L_i(j)$, that is, the j'th neighbor of vertex i if it is defined and a special symbol $\perp$ otherwise. In a few situations, the representation may be more ad hoc, so that a query returns more elaborate information, e.g., the degree of a node in a graph (see the general graph model in Chapter 5).

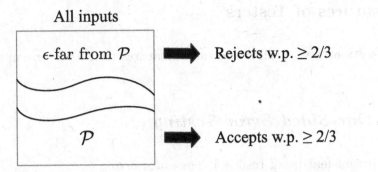

Fig. 1.1: Tester accepts inputs satisfying $\mathcal{P}$ with probability at least 2/3 and rejects inputs ϵ-far from $\mathcal{P}$ with probability at least 2/3. We do not care the outputs of the tester for other inputs.

One reason to focus on the query complexity is that analyzing both query complexity and time complexity complicates the arguments. The other, more important, reason is that we have a better understanding of query complexity than time complexity. For example, we can show lower bounds on query complexity by information-theoretic arguments. However, we typically need assumptions from computational complexity such as $P \neq NP$ to obtain non-trivial lower bounds on time complexity.

1.3.3 Testers

Given the discussion in the last two subsections, we can finally define the notion of a tester rigorously:

Definition 1.1 (Tester). An algorithm is said to be a *(property) tester* for a property $\mathcal{P}$, if the following holds:

- The input consists of an integer $n \in \mathbb{Z}_{>0}$, an error parameter $\epsilon \in (0, 1)$, and query access to the input of size n.
- It accepts with probability at least 2/3 if the input satisfies $\mathcal{P}$.
- It rejects with probability at least 2/3 if the input is ϵ-far from satisfying $\mathcal{P}$.

tester

See Figure 1.1 for a schematic. The probability threshold of 2/3 is not that important: We can improve the probability to $1 - \delta$ by running the algorithm $O(\log(1/\delta))$ times and outputting the majority of the outputs (see Problem 1.2).

1.4 Features of Testers

In this section, we overview additional features that a tester can possess.

1.4.1 One-Sided Error Testing

one-sided error

An important feature of testers is *one-sided error*:

> **Definition 1.2** (One-sided error tester). We say that a tester for a property $\mathcal{P}$ is a *one-sided error* tester if it always accepts inputs that satisfy $\mathcal{P}$.

two-sided error

In contrast, we sometimes say that a tester has *two-sided error* if it may reject inputs that satisfy $\mathcal{P}$ (but it should accept them with probability at least 2/3). If a one-sided error tester rejects, then we are sure that the input does not satisfy the property, and hence its decision is more reliable in this sense than two-sided testers. However, one-sided error testers may require many more queries than two-sided error testers.

Analyzing query complexity for one-sided error testers is often much easier than that for two-sided error testers. A one-sided error tester for a property $\mathcal{P}$ should accept inputs satisfying $\mathcal{P}$ by definition, and hence we only have to analyze its behavior on inputs that are ϵ-far from satisfying $\mathcal{P}$. When showing lower bounds on the query complexity, we can use the observation that a one-sided error tester never rejects until it finds a witness with which we are sure that the input does not satisfy $\mathcal{P}$. In other words, it never rejects until there is no object satisfying $\mathcal{P}$ that is consistent with the queried part of the input object. For example, for the all-one string case, a one-sided error tester never rejects until it finds a bit 0. Hence, we can show a lower bound for one-sided query complexity by creating a single ϵ-far input such that any small part of it can be extended to an object satisfying $\mathcal{P}$. In contrast, we need more sophisticated arguments to show lower bounds on the query complexity of two-sided error testers.

1.4.2 Non-adaptivity

Another important feature of a tester is non-adaptivity:

non-adaptive tester

> **Definition 1.3** (Non-adaptive tester). We say that a tester for a property $\mathcal{P}$ is a *non-adaptive tester* if the queries are determined independently of the answers provided by the query access.

In other words, a non-adaptive tester first determines the query set before accessing the input object. Note that the query set may depend on the internal randomness of the tester. In contrast, a tester whose queries may depend on the answers to previous queries is called an *adaptive tester*.

adaptive tester

> **Exercise 1.1.** Let $\mathcal{P}$ be a property of functions $f\colon [n] \to [d]$. Then show that if there is an adaptive tester T_a for $\mathcal{P}$ with query complexity $q(n, \epsilon)$, then there is a non-adaptive tester T_{na} with query complexity $d^{q(n,\epsilon)}$.

Hence, if there is a constant-query (adaptive) tester for a property $\mathcal{P}$, then there is a constant-query non-adaptive tester for $\mathcal{P}$. This means that, when we only care about constant-query testability of a property, adaptivity does not help much. However, when the dependency on ϵ is critical or when we care about sublinear-query testability, adaptivity should be considered.

1.5 Variations of Property Testing

Most studies on property testing are based on the notion of a tester given in Definition 1.1. However, several variations have been proposed in the literature, and we briefly discuss a few significant ones.

1.5.1 Tolerant Tester

A natural variation of a tester is an algorithm that accepts if the input is close to satisfying the property and rejects if the input is far from satisfying the property. If ϵ-*close* is defined as the complement of the event ϵ-far, then tolerant tester is defined thus:

ϵ-closeness

> **Definition 1.4** (Tolerant tester). We say that an algorithm is a *tolerant tester* for a property $\mathcal{P}$ if, given $n \in \mathbb{Z}_{>0}$, $\epsilon_1, \epsilon_2 \in (0, 1)$ with $\epsilon_1 < \epsilon_2$, and query access to the input, it accepts with probability at least $2/3$ if the input is ϵ_1-close to $\mathcal{P}$, and rejects with probability at least $2/3$ if the input is ϵ_2-far from $\mathcal{P}$.

tolerant tester

From a tolerant tester for a property $\mathcal{P}$, we can obtain a tester for $\mathcal{P}$ by setting $\epsilon_1 = 0$ and $\epsilon_2 = \epsilon$. Besides tolerant testing being a natural generalization of standard testing, it is a desirable notion in many settings. For example, consider the property that points in a Euclidean space forms a good clustering. Then, we want an algorithm that accepts with high probability when there is a good clustering of all but a small fraction of the points, not necessarily of all points.

Although tolerant testing is a much harder task than the usual testing in general, in some setting surprisingly, a property is tolerantly testable with a constant number of queries if and only if it is testable with a constant number of queries, and this equivalence is a crucial component to obtain characterizations of constant-query testable properties (see Chapters 9 and 11).

1.5.2 Distribution-Free Testing and Sample-Based Testing

Let $f, g \colon [n] \to R$ be two functions. Then, the relative Hamming distance $\delta_H(f, g)$ can be regarded as the probability that $f(i)$ and $g(i)$ disagrees when i is sampled from the uniform distribution over $[n]$, that is:

$$\delta_H(f, g) = \Pr_{i \sim [n]}[f(i) \neq g(i)].$$

Naturally, we can replace the uniform distribution by an arbitrary distribution $\mathcal{D}$ over $[n]$. That is, we define the relative distance between f and g with respect to $\mathcal{D}$ as:

$$\delta_{\mathcal{D}}(f, g) = \Pr_{i \sim \mathcal{D}}[f(i) \neq g(i)].$$

ϵ-farness

We say that f is ϵ-far from a property $\mathcal{P}$ with respect to $\mathcal{D}$ if $\delta_{\mathcal{D}}(f, g) > \epsilon$ for every $g \colon [n] \to R$ satisfying $\mathcal{P}$.

distribution-free tester

Definition 1.5 (Distribution-free tester). An algorithm is called a *distribution-free tester* for a property $\mathcal{P}$, if given an integer $n \in \mathbb{Z}_{>0}$, an error parameter $\epsilon \in (0, 1)$, query access to the input $f \colon [n] \to R$, and a device that samples i from an unknown distribution $\mathcal{D}$ over $[n]$, it accepts with probability at least $2/3$ if f satisfies $\mathcal{P}$ and rejects with probability at least $2/3$ if f is ϵ-far from satisfying $\mathcal{P}$ with respect to $\mathcal{D}$.

This notion was inspired by similar models in computational learning theory such as PAC learning.

sample-based tester

A restriction of a distribution-free tester is a *sample-based tester*, which is not given query access to the input function $f \colon [n] \to R$, but can only sample i according to some distribution $\mathcal{D}$ over $[n]$ and obtain the value $f(i)$. Typically, $\mathcal{D}$ is chosen to be the uniform distribution over $[n]$. In this setting, we focus on

sample complexity

the *sample complexity*, which is the number of samples. Although sampled-based testers are quite restrictive compared to query-based testers, they are desirable in some applications where obtaining samples is more feasible than getting answers to specific queries.

1.6 Analysis for Monotonicity Testing

To illustrate how to rigorously analyze testers, we return to the problem with which we began the chapter: testing monotonicity of arrays. For convenience, in this section, we switch to representing the input data in terms of functions instead of arrays. Thus, a function $f: [n] \to \mathbb{R}$ is *monotone* if $f(i) \le f(i+1)$ for all $i \in [n-1]$. Distance from monotonicity is in terms of Hamming distance, as discussed in Section 1.3.1, and queries are defined as in Section 1.3.2.

monotonicity

1.6.1 Real-valued Functions

We now analyze the tester from Section 1.1. Recall that we have assumed without loss of generality that each $f(i)$ is distinct.

For a function $f: [n] \to \mathbb{R}$, we say $i \in [n]$ is *searchable* if a binary search for $f(i)$ indeed ends at i. If f is monotone, obviously every i is searchable. Additionally, we see that:

searchable

> **Lemma 1.1.** *If i and j are both searchable, and $i < j$, then $f(i) < f(j)$.*

Proof. Suppose to the contrary that $f(j) < f(i)$. Let $i_1, i_2, \ldots, i_s$ and $j_1, j_2, \ldots, j_t$ be the sequence of queries made for searching $f(i)$ and $f(j)$ respectively using the binary search algorithm. Note that $i_1 = j_1 = \lceil n/2 \rceil$, $i_s = i$ and $j_t = j$. Let ℓ^* be the largest integer ℓ such that $i_\ell = j_\ell$. Clearly, either $s > \ell^*$ or $t > \ell^*$ because otherwise, $f(i) = f(i_s) = f(j_t) = f(j)$.

Suppose $s > \ell^*$. It must be that $f(j) \le f(i_{\ell^*}) < f(i)$, because if $f(i)$ and $f(j)$ were both less than or greater than $f(i_{\ell^*})$, then $i_{\ell^*+1} = j_{\ell^*+1}$ holds. Since $f(j) \le f(i_{\ell^*})$, $j_t \le i_{\ell^*}$ holds, and since $f(i_{\ell^*}) < f(i)$, $i_{\ell^*} < i_s$ holds. Therefore, $j = j_t < i_s = i$, a contradiction. The case when $t > \ell^*$ is similar. $\qquad\square$

This immediately implies the following.

> **Corollary 1.1.** *If f is ϵ-far from being monotone, then there are more than ϵn i's that are not searchable.*

Proof. By Lemma 1.1, f restricted to the searchable indices is monotone. If there are at most ϵn non-searchable i's, then the value of f on these i's can be modified to make all of f monotone (e.g., for any non-searchable i, we can modify $f(i)$ to $f(j)$ where j is the integer closest to i that is searchable). $\qquad\square$

We can now see that the Binary Search-based Tester (Algorithm 1.1) is a one-sided error tester for monotonicity using $O(\epsilon^{-1} \log n)$ queries. The query complexity is obvious, as each binary search uses $O(\log n)$ queries. When f is monotone, each binary search succeeds. When f is ϵ-far from being monotone, the probability of picking a searchable i is at most $1-\epsilon$ by Corollary 1.1, and so the probability of the tester accepting is $(1-\epsilon)^q \le 1/3$ when $q = \Theta(\epsilon^{-1})$. Note that the tester is adaptive; we describe in Chapter 3 a non-adaptive tester for the same property.

1.6.2 Boolean-valued functions

To get more intuition on property testing, let us consider the problem of testing monotonicity of Boolean functions $f\colon [n] \to \{0,1\}$. The algorithm to test this property is a very natural sample-based tester. Let S be a random sample of $\Theta(\epsilon^{-1})$ indices. The tester rejects if and only if there exist two indices $i, j \in S$ with $i < j$ such that $f(i) = 1$ and $f(j) = 0$. The details are provided in Algorithm 1.2.

Algorithm 1.2 Tester for monotonicity of Boolean-valued functions

---

Input: An integer $n \in \mathbb{Z}_{>0}$, $\epsilon \in (0,1)$, and query access to $f\colon [n] \to \{0,1\}$.
1: Let S be a set of $6\epsilon^{-1}$ indices sampled independently and uniformly from $[n]$.
2: **if** there exist $i, j \in S$ with $i < j$, $f(i) = 1$, and $f(j) = 0$ **then**
3:     Reject.
4: **end if**
5: Accept.

Now we see the correctness of Algorithm 1.2.

Theorem 1.2. *Algorithm 1.2 is a one-sided error tester for monotonicity with query complexity $O(\epsilon^{-1})$.*

Proof. It is easy to see that the query complexity of Algorithm 1.2 is $O(\epsilon^{-1})$. Also, it always accepts when f is monotone. Hence, the question is whether it rejects with probability at least $2/3$ when f is ϵ-far from being monotone. For simplicity, we assume that $\epsilon n/2$ is an even integer.

Fix a function $f\colon [n] \to \{0,1\}$ that is ϵ-far from being monotone. For an integer $i \in \{0, 1, \ldots, n\}$, let $O_{\le i}$ be the number of ones in $f(1), \ldots, f(i)$ and let $Z_{>i}$ be the number of zeros in $f(i+1), \ldots, f(n)$. For an integer $i \in \{0, 1, \ldots, n\}$, we define $g_i\colon [n] \to \{0,1\}$ as:

$$g_i(j) = \begin{cases} 0 & \text{if } j \le i \\ 1 & \text{otherwise.} \end{cases}$$

Note that the $d_{\mathrm{H}}(f, g_i) = O_{\le i} + Z_{>i}$. Since g_i is monotone, we have $d_{\mathrm{H}}(f, g_i) = O_{\le i} + Z_{>i} > \epsilon n$ for every $i \in \{0, 1, \ldots, n\}$.

Since $O_{\leq 0} = 0$ and $Z_{>n} = 0$, we have $O_{\leq n} > \epsilon n$ and $Z_{>0} > \epsilon n$. As $O_{\leq i}$ increases by at most one (as a function of i), there exists some i^* such that $O_{\leq i^*} = \epsilon n/2$. For such i^*, we have $Z_{>i^*} > \epsilon n/2$.

Then, the probability that a particular sample is $i \leq i^*$ with $f(i) = 1$ is at least $\epsilon/2$. Hence, the probability that the set S contains some $i \leq i^*$ with $f(i) = 1$ is at least:

$$1 - \left(1 - \frac{\epsilon}{2}\right)^{6/\epsilon} \geq 1 - \exp\left(-\frac{\epsilon}{2} \cdot \frac{6}{\epsilon}\right) \geq \frac{9}{10}.$$

Similarly, the probability that the set S contains some $j > i^*$ with $f(j) = 0$ is at least $9/10$. Hence, by the union bound, the probability that the set S contains such i and j simultaneously is at least $8/10 > 2/3$. In such a case, we reject f.   □

We have two lessons from the examples above.

- In both the real-valued and Boolean-valued cases, the algorithms themselves are quite simple while the analysis is somewhat involved. The hardest part is showing that the tester rejects inputs that are far from the property with sufficient probability. This phenomenon is widely observed in the study of property testing. Indeed, it can be regarded as a virtue of property testing because, once the analysis is done, the implementation is quick and easy.
- The other lesson is that property testing reveals the relation between global and local structures. The property of being monotone is a global property. However, the analysis of Algorithm 1.1 or 1.2 suggests that, in a function far from being monotone, there are many local witnesses of non-monotonicity. Developing testers often boils down to revealing such a relation in a property.

1.7 Connections to Other Areas

In this section, we discuss connections of property testing with other areas studied in theoretical computer science.

Approximation

Sometimes, property testing algorithms can be used to derive *approximation algorithms* for optimization problems. For example, let us consider the *maximum cut problem* in which we want to find a cut with the maximum number of edges in a graph. In Chapter 4, we will see a constant-query tester

approximation algorithms

maximum cut

for the property of having a cut of at least ρn^2 edges in an n-vertex graph, where $\rho \in (0, 1)$ is a parameter. This tester distinguishes the case that the maximum size of a cut is at least ρn^2 from the ϵ-far case that it is less than $(\rho - \epsilon)n^2$. Since the maximum size of a cut in a dense graph is $\Omega(n^2)$, we **constant-time** can use the tester to derive a *constant-time approximation scheme*, that is, **approximation scheme** constant-time $(1-\epsilon)$-approximation algorithm, for the maximum cut problem on dense graphs.

maximum clique As another example, let us consider the *maximum clique problem* in which we want to find a clique of the maximum number of vertices in a graph. The traditional notion of approximation for this problem corresponds to distinguishing the case that the maximum size of a clique is at least ρn from, say, the case that it is at most $\rho n/2$. In Chapter 4, we will see a constant-query tester for the property of having a clique of at least ρn^2 vertices in an n-vertex graph, where $\rho \in (0, 1)$ is a parameter. This tester distinguishes the case that an n-vertex graph has a clique of size ρn from the case in which any subset of ρn vertices misses at least ϵn^2 edges. Although the former problem is NP-Hard when $\rho < 1/4$, the latter problem can be solved in constant time. As which notion of approximation is relevant largely depends on applications, there will be a situation that property testing is useful to solve the maximum clique problem.

Building on the techniques developed in property testing, sublinear-time approximation algorithms have been developed for basic graph parameters. For example, it is known that, given some suitable query access to the input graph, there is a $(1 \pm \epsilon)$-approximation algorithm for the average degree that runs in $\widetilde{O}(\sqrt{n})$[6] time and a $(1 \pm \epsilon)$-approximation algorithm for the number of triangles that runs in $\widetilde{O}(m^{3/2}/t)$ time, where n, m, and t are the number of vertices, edges, and triangles, respectively, in the input graph. The latter algorithm runs in sublinear time when $t = \Omega(m^{1/2+\delta})$ for any $\delta > 0$. See Section 5.9 for more detailed discussion.

Computational Learning Theory

PAC learning One of the most basic frameworks in computational learning theory is *probably approximately correct (PAC) learning*. In this framework, for some unknown function $f \colon \{0, 1\}^n \to \{0, 1\}$ in a class $\mathcal{C}$ of functions, we are given a small number of samples of the form $(x, f(x))$, where x is drawn from some distribution $\mathcal{D}$, and the goal is to output a hypothesis function **concept class** $h \colon \{0, 1\}^n \to \{0, 1\}$ such that the probability that h disagrees with f according to $\mathcal{D}$ is small. We call $\mathcal{C}$ a *concept class*. To see the connection with property testing, we consider the following variant:

---

[6] $\widetilde{O}(\cdot)$ suppresses polylogarithmic factors.

Definition 1.6 (An inefficient variant of PAC learning). Let $\mathcal{C}$ be a class of functions $f\colon \{0,1\}^n \to \{0,1\}$. Then, we say that an algorithm is a *learner* for $\mathcal{C}$ if, given $\epsilon, \delta \in (0,1)$ and access to vectors distributed according to a fixed distribution $\mathcal{D}$ over $\{0,1\}^n$ and labeled by an unknown function $f \in \mathcal{C}$, it outputs a hypothesis function $h\colon \{0,1\}^n \to \{0,1\}$ such that

$$\Pr_{x \sim \mathcal{D}}[h(x) \neq f(x)] \leq \epsilon.$$

with probability at least $1 - \delta$.

The algorithm may also have access to a value oracle, that is, we get the value of $f(x)$ if we specify a vector $x \in \{0,1\}^n$. In this case, we refer to the learning model as *learning with queries*. If the hypothesis function h always belongs to $\mathcal{C}$, we say that $\mathcal{C}$ is *properly learnable*.

learner

learning with queries
proper learning

In standard PAC learning, we also require that the algorithm only draw $\mathrm{poly}(n, \epsilon^{-1}, \delta^{-1})$ samples.

We can look at property testing as a relaxation of learning with queries and under the uniform distribution. Namely, instead of asking that the algorithm outputs a hypothesis function, we only require that the algorithm decide whether the function belongs to $\mathcal{C}$ or is far from any function in $\mathcal{C}$. In this view, we can use property testing as a pruning step when learning an unknown function: we first run the tester for $\mathcal{C}$ to decide whether to use $\mathcal{C}$ as our concept class of learning, as testers are often more efficient than learners.

Problem 1.7 shows that property testing is no harder than proper learning. Namely, if we have a proper learner for a concept class $\mathcal{C}$ (with or without queries), then we can use it as a subroutine to test the property of belonging to $\mathcal{C}$, with a small loss in the query complexity.

Distributed Algorithms

In distributed computing for graph problems, we have a processor for each vertex, and they communicate with each other through edges. In the *LOCAL model* for distributed algorithms, every vertex can send messages to all of its neighbors in each round of communication, and there is no restriction on the lengths of the messages. Distributed algorithms in this model imply sublinear-time approximation algorithms for graphs when they are represented as incidence lists. For example, this connection has been used to devise sublinear-time approximation algorithms for the minimum vertex cover and maximum matching problems (see Chapter 5).

LOCAL model

Communication Complexity

communication
complexity

Communication complexity is a mathematical abstraction to study the situation where there are a small number of parties communicating among themselves in order to jointly solve a problem. The parties can be actual physical parties or virtual parties corresponding to different parts of a computing device. The study of communication complexity has been extensive and successful, with satisfactory (and beautiful) solutions having been found for most of the important problems in this area.

It turns out that there is a surprising connection between communication complexity and property testing, which we explore in Chapter 6. In particular, low-query testers for properties of interest (e.g., monotonicity of arrays) yields low-cost protocols for natural problems in communication complexity (e.g., indexing). Thus, a lower bound on the cost of solving the communication problem implies a lower bound on the query complexity of the testing problem.

Coding Theory

linear code

locally testable code

A very natural and well-studied class of properties is membership in vector subspaces. Vector subspaces over finite fields can also be viewed as *linear codes*. Linear codes which can be tested with a constant number of queries (independent of the code length) are called *locally testable codes*, and these have intimate connections with constructions of probabilistically checkable codes in complexity theory. Locally testable codes with good parameters have been built using powerful results in coding theory which relate algebraic, combinatorial and algorithmic properties of linear codes. We will turn to these topics in Chapter 12.

1.8 Organization

The subsequent chapters are organized as follows.

Chapter 2: Basic Techniques

In this chapter, we introduce common techniques used throughout this book. First, we explain useful procedures such as those detecting a particular element in an array and estimating the number of times that a particular element appears in an array. Then, we discuss reductions between testing problems that preserves testability, and we provide its applications. Then, we introduce Yao's minimax principle, which is the most basic technique for showing lower bounds on the query complexity in property testing.

Part II

In this part, we consider testability of specific properties and overview basic results in property testing.

Chapter 3: Strings

Strings are arguably one of the simplest objects, and hence we start with testing properties on strings. In this chapter, we start with studying concrete properties such as being a palindrome, being a concatenation of two palindromes, and being a sequence of properly matched parenthesis. Then, we move on to testing monotonicity and its generalization assuming a total order on the characters (e.g., the characters are integers). A notable result is that the monotonicity tester given in Section 1.1 can be made non-adaptive. Although the object we study in this chapter is a string, we will make use of several notions from graph theory such as matching and transitive-closure-spanner.

Chapter 4: Graphs in the Adjacency Matrix Model

This chapter is devoted to testing properties of graphs when the graph is represented by an adjacency matrix. As the size of an adjacency matrix is n^2, roughly speaking, ϵ-farness means that we need to add or remove more than ϵn^2 edges to make the input graph satisfy the property of interest. First, we show that partition properties such as k-colorability are constant-query testable. The highlight of this chapter is constant-query testability of H-freeness, which is a property of having no isomorphic copy of a graph H as a subgraph. We mainly focus on the case that H is a triangle, a cycle of length three. To show that triangle-freeness is constant-query testable, we make use of the celebrated Szemerédi's regularity lemma, which says that any graph can be partitioned into a constant number of parts so that each pair of parts looks like a random bipartite graph. Szemerédi's regularity lemma will also play an important role to obtain characterizations of constant-query testable properties in Chapter 9. Finally, we observe that several properties such as connectivity are trivial to test in this model, which motivates us to consider another model, and it is the main topic of the next chapter.

Chapter 5: Graphs in the Bounded-Degree Model

In this chapter, we study testing properties of graphs in the bounded-degree model. This model is parameterized by an integer $d \in \mathbb{Z}_{>0}$, and we only consider graphs of maximum degree at most d. As the maximum number of edges in such graphs is dn, we define ϵ-farness as having to add or remove more than ϵdn edges. Because of this difference from the adjacency matrix model, some of the properties that were trivially testable in the adjacency matrix model become relevant. First, we show that H-freeness is constant-query testable without using Szemerédi's regularity lemma. Then, we show that various connectivity properties such as k-edge-connectivity and k-vertex-connectivity are constant-query testable with one-sided error, using results from edge augmentation theory to show that ϵ-far graphs have many small witnesses of not satisfying the property. We then discuss cycle-freeness as a representative example that requires the two-sided error property to achieve constant-query testability. Next, we consider k-colorability and show that, as opposed to the adjacency matrix model, testing 2-colorability, or bipartiteness, requires $\widetilde{\Theta}(\sqrt{n})$ queries, and testing 3-colorability requires $\Omega(n)$ queries. We then show constant-query approximation algorithms for several optimization problem such as the minimum spanning tree problem and the maximum matching problem.

Chapter 6: Functions over Hypercubes

The primary focus of this chapter is testing properties of Boolean functions, that is, $f \colon \{0,1\}^n \to \{0,1\}$. Just as a course on standard algorithms often starts with a discussion of sorting, we begin with algorithms for testing monotonicity of Boolean functions. Next, we develop some basic results in Fourier analysis for Boolean functions which are useful for many problems in the area. Then, we analyze the so-called Blum-Luby-Rubinfeld (BLR) tester for linearity, both using Fourier analysis as well as a "self-correcting" approach. Also, we study another classic problem called junta testing, that is, testing whether the input function depends only on a constant number of the variables. Then, we move on to showing lower bounds for the query complexity of these testing problems. In this context, we also look at a simple and powerful connection to communication complexity.

Chapter 7: Massively Parameterized Model

Massively parameterized model is different from the models discussed so far in the sense that the property to be tested is determined by a large number of parameters. For example, suppose that we are given a bipartite graph $G = (V, E)$ on n vertices and a labeling $f \colon V \to \{0, 1\}$ on vertices, and we want to test f is a proper 2-coloring of G. Then, the property to be tested is determined by the graph G, which has $O(n^2)$ parameters. Sublinear-time testers do not exist by definition because G is a part of the input and it requires $\Omega(n)$ time to read the whole input. Hence, the main focus of this model is whether we can test properties making a sublinear number of queries to the labeling f.

We first consider whether a labeling is a 2-coloring on a given bipartite graph, whether a labeling is monotone on a given directed acyclic graph, and whether a vector is a member of a given subspace. We then see that these results can be seen as special cases of a more general problem of testing whether the assignment given through query access is a satisfying assignment of the given CSP instance.

Chapter 8: Vectors and Matrices over the Reals

In this chapter, we shift our focus on objects with a continuous nature, or more specifically, vectors and matrices over $\mathbb{R}$. We first consider testing whether the input matrix has a low rank. We then consider testing whether a given vector belongs to a fixed low-dimensional subspace. This problem is different from the one in the previous chapter in that the underlying field is $\mathbb{R}$ instead of $\mathbb{F}_2$ and that the fixed subspace is low-dimensional. We will see that linear algebraic tools are useful to solve these problems.

Part III

In this part, we discuss more advanced topics, and in particular we will be interested in providing general conditions that lead to constant- or sublinear-query testability.

Chapter 9: Graphs in the Adjacency Matrix Model

This chapter is devoted to showing characterizations of constant-query testable properties in the adjacency matrix model. We first show that every monotone property, that is, properties closed under taking subgraphs, is constant-query testable with one-sided error. Then, we show that every hereditary property, that is, properties closed under taking induced subgraphs, is constant-query testable with one-sided error. It turns out that property is constant-query testable if and only if it is (essentially) hereditary. The essential tools to show these results are variants of Szemerédi's regularity lemma. Then, we move on to the characterization of constant-query testable properties (with two-sided error). Roughly speaking, a property is constant-query testable if and only if whether it is satisfied or not is determined by the densities between parts in the partition obtained by Szemerédi's regularity lemma.

Chapter 10: Graphs in the Bounded-Degree Model

In this chapter, we provide several general conditions on properties that makes them constant-query testable in the bounded-degree model. We first consider properties closed under adding edges. More specifically, we show that a property called (k, ℓ)-fullness, which unifies several interesting properties, is constant-query testable with two-sided error. Here, matroid theory plays a crucial role. Then, we consider properties closed under removing edges. More specifically, we show that every minor-closed property, that is, properties closed under taking subgraphs and contracting edges, is constant-query testable with two-sided error. The full characterization of constant-query testable properties is out of reach at the time of writing.

Chapter 11: Affine-Invariant Properties of Functions

In this chapter, we explain general results on testing affine-invariant properties of functions $f \colon \mathbb{F}^n \to \mathbb{F}$, where $\mathbb{F}$ is a finite field and a property $\mathcal{P}$ is said to be affine-invariant if, for any $f \in \mathcal{P}$ and an affine transformation A over $\mathbb{F}^n$, we have $f \circ A \in \mathcal{P}$. The goal of this chapter is to characterize constant-query testability of affine-invariant properties, and the argument is somehow similar to the one in Chapter 9. The techniques we use are collectively called "higher-order Fourier analysis" and it has clear parallels to Szemerédi 's regularity lemma and the associated apparatus.

Chapter 12: Linear Properties of Functions

This chapter is focused on linear affine-invariant properties of functions $f \colon \mathbb{F}^n \to \mathbb{F}$ where $\mathbb{F}$ is a finite (but often large) field. Such properties naturally arise in the form of error-correcting codes. We show the testability of very general classes of such properties, obtained by tensor products or 'lifts' of base codes. We end the chapter by discussing how to construct locally testable codes, which enjoy not only small query complexity but also other good coding-theoretic properties, such as rate and distance.

Chapter 13: Massively Parameterized Model

In this chapter, we focus on the CSP perspective of the massively parameterized model. Specifically, we classify Boolean CSPs into three categories in terms of their testability: (i) CSPs that are constant-query testable, (ii) CSPs that are not constant-query testable but are sublinear-query testable, and (iii) CSPs that are not sublinear-query testable. To obtain such a classification, we make use of results from universal algebra, which has been crucially used to study the computational complexity of CSPs.

1.9 Bibliographic Notes

Property testing naturally emerged in the context of program checking and probabilistically checkable proofs. In the context of *program checking* [94, 368], as it is often tough to exactly check whether a given program computes a specified function, we may choose to test it satisfy some closely related property. In the context of *probabilistically checkable proofs (PCPs)* [32, 31], the property tested is being a codeword with respect to a specific code. The notion of property testing was first formulated by Rubinfeld and Sudan [368]. Goldreich, Goldwasser, and Ron [209] extended the notion to combinatorial objects such as graphs.

program checking

probabilistically checkable proofs

Parnas, Ron and Rubinfeld [347] introduced the notion of tolerant testing, which has since been intensively studied. Tolerant testing has been shown to be possible for large classes of graph and function properties, a topic that we will return to in Chapters 9 and 11.

PAC learning was defined in the seminal work of [386]. The notion of distribution-free testing was introduced in [209] and has been intensively studied [3, 160, 204, 240, 241, 242, 303]. Goldreich, Goldwasser, and Ron [209] showed that any proper PAC learning algorithm can be used to construct a distribution-free tester for the same class.

The notion of a sample-based tester was introduced in an early work of property testing [209], but was largely ignored until a subsequent work [218]. Fischer, Lachish, and Vasudev [181] showed that every non-adaptive property tester with a constant number of queries can be converted to a sample-based tester with $O(n^c)$ samples for some $c < 1$. Blais and Yoshida [92] gave a characterization of properties that can be tested with a constant number of samples.

As sample-based testers are too restrictive, a notion called *active testing* [39] has been considered, which is inspired from a machine learning concept called *active learning*. The idea is that the tester samples a large number, say, $\Theta(\log n)$ or $\Theta(\sqrt{n})$, of indices from $[n]$, and then queries only on a subset of a small size, say, $O(1)$. It is shown in [39] that several properties for which sample-based testers require $\omega(1)$ samples can be actively tested with $O(1)$ queries.

active testing

active learning

The monotonicity tester for real-valued functions explained in Section 1.6.1 is due to Ergun, Kannan, Kumar, Rubinfeld, and Viswanathan [171], and that for Boolean-valued functions explained in Section 1.6.2 is folklore.

Problems

1.1. For a property $\mathcal{P}$, suppose there is a one-sided error tester T as in Definition 1.2 that makes $q(n, \epsilon)$ queries on inputs of size n. Show that for any $\delta > 0$, there is a one-sided error tester T' making $O(q(n, \epsilon) \cdot \log \delta^{-1})$ queries that rejects inputs ϵ-far from satisfying $\mathcal{P}$ with probability at least $1 - \delta$.

1.2. For a property $\mathcal{P}$, suppose there is a tester T as in Definition 1.1 that makes $q(n, \epsilon)$ queries on inputs of length n. Show that for any $\delta > 0$, there is a tester T' making $O(q(n, \epsilon) \cdot \log \delta^{-1})$ queries that accepts inputs satisfying $\mathcal{P}$ with probability at least $1 - \delta$ and rejects inputs ϵ-far from satisfying $\mathcal{P}$ with probability at least $1 - \delta$.

Hint: Recall the Chernoff and Hoeffding bounds (see Appendix A). They will be used throughout this book, often without mention.

1.3. (a) Show that for events X and B:

$$\Pr[X] \leq \Pr[B] + \Pr[X \mid \bar{B}]$$

Usually, when applying this inequality, B is taken to be a "bad event". Then, assuming B is a low probability event, it suffices to upper bound the probability conditioning on B not occurring.

(b) Modify Algorithm 1.2 so that S is constructed by independently adding every $i \in [n]$ to S with probability $10/\epsilon n$. Argue the correctness of this modified tester.

1.4. Let $\mathcal{P}_n = \{\mathcal{P}_n\}_{n \in \mathbb{Z}_{>0}}$ and $\mathcal{P}' = \{\mathcal{P}'_n\}_{n \in \mathbb{Z}_{>0}}$ be properties of functions $f \colon [n] \to \{0, 1\}$ that are testable with $q(\epsilon, n)$ and $q'(\epsilon, n)$ queries, respectively. Show that the property $\mathcal{P}'' = \{\mathcal{P}_n \cup \mathcal{P}'_n\}_{n \in \mathbb{Z}_{>0}}$ is testable with $O(q(\epsilon, n) + q'(\epsilon, n))$ queries.

1.5. Show that there does not exist a deterministic tester (adaptive or non-adaptive) for monotonicity of functions $f \colon [n] \to \{0, 1\}$ with $o(n)$ query complexity.

same-signed
1.6. A function $f \colon [n] \to \mathbb{R}$ is *same-signed* if $f(i) \geq 0$ for all $i \in [n]$ or $f(i) < 0$ for all $i \in [n]$. Design and analyze a tester for same-signedness that makes $O(\epsilon^{-1})$ queries.

1.7. (a) Show that if there is a proper learning algorithm for $\mathcal{P}$ that makes $q(n, \epsilon, \delta)$ queries, then there is a tester for $\mathcal{P}$ that makes at most $q(n, \frac{\epsilon}{2}, \frac{1}{6}) + O(\epsilon^{-1})$ queries. (**Hint**: Apply the learner and then estimate the distance between the input and the learner's output.)

(b) Show that if there is a proper learning algorithm for $\mathcal{P}$ that uses $s(n, \epsilon, \delta)$ samples, then there is a sample-based tester for $\mathcal{P}$ with sample complexity at most $s(n, \epsilon/2, 1/6) + O(\epsilon^{-1})$.

1.8. Let $\mathcal{P}$ be a property of functions $f \colon [n] \to R$. A *distance approximation* algorithm for a property $\mathcal{P}$ acts as follows: given integer n, parameter α and access to an input f, it makes $q(n, \alpha)$ queries to f and returns $\hat{\delta}$ which satisfies:

$$\delta_H(f, \mathcal{P}) - \alpha \le \hat{\delta} \le \delta_H(f, \mathcal{P}) + \alpha$$

with probability at least 2/3.

(a) Given a distance approximation algorithm for $\mathcal{P}$ with query complexity $q(n, \alpha)$, construct a tolerant tester for $\mathcal{P}$ with query complexity $q(n, (\epsilon_2 - \epsilon_1)/2)$ (recall the notation in Definition 1.4).

(b) Given a tolerant tester for $\mathcal{P}$ with query complexity $q(n, \epsilon_2 - \epsilon_1)$, construct a distance approximation algorithm for $\mathcal{P}$ with query complexity $O(q(n, 2\alpha) \cdot \log \alpha^{-1} \cdot \log \log \alpha^{-1})$.

1.9. Suppose there is an election with m candidates and n voters. We define an ϵ-*winner* to be a candidate who gets the most votes and has at least ϵn votes more than the candidate with the second-highest number of votes. Show that with probability at least 2/3, the ϵ-winner (if it exists) gets the most votes in a random poll of size $O(\epsilon^{-2})$. Note that there is no dependence on either m or n. (**Hint**: Use the *Dvoretzky–Kiefer–Wolfowitz (DKW) inequality*: if μ is a probability distribution over the reals with cumulative distribution function $F(z) = \mu((-\infty, z])$, and if $X_1, \ldots, X_n$ are random variables each i.i.d. from μ, then:

$$\Pr\left[\sup_z \left| \frac{1}{n} \sum_{i=1}^{n} 1_{\{X_i \le z\}} - F(z) \right| > \epsilon \right] \le 2e^{-2n\epsilon^2}$$

for any $\epsilon > 0$.)

1.10. A function $f \colon [n] \times [n] \to \mathbb{R}$ is said to be monotone over the grid if $f(i, j) \le f(i', j')$ whenever $i \le i'$ and $j \le j'$. Show that monotonicity over the grid can be tested using $O(\epsilon^{-1} \log^2 n)$ queries.

1.11. Show that any one-sided error tester for a property $\mathcal{P}$ with query complexity $q(\epsilon, n)$ is a tolerant tester for $\mathcal{P}$ that accepts $1/(3q(\epsilon, n))$-close inputs with probability at least 2/3 (and rejects ϵ-far inputs with probability at least 2/3).

Chapter 2
Basic Techniques

This chapter describes basic techniques that will be frequently used throughout this book. Section 2.1 studies some common problems arising in the analysis of testers: finding a particular character in a string, estimating the sum of a sequence of real numbers, and bounding the number of successful iterations where each iteration is successful with a certain probability. The latter bound will be useful to analyze testers that have an iterative nature.

In Section 2.2, we formally define gap-preserving local reductions, and show that they allow one to convert testers for one property into testers for a different property of interest. Just as for standard algorithms, reductions can also be used to prove impossibility results. In the context of property testing, they imply query complexity lower bounds.

The most widely used tool used to show lower bounds on query complexity though is Yao's minimax principle, described in Section 2.3. The technique uses a simple but powerful duality that arises from viewing the task of testing as a game played between the tester and a player who provides the inputs.

There is a third approach towards proving lower bounds on query complexity: the communication complexity methodology. We describe this technique later in Chapter 6.

2.1 Common Analysis Tools

2.1.1 Value Detection

Consider the problem of finding a particular value $r \in R$ from a function $f : [n] \to R$ in constant time when f has many copies of r.

© The Author(s), under exclusive license to Springer Nature Singapore Pte Ltd 2022
A. Bhattacharyya and Y. Yoshida, *Property Testing*,
https://doi.org/10.1007/978-981-16-8622-1_2

Lemma 2.1. *For any $\epsilon, \delta \in (0, 1)$, there is an algorithm that, given query access to $f: [n] \to R$ and a value $r \in R$, makes $O\left(\epsilon^{-1} \log \delta^{-1}\right)$ many queries to f, and finds $i \in [n]$ with $f(i) = r$ with probability at least $1 - \delta$, provided that $|f^{-1}(r)| \geq \epsilon n$.*

Proof. The algorithm samples $i_1, \ldots, i_q$ from $[n]$ uniformly at random, where $q = \Theta\left(\epsilon^{-1} \log \delta^{-1}\right)$. Then, the probability that $f(i_j) \neq r$ for every $j \in [q]$ is at most:

$$\left(\frac{n - \epsilon n}{n}\right)^q = (1 - \epsilon)^q \leq \exp(-\epsilon q),$$

where the inequality uses the fact $1 - x \leq e^{-x}$ for any $x \in \mathbb{R}$. By choosing the hidden constant in q large enough, we can make this probability at most δ. $\square$

Lemma 2.1 is flexible and can be used for various objects. For example, it can be used to find a character $\sigma \in \Sigma$ in a string $s \in \Sigma^n$ when s has at least ϵn copies of σ and to find $x \in \{0, 1\}^n$ with $f(x) = 1$ in a Boolean function $f: \{0, 1\}^n \to \{0, 1\}$ when $|f^{-1}(1)| \geq \epsilon 2^n$.

2.1.2 Sum Estimation

The second technique is estimating the sum of values in a sequence of bounded real numbers with a constant number of queries to the sequence.

Lemma 2.2. *For any $\epsilon, \delta \in (0, 1)$, there is an algorithm that, given query access to $f: [n] \to [a, b]$ for $a, b \in \mathbb{R}$ with $a < b$, queries f $O\left(\epsilon^{-2} \log \delta^{-1}\right)$ times, and outputs a value $X \in \mathbb{R}$ such that:*

$$\left| X - \sum_{i \in [n]} f(i) \right| \leq \epsilon(b - a)n$$

with probability at least $1 - \delta$.

Proof. The algorithm first samples $i_1, \ldots, i_q$ from $[n]$ uniformly at random, where $q = \Theta\left(\epsilon^{-2} \log \delta^{-1}\right)$. Then, it outputs the normalized empirical sum:

$$X := \frac{n}{q} \sum_{j \in [q]} f(i_j).$$

Clearly, the number of queries is as stated.

Now we show that X is a good approximation to the true sum with high probability. From Hoeffding's inequality (see Appendix A), we have:

$$\Pr\left[\left|X - \frac{n}{q}\sum_{j\in[q]} f(i_j)\right| \geq \epsilon(b-a)n\right] \leq 2\exp(2q\epsilon^2) \leq \delta$$

by choosing the hidden constant in q large enough. $\square$

Exercise 2.1. Construct a tester that given n, ϵ and access to a function $f\colon [n] \to \{0,1\}$ accepts with probability $1 - \delta$ if $|f^{-1}(1)| \geq n/2$, rejects with probability $1 - \delta$ if $|f^{-1}(1)| < (1-\epsilon)n/2$ and makes $O\left(\epsilon^{-2}\log\delta^{-1}\right)$ queries.

You will be asked to show that the bound in Lemma 2.2 is tight in Problem 2.4. In subsequent chapters, we often use Lemma 2.2 without mentioning it.

2.1.3 Concentration Bound on the Number of Successful Iterations

When analyzing the success probability of a tester, we often encounter the following situation: The tester is iterative, and each iteration is "successful" with probability at least $\eta > 0$. How many iterations do we need to get the desired number of successful iterations?

Lemma 2.3. *Suppose we have ℓ iterations and each iteration is successful with probability at least $\eta > 0$. Then for any $\delta \in (0,1)$, the total number of successful iterations in the end is at least $\eta\ell - \sqrt{2\ell\log\delta^{-1}}$ with probability at least $1 - \delta$.*

Proof. Let $\eta_i \geq \eta$ be the probability that the i-th iteration is successful. Let Y_i be the random variable such that:

$$Y_i = \begin{cases} 1 - \eta_i^{-1} & \text{if the } i\text{-th iteration is successful,} \\ 1 & \text{otherwise.} \end{cases}$$

Let $Z_i = \sum_{j\in[i]} Y_j$. Then, $\mathbf{E}[Z_i \mid Z_1, \ldots, Z_{i-1}] = Z_{i-1} + 1 \cdot (1 - \eta_i) + (1 - \eta_i^{-1}) \cdot \eta_i = Z_{i-1}$ and $|Z_i - Z_{i-1}| \leq \eta_i^{-1} \leq \eta^{-1}$ for every $i \in [\ell]$. By Azuma's inequality (Lemma A.2), we obtain that:

$$\Pr[Z_\ell \geq t] \leq \exp\left(-\frac{t^2\eta^2}{2\ell}\right)$$

for any t. Setting $t = \sqrt{2\ell\log\delta^{-1}} \cdot \eta^{-1}$, we obtain that $Z_\ell \leq \sqrt{2\ell\log\delta^{-1}} \cdot \eta^{-1}$ with probability at least $1 - \delta$. For the number of successful iterations s, we have $Z_\ell = (\ell - s) + s(1 - \eta^{-1}) = \ell - s\eta^{-1}$. Thus, we obtain that $s \geq \eta\ell - \sqrt{2\ell \log \delta^{-1}}$. $\square$

Exercise 2.2. Show that we can test whether a given function $f: [n] \to \mathbb{Z}$ has at most k values, that is, $|\{f(i) : i \in [n]\}| \leq k$, with $O(k/\epsilon)$ queries, when ϵ is sufficiently small.

2.2 Gap-Preserving Local Reductions

In this section, we consider reductions between two testing problems. To make a reduction useful in the context of property testing, the reduction should preserve the distance to the property, and the function made by the reduction must be efficiently constructed from the original function. More specifically, we consider the following:

gap-preserving local reduction

Definition 2.1 (Gap-preserving local reduction). Let $\mathcal{P}$ and $\mathcal{Q}$ be properties on functions. We say that a mapping φ from a function $f: [n] \to R$ to a function $g: [n'] \to R'$ is a *gap-preserving local reduction* from $\mathcal{P}$ to $\mathcal{Q}$ if there exist functions $s: \mathbb{Z}_{>0} \to \mathbb{Z}_{>0}, d: (0,1) \to (0,1)$ and a constant $c \in \mathbb{Z}_{>0}$ such that the following properties hold:

- $n' \leq s(n)$.
- If f satisfies $\mathcal{P}$, then $\varphi(f)$ satisfies $\mathcal{Q}$.
- If f is ϵ-far from satisfying $\mathcal{P}$, then $\varphi(f)$ is $d(\epsilon)$-far from satisfying $\mathcal{Q}$.
- The answer to a query to $\varphi(f)$ can be computed by making at most c oracle queries to f.

Theorem 2.1. *Suppose there is a gap-preserving local reduction from a property $\mathcal{P}$ to another property $\mathcal{Q}$. Then, if $\mathcal{Q}$ is testable with $q(n,\epsilon)$-queries for some function $q: \mathbb{Z}_{>0} \times (0,1) \to \mathbb{Z}_{>0}$, then $\mathcal{P}$ is testable with $c \cdot q(s(n), d(\epsilon))$ queries.*

Proof. Let A be a tester with query complexity $q(n,\epsilon)$ for the property $\mathcal{Q}$, whose existence is guaranteed by the assumption. Let $f: [n] \to R$ be a function for which we want to test the property $\mathcal{P}$ is satisfied. Then, we apply A on $\varphi(f)$ with an error parameter $d(\epsilon)$.

If f satisfies $\mathcal{P}$, then $\varphi(f)$ satisfies $\mathcal{Q}$ and hence the algorithm A accepts with probability at least $2/3$. If f is ϵ-far from satisfying $\mathcal{P}$, then $\varphi(f)$ is $d(\epsilon)$-far from satisfying $\mathcal{Q}$ and hence the algorithm A rejects with probability at least $2/3$. Finally, the number of queries made to f is $c \cdot q(s(n), d(\epsilon))$. $\square$

Theorem 2.1 can be used both in a positive sense and a negative sense:

- If $\mathcal{Q}$ is constant-query testable, that is, $q(n, \epsilon) = q'(\epsilon)$ for some $q' \colon (0, 1) \to \mathbb{Z}_{>0}$, then the existence of a gap-preserving local reduction from $\mathcal{P}$ to $\mathcal{Q}$ implies that $\mathcal{P}$ is also constant-query testable.
- The non-existence of a tester for $\mathcal{P}$ with query complexity $q(s(n), d(\epsilon))$ implies that the query complexity of testing $\mathcal{Q}$ is lower bounded by $\Omega(q(n, \epsilon))$.

We provide concrete examples in the following two sections.

2.2.1 Testing $\mathcal{P}$ via Reduction to $\mathcal{Q}$

As a positive application of Theorem 2.1, we consider testing monotonicity of a $\{0, 1, 2\}$-valued function. We say that a function $f \colon [n] \to \{0, 1, 2\}$ is *monotone* if for every $i \in [n - 1]$ we have $f(i) \le f(i + 1)$.

monotonicity

> **Theorem 2.2.** *We can test monotonicity of a function $f \colon [n] \to \{0, 1, 2\}$ with $O(\epsilon^{-1})$ queries.*

Proof. Recall that the monotonicity of $\{0, 1\}$-valued function is testable with $O(\epsilon^{-1})$ queries (see Section 1.6). We show a gap-preserving local reduction from monotonicity of functions $f \colon [n] \to \{0, 1, 2\}$ to monotonicity of pairs (g, h) of functions, where $g, h \colon [n] \to \{0, 1\}$. Here, we say that a pair (g, h) is *monotone* if both g and h are monotone and is *ϵ-far from being monotone* if we must modify more than $2\epsilon n$ values of g and h to make both of them monotone ($2\epsilon n$ instead of ϵn because the total domain size is $2n$). Note that the monotonicity of a pair (g, h) is testable with $O(\epsilon^{-1})$ queries by testing both g and h with $O(\epsilon^{-1})$ queries with success probability $5/6$ and then by accepting if and only if both tests accept, because if the pair (g, h) is ϵ-far then at least one of g and h must be ϵ-far. Then, the claim holds by Theorem 2.1.

Now, we explain how we construct g and h from f. We define:

$$g(i) = \begin{cases} 0 & \text{if } f(i) = 0, \\ 1 & \text{if } f(i) = 1 \text{ or } f(i) = 2. \end{cases}$$

$$h(i) = \begin{cases} 0 & \text{if } f(i) = 0 \text{ or } f(i) = 1, \\ 1 & \text{if } f(i) = 2. \end{cases}$$

for every $i \in [n]$.

Now, we check the conditions required by gap-preserving local reduction.

1. The domain size of (g, h) is precisely twice the domain size of f.
2. If f is monotone, then clearly g and h are monotone.
3. Suppose that (g, h) is $\epsilon/2$-close to monotonicity. The goal is to show that f is ϵ-close to monotonicity. First, note that we have the following relation between f and (g, h):

$$f(i) = \begin{cases} 0 & \text{if } g(i) = h(i) = 0, \\ 1 & \text{if } g(i) = 1 \text{ and } h(i) = 0, \\ 2 & \text{if } g(i) = h(i) = 1. \end{cases}$$

For a set $I \subseteq [n]$ of indices, we define g_I (resp., h_I) to be the function obtained from g (resp., h) by flipping values of $g(i)$ (resp., $h(i)$) for every $i \in I$. Let $I \subseteq [n]$ and $J \subseteq [n]$ be the set of indices such that g_I and h_J are monotone and $|I| + |J| \le \epsilon n$, whose existence is guaranteed by the assumption. Then, we define $f' : [n] \to R$ according to the following rule:

$$f'(i) = \begin{cases} 0 & \text{if } g_I(i) = h_J(i) = 0, \\ 1 & \text{if } (g_I(i) = 1 \text{ and } h_J(i) = 0) \text{ or } (g_I(i) = 0 \text{ and } h_J(i) = 1) \\ 2 & \text{if } g_I(i) = h_J(i) = 1. \end{cases}$$

It is easy to see that f' is monotone. The number of modified values when constructing f' from f is at most $|I| + |J| \le \epsilon n$.

4. We can answer to a query to g and that to h by querying f once.

Hence, the reduction above is a gap-preserving local reduction with $s(n) = 2n$, $d(\epsilon) = \epsilon/2$, and $c = 1$. By Theorem 2.1, we can test the monotonicity of $\{0, 1, 2\}$-valued functions with $O(\epsilon^{-1})$ queries. $\square$

Exercise 2.3. Show that monotonicity of functions $f \colon [n] \to [k]$ is testable with $O(\epsilon^{-1}k)$ queries.

2.2.2 Lower Bound for $\mathcal{Q}$ via Reduction from $\mathcal{P}$ to $\mathcal{Q}$

The next example shows a simple application of gap-preserving local reduction for proving query complexity lower bounds.

Theorem 2.3. *As in Problem 1.6, call a function $f \colon [n] \to \mathbb{R}$ same-signed if $f(i) \ge 0$ for all $i \in [n]$ or $f(i) < 0$ for all $i \in [n]$. Then, for any[a] $0 < \epsilon < 1/2$, testing whether a function is same-signed requires $\Omega(\epsilon^{-1})$ queries.*

[a] No function is 1/2-far from same-signed, making the problem trivial in this case.

Proof. Let L_{one} be the property satisfied only by the all-ones string, that is, $L_{\mathrm{one}} = \{1^n : n \in \mathbb{Z}_{>0}\}$. We show later in Section 2.3 that testing L_{one} requires $\Omega(\epsilon^{-1})$ queries.

We now give a gap-preserving local reduction from L_{one} to being same-signed. Given a string $s \in \{0, 1\}^n$, let $f : [2n] \to \mathbb{Z}$ be defined as: (i) if

$i \in [n]$, then $f(i) = +1$ if $s_i = 1$ and $f(i) = -1$ if $s_i = 0$, and (ii) $f(i) = +1$ for $n + 1 \leq i \leq 2n$. We can easily check that this is a gap-preserving local reduction.

1. The length of f is twice the length of s.
2. If $s = 1^n$, then $f \equiv 1$ and is clearly same-signed.
3. Suppose $\epsilon \in (0, 1)$. If s is ϵ-far from L_{one}, then $s_i = 0$ at more than ϵn positions i. Correspondingly, $f(i) = -1$ for more than $\epsilon/2 \cdot 2n$ values of i. Also, by construction, f is 1 on the last $n > \epsilon \cdot 2n$ coordinates. Hence, f is $\epsilon/2$-far from being same-signed.
4. A query to f can be answered by querying s at most once.

Therefore, a tester for being same-signed that makes $q(\epsilon)$ queries implies a tester for L_{one} making $q(\epsilon/2)$ queries. Given the lower bound $q(\epsilon/2) = \Omega(\epsilon^{-1})$ from Section 2.3, we get $q(\epsilon) = \Omega(\epsilon^{-1})$. $\square$

2.3 Yao's Minimax Principle

The most general purpose and widely used method for showing lower bounds on query complexity is *Yao's minimax principle*. For concreteness, we focus here on properties of functions $f \colon [n] \to R$, where R is a set. However, we can easily extend the argument to strings and other objects and will apply results in this section on those objects in subsequent chapters.

Let A be a deterministic algorithm that accepts or rejects, given an integer $n \in \mathbb{Z}_{>0}$, an error parameter $\epsilon \in (0, 1)$, and a function $f \colon [n] \to R$. As A is deterministic, we can regard A as a function, and we often denote that $A(n, \epsilon, f) = 1$ (resp., 0) when A accepts (resp., rejects). Let $\mathcal{P}$ be a property over functions $f \colon [n] \to R$ for which ϵ-farness is defined as in Section 1.3. We say that A *errs in testing* $\mathcal{P}$ on the input (n, ϵ, f) if f satisfies $\mathcal{P}$ and $A(n, \epsilon, f) = 0$, or f is ϵ-far from satisfying $\mathcal{P}$ and $A(n, \epsilon, f) = 1$.

Note that a tester of sublinear query complexity should be randomized. An observation that facilitates the analysis of a randomized algorithm is that any randomized algorithm can be viewed as a distribution over deterministic algorithms. Hence, a (randomized) tester for $\mathcal{P}$ can be regarded as a distribution $\mathcal{A}$ over algorithms such that, for any function $f \colon [n] \to R$, the following hold:

- $\Pr_{A \sim \mathcal{A}}[A(n, \epsilon, f) = 1] \geq 2/3$ if f satisfies $\mathcal{P}$.
- $\Pr_{A \sim \mathcal{A}}[A(n, \epsilon, f) = 0] \geq 2/3$ if f is ϵ-far from satisfying $\mathcal{P}$.

Yao's minimax principle states that, in order to show a lower bound on query complexity, it suffices to find a single distribution $\mathcal{F}$ over functions such that any deterministic algorithm A errs on f sampled from $\mathcal{F}$ (denoted by $f \sim \mathcal{F}$) with high probability.

Yao's minimax
principle

Theorem 2.4 (Yao's minimax principle in the context of property testing). *Let $\mathcal{P}$ be a property over functions $f\colon [n] \to R$, and let $q\colon \mathbb{Z}_{>0} \times (0,1) \to \mathbb{Z}_{>0}$ be a function. Suppose that for some $n \in \mathbb{Z}_{>0}$ and $\epsilon \in (0,1)$, there exists a distribution $\mathcal{F}$ over functions such that, for every deterministic algorithm A that makes at most $q(n,\epsilon)$ queries to the input function, it holds that*

$$\Pr_{f \sim \mathcal{F}}[A \text{ errs in testing } \mathcal{P} \text{ on } (n,\epsilon,f)] > \frac{1}{3}.$$

Then, the query complexity to test $\mathcal{P}$ on an error parameter ϵ and a function $f\colon [n] \to R$ is more than $q(n,\epsilon)$.

Moreover, if we only consider non-adaptive/one-sided error algorithms in the assumption, then the lower bound applies to non-adaptive/one-sided error testing.

Proof. Suppose that $\mathcal{A}$ is a tester that, given query access to $f\colon [n] \to R$, distinguishes the case f satisfies $\mathcal{P}$ from the case f is ϵ-far from satisfying $\mathcal{P}$. Then, we have $\Pr_{A \sim \mathcal{A}}[A \text{ errs on } f] \leq 1/3$. It follows that:

$$\Pr_{f \sim \mathcal{F}, A \sim \mathcal{A}}[A \text{ errs on } f] \leq \max_{f\colon [n] \to R} \Pr_{A \sim \mathcal{A}}[A \text{ errs on } f] \leq \frac{1}{3}.$$

Then, there exists a deterministic algorithm $A \in \mathrm{supp}(\mathcal{A})$ such that:

$$\Pr_{f \sim \mathcal{F}}[A \text{ errs on } f] \leq \frac{1}{3},$$

which contradicts the assumption.

The applicability to non-adaptive/one-sided error testing can be shown by considering non-adaptive/one-sided error tester $\mathcal{A}$ in the argument above. $\square$

Without Yao's minimax principle, we need to come up with a hard function for each randomized algorithm. As we cannot enumerate randomized algorithms, this essentially means that we need to find a generic transformation from a randomized algorithm to a function so that it errs on the function with high probability, which seems like a daunting task. On the other hand, by Yao's minimax principle, we only need to find a *single distribution over functions* for which any *deterministic* algorithm errs with high probability. Also, note that the lower bound derived by Theorem 2.4 is information theoretic and unconditional, unlike the situation in standard computational complexity where assumptions are needed such as $\mathsf{P} \neq \mathsf{NP}$.

An interesting way to state Yao's minimax principle is in the language of game theory. Consider a 2-player game between Alice and Bob, where Alice chooses a deterministic algorithm with query complexity q and Bob chooses an input instance. A randomized algorithm of query complexity q corresponds to a *strategy* by Alice, meaning that Alice chooses from a distribution $\mathcal{A}$

strategy

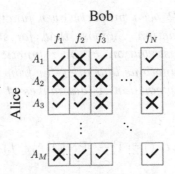

Fig. 2.1: A cross (resp., check) mark on the (i, j)-th entry indicate that the algorithm A_i on the function f_j errs (resp., does not err). The strategy of Alice (resp., Bob) is a distribution over algorithms (resp., functions), that is, that over rows (resp., columns).

supported on deterministic algorithms of query complexity q. Similarly, a distribution $\mathcal{F}$ over inputs f corresponds to a strategy by Bob. For every input provided by Bob, Alice either errs or doesn't. See Figure 2.1 for an illustration.

Now, the hypothesis of Yao's minimax principle can be stated this way: there exists a strategy $\mathcal{F}$ for Bob such that even if Alice can tailor her strategy $\mathcal{A}$ according to[1] $\mathcal{F}$, the probability that she errs is more than $1/3$. It is then intuitively obvious that if Alice has to come up with a strategy $\mathcal{A}$ without knowing $\mathcal{F}$, she can only fare worse. That is, for any randomized algorithm $\mathcal{A}$ making q queries, there is an input f such that $\Pr_{A \sim \mathcal{A}}[A \text{ errs on } f] > 1/3$, that is, no tester with query complexity q exists.

2.3.1 Useful Reformulations

Let $\mathcal{F}$ be a distribution such that $f \sim \mathcal{F}$ satisfies $\mathcal{P}$ with probability half and is ϵ-far from satisfying $\mathcal{P}$ with the complement probability half. We can reformulate Theorem 2.4 when $\mathcal{F}$ is of this form:

---

[1] Since Alice knows $\mathcal{F}$, her best strategy is to fix a deterministic algorithm A of query complexity q that minimizes the chance of her erring.

Theorem 2.5. *Let $\mathcal{P}$ be a property over functions and let $q \colon \mathbb{Z}_{>0} \times (0,1) \to \mathbb{Z}_{>0}$ be a function. Suppose that, for some $n \in \mathbb{Z}_{>0}$ and $\epsilon \in (0,1)$, there exist a distribution $\mathcal{F}_1$ over functions satisfying $\mathcal{P}$ and a distribution $\mathcal{F}_0$ over functions that are ϵ-far from satisfying $\mathcal{P}$ such that, for any deterministic algorithm A that makes at most $q(n, \epsilon)$ queries, it holds that*

$$\left| \Pr_{f \in \mathcal{F}_1} [A(n, \epsilon, f) = 1] - \Pr_{f \in \mathcal{F}_0} [A(n, \epsilon, f) = 1] \right| < \frac{1}{3}.$$

Then, the query complexity to test $\mathcal{P}$ on an error parameter ϵ and a function $f \colon [n] \to R$ is more than $q(n, \epsilon)$.

  Moreover, if we only consider non-adaptive/one-sided error algorithms in the assumption, then the lower bound applies to non-adaptive/one-sided error testing.

Proof. Let A be an arbitrary deterministic algorithm of query complexity at most $q(n, \epsilon)$. Let $p_1 = \Pr_{f \in \mathcal{F}_1}[A(n, \epsilon, f) = 1]$ and $p_0 = \Pr_{f \in \mathcal{F}_0}[A(n, \epsilon, f) = 1]$.

Let $\mathcal{F}$ be a distribution over functions in which we sample a function from $\mathcal{F}_1$ with probability half and sample a function from $\mathcal{F}_0$ with the complement probability half. Then, the probability that A errs is:

$$\frac{1}{2}(1 - p_1) + \frac{1}{2}p_0 = \frac{1}{2} - \frac{1}{2}(p_0 - p_1) \geq \frac{1}{2} - \frac{1}{2}|p_0 - p_1| > \frac{1}{3}.$$

Hence, $\mathcal{F}$ satisfies the assumption of Theorem 2.4, and we get the claim. $\square$

When designing distributions $\mathcal{F}_1$ and $\mathcal{F}_0$, it is convenient if we can add functions not satisfying $\mathcal{P}$ to $\mathcal{F}_1$ (with a small probability mass) and functions not ϵ-far from satisfying $\mathcal{P}$ to $\mathcal{F}_0$.

Corollary 2.1. *Let $\mathcal{P}$ be a property over functions and let $q \colon \mathbb{Z}_{>0} \times (0, 1) \to \mathbb{Z}_{>0}$ be a function. Suppose that, for some $n \in \mathbb{Z}_{>0}$ and $\epsilon, \eta_0, \eta_1, \eta_2 \in (0, 1)$, there exist distributions $\mathcal{F}_1$ and $\mathcal{F}_0$ over functions such that*

- *The probability that $f \sim \mathcal{F}_1$ satisfies $\mathcal{P}$ is at least $1 - \eta_1$.*
- *The probability that $f \sim \mathcal{F}_0$ is ϵ-far from satisfying $\mathcal{P}$ is at least $1 - \eta_0$.*
- *For every deterministic algorithm A that makes at most $q(n, \epsilon)$ queries to the input function, we have*

$$\left| \Pr_{f \in \mathcal{F}_1} [A(n, \epsilon, f) = 1] - \Pr_{f \in \mathcal{F}_0} [A(n, \epsilon, f) = 1] \right| \le \eta_2.$$

If $\eta_0 + \eta_1 + \eta_2 < 1/3$, then the query complexity of testing $\mathcal{P}$ on an error parameter ϵ and a function $f \colon [n] \to R$ is more than $q(n, \epsilon)$.

Moreover, if we only consider non-adaptive/one-sided error algorithms in the assumption, then the lower bound applies to non-adaptive/one-sided error testing.

Proof. Let $\mathcal{F}_1'$ (resp., $\mathcal{F}_0'$) denote the distribution of a function $f \sim \mathcal{F}_1$ (resp., $f \sim \mathcal{F}_0$), conditioned on that f satisfies $\mathcal{P}$ (resp., f is ϵ-far from satisfying $\mathcal{P}$). Then, we have:

$$\left| \Pr_{f \in \mathcal{F}_1'} [A(n, \epsilon, f) = 1] - \Pr_{f \in \mathcal{F}_0'} [A(n, \epsilon, f) = 1] \right|$$

$$\le \left| \Pr_{f \in \mathcal{F}_1} [A(n, \epsilon, f) = 1] - \Pr_{f \in \mathcal{F}_1'} [A(n, \epsilon, f) = 1] \right|$$

$$+ \left| \Pr_{f \in \mathcal{F}_0} [A(n, \epsilon, f) = 1] - \Pr_{f \in \mathcal{F}_0'} [A(n, \epsilon, f) = 1] \right|$$

$$+ \left| \Pr_{f \in \mathcal{F}_1} [A(n, \epsilon, f) = 1] - \Pr_{f \in \mathcal{F}_0} [A(n, \epsilon, f) = 1] \right|$$

$$= \eta_1 + \eta_0 + \eta_2 < \frac{1}{3}.$$

Hence, the claim holds by Theorem 2.5. $\qquad\qquad \square$

2.3.2 Applications

We see several applications of Yao's minimax principle.

Testing all-one strings

Let us start with a simple problem. Let $L_{\text{one}} = \{1^n : n \in \mathbb{Z}_{>0}\} \subseteq \{0,1\}^*$ be the language of all-one strings. We have the following lower bound for testing L_{one}.

Theorem 2.6. *Any tester for L_{one} requires $\Omega(\epsilon^{-1})$ queries.*

Proof. Fix $n \in \mathbb{Z}_{>0}$ and $\epsilon \in (0,1)$. For simplicity, we assume that ϵ^{-1} and ϵn are integers.

Let $\mathcal{F}_1$ be the distribution from which we always sample the string 1^n. We divide $[n]$ into ϵ^{-1} blocks each of which has size ϵn. For $i \in [\epsilon^{-1}]$, let s_i be the n-bit string obtained from 1^n by flipping the 1's in the i-th block to 0's. Then, let $\mathcal{F}_0$ be the uniform distribution over $s_1, \ldots, s_{\epsilon^{-1}}$.

Now, we check $\mathcal{F}_1$ and $\mathcal{F}_0$ satisfy the assumptions of Theorem 2.5. First, the unique string sampled from $\mathcal{F}_1$ satisfies L_{one}. Second, every string sampled from $\mathcal{F}_0$ is ϵ-far from L_{one}. To check the third condition, let A be a deterministic algorithm, which queries at most $o(\epsilon^{-1})$ indices. The algorithm A on the input $(n, \epsilon, 1^n)$ always obtains 1's from the query access, and let S be the set of queried indices along the way. Note that $|S| = o(\epsilon^{-1})$. Now, consider the behavior of the A on the input (n, ϵ, s_i). If S does not have an index in the i-th block, then A always obtains 1's from the query access, and it follows that $A(n, \epsilon, s_i) = A(n, \epsilon, 1^n)$. The probability that S has an index in the i-th block is at most:

$$1 - (1 - \epsilon)^{|S|} < \frac{1}{3}.$$

This means that:

$$\left| \Pr_{s \in \mathcal{F}_1} [A(n, \epsilon, s) = 1] - \Pr_{s \in \mathcal{F}_0} [A(n, \epsilon, s) = 1] \right| < \frac{1}{3}.$$

By Theorem 2.5, we get a lower bound of $\Omega(\epsilon^{-1})$. $\square$

Recalling that we can design a tester with $O(\epsilon^{-1})$ queries for L_{one} using Lemma 2.1, Theorem 2.6 implies that the bound with respect to ϵ is tight.

Testing Monotonicity on a Hypercube

monotonicity   We say that a function $f \colon \{0,1\}^n \to \{0,1\}$ is *monotone* if $f(x) \le f(y)$ whenever $x \le y$, that is, $x_i \le y_i$ for every $i \in [n]$. As another application of Yao's minimax lemma, we show a lower bound for testing monotonicity.

Theorem 2.7. *Every one-sided error non-adaptive tester for monotonicity of functions $f \colon \{0,1\}^n \to \{0,1\}$ requires $\Omega(\sqrt{n})$ queries.*

We say that a pair $(x, y) \in \{0, 1\}^n \times \{0, 1\}^n$ is a *violating pair* if $x \leq y$ and   *violating pair*
$f(x) > f(y)$. Furthermore, we say that it is a *violating edge* if $\|x\|_1 + 1 = \|y\|_1$.   *violating edge*
A one-sided error tester rejects a function f if and only if it detects a violating
pair (otherwise, we can make up a monotone function whose values match
on queried vectors).

For $i \in [n]$, we define a function $f_i \colon \{0, 1\}^n \to \{0, 1\}$ as follows:

$$f_i(x_1, \ldots, x_n) = \begin{cases} 1 & \text{if } \|x\|_1 > n/2 + \sqrt{n}, \\ 0 & \text{if } \|x\|_1 < n/2 - \sqrt{n}, \\ 1 - x_i & \text{otherwise.} \end{cases}$$

We say that a vector $x \in \{0, 1\}^n$ is in the *middle region* if $n/2 - \sqrt{n} \leq \|x\|_1 \leq$ *middle region*
$n/2 + \sqrt{n}$.

Consider an edge from:

$$x = (x_1, \ldots, x_{i-1}, 0, x_{i+1}, \ldots, x_n)$$

to

$$x' = (x_1, \ldots, x_{i-1}, 1, x_{i+1}, \ldots, x_n).$$

It is easy to verify that this edge is violating in f_i if (and only if) both x and x'
are in the middle region. As the set of vectors in the middle region amounts
to a constant fraction of the hypercube $\{0, 1\}^n$ (by Chernoff's bound), we
can take a set of ϵn violating edges that are disjoint to each other for some
constant $\epsilon > 0$. This means that each f_i's is ϵ-far from being monotone for
some $\epsilon > 0$.

Let $\mathcal{F}$ be the uniform distribution over f_i's. Then, the following lemma
combined with Yao's minimax principle immediately implies Theorem 2.7.

> **Lemma 2.4.** *Let A be a (deterministic) non-adaptive tester for mono-*
> *tonicity of functions $f \colon \{0, 1\}^n \to \{0, 1\}$ with query complexity q. Then,*
> *the probability that A detects a violating pair in a function sampled from*
> *$\mathcal{F}$ is at most $O(q/\sqrt{n})$.*

Proof. Let Q denote the set of queried vectors of size at most q in the middle
region. We may regard Q as a graph where two vectors $u, v \in Q$ are connected
by an edge if $u \leq v$, and let F be its arbitrary spanning forest. If the input
function is f_i and Q reveals a violation in f_i, then there must exist an edge
(u, v) in F such that $u_i = 0$ and $v_i = 1$. Recalling that $\|v\|_1 - \|u\|_1 \leq 2\sqrt{n}$ for
every edge (u, v) in F, the number of f_i's for which Q can reveals a violation
is at most:

$$|E(F)| \cdot 2\sqrt{n} \leq 2(q - 1)\sqrt{n} = O(q\sqrt{n}).$$

As the number of f_i's is n, the claim holds. $\qquad\square$

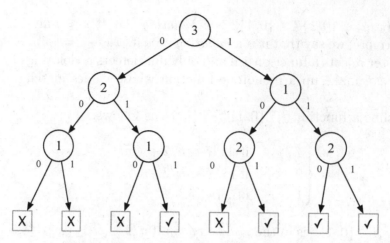

Fig. 2.2: Binary tree representing a tester for 3-bit strings in L_{maj}. The value on a node represents the index that the algorithm queries. The value on an arc represnet the answer from the query access. A cross (resp., check) mark represents that the algorithm will reject (resp., accept) upon reaching there.

Testing Majority

Let $L_{\mathrm{maj}} = \{x \in \{0,1\}^n : \sum_i x_i > n/2\}$. We have established in Exercise 2.1 that L_{maj} is testable using $O(\epsilon^{-2})$ queries. We will now prove that this bound is tight. Along the way, we will describe a framework for showing statistical indistinguishability that is useful in many other settings.

Theorem 2.8. *The query complexity of testing L_{maj} is $\Omega(\epsilon^{-2})$.*

Proof. Let P_1 be the distribution on $\{0,1\}$ defined by $P_1(1) = 1/2 + 2\epsilon$ and $P_1(0) = 1/2 - 2\epsilon$. Also, let P_0 be the distribution defined by $P_0(1) = 1/2 - 2\epsilon$ and $P_0(0) = 1/2 + 2\epsilon$. Let $\mathcal{F}_1 = P_1^n$ be the distribution on strings $x \in \{0,1\}^n$ obtained by setting each $x_i \sim P_1$ independently. Similarly, let $\mathcal{F}_0 = P_0^n$. Using Hoeffding's inequality (see Appendix A), when n is large enough, $x \sim \mathcal{F}_1$ satisfies L_{maj} with probability 0.99 and $x \sim \mathcal{F}_0$ is ϵ-far from satisfying L_{maj} with probability 0.99. So, in Corollary 2.1, we can set $\eta_1 = \eta_0 = 0.01$.

Let A be a deterministic tester for L_{maj} with query complexity q. It is intuitively clear that adaptivity does not help in distinguishing between $\mathcal{F}_1$ and $\mathcal{F}_0$. To see why, let us view A as a binary tree of depth at most q in which each node is labeled with a query in $[n]$, and depending on whether the answer to a node's query is 0 or 1, the next query is determined using the label of the left or right child respectively; see Figure 2.2. We can naturally associate to each leaf ℓ of the tree a pair of probabilities (p_1^ℓ, p_0^ℓ) corresponding to the probability that a random input from $\mathcal{F}_1$ and $\mathcal{F}_0$ respectively follows the path to ℓ. The success probability of the algorithm is entirely determined by these probabilities and the corresponding decision made by the algorithm. Now, because in both $\mathcal{F}_1$ and $\mathcal{F}_0$, each bit of the input is distributed identically, we can relabel the tree nodes so that each path is a prefix of the same sequence of queries $1, 2, \ldots, q$ without affecting the value of (p_1^ℓ, p_0^ℓ) for any leaf ℓ. The resulting algorithm is now non-adaptive and queries $x_1, \ldots, x_q$.

To apply Corollary 2.5, we need that no deterministic algorithm can distinguish between $(x_1, \ldots, x_q)$ when x is sampled from $\mathcal{F}_1$ versus $\mathcal{F}_0$ with probability more than $1/4$. Equivalently, we need that:

$$d_{\text{TV}}(P_1^q, P_0^q) = \max_{S \subseteq \{0,1\}^q} |P_1^q(S) - P_0^q(S)| < \frac{1}{4}$$

where S corresponds to the subset of inputs on which A accepts. It is tricky to get a handle on d_{TV} directly but we can bound it in terms of the *KL divergence*. Namely, we can use *Pinsker's inequality*:

KL divergence

Pinsker's inequality

> **Theorem 2.9** (Pinsker's inequality). *For any two distributions P and Q on finite domains,*
>
> $$d_{\text{TV}}(P, Q) \leq \sqrt{\frac{1}{2} d_{\text{KL}}(P \| Q)}$$

It remains to bound $d_{\text{KL}}(P_1^q \| P_0^q)$:

$$d_{\text{KL}}(P_1^q \| P_0^q) = \sum_{x_1, \ldots, x_q} P_1(x_1) \cdots P_1(x_q) \ln \frac{P_1(x_1) \cdots P_1(x_q)}{P_0(x_1) \cdots P_0(x_q)}$$

$$= \sum_{x_1, \ldots, x_q} P_1(x_1) \cdots P_1(x_q) \sum_{i=1}^{q} \ln \frac{P_1(x_i)}{P_0(x_i)}$$

$$= q \cdot \left(P_1(0) \ln \frac{P_1(0)}{P_0(0)} + P_1(1) \ln \frac{P_1(1)}{P_0(1)} \right)$$

$$= q \cdot \left(\left(\frac{1}{2} - 2\epsilon \right) \ln \frac{1/2 - 2\epsilon}{1/2 + 2\epsilon} + \left(\frac{1}{2} + 2\epsilon \right) \ln \frac{1/2 + 2\epsilon}{1/2 - 2\epsilon} \right)$$

$$= 4\epsilon q \ln \frac{1/2 + 2\epsilon}{1/2 - 2\epsilon}$$

$$\leq 4\epsilon q \cdot \frac{4\epsilon}{1/2 - 2\epsilon} \leq 64\epsilon^2 q,$$

where in the last line, we used the inequality $\ln(1 + x) \leq x$ and assumed $\epsilon \leq 1/8$. If $q < \epsilon^{-2}/512$, Pinsker's inequality implies $d_{\text{TV}}(P_1^q, P_0^q) < 1/4$, and hence, the conclusion of Corollary 2.5 follows. $\qquad\square$

2.4 Bibliographic Notes

The bound of Lemma 2.2 was shown to be tight with respect to both ϵ and δ in [113]. The argument in Lemma 2.3 was used in [300].

Theorem 2.4 suggests the methodology of proving lower bounds on the worst-case complexity of randomized algorithms by proving lower bounds on the average case complexity of deterministic algorithms. This methodology is often attributed to Yao [397], who exploited it to prove lower bounds on Boolean circuits and communication complexity. It was first applied to property testing by Goldreich, Goldwasser, and Ron [209]. Although it is not very important in property testing, Theorem 2.4 is merely one direction of Yao's minimax principle. The other direction states that if testing $\mathcal{P}$ requires a query complexity more than q, then there exists a distribution as in the assumption of Theorem 2.4. The proof requires von Neumann's minimax theorem from game theory and is more involved.

The notion of gap-preserving local reduction has been used implicitly in the literature and is formally introduced in [97] to show a lower bound for testing 3-colorability in the bounded-degree model. (See Section 5.6 for details.)

Problems

2.1. Show that if an array A of numbers is ϵ-far from having median μ, then the median of $O(\epsilon^{-2})$ random samples from A is not μ with high probability.

2.2. (a) Let $X_1, \ldots, X_n$ be a sequence of i.i.d. random variables, where each X_i is 1 with probability 2/3 and 0 with probability 1/3. Show that for $n = \Theta(\log \delta^{-1})$, a variable Y can be defined in terms of $X_1, \ldots, X_n$ that is 1 with probability $1 - \delta$ and 0 with probability δ.
(b) Let μ be an *unknown* real number. Suppose $X_1, \ldots, X_n$ are a sequence of i.i.d. random variables, where for each i, $|X_i - \mu| \leq \epsilon$ with probability 2/3 and $|X_i - \mu| > \epsilon$ with probability 1/3. Show that for $n = \Theta(\log \delta^{-1})$, a variable Y can be defined in terms of $X_1, \ldots, X_n$ such that $|Y - \mu| \leq \epsilon$ with probability $1 - \delta$ and $|Y - \mu| > \epsilon$ with probability δ.

2.3. Use Yao's minimax principle to show that testing monotonicity of functions $f : [n] \to \{0, 1\}$ requires $\Omega(\epsilon^{-1})$ queries.

2.4. Let $\mathcal{F}_1$ be the distribution on $\{0, 1\}^n$ where each coordinate is independently 1 with probability $\alpha(1 + \epsilon)$ and 0 with the rest. Similarly, let $\mathcal{F}_0$ be the distribution where each coordinate is independently 1 with probability $\alpha(1 - \epsilon)$. Show that any deterministic tester needs $\Omega(\alpha^{-1}\epsilon^{-2})$ queries to distinguish $\mathcal{F}_1$ and $\mathcal{F}_0$ with success probability 2/3. (**Hint:** Recall the technique used to lower bound the query complexity of L_{maj}.)

2.5. Prove that any one-sided error non-adaptive tester for monotonicity of functions $f\colon [n] \to \mathbb{R}$ requires $\Omega(\log n)$ queries even when ϵ is constant. (**Hint:** Construct a family of $t = O(\log n)$ functions $f_1, \ldots, f_t\colon [n] \to \mathbb{R}$ such that for any $x, y \in [n]$ with $x < y$, there exists exactly one $i \in [t]$ satisfying $f_i(x) > f_i(y)$.)

2.6. In this problem, you will argue probabilistically that there exists a property requiring $\Omega(n)$ queries to test.

(a) Suppose $\mathcal{P}$ is a family of $2^{n/10}$ many functions $f\colon [n] \to \{0, 1\}$. Let $\mathcal{F}_1$ be a random function from $\mathcal{P}$, and $\mathcal{F}_0$ be a random function from the set of all functions $f\colon [n] \to \{0, 1\}$. Show using Chernoff's bound that $f \sim \mathcal{F}_0$ is $1/8$-far from $\mathcal{P}$ with probability at least $99/100$.

(b) Let $q = n/100$, and $\delta = 2^{-2^{n/30}}$. Show that if $\mathcal{P}$ is a random family of $2^{n/10}$ functions, with probability at least $1 - \delta$ over the choice of $\mathcal{P}$, for any fixed set T of inputs of size at most q, the total variation distance between the distributions $(f(x)\colon x \in T)_{f \sim \mathcal{F}_1}$ and $(f(x)\colon x \in T)_{f \sim \mathcal{F}_0}$ is less than $1/4$.

(c) Show that if $\mathcal{P}$ is a random family of $2^{n/10}$ functions, with probability at least $1 - 2^q \delta$ over the choice of $\mathcal{P}$, for any fixed deterministic adaptive tester A of query complexity q:

$$\left| \Pr_{f \sim \mathcal{F}_1}[A(f) = 1] - \Pr_{f \sim \mathcal{F}_0}[A(f) = 1] \right| < \frac{1}{4}$$

(d) Show that if $\mathcal{P}$ is a random family of $2^{n/10}$ functions, with probability at least $1 - n^{2^q} 2^q \delta > 0$ over the choice of $\mathcal{P}$, no deterministic adaptive tester of query complexity q distinguishes between $\mathcal{F}_1$ and $\mathcal{F}_0$ with probability $> 1/4$. Finish the argument that there exists a property $\mathcal{P}$ that requires $\Omega(n)$ queries to test.

2.7. Show that there exist two properties $\mathcal{P} = \{\mathcal{P}_n\}_{n \in \mathbb{Z}_{>0}}$ and $\mathcal{P}' = \{\mathcal{P}'_n\}_{n \in \mathbb{Z}_{>0}}$ of functions $f\colon [n] \to \{0, 1\}$ that are both trivially testable (by the algorithm that always accepts, provided n is large enough as a function of ϵ^{-1}), whereas the property $\mathcal{P}'' = \{\mathcal{P}_n \cap \mathcal{P}'_n\}_{n \in \mathbb{Z}_{>0}}$ is not testable with $o(n)$ queries. (**Hint:** Use the property shown in Problem 2.6.)

2.8. Show that there exists a property $\mathcal{P} = \{\mathcal{P}_n\}_{n \in \mathbb{Z}_{>0}}$ of functions $f\colon [n] \to \{0, 1\}$ such that $\mathcal{P}$ is trivially testable (by an algorithm that always accepts, provided n is large enough as a function of ϵ^{-1}) whereas $\overline{\mathcal{P}} = \{\overline{\mathcal{P}}_n\}$ is not testable with $o(n)$ queries. (**Hint:** Show that in constructing the property in Problem 2.6, you can additionally ensure that every $f \in \mathcal{P}$ is $\exp(-n)$-close to a function $g \notin \mathcal{P}$.)

Part II

Chapter 3
Strings

We start our detailed study of property testing with strings, because their analysis is mostly accessible using only elementary techniques. First, we introduce basic operations on strings and then define the testing model for string properties in Section 3.1. We show that the property of being a palindrome, that is, a string that reads the same forward and backward, is constant-query testable with one-sided error in Section 3.2. Then, we show that the property of being the concatenation of two palindromes is one-sided error testable with $\widetilde{O}(\sqrt{n})$ queries in Section 3.3. We see that the property of belonging to the Dyck language, a language consisting of matched parentheses, is constant-query testable with two-sided error in Section 3.4. The monotonicity we have studied in Section 1 can be seen as a property a string if there is a total ordering over the characters in the string. We discuss non-adaptive testers for monotonicity and its generalization in Section 3.5.

Our goal in this chapter is to give a flavor of techniques used in testing string properties. There has been work in building an overarching theory that relates the query complexity of string properties to other characterizations (e.g., whether the property can be recognized by a finite automaton or by a context-free grammar). See the bibliographic notes (Section 3.6) of this chapter for pointers to such work.

3.1 Model

Before describing the testing model, we first introduce some operations on strings. Let Σ be a set of characters. For a string $s \in \Sigma^n$ and an index $i \in [n]$, $s[i] \in \Sigma$ denotes the i-th character of s. For a string $s \in \Sigma^n$ and indices $i, j \in [n]$ with $i \leq j$, let $s[i, j] \in \Sigma^{j-i+1}$ denote the substring of s obtained by taking from the i-th character to the j-th character (inclusively). Similarly, for a string $s \in \Sigma^n$ and a set of indices $I \subseteq [n]$, let $s[I] \in \Sigma^{|I|}$ denote the subsequence obtained from s by taking $s[i]$ for each $i \in I$, preserving the order. For a string $s \in \Sigma^n$, $s^R \in \Sigma^n$ denotes its reversed strings, that is, $s^R[i] = s[n - i + 1]$ for $i \in [n]$. For two strings $s, t \in \Sigma^*$, st denotes the string obtained by concatenating s and t in this order.

language

Let Σ be a set of characters and $L \subseteq \Sigma^*$ be a *language*. Then, the most basic question about strings is whether the given string $s \in \Sigma^n$ belongs to L. In order to put this problem into the testing framework, let us consider the following scenario. We know the length n of the input string s. Also, we are given query access to s, that is, we can obtain the character $s[i] \in \Sigma$ by specifying the index $i \in [n]$. For the distance measure, we use the Hamming distance: For two strings $s, t \in \Sigma^n$ of the same length, the Hamming distance denoted by $d_{\mathrm{H}}(s, t)$ is defined as:

$$d_{\mathrm{H}}(s, t) = |\{i \in [n] : s[i] \neq t[i]\}|.$$

ϵ-farness

tester

Then, we define the Hamming distance of a string $s \in \Sigma^n$ and a language $L \subseteq \Sigma^*$, denoted by $d_{\mathrm{H}}(s, L)$, as $\min_{t \in L \cap \Sigma^n} d_{\mathrm{H}}(s, t)$. For $\epsilon \in (0, 1)$, we say that $s \in \Sigma^n$ is ϵ-*far* from L if $d_{\mathrm{H}}(s, L) > \epsilon n$. For a language $L \subseteq \Sigma^*$, we say that an algorithm is a *tester for (the property of belonging to)* L if, given $n \in \mathbb{Z}_{>0}$, $\epsilon \in (0, 1)$, and query access to a string $s \in \Sigma^n$, it accepts with probability at least $2/3$ if $s \in L$ and rejects with probability at least $2/3$ if s is ϵ-far from L.

3.2 Palindromes

palindrome

For $n \in \mathbb{Z}_{>0}$, we say that a string s is a *palindrome* if it reads the same backward or forward. For example:

"civic", "madam", "noon", "radar", and "redder"

are palindromes whereas:

"property", "testing", and "palindrome"

are not.

In this section, we show that palindromes are constant-query testable with one-sided error. For mathematical simplicity, we restrict our attention to palindromes of even lengths. Namely, we define:

$$L_{\mathrm{Pal}} = \{s \in \Sigma^* : \exists w \in \Sigma^*, s = ww^R\},$$

and design a tester for L_{Pal}. However, it is easy to extend the tester and its analysis to all palindromes (Exercise 3.1).

violating index

For a string $s \in \Sigma^n$ (of an even length), we say that an index $i \in [n/2]$ is *violating* if $s[i] \neq s[n - i + 1]$. The following proposition is immediate.

Proposition 3.1. *A string $s \in \Sigma^n$ is a palindrome if and only if there is no violating index.*

Our strategy is checking this condition in a small part of the input string. That is, we sample a constant number of indices in $[n/2]$, and check whether there is a violating index or not (by querying s). We immediately reject when a violating index is found, and accept when all the sampled indices are not violating. The details are given below.

Algorithm 3.1 Tester for L_{Pal}

Input: An even integer n, $\epsilon \in (0,1)$, and query access to a string $s \in \Sigma^n$.
1: **for** $q := \Theta(\epsilon^{-1})$ times **do**
2:     Sample i from $[n/2]$ uniformly at random.
3:     **if** $s[i] \neq s[n - i + 1]$ **then**
4:         Reject.
5:     **end if**
6: **end for**
7: Accept.

Theorem 3.1. *Algorithm 3.1 is a one-sided error tester for L_{Pal} with $O(\epsilon^{-1})$ queries.*

Proof. The query complexity of Algorithm 3.1 is clearly $2q = O(\epsilon^{-1})$. Also, it never rejects palindromes, and hence it is a one-sided error tester.

Now we show that for any string $s \in \Sigma^n$ that is ϵ-far from L_{Pal}, the tester rejects with probability at least $2/3$. Let:

$$S = \big\{ i \in [n/2] : s[i] \neq s[n - i + 1] \big\}$$

be the set of violating indices. Then, we observe that $|S| > \epsilon n$. Otherwise, we can obtain a palindrome by replacing $s[n - i + 1]$ with $s[i]$ for each $i \in S$, which results in at most $|S| \leq \epsilon n$ changes, contradicting the ϵ-farness of s.

Note that the tester rejects s if and only if it samples a violating index $i \in S$. Then, we apply Lemma 2.1 on a function $f \colon [n/2] \to \{0,1\}$ defined as $f(i) = 1$ if and only if $i \in S$. Then, the probability that we do not hit any index $i \in [n/2]$ with $f(i) = 1$ can be made at most $1/3$ by choosing the hidden constant in q large enough. This means that the probability that we miss violating indices is at most $1/3$. $\qquad\square$

The key points of this proof can be summarized as follows:

- There are many witnesses of not being a palindrome, that is, violating indices, in a string that is ϵ-far from palindromes.
- We can easily find a witness if there are many witnesses in a string.

The second point almost automatically holds no matter how we define a witness as long as each witness is of a constant size. To ensure the first point, however, we need to define a witness carefully. The definition of a violating index is helpful because we can fix a violating index independently of other violating indices. Because of this feature, we have at least ϵn violating indices in a string that is ϵ-far from palindromes.

Exercise 3.1. Extend Algorithm 3.1 so that it can handle strings of odd lengths.

Remark 3.1. Let $\overline{L}_{\mathrm{Pal}}$ be the complement of L_{Pal}, that is,

$$\overline{L}_{\mathrm{Pal}} = \{s \in \Sigma^* : \forall w \in \Sigma^*, s \neq ww^R\}.$$

The question of testing $\overline{L}_{\mathrm{Pal}}$ is natural but is almost nonsense. This is because, for any string $s \in \Sigma^n$, we can get a string in $\overline{L}_{\mathrm{Pal}}$ by changing only one character of s. This means that s is always $1/n$-close to $\overline{L}_{\mathrm{Pal}}$. In particular, when $\epsilon \geq 1/n$, we can always accept the input string as every string is ϵ-close to $\overline{L}_{\mathrm{Pal}}$. Then, we can test $\overline{L}_{\mathrm{Pal}}$ as follows:

- If $n < \epsilon^{-1}$, then we (correctly) decide whether $s \in \overline{L}_{\mathrm{Pal}}$ by running a standard linear-time algorithm on s;
- Otherwise, we always accept.

We can verify this algorithm is a valid tester with query complexity $O(\epsilon^{-1})$.

This example shows that to make a testing problem meaningful, we need to ensure that, for any constant $\epsilon > 0$ and (infinitely many) $n \in \mathbb{Z}_{>0}$, there exists a string of length n that is ϵ-far from satisfying the considered property.

3.3 Two Palindromes

Let $L_{\mathrm{Rev}} = \{uu^R vv^R : u, v \in \Sigma^*\}$ denote the set of strings that consists of two (even-length) palindromes. Compared to palindromes, testing L_{Rev} is more involved. In this section, we show an upper bound of $O(\epsilon^{-1}\sqrt{n}\log n)$ in Section 3.3.1 and an almost matching lower bound of $\Omega(\sqrt{n})$ in Section 3.3.2.

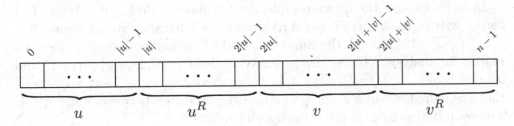

Fig. 3.1: Configuration of u and v in a string in L_{Rev}. The pairs $(0, 2|u| - 1)$, $(|u| - 1, |u|)$, $(2|u|, n - 1)$, and $(2|u| + |v| - 1, 2|u| + |v|)$ are paired.

3.3.1 Upper Bound

If the input string has an odd length, then we can immediately reject. Hence in what follows, we assume that the input length n is even. Also, it is convenient that a string $s \in \Sigma^n$ is indexed as $s[0], \ldots, s[n - 1]$ instead of $s[1], \ldots, s[n]$.

Suppose $s \in L_{\text{Rev}}$ can be written as $s = uu^R vv^R$. We say that indices $i, j \in \{0, \ldots, n - 1\}$ are *paired* in s if $i + j = 2|u| - 1 \pmod{n}$. In other words, if i and j are either in symmetric positions with respect to uu^R, or with respect to vv^R (see Figure 3.1). We note that i and j are always distinct because $i + j$ is odd. A crucial fact for designing a tester for two palindromes is the following:

paired indices

Proposition 3.2. *Let $s \in L_{\text{Rev}}$ and (i, j) be paired indices with respect to s. Then, for every $p \in \mathbb{Z}_{\geq 0}$, we have $s[(i - p) \bmod n] = s[(j + p) \bmod n]$.*

For a set of offsets $P = \{p_1, \ldots, p_m\}$, we define the *backward pattern* of an index i with respect to P as the subsequence $s[(i - p_1) \bmod n], \ldots, s[(i - p_m) \bmod n]$ and the *forward pattern* of an index j with respect to P as the subsequence $s[(i + p_1) \bmod n], \ldots, s[(i + p_m) \bmod n]$. From Proposition 3.2, we immediately have the following.

backward pattern

forward pattern

Corollary 3.1. *Let $s \in L_{\text{Rev}}$ and (i, j) be paired indices in s. The backward pattern of i and the forward pattern of j both with respect to P are identical for any choice of P.*

Our algorithm exploits Corollary 3.1: it first finds paired indices (i, j) and then checks whether the forward pattern of i and the backward pattern of j are identical for sufficiently large P. However, as we do not know the value of $2|u| - 1 \pmod{n}$ beforehand, it is not trivial to find paired indices. Regarding that $2|u| - 1 \pmod{n}$ ranges between 1 and $n - 1$, the simplest way of finding paired indices is fixing $i = 0$ and enumerating j from 1 to $n - 1$. However, this method requires $O(n)$ queries.

In order to save the query complexity, we observe that $2|u| - 1 \pmod{n}$ can be written as $a\lceil\sqrt{n}\rceil + b \pmod{n}$ (where not both are zeros), for some $0 \le a, b \le \lceil\sqrt{n}\rceil - 1$. (Though the choice of a and b may not be unique, it does not matter for analysis.) To use this property, we let $I = \{0, 1, \ldots, \lceil\sqrt{n}\rceil - 1\}$ and $J = \{0, \lceil\sqrt{n}\rceil, \ldots, \lceil\sqrt{n}\rceil(\lceil\sqrt{n}\rceil - 1)\}$. Then, there exists $a \in I$ and $b\lceil\sqrt{n}\rceil \in J$ that are paired because $a + b\lceil\sqrt{n}\rceil$ runs over all values between 1 and $n - 1$. The overall algorithm is given in Algorithm 3.2.

Algorithm 3.2

Input: An even integer $n \in \mathbb{Z}_{>0}$, $\epsilon \in (0, 1)$, and query access to a string $s \in \Sigma^n$.
1: Pick a set $P = \{p_1, \ldots, p_m\}$ of indices uniformly at random from $\{0, \ldots, n - 1\}$, where $m = \Theta(\epsilon^{-1} \log n)$.
2: $I := \{0, 1, \ldots, \lceil\sqrt{n}\rceil - 1\}$.
3: $J := \{0, \lceil\sqrt{n}\rceil, \ldots, \lceil\sqrt{n}\rceil(\lceil\sqrt{n}\rceil - 1)\}$.
4: **if** there exists a pair $i \in I$ and $j \in J$ (where not both are zeros) such that the backward pattern of i and the forward pattern of j both with respect to P are the same **then**
5:　　Accept.
6: **else**
7:　　Reject.
8: **end if**

To show that Algorithm 3.2 rejects strings that are ϵ-far from L_{Rev}, we introduce the notion of a compatible pair. We say that a pair of indices (i, j) is an $(1 - \epsilon)$-*compatible pair* with respect to s if $(i + j) \bmod n$ is odd, and if $s[(i - p) \bmod n] = s[(j + p) \bmod n]$ for more than a $(1 - \epsilon)$-fraction of the indices $p \in \{0, \ldots, n - 1\}$. The following lemma says that we can construct a string in L_{Rev} by a small number of changes if there is $(1 - \epsilon)$-compatible pair:

> **Lemma 3.1.** *If there exists a $(1 - \epsilon)$-compatible pair (i, j) with respect to s, then s is ϵ-close to L_{Rev}.*

Proof. Let $\ell_u = \lfloor(i + j \bmod n)/2\rfloor$ and $\ell_v = (n - 2\ell_u)/2$. Then, let $u = s[0, \ell_u - 1]$ and $v = s[2\ell_u, 2\ell_u + \ell_v - 1]$. It is immediate that s is ϵ-close to $uu^R vv^R$. □

Now we analyze Algorithm 3.2.

> **Theorem 3.2.** *Algorithm 3.2 is a one-sided error tester for L_{Rev} with query complexity $O(\epsilon^{-1}\sqrt{n}\log n)$.*

Proof. We first show that Algorithm 3.2 always accepts if $s \in L_{\text{Rev}}$. Let $s = uu^R vv^R$. By our selection of I and J, there must exist $i \in I$ and $j \in J$ that are paired in s. For such i and j, the tester accepts s.

compatible pair

Next, we show that Algorithm 3.2 rejects with probability at least 2/3 if s is ϵ-far from L_{Rev}. By Lemma 3.1, there is no $(1 - \epsilon)$-compatible pair in s. It follows that for every fixed pair $i \in I$ and $j \in J$ (that are necessarily not compatible), the probability that the backward pattern of i is identical to the forward pattern of j is at most:

$$(1 - \epsilon)^m < \frac{1}{3|I||J|}.$$

by setting the hidden constant in m to be large enough. Applying the union bound, the probability that the test accepts s by mistake is smaller than 1/3.

The query complexity is $O(|I|m + |J|m) = O(\epsilon^{-1}\sqrt{n}\log n)$. $\qed$

Compared to the palindrome case, a tricky part was guaranteeing that we do not reject strings in L_{Rev}. To this end, we needed to find paired indices (i, j) and this part took $O(\sqrt{n})$ queries. Rejecting strings that are ϵ-far from L_{Rev} was rather easy because any pair (i, j) is non-compatible and we can easily find a witness offset p such that $s[(i - p) \bmod n] \neq s[(j + p) \bmod n]$.

3.3.2 Lower Bound

In this section, we show a lower bound almost matches Theorem 3.2:

Theorem 3.3. *Any tester for* L_{Rev} *requires* $\Omega(\sqrt{n})$ *queries.*

We consider the case that n is divisible by 6 and $\Sigma = \{0, 1\}$. We say that a string is *positive* if it belongs to L_{Rev} and is *negative* if it is ϵ-far from L_{Rev}. We define two distributions $\mathcal{D}_1$ and $\mathcal{D}_0$ consisting of positive and negative strings, respectively. A positive string in $\mathcal{D}_1$ is chosen by picking uniformly at random an integer k in the interval $[n/6 + 1, n/3]$ and then by selecting a positive string uniformly among strings $uu^R vv^R$ with $|u| = k$. A negative string in $\mathcal{D}_0$ is chosen uniformly at random from among all negative strings.

Let A be a deterministic tester for L_{Rev}. To apply Yao's minimax principle (Theorem 2.5), we show that, if its maximum number of queries is $d = o(\sqrt{n})$, then the difference between the probability that A accepts on a string sampled from $\mathcal{D}_1$ and that on a string sampled from $\mathcal{D}_0$ is less than 1/3.

We can view A as a binary decision tree, where each node represents a query to a certain place, and the two outgoing edges, labeled with 0 or 1, represent possible answers. Each leaf represents the end of a possible computation and is labeled "accept" or "reject" according to the decision of the algorithm. Tracing the path from the root to a node of A, we can associate with each node t of A a pair (Q_t, f_t), where $Q_t \subseteq [n]$ is a set of queries to the input string, and $f_t : Q_t \to \{0, 1\}$ is a vector of answers received by the

positivity/negativity

algorithm. We may obviously assume that A is a full binary tree of height d and has thus 2^d leaves. Then $|Q_t| = d$ for each leaf t of A.

We will use the following notation. For a subset $Q \subseteq [n]$ and a function $f : Q \to \{0, 1\}$, let:

$$E_0(Q, f) = \left\{ s \in \{0, 1\}^n : d_H(s, L_{\text{Rev}}) > \epsilon n, s \text{ coincides with } f \text{ on } Q \right\},$$
$$E_1(Q, f) = \left\{ s \in \{0, 1\}^n \cap L_{\text{Rev}} : s \text{ coincides with } f \text{ on } Q \right\},$$

that is, $E_0(Q, f)$ (resp., $E_1(Q, f)$) is the set of all negative (resp., positive) strings of length n consistent with the pair (Q, f). Also, for a probability distribution $\mathcal{D}$ over binary strings of length n and a subset $E \subseteq \{0, 1\}^n$, we define $\mu_{\mathcal{D}}(E) = \sum_{s \in E} \Pr_{s \sim \mathcal{D}}[s \in E]$.

The theorem follows from the following two lemmas.

Lemma 3.2. *For every subset $Q \subseteq [n]$ of size $o(n)$ and function $f : Q \to \{0, 1\}$,*

$$\mu_{\mathcal{D}_0}(E_0(Q, f)) \geq \left(1 - o(1)\right) 2^{-|Q|}.$$

Proof. We first note that L_{Rev} has at most $2^{n/2} n/2$ strings of length n. (First choose a string of length $n/2$, and then cut it into two parts u and v, thus getting a string $s = uu^R vv^R \in L_{\text{Rev}}$.) Therefore, the number of strings of length n at a distance at most ϵn from L_{Rev} is at most

$$|L_{\text{Rev}} \cap \{0, 1\}^n| \cdot \sum_{i=0}^{\epsilon n} \binom{n}{i} \leq \frac{2^{n/2} n}{2} \cdot \left(\frac{en}{\epsilon n}\right)^{\epsilon n} \leq 2^{n/2 + 2\epsilon \log \epsilon^{-1} \cdot n},$$

where the first inequality used the fact $\sum_{i=0}^{k} \binom{n}{i} \leq (en/k)^k$. We mean by $s[Q] = f$ that $s[i] = f(i)$ for every $i \in Q$. We get:

$$|E_0(Q, f)| \geq \left|\left\{ s \in \{0, 1\}^n : s[Q] = f \right\}\right| - \left|\left\{ s \in \{0, 1\}^n : d_H(s, L_{\text{Rev}}) < \epsilon n \right\}\right|$$
$$\geq 2^{n - |Q|} - 2^{n/2 + 2\epsilon \log \epsilon^{-1} \cdot n} = (1 - o(1)) 2^{n - |Q|}.$$

Then, we have:

$$\mu_{\mathcal{D}_0}(E_0(Q, f)) \geq \frac{|E_0(Q, f)|}{2^n} \geq \left(1 - o(1)\right) 2^{-|Q|}. \qquad \square$$

Lemma 3.3. *For every subset $Q \subseteq [n]$ of cardinality $o(\sqrt{n})$ and function $f : Q \to \{0, 1\}$,*

$$\mu_{\mathcal{D}_1}(E_1(Q, f)) \geq \left(1 - o(1)\right) 2^{-|Q|}.$$

Proof. From the definition of the distribution $\mathcal{D}_1$, for a string $s \in L_{\text{Rev}} \cap \{0, 1\}^n$, we have:

$$\mu_{\mathcal{D}_1}(\{s\}) = \frac{\left|\left\{s = uu^R vv^R : |u| = k, \frac{n}{6} + 1 \le k \le \frac{n}{3}\right\}\right|}{\frac{n}{6} 2^{n/2}}.$$

Then, we have:

$$\mu_{\mathcal{D}_1}(E_1(Q, f)) = \frac{1}{\frac{n}{6} 2^{n/2}} \sum_{k=n/6+1}^{n/3} \left|\left\{s \in \{0,1\}^n : s[Q] = f, s = uu^R vv^R, |u| = k\right\}\right|.$$

Now observe that, for each of the $\binom{d}{2}$ pairs of indices in Q, there are at most two choices of k for which the pair is symmetric with respect to k or to $n/2 + k$. This implies that for $n/6 - 2\binom{d}{2} = (1 - o(1))n/6$ choices of k, the set Q does not contain a pair symmetric with respect to k or $n/2 + k$. For each such k, we have:

$$\left|\left\{s \in \{0,1\}^n : s[Q] = f, s = uu^R vv^R, |u| = k\right\}\right| = 2^{n/2 - |Q|}.$$

Therefore:

$$\mu_{\mathcal{D}_1}(E_1(Q, f)) \ge \frac{(1 - o(1))\frac{n}{6} 2^{n/2 - |Q|}}{\frac{n}{6} 2^{n/2}} = (1 - o(1))2^{-|Q|}. \qquad \square$$

Proof of Theorem 3.3. Let T_0 and T_1 be the sets of all leaves of A labeled "reject" and "accept", respectively. By Lemmas 3.2 and 3.3, we have:

$$\left| \Pr_{s \sim \mathcal{D}_1}[A \text{ accepts on } s] - \Pr_{s \sim \mathcal{D}_0}[A \text{ accepts on } s] \right|$$

$$= \left| \sum_{t \in T_1} \mu_{\mathcal{D}_1}(E_1(Q_t, f_t)) - \sum_{t \in T_1} \mu_{\mathcal{D}_0}(E_0(Q_t, f_t)) \right|$$

$$= \left| \sum_{t \in T_1} \mu_{\mathcal{D}_1}(E_1(Q_t, f_t)) + \sum_{t \in T_0} \mu_{\mathcal{D}_0}(E_0(Q_t, f_t)) - 1 \right|$$

$$\le \left| (|T_1| + |T_0|)(1 - o(1))2^{-d} - 1 \right| = o(1).$$

Hence, the claim holds. $\qquad \square$

3.4 The Dyck Language

The *Dyck language* is a language that consists of perfectly matched parentheses. For example, "()()" and "(()())" are strings in the Dyck Language while ")()" and "(())(" are not. Formally, the Dyck Language is defined by the following context-free grammar:

Dyck language

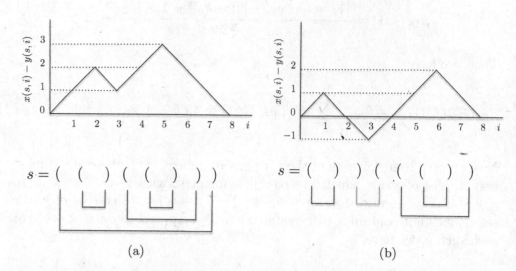

Fig. 3.2: Function $x(s,i) - y(s,i)$ and matchings. The red pair in (b) violates the condition of a proper matching.

$$S \to (S)$$
$$S \to SS$$
$$S \to \gamma,$$

where γ denotes the empty string. In this section, we show that the Dyck language is constant-query testable with two-sided error whereas any one-sided error tester requires $\Omega(n)$ queries. When a string belongs to the Dyck language, we just say that the string is *Dyck*. Also, we define L_{Dyck} as the Dyck language.

Dyck

3.4.1 Two-sided Error Constant-Query Tester

We can immediately reject the input string s if its length n is odd. Hence, in what follows, we assume that n is even. For notational simplicity, we identify the characters '(' and ')' with the digits 0 and 1, respectively. For $i \in [n]$, we denote by $x(s,i)$ and $y(s,i)$ the number of 0's and 1's, respectively, in the substring $s[1,i]$. (Here, we again use the convention that $s \in \{0,1\}^n$ is indexed as $s[1], \ldots, s[n]$.)

The function $x(s,i) - y(s,i)$ is drawn for two strings, one being Dyck (Figure 3.2a) and the other being non-Dyck (Figure 3.2b). From the figure, it is almost immediate that the condition of belonging to the Dyck language can be restated as follows:

Proposition 3.3. *A string $s \in \{0,1\}^n$ is Dyck if and only if the following two conditions hold:*

(a) $x(s,i) \geq y(s,i)$ for every $i \in [n]$.
(b) $x(s,n) = y(s,n)$.

Exercise 3.2. Prove Proposition 3.3.

---

matching
properness

A *matching* in a string $s \in \Sigma^n$ of even length is a partition of $[n]$ into pairwise disjoint pairs. We say that a matching is *proper* if, in each pair of the matching, the left character is 0 and the right character is 1.

Examples of matchings are depicted in Figure 3.2. The matching for the Dyck string in Figure 3.2a is proper whereas the matching for the other non-Dyck string in Figure 3.2b is improper. This is not a coincidence, and we can further restate Proposition 3.3 as follows.

Corollary 3.2. *A string $s \in \{0,1\}^n$ is Dyck if and only if there is a proper matching of size $n/2$.*

Proof. If s is Dyck, by pairing matched parenthesis, we can obtain the desired matching.

Suppose there is a proper matching. Let $i \in [n]$ be an arbitrary index. Then, for any pair in the matching, only the left character or both the characters lie in the substring $s[1,i]$. This means that $s[1,i]$ have more 0's than 1's, and condition (a) of Proposition 3.3 is satisfied. Condition (b) of Proposition 3.3 is also satisfied because each pair in the matching has one 0 and one 1. Hence, s is Dyck. □

Proposition 3.3 uses $x(s,i)$ and $y(s,i)$ for characterizing Dyck strings, that is, strings that have the distance 0 to the Dyck language. Indeed, we can use $x(s,i)$ and $y(s,i)$ for estimating the distance to the Dyck language.

Hall's theorem
matching

Before stating the relations, we need to introduce *Hall's theorem* from graph theory. For a bipartite graph (U, V, E), a *matching* is a set of disjoint edges. More formally, a set of edges $\{(u_1, v_1), \dots, (u_m, v_m)\}$, where $u_i \in U$ and $v_i \in V$ for $i \in [m]$, is called a matching if $(u_i, v_i) \in E$ for each $i \in [m]$, $u_i \neq u_j$ for every $i \neq j$, and $v_i \neq v_j$ for every $i \neq j$. For $S \subseteq V$, let $\Gamma(S) \subseteq U$ be the set of neighbors of vertices in S. Then, we have the following.

Theorem 3.4 (Defect form of Hall's theorem). *Let (U, V, E) be a bipartite graph. If there exists $\ell \in \mathbb{Z}_{\geq 0}$ such that $|\Gamma(S)| \geq |S| - \ell$ holds for any $S \subseteq V$, then there is a matching of size $|V| - \ell$.*

We can obtain an upper bound on $d_H(s, L_{Dyck})$ using $x(s,i)$ and $y(s,i)$:

Lemma 3.4. *If a string $s \in \{0,1\}^n$ satisfies*

(a) $y(s,i) - x(s,i) \le d_1$ *for every $i \in [n]$ and*
(b) $x(s,n) - y(s,n) \le d_2$,

then $d_H(s, L_{Dyck}) \le d_1 + d_2/2 + 2$.

Proof. Consider the bipartite graph (U, V, E), where:

$$U = \{i \in [n] : s[i] = 0\},$$
$$V = \{i \in [n] : s[i] = 1\},$$
$$E = \{(i,j) \in U \times V : i < j\}.$$

Note that for any subset $S \subseteq V$, we have:

$$
\begin{aligned}
|\Gamma(S)| = |\{i \in [n] : s[i] = 0 \wedge i < \max S\}| \quad &(\max S := \max\{v \in S\}) \\
= x(s, \max S - 1) \\
= x(s, \max S) \\
\ge y(s, \max S) - d_1 \\
= |S| - d_1,
\end{aligned}
$$

where the third equality holds because $s[\max S] = 1$ and the inequality is due to assumption (a). By Theorem 3.4, G contains a proper matching of size at least $y(s,n) - d_1$. By assumption (b) and the fact that $x(s,n) + y(s,n) = n$, we have $y(s,n) \ge n/2 - d_2/2$. Therefore, there is a proper matching of size at least $n/2 - d_2/2 - d_1$ in s. Let us pair the remaining elements of s arbitrarily, where all pairs but at most one consist of either two 0's or two 1's. By changing, when needed, the left entry of each such pair to 0 and its right entry to 1 we obtain a Dyck string. The total number of changes is at most $n/2 - (n/2 - d_2/2 - d_1) + 2 = d_1 + d_2/2 + 2$, which means that $d_H(s, L_{Dyck}) \le d_1 + d_2/2 + 2$. $\square$

We can also obtain lower bounds of $d_H(s, L_{Dyck})$ using $x(s,i)$ and $y(s,i)$:

Proposition 3.4. *The following hold:*

(a)   *If $y(s,i) - x(s,i) \ge d$ for some $i \in [n]$, then $d_H(s, L_{Dyck}) \ge d/2$.*
(b)   *If $x(s,n) - y(s,n) \ge d$, then $d_H(s, L_{Dyck}) \ge d/2$.*

Proof. By observing that the absolute value of $y(s,i) - x(s,i)$ change by at most two by flipping a character in s, the claim immediately follows from Proposition 3.3. $\square$

In order to test L_{Dyck}, we sample a subsequence $\tilde{s}$ of constant length from s, and then test whether $\tilde{s}$ is close to being Dyck by using $d_H(\tilde{s}, L_{Dyck})$. Note that $d_H(\tilde{s}, L_{Dyck})$ is computable in $O(|\tilde{s}|^3)$ time by dynamic programming.

To formalize the idea, we set:

$$\ell = \frac{C \log \epsilon^{-1}}{\epsilon^2}, \qquad \Delta = \frac{C \log \epsilon^{-1}}{\epsilon}, \qquad \text{and} \qquad p = \frac{\ell}{n},$$

where $C > 0$ is a sufficiently large constant, whose value will be determined later. The algorithm for testing L_{Dyck} is given in Algorithm 3.3.

Algorithm 3.3

Input: An even integer $n \in \mathbb{Z}_{>0}$, $\epsilon \in (0, 1)$, and query access to a string $s \in \{0,1\}^n$.
1: Choose a subsequence $\tilde{s}$ of s in the following way: For each character of s, add it to $\tilde{s}$ with probability p independently from others.
2: **if** $\tilde{s}$ contains more than $\ell + \Delta/4$ characters **then**
3:     Accept without querying any character.
4: **else if** $d_{\text{H}}(\tilde{s}, L_{\text{Dyck}}) \leq \Delta$ **then**
5:     Accept.
6: **else**
7:     Reject.
8: **end if**

Note that ℓ is the expected length of the subsequence $\tilde{s}$. Remark that we accept when $d_{\text{H}}(\tilde{s}, L_{\text{Dyck}}) \leq \Delta$ but not when $d_{\text{H}}(\tilde{s}, L_{\text{Dyck}}) = 0$. This is because, even if s itself is Dyck, its subsequence $\tilde{s}$ may not be exactly Dyck. This makes Algorithm 3.3 a two-sided error tester.

The query complexity is clearly $O(\ell + \Delta) = O(\epsilon^{-2} \log \epsilon^{-1})$. The following two lemmas achieve the correctness of Algorithm 3.3.

Lemma 3.5. *For any string $s \in L_{\text{Dyck}}$, Algorithm 3.3 accepts with probability at least $2/3$.*

Lemma 3.6. *For any string s that is ϵ-far from L_{Dyck}, Algorithm 3.3 rejects with probability at least $2/3$.*

Proof of Lemma 3.5. Set $t = C\epsilon^{-1}$, and assume for simplicity that t as well as n/t are integers. For $j \in [t]$, let X_j be the number of 0's in $\tilde{s}$, sampled from the interval $[1, nj/t]$. Let also Y_j denote the number of 1's in $\tilde{s}$, sampled from the same interval. Both X_j and Y_j are binomial random variables with the number of trials $x(s, nj/t)$ and $y(s, nj/t)$, respectively, and success probabilities p. As $s \in L_{\text{Dyck}}$, we have by Proposition 3.3 that $x(s, nj/t) \geq y(s, nj/t)$, implying $\mathbf{E}[X_j] \geq \mathbf{E}[Y_j]$. Applying Chernoff's bound, we obtain:

$$\Pr\left[Y_j \geq X_j + \frac{\Delta}{2}\right] \leq \Pr\left[X_j \leq \mathbf{E}[X_j] - \frac{\Delta}{4}\right] + \Pr\left[Y_j \geq \mathbf{E}[Y_j] + \frac{\Delta}{4}\right]$$

$$\leq \exp\left(-\Omega\left(\frac{\Delta^2}{x(s, nj/t)p}\right)\right) + \exp\left(-\Omega\left(\frac{\Delta^2}{y(s, nj/t)p}\right)\right)$$

$$\leq 2 \cdot \exp\left(-\Omega\left(\frac{\Delta^2}{\ell}\right)\right) = \exp\left(-\Omega\left(C\log\frac{1}{\epsilon}\right)\right). \quad (3.1)$$

For $j \in [t - .1]$, set $Z_j = Y_{j+1} - Y_j$. Note that $\mathbf{E}[Z_j] \leq \ell/t$. Using a similar argument as above, we get:

$$\Pr\left[Z_j \geq \frac{2\ell}{t}\right] \leq \exp\left(-\Omega\left(\frac{\ell}{t}\right)\right) = \exp\left(-\Omega\left(\frac{\log\epsilon^{-1}}{\epsilon}\right)\right) \quad (3.2)$$

As $s \in L_{\text{Dyck}}$, we have by Proposition 3.3 that $x(s, n) = y(s, n) = n/2$. Hence:

$$\Pr\left[X_t \geq \frac{\ell}{2} + \frac{\Delta}{8}\right] \leq \exp\left(-\Omega\left(\frac{\Delta^2}{\ell}\right)\right) = \exp\left(-\Omega\left(C\log\frac{1}{\epsilon}\right)\right). \quad (3.3)$$

Finally, we have the following estimate on the distribution of the sample size $|\tilde{s}|$:

$$\Pr\left[||\tilde{s}| - \ell| \geq \frac{\Delta}{4}\right] \leq \exp\left(-\Omega\left(\frac{\Delta^2}{\ell}\right)\right) = \exp\left(-\Omega\left(C\log\frac{1}{\epsilon}\right)\right). \quad (3.4)$$

Setting C to be large enough and recalling the definition of t, by the union bound, we derive from (3.1)–(3.4) that with probability at least $2/3$ the following events hold simultaneously:

1. $\max_{j \in [t]}(Y_j - X_j) \leq \dfrac{\Delta}{2}$,

2. $\max_{j \in [t-1]} Z_j \leq \dfrac{2\ell}{t}$,

3. $X_t \leq \dfrac{\ell}{2} + \dfrac{\Delta}{8}$, and

4. $|\tilde{s}| \geq \ell - \dfrac{\Delta}{4}$.

Assume that the above four conditions are satisfied. Then we claim that $d_{\text{H}}(\tilde{s}, L_{\text{Dyck}}) \leq \Delta$. Indeed, the first two conditions guarantee that, for all $i \in [|\tilde{s}|]$, we have $y(\tilde{s}, i) - x(\tilde{s}, i) \leq \Delta/2 + 2\ell/t \leq 2\Delta/3$ by setting C to be large enough. The last two conditions provide that $x(\tilde{s}, |\tilde{s}|) - y(\tilde{s}, |\tilde{s}|) = X_t - Y_t = 2X_t - |\tilde{s}| \leq \Delta/2$. Therefore, by Lemma 3.4, we have $d_{\text{H}}(\tilde{s}, L_{\text{Dyck}}) \leq \Delta$ (assuming that Δ is sufficiently large so that the additive term of 2 does not affect the argument). Thus, Algorithm 3.3 accepts s with probability at least $2/3$. $\qquad\square$

Proof of Lemma 3.6. When the string s is ϵ-far from being Dyck, by Lemma 3.4, at least one of the following two cases happens:

(a) There exists an index $i \in [n]$ such that $y(s,i) - x(s,i) > \epsilon n/2$;

(b) $x(s,n) - y(s,n) > \epsilon n/2$.

Suppose that the case (a) happened. Let X, Y be the number of 0's, 1's, respectively, of $\tilde{s}$, sampled from the interval $[1, i]$. Let also k be the number of elements from $[1, i]$ chosen to $\tilde{s}$. Then $X = x(\tilde{s}, k)$, $Y = y(\tilde{s}, k)$. Both X and Y are binomially distributed with parameters $x(s, i)$ and p, and $y(s, i)$ and p, respectively. It follows from the definition of i that $\mathbf{E}[Y] - \mathbf{E}[X] \geq \epsilon \ell / 2$. However, then we have:

$$\Pr[y(\tilde{s}, k) - x(\tilde{s}, k) \leq 2\Delta]$$
$$= \Pr[Y - X \leq 2\Delta]$$
$$\leq \Pr\left[X \geq \mathbf{E}[X] + \left(\frac{\epsilon \ell}{4} - \Delta \right) \right] + \Pr\left[Y \geq \mathbf{E}[Y] + \left(\frac{\epsilon \ell}{4} - \Delta \right) \right]$$
$$= \exp\left(-\Omega\left(\frac{(\epsilon \ell / 4 - \Delta)^2}{\ell} \right) \right).$$

Setting the constant C to be sufficiently large and recalling the definitions of p and Δ, we see that the above probability is at most $1/6$. But if $y(\tilde{s}, k) - x(\tilde{s}, k) > 2\Delta$, it follows from Proposition 3.4 that $d_{\mathrm{H}}(\tilde{s}, L_{\mathrm{Dyck}}) > \Delta$.

Suppose that the case (b) happened. Using similar arguments to the case above, we have:

$$\Pr[x(\tilde{s}, |\tilde{s}|) - y(\tilde{s}, |\tilde{s}|) \leq 2\Delta] = \exp\left(-\Omega\left(\frac{(\epsilon pn/4 - \Delta)^2}{pn} \right) \right).$$

The above probability can be made at most $1/6$ by the choice of C. But if $x(\tilde{s}, |\tilde{s}|) - y(\tilde{s}, |\tilde{s}|) > 2\Delta$, it follows from Proposition 3.4 that $d_{\mathrm{H}}(\tilde{s}, L_{\mathrm{Dyck}}) > \Delta$.

Thus in both cases, our algorithm accepts s with probability at most $1/6$. In addition, the algorithm may accept s (in each of the cases) when $|\tilde{s}| > d + \Delta/4$. However, by (3.4) this is bounded by $1/6$ (by choosing C large enough). Hence Algorithm 3.3 rejects s with probability at least $2/3$.   □

To summarize, we obtain the following theorem.

Theorem 3.5. *The Dyck language is testable with $O(\epsilon^{-2} \log \epsilon^{-1})$ queries.*

The key idea behind the analysis for the Dyck language tester was introducing surrogate parameters, that is, $x(s, i)$ and $y(s, i)$, to roughly estimate the distance to the Dyck language. To relate those parameters with the distance, we explicitly constructed a string in the Dyck language and analyzed the number of modifications by using $x(s, i)$ and $y(s, i)$. Since we could estimate $x(s, i)$ and $y(s, i)$ for $i \in [n]$ from a subsequence of a constant size made from s, we could compute a rough estimate of the distance to the Dyck language.

3.4.2 Linear Lower Bound for One-sided Error Testers

We have seen that the Dyck language is constant-query testable with two-sided error. For one-sided error testers, we can show a linear lower bound:

> **Theorem 3.6.** *Any one-sided error tester for the Dyck language requires* $\Omega(n)$ *queries.*

Proof. Assume that there exists one-sided error $(\epsilon/2)$-tester $\mathcal{A}$ for the Dyck language. Consider its execution on the input string $u = 0^{n/2+\epsilon n}1^{n/2-\epsilon n}$. It is easy to see that $d_{\mathrm{H}}(u, L_{\mathrm{Dyck}}) > \epsilon n/2$. Therefore, $\mathcal{A}$ must reject u with probability at least $2/3$.

Fix any sequence of coin tosses which makes $\mathcal{A}$ reject u, and denote by Q the corresponding set of queried characters of u. We claim that if $|Q \cap [n/2 + \epsilon n]| \leq n/2 - \epsilon n$, then there exists a string s of length n from L_{Dyck} for which $s[i] = u[i]$ for all $i \in Q$. To prove this claim, we may assume that $|Q \cap [n/2 + \epsilon n]| = n/2 - \epsilon n$. Define s as follows. For all $i > n/2 + \epsilon n$ we set $s[i] = 1$. Now, we take the first ϵn indices i in $[n/2 + \epsilon n] \setminus Q$ and set $s[i] = 0$. For the last ϵn indices i in $[n/2 + \epsilon n] \setminus Q$, we set $s[i] = 1$. Also, $s[i] = u[i]$ for all $i \in Q$. Now, s satisfies the sufficient condition for belonging to L_{Dyck}, given by Proposition 3.3. Indeed, at any point j in $[n/2 + \epsilon n]$, the number of 0's in the first j characters of s is at least as large as the number of 1's. Also, for $j \geq n/2 + \epsilon n$ we have $x(s, j) = n/2$ and $y(s, j) = \epsilon n + (j - n/2 - \epsilon n) = j - n/2$. Therefore, $s \in L_{\mathrm{Dyck}}$.

As $\mathcal{A}$ is assumed to be a one-sided error tester, it should always accept every $s \in L_{\mathrm{Dyck}}$. But then we must have $|Q \cap [n/2 + \epsilon n]| > n/2 - \epsilon n$, which implies that $\mathcal{A}$ queries at least $\Omega(n)$ characters. $\square$

3.5 Monotonicity and Permutation-Freeness

monotonicity

We began Chapter 1 by discussing the problem of testing *monotonicity* of an array. Monotonicity can be naturally viewed as a property of strings. Given a total ordering $\leq$ on Σ, a string $s \in \Sigma^n$ is said to be monotone if $s_i \leq s_{i+1}$ for all $i \in [n-1]$. Equivalently, there do not exist any $i < j$ such that $s_j < s_i$. Section 1.1 described a one-sided error adaptive tester for monotonicity with query complexity $O(\epsilon^{-1} \log n)$.

More generally, one can define *permutation-freeness* properties. As before, suppose Σ is endowed with a total ordering $\leq$. Given a positive integer $k \leq n$ and a permutation $\pi \colon [k] \to [k]$, a string $s \in \Sigma^n$ is said to *contain* π if there exist indices $i_1 < i_2 < \cdots < i_k$ in $[n]$ such that for all $a, b \in [k]$, $s[i_a] < s[i_b]$ if and only if $\pi(a) < \pi(b)$. If the string s does not contain π, then it is said to be π-*free*. For example, if $k = 2$ and[1] $\pi_{\mathrm{mon}} = (2, 1)$, then monotonicity is equivalent to π_{mon}-freeness.

We note that permutation-freeness is a natural property of a sequence that has a lot of applications in combinatorics. For example, the permutations that can be obtained from the identity permutation using a Gilbreath shuffle are exactly those are $(1, 3, 2)$-free and $(3, 1, 2)$-free. A Gilbreath shuffle is a two step shuffling procedure for a deck of cards, where the deck is first cut into two piles putting the second one in a reverse order, and then riffling the piles together.

In this section, we describe a non-adaptive tester for monotonicity with the same query complexity as the adaptive one, $O(\epsilon^{-1} \log n)$. In the problems at the end of the chapter, we guide the reader to a tester for monotone permutation-freeness making $\mathrm{poly}(\epsilon^{-1} \log n)$ where the degree of the polynomial depends on the length of the permutation. In Section 3.6, we discuss the state-of-the-art results on testing π-freeness.

Non-adaptive Tester for Monotonicity

The tool we use to design a non-adaptive tester for monotonicity of strings $s \in \Sigma^n$ is a graph-theoretic object called a *spanner*. For a directed graph $G = (V, E)$ and an integer $k \geq 1$, a subgraph $H = (V, E_H)$ of G is called a k-*spanner* of G if for every pair of vertices $u, v \in V$, the shortest path distance $d_H(u, v)$ (do not confuse with the Hamming distance d_H) from u to v in H is at most $k \cdot d_G(u, v)$. The parameter k is called the *stretch* of the spanner.

The *transitive closure* of a directed graph $G = (V, E)$, denoted by $\mathrm{TC}(G)$, is the supergraph $H = (V, E_H)$ of G such that $(u, v) \in E_H$ if and only if v is reachable from u, that is, there is a path from u to v. The following is the key notion for our argument.

Definition 3.1 (TC-spanner). Let $G = (V, E)$ be a directed graph and $k \geq 1$ be an integer. A k-*transitive-closure-spanner* (k-TC-spanner) of G is a directed graph $H = (V, E_H)$ with the following properties:

- E_H is a subset of the arcs in $\mathrm{TC}(G)$.
- For any pair of vertices $u, v \in V$, if $d_G(u, v) < \infty$, then $d_H(u, v) \leq k$.

Notice that a k-TC-spanner of G is just a k-spanner of $\mathrm{TC}(G)$.

---

[1] $\pi = (i_1, \ldots, i_k)$ is shorthand for the permutation defined by $\pi(j) = i_j$ for all $j \in [k]$.

The following lemma constructs 2-TC-spanners for the directed path.

> **Lemma 3.7.** *Let $G = ([n], E)$ be the directed path graph on n vertices, where $E = \{(i, i+1) : i \in [n-1]\}$. Then, G has a 2-TC-spanner of size $O(n \log n)$.*

Proof. As long as $n \geq 2$, we add to H arcs of the form (i, p) for $1 \leq i < p$ and (p, i) for $p < i \leq n$, where $p = \lfloor n/2 \rfloor$, and then recursively process the subgraph on the vertex set $\{1, \ldots, p-1\}$ and the subgraph on the vertex set $\{p+1, \ldots, n\}$. From the construction, for any $x, y \in [n]$, there exists an arc (x, y) in H, or there exists an index $x < p < y$ such that there are arcs (x, p) and (p, y) in H. Hence H is a 2-TC-spanner of G.

Let $T(n)$ be the number of arcs we add for a path graph on n vertices. Then, we have:

$$T(n) \leq n + 2T(\lfloor n/2 \rfloor)$$

and $T(1) = 0$. Solving this recursion, we obtain that $T(n) = O(n \log n)$. □

Exercise 3.3. Let $G = ([n]^2, E)$ be the directed grid graph on n^2 vertices, where $E = \{((i,j), (i+1,j)) : i \in [n-1], j \in [n]\} \cup \{((i,j), (i,j+1)) : i \in [n], j \in [n-1]\}$. Show that G has a 2-TC-spanner of size $O(n^2 \log^2 n)$ arcs.

We now show 2-TC-testers can be used to test a very general notion of monotonicity. For a directed acyclic graph $G = (V, E)$ where the vertex set V is identified with $[n]$, we say that a string $s \in \Sigma^n$ is *monotone with respect to G*, if $s_i \leq s_j$ whenever $(i, j) \in E$. A string is *ϵ-far from being monotone* if for any monotone s', we have $d_H(s, s') > \epsilon n$. We will study this problem in more detail in Section 7.2. Here, we show that the existence of a small 2-TC-spanner implies an efficient monotonicity tester.

monotonicity
ϵ-farness

> **Lemma 3.8.** *If a directed acyclic graph G on n vertices has a 2-TC-spanner H with m arcs, then there exists a one-sided error non-adaptive tester for monotonicity with respect to G that runs with $O\left(\frac{m}{\epsilon n}\right)$ queries.*

Combining Lemmas 3.7 and 3.8, we get a non-adaptive tester for (the standard notion of) monotonicity with query complexity $O(\epsilon^{-1} \log n)$. We turn to the proof of Lemma 3.8.

Proof. The tester selects $4m/(\epsilon n)$ arcs of the 2-TC-spanner H uniformly at random. It queries the input string s on the endpoints of all the selected arcs and rejects if and only if one of the selected arcs is *violating*, that is, $s_i > s_j$ for an arc (i, j).

violating arc

If the string s is monotone with respect to G, the algorithm always accepts. Hence, it suffices to show that inputs that are ϵ-far from being monotone are rejected with probability at least $2/3$. Suppose s is ϵ-far from being monotone.

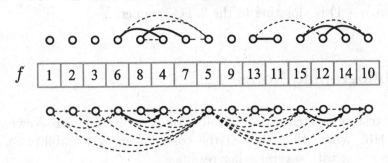

H and M being mapped

Fig. 3.3: The middle array represents a function $f: [15] \to \Sigma$, where $\Sigma = \{1, \ldots, 15\}$. The graph above is an undirected graph G' consisting of violating arcs (being regarded as undirected) and the bold edges form a maximum matching M in G'. The graph below is a 2-TC-spanner of the path graph and the bold arcs are being mapped from M.

It is enough to demonstrate that s violates at least $\epsilon n/2$ arcs in H: Then, each selected arc is violated with probability $\epsilon n/2m$, and the lemma follows.

Let E' be the set of violating arcs in $TC(G)$. Let $G' = (V, E')$ be an *undirected* graph, where we regard each arc in E' as undirected. Then, we will prove[2] in Lemma 7.5 that the minimum size of a *vertex cover* in G' is at least ϵn. Here, we just assume this claim.

From the well known relation between the minimum size of a vertex cover and the maximum size of a *matching*, there is a matching M of $\epsilon n/2$ edges in G'. To bound the number of violating arcs, we show an injective mapping from the set of edges in M to the set of violating arcs in H (see Figure 3.3). For each edge $\{i, j\}$ in the matching, where j is reachable from i in G, consider the corresponding path P from i to j of length at most 2 in the 2-TC-spanner H. If P is of length 1, (i, j) is the violating arc in H corresponding to the edge $\{i, j\}$ in the matching. Otherwise, let $P = (i, i', j)$ be the path of length 2. At least one of the arcs, (i, i') or (i', j), is violating, and we map $\{i, j\}$ to that arc. As all edges in M have distinct endpoints, each edge in M is mapped to a unique violating arc in $TC(G)$. Thus, the 2-TC-spanner H has at least $\epsilon n/2$ violating arcs, as required. $\square$

The fact that H is a 2-TC-spanner is crucial for the proof. If it was a k-TC-spanner for $k > 2$, the path of length k from i to j might not have any violating arcs incident to i or j, even if $s_i > s_j$. Consider $G = (V, E)$, where $V = \{1, \ldots, 2n\}$, $E = \{(i, n) : i < n\} \cup (n, n+1) \cup \{(n+1, j) : j > n+1\}$. G is a 3-TC-spanner for itself. Now set $s_i = 1$ for $i \le n$ and $s_i = 0$

(margin notes: vertex cover; matching)

---

[2] The proof is simple, and the reader is encouraged to prove it himself at this point.

otherwise. Clearly, this function is 1/2-far from being monotone, but only one arc $(n, n+1)$ is violating in the 3-TC-spanner.

3.6 Bibliographic Notes

Property testing on strings was initiated by Alon, Krivelevich, Newman, and Szegedy [16], where they showed the constant-query testability of regular languages along with several other results.

The constant-query tester for palindromes discussed in Section 3.2 is folklore. A related result is testing periodicity, that is, $s[i] = s[j]$ whenever $i \equiv j$ (mod p), where p is the parameter of the property. Lachish and Newman [295] showed that, when $p = O(\log n)$, there exists a non-adaptive one-sided error tester with a polylogarithmic number of queries in p, and that, when $p = \omega(\log n)$, every adaptive two-sided error tester requires a polynomial number of queries in p. The tester for two palindromes given in Section 3.3.1 is due to Parnas, Ron, and Rubinfeld [346] and the lower bound discussed in Section 3.3.2 is due to Alon, Krivelevich, Newman, and Szegedy [16].

The tester for the Dyck language given in Section 3.4 is due to Alon, Krivelevich, Newman, and Szegedy [16]. As an extension of the Dyck language, it is natural to consider languages with k kinds of parentheses, where the open parenthesis of the i-th kind must matches the closed parenthesis of the i-th kind. Such a language is called the *Dyck language of order k*. Parnas, Ron, and Rubinfeld [346] showed that testing the Dyck language of order k for $k \geq 2$ can be done with $\widetilde{O}(\epsilon^{-3} n^{2/3})$ queries and requires $\Omega(n^{1/11})$ queries. The upper and lower bounds were improved to $\widetilde{O}(n^{2/5})$ and $\Omega(n^{1/5})$, respectively [183].

Some efforts have been made to show a broad class of languages is constant-query testable. First, as we mentioned, Alon, Krivelevich, Newman, and Szegedy [16] showed that every *regular language* is constant-query testable. However, the next larger class of languages in the Chomsky hierarchy [133], *context-free languages*, are not constant-query testable in general as the Dyck language, a context-free language, is not.

It is shown that any language recognizable by an oblivious read-once constant-width *branching program* is constant-query testable [331]. However, there is a language that is recognizable by an oblivious read-*twice* constant-width branching program but is not constant-query testable [186].

As another general result, Lachish, Newman, and Shapira [296] showed that, for any function $\log \log n \leq s(n) \leq \log n / 10$, there is a language that is recognizable in $O(s(n))$ space whereas testing the language requires $2^{\Omega(s(n))}$ queries, which in particular means the language is not constant-query testable. This result is interesting because any language that is recognizable in $o(\log \log n)$ space is regular and hence is constant-query testable.

Dyck language

regular language

context-free languages

branching program

The notion of transitive-closure spanner and the monotonicity tester based on it explained in Section 3.5 are due to Bhattacharyya, Grigorescu, Jung, Raskhodnikova, and Woodruff [78].

The example about a Gilbreath shuffle in Section 3.5 is taken from [332]. A database of more applications can be found online [382]. For monotone permutations, that is, $\pi = (k, k-1, \ldots, 1)$ or $\pi = (1, 2, \ldots, k)$, there is a non-adaptive one-sided error ϵ-tester with $(\epsilon^{-1} \log n)^{O(\log_2 k)}$ queries, which is known to be tight for non-adaptive testers [53]. This result improves on the algorithm sketched in Problem 3.11, due to [332], which only achieves $(\epsilon^{-1} \log n)^{\tilde{O}(k^2)}$ query complexity. For monotone permutations, there is an adaptive one-sided error ϵ-tester using $(k/\epsilon)^{O(k)} \cdot \log n$ queries, a strict improvement over the non-adaptive result [56]. For general permutations, any non-adaptive one-sided error ϵ-tester requires at least $\Omega(\sqrt{n})$ queries [332]. Ben-Eliezer and Canonne [52] showed a non-adaptive one-sided error ϵ-tester with $O\left(\epsilon^{-\frac{1}{k-1}} n^{1-\frac{1}{k-1}}\right)$ queries, where k is the length of the permutation, and most permutations require that many queries. It is conjectured in [332] that for any fixed-length permutation π, there exists an adaptive tester making only polylogarithmic in n many queries!

Problems

3.1. Show that Algorithm 3.1 is a *tolerant tester* (see Section 1.5) for L_{Pal}. What is its query complexity in terms of ϵ_1 and ϵ_2?

tolerant tester

3.2. Suppose Algorithm 3.2 for L_{Rev} is modified so that in lines 2 and 3, I and J are chosen to be two random subsets of size $\Theta(\sqrt{n})$. Show that the resulting algorithm is a two-sided error tester for L_{rev}.

3.3. Let L_{Dyck}^k denote the Dyck language of order k. We say that a string s is consistent with L_{Dyck}^k if s is a substring of a string in L_{Dyck}^k. Show that, if consistency with L_{Dyck}^k is testable with $q(\epsilon, n)$ queries, then L_{Dyck}^k is testable with $q(\epsilon, n) + O(\epsilon^{-2} \log \epsilon^{-1})$ queries. (**Hint:** Use the tester for the Dyck language of order 1.)

3.4. Show that, for any permutation π of length k, we can test π-freeness of a function $f: [n] \to \mathbb{R}$ using $O(\epsilon^{-1/k} n^{1-1/k})$ queries.

3.5. Let $L_{010} = \{0^a 1^b 0^c : a, b, c \geq 0\}$. If $x \in \{0, 1\}^n$ is ϵ-far from L_{010}, argue that there exist $\epsilon n/3$ many i's such that: (i) $x_i = 0$, (ii) $|\{j : j < i, x_j = 1\}| \geq \epsilon n/3$, and (iii) $|\{j : j > i, x_j = 1\}| \geq \epsilon n/3$. Use this fact to devise a tester for L_{010} with query complexity $O(\epsilon^{-1})$.

3.6. Suppose L and L' are languages closed under taking (contiguous) substrings[3]. Show that if L and L' are constant-query testable, then so is $L'' = \{ss' : s \in L, s' \in L'\}$.

3.7. Show that if a language L is testable with respect to the Hamming distance, it is also testable with respect to the *edit distance*.

edit distance

3.8. Let $c_1, \ldots, c_k$ be distinct symbols from Σ. Let $L_{\text{seq}} = \{c_1^{n_1} c_2^{n_2} \cdots c_k^{n_k} : n_1, \ldots, n_k \geq 0\}$. Show that L_{seq} is testable using $O(k\epsilon^{-1})$ queries. (**Hint:** Reduce to testing monotonicity.)

3.9. Show that the monotonicity of a function $f \colon [n] \to [k]$ is testable with $O(\epsilon^{-1} \log k)$ queries. (This improves on the bound in Exercise 2.3.)

3.10. In this problem, you will devise yet another one-sided monotonicity tester. It has sub-optimal query complexity but will be useful as a stepping stone to testing more complicated properties (see Problem 3.11).

Let $s \in \Sigma^n$ be ϵ-far from being monotone. As in the proof of Lemma 3.8, let M denote a matching of $\epsilon n/2$ disjoint pairs (i, j) such that $i < j$ but $s_i > s_j$. For $d \in \{0, 1, \ldots, \lfloor \log n \rfloor - 1\}$, let:

$$M_d = \{(i, j) \in M : 2^d \leq j - i < 2^{d+1}\}.$$

For $\ell \in [n]$, let $M_{\ell, d}$ denote those pairs (i, j) in M_d where $i \leq \ell \leq j$, and let $\delta_d(\ell)$ denote the fraction of elements in $[\ell - 2^{d+1}, \ell + 2^{d+1}]$ that belong to pairs in $M_{\ell, d}$.

(a) Show that:

$$\mathbf{E}_{\ell} \left[\sum_d \delta_d(\ell) \right] \geq \Omega(\epsilon)$$

where ℓ is sampled uniformly from $[n]$.

(b) Prove that:

$$\Pr_{\ell} \left[\exists d : \delta_d(\ell) \geq \Omega\left(\frac{\epsilon}{\log n}\right) \right] \geq \Omega\left(\frac{\epsilon}{\log n}\right).$$

(c) Suppose for some particular d and ℓ, $\delta_d(\ell) = \eta$. Argue that if S is a set of $O(1/\eta)$ uniformly chosen random samples from $[\ell - 2^{d+1}, \ell + 2^{d+1}]$, then with constant probability, there exist $(i, j), (i', j') \in M_{\ell, d}$ such that $i, j' \in S$ and $s_i \geq s_{i'}$. Observe that this implies $i < j'$ but $s_i > s_{j'}$, and hence, $(i, j') \in S^2$ is a violating pair.

(d) Put together the parts above to design an $O(\epsilon^{-2} \log^3 n)$-query one-sided monotonicity tester.

---

[3] In other words, if $x \in L \cap \Sigma^n$ and $I \subseteq [n]$ is an interval, then $x|_I \in L$. Same for L'.

3.11. This problem asks you to extend the ideas described in Problem 3.10 in order to test arbitrary monotone permutation-freeness. Let id_k denote the identity permutation on $[k]$. Then, a string $s \in \Sigma^n$ is id_k-free if for all $i_1 < i_2 < \cdots < i_k$, it is not the case that $s_{i_1} < s_{i_2} < \cdots < s_{i_k}$; otherwise, such a tuple $(i_1, \ldots, i_k)$ is called violating.

(a) Show that if s is ϵ-far from id_k-freeness, then there exists a set M of $\epsilon n/k$ disjoint k-tuples $(i_1, \ldots, i_k)$ that are violating.

(b) For a tuple $(i_1, \ldots, i_k) \in M$, define:

$$\mathsf{Gap}(i_1, \ldots, i_k) = \max_{1 \leq t < k} \lfloor \log_2(i_{t+1} - i_t) \rfloor$$

Define $\mathsf{GapIndex}(i_1, \ldots, i_k)$ to be the smallest value of t for which $\lfloor \log_2(i_{t+1} - i_t) \rfloor$ equals the Gap. From part (a), there exists t such that the number of tuples in M whose $\mathsf{GapIndex}$ is t is at least $\Omega(\epsilon n/k^2)$; fix this value of t. Extending Problem 3.10, for $d \in \{0, 1, \ldots, \lfloor \log n \rfloor - 1\}$ and $\ell \in [n]$, we set:

$$M_d = \{(i_1, \ldots, i_k) \in M : \mathsf{Gap}(i_1, \ldots, i_k) = d\}$$
$$M_{\ell,d} = \{(i_1, \ldots, i_k) \in M_d : i_t \leq \ell \leq i_{t+1}\}$$

Finally, let $\delta_d(\ell)$ denote the fraction of elements in $[\ell - k2^{d+1}, \ell + k2^{d+1}]$ that belong to tuples in $M_{\ell,d}$.

Redo parts (a) and (b) of the earlier problem to show that:

$$\Pr_\ell \left[\exists d : \delta_d(\ell) \geq \Omega\left(\frac{\epsilon}{\log n}\right) \right] \geq \Omega\left(\frac{\epsilon}{\log n}\right),$$

where ℓ is sampled uniformly from $[n]$ and the Ω notation hides constants depending on k.

(c) Let ℓ, d be such that $\delta_d(\ell) = \eta$. Argue that there must exist two (not necessarily disjoint) sets of violating tuples $M_{\ell,d}^0, M_{\ell,d}^1 \subseteq M_{\ell,d}$ such that for any $(i_1, \ldots, i_k) \in M_{\ell,d}^0$ and $(i_1', \ldots, i_k') \in M_{\ell,d}^1$, it holds that $s_{i_t} \leq s_{i_t'}$. Moreover, both $|M_{\ell,d}^0|$ and $|M_{\ell,d}^1|$ are at least $\Omega(\eta 2^d)$.

(d) If $(i_1, \ldots, i_k) \in M_{\ell,d}^0$ and $(i_1', \ldots, i_k') \in M_{\ell,d}^1$, why does $(i_1, \ldots, i_t, i_{t+1}', \ldots, i_k')$ violate id_k-freeness?

(e) Show that if ℓ and d are such that $\delta_d(\ell) = \Omega(\epsilon/\log n)$, then $s|_{[\ell - k2^{d+1}, \ell]}$ contains $\Omega(\epsilon 2^d/\log n)$ tuples from the restriction of $M_{\ell,d}^0$ to the first t coordinates, and similarly $s|_{[\ell, \ell + k2^{d+1}]}$ contains $\Omega(\epsilon 2^d/\log n)$ tuples from the restriction of $M_{\ell,d}^1$ to the last $k - t$ coordinates

(f) Design a recursive algorithm to test id_k-freeness using the above ideas. Namely, sample ℓ and d so that $\delta_d(\ell) \geq \Omega(\epsilon/\log n)$ and then recursively test the substrings defined in part (e) in order to get a prefix of a string in $M_{\ell,d}^0$ and the suffix of a string in $M_{\ell,d}^1$, so as to get a string in M by part (d). The query complexity of your tester should be $\mathrm{poly}(\epsilon^{-1} \log n)$ where the degree depends on k.

Chapter 4
Graphs in the Adjacency Matrix Model

In this chapter, we study testing properties of graphs in the *adjacency matrix* *model*. In this model, we have query access to the adjacency matrix of the input graph and, roughly speaking, a tester aims to distinguish the case that the input graph G on n vertices satisfies a predetermined property $\mathcal{P}$ from the case that we need to modify more than ϵn^2 edges to make G satisfy $\mathcal{P}$. Testing graph properties in the adjacency matrix model is one of the highlights of property testing because elegant mathematical tools from graph theory and additive combinatorics have been exploited to analyze testers and to obtain characterizations of constant-query testable properties. In this chapter, we consider specific properties and glimpse how these mathematical tools are used. We look at deeper and more general results later in Chapter 9.

adjacency matrix model

We first review basic terminology in graph theory in Section 4.1. In Section 4.2, we formally define the adjacency matrix model. There are two major classes of properties that are testable with a constant number of queries: partition properties and subgraph freeness. Partition properties include being a clique, k-colorability, and having a cut of size at least ρn^2 for a parameter $\rho \in (0, 1)$. We will see that these properties are testable with a constant number of queries in Section 4.3. In Section 4.4, we introduce a "canonical" form of a tester, which will be useful to show lower bounds. Then, we proceed to study subgraph freeness, which is the property of not having a particular graph H as its subgraph. We mainly focus on the case that H is a square and triangle, that is, a cycle of length four and three, respectively. Although the tester for square-freeness is simple, to test triangle-freeness, we require Szemerédi's regularity lemma, which is a cornerstone result in graph theory. We will see these results in Section 4.5. In Section 4.6, we explain that some properties are trivial to test in the adjacency matrix model, which motivates us to study another model called the bounded-degree model. We will study that model in Chapter 5.

A. Bhattacharyya and Y. Yoshida, *Property Testing*,
https://doi.org/10.1007/978-981-16-8622-1_4

4.1 Terminology

Let $G = (V, E)$ be an undirected graph. For a vertex $v \in V$, $\Gamma_G(v)$ denotes the set of neighbors of v, that is:

$$\Gamma_G(v) = \big\{ w \in V : \{v, w\} \in E \big\}.$$

For a vertex set $S \subseteq V$, $\Gamma(G)$ denotes the set of neighbors of S, that is:

$$\Gamma_G(S) = \big\{ w \in V : \{v, w\} \in E \big\} \setminus S.$$

induced subgraph   For a vertex set $S \subseteq V$, the *subgraph of G induced by S*, denoted by $G[S]$, is the graph $\big(S, E \cap \binom{S}{2}\big)$. For vertex sets $S, T \subseteq V$, we denote by $E_G(S, T)$ the set of edges between S and T:

$$E_G(S, T) = \big\{ \{u, v\} \in E : u \in S, v \in T \big\}.$$

When $S = T$, we simply write $E_G(S)$. We omit subscripts G if they are clear from the context.

4.2 Adjacency Matrix Model

Let $G = (V, E)$ be a graph and $\pi \colon V \to V$ be a bijection. Then, we define $\pi(G)$ as the graph $(V, \pi(E))$, where:

$$\pi(E) = \big\{ \{\pi(u), \pi(v)\} : \{u, v\} \in E \big\}.$$

isomorphism   We say that two graphs G and H on the same vertex set V are *isomorphic* if there exists a bijection $\pi \colon V \to V$ such that $H = \pi(G)$. Isomorphism can be understood as the renaming of vertices. We are interested in properties invariant under isomorphisms.

graph property

> **Definition 4.1.** A *graph property* is a set of graphs that is closed under isomorphism. That is, if a graph G satisfies a graph property $\mathcal{P}$, then for every bijection $\pi \colon V \to V$, the graph $\pi(G)$ also satisfies $\mathcal{P}$.

In this section, we only consider simple graphs, that is, graphs with no self-loop and no parallel edge.

In the adjacency matrix model, we regard a graph $G = (V, E)$ as being represented by an adjacency matrix (function) $A_G \colon V \times V \to \{0, 1\}$, where:

$$A_G(u, v) = \begin{cases} 1 & \text{if } \{u, v\} \in E, \\ 0 & \text{otherwise.} \end{cases}$$

Hence, query access to G means query access to A_G. We assume that $V = [n]$, where n is the number of vertices. Then, the vertex set V does not have to be provided explicitly because we can access A_G by specifying a pair of integers in $[n]$.

We define the *distance* between two graphs G and H on the same vertex set V as the size of the symmetric difference of the edge set, namely:

distance

$$d(G, H) = |E(G) \triangle E(H)|.$$

This can be equivalently defined using their adjacency matrices, that is:

$$d(G, H) = \left| \left\{ \{u, v\} \in \binom{V}{2} : A_G(u, v) \neq A_H(u, v) \right\} \right|.$$

Then, we define the distance between a graph G on n vertices and a graph parameter $\mathcal{P}$ as:

$$d(G, \mathcal{P}) = \min_{H \in \mathcal{P}_n} d(G, H),$$

where $\mathcal{P}_n$ is the subset of $\mathcal{P}$ consisting of graphs on n vertices. If $\mathcal{P}_n$ is empty, we define $d(G, \mathcal{P}) = \infty$. We note that $d(G, \mathcal{P}) = d(\pi(G), \mathcal{P})$ holds for any bijection $\pi \colon V \to V$.

We say that G on n vertices is ϵ-*far from* $\mathcal{P}$ if $d(G, \mathcal{P}) > \epsilon n^2$. An algorithm is said to be a *tester* for $\mathcal{P}$ if, given an integer $n \in \mathbb{Z}_{>0}$, an error parameter $\epsilon \in (0, 1)$, and query access to a graph G on n vertices, it accepts with probability at least $2/3$ if G satisfies $\mathcal{P}$, and rejects with probability at least $2/3$ if G is ϵ-far from $\mathcal{P}$. Intuitively speaking, ϵ-farness means that we need to modify an $\Omega(\epsilon)$-fraction of all possible (potential) edges because the maximum number of edges in an n-vertex simple graph is $\binom{n}{2} = \Theta(n^2)$. In this sense, one may think it is more natural to define ϵ-farness as $d(G, \mathcal{P}) > \epsilon\binom{n}{2}$, but we use the present definition to avoid cumbersome constants.

ϵ-farness
tester

We finally note that this notion of distance between graphs is most meaningful when the graphs are dense, that is, they have $\Omega(n^2)$ edges because then ϵ-farness means that we need to modify an $\Omega(\epsilon)$-fraction of *existing* edges. Thus, the adjacency matrix model is often called the *dense graph model*. We come back to this issue in Section 4.6.

dense graph model

4.3 Partition Properties

In this section, we consider *partition properties*. Roughly speaking, partition properties refer to properties for which the vertex set of a graph can be partitioned into a constant number of parts so that the sizes of those parts and edge densities between those parts are within specified ranges. Although we will give the formal definition of a partition property in Section 4.3.3, let us mention that partition properties encompass the following properties:

partition property

biclique

- **Biclique**: A graph $G = (V, E)$ is a *biclique* (also known as a complete bipartite graph) if there exists a bipartition (V_1, V_2) of V such that $E = \{\{u, v\} : (u, v) \in V_1 \times V_2\}$.

bipartiteness

- **Bipartiteness**: A graph $G = (V, E)$ satisfies *bipartiteness* if there exists a bipartition (V_1, V_2) of V such that V_1 and V_2 are independent sets. In other words, G is bipartite if every edge is incident to exactly one vertex in V_1 and exactly one vertex in V_2. Note that a biclique is bipartite.

k-colorability

- **k-colorability**: For an integer $k \in \mathbb{Z}_{>0}$, a graph $G = (V, E)$ is *k-colorable* if there exists a partition $(V_1, V_2, \ldots, V_k)$ of V such that each V_i is an independent set. Note that a graph is bipartite if and only if it is 2-colorable.

ρ-cut

Turán's theorem

ρ-bisection

- **ρ-cut**: For $\rho \in (0, 1/4]$, a graph $G = (V, E)$ has a *ρ-cut* if there exists a bipartition (V_1, V_2) of V such that the number of edges between V_1 and V_2 is at least ρn^2. The upper bound of $1/4$ comes from the fact that any bipartite graph can have at most $n^2/4$ edges by *Turán's theorem*..

- **ρ-bisection**: For $\rho \in (0, 1/4]$, a graph $G = (V, E)$ has a *ρ-bisection* if there exists a bipartition (V_1, V_2) of V into two equal sized sets such that the number of edges between V_1 and V_2 is at most ρn^2.

clique

- **ρ-clique**: For $\rho \in (0, 1]$, a graph $G = (V, E)$ has a *ρ-clique* if there exists a bipartition (V_1, V_2) of V such that $|V_1| = \lceil \rho n \rceil$ and the subgraph induced by V_1 is a clique.

It turns out that all of these properties are testable with $\text{poly}(\epsilon^{-1})$ queries. In this section, as illustrative examples, we see that the property of being a biclique and bipartiteness are constant-query testable (with one-sided error) in Section 4.3.1 and Section 4.3.2, respectively, and then briefly discuss general results in Section 4.3.3.

4.3.1 Biclique

biclique

In this section, we show that the property of being a *biclique* is constant-query testable with one-sided error. We note that an empty graph $G = (V, \emptyset)$ is considered as a biclique because of the trivial bipartition $(V, \emptyset)$.

The following exercise shows that we indeed need *queries* instead of *samples*:

> **Exercise 4.1.** Show that any sample-based tester, that is, at each time pick a pair of vertices uniformly at random and then see whether they span an edge, for the property of being a biclique requires $\Omega(\sqrt{n})$ samples.

Our algorithm is straightforward: We sample a set $S \subseteq V$ of a constant number of vertices, obtain the induced subgraph $G[S]$ by querying all pairs of vertices in S, and then check whether the induced subgraph $G[S]$ is a biclique. See Algorithm 4.1 for details.

Algorithm 4.1 One-sided error tester for the property of being a biclique

---

Input: An integer $n \in \mathbb{Z}_{>0}$, $\epsilon \in (0, 1)$, and query access to a graph $G = (V, E)$ on n vertices.
1: Pick a set $S \subseteq V$ of $\Theta(\epsilon^{-1})$ vertices uniformly at random.
2: Query all pairs of vertices (u, v) for $u, v \in S$.
3: **if** $G[S]$ is a biclique **then**
4:     Accept.
5: **else**
6:     Reject.
7: **end if**

Before analyzing Algorithm 4.1, we introduce one notion: We say that an edge $\{u, v\} \in E$ is *violating* with respect to a bipartition (V_1, V_2) of V if either $u, v \in V_1$ or $u, v \in V_2$ holds. Similarly, we say that a non-edge $\{u, v\} \in \binom{V}{2} \setminus E$ is *violating* if either $(u, v) \in V_1 \times V_2$ or $(u, v) \in V_2 \times V_1$ holds.

violating edge

violating non-edge

> **Theorem 4.1.** *Algorithm 4.1 is a one-sided error tester for the property of being a biclique with query complexity $O(\epsilon^{-2})$.*

Proof. The query complexity is $O(\epsilon^{-2})$ because the number of edges in $G[S]$ is $O(\epsilon^{-2})$. If $G = (V, E)$ is a biclique, then any induced subgraph is a biclique, and hence the algorithm always accepts.

Suppose that $G = (V, E)$ is ϵ-far from being a biclique. Fix the first vertex $u \in V$ that is selected by the algorithm. Then u defines a bipartition (V_1, V_2) of V, where $V_1 = \Gamma(u)$ and $V_2 = V \setminus \Gamma(u)$. Note that $\Gamma(u)$ excludes u and hence $u \in V_2$. Since G is ϵ-far from being a biclique, there are more than ϵn^2 violating pairs with respect to this bipartition. It follows that there are at least $\epsilon n^2 / 2$ violating edges or at least $\epsilon n^2 / 2$ violating non-edges.

Suppose that there are at least $\epsilon n^2 / 2$ violating edges. Note that if the vertex set S contains both endpoints of a violating edge $\{v, w\} \in E$, then the algorithm rejects because the induced subgraph $G[\{u, v, w\}]$ is not a biclique, and hence the induced subgraph $G[S]$ is not a biclique. Think of the vertex set S as consisting of u followed by $(|S| - 1)/2$ pairs of vertices. Each of these pairs is a violating edge with probability at least[1] $\epsilon/2$, and hence the probability we miss a violating edge is at most:

$$\left(1 - \frac{\epsilon}{2}\right)^{(|S|-1)/2} \leq \frac{1}{3}$$

by setting the hidden constant in S to be large enough.

---

[1] Here, we are assuming that each vertex in S is uniformly and independently chosen at random from V. This is not exactly true, as Line 1 in Algorithm 4.1 asks for a specific number of vertices. However, it is true with probability $1 - o(1)$ that $\Theta(\epsilon^{-1})$ vertices chosen independently and uniformly at random from V are all distinct, and so, we might as well assume that this is how S is generated. In the future, we will overlook these minor issues for the sake of simplicity.

Suppose that there at least $\epsilon n^2/2$ violating non-edges. Note that if the vertex set S contains both endpoints of a violating non-edge $\{v, w\} \in \binom{V}{2} \setminus E$, then the algorithm rejects because the induced subgraph $G[\{u, v, w\}]$ is not a biclique, and hence the induced subgraph $G[S]$ is not a biclique. The probability we miss a violating non-edge is again at most $1/3$ by setting the hidden constant in S to be large enough.

$\square$

Exercise 4.2. Note that the above analysis depends on the value of the adjacency matrix at only $\Theta(\epsilon^{-1})$ locations. Hence, argue that the query complexity can be made $\Theta(\epsilon^{-1})$.

The point in the proof of Theorem 4.1 is that the first vertex induces a bipartition of the whole vertex set and then we only have to check whether other edges are consistent with the bipartition using remaining queries. This principle is also used in the analysis of testing bipartiteness in the next section, but the way we get a bipartition is more complicated.

4.3.2 Bipartiteness

bipartiteness

In this section, we show that *bipartiteness* is constant-query testable. Our algorithm is again straightforward: We sample a set $S \subseteq V$ of a constant number of vertices, obtain the induced subgraph $G[S]$ by querying all pairs of vertices in S, and then check whether the induced subgraph $G[S]$ is bipartite. See Algorithm 4.2 for details.

Algorithm 4.2 One-sided error tester for bipartiteness

Input: An integer $n \in \mathbb{Z}_{>0}$, $\epsilon \in (0, 1)$, and query access to a graph $G = (V, E)$ on n vertices.
1: Pick a set S of vertices uniformly at random, where $|S| = \Theta(\epsilon^{-2} \log \epsilon^{-1})$.
2: Query all pairs of vertices (u, v) for $u, v \in S$.
3: **if** $G[S]$ is bipartite **then**
4:     Accept.
5: **else**
6:     Reject.
7: **end if**

It is clear that Algorithm 4.2 has query complexity $O(\epsilon^{-4} \log^2 \epsilon^{-1})$ and always accepts bipartite graphs because, if a graph is bipartite, then its induced subgraph is always bipartite. Hence, what is remaining is to show that Algorithm 4.2 rejects with high probability when G is ϵ-far from bipartiteness. In what follows, we fix the number of vertices n and the input graph $G = (V, E)$ on n vertices that is ϵ-far from bipartiteness.

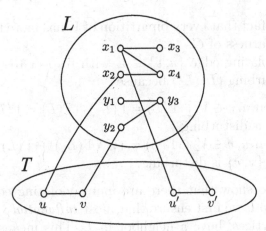

Fig. 4.1: The edges $\{u,v\}$ and $\{u',v'\}$ in T are disturbing the bipartitions $(\{x_1,x_2,y_1,y_2\},\{x_3,x_4,y_3\})$ and $(\{x_1,x_2,y_3\},\{x_3,x_4,y_1,y_2\})$, respectively, of L. We can observe that $G[L \cup T]$ is not bipartite due to the odd-cycle $x_1u'v'y_3y_2vux_2x_4$.

Before starting the analysis, we introduce several useful definitions:

Definition 4.2 (Violating edges and good bipartitions).

- We say that an edge $\{u,v\} \in E$ is a *violating edge* with respect to a bipartition (V_1, V_2) of V if either $u, v \in V_1$ or $u, v \in V_2$.
- If a bipartition (V_1, V_2) has at most ϵn^2 violating edges, then we say that it is ϵ-*good*. Otherwise, it is ϵ-*bad*.

violating edge

ϵ-goodness/badness

Thus, every bipartition of G is ϵ-bad.

We view the set of sampled vertices S as a union of two sets L and T, where:
$$|L| = \Theta\left(\frac{1}{\epsilon}\log\frac{1}{\epsilon}\right) \quad \text{and} \quad |T| = \Theta\left(\frac{1}{\epsilon^2}\log\frac{1}{\epsilon}\right).$$

Here, 'L' stands for *learning* a bipartition and 'T' stands for *testing* the bipartition. To show that the subgraph $G[S]$ is not bipartite with high probability, we consider all possible bipartitions (L_1, L_2) of L. We say that an edge $\{u,v\} \in E$ *disturbs* a bipartition (L_1, L_2) of L if $u,v \in \Gamma(L_1)$ or $u,v \in \Gamma(L_2)$. We will show that with high probability, for every bipartition (L_1, L_2) of L, there is a disturbing edge in T. This means that $G[S]$ is not bipartite, and hence the algorithm rejects. See Figure 4.1 for a schematic.

disturbance

Exercise 4.3. Formalize the argument above that $G[S]$ is not bipartite when all the bipartitions of L are disturbed.

Fix a bipartition (L_1, L_2) of L. To show that there are many disturbing edges of (L_1, L_2), we use the fact that there are more than ϵn^2 violating edges with respect to the bipartition (V_1, V_2), where $V_1 = \Gamma(L_2)$ and $V_2 = V \setminus \Gamma(L_2)$.

Here, we used the fact that every bipartition of V has more than ϵn^2 violating edges from the ϵ-farness of G.

Note that a violating edge $\{u, v\} \in E$ with respect to (V_1, V_2) contained in $G[\Gamma(L)]$ is disturbing (L_1, L_2) because

- if $u, v \in V_1$, then $u, v \in V_1 \cap \Gamma(L) = \Gamma(L_2) \cap \Gamma(L) = \Gamma(L_2) \setminus L$ and hence the edge $\{u, v\}$ is disturbing.
- if $u, v \in V_2$, then $u, v \in V_2 \cap \Gamma(L) = (V \setminus \Gamma(L_2)) \cap \Gamma(L) = \Gamma(L_1) \setminus L$ and hence the edge $\{u, v\}$ is disturbing.

Hence, we want to show that there are many violating edges contained in $G[\Gamma(L)]$. To this end, we first ensure that most *influential* vertices in V, that is, high degree vertices, have a neighbor in L. This means that only a few edges are disjoint from L, and those edges do not affect the analysis much.

Definition 4.3 (Influential vertices and covering sets).

- A vertex $v \in V$ is called *influential* if it has degree at least $\epsilon n/3$.
- A vertex set $U \subseteq V$ is called a *covering set* if all but at most $\epsilon n/3$ of the influential vertices in V have a neighbor in U.

Lemma 4.1. *The set L is a covering set with probability at least $5/6$.*

Proof. The probability that an influential vertex v does not have any neighbor in L is at most:

$$\left(1 - \frac{\epsilon}{3}\right)^{|L|} \leq \exp\left(-\frac{\epsilon |L|}{3}\right) < \frac{\epsilon}{18},$$

by setting the hidden constant in $|L|$ to be large enough. Hence, the expected number of influential vertices non-adjacent to L is at most $\epsilon n/18$, and by Markov's inequality, the probability that there are more than $\epsilon n/3$ such vertices is at most $1/6$. $\square$

Now we count the number of disturbing edges, assuming that L is a covering set.

Lemma 4.2. *If L is a covering set, any bipartition (L_1, L_2) of L has at least $\epsilon n^2/3$ disturbing edges.*

Proof. Consider the bipartition (V_1, V_2), where $V_1 = \Gamma(L_2)$ and $V_2 = V \setminus V_1$. From the argument above, the number of edges disturbing (L_1, L_2) is at least the number of violating edges with respect to (V_1, V_2) contained in $G[\Gamma(L)]$. To bound the latter from below, we consider the following two cases for (violating) edges incident to $V \setminus \Gamma(L)$:

- Edges incident to non-influential vertices: There are at most n such vertices and by definition each has at most $\epsilon n/3$ incident edges, giving a total of $\epsilon n^2/3$ edges.

influential vertex
covering set

- Edges incident to influential vertices in $V \setminus \Gamma(L)$: Since L is a covering set, there are at most $\epsilon n/3$ such influence vertices and each has at most n incident edges, giving a total of $\epsilon n^2/3$ edges.

Hence, the number of violating edges with respect to (V_1, V_2) contained in $G[\Gamma(L)]$ is at least:

$$\epsilon n^2 - \frac{\epsilon n^2}{3} - \frac{\epsilon n^2}{3} = \frac{\epsilon n^2}{3},$$

which lower bounds the number of edges disturbing the bipartition (L_1, L_2). $\qquad\square$

Lemma 4.3. *If G is ϵ-far from bipartiteness, then Algorithm 4.2 rejects with probability at least $2/3$.*

Proof. The lemma follows by observing that $G[S]$ is bipartite only if either (i) the set L is not a covering set, or (ii) the set L is a covering set but there exists a bipartition (L_1, L_2) such that no disturbing edge occurs in T.

The probability that (i) happens is at most $1/6$ by Lemma 4.1. We now bound the probability that (ii) happens. For any fixed bipartition (L_1, L_2), the number of disturbing edges is at least $\epsilon n^2/3$ from Lemma 4.2. This means that the probability that no disturbing edge occurs in T is at most:

$$\left(1 - \frac{\epsilon}{3}\right)^{|T|/2} \leq \frac{2^{-|L|}}{6}$$

by setting the hidden constant in $|T|$ to be large enough. By the union bound, the probability that (ii) occurs is bounded by $1/6$.

Again by the union bound over the $2^{|L|}$ bipartitions of L, the probability that $G[S]$ becomes bipartite is at most $1/3$, and hence the algorithm rejects with probability at least $2/3$. $\qquad\square$

Note that a graph is bipartite if and only if there is no odd-cycle, that is, a cycle of odd length. Hence, Lemma 4.3 is implicitly stating that, if a graph G is ϵ-far from bipartiteness, then there exists an odd-cycle of length $O(|S|) = O(\epsilon^{-2} \log \epsilon^{-1})$. This fact is not trivial at all.

To summarize, we get the following:

Theorem 4.2. *Bipartiteness has a one-sided error tester with query complexity $O(\epsilon^{-4} \log^2 \epsilon^{-1})$.*

We can save a factor of ϵ^{-1} in the query complexity of the testing algorithm. This is done by merely observing that we do not need to perform queries for all pairs of vertices in T. Instead, we can choose T to be the union of uniformly chosen $\Theta(\epsilon^{-2} \log \epsilon^{-1})$ pairs of vertices. We then need only to query which of these $|T|/2$ pairs are edges, as well as query all $|L||T|$ pairs (u, v) where $u \in L$ and $v \in T$. Note that the proof of Lemma 4.3 does not refer to any edge between vertices in T, except for the $|T|/2$ pairs.

> **Exercise 4.4.** Show that bipartiteness cannot be tested by an algorithm that looks at the subgraph induced by $o(\epsilon^{-1})$ vertices that are chosen uniformly at random.

4.3.3 General Partition Property

partition property

We now formally define partition properties. A *partition property* refers to a property for which the vertex set V of a graph can be partitioned into a constant number of parts $V_1, \ldots, V_t$ so that the sizes of those parts and edge densities between those parts are within specified ranges. Hence, a partition property is determined by a sequence of parameters. The first parameter $t \in \mathbb{Z}_{>0}$ determines the number of parts in the partition. For each $i \in [t]$, the parameters ℓ_i and h_i with $0 \le \ell_i \le h_i \le 1$ are the lower and upper bounds, respectively, on the size of V_i relative to the size of V. For each pair $(i,j) \in [t] \times [t]$, the parameters $\ell_{i,j}$ and $h_{i,j}$ with $0 \le \ell_{i,j} \le h_{i,j} \le 1$ are the lower and upper bounds, respectively, on the size of edge set $E(V_i, V_j)$ relative to $|V|^2$. As our focus is undirected graphs, we assume that $\ell_{i,j} = \ell_{j,i}$ and $h_{i,j} = h_{j,i}$ for every $(i,j) \in [t] \times [t]$. Formally, we define a partition property as follows:

> **Definition 4.4** (Partition property). A partition property is parameterized by a sequence:
>
> $$\left(t, \{\ell_i\}_{i \in [t]}, \{h_i\}_{i \in [t]}, \{\ell_{i,j}\}_{i,j \in [t]}, \{h_{i,j}\}_{i,j \in [t]}\right),$$
>
> where $t \in \mathbb{Z}_{>0}$, $0 \le \ell_i \le h_i \le 1$ for each $i \in [t]$, $0 \le \ell_{i,j} \le h_{i,j} \le 1$ for each $i, j \in [t]$. The property consists of all graphs $G = (V, E)$ such that there exists a partition $(V_1, \ldots, V_t)$ of V into t sets that satisfies the following conditions:
>
> - For every $i \in [t]$:
>
> $$\ell_i \le \frac{|V_i|}{|V|} \le h_i.$$
>
> - For every $1 \le i \le j \le t$:
>
> $$\ell_{i,j} \le \frac{|E(V_i, V_j)|}{|V|^2} \le h_{i,j}.$$

> **Remark 4.1.** The definition above has the following issue when $\ell_i = h_i$ for some $i \in [t]$ or $\ell_{i,j} = h_{i,j}$ for some $1 \le i \le j \le t$. For example, suppose that $\ell_1 = h_1 = 1/3$. In such a case, in order for a graph to admit a partition $V_1, \ldots, V_t$ with $|V_i|/|V| = 1/3$, the value of n must

be a multiple of 3. Hence, the tester for such a partition property must reject when n is not a multiple of 3. We want to avoid such uninteresting technicality, and instead we allow (fractional) partition in which up to $t - 1$ vertices may be split among several parts.

Every partition property is testable with a constant number of queries:

Theorem 4.3. *Every partition property with the first parameter t is testable with* $\mathrm{poly}(t\epsilon^{-1})^t$ *queries, where the polynomial does not depend on the parameters of the property.*

The algorithm used to show Theorem 4.3 is too complicated to describe here. In particular, it is not enough to sample a small induced subgraph, and check whether it satisfies the partition property[2].

We can formulate many properties using partition properties and they can be tested using Theorem 4.3:

- *Bipartiteness*: We choose $t = 2$ and $h_{1,1} = h_{2,2} = 0$. All other parameters are trivial, that is, lower bounds are set to zero and upper bounds are set to one. Note that this partition property consists of graphs with a bipartition (V_1, V_2) such that the induced subgraphs $G[V_1]$ and $G[V_2]$ are independent, that is, bipartite graphs. bipartiteness
- *k-colorability*: We choose $t = k$ and $h_{i,i} = 0$ for every $i \in [k]$. All other parameters are trivial. colorability
- *ρ-cut*: We choose $t = 2$ and $\ell_{1,2} = \rho$. All other parameters are trivial. cut
- *ρ-bisection*: We choose $t = 2$ and $h_{1,2} = \rho$ and $\ell_1 = h_1 = \ell_2 = h_2 = \frac{1}{2}$. bisection
- *ρ-clique*: We choose $t = 1$ and $\ell_1 = \rho$ and $\ell_{1,1} = \frac{\rho(\rho - 1/n)}{2}$. As the parameter $\ell_{1,1}$ depends on n, we cannot express ρ-clique as a single partition property. Hence, in order to test ρ-clique using the tester provided in Theorem 4.3, we need to change the partition property to test depending on the number of vertices. clique
- *Biclique* cannot be expressed as a single partition property. However, we can test it by running the algorithm given in Theorem 4.3 multiple times as follows: For each multiples ρ_1 and ρ_2 of $\epsilon/2$, we test with the error parameter $\epsilon/2$ whether the input graph G satisfies the partition property with $t = 2$, $\ell_1 = \rho$, $h_1 = \rho_1 + \epsilon$, $\ell_2 = \rho_2$, $h_2 = \rho_2 + \epsilon$, and $\ell_{1,2} = \rho_1 \rho_2$, and $h_{1,2} = 1$. We accept if some of the tests accepts, and reject otherwise. We can verify the correctness of this algorithm as follows: Suppose that G is a biclique with a bipartition (V_1, V_2). Then, the algorithm above accepts (with high probability) when ρ_1 and ρ_2 are the largest multiples of $\epsilon/2$ no more than $|V_1|/|V|$ and $|V_2|/|V|$, respectively. On the other hand, if the biclique

---

[2] The canonical tester that will be described in Section 4.4 samples a small induced subgraph and checks it satisfies some particular property. But the property will not be the partition property of interest.

algorithm accepts with high probability for some choice of ρ_1 and ρ_2, then G is $\epsilon/2$-close to having a bipartition (V_1, V_2) such that:

$$|E(V_1, V_2)| \geq \rho_1\rho_2|V|^2 \geq \left(|V_1| - \frac{\epsilon|V|}{2}\right)\left(|V_2| - \frac{\epsilon|V|}{2}\right)$$

$$= |V_1||V_2| - \left(\frac{\epsilon}{2} - \frac{\epsilon^2}{4}\right)|V|^2,$$

which is $(\epsilon/2 - \epsilon^2/4)$-close to being a biclique. This mean that G is $\epsilon/2 + \epsilon/2 - \epsilon^2/4 = \epsilon - \epsilon^2/4$-close to being a biclique.

The generality of Theorem 4.3 comes at the cost of efficiency. As we have seen, however, more efficient testing is possible for some specific properties such as being a biclique and bipartiteness.

4.4 Canonical Tester

When showing a lower bound on the query complexity for testing a particular property, it is convenient if there is a canonical form of a tester because we can concentrate on such a tester instead of considering all possible testers. For graph properties in the adjacency matrix model, we consider the following form of a canonical tester:

canonical tester

> **Definition 4.5.** A tester is *canonical* if there exists a function $s\colon \mathbb{Z}_{>0} \times (0,1) \to \mathbb{Z}_{>0}$ such that, given $n \in \mathbb{Z}_{>0}$, $\epsilon \in (0,1)$, and query access to a graph G on n vertices, it uniformly selects a set of $s(n, \epsilon)$ vertices and accepts if and only if the induced subgraph obtained through the query access has some fixed property $\mathcal{P}$.

Note that the property $\mathcal{P}$ may be different from the property we want to test.

The following theorem states that, if there is a tester for a property $\mathcal{P}$, then there is a canonical tester.

> **Theorem 4.4.** *Let $\mathcal{P}$ be any graph property. If there exists a tester with query complexity $q(n, \epsilon)$ for $\mathcal{P}$, then there exists a canonical tester for $\mathcal{P}$ that samples $O(q(n, \epsilon))$ vertices. Furthermore, if the original tester has one-sided error then so does the new tester.*

Note that the query complexity of the canonical tester is $O\left(q(n, \epsilon)^2\right)$. Hence, by blowing up the number of queries quadratically, we can canonicalize a tester. The proof of Theorem 4.4 is a bit technical, and we only provide a sketch.

vertex-uncovering tester

Proof sketch of Theorem 4.4. First, we say that a tester is *vertex-uncovering* if in each step, depending on its internal randomness and the answers obtained in previous steps, it selects a new vertex $v \in V$ and makes queries to all pairs (v, w), where $w \in V$ is a vertex selected in some prior step. Clearly, any tester A can be simulated by a vertex-uncovering tester A_1, albeit the query complexity quadratically increases.

Next, to suppress non-adaptiveness, we consider a tester A_2 that randomly samples a permutation $\pi \colon V \to V$ and then apply A_1 on $\pi(G)$. We note that A_2 is a valid tester for $\mathcal{P}$ because A_1 is a tester for $\mathcal{P}$, $\pi(G)$ satisfies $\mathcal{P}$ if G satisfies $\mathcal{P}$, and $\pi(G)$ is ϵ-far from $\mathcal{P}$ if G is ϵ-far from $\mathcal{P}$, and hence satisfies the conditions of a (randomized) gap-preserving local reduction (from $\mathcal{P}$ to itself). Looking at the process of A_2, it non-adaptively samples an induced subgraph and then decides based on the induced subgraph and its internal randomness.

Using a similar argument, we can show that we can simulate A_2 by another tester A_3 that samples an induced subgraph uniformly at random and decides based on the induced subgraph without the label information on vertices and its internal randomness independent from the randomness used to sample the induced subgraph.

Finally, we can show that we can simulate A_3 by another non-adaptive tester A_4 that samples an induced subgraph uniformly at random and deterministically decides based solely on the induced subgraph without the label information on vertices. To get rid of the internal randomness, we design A_4 so that A_4 always accepts when having sampled an induced subgraph isomorphic to a graph H when the probability that A_3 accepts is at least half when having sampled an induced subgraph isomorphic to H and vice versa. Note that the resulting tester A_4 is canonical. $\qquad\square$

We will utilize Theorem 4.4 later in Section 4.5.3 to show a super-polynomial lower bound in ϵ^{-1} for a specific property. Also, Theorem 4.4 is useful when characterizing constant-query testable properties because we only have to consider constant-query testability by canonical testers.

4.5 Subgraph Freeness

Let H be a connected graph. We say that a graph G is H-*free* if G does not have a subgraph isomorphic to H. In this section, we study specific choices of H, namely, a cycle of length three (denoted C_3 or a *triangle*) and a cycle of length four (denoted C_4 or a *square*). Indeed, H-freeness is constant-query testable for any fixed H. We will cover this general result in Chapter 9.

We start with a simple general framework that can be applied to any H (although it may not yield the optimal sample complexity). Specifically, we repeat the following process $q_H(\epsilon)$ times for some function $q_H \colon (0, 1] \to \mathbb{Z}_{>0}$: Sample a set S of $|V(H)|$ vertices uniformly at random, and reject if the

H-freeness

triangle
square

subgraph induced by S contains H as its subgraph, and accept otherwise. See Algorithm 4.3 for details.

Algorithm 4.3 One-sided error tester for H-freeness

Input: An integer $n \in \mathbb{Z}_{>0}$, $\epsilon \in (0, 1)$, and query access to a graph $G = (V, E)$ on n vertices.
1: **for** $q_H(\epsilon)$ times **do**
2:     Pick a set S of $|V(H)|$ vertices uniformly at random.
3:     **if** The induced subgraph $G[S]$ contains H as its subgraph **then**
4:         Reject.
5:     **end if**
6: **end for**
7: Accept.

It is clear that the algorithm always accepts if G is H-free and the query complexity is $|V(H)|^2 \cdot q_H(\epsilon)$. Hence, the question is whether the algorithm rejects graphs that are ϵ-far from H-freeness. This question is addressed by considering the following:

Question 4.1. In a graph $G = (V, E)$ that is ϵ-far from H-freeness, how many vertex sets $S \subseteq V$ of size $|V(H)|$ have H as a subgraph of $G[S]$?

In order to address Question 4.1, it suffices to consider the following problem:

Question 4.2. In a graph $G = (V, E)$ that is ϵ-far from H-freeness, how many isomorphic copies of H do there exist?

The difference between Question 4.1 and Question 4.2 is that the latter counts a single vertex set $S \subseteq V$ several times if $G[S]$ contains several isomorphic copies of H. However, for a fixed H, they are only different by a constant factor because the number of isomorphic copies of H in $G[S]$ is bounded by a constant.

In turns out that, for any graph H, there exists $\delta_H(\epsilon)$ such that, a graph G that is ϵ-far from H-freeness contains $\delta_H(\epsilon) \cdot \binom{|V(G)|}{|V(H)|}$ isomorphic copies of H. Then, we can set $q_H(\epsilon) = \Theta(\frac{1}{\delta_H(\epsilon)})$ because then with high probability we hit a vertex set S that contains H as its subgraph.

Interestingly, the analysis for testing square-freeness is much easier than that for testing triangle-freeness and the known bound on $\delta_H(\epsilon)$ for squares is much larger than that for triangles. The analysis for squares only requires an elementary argument whereas that for triangles involves a deep result in graph theory. We study square-freeness and triangle-freeness in more detail in Section 4.5.1 and Section 4.5.2, respectively.

4.5.1 Square-Freeness

A *homomorphism* of a graph H into a graph G is a mapping $f \colon V(H) \to V(H)$ such that $\{f(u), f(v)\} \in E(G)$ whenever $\{u, v\} \in E(H)$. Note that a homomorphism does not have to be injective. For example, every bipartite graph can be homomorphically mapped into an edge and a square can be homomorphically mapped into a path of length two.

homomorphism

We start with counting the number of homomorphisms from a square to G instead of counting the number of isomorphic copies of a square in G because the former is an easier task and gives a bound on the number of isomorphic copies as well. The next lemma shows that every dense graph contains many copies of a square.

Lemma 4.4 (Square removal lemma). *Let $\epsilon > 0$ and let $G = (V, E)$ be a graph on n vertices and at least ϵn^2 edges. Then, the number of homomorphisms from a square into G is at least $16\epsilon^4 n^4$.*

Proof. Let $d_1 \geq d_2 \geq \cdots \geq d_n$ be the degrees of the vertices of G. Let $\bar{d} = (\sum_{i \in [n]} d_i)/n$ denote the average degree. Note that we have $\bar{d} \geq 2\epsilon n$. The number of homomorphisms from a path of length two into G is:

$$\sum_{i \in [n]} d_i^2 \geq n\bar{d}^2 \geq n(2\epsilon n)^2 = 4\epsilon^2 n^3,$$

where the first inequality follows from Jensen's inequality. Let $N = n^2$ and we classify the homomorphisms above into N classes, according to the ordered set of images of the two endpoints of the path. Let $D_1, D_2, \ldots, D_N$ be the numbers of homomorphisms of the N possible types. Note that each ordered 2-tuple of (not necessarily distinct) homomorphisms of the same type defines a homomorphism of a square into G.

Let $\bar{D} = (\sum_{i \in [N]} D_i)/N$ denote the average of $D_1, D_2, \ldots, D_N$. Note that we have $\bar{D} \geq 4\epsilon^2 n$. Then, the total number of homomorphisms from a square into G is at least:

$$\sum_{i \in [N]} D_i^2 \geq N\bar{D}^2 \geq N(4\epsilon^2 n)^2 = 16\epsilon^4 n^4,$$

where the first inequality follows again from Jensen's inequality. $\square$

An isomorphism from H to itself is called an *automorphism*. We can verify that the number of automorphism from a square to itself is eight. Then, we have the following:

automorphism

Corollary 4.1. *Let $\epsilon > 0$ and G be a graph on n vertices with at least ϵn^2 edges. Then, the number of subgraphs of G isomorphic to a square is at least:*

$$\delta_\square(\epsilon) \binom{n}{4},$$

where $\delta_\square(\epsilon) = \Omega(\epsilon^4)$.

Proof. The number of homomorphisms of a square into G which are not injective is at most $O(n^{4-1}) = o(n^4)$, and the result thus follows from Lemma 4.4, after dividing by the number of automorphisms of H, that is, eight. $\square$

It is worth noting that, for the random graph $G(n, 2\epsilon)$ on n vertices, in which each pair of vertices forms an edge with probability 2ϵ independently from others, the assertion of Corollary 4.1 is tight.

From Corollary 4.1, we get the following:

Theorem 4.5. *Algorithm 4.3 with H being a square and $q_H(\epsilon) = \Theta(1/\delta_\square(\epsilon))$ is a one-sided error tester for square-freeness with query complexity $O(\epsilon^{-4})$.*

Proof. We have already seen that Algorithm 4.3 is a one-sided error tester. When G is ϵ-far from square-freeness, G should have at least ϵn^2 edges (Otherwise, by removing at most ϵn^2 edges, we can get an empty graph, which is square-free.) Then, by Corollary 4.1, G contains at least $\delta_\square(\epsilon)$ subgraphs isomorphic to a square. Hence, Algorithm 4.3 with H being a square rejects with probability at least $2/3$ by setting the hidden constant in $q_H(\epsilon)$ to be large enough. The query complexity is $\binom{4}{2} \cdot q_H(\epsilon) = O(\epsilon^{-4})$. $\square$

A couple of remarks are relevant here:

- We note that there is a simple two-sided error tester for square-freeness with query complexity $O(\epsilon^{-1})$. It merely estimates the number of edges in the input graph by using Lemma 2.2 to within $\epsilon n^2/2$, and accepts if and only if the estimation is at most ϵn^2. If G is square-free, then the number of edges in G is $o(n^2)$ by Lemma 4.4, and the algorithm accepts with high probability (assuming that n is sufficiently large.) If G is ϵ-far, then it must have ϵn^2 edges, and the algorithm rejects with high probability.
- Corollary 4.1 and Theorem 4.5 can be generalized to bipartite graphs:

Exercise 4.5. Let $s \geq t \geq 1$ be integers. Show that, for every graph $G = (V, E)$ on n vertices with at least ϵn^2 edges, the number of homomorphisms from complete bipartite graph $K_{s,t}$ into G is at least $(2\epsilon)^{st} n^{s+t}$. Using this fact, show that there is a one-sided error tester for H-freeness with $(1/\epsilon)^{O(st)}$ queries.

The query complexity bound $(1/\epsilon)^{O(st)}$ is not tight in the exponent of $1/\epsilon$; see the discussion in Section 4.5.4.

4.5.2 Triangle-Freeness and Regularity Lemma

Define T: $\mathbb{Z}_{>0} \to \mathbb{Z}_{>0}$ as the tower of twos, that is, $T(1) = 2$ and $T(k+1) = 2^{T(k)}$ for $k \in \mathbb{Z}_{>0}$, or more pictorially:

$$T(k) = 2^{2^{2^{\cdot^{\cdot^{2}}}}},$$

where the number of twos is k. The following theorem on testing triangle-freeness is the main result of this section:

Lemma 4.5 (Triangle removal lemma). *Let $\epsilon > 0$ and let G be a graph on n vertices that is ϵ-far from triangle-freeness, then G contains at least $\delta_\triangle(\epsilon)\binom{n}{3}$ triangles, where:*

$$\delta_\triangle(\epsilon) \geq \frac{1}{T(\text{poly}(\epsilon^{-1}))}.$$

As opposed to Lemma 4.4, we cannot guarantee that there are many copies of a triangle just by assuming that the graph is dense. For example, a complete bipartite graph G on the bipartition (V_1, V_2) with $|V_1| = |V_2| = n/2$ has $n^2/4$ edges whereas G has no triangle.

Although $\delta_\triangle$ is a tiny function of ϵ, it is a positive value independent of the graph size. Hence, we get the following:

Theorem 4.6. *Algorithm 4.3 with H being a triangle and $q_H(\epsilon) = \Theta(\delta_\triangle(\epsilon)^{-1})$ is a one-sided error tester for triangle-freeness with query complexity $O(T(\text{poly}(\epsilon^{-1})))$.*

The proof is very similar to Theorem 4.5 and we omit it. The main reason that the bounds on a square and a triangle are so different is that the former is bipartite whereas the latter is not. We will discuss this issue later in Section 4.5.4.

To prove Lemma 4.5, we use the celebrated Szemerédi's regularity lemma from graph theory. We introduce Szemerédi's regularity lemma in Section 4.5.2.1 and prove the triangle removal lemma in Section 4.5.2.2.

4.5.2.1 Szemerédi's regularity lemma

Szemerédi's regularity lemma roughly states that any graph can be partitioned into a constant number of parts so that almost all pairs look random bipartite graphs. In order to formally state Szemerédi's regularity lemma, we need several definitions.

density

Definition 4.6 (Density). Let $G = (V, E)$ be a graph, and (S, T) be a pair of non-empty disjoint subsets of V. The *density* of the bipartite subgraph induced by S and T is:

$$d(S, T) = \frac{|E(S, T)|}{|S||T|}.$$

In what follows, we always consider pairs non-empty disjoint subsets, unless stated otherwise.

γ-regularity

Definition 4.7 (γ-regularity). Let $G = (V, E)$ be a graph. For $\gamma > 0$, a pair (S, T) of subsets of V is said to be γ-*regular* if, for every $S' \subseteq S$ and $T' \subseteq T$ with $|S'| > \gamma|S|$ and $|T'| > \gamma|T|$, the following holds:

$$|d(S, T) - d(S', T')| < \gamma.$$

A regular pair in a graph looks like a random bipartite graph of the same edge density; one may think of and analyze a regular pair as if it was a random bipartite graph, and the conclusion reached would typically hold for the regular pair.

> **Exercise 4.6.** Let (S, T) be a pair of vertex subsets. Show that, if $|d(S', T') - d(S, T)| < \gamma$ for sets $S' \subseteq S$ and $T' \subseteq T$ of sizes $|S'| = \lceil \gamma|S| \rceil$ and $|T'| = \lceil \gamma|T| \rceil$, then the pair (S, T) is γ-regular.

equipartition

Definition 4.8 (Equipartition). A partition $(V_1, \ldots, V_t)$ is an *equipartition* of V if:

$$\left\lfloor \frac{|V|}{t} \right\rfloor \leq |V_i| \leq \left\lceil \frac{|V|}{t} \right\rceil$$

for every $i \in [t]$.

refinement

A partition $\mathcal{B}$ is a *refinement* of another partition $\mathcal{A}$ if $\mathcal{B}$ is obtained from $\mathcal{A}$ by further partitioning sets in $\mathcal{A}$.

Szemerédi's regularity lemma states that, given any equipartition, one can always refine it to get a new equipartition so that almost all pairs are regular.

Szemerédi's regularity lemma

Lemma 4.6 (*Szemerédi's regularity lemma* [377]). *For any $m \in \mathbb{Z}_{>0}$ and $\gamma \in (0, 1)$, there exists $T = T_{4.6}(m, \gamma)$ such that if $G = (V, E)$ is a graph with more than T vertices and $\mathcal{A}$ is an equipartition of V into m sets, then there is an equipartition $\mathcal{B}$ of V with $|B| = k$ that is a refinement of $\mathcal{A}$ with the following property:*

- $m \leq k < T$;
- *All but at most $\gamma \binom{k}{2}$ pairs of sets in $\mathcal{B}$ are γ-regular.*

See Figure 4.2 for a schematic. A useful feature of Szemerédi's regularity lemma is that the parameter T does not depend on the graph size. However,

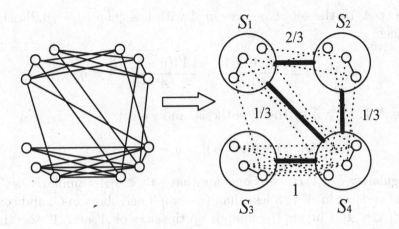

Fig. 4.2: Regular partition of a graph with $\mathcal{A} = \{V\}$ and $\mathcal{B} = \{S_1, S_2, S_3, S_4\}$. The value on the bold edge between parts represent the density between the parts.

the dependence of T on γ is prohibitively large for any practical applications because even $T(2, \gamma)$ grows as $\mathrm{T}(\gamma^{-5})$. Indeed, this huge upper bound cannot be significantly improved because $\mathrm{T}(\gamma^{-1/16})$ is a lower bound on $T(2, \gamma)$. Nevertheless, Szemerédi's Regularity Lemma has a large number of theoretical applications.

4.5.2.2 Proof of the triangle removal lemma

Before proving the triangle removal lemma (Lemma 4.5), we first see that three disjoint sets, each of which is regular and have a reasonably large density, contain many triangles:

Lemma 4.7. *Let $G = (V, E)$ be a graph. For any $\eta > 0$, there exists $\gamma = \gamma_{4.7}(\eta) > 0$ and $\delta_{4.7} = \delta(\eta) > 0$ such that if A, B, C are disjoint subsets of V and each pair of them is γ-regular with density at least η, then G contains at least $\delta|A||B||C|$ distinct triangles with a vertex from each set. Furthermore, $\gamma = \eta/2$ and $\delta = (1 - \eta)\eta^3/8$.*

Note that, if G were a random graph with edge density η, then the expected number of distinct triangles spanning A, B, and C is $\eta^3|A||B||C|$. Lemma 4.7 claims that we can guarantee a similar number of distinct triangles in a γ-regular graph.

Proof of Lemma 4.7. Let A^* be the set of vertices in A with at least $(\eta - \gamma)|B|$ neighbors in B and at least $(\eta - \gamma)|C|$ neighbors in C.

Claim 4.1. $|A^*| \geq (1 - 2\gamma)|A|$.

Proof. Let A' be the set of vertices in A with less than $(\eta - \gamma)|B|$ neighbors in B. Then:

$$d(A', B) = \frac{|E(A', B)|}{|A'||B|} < \frac{|A'|(\eta - \gamma)|B|}{|A'||B|} = \eta - \gamma.$$

We have $d(A, B) \geq \eta$ by the hypothesis, and we get:

$$|d(A, B) - d(A', B)| > \eta - (\eta - \gamma) = \gamma.$$

By γ-regularity of (A, B), we conclude that $|A'| < \gamma|A|$. Similarly, let A'' be the set of vertices in A with less than $(\eta - \gamma)|C|$ neighbors in C, and conclude that $|A''| < \gamma|A|$. Putting the bounds on the sizes of A' and A'' together, we get:

$$|A^*| = |A \setminus (A' \cup A'')| \geq (1 - 2\gamma)|A|,$$

as required.   □

Now we get back to the proof of Lemma 4.7. For a vertex $v \in A^*$, let $B_v = B \cap \Gamma(v)$ and $C_v = C \cap \Gamma(v)$. Since we set $\gamma = \eta/2$:

$$|B_v| \geq (\eta - \gamma)|B| = \gamma|B|.$$

Similarly, we have $|C_v| \geq \gamma|C|$. Each edge between B_v and C_v contributes a triangle (with the vertex v). So, the question is how many edges there are between B_v and C_v. The pair (B, C) is γ-regular with density $d(B, C) \geq \eta$. Therefore, $d(B_v, C_v) \geq \eta - \gamma$ and we get:

$$|E(B_v, C_v)| = d(B_v, C_v) \cdot |B_v| \cdot |C_v| \geq (\eta - \gamma)^3|B||C| = \left(\frac{\eta}{2}\right)^3 |B||C|.$$

By the claim:

$$|A^*| \geq (1 - 2\gamma)|A| = (1 - \eta)|A|.$$

Setting $\delta = (1 - \eta)\eta^3/8$ gives that the number of distinct triangles with a vertex from each set is at least:

$$(1 - \eta)|A|\left(\frac{\eta}{2}\right)^3 |B||C| = \frac{(1 - \eta)\eta^3}{8}|A||B||C| = \delta|A||B||C|,$$

as required.   □

Now we prove the triangle removal lemma. Consider a graph $G = (V, E)$ that is ϵ-far from being triangle-free, and let $\mathcal{A}$ be an arbitrary equipartition of V into $\lceil 5\epsilon^{-1} \rceil$ sets. Set $\gamma = \min\{\epsilon/5, \gamma_{4.7}(\epsilon/5)\} = \epsilon/10$.

Apply the regularity Lemma with $m := \lceil 5\epsilon^{-1} \rceil$ and γ. Then, we get $T = T(\lceil 5\epsilon^{-1} \rceil, \gamma)$ and an equipartition $\mathcal{B} = \{B_1, \ldots, B_k\}$ that is a refinement of $\mathcal{A}$ such that:

- $\lceil 5\epsilon^{-1} \rceil \leq k \leq T$;

- All but at most $\gamma\binom{k}{2}$ pairs of $\{B_1, B_2, \ldots, B_k\}$ are γ-regular;
- $|B_i| \in [\lfloor n/T \rfloor, \epsilon n/5]$ for $i \in [k]$.

To show that there are many triangles, we remove all the "non-useful" edges, which connect pairs violating the condition of Lemma 4.7. The number of removed edges turns out to be small, and hence a triangle still exists in the resulting graph. Then, we apply Lemma 4.7 on the three sets spanning the triangle to show that there are many triangles among the sets.

Now, we formalize the notion of a useful edge:

Definition 4.9 (Useful edge). An edge $\{u, v\}$ with $u \in B_i$ and $v \in B_j$ is *useful* if it satisfies the following three conditions: useful edge

- $i \neq j$.
- (B_i, B_j) is γ-regular.
- The density $d(B_i, B_j) \geq \epsilon/5$.

We can show that G does not contain many non-useful edges. The proof is by simply counting the number of edges which violate the three conditions respectively.

Lemma 4.8. *G has at most $\epsilon n^2/2$ non-useful edges with respect to the equipartition $\mathcal{B}$.*

Proof. Let m_1 be the number of edges violating the first condition. Each vertex in G can have at most $n/k - 1$ neighbors in the same partition. Hence:

$$m_1 \leq \left(\frac{n}{k} - 1\right) n \leq \frac{(n-1)n}{k} \leq \frac{n^2}{k} \leq \frac{\epsilon n^2}{5}.$$

Let m_2 be the number of edges violating the second condition. By the regularity Lemma, there are at most $\gamma\binom{k}{2}$ pairs of parts in $\mathcal{B}$ which are not γ-regular. Each of the pairs contributes at most $(n/k)^2$ cross edges. Hence, we have:

$$m_2 \leq \gamma\binom{k}{2}\left(\frac{n}{k}\right)^2 \leq \gamma\frac{k(k-1)}{2}\frac{n(n-1)}{k(k-1)} \leq \frac{\gamma n^2}{2} \leq \frac{\epsilon n^2}{10}.$$

Let m_3 be the number of edges violating the third condition.

$$m_3 < \frac{\epsilon}{5}\left(\frac{n}{k}\right)^2\binom{k}{2} \leq \frac{\epsilon n^2}{10}.$$

Hence, $m_1 + m_2 + m_3 \leq 4\epsilon/10 \cdot n^2 < \epsilon n^2/2$, which gives the lemma. □

Now, we prove the triangle removal lemma.

Proof of Lemma 4.5. We remove all the non-useful edges in G. Note that the number of removed edges is only $\epsilon n^2/2$, which is smaller than ϵn^2. Since G is

ϵ-far from being triangle-free, there exists a triangle (u, v, w), where $u \in B_{i_1}$, $v \in B_{i_2}$, $w \in B_{i_3}$ for some $i_1, i_2, i_3 \in [k]$.

By applying Lemma 4.7 on the sets B_{i_1}, B_{i_2}, and B_{i_3}, the number of triangles in G is at least $\delta_{4.7}(\epsilon/5)|B_{i_1}||B_{i_2}||B_{i_3}|$, which is at least $\delta_{4.7}(\epsilon/5) \cdot (\lfloor n/T \rfloor)^3$. $\qquad\qquad\square$

Clearly, the reason that the enormous tower function T appears in the query complexity above is due to the use of Szemerédi's regularity lemma. It is known that the bound on $\delta_\triangle(\epsilon)$ can be improved to $1/T(O(\log \epsilon^{-1}))$ by bypassing the use of Szemerédi's regularity lemma; see Section 4.8.

4.5.3 Lower Bounds for Triangle-Freeness

We have seen that triangle-freeness is testable with $O(T(\text{poly}(\epsilon^{-1})))$ queries. A natural question is whether we can improve this query complexity. The following theorem shows that any one-sided error tester needs at least a super-polynomial number of queries in ϵ.

> **Theorem 4.7.** *Every one-sided error tester for triangle-freeness requires at least:*
> $$\left(\frac{1}{\epsilon}\right)^{\Omega(\log \epsilon^{-1})}$$
> *queries.*

This lower bounds is the current best although it is far apart from the upper bound of $T(\text{poly}(\epsilon^{-1}))$.

By Theorem 4.4, we can restrict our attention to a one-sided error *canonical tester*. Recall that a canonical tester samples a vertex set $S \subseteq V$ of a fixed size uniformly at random, and then decides its output solely depending on the induced subgraph $G[S]$. Hence, for a one-sided error canonical tester to reject a graph, it must be the case that the induced subgraph $G[S]$ cannot be extended to a triangle-free graph, or in other words, $G[S]$ must contain a triangle as its subgraph. This motivates us to show the following graph construction.

canonical tester

> **Lemma 4.9.** *For any $\epsilon \in (0, 1)$ and infinitely many $n \in \mathbb{Z}_{>0}$, there exists a graph G on n vertices with the following property:*
> - *G is ϵ-far from triangle-freeness.*
> - *The number of triangles in G is only $\epsilon^{\Omega(\log \epsilon^{-1})} \binom{n}{3}$.*

If such an ϵ-far graph G exists, in order to reject it, a canonical tester must sample $(1/\epsilon)^{\Omega(\log \epsilon^{-1})}$ vertices because the probability that $G[S]$ contains a triangle is:

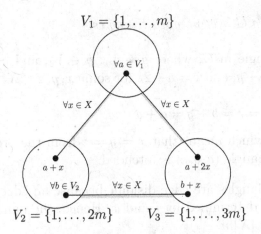

Fig. 4.3: Graph construction

$$\Pr_{S}\big[G[S] \text{ contains a triangle as a subgraph}\big]$$

$$= \Pr_{\{v_1,\ldots,v_s\}\sim\binom{V}{s}}\big[\exists i,j,k \in [s], G[\{v_i, v_j, v_k\}] \text{ is isomorphic to a triangle}\big]$$

$$\leq \sum_{i,j,k\in[s]} \Pr_{\{v_1,\ldots,v_s\}\sim\binom{V}{s}}\big[G[\{v_i, v_j, v_k\}] \text{ is isomorphic to a triangle}\big]$$

(by the union bound)

$$\leq s^3\epsilon^{\Omega(\log\epsilon^{-1})},$$

where $s = |S|$. In order to make this probability more than $2/3$, we must have $s = (1/\epsilon)^{\Omega(\log\epsilon^{-1})}$ and Theorem 4.7 follows.

Now we turn to proving Lemma 4.9. To this end, we use the following number theoretic theorem.

Theorem 4.8 (Behrend's theorem). *For any $m \in \mathbb{Z}_{>0}$, there exists a set $X \subseteq [m]$ such that:*

$$|X| \geq \frac{m}{e^{10\sqrt{\log m}}}$$

and the only solution to $x + y = 2z$ for $x, y, z \in X$ is $x = y = z$.

Proof of Lemma 4.9. Let us fix m and X be the set constructed by Theorem 4.8. Our graph $G = (V, E)$ is a tripartite graph on vertex sets $V_1 = [m]$, $V_2 = [2m]$, $V_3 = [3m]$. Then, we add edges as follows (Figure 4.3):

- For each $a \in V_1$, $b \in V_2$, and $x \in X$, add an edge (a, b) if $b = a + x$.
- For each $b \in V_2$, $c \in V_3$, and $x \in X$, add an edge (b, c) if $c = b + x$.
- For each $a \in V_1$, $c \in V_3$, and $x \in X$, add an edge (a, c) if $c = a + 2x$.

It is easy to see that $|V| = 6m$ and $|E| = 4|X|m$.

We say that a triangle of the form $(i, i + x, i + 2x)$ for $i \in [m]$ and $x \in X$ is an *intended triangle*.

intended triangle

Claim 4.2. *All triangles in G are intended triangles.*

Proof. Let (a, b, c) be a triangle in G, where $a \in V_1$, $b \in V_2$, and $c \in V_3$. Suppose that $b = a + x$, $c = b + y$, and $c = a + 2z$ for some $x, y, z \in X$. Then, we have:

$$a + 2z = c = b + y = a + x + y.$$

Hence, we have $x + y = 2z$, which means that $x = y = z$ from the property of X. This means that the triangle (a, b, c) is intended.   □

Note that all the intended triangles are edge-disjoint because an edge in an intended triangle is uniquely determined by i and x. Hence, the number of edge-disjoint triangles in G is $|X|m$.

In order to make G triangle-free, we need to remove at least one edge from each triangle. Hence, the farness of G from triangle-freeness is at least:

$$\frac{|X|m}{36m^2} \geq \frac{1}{36e^{10\sqrt{\log m}}}.$$

In order to make G ϵ-far from triangle-freeness, it suffices to choose:

$$m = \left(\frac{1}{\epsilon}\right)^{\Omega(\log \epsilon^{-1})}.$$

The number of triangles is:

$$|X|m = \frac{m^2}{e^{10\sqrt{\log m}}} = O\left(\frac{1}{me^{10\sqrt{\log m}}}\binom{|V|}{3}\right) = \epsilon^{\Omega(\log \epsilon^{-1})}\binom{|V|}{3}.$$

The only problem in the previous construction is that the number of vertices of G is bounded by $6m$, which is a function of ϵ^{-1}. In order to make the number of vertices arbitrarily large, we modify the construction of our graph by adding gadgets. That is, we replace each vertex v with a gadget v containing s vertices, where s is a parameter. Then, if there was an edge (u, v) in G, we create an edge between all vertices in gadget u and all vertices in gadget v. Let $G' = (V', E')$ be the obtained graph. Then, we have $|V'| = 6ms$ and $|E'| = 3|X|ms^2$. The number of triangles in G' is $\Theta(m|X|s^3)$ because for each triangle in G, there are now $\binom{s}{3}$ triangles, and the number of edge-disjoint triangles is $\Theta(m|X|s^2)$ because for each triangle in G, there are s choices for the first, s choices for the second, and only one possibility for the third; otherwise they are not edge-disjoint. Then, the farness of G' from triangle-freeness is:

$$\Omega\left(\frac{m|X|s^2}{(6ms)^2}\right) = \Omega\left(\frac{1}{36e^{10\sqrt{\log m}}}\right) \geq \epsilon.$$

The number of triangles is:

$$O(m|X|s^3) = O\left(\frac{m^2 s^3}{e^{10\sqrt{\log m}}}\right) = O\left(\frac{1}{me^{10\sqrt{\log m}}}\binom{|V'|}{3}\right) = \epsilon^{\Omega(\log \epsilon^{-1})}\binom{|V'|}{3}.$$
$\square$

4.5.4 Testing H-Freeness

Recall that, for a connected graph H, $\delta_H(\epsilon)$ denotes the minimum fraction of isomorphic copies of H (with respect to the number of all possible subgraphs) in a graph that is ϵ-far from H-freeness. The following is a summary of known upper and lower bounds on $\delta_H(\epsilon)$ for general H.

Theorem 4.9 (Upper bound and lower bounds on $\delta_H(\epsilon)$). *Let H be a connected graph on h vertices. If H is bipartite, then:*

$$\epsilon^{O(h^2)} \leq \delta_H(\epsilon) \leq \epsilon^{\Omega(h^2)}.$$

Else if H is non-bipartite:

$$\frac{1}{\mathrm{T}\left(O(h^4 \log \epsilon^{-1})\right)} \leq \delta_H(\epsilon) \leq \epsilon^{\Omega(\log \epsilon^{-1})}$$

The inequalities of the bipartite case is obtained by extending the argument for the square case. The left and right inequalities of the non-bipartite case is obtained by extending the arguments for the triangle case.

We can also obtain the following testability results.

Theorem 4.10. *Let H be a connected graph on h vertices. Then, the following hold:*

- *If H is bipartite, then there is a one-sided error tester for H-freeness with $(1/\epsilon)^{O(h)}$ queries and any one-sided error tester for H-freeness requires $(1/\epsilon)^{\Omega(h)}$ queries.*
- *Else if H is non-bipartite, there is a one-sided error tester for H-freeness with $\mathrm{T}\left(O(h^4 \log \epsilon^{-1})\right)$ queries and any one-sided error tester for H-freeness requires $(1/\epsilon)^{\Omega(\log \epsilon^{-1})}$ queries.*

The result for non-bipartite H follows as a direct corollary from the above Theorem 4.9. We need to prove the first part.

Proof. Suppose that $H = K_{s,t}$ with $s \leq t$. Consider the canonical tester that samples a random subset of vertices S of size $O(\epsilon^{-s})$ and rejects if $G[S]$ contains H. We show that if G has ϵn^2 edges, the canonical tester rejects with probability at least 2/3. For the analysis, let us view S as the union of sets $L_1, \ldots, L_k, R$ where each $|L_i| = s$, $k = 10(2\epsilon)^{-s}$ and $|R| = 12t(2\epsilon)^{-s}$, and each of these sets consists of vertices uniformly chosen at random.

We claim that with probability $5/6$, there exists an $i^* \in [k]$ such that $(2\epsilon)^s n/2$ vertices are adjacent to all the s vertices in L_{i^*}. Suppose this was the case. Then if we choose $2t(2\epsilon)^{-s}$ further random vertices, in expectation, t of them are adjacent to all the s vertices in L_{i^*}. Hence, if $|R| = 12t(2\epsilon)^{-s}$, by Markov's inequality, with probability at least $5/6$, $L_{i^*} \cup R$ induces a copy of $K_{s,t}$. Thus, overall with probability at least $2/3$, the test rejects.

To prove the claim, observe that for any $i \in [k]$:

$$\mathbf{E}[\#v \text{ adjacent to all of } L_i] = \sum_v \Pr[v \text{ adjacent to all of } L_i]$$

$$= \sum_v \left(\frac{\deg(v)}{n} \right)^s \geq \frac{1}{n^{s-1}} \left(\sum_v \frac{\deg(v)}{n} \right)^s \geq (2\epsilon)^s n,$$

where the first inequality used the convexity of the map $x \mapsto x^s$ and the second inequality used the lower bound of ϵn^2 on the number of edges. Therefore:

$$\Pr\left[\geq \frac{1}{2}(2\epsilon)^s n \text{ vertices adjacent to all of } L_i \right] \geq \frac{1}{2}(2\epsilon)^s$$

So, the probability that for all $i \in [k]$, there are less than $(2\epsilon)^s n/2$ vertices adjacent to all of L_i is at most $(1 - (2\epsilon)^s/2)^{10(2\epsilon)^{-s}} < 1/6$.

We leave the lower bound in Theorem 4.10 as Problem 4.12 for the reader.

$\square$

4.6 Trivial Properties

In this section, we see that, in some cases, properties are constant-query testable because of some trivial reasons.

The first such case is when we can make any graph satisfy the property by adding or removing a small number of edges:

sensitive property

Definition 4.10. A graph property $\mathcal{P}$ is *sensitive* if there exist some $C > 0$ and $c < 2$ such that, for any graph G on n vertices, we have:

$$d(G, \mathcal{P}) < Cn^c.$$

For example, connectivity, Hamiltonian and Eulerian are sensitive properties with $c = 1$ because we can make a graph satisfy them by adding $O(n)$ edges.

The following lemma shows that sensitive properties are constant-query testable.

Lemma 4.10. *Let $\mathcal{P}$ be a sensitive property with parameters C and c. Then, we can test $\mathcal{P}$ with $O((C\epsilon^{-1})^{2/(2-c)})$ queries with one-sided error.*

Proof. Let G be the input graph on n vertices and $\epsilon > 0$ be the error parameter. We define n_0 as the smallest number such that $Cn_0^c \leq \epsilon n_0^2$. Note that $n_0 = \Theta((C\epsilon^{-1})^{1/(2-c)})$.

If $n \leq n_0$, then we query all the edges of G, and check whether G satisfies $\mathcal{P}$. In this case, the query complexity is at most n_0^2, which is a function of ϵ, and the output is always correct.

If $n > n_0$, then we accept without querying G. In this case, the query complexity is zero, and the output is correct because we have $d(G, \mathcal{P}) < Cn^c \leq \epsilon n^2$, which means that G is ϵ-close to $\mathcal{P}$. □

Another case that makes testing easy is when only sparse graphs can satisfy the property.

> **Definition 4.11.** A graph property $\mathcal{P}$ is *sparse* if there exist some $C > 0$ and $c < 2$ such that any graph satisfying $\mathcal{P}$ has at most Cn^c edges.

sparse property

For example, cycle-freeness and planarity are sparse properties with $c = 1$. Sparse properties are also easy to test:

> **Lemma 4.11.** *Let $\mathcal{P}$ be a sparse property with parameters C and c. Then, we can test $\mathcal{P}$ with $O((C\epsilon^{-1})^{2/(2-c)})$ queries.*

Proof. Let G be the input graph on n vertices and $\epsilon > 0$ be the error parameter. We define n_0 as the smallest number such that $Cn_0^c \leq \epsilon n_0^2/5$. Note that $n_0 = \Theta((C\epsilon^{-1})^{1/(2-c)})$.

If $n \leq n_0$, then we query all the edges of G, and check whether G satisfies $\mathcal{P}$. In this case, the query complexity is at most n_0^2, which is a function of ϵ, and the output is always correct.

If $n > n_0$, then we estimate the number of edges in G to within $\epsilon n^2/5$ by using Lemma 2.2. We accept if and only if the estimate is at most $3\epsilon n^2/5$. The query complexity is $O(\epsilon^{-2})$. In what follows, we show the correctness of the algorithm when the estimation has succeeded.

If G satisfies $\mathcal{P}$, then the number of edges is at most $Cn^c \leq \epsilon n^2/5$, and the estimate is at most $2\epsilon n^2/5 < 3\epsilon n^2/5$. Hence, we accept G with probability at least $2/3$.

If G is ϵ-far from satisfying $\mathcal{P}$, then we must have at least ϵn^2, and the estimate is at least $4\epsilon n^2/5 > 3\epsilon n^2/5$. Hence, we reject G with probability at least $2/3$. □

Although Lemmas 4.10 and 4.11 state that all the sensitive and sparse properties are testable with a constant number of queries, it is mostly because we are abusing the definition of ϵ-farness, which requires ϵn^2-edge modifications. In Chapter 5, we consider the bounded-degree model, in which a graph is said to be ϵ-far from a property if $O(\epsilon n)$ modifications of edges do not make the graph satisfy the property. This difference of the definition of ϵ-farness makes testing of sensitive properties and sparse properties more interesting.

Table 4.1: Known results for testing graph isomorphism

	One graph known	Both graphs unknown
One-sided Error	$\widetilde{O}(n)$, $\Omega(n)$ [184]	$\widetilde{O}(n^{3/2})$, $\Omega(n^{3/2})$ [184]
Two-sided error	$\widetilde{O}(n^{1/2})$, $\Omega(n^{1/2})$ [184]	$O(n) \cdot 2^{\widetilde{O}(\sqrt{\log n})}$ [338], $\Omega(n)$ [184]

4.7 Additional Topics

Isomorphism

The graph isomorphism problem is a fundamental problem in graph theory, which asks whether two graphs G and H on the same number of vertices are isomorphic. This problem clearly belongs to NP, but it is not known to belong to either of P and NP-complete. The current best time complexity is quasi-polynomial ($\exp(\text{poly} \log(n))$), due to Babai [37].

Fischer and Matsliah [184] studied testing graph isomorphism. Here, we can think about two models, that is, the model with one graph known and the model with both graphs unknown. In the former model, we have full access to a graph H on, say, n vertices and query access to another n-vertex graph G, and we want to test whether G is isomorphic to H. In the latter model, we have query accesses to two graphs G and H on the same number of vertices, and we want to test whether G is isomorphic to H.

For the former model, Fischer and Matsliah [184] showed a one-sided error tester with $\widetilde{O}(n)$ queries and a two-sided error tester with $\widetilde{O}(\sqrt{n})$ queries, both being tight up to polylogarithmic factors. For the latter model, they showed a one-sided error tester with $\widetilde{O}(n^{3/2})$ queries, which is tight up to a polylogarithmic factor, and a two-sided error tester with $\widetilde{O}(n^{5/4})$ queries, where they only showed a lower bound of $\Omega(n)$. Onak and Sun [338] improved the query complexity for the last case to $O(n) \cdot 2^{\widetilde{O}(\sqrt{\log n})}$. Known results for testing graph isomorphism are summarized in Table 4.1.

Optimization

Sometimes property testers can be used to solve optimization problems approximately. For example, any tester for ρ-cut with time complexity $T(n, \epsilon)$ yields an algorithm that approximates the size of the maximum cut with an additive error ϵn^2 in $T(n, \epsilon) \cdot \widetilde{O}(\log \epsilon^{-1})$ time. To see this, observe that any graph G that is ϵ-close to having a ρ-cut must have a cut of size at least $(\rho - \epsilon)n^2$. Hence, by using the tester for ρ-cut, we can distinguish the case that G has ρ-cut from the case that G has no $(\rho - \epsilon)$-cut (with high probability). To get an additive error of ϵn^2, it suffices to perform a binary search on ρ.

By combining Theorem 4.3 with the argument above, we obtain an algorithm that approximates the size of the maximum cut to within ϵn^2 in constant time for any constant $\epsilon > 0$. Indeed, we can modify the algorithm in Theorem 4.3 so that we can also find such a cut in linear time in n [209].

Digraphs

The adjacency matrix model for digraphs (directed graphs) has also been studied in the literature. The model is almost the same as that for undirected graphs. First, observe that a digraph $G = (V, E)$ can be represented as an adjacency matrix $A_G \colon V \times V \to \{0, 1\}$, where $A_G(u, v) = 1$ if and only if $(u, v) \in E$. Then, we define $d(G, H)$ for two digraphs G and H on the same vertex set V using their adjacency matrices, that is:

$$d(G, H) = \left| \left\{ (u, v) \in V \times V : A_G(u, v) \neq A_H(u, v) \right\} \right|.$$

The distance from a property $\mathcal{P}$ and a tester for $\mathcal{P}$ are defined as in the undirected case.

The study of the adjacency matrix model for digraph is initiated by Bender and Ron [71]. They showed a $\mathrm{poly}(\epsilon^{-1})$-query tester for *acyclicity*, that is, the property of having no directed cycles. Testing subgraph-freeness is also studied in [19].

acyclicity

Hypergraphs

A *hypergraph* $G = (V, E)$ is pair of a vertex set V and a set of hyperedges $E \subseteq 2^V$. When each hyperedge $e \in E$ is of size k, the hypergraph G is called k-uniform.

hypergraph

We can consider a testing model for hypergraphs that generalizes the adjacency matrix model for graphs. Observe that a k-uniform hypergraph $G = (V, E)$ can be represented as a tensor $A_G \colon V^k \to \{0, 1\}$, where $A_G(v_1, \ldots, v_k) = 1$ if and only if $\{v_1, \ldots, v_k\} \in E$. Then, we define $d(G, H)$ for two hypergraphs G and H on the same vertex set V using their associated tensors, that is:

$$d(G, H) = \left| \left\{ v_1, \ldots, v_k \in V : A_G(v_1, \ldots, v_k) \neq A_H(v_1, \ldots, v_k) \right\} \right|.$$

The distance from a property $\mathcal{P}$ and a tester for $\mathcal{P}$ are defined as in the undirected case and we say that a hypergraph G on n vertices is ϵ-far from $\mathcal{P}$ if $d(G, \mathcal{P}) > \epsilon n^k$.

Szemerédi's regularity lemma and the removal lemma for k-uniform hypergraphs have been intensively studied and have been successfully applied to testing properties of hypergraphs [194, 229, 230, 326, 359, 359, 361].

4.8 Bibliographic Notes

Testing graph properties in the adjacency matrix model was initiated by Goldreich, Goldwasser, and Ron [209].

Deciding (or recognizing) graph properties [308] by examining entries of the adjacency matrix of a graph has been received much attention before the study of property testing had begun. Rivest and Vuillemin [355] resolved the Aanderaa–Rosenberg Conjecture [364], showing that any deterministic algorithm for deciding any nontrivial monotone n-vertex graph property must examine $\Omega(n^2)$ entries. The query complexity of randomized algorithms was conjectured to also be $\Omega(n^2)$ by Yao [398] and the current best lower bound is $\Omega(n^{4/3})$ due to Hajnal [239].

The algorithm for testing biclique in Section 4.3.1 is folklore. The algorithm for testing bipartiteness and its analysis in Section 4.3.2 is due to [209]. Alon and Krivelevich [15] showed that Algorithm 4.2 is actually a tester for bipartiteness even when $|S| = \Theta(\epsilon^{-1} \log \epsilon^{-1})$, which leads to non-adaptive testing with $\widetilde{O}(\epsilon^{-2})$ queries. For non-adaptive testers, an almost matching lower bound of $\Omega(\epsilon^{-2})$ is known [98]. For adaptive testers, although the current best lower bound is merely $\Omega(\epsilon^{-3/2})$ [98], it is not known whether we can test with $O(\epsilon^{-c})$ queries for some $c < 2$. The constant-query testability of k-colorability was implicitly proven already in [99] for $k = 2$ and in [357] for general k. However, much more efficient testers have been devised [15, 209] and the current best upper bound is $O(\epsilon^{-2})$ [374]. General partition properties are shown to be testable with a constant number of queries in [209] and further generalization of partition properties has been studied by Nakar and Ron [327].

Goldreich and Trevisan [222] introduced the notion of canonical testers. It is known that there are gaps in query complexity between canonical testers and general non-adaptive testers, and those between the latter and general adaptive testers [215]. Canonical testers have been studied in various other contexts such as linear-invariant properties of a function on a finite field [79] and permutation-invariant properties of a Boolean function [146].

The tester for square-freeness and its analysis presented in Section 4.5.1 is based on [5]. Its extension to general bipartite graphs can also be found in [5].

The tester for triangle-freeness and more generally for H-freeness were (implicitly) given in [4] (see also [10]). A version of Lemma 4.7 for a general graph H can be found in [285]. For the triangle removal lemma, Fox [190] showed that the bound on $\delta_{\triangle}(\epsilon)$ can be improved to $1/\mathrm{T}\big(O(\log \epsilon^{-1})\big)$ by bypassing the use of Szemerédi's regularity lemma. The function $\delta_{\triangle}(\epsilon)$ is related to the maximum possible density of a subset of $[n]$ with no three-term arithmetic progression, and the latter problem has attracted much attention in additive combinatorics [103, 105, 365, 378].

Szemerédi's regularity lemma [377] has found numerous applications in extremal graph theory, Ramsey theory, and graph algorithms. The lower bound of $\mathrm{T}(\gamma^{-1/16})$ on $T(2, \gamma)$ has been shown in a sequence of works [135, 227, 323]. See [136, 285] for extensive surveys on regularity lemma.

The construction of a graph that is ϵ-far from triangle-freeness yet has only a small number of triangles is due to [5]. Theorem 4.8 is due to Behrend [45].

Theorem 4.9 states that the removal lemma for a graph H has a polynomial bound in ϵ if and only if H is bipartite. Alon and Shapira [19] considered the directed version of this problem and showed that the removal lemma for a directed graph H has a polynomial bound in ϵ if and only if the core of H, which is the smallest subgraph K of H for which there is a homomorphism from H into K, is an oriented tree or a directed cycle of length 2.

Problems

4.1. Show that the property of being a complete graph is testable with one-sided error and query complexity $O(\epsilon^{-1})$.

4.2. Show that the property of directed graphs having a bipartition of the vertex set such that all the directed edges go from one part to the other is testable with one-sided error and query complexity $O(\epsilon^{-1})$.

4.3. Show a constant-query two-sided error tester for the property of a graph being a balanced biclique. A *balanced biclique* is a biclique where the two parts of the bipartition have equal size.

balanced biclique

4.4. Show a constant-query two-sided error tester for the property of a graph being a bisection. A *bisection* is a bipartite graph where the two parts of the bipartition have equal size.

bisection

4.5. (a) Say that $x \in \{0,1\}^{n \times n}$ satisfies the AND-product property if there exists $y \in \{0,1\}^{n}$ such that for all $i, j \in [n]$, $x_{ij} = y_i y_j$. Design a tester for the AND-product property.

(b) Say that $x \in \{0,1\}^{n \times n}$ satisfies the OR-product property if there exists $y \in \{0,1\}^{n}$ such that for all $i, j \in [n]$, $x_{ij} = y_i \vee y_j$. Design a tester for the OR-product property.

Hint: Reduce these problems to testing graph properties.

4.6. Explain why it is unlikely that there is an algorithm that approximates the maximum cut size to within ϵn^2 with query complexity polynomial in $1/\epsilon$. (**Hint**: it would imply NP $\subseteq$ BPP.)

hereditary property

4.7. A graph property $\mathcal{P}$ is said to be *hereditary* if, for every graph G satisfying $\mathcal{P}$, every induced subgraph of G satisfies $\mathcal{P}$. For example, k-colorability is hereditary property whereas connectivity is not.

Let $\mathcal{P}$ be a hereditary property and supposed that $\mathcal{P}$ is testable with $q(\epsilon)$ queries. Then, show that $\mathcal{P}$ is testable by inspecting a random induced subgraph of size $O(q(\epsilon))$ and accepting if and only if it satisfies $\mathcal{P}$.

4.8. Let A and B be disjoint sets of size n. Show that, for arbitrary η, a random bipartite graph between A and B of density η is γ-regular with probability at least $1 - \exp(-\Omega(\gamma n^2 + n))$.

4.9. Let A, B is a γ-regular pair with density η, and let $A' \subseteq A$ and $B' \subseteq B$ be subsets with $|A'| \geq \delta|A|$ and $|B'| \geq \delta|B|$ for some $\delta \geq \gamma$. Then show that A', B' is a $\max\{2, \delta^{-1}\}\gamma$-regular pair, with density at least $\eta - \gamma$ and at most $\eta + \gamma$.

4.10. Show that, for any $\delta \in (0, 1)$, there exists $\gamma = \gamma_{4.10}(\delta)$ such that the following holds: Let $G = (V_1 \cup V_2 \cup V_3, E)$ be a graph such that each V_i has size m and every pair (V_i, V_j) is γ-regular. Then, the number of triangles in G, which have precisely one vertex in each of the sets V_1, V_2, V_3 is at least:

$$\left(d(V_1, V_2)d(V_2, V_3)d(V_3, V_1) - \delta\right) m^3.$$

(**Hint**: Show that there is a large subset of vertices in V_3 having approximately $\eta_{13}|V_1|$ neighbors in V_1 and $\eta_{23}|V_2|$ neighbors in V_2. Then apply Problem 4.9 on those neighbors.)

4.11. Show that the following problem is co-NP-complete: Given $\gamma > 0$ and a bipartite graph G with vertex classes A, B such that $|A| = |B| = n$, determine if G is γ-regular. You can use the fact that the following problem is NP-complete: Given a bipartite graph G with vertex classes A, B such that $|A| = |B| = n$ and $|E(G)| = n^2/2 - 1$ contains a subgraph isomorphic to $K_{n/2,n/2}$.

4.12. Let H be a fixed bipartite graph of size h. Show that any one-sided tester for H-freeness requires $1/\epsilon^{\Omega(h)}$ queries. (**Hint**: Consider the random graph where each pair is an edge with probability $\Theta(\epsilon)$. Show that on one hand, it is ϵ-far from being H-free and on the other hand, the probability that a random subset of size $O(h)$ contains a copy of H is less than $1/3$.)

4.13. Show that cycle-freeness is testable with one-sided error with $O(\epsilon^{-2})$ queries, by arguing that a random subset of $t = \Theta(\epsilon^{-1})$ vertices induces $> t$ edges with probability at least $2/3$.

Chapter 5
Graphs in the Bounded-Degree Model

We have seen that sensitive and sparse properties are trivial to test in the adjacency matrix model in Section 4.6. This fact does not mean those properties are uninteresting, but it is merely an artifact of the adjacency matrix model. To cope with this issue, we consider another model, called the bounded-degree model, in which the maximum degree of the input graph is bounded by some constant.

In Section 5.1, we formally define the bounded-degree model. We show that subgraph freeness, connectivity properties, and cycle-freeness are testable with a constant number of queries in Sections 5.2, 5.3, and 5.4, respectively. Then, we briefly discuss that bipartiteness is testable with $\widetilde{O}(\sqrt{n})$ queries and that testing bipartiteness requires $\Omega(\sqrt{n})$ queries in Section 5.5. Note that bipartiteness can be seen as 2-colorability. In Section 5.6, we will see testing 3-colorability requires $\Omega(n)$ queries. Finally, we describe constant-time approximation algorithms for several optimization problems. More specifically, we consider the minimum spanning tree problem and the minimum vertex cover problem in Sections 5.7 and 5.8, respectively. We will study more advanced and general results based on matroid and graph minor theory in Chapter 10.

Recall that, in the adjacency matrix model, any tester can be simulated by a canonical tester by quadratically blowing up the query complexity (Theorem 4.4). This means that, when we aim for query complexity polynomial in ϵ, it suffices to consider canonical testers and we do not need any effort to design testers. On the other hand, no such efficient canonical testers are known in the bounded-degree model; in general, the query complexity exponentially blows up. Hence, we need more algorithmic techniques to obtain efficient testers, which makes the bounded-degree model interesting.

A. Bhattacharyya and Y. Yoshida, *Property Testing*,
https://doi.org/10.1007/978-981-16-8622-1_5

5.1 Bounded-Degree Model

bounded-degree model

We introduce the *bounded-degree model*, in which the maximum degree of the input graph is bounded by a fixed constant $d \in \mathbb{Z}_{>0}$. Note that d is a parameter of the model but is not the part of the input.

A graph $G = (V, E)$ with a degree bound d is provided as query access $\mathcal{O}_G : V \times [d] \to V \cup \{\bot\}$. Here, for each vertex $u \in V$, the set:

$$\{\mathcal{O}_G(u, i) : i \in [d]\}$$

contains each neighbor of u exactly once and $d - \deg(u)$ many $\bot$'s, where $\deg(u)$ is the degree of u. If $\mathcal{O}_G(u, i) = v$ for some $i \in [d]$ (unique if existed),

i-th neighbor

then we say that v is the *i-th neighbor* of u. If $\mathcal{O}_G(u, i) = \bot$, then it means that there is no i-th neighbor of u.

For a graph $G = (V, E)$ on n vertices, as with the adjacency matrix model, we assume $V = [n]$ so that we can specify vertices without knowing the vertex set V explicitly.

Recall that for two graphs G and H on the same vertex set, we defined (in Section 4.2) the distance between them as:

$$d(G, H) = |E(G) \triangle E(H)|,$$

ϵ-farness

where $\triangle$ is the symmetric difference. In the bounded-degree graph model with a degree bound $d \in \mathbb{Z}_{>0}$, we say that a graph $G = (V, E)$ is ϵ-far from satisfying a property $\mathcal{P}$ if $d(G, \mathcal{P}) > \epsilon dn$. It might be more natural to define ϵ-farness as $d(G, \mathcal{P}) \geq \epsilon dn/2$ because the number of edges in a simple graph of the maximum degree d is $dn/2$. However, we adopt the present definition in order to avoid the cumbersome coefficient.

tester

An algorithm is said to be a *tester* for a property $\mathcal{P}$ if, given an integer $n \in \mathbb{Z}_{>0}$, $\epsilon \in (0, 1)$, and query access to a graph G on n vertices, it accepts with probability at least $2/3$ if G satisfies $\mathcal{P}$ and rejects if G is ϵ-far from $\mathcal{P}$.

Remark 5.1. If we regard that the graph G with a degree bound d is given as a function $\mathcal{O}_G(u, i)$, then it is also natural to define ϵ-farness

ϵ-farness

in the following way: We say that G is ϵ-far from a property $\mathcal{P}$ if for any $H \in \mathcal{P}$, the Hamming distance between $\mathcal{O}_G : V \times [d] \to V$ and $\mathcal{O}_H : V \times [d] \to V$, that is:

$$|\{(u, i) \in V \times [d] : \mathcal{O}_G(u, i) \neq \mathcal{O}_H(u, i)\}|,$$

is at least ϵdn. A subtle difference from the former definition of ϵ-farness is that the maximum degree of the resulting graph H must be less than or equal to d. Although choosing which ϵ-farness is just a matter of taste, the latter definition sometimes makes the analysis quite involved because we need to modify the input graph so as to satisfy $\mathcal{P}$ while bounding its maximum degree. Hence, we will take the former definition.

5.2 *H*-Freeness

Recall that, for a connected graph H, we say that a graph G is *H-free* if G does not contain H as its subgraph. In this section, we show that H-freeness is constant-query testable for any fixed H in the bounded-degree model.

The tester samples merely a constant number of vertices and detects whether there is a copy of H around those vertices. In this sense, the strategy of the tester is similar to that for the adjacency matrix model given in Section 4.5.4. However, the analysis is much simpler. In particular, we do not need Szemerédi's regularity lemma.

Now, we formally describe the tester. Let $r(H)$ denote the *radius* of H, that is, $r(H)$ is the smallest integer r such that there exists a vertex v in H such that all vertices in H are at distance at most r from v. Such a vertex v is called a *center* of H (there may be several centers in H). The tester for H-freeness is given in Algorithm 5.1.

H-freeness

radius

center

Algorithm 5.1 (Tester for *H*-freeness)

Input: An integer $n \in \mathbb{Z}_{>0}$, $\epsilon \in (0, 1)$, and query access to a graph G on n vertices.
1: **for** $s := \Theta(\epsilon^{-1})$ times **do**
2:     Uniformly select a vertex $v \in V$.
3:     Conduct a BFS of depth $r(H)$ starting from v.
4:     **if** the explored subgraph contains a copy of H as its subgraph **then**
5:         Reject.
6:     **end if**
7: **end for**
8: Accept.

Theorem 5.1. *For any connected graph H, H-freeness is one-sided error testable with query complexity $O(\epsilon^{-1}d^{r(H)})$.*

Proof. Algorithm 5.1 never rejects H-free graphs, and the query complexity is $O(\epsilon^{-1}d^{r(H)})$.

Now we show that the algorithm rejects with probability at least 2/3 when G is ϵ-far from H-freeness. We call a vertex $v \in V$ a *witness* if it is a center of a copy of H that resides in G. Note that, if we sample a witness vertex in Algorithm 5.1, then we reject the graph. Hence, we consider the probability of sampling a witness vertex.

Since removing all edges incident to witness vertices makes the graph H-free, G must have at least ϵn witness vertices. Then, by Lemma 2.1, the

witness

probability of sampling a witness vertex becomes at least $2/3$ by setting the hidden constant in s used in Algorithm 5.1 to be large enough.   □

Note that, in the adjacency matrix model, obtaining a set of neighbors of a vertex already requires $\Omega(n)$ queries. On the other hand, as we have seen in Algorithm 5.1, we can explore the subgraph of a constant radius from a vertex in the bounded-degree model. This makes testers in the bounded-degree model very different from those in the adjacency matrix model.

5.3 Connectivity Properties

u-v path
edge-disjoint path
k-edge-connectivity
vertex-disjoint path

k-vertex-connectivity

A path connecting two vertices u and v is called a *u-v path*. We say that two *u-v* paths are *edge-disjoint* if they do not share edges. Then, a graph G is *k-edge-connected* if, for any two vertices $u, v \in V$, there are k mutually edge-disjoint *u-v* paths. We say that two *u-v* paths are *(internally) vertex-disjoint* if they do not share vertices except for u and v. Then, a graph G is *k-vertex-connected* if, for any two vertices $u, v \in V$, there are k mutually (internally) vertex-disjoint *u-v* paths. When $k = 1$, k-edge-connectivity and k-vertex-connectivity coincide with the usual connectivity.

In this section, we see that for any fixed $k \in \mathbb{Z}_{>0}$, k-edge-connectivity and k-vertex-connectivity are one-sided error testable with a constant number of queries. We note that those properties are sparse and are trivial to test in the adjacency matrix model (see Section 4.6). However, the analysis in the bounded-degree model is no longer trivial. A general theme underlying testing a connectivity property $\mathcal{P}$ is the relation between the distance from $\mathcal{P}$ and the number of small disjoint witnesses of not satisfying $\mathcal{P}$. For example, when $\mathcal{P}$ is connectivity, then a witness is a connected component of size less than n; If there exists such a connected component, then the graph should be disconnected. If we can show that there are many small witnesses in a graph that is far from satisfying $\mathcal{P}$, then we could reject the graph by finding one of the witnesses by local search. In order to derive such a bound, we consult results from *edge augmentation theory*, which aims at characterizing the number of edges to be added in order to make a graph satisfy the property of interest.

edge augmentation
theory

5.3.1 Connectivity

First, we consider the simplest case of $k = 1$, that is, connectivity. We start with the following simple observation.

Proposition 5.1. *If a graph G is ϵ-far from being connected, then the number of connected components in G is at least ϵdn.*

Proof. Suppose that the number of connected components is at most ϵdn. Then, we can obtain a connected graph by adding $\epsilon dn - 1$ edges to G, which contradicts the ϵ-farness of G. $\qquad\square$

Recall that we allowed making a graph with the maximum degree more than d after edge modifications. We can remove this assumption (by slightly worsening the bound), but the analysis becomes more technical, and we do not go into that direction.

We have the following corollary of Proposition 5.1.

Corollary 5.1. *If a graph G is ϵ-far from being connected, then the number of connected components of size at most $\frac{2}{\epsilon d}$ in G is at least $\epsilon dn/2$.*

Proof. By Proposition 5.1, the graph G has at least ϵdn connected components. If the claim does not hold, then there are at least $\epsilon dn/2$ connected components of more than $\frac{2}{\epsilon d}$ vertices. This means that there are more than n vertices, which is a contradiction. $\qquad\square$

Note that we can reject if we detect a connected component (of size less than n). Corollary 5.1 states that, if the input graph is ϵ-far from being connected, then there are $\Omega(n)$ many small connected components, where we say that a connected component is *small* if its size is at most $\frac{2}{\epsilon d}$. In particular, this means that we can easily obtain a vertex in a small connected component by sampling vertices uniformly at random. Also, we can easily detect that the obtained vertex belongs to a small connected component by conducting a BFS. The discussion above suggests the following algorithm.

small component

Algorithm 5.2 (Tester for connectivity)

Input: An integer $n \in \mathbb{Z}_{>0}$, $\epsilon \in (0,1)$, and query access to a graph G on n vertices.
1: **for** $s := \Theta(\frac{1}{\epsilon d})$ times **do**
2:     Sample a vertex $v \in V$ uniformly at random.
3:     Conduct a BFS from v until it reaches $\frac{2}{\epsilon d}$ vertices or no more new vertices can be reached.
4:     **if** we have found a connected component (of size less than n) **then**
5:         Reject.
6:     **end if**
7: **end for**
8: Accept.

Lemma 5.1. *Algorithm 5.2 is a one-sided error tester for connectivity with query complexity $O(\frac{1}{\epsilon^2 d})$.*

Proof. It is clear that Algorithm 5.2 always accepts connected graphs because they have no connected components of size less than n.

Suppose that G is ϵ-far from being connected. By Corollary 5.1, the number of small connected components is at least $\epsilon dn/2$. Hence, the number of vertices in a small connected component is also at least $\epsilon dn/2$. By setting the hidden constant in s to be large enough, the probability that we do not sample a vertex in a small connected component is at most:

$$\left(1 - \frac{\epsilon d}{2}\right)^s \leq \frac{1}{3}.$$

Because we can correctly reject when we sample a vertex in a small connected component, the probability that we reject is at least $\frac{2}{3}$.

Finally, we analyze the query complexity. We conduct BFSes $s = O(\frac{1}{\epsilon d})$ times and each BFS stops when it reaches $\frac{2}{\epsilon d}$ vertices. When exploring a vertex in a BFS, we query d times in order to get its neighbors. Hence, the total query complexity is $O(\frac{1}{\epsilon d} \cdot \frac{2}{\epsilon d} \cdot d) = O(\frac{1}{\epsilon^2 d})$. □

Remark 5.2. It might be curious that the query complexity decreases as d increases because more input graphs are taken into consideration as d increases, and seemingly the problem becomes harder. The reason that the query complexity decreases is that the definition of ϵ-farness also changes as d changes. Indeed, when $d = n$, the model almost coincides with the adjacency matrix model, in which testing connectivity is trivial (for large n).

5.3.2 Improved Tester for Connectivity

Before getting into k-edge-connectivity, we look that we can improve the query complexity in terms of ϵ from $O(\frac{1}{\epsilon^2 d})$ to $\tilde{O}(\epsilon^{-1})$. This is indeed an improvement because we can assume $\epsilon d \leq 1$; if $\epsilon d > 1$, then any graph can be made connected by adding $n - 1 \leq \epsilon dn$ edges, and hence no graph is ϵ-far from connectivity.

The idea of the new tester is classifying connected components using their sizes more finely instead of classifying them into small and large ones. Let B_i be the set of connected components of size at most $2^i - 1$ vertices and at least 2^{i-1} vertices. Let $\ell = \lceil \log(\frac{2}{\epsilon d} + 1) \rceil$. We start with the following observation.

Proposition 5.2. *Let G be a graph ϵ-far from being connected. Then, there exists $i \in [\ell]$ such that $|B_i| \geq \frac{\epsilon dn}{2\ell}$.*

Proof. By Corollary 5.1, we know that $\sum_{i=1}^{\ell} |B_i| \geq \epsilon dn/2$. Hence, the claim follows. $\square$

Suppose that a graph G is ϵ-far from being connected and fix $i \in [\ell]$ such that $|B_i| \geq \frac{\epsilon dn}{2\ell}$. Then, given a vertex $v \in V$ belonging to a connected component in B_i, the query complexity to detect that v is in a connected component of size less than n is proportional to 2^i. However, the number of vertices in a connected component in B_i is also proportional to 2^i, and hence we only need to sample fewer vertices when i is large. The improved tester is given below.

Algorithm 5.3 (Improved tester for connectivity)

Input: An integer $n \in \mathbb{Z}_{>0}$, $\epsilon > 0$, and query access to a graph G on n vertices.
1: $\ell := \lceil \log(\frac{2}{\epsilon d} + 1) \rceil$.
2: **for** $i = 1$ to ℓ **do**
3:      **for** $s_i := \Theta(\frac{\ell}{2^i \epsilon d})$ **do**
4:          Sample a vertex $v \in V$ uniformly at random.
5:          Conduct a BFS from v until it reaches 2^i vertices or no new vertices can be reached.
6:          **if** we have found a connected component (of size less than n) **then**
7:              Reject.
8:          **end if**
9:      **end for**
10: **end for**
11: Accept.

Theorem 5.2. *Algorithm 5.3 is a one-sided error tester for connectivity with query complexity $O(\epsilon^{-1} \log^2 \frac{1}{\epsilon d})$.*

Proof. It is clear that Algorithm 5.2 always accepts any connected graph because such a graph has no connected components of size less than n.

Suppose that the graph G is ϵ-far from being connected. By Proposition 5.2, there exists $i \in [\ell]$ such that $|B_i| \geq \frac{\epsilon dn}{2\ell}$. Then, the number of vertices in connected components belonging to B_i is at least $2^{i-1}|B_i|$. It follows that the probability that we sample a vertex belonging to a connected component in B_i is at least:

$$\frac{2^{i-1}|B_i|}{n} \geq \frac{2^{i-2}\epsilon d}{\ell} \geq \frac{2}{s_i}$$

by setting the hidden constant in s_i to be large enough. Thus, with probability at least $1 - (1 - 2/s_i)^{s_i} > 1 - e^{-2} > 2/3$, a vertex v belonging to a connected component in B_i is sampled. In such a case, we can reject the graph because we will find a connected component of size less than 2^i containing v.

The query complexity of the algorithm is bounded by:

$$\sum_{i=1}^{\ell} s_i 2^i d = O\left(\frac{\log^2 \frac{1}{\epsilon d}}{\epsilon}\right). \qquad \Box$$

5.3.3 k-Edge-Connectivity

Now, we move on to k-edge-connectivity. When testing connectivity, we observed that a constant-size connected component can be used as a witness of disconnectivity and that there are many small connected components in a graph that is ϵ-far from being connected. The key to design testers for k-edge-connectivity is introducing a suitable notion of a witness for k-edge-connectivity with such properties.

For a vertex set $S \subseteq V$, let $d_G(S)$ denote the number of edges leaving S, that is, $d_G(S) = |\{\{u,v\} \in E : u \in S, v \notin S\}|$. We say that a vertex set
violating set
$S \subsetneq V$ is a *violating set* if $d_G(S) < k$. A graph is k-edge-connected if and
Menger's theorem
only if there is no violating set by *Menger's theorem*. Clearly, the existence of a violating set implies that the whole graph is not k-edge-connected. Hence, we can use violating sets as witnesses of not being k-edge-connected. The question is whether there are many such vertex sets in a graph that is ϵ-far from being k-edge-connected. To answer this question, we exploit the Watanabe-Nakamura theorem, which is a cornerstone in edge augmentation
subpartition
theory. We call a family of vertex sets $\mathcal{S} = \{S_1, \ldots, S_t\}$ a *subpartition* of V if $S_i \subseteq V$ for every $i \in [t]$ and $S_i \cap S_j = \emptyset$ for every $i, j \in [t]$ with $i \neq j$. (When
partition
$\bigcup_{i \in [t]} S_i = V$, it is called a *partition*.) Let $\gamma_k(G)$ be the minimum number of edges that have to be added to G to make it k-edge-connected. Let $t_k(G)$ be defined as:

$$t_k(G) = \max_{\mathcal{S}} \sum_{S \in \mathcal{S}} \big(k - d_G(S)\big),$$

where the maximum is over subpartitions $\mathcal{S}$ of V. Note that a graph G is k-edge-connected if and only if $t_k(G) = 0$. Also, it is immediate that $\gamma_k(G) \geq \lceil t_k(G)/2 \rceil$ because we can decrease the value of $t_k(G)$ by at most two by adding an edge. Indeed, the converse also holds:

Watanabe-Nakamura theorem

Theorem 5.3 (*Watanabe-Nakamura theorem*). *Let $G = (V, E)$ be a graph and $k \geq 2$ be an integer. Then, we have:*

$$\gamma_k(G) = \left\lceil \frac{t_k(G)}{2} \right\rceil.$$

In what follows, we assume a technical condition $\epsilon d n \geq 2$. (If this is not the case, $n \leq \frac{2}{\epsilon d}$ and the problem becomes trivial.) Then, we have the following corollary.

Corollary 5.2. *If $G = (V, E)$ is ϵ-far from being k-edge-connected. Then, there are at least $\frac{\epsilon dn}{2k}$ disjoint violating sets of size at most $\frac{2k}{\epsilon d}$.*

Proof. By Theorem 5.3, we have:

$$\sum_{S \in \mathcal{S}} (k - d_G(S)) \geq 2(\epsilon dn - 1) \geq \epsilon dn$$

for some subpartition $\mathcal{S}$ of V. We can assume that each $S \in \mathcal{S}$ is a violating set because the left-hand side never decreases by removing non-violating sets from $\mathcal{S}$. Since each summand contributes by at most k, we must have $|\mathcal{S}| \geq \frac{\epsilon dn}{k}$.

Suppose that the number of sets with size at most $\frac{2k}{\epsilon d}$ in $\mathcal{S}$ is at most $\frac{\epsilon dn}{2k}$. This means that there are at least $\frac{\epsilon dn}{2k}$ sets of size larger than $\frac{2k}{\epsilon d}$. It follows that the number of vertices is more than n, which is a contradiction. □

We say that a vertex set S is *small* if $|S| \leq \frac{2k}{\epsilon d}$. Corollary 5.2 states that there are $\Omega(n)$ small violating sets in a graph that is ϵ-far from being k-edge-connected. This fact suggests us to consider the following algorithm (Algorithm 5.4).

small vertex set

Algorithm 5.4 (One-sided error tester for k-edge-connectivity)

Input: An integer $n \in \mathbb{Z}_{>0}$, $\epsilon \in (0, 1)$, and query access to a graph $G = (V, E)$ on n vertices.

1: **for** $s := \Theta(\frac{k}{\epsilon d})$ times **do**
2:     Sample a vertex $v \in V$ uniformly at random.
3:     Conduct a BFS starting from v with a radius $\frac{2k}{\epsilon d}$.
4:     **if** there exists a subset S in the explored subgraph with $d_G(S) < k$ **then**
5:         Reject.
6:     **end if**
7: **end for**
8: Accept.

Theorem 5.4. *Algorithm 5.4 is a one-sided error tester for k-edge-connectivity of query complexity $d^{O(k/(\epsilon d))}$.*

Proof. Algorithm 5.4 accepts any k-edge-connected graph because such a graph has no cut of size less than k.

Suppose that G is ϵ-far from being k-edge-connected. By Corollary 5.2, there are at least $\frac{\epsilon dn}{2k}$ disjoint small violating sets. The number of vertices in those violating sets is at least $\frac{\epsilon dn}{2k}$. Hence, by setting the hidden constant in s to be large enough, the probability that we do not sample any vertex in those violating sets is at most:

$$\left(1 - \frac{\epsilon d}{2k}\right)^s \le \frac{1}{3}.$$

Once we have sampled a vertex in a vertex set in a violating set, we can correctly reject the input graph. Hence, the rejection probability is at least 2/3.

Finally, we analyze the query complexity. We conduct BFSes $s = O(\frac{k}{\epsilon d})$ times and each BFS reaches at most $d^{O(k/(\epsilon d))}$ vertices. When exploring a vertex in a BFS, we query d times in order to get its neighbors. Hence, the total query complexity is $O(\frac{k}{\epsilon d}) \cdot d^{O(k/(\epsilon d))} \cdot d = d^{O(k/(\epsilon d))}$.   □

In retrospect, the proof is almost the same as that for connectivity except that we need the Watanabe-Nakamura theorem instead of Proposition 5.1.

Having seen that the tester provided by Theorem 5.4 has an exponential query complexity in ϵ^{-1}, a natural question is whether we can improve it. In the next section, we show that this is the case and it can be improved to polynomial in ϵ^{-1}.

5.3.4 Improved Tester for k-Edge-Connectivity

In this section, we show a tester for k-edge-connectivity whose query complexity is polynomial in ϵ^{-1}.

To see the idea, recall Corollary 5.2, stating that, if a graph is ϵ-far from k-edge-connectivity, then there exist $\Omega(\epsilon n)$ many disjoint violating sets of size $O(\epsilon^{-1})$. (We omitted the factor depending on k and d for simplicity.) Hence, we can find a vertex in a violating set (with high probability) just by sampling $\Omega(\epsilon^{-1})$ vertices. The problem in Algorithm 5.4 is that detecting a violating set from a vertex in it requires $O(d^{O(\epsilon^{-1})})$ queries because it conducts a BFS of radius $\Theta(\epsilon^{-1})$. Hence, in order to get a query complexity polynomial in ϵ^{-1}, we need an algorithm that detects a violating set more quickly.

In Algorithm 5.5, we show an efficient algorithm that, given a vertex s and a size upper bound t, detects a violating set containing s of size at most t with high probability (if exists). It first selects a random permutation $\pi: E \to [m]$, where $m = |E|$ is the number of edges. For an edge $e \in E$, we call $\pi(e)$ the *rank* of e (with respect to π). Then, starting with a vertex set $S = \{s\}$, the algorithm iteratively augments S by traversing the edge with the smallest rank leaving S. As selecting π requires $\Omega(m)$ time, this algorithm is not a constant-time algorithm as is (even when t is constant). We come back to this issue later.

We refer to the process from Line 2 to Line 10 as an *expanding process*. An example of an expanding process is schematically given in Figure 5.1. In Figure 5.1a, starting from the vertex s, we search for the cut $E(C, \bar{C})$, which has size two. The integer values on edges represent the relative ordering of

---

Algorithm 5.5 (Violating set detection algorithm)

Input: An integer $n \in \mathbb{Z}_{>0}$, a vertex $s \in V$, a size upper bound $t \in \mathbb{Z}_{>0}$, and query access to a graph $G = (V, E)$ on n vertices.

1: **for** $\Theta(t^2)$ times **do**
2:     $\pi \leftarrow$ a random permutation over E.
3:     $S \leftarrow \{s\}$.
4:     **while** $|S| < t$ and $d_G(S) \geq k$ **do**
5:         Select the edge $e = \{u, v\}$ with the smallest rank among edges in $E(S, \bar{S})$.
6:         $S \leftarrow S \cup \{v\}$, assuming $u \in S$ and $v \in \bar{S}$.
7:     **end while**
8:     **if** S is a violating set, that is, $S \subsetneq V$ and $d_G(S) < k$ **then**
9:         Reject.
10:     **end if**
11: **end for**
12: Accept.

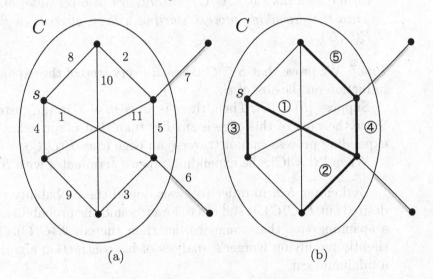

Fig. 5.1: Expanding process

their ranks with respect to the permutation π. In Figure 5.1b, the exploration ordering is given by the circled numbers on edges, and the expanding process succeeded in founding the cut $E(C, \bar{C})$.

There are two issues regarding the random permutation π. The first one is generating π requires (at least) $O(|E|)$ time. Although this is not problematic if we only care about query complexity, a smaller (say, constant) time complexity, is desirable. The other issue is that we do not know the number of edges and hence we cannot generate a bijection $\pi \colon E \to [m]$. We will address these issue at the end of this section, but for now, let us assume that we have a permutation π at hand (and can compare the ranks of edges in constant time).

The query complexity of Algorithm 5.5 is $O(t^2 \cdot dt)$. If the graph G is k-edge-connected, then for any starting vertex s, Algorithm 5.5 always accepts because there is no violating set in the graph.

Below, we show that if s belongs to a violating set of size at most t, then Algorithm 5.5 rejects with high probability. We say that a violating set C is *minimal* if there is no other violating set C' with $C' \subsetneq C$.

Let $\pi\colon E \to [m]$ be an arbitrary permutation over edges. A spanning tree T of the subgraph $G[C]$ induced by C is said to *come earlier* than the cut $E(C, \bar{C})$ (with respect to π) if the largest rank of an edge in T (with respect to π) is smaller than the smallest rank of an edge in the cut $E(C, \bar{C})$ (with respect to π). An example of a spanning tree that comes earlier than the cut appears in Figure 5.1b as the tree formed by bold edges.

Lemma 5.2. *Suppose that C contains a spanning tree T that comes earlier than the cut $E(C, \bar{C})$ with respect to a permutation $\pi\colon E \to [m]$. Then the expanding process starting with π succeeds in finding the cut $E(C, \bar{C})$.*

Proof. We prove that $S \subseteq C$ holds at every step of the expanding process by induction on the size of S.

Suppose $|S| < |C|$. Then, there is an edge of T in the current cut $E(S, \bar{S})$. Since the rank of this edge is smaller than that of any edge in $E(C, \bar{C})$, the expanding process cannot traverse an edge from $E(C, \bar{C})$.

When $|S| = |C|$, the expanding process terminates with $S = C$.   □

By Lemma 5.2, in order to lower bound the probability that we find the desired cut $E(C, \bar{C})$, it suffices to lower bound the probability that C contains a spanning tree that comes earlier than the cut $E(C, \bar{C})$. This is done by slightly modifying Karger's analysis of his contraction algorithm for finding a minimum cut.

Lemma 5.3. *Let C be a minimal violating set with at most t vertices and $\pi\colon E \to [m]$ be a random permutation. Then, C contains a spanning tree that comes earlier than the cut $E(C, \bar{C})$ with respect to π with probability $\Omega(1/t^2)$.*

Proof. We consider an auxiliary graph G', in which all vertices in $\bar{C}$ are contracted to a single vertex, denoted by x. That is, $V(G') = C \cup \{x\}$ and $E(G')$ contains all edges inside $G[C]$ and an edge $\{u, x\}$ for every edge $\{u, v\}$ such that $u \in C$ and $v \in \bar{C}$. Since C is a minimal violating set in G, the graph G' has a single minimum cut of size less than k; that is, the cut $E(C, \{x\})$.

We now introduce Karger's contraction algorithm. Given a graph, the contraction algorithm iteratively performs the following step until two vertices are left: it selects an edge at random from the current graph (which is initially the original graph) and contracts its endpoints. Note that the resulting graph may have multiple edges, and the number of vertices decreases by one in each step. An alternative way of looking at this contraction algorithm is to sample a random permutation over edges and to contract the edge with the smallest rank at each step. We can observe that, if the contraction algorithm succeeds in finding the cut $E(C, \bar{C})$, then the contracted edges form a spanning tree that comes earlier than the cut $E(C, \bar{C})$. Hence, it suffices to lower bound the probability that the contraction algorithm succeeds.

We consider a $(|C|+1)$-vertex graph with a minimum cut of size $c \leq k-1$. Note that, as long as the contraction algorithm does not contract the edge in the cut $E(C, \{x\})$, except for x, the degree of every vertex in the current graph at any step is at least k. The degree of x remains c. Hence, at the i-th step of the algorithm, the probability of contracting a cut edge is at most:

$$\frac{c}{((|C| - i + 1)k)/2} \leq \frac{2}{|C| - i + 1}.$$

Then, the probability that no edge in $E(C, \{x\})$ is contracted in any step of the algorithm is at least:

$$\prod_{i=1}^{|C|-1} \left(1 - \frac{2}{|C| - i + 1}\right) = \prod_{i=2}^{|C|} \frac{i - 2}{i} = \frac{2}{|C|(|C| - 1)} = \Omega\left(\frac{1}{t^2}\right). \qquad \square$$

Lemma 5.4. *Let C be a minimal violating set with at most t vertices, and let s be an arbitrary vertex in C. Then, Algorithm 5.5 finds the cut $E(C, \bar{C})$ with probability at least $2/3$.*

Proof. By Lemma 5.3, each expanding process finds the cut $E(C, \bar{C})$ with probability at least $\Omega(t^{-2})$. Then, by setting the hidden constant in s to be large enough, we can find the cut $E(C, \bar{C})$ with probability at least $2/3$. $\quad\square$

Now, we explain how we can avoid generating a permutation $\pi \colon E \to [m]$ explicitly. First, notice that a random permutation π can be generated by assigning each edge e a random value r_e sampled from $[0, 1]$ uniformly and independently and by ordering edges in increasing order of the random values. To avoid sampling all the r_e's, which still takes $\Omega(m)$ time, we generate r_e's on the fly in the expanding process. That is, when we encounter an edge e for the first time, we assign e a value sampled from $[0, 1]$ uniformly at random. If r_e is already assigned, we use that value. Then, we can select the edge with the smallest rank by merely selecting the edge with the smallest assigned value.

Combining Lemma 5.4 with the fact that there are many small disjoint violating sets, we get an efficient tester for k-edge-connectivity:

Theorem 5.5. *For any $k \in \mathbb{Z}_{>0}$, k-edge-connectivity is one-sided error testable with $O\left(\frac{k^4}{\epsilon^4 d^3}\right)$ queries.*

Proof. Our algorithm is obtained from Algorithm 5.4 by replacing the BFS part with Algorithm 5.5.

This algorithm accepts any k-edge-connected graph, and by Lemma 5.4, rejects graphs that are ϵ-far from being k-edge-connected with probability at least $2/3$. Hence, it is a one-sided error tester for k-edge-connectivity.

Finally, we check its query complexity. We randomly sample $O(\frac{k}{\epsilon d})$ vertices, and for each sampled vertex, we perform Algorithm 5.5 with $t = O(\frac{k}{\epsilon d})$. Then, the query complexity is:

$$O\left(\frac{k}{\epsilon d} \cdot t^2 \cdot td\right) = O\left(\frac{kt^3}{\epsilon}\right) = O\left(\frac{k^4}{\epsilon^4 d^3}\right). \qquad \square$$

Exercise 5.1. Show that k-edge-connectivity is testable with query complexity $\widetilde{O}\left(\frac{k^4}{\epsilon^3 d^2}\right)$. (**Hint**: Use the technique of classifying small violating sets more finely, used in Section 5.3.2)

5.3.5 k-Vertex-Connectivity

Next, we show a constant-query tester for k-vertex-connectivity. Although the argument is slightly more complicated than that for k-edge-connectivity, the outline is almost the same.

violating set   Let $G = (V, E)$ be a graph. We say that a vertex set $S \subsetneq V$ is a *violating set* if $|\Gamma_G(S)| < k$. Note that, by Menger's theorem for vertex connectivity, a graph is k-vertex-connected if and only if there is no violating set.

The algorithm for testing k-vertex-connectivity is very similar to that for k-edge-connectivity (Algorithm 5.6).

Algorithm 5.6 (One-sided error tester for k-vertex-connectivity)

Input: An integer $n \in \mathbb{Z}_{>0}$, $\epsilon \in (0, 1)$, and a graph $G = (V, E)$ on n vertices.
1: **for** $s := \Theta(\frac{k}{\epsilon d})$ times **do**
2:     Sample a vertex $v \in V$ uniformly at random.
3:     Conduct a BFS starting from v with a radius $\frac{2k}{\epsilon d}$.
4:     **if** there exists a subset S in the explored subgraph with $|\Gamma_G(S)| < k$ **then**
5:         Reject.
6:     **end if**
7: **end for**
8: Accept.

In order to prove that Algorithm 5.6 rejects graphs ϵ-far from being k-vertex connected, we need to show that there are many small violating sets. To this end, we consult a theorem by Jordan and Jackson, which is a counterpart of the Watanabe-Nakamura theorem for k-vertex connectivity. Before stating the Jordan-Jackson theorem, we introduce several definitions.

Let $\bar{\gamma}_k(G)$ denote the minimal number of edges that have to be added to the graph to make it k-vertex-connected. Let $\bar{t}_k(G)$ be defined as:

$$\bar{t}_k(G) = \max_{\mathcal{S}} \sum_{S \in \mathcal{S}} (k - |\Gamma_G(S)|),$$

where the maximum is over subpartitions $\mathcal{S}$ of V. This is a vertex-connectivity version of the parameter $t_k(G)$. As G is k-vertex-connected if and only if $\bar{t}_k(G) = 0$ and we can decrease the value of $\bar{t}_k(G)$ by at most two by adding an edge, we have $\bar{\gamma}_k(G) \geq \lceil \bar{t}_k(G)/2 \rceil$.

In the case of k-edge-connectivity, we can characterize $\gamma_k(G)$ by using $t_k(G)$ only. In the case of k-vertex-connectivity, however, we need an additional parameter. For a vertex set $S \subseteq V$, let $b_k(S)$ denote the number of connected components in the subgraph $G[V \setminus S]$. In order for a graph G to be k-vertex connected, $G[V \setminus S]$ must be connected for any vertex set $S \subseteq V$ of size at most $k - 1$. Hence, by letting:

$$b_k(G) = \max\{b_k(S) : S \subseteq V, |S| = k - 1\},$$

we obtain another lower bound $\bar{\gamma}_k(G) \geq b_k(G) - 1$.

Unfortunately, $\bar{t}_k(G)$ and $b_k(G)$ are not sufficient to give a characterization of $\bar{\gamma}_k(G)$, and we introduce another notion. Let $\delta_k(S) = \max\{0, \max_{u \in S}(k - d_G(u))\}$ for a vertex set $S \subseteq V$, and we define:

$$b_k^*(G) = \max\{b_k(S) + \delta_k(S) : S \subseteq V, |S| = k - 1\}.$$

Then, we have the following:

Theorem 5.6 (*Jordan-Jackson theorem*). *Let $G = (V, E)$ be a graph. If $\bar{\gamma}_k(G) \geq 10(k + 1)^6$, then:*

$$\bar{\gamma}_k(G) = \max\left\{ b_k^*(G) - 1, \left\lceil \frac{\bar{t}_k(G)}{2} \right\rceil \right\}.$$

Jordan-Jackson theorem

Corollary 5.3. *Let $G = (V, E)$ be a graph ϵ-far from being k-vertex-connected such that $\epsilon dn \geq 10(k + 1)^6$. Then, we have at least $\frac{\epsilon dn}{2k}$ disjoint violating sets of size at most $\frac{2k}{\epsilon d}$.*

Proof. We apply Theorem 5.6 to G. We have two cases to consider:

- $\bar{\gamma}_k(G) = b_k^*(G) - 1$: This mean that there is a set of vertices S with $|S| = k - 1$ for which $b_k(S) + \delta_k(S) - 1 \geq \epsilon dn$. Since $\delta_k(S) \leq k$, we have $b_k(S) \geq \epsilon dn + 1 - k$. According to the definition of $b_k(S)$, there are $\epsilon dn + 1 - k$ connected components in $G \setminus S$. This means that the number of disjoint violating sets in G is at least $\epsilon dn + 1 - k \geq \epsilon dn/2$ (the inequality is by $\epsilon dn \geq 10(k+1)^6$). By an argument similar to that used in the proof of Corollary 5.2, there are at least $\epsilon dn/4$ violating sets of size at most $\frac{2}{\epsilon d}$.

- $\bar{\gamma}_k(G) = \lceil \bar{t}_k(G)/2 \rceil$: By an argument similar to that used in the proof of Corollary 5.2, there are at least $\frac{\epsilon dn}{2k}$ violating sets of size at most $\frac{2k}{\epsilon d}$.

Combining these two cases, we get the claim.   □

> **Theorem 5.7.** *Algorithm 5.6 is a one-sided error tester for k-vertex-connectivity of query complexity $d^{O(k/(\epsilon d))}$.*

Proof. Algorithm 5.6 accepts any k-vertex-connected graph because such a graph has no vertex cut of size less than k.

Suppose that G is ϵ-far from being k-vertex-connected. By Corollary 5.3, there are at least $\frac{\epsilon dn}{2k}$ disjoint small violating sets. The number of vertices in those violating sets is at least $\frac{\epsilon dn}{2k}$. Hence, by setting the hidden constant in s to be large enough, the probability that we do not sample any vertex in those violating sets is at most:

$$\left(1 - \frac{\epsilon d}{2k}\right)^s \leq \frac{1}{3}.$$

Once we have sampled a vertex in a vertex set in a violating set, we can correctly reject the input graph. Hence, the rejection probability is at least $2/3$.

Finally, we analyze the query complexity. We conduct BFSes $s = O(\frac{k}{\epsilon d})$ times and each BFS explores at most $d^{O(k/(\epsilon d))}$ vertices. When exploring a vertex in a BFS, we query d times in order to get its neighbors. Hence, the total query complexity is $O(\frac{k}{\epsilon d}) \cdot d^{O(k/(\epsilon d))} \cdot d = d^{O(k/(\epsilon d))}$.   □

As contraction-type algorithms such as Karger's algorithm are not known for vertex-connectivity, we cannot use the strategy in Section 5.3.4 to improve the query complexity to polynomial in ϵ^{-1}. However, another one-sided error tester for k-vertex connectivity with $\widetilde{O}(\epsilon^{-1}k\epsilon)$ queries.

5.4 Cycle-Freeness

cycle-freeness
forest

We say that a graph G is *cycle-free* if it has no cycle. A cycle-free graph is often called a *forest*. In this section, we show that cycle-freeness is constant-query testable with two-sided error.

There is a simple characterization of cycle-freeness:

> **Lemma 5.5.** *A graph G of n vertices, m edges, and c connected components is cycle-free if and only if $m - n + c = 0$.*

Proof. Suppose that G is cycle-free and let $S_1, \ldots, S_c$ be its connected components. Then, $m = \sum_{i=1}^{c}(|S_i| - 1) = n - c$ holds because each S_i is a tree, and it follows that $m - n + c = 0$.

Suppose that $m - n + c = 0$ and let $S_1, \ldots, S_c$ be the connected components of G. Let m_i be the number of edges in S_i. Then, in order to make S_i connected, we must have $m_i \geq |S_i| - 1$. Hence, $m = \sum_{i=1}^{c} m_i \geq \sum_{i=1}^{c}(|S_i| - 1) = n - c$. As $m - n + c = 0$ from the assumption, we must have $m_i = |S_i| - 1$ for every $i \in [c]$. This means that each S_i is a tree, and hence G is cycle-free. □

Indeed, the quantity $m - n + c$ characterizes the distance to cycle-freeness, as stated in the following lemma.

Lemma 5.6. *Let G be a graph of n vertices, m edges, and c connected components. The distance of G from cycle-freeness is exactly $m - n + c$. In particular, if G is ϵ-far from being connected, then $m - n + c \geq \epsilon dn$.*

Exercise 5.2. Prove Lemma 5.6.

By Lemma 5.6, in order to test cycle-freeness, it suffices to calculate $m - n + c$.

An issue here is that, although the value of n is given as a part of the input, we do not know the values of m and c. Indeed, it is impossible to efficiently compute the exact values of m and c using the query access to the input graph. For example, consider a graph consisting of a path of length n and another graph consisting of two paths of length $n/2$. The numbers of connected components of the former and the latter graphs are 1 and 2, respectively. However, they look the same as long as we do not hit an end vertex of the paths. Indeed, it is not hard to formally show that we need $\Omega(n)$ queries to distinguish these two graphs.

Thus, instead of exactly computing m and n, we try to estimate m and n to within, say, $\epsilon dn/10$. This is sufficient to distinguish cycle-free graphs from graphs that are ϵ-far from being cycle-free.

The following two lemmas show that we can estimate m and c with a constant number of queries.

Lemma 5.7. *Let $G = (V, E)$ be a graph of m vertices. There is an algorithm that, given $\epsilon, \delta \in (0, 1)$ and query access to G, outputs an estimation $\tilde{m}$ to m such that:*

$$|\tilde{m} - m| \leq \frac{\epsilon dn}{10}$$

with probability at least $1 - \delta$. The query complexity of the algorithm is $O(\frac{d \log \delta^{-1}}{\epsilon^2})$.

Proof. We define a function $f \colon V \to [0,1]$ as $f(u) = \frac{\deg(u)}{2d}$. Our algorithm first obtains a value X by applying Lemma 2.2 with f, $\epsilon/10$, and δ, and then returns the value dX.

Since $\sum_{u \in V} f(u) = m/d$, the value dX satisfies $|dX - m| \le \epsilon dn/10$ with probability at least $1 - \delta$.

As the number of queries to f is $O(\epsilon^{-2} \log \delta^{-1})$ and each query to f can be answered by querying G d times, the total query complexity to G is $O(\epsilon^{-2} d \log \delta^{-1})$. $\square$

Lemma 5.8. *Let $G = (V, E)$ be a graph of c connected components. There is an algorithm that, given $\epsilon, \delta \in (0,1)$ and query access to G, outputs an estimation $\tilde{c}$ to c such that:*

$$|\tilde{c} - c| \le \frac{\epsilon dn}{10}$$

with probability at least $1 - \delta$. The query complexity of the algorithm is $O(\frac{\log(1/\delta)}{\epsilon^3 d^2})$.

Proof. Let $t = \frac{20}{\epsilon d}$. We define a function $f \colon V \to [0,1]$ as:

$$f(v) = \begin{cases} \frac{1}{|S|} & \text{if } v \text{ belongs to a connected component } S \text{ of size at most } t. \\ 0 & otherwise \end{cases}$$

Our algorithm first obtains a value X by applying Lemma 2.2 with f, $\epsilon d/20$ and δ, and then returns the value X.

We have $|X - \sum_{v \in V} f(v)| \le \epsilon dn/20$ with probability at least $1 - \delta$. Also, the number of connected components of size more than t is at most $\epsilon dn/20$. Hence, we have $|\sum_{v \in V} f(v) - c| \le \epsilon dn/20$. It follows that:

$$|X - c| \le \left| X - \sum_{v \in V} f(v) \right| + \left| \sum_{v \in V} f(v) - c \right| \le \frac{\epsilon dn}{10}$$

holds with probability at least $1 - \delta$.

We can implement query access to f as follows: For a given vertex $v \in V$, we perform a BFS until it reaches t vertices or no more new vertices can be reached. If the explored subgraph S forms a connected component of size at most t, then we return $1/|S|$, and otherwise we return zero.

The total query complexity is $O(\frac{\log(1/\delta)}{\epsilon^2 d^2} \cdot dt) = O(\frac{\log(1/\delta)}{\epsilon^3 d^2})$. $\square$

Using these two lemmas, we can straightforwardly test cycle-freeness: First, we estimate m and c, and then accept if and only if the estimated value of $m - n + c$ is close to zero. The details are shown in Algorithm 5.7.

Algorithm 5.7 (Tester for cycle-freeness)

Input: An integer $n \in \mathbb{Z}_{>0}$, $\epsilon \in (0,1)$, and query access to a graph G on n vertices.

1: $\tilde{m} \leftarrow$ Estimate obtained by using Lemma 5.7 with ϵ and $\delta = 1/6$.
2: $\tilde{c} \leftarrow$ Estimate obtained by using Lemma 5.8 with ϵ and $\delta = 1/6$.
3: **if** $\tilde{m} - n + \tilde{c} \geq \epsilon dn/2$ **then**
4:     Reject.
5: **else**
6:     Accept.
7: **end if**

Theorem 5.8. *Algorithm 5.7 is a tester for the cycle-freeness with query complexity* $O(\frac{1}{\epsilon^3 d^2} + \frac{d}{\epsilon^2})$.

Proof. First, we see the correctness of the tester. By the union bound, with probability at least $2/3$, we have $|\tilde{m} - m| \leq \epsilon dn/10$ and $|\tilde{c} - c| \leq \epsilon dn/10$. We assume that this is the case. If G is connected, then by Lemma 5.5, we have:

$$\tilde{m} - n + \tilde{c} \leq m - n + c + \frac{\epsilon dn}{5} = \frac{\epsilon dn}{5},$$

and hence we accept. If G is ϵ-far from being connected, then by Lemma 5.6, we have:

$$\tilde{m} - n + \tilde{c} \geq \epsilon dn - \frac{\epsilon dn}{5} \geq \frac{4\epsilon dn}{5},$$

and hence we reject.

The query complexity follows from Lemmas 5.7 and 5.8.   □

Cycle-freeness is equivalent to C_3-minor-freeness, where C_3 is the cycle of length 3. In Section 10.3, we will see that H-minor-freeness is constant-query testable for any fixed graph H.

Note that Algorithm 5.7 is a two-sided error tester. Indeed, any one-sided error for cycle-freeness requires $\Omega(\sqrt{n})$ queries. Although the formal proof, based on Yao's minimax principle, is somewhat cumbersome and is omitted, we can give some intuition why it is hard. First, notice that one-sided error testers can reject only when a cycle is found. Think of a random 3-regular graph G. Then, it is far from being cycle-free because the number of edges in G is $3n/2$ whereas any cycle-free graph can have at most $n - 1$ edges. However, when we look at a small part of the graph, what we observe is just a tree (with high probability), and hence we cannot reject.

5.5 Bipartiteness

So far, we have seen that several properties are constant-query testable in the bounded-degree model. In this section, we see that testing bipartiteness requires $\Omega(\sqrt{n})$ queries but is testable with $\widetilde{O}(\sqrt{n})$ queries, which is sublinear in n. This illustrates the difference between the adjacency matrix model and the bounded-degree model as bipartiteness is constant-query testable in the adjacency matrix model (Section 4.3.2).

5.5.1 Upper Bound

Here, we consider testing bipartiteness with $\widetilde{O}(\sqrt{n})$ queries. The tester itself is quite simple: After fixing a starting vertex $s \in V$, we perform $\widetilde{O}(\sqrt{n})$ many random walks of length poly $\log n$ from s. We accept if and only if the graph induced by these walks is bipartite. It is clear that the tester is a one-sided error tester and has query complexity $\widetilde{O}(\sqrt{n})$. Hence, the question is whether it rejects when the input graph is ϵ-far from being bipartite.

lazy random walk

parity

For the ease of analysis, we use *lazy random walk* instead of standard random walk. In a lazy random walk, in each step, each neighbor is selected with probability $\frac{1}{2d}$ and the walk proceeds to the vertex, and otherwise (with probability at least $1/2$) the walk remains in the present vertex. The *parity* of a random walk is the parity of the number of steps ignoring self-loops. Algorithm 5.8 shows a tester for bipartiteness.

Algorithm 5.8

Input: $n \in \mathbb{Z}_{>0}$, $\epsilon \in (0, 1)$, and query access to a graph $G = (V, E)$ on n vertices.
1: **for** $\Theta(\epsilon^{-1})$ times **do**
2:     Sample a vertex $s \in V$ uniformly at random.
3:     Perform $k := \sqrt{n} \cdot \text{poly}(\epsilon^{-1} \log n)$ lazy random walks from s, each of length $\ell := \text{poly}(\epsilon^{-1} \log n\epsilon)$.
4:     Let R_0 (resp., R_1) denote the vertex set reached from s with even (resp., odd) parity in any of these walks.
5:     **if** $R_0 \cap R_1 \neq \emptyset$ **then**
6:         Reject.
7:     **end if**
8: **end for**
9: Accept.

Theorem 5.9. *Algorithm 5.8 is a one-sided error tester for bipartiteness with query complexity $\sqrt{n} \cdot \text{poly}(\epsilon^{-1} \log n)$.*

The proof of Theorem 5.9 is quite involved, and here we consider only the "rapidly mixing" case, which we describe below. For the rapidly mixing case, it suffices to focus on a single starting vertex, say, $s \in V$. Let $p_0(v)$ (resp., $p_1(v)$) denote the probability that a lazy random walk of length ℓ, starting at s, reaches v with even (resp., odd) parity. When we want to stress the dependency on ℓ, we write $p_0^\ell(v)$ and $p_1^\ell(v)$. We assume that:

$$\frac{1}{2n} < p_0(v) + p_1(v) < \frac{2}{n}. \tag{5.1}$$

holds for every $v \in V$. We note that a d-regular random graph for $d \geq 3$ satisfies this property with high probability. (See Problem 5.5.) In general, even when the graph is connected and regular where $\lim_{\ell \to \infty}(p_0^\ell(v) + p_1^\ell(v)) = 1/n$, we need a polynomial number of steps in n to satisfy (5.1) with high probability, say, 2/3.

Exercise 5.3. Construct a graph $G = (V, E)$ such that for some particular vertex $s \in V$, we need $\ell = \Omega(n^2)$ to satisfy (5.1) with probability at least 2/3. for which $\ell = \Omega(n^2)$,

---

We consider two cases regarding the sum $\sum_{v \in V} p_0(v)p_1(v)$. If the sum is small, we show that V can be partitioned into two parts so that there are few edges between vertices in the same part, which implies that G is close to being bipartite (Lemma 5.9). Otherwise, we show that with a high probability, we reject G (Lemma 5.10). This completes the proof of Theorem 5.9 for the rapidly mixing case.

Lemma 5.9. *Suppose $\sum_{v \in V} p_0(v)p_1(v) \leq \frac{\epsilon}{100n}$. Let $V_0 = \{v \in V : p_0(v) < p_1(v)\}$ and $V_1 = V \setminus V_0$. Then, the number of edges with both endpoints in the same V_i is less than ϵdn.*

Proof sketch. Consider an edge $\{u, v\} \in \binom{V_0}{2}$. Then, both $p_1(u)$ and $p_1(v)$ are greater than $\frac{1}{2} \cdot \frac{1}{2n} = \frac{1}{4n}$. We can also show that $p_0(v)$ is high. To see this, we first note that $p_1^{\ell-1}(u) \geq p_1^\ell(u)/2 \geq \frac{1}{8n}$ since at least half of the probability $p_1^\ell(u)$ is contributed by walking along the self-loop at u after an $(\ell - 1)$-step walk of odd parity ending at u. Once an $(\ell - 1)$-step walk reaches u, with probability exactly $\frac{1}{2d}$, it continues to v in the next step. Thus, the edge $\{u, v\}$ contributes at least $\frac{1}{8n}\frac{1}{2d}\frac{1}{4n} = \frac{1}{64dn^2}$ to the sum $\sum_{w \in V} p_0(w)p_1(w)$. The same argument holds for edges in $\binom{V_1}{2}$. It follows that we can have at most $\frac{\epsilon}{100n} / \frac{1}{64dn^2}$ such edges, and the claim follows. $\square$

Lemma 5.10. *Suppose $\sum_{v \in V} p_0(v)p_1(v) \geq \frac{\epsilon}{100n}$. Then, with probability at least 2/3, the set $R_0 \cap R_1$ is not empty (and Algorithm 5.8 rejects).*

Proof sketch. For every $i \neq j$ with $i, j \in [k]$, we define an indicator random variable X_{ij} representing the event that the vertex encountered in the ℓ-th step of the i-th walk equals the vertex encountered in the ℓ-th step of the j-th walk, and that the i-th walk has an even parity and j-th walk has an odd parity. Then, we have:

$$\mathbf{E}[|R_0 \cap R_1|] = \sum_{i \neq j} \mathbf{E}[X_{ij}] = k(k-1) \sum_{v \in V} p_0(v) p_1(v)$$

$$> \frac{1000n}{\epsilon} \sum_{v \in V} p_0(v) p_1(v) \geq 10,$$

where the second inequality is due to the choice of k, and the third to the assumption.

To show that $|R_0 \cap R_1| > 0$ holds with high probability, we exploit Chebyshev's inequality. (Note that X_{ij}'s are not independent and we cannot apply Chernoff's bound.) Let $\mu := \sum_{v \in V} p_0(v) p_1(v)$ $(= \mathbf{E}[X_{ij}]$ for arbitrary $i \neq j)$, and $\bar{X}_{ij} := X_{ij} - \mu$. Then, we have:

$$\Pr\left[\sum_{i \neq j} X_{ij} = 0\right] < \frac{\mathbf{Var}\left[\sum_{i \neq j} X_{ij}\right]}{\left(k^2 \mu\right)^2} \leq \frac{1}{k^4 \mu^2} \mathbf{E}\left[\left(\sum_{i \neq j} \bar{X}_{ij}\right)^2\right]$$

$$= \frac{1}{k^4 \mu^2} \left(\sum_{\substack{i \neq j, i' \neq j': \\ |\{i,j,i',j'\}| \leq 2}} \mathbf{E}\left[\bar{X}_{ij} \bar{X}_{i'j'}\right] + \right.$$

$$\left. \sum_{\substack{i \neq j, i' \neq j': \\ |\{i,j,i',j'\}| = 3}} \mathbf{E}\left[\bar{X}_{ij} \bar{X}_{i'j'}\right] + \sum_{\substack{i \neq j, i' \neq j': \\ |\{i,j,i',j'\}| = 4}} \mathbf{E}\left[\bar{X}_{ij} \bar{X}_{i'j'}\right] \right). \qquad (5.2)$$

Note that $\mathbf{E}[\bar{X}_{ij} \bar{X}_{ji}] = 0$ because $X_{ij} X_{ji} = 0$, and that $\mathbf{E}[\bar{X}_{ij} \bar{X}_{i'j'}] = 0$ when $|\{i, j, i', j'\}| = 4$ because X_{ij} and $X_{i'j'}$ are independent in that case. Then, we have:

$$(5.2) = \frac{1}{k^4 \mu^2} \left(\sum_{i \neq j} \mathbf{E}[\bar{X}_{ij}^2] + \sum_{i \neq j \neq k \neq i} \mathbf{E}[\bar{X}_{ij} \bar{X}_{ik}] + \sum_{i \neq j \neq k \neq i} \mathbf{E}[\bar{X}_{ij} \bar{X}_{kj}] \right)$$

$$< \frac{1}{k^2 \mu} + \frac{2}{k \mu^2} \mathbf{E}[X_{12} X_{13}].$$

For the second term, we observe that $\Pr[X_{12} = X_{13} = 1]$ is upper bounded by $\Pr[X_{12} = 1] = \mu$ times the probability that the ℓ-th vertex of the first walk appears as the ℓ-th vertex of the third walk. Using the rapid mixing hypothesis, we upper bound the latter probability by $2/n$, and obtain:

$$\Pr[|R_0 \cap R_1| = 0] < \frac{1}{k^2 \mu} + \frac{2}{k \mu^2} \cdot \mu \cdot \frac{2}{n} < \frac{1}{3},$$

by setting the hidden constant in k to be large enough. $\square$

In the general case, we partition the input graph into expanders by removing a small number of edges and apply the analysis above to each of those expanders. However, as we cannot compute the partition in sublinear time and a random walk can enter and leave several parts of the partition, the analysis is quite involved and is beyond the scope of this book.

5.5.2 Lower Bound

In this section, we consider lower bounds for testing bipartiteness. Specifically, we show the following:

Theorem 5.10. *Any (possibly two-sided) tester for bipartiteness requires* $\Omega(\sqrt{n})$ *queries.*

By Yao's minimax principle, it is sufficient to construct two graph distributions $\mathcal{G}_N$ and $\mathcal{G}_Y$ with the following properties:

- (Almost) all graphs in the support of $\mathcal{G}_N$ are far from being bipartite;
- All graphs in the support of $\mathcal{G}_Y$ are bipartite.
- Any deterministic $O(\sqrt{n})$-query algorithm cannot distinguish a graph chosen randomly from $\mathcal{G}_N$ and a graph chosen randomly from $\mathcal{G}_Y$ with high probability.

We start with the construction of both distributions: Let n be an even integer.

- The distribution $\mathcal{G}_N$ is a uniform distribution over all 3-regular graphs that are composed of the union of a Hamiltonian cycle and a perfect matching. That is, there are n edges connecting the vertices in a cycle, and the other $n/2$ edges form a perfect matching.
- The distribution $\mathcal{G}_Y$ is the same as the first except that the perfect matchings are restricted as follows: the distance on the cycle between the endpoints of an edge in the perfect matching must be odd.

In both cases, we assume that the edges incident to any vertex are labeled in the following fixed manner: Each cycle edge is labeled 1 in one endpoint and 2 in the other. This labeling forms an orientation of the cycle. The matching edges are labeled 3. Clearly, all graphs in $\mathcal{G}_Y$ are bipartite because all cycles in the graph are of even length.

> **Exercise 5.4.** Show that a graph sampled from $\mathcal{G}_N$ is 0.01-far from being bipartite with probability at least $1 - \exp(-n)$.

Now, we turn to show that any deterministic algorithm that performs $o(\sqrt{n})$ queries cannot distinguish between a graph sampled from $\mathcal{G}_N$ and a graph sampled from $\mathcal{G}_Y$.

Let $\mathcal{A}$ be a deterministic algorithm for testing bipartiteness using $Q = Q(n)$ queries. Namely, $\mathcal{A}$ is a mapping from a *query-answer history*:

query-answer history

$$(q_1, a_1), \ldots, (q_t, a_t)$$

to $q_{t+1} \in V \times \{1, 2, 3\}$, for every $t < Q$, and to $\{\textbf{accept}, \textbf{reject}\}$, for $t = Q$. A query q_t is a pair (v_t, i_t), where $v_t \in V$ and $i_t \in \{1, 2, 3\}$, and an answer a_t is simply a vertex.

We assume that the mapping is defined only on histories which are consistent with some graph. Then, any query-answer history of length $t - 1$ can be used to define a *knowledge graph*, H_{t-1}, at time $t - 1$ (that is, before the t-th query). The vertex set of H_{t-1} contains all vertices which appeared in the history (either in queries or in answers), and its edge set contains the edges between $v_{t'}$ and $a_{t'}$ for all $t' < t$ (with the appropriate labelings $i_{t'}$ at vertex $v_{t'}$). Thus, H_{t-1} is a labeled subgraph of the labeled graph tested by $\mathcal{A}$.

knowledge graph

Let $\mathcal{D}_Y^{\mathcal{A}}$ and $\mathcal{D}_N^{\mathcal{A}}$ denote the distributions over query-answer histories (of length Q), or in other words, knowledge graphs, induced by the execution of $\mathcal{A}$ on a graph sampled from $\mathcal{G}_Y$ and $\mathcal{G}_N$, respectively. Now, we bound the statistical distance between $\mathcal{D}_Y^{\mathcal{A}}$ and $\mathcal{D}_N^{\mathcal{A}}$.

Lemma 5.11. *Let $\alpha < 1/2$, $Q \leq \alpha\sqrt{n}$ and $n \geq 8Q$. Then, the statistical distance between $\mathcal{D}_N^{\mathcal{A}}$ and $\mathcal{D}_Y^{\mathcal{A}}$ is at most $4\alpha^2$. Furthermore, for both distributions, with probability at least $1 - 4\alpha^2$ the knowledge graph at the end of the execution of $\mathcal{A}$ contains no cycles.*

Proof. We assume without loss of generality that $\mathcal{A}$ does not ask queries whose answer can be derived from the knowledge graph since those give no new information. Under this assumption, we first prove the following.

Claim 5.1. *In both $\mathcal{D}_N^{\mathcal{A}}$ and $\mathcal{D}_Y^{\mathcal{A}}$, the total probability mass assigned to query-answer histories in which a vertex in H_{t-1} is returned as an answer to the t-th query for some $t \leq Q$ is at most $4\alpha^2$.*

Proof. We show that for every t the probability that the t-th answer is in H_{t-1} (that is, $a_t = v_{t'}$ or $a_t = a_{t'}$ for some $t' < t$) is at most $8(t-1)/n$. To simplify the analysis, we regard that the distributions $\mathcal{D}_N^{\mathcal{A}}$ and $\mathcal{D}_Y^{\mathcal{A}}$ first assign parities to vertices and then generate a graph such that even-parity vertices and odd-parity vertices alternate in the cycle uniformly at random. Fixing t, there are two cases in which the event a_t belongs to H_{t-1} might occur:

1. $i_t = 3$, and v_t is matched to a vertex in the knowledge graph H_{t-1}. Since the number of vertices in H_{t-1} is at most $2(t-1)$, this event occurs with probability at most $\frac{2(t-1)}{n-2(t-1)}$ for $\mathcal{D}_N^{\mathcal{A}}$, and at most $\frac{2(t-1)}{n/2-2(t-1)}$ for $\mathcal{D}_Y^{\mathcal{A}}$. Note that, in $\mathcal{D}_Y^{\mathcal{A}}$, v_t can be matched only to a vertex with the opposite parity.
2. $i_t \in \{1, 2\}$ and a_t is chosen in H_{t-1}. Because a vertex can be connected only to a vertex with the opposite parity, this event occurs with probability at most $\frac{2(t-1)}{n/2-2(t-1)}$.

Thus, in both cases, the probability that a_t belongs to H_{t-1} is at most $\frac{2(t-1)}{n/2-2(t-1)} < 8(t-1)/n$ (as $n \geq 8t$). The probability that such an event occurs in any sequence of $\alpha\sqrt{n}$ queries is at most $\sum_{t=1}^{\alpha\sqrt{n}} 8(t-1)/n \leq 4\alpha^2$ by the union bound. $\qquad\square$

The claim implies that with probability at least $1 - 4\alpha^2$ the knowledge graph of $\mathcal{A}$ contains no cycle.

Observe that whenever the vertex returned as an answer to a query is not in the current knowledge graph, it is uniformly distributed among the vertices not in that graph. Since the queries of $\mathcal{A}$ depend only on the query-answer history, conditioned on that we have never get a vertex in the current knowledge graph as an answer to a query, the distribution of answers are the same between $\mathcal{D}_N^{\mathcal{A}}$ and $\mathcal{D}_Y^{\mathcal{A}}$. $\qquad\square$

Proof of Theorem 5.10. Fix $\epsilon = 0.01$. Instantiating Lemma 5.11 with $\alpha = 1/2$, for any algorithm $\mathcal{A}$ that makes $\alpha\sqrt{N}$ queries, the statistical distance between $\mathcal{D}_N^{\mathcal{A}}$ and $\mathcal{D}_Y^{\mathcal{A}}$ is at most $4 \cdot (1/4)^2 = 1/4$.

Since all graphs in $\mathcal{G}_Y$ are bipartite and $\mathcal{A}$ is a tester for bipartiteness, we have:

$$\Pr_{G \sim \mathcal{G}_Y} [\mathcal{A} \text{ accepts } G] = \Pr_{H \sim \mathcal{D}_Y^{\mathcal{A}}} [\mathcal{A} \text{ accepts on } H] \geq \frac{2}{3}. \qquad (5.3)$$

Combining (5.3) with the bound of 1/4 on the statistical distance between $\mathcal{D}_N^{\mathcal{A}}$ and $\mathcal{D}_Y^{\mathcal{A}}$, we have:

$$\Pr_{G \sim \mathcal{G}_N} [\mathcal{A} \text{ accepts } G] = \Pr_{H \sim \mathcal{D}_N^{\mathcal{A}}} [\mathcal{A} \text{ accepts on } H] \geq \frac{2}{3} - \frac{1}{4} > 0.4. \qquad (5.4)$$

However, by Exercise 5.4, at least 99% of the graphs in $\mathcal{G}_N$ are 0.01-far from being bipartite and thus must be rejected. This means that:

$$\Pr_{G \sim \mathcal{G}_N} [\mathcal{A} \text{ accepts } G] \leq 0.99 \cdot \frac{1}{3} + 0.01 < 0.35,$$

contradicting with (5.4). $\qquad\square$

5.6 3-Colorability

Having seen that the query complexity for testing bipartiteness, that is, 2-colorability, is $\widetilde{\Theta}(\sqrt{n})$, it is natural to ask whether we can test k-colorability for $k \geq 3$ with a sublinear number of queries. In this section, we answer this question in the negative by showing the following:

Theorem 5.11. *There exists a universal constant $d \in \mathbb{Z}_{>0}$ such that testing 3-colorability with a degree bound d requires $\Omega(n)$ queries.*

The $\Omega(n)$ lower bound for testing 3-colorability is obtained via gap-preserving local reductions. First, let us introduce some source problems:

conjunctive normal form

literal

3-CNF

- **3-SAT**: A Boolean formula is in *conjunctive normal form* (CNF) if it consists of clauses joined by $\wedge$'s, where each clause is an $\vee$ of literals. Here, a *literal* is a Boolean variable or a negated Boolean variable. If all clauses have exactly three literals, the formula is said to be a *3-CNF*. The following is an example of a 3-CNF on a variable set $\{x, y, z, w\}$:

$$(x \vee y \vee z) \wedge (\bar{x} \vee y \vee w) \wedge (x \vee \bar{z} \vee \bar{w}) \wedge (\bar{y} \vee z \vee w).$$

SAT

system of linear equations

  3-SAT is the problem of finding a satisfying assignment to a given 3-CNF.
- **3-LIN**: 3-LIN is the problem of finding a solution to a system of linear equations on $\mathbb{F}_2$ for which each equation involves exactly three variables. The following is an example of an instance of 3-LIN on a variable set $\{x, y, z, w\}$:

$$x + y + z = 0 \bmod 2,$$
$$x + y + w = 1 \bmod 2,$$
$$y + z + w = 1 \bmod 2.$$

degree

ϵ-farness

For these problems, we can consider the following testing problems (in the bounded-degree model). Let d be a parameter of the model, which defines an upper bound on the *degree*, that is, the number of constraints in which a variable can appear. An instance $\mathcal{I} = (V, \mathcal{C})$ with a degree bound d of 3-SAT or 3-LIN, where V is a variable set and $\mathcal{C}$ is a constraint set, is provided through query access $\mathcal{O}_{\mathcal{I}} : V \times [d] \to \mathcal{C} \cup \{\bot\}$. Here, $\mathcal{O}_{\mathcal{I}}(v, i)$ returns the i-th constraint in which v appears if it exists and a special symbol $\bot$ otherwise. For $\epsilon > 0$, we say that an instance of 3-SAT or 3-LIN is ϵ-*far* from being satisfiable if removing at most ϵdn constraints do not make it satisfiable. Then, a tester for 3-SAT (resp., 3-LIN) is an algorithm that, given $n \in \mathbb{Z}_{>0}$, $\epsilon \in (0, 1)$, and query access to an instance $\mathcal{I}$ of 3-SAT (resp., 3-LIN) on n variables with a degree bound d, accepts with probability at least $2/3$ if $\mathcal{I}$ is satisfiable and rejects with probability at least $2/3$ if $\mathcal{I}$ is ϵ-far from being satisfiable.

Before considering 3-colorability, we show an $\Omega(n)$ lower bound for 3-LIN. To this end, we use the following construction of a matrix, which is obtained from a random hypergraph.

Lemma 5.12. *For every $c \in \mathbb{Z}_{>0}$, there exists $\delta > 0$ such that, for every n, there exists a matrix $A \in \{0,1\}^{cn \times n}$ with the following properties:*

- *each row has exactly three non-zero entries,*
- *each column has exactly $3c$ non-zero entries, and*
- *every collection of δn rows is linearly independent.*

By Yao's minimax principle, it suffices to construct two distributions $\mathcal{D}_{\mathrm{far}}$ and $\mathcal{D}_{\mathrm{sat}}$ that cannot be distinguished by an $o(n)$-query deterministic algorithm with high probability such that an instance sampled from $\mathcal{D}_{\mathrm{far}}$ is almost always far from being satisfiable whereas an instance sampled from $\mathcal{D}_{\mathrm{sat}}$ is satisfiable. Let $c \in \mathbb{Z}_{>0}$ be an integer that we will determine later. Using the matrix $A \in \{0,1\}^{cn \times n}$ given by Lemma 5.12, we consider the following two distributions on instances of 3-LIN with n variables, cn equations, and each variable appearing in exactly $3c$ equations:

- The distribution $\mathcal{D}_{\mathrm{far}}$ consists of instances $Ax = b$, where $b \in \{0,1\}^{cn}$ is chosen uniformly at random.
- The distribution $\mathcal{D}_{\mathrm{sat}}$ consists of instances $Ax = Az$, where $z \in \{0,1\}^n$ is chosen uniformly at random.

By construction, every instance in $\mathcal{D}_{\mathrm{sat}}$ is satisfiable. On the other hand, instances in $\mathcal{D}_{\mathrm{far}}$ are far from satisfiable with high probability:

Lemma 5.13. *For a sufficiently large $c \in \mathbb{Z}_{>0}$, with probability $1 - o(1)$, an instance sampled from $\mathcal{D}_{\mathrm{far}}$ is $\Omega(1)$-far from satisfiable.*

Proof. For a fixed assignment x, the vector $Ax - b$ is uniformly distributed in $\{0,1\}^{cn}$. By Chernoff's bound, with probability $1 - \exp(-\Omega(cn))$, $Ax - b$ has Hamming weight at least $\Omega(cn)$. A union bound over all 2^n possible assignments for x yields the desired result, as long as c is sufficiently large. $\square$

In what follows, we fix c so that the consequence of Lemma 5.13 holds. Also, we fix δ determined from c by Lemma 5.12. Note that every instance generated by $\mathcal{D}_{\mathrm{far}}$ and $\mathcal{D}_{\mathrm{sat}}$ fits in the bounded-degree model with a degree bound $3c$. Then, we have the following:

Theorem 5.12. *There exists a universal constant $d \in \mathbb{Z}_{>0}$ such that testing 3-LIN with a degree bound d requires $\Omega(n)$ queries.*

Proof. Let A' be an arbitrary set of δn rows of A. By Lemma 5.12, the rows of A' are linearly independent. Therefore, for a uniformly random $z' \in \{0,1\}^n$, $A'z'$ is uniformly distributed in $\{0,1\}^{\delta n}$. In particular, the distribution of $A'z'$ is the same as the distribution of a vector $b' \in \{0,1\}^{\delta n}$ chosen uniformly at random. This means that any tester of query complexity at most δn cannot distinguish instances from $\mathcal{D}_{\mathrm{sat}}$ and those from $\mathcal{D}_{\mathrm{far}}$. $\square$

Consider the canonical reduction from 3-LIN to 3-SAT, that is:

$$x + y + z = 0 \bmod 2 \Rightarrow (\bar{x} \vee y \vee z) \wedge (x \vee \bar{y} \vee z) \wedge (x \vee y \vee \bar{z}) \wedge (\bar{x} \vee \bar{y} \vee \bar{z}),$$
$$x + y + z = 1 \bmod 2 \Rightarrow (x \vee y \vee z) \wedge (\bar{x} \vee \bar{y} \vee z) \wedge (x \vee \bar{y} \vee \bar{z}) \wedge (\bar{x} \vee y \vee \bar{z}).$$

This reduction is a gap-preserving local reduction (with constant parameters), and by Theorem 5.12, we immediately have the following lower bound for 3-SAT:

Theorem 5.13. *Testing* 3-*SAT requires* $\Omega(n)$ *queries.*

The proof of Theorem 5.11 follows from Theorem 7.2 and a reduction from 3-SAT to 3-colorability. The reduction is almost identical to the standard one used to show the NP-completeness of 3-colorability, but we need to slightly modify it in order to bound the maximum degree of the resulting graph.

Using gap-preserving local reductions from 3-SAT, several other NP-complete problems such as 3-edge-colorability, having a Hamilton path, and 3-dimensional matching have been shown to have linear lower bounds in the bounded-degree model. Although linear lower bounds of those problems are shown through reductions (with slight modifications if required) used to show NP-hardness of those problems, it is interesting that the source of hardness is 3-LIN, which is solvable in polynomial time by using Gaussian elimination. This illustrates the difference between property testers and polynomial-time algorithms: A problem can be difficult for the former if we need to exploit some global structure to solve it, whereas the latter can sometimes handle such a global structure efficiently.

5.7 Minimum Spanning Trees

The techniques we have seen so far can also be used to solve optimization problems. As a simple example, in this section, we consider approximating the weight of a minimum spanning tree.

weight
spanning tree
minimum spanning
tree

Let $G = (V, E, w)$ be a weighted graph, where $w \colon E \to \mathbb{R}$ is a weight function on edges. The *weight* of a tree $T \subseteq E$ is defined as $\sum_{e \in T} w(e)$. A tree $T \subseteq E$ is called a *spanning tree* if T is incident to all the vertices in V. We say that a spanning tree $T \subseteq E$ is a *minimum spanning tree* (MST) of G if it has the smallest weight among all the spanning trees of G. Then, let $\mathrm{mst}(G)$ be the weight of an MST. The goal is to estimate $\mathrm{mst}(G)$ to within ϵn, where ϵ is an error parameter. To this end, we require the following three assumptions.

- The input graph G is connected. Otherwise, the problem of computing $\mathrm{mst}(G)$ is not well defined.
- The range of the weight function w is a finite set $[W]$, where $W \in \mathbb{Z}_{>0}$ is a fixed integer.

- When we obtain a vertex v as a neighbor of a vertex u from the query access, we also obtain the weight $w(\{u, v\})$.

We reduce the problem of estimating $\mathrm{mst}(G)$ to estimating the number of connected components in a series of graphs made from G. To see the idea, consider the case that every edge in G has a weight one or two. Let G_1 be the subgraph of G consisting of edges of weight one, and let c_1 be the number of connected components in G_1. Then, any MST in G must use $c_1 - 1$ edges of weight two, and all the other edges are of weight one. Hence, $\mathrm{mst}(G) = ((n-1) - (c_1 - 1)) + 2(c_1 - 1) = n - 2 + c_1$.

We generalize this idea to the case that weights are chosen from $[W]$. For $w \in [W]$, let G_i be the subgraph of G consisting of edges of weight at most i. Let c_i be the number of connected components in G_i, and we define $c_0 = n$ for convenience. Note that $c_W = 1$ from the assumption. Then, we have the following:

Lemma 5.14.

$$\mathrm{mst}(G) = n - W + \sum_{i=1}^{W-1} c_i.$$

Proof. Let m_i be the number of edges of weight i in an MST of G. Note that m_i is independent of the choice of the MST. Observe that for all $0 \le \ell \le W - 1$, $\sum_{i > \ell} m_i = c_\ell - 1$. Therefore:

$$\mathrm{mst}(G) = \sum_{i=1}^{W} i m_i = \sum_{\ell=0}^{W-1} \sum_{i=\ell+1}^{W} m_i = -W + \sum_{\ell=0}^{W-1} c_\ell = n - W + \sum_{i=1}^{W} c_\ell,$$

which completes the proof.   □

By Lemma 5.8, we can approximate $\mathrm{mst}(G)$ using the following algorithm.

Algorithm 5.9 Approximation algorithm for the weight of an MST

Input: Integers $n, W \in \mathbb{Z}_{>0}$, $\epsilon \in (0, 1)$, and query access to a weighted graph G on n vertices with the maximum edge weight at most W.

1: **for** $i = 1$ to $W - 1$ **do**
2:      Apply Lemma 5.8 with query access to G_i, $\frac{\epsilon}{dW}$, and $\frac{1}{3W}$.
3:      Let $\tilde{c}_i$ be the obtained estimation.
4: **end for**
5: Return $\nu := n - W + \sum_{i=1}^{W-1} \tilde{c}_i$.

We mention how to implement query access to G_i. Suppose that we want to know the j-th neighbor of a vertex $u \in V$. If $\mathcal{O}_G(u, j) = \bot$, then we simply return $\bot$. If $\mathcal{O}_G(u, j)$ returns a vertex v and the weight $w(\{u, v\})$, then we return v if $w(\{u, v\}) \le i$ and return $\bot$ otherwise.

Now we show the correctness of Algorithm 5.9.

Theorem 5.14. *Algorithm 5.9 approximates* $\mathrm{mst}(G)$ *to within* ϵn *with probability at least* $2/3$. *The query complexity is* $O(\epsilon^{-3}dW^4 \log W)$.

Proof. By the union bound, with probability at least $2/3$, we have $|\tilde{c}_i - c_i| \leq \frac{\epsilon n}{W}$ for every $i \in [W]$. Then, we have:

$$|\nu - \mathrm{mst}(G)| = \left| \sum_{i=1}^{W-1} (\tilde{c}_i - c_i) \right| \leq \sum_{i=1}^{W-1} |\tilde{c}_i - c_i| \leq \epsilon n.$$

The query complexity is:

$$O\left(W \cdot \frac{d^3 W^3 \log(1/3W)}{\epsilon^3 d^2} \right) = O\left(\frac{dW^4 \log(1/W)}{\epsilon^3} \right),$$

which completes the proof. $\qquad\square$

Remark 5.3. Suppose that the weights of G are all in the range $[1, w]$, for some real value $w \in \mathbb{R}$. To extend Algorithm 5.9 to this case, we can multiply all the weights by ϵ^{-1} and round each weight to the nearest integer. Then, we run Algorithm 5.9 with error parameter $\epsilon/2$ and with a new range of weights $[1, \lceil \epsilon^{-1}w \rceil]$ to get a value ν. Finally, output $\epsilon\nu$. The additive error introduced by the rounding is at most $\epsilon/2$ per edge in the MST and hence $\epsilon n/2$ for the whole MST, which gives a total additive error of at most ϵn. The query complexity of the algorithm is increased by a factor of ϵ^{-1}.

5.8 1/2-Approximation to Maximum Matching

matching

maximum matching

approximation

A *matching* in a graph G is a set of edges whose endpoints are distinct. A *maximum matching* is a matching of the largest size. Let $\mathrm{mm}(G)$ denote the maximum size of a matching. We say that an algorithm is an $(\alpha, \epsilon n)$-*approximation algorithm* to the maximum size of a matching if, given (query access to) a graph G, it returns a value ν such that:

$$\alpha \cdot \mathrm{mm}(G) - \epsilon n \leq \nu \leq \mathrm{mm}(G)$$

with probability at least $2/3$. In this section, we show a constant-query $(1/2, \epsilon n)$-approximation algorithm to the maximum size of a matching.

maximal matching

A matching is *maximal* if it can not be extended by adding edges to it. The sizes of maximal matchings vary, but it is well known the size of any maximal matching is at least half the maximum size of a matching. Hence, in order to get $(1/2, \epsilon n)$-approximation to the maximum size of a matching, it suffices to estimate the size of *some particular* maximal matching to within ϵn. To this end, we develop query access $\mathcal{O}_G^{\mathrm{mat}}$ to a fixed maximal matching M in a graph $G = (V, E)$, that is, when we specify an edge $e \in E$, it returns whether e is a member of M. Here, the maximal matching M will be determined by internal randomness of $\mathcal{O}_G^{\mathrm{mat}}$. If there were such query access, then we can easily approximate the size of the maximal matching by using Lemma 2.2.

In Section 5.8.1, we develop query access to a maximal matching that is obtained by a naive greedy algorithm whose expected query complexity is $2^{O(d)}$. In Section 5.8.2, we briefly describe a more efficient implementation of the query access whose expected query complexity is polynomial in d.

5.8.1 Simulation of the Greedy Algorithm

Before considering constant-query algorithms, let us consider a global greedy algorithm that constructs a maximal matching (Algorithm 5.10). It takes a graph $G = (V, E)$ and a permutation $\pi \colon E \to [m]$, where $m = |E|$ is the number of edges. For an edge $e \in E$, we call $\pi(e)$ its *rank*. Let $e_1, \ldots, e_m$ be the ordering of edges in E increasingly sorted according to their ranks. Then, starting with an empty matching M, for each $i \in [m]$, we greedily add e_i to M if neither of its endpoints appears in the current M. It is clear that the resulting matching M is maximal. The permutation π can be fixed just to obtain a maximal matching, but it will play an important role when bounding the query complexity of the final algorithm.

rank

Algorithm 5.10 (Global algorithm for computing a maximal matching)

Input: A graph $G = (V, E)$ on m edges and a permutation $\pi \in E \to [m]$.
1: $M \leftarrow$ an empty edge set.
2: Let $e_1, \ldots, e_m$ be edges increasingly sorted according to their ranks.
3: **for** $i = 1$ to m **do**
4:     **if** neither endpoints of e_i appears in M **then**
5:         Add e_i to M.
6:     **end if**
7: **end for**
8: Output M.

Now, we transform Algorithm 5.10 to a local algorithm with which we can access a maximal matching. Let $\mathfrak{S}_E$ be the set of all permutations $\pi \colon E \to [m]$. Then, we want to construct an efficient query access $\mathcal{O}_G^{\mathrm{mat}} \colon \mathfrak{S}_E \times E \to \{\mathbf{true}, \mathbf{false}\}$ such that

- $\mathcal{O}_G^{\mathrm{mat}}(\pi, e) = \mathbf{true}$ if and only if e belongs to the matching determined by π.
- The (expected) number of queries to G made by $\mathcal{O}_G^{\mathrm{mat}}$ is constant.

Note that, we do not want to explicitly specify the permutation $\pi\colon E \to [m]$ because generating π requires $\Omega(n)$ time. We will discuss this issue later, and in what follows, we assume that we can freely access π.

First, $\mathcal{O}_G^{\mathrm{mat}}(\pi, e)$ collects values of $\mathcal{O}_G^{\mathrm{mat}}(\pi, e')$ for e' incident to e whose rank is lower than that of e. If $\mathcal{O}_G^{\mathrm{mat}}(\pi, e')$ is **true** for some e', then $\mathcal{O}_G^{\mathrm{mat}}(\pi, e)$ returns **false**. Otherwise, it returns **true**. It is easy to see that $\mathcal{O}_G^{\mathrm{mat}}$ locally simulates the greedy algorithm and correctly decides whether e is in the maximal matching determined by π. Also, since the rank of the current edge always decreases when calling $\mathcal{O}_G^{\mathrm{mat}}$ recursively, $\mathcal{O}_G^{\mathrm{mat}}$ always stops. Our implementation of $\mathcal{O}_G^{\mathrm{mat}}$ is summarized in Algorithm 5.11.

Algorithm 5.11 Query access $\mathcal{O}_G^{\mathrm{mat}}$ to a maximal matching

---

Input: A permutation $\pi \in \mathfrak{S}_E$ and an edge $e = \{u, v\} \in E$.
1: **for** each edge e' incident to u or v other than e whose rank is smaller that of e
    do
2:     **if** $\mathcal{O}_G^{\mathrm{mat}}(\pi, e')$ returns **true then**
3:         **return false.**
4:     **end if**
5: **end for**
6: **return true.**

In general, we cannot bound the number of recursive calls of $\mathcal{O}_G^{\mathrm{mat}}$ and its query complexity to G in the worst case. To see this, consider a path $P = (e_1, \ldots, e_k)$ of length $k = \Omega(n)$ and a permutation π for which the ranks of $e_1, \ldots, e_k$ are in decreasing order. Then, $\mathcal{O}_G^{\mathrm{mat}}(\pi, e_1)$ must traverse all the edges along P, and the resulting number of recursive calls is k.

However, notice that the probability that such a situation occurs is very tiny if the permutation π is chosen uniformly at random. Indeed, the expected number of queries to G of Algorithm 5.11 over uniformly sampled permutation π is small:

Lemma 5.15. *For any $e \in E$, the expected query complexity of $\mathcal{O}_G^{\mathrm{mat}}(\pi, e)$ over permutations $\pi\colon E \to [m]$ is $2^{O(d)}$.*

Proof. The probability that we traverse a path $P = (e_1, e_2, \ldots, e_k)$ of length k starting with $e_1 = e$ is:

$$\Pr_{\pi}[\text{all the edges in } P \text{ are explored}] = \Pr_{\pi}[r_{e_1} > r_{e_2} > \cdots > r_{e_k}] = \frac{1}{k!}.$$

Since the number of paths of length k starting with e is at most d^k, the expected total number of edges to be explored is at most:

$$\sum_{k=0}^{\infty} \frac{d^k}{k!} = e^d = 2^{O(d)}.$$

Then, the total number of queries to G is $2^{O(d)} \cdot d = 2^{O(d)}$. □

Notice that we only require uniformly sampled permutation in Lemma 5.15. Hence, by using the technique described in Section 5.3.4, we can generate a permutation π "on the fly" and we do not need to generate the whole π.

Theorem 5.15. *There is a $(1/2, \epsilon n)$-approximation algorithm for the maximum size of a matching with query complexity $\epsilon^{-2} 2^{O(d)}$.*

Proof. Our algorithm first obtains a value X by applying Lemma 2.2 on the query access $\mathcal{O}_G^{\text{mat}}$ with a random permutation $\pi \colon E \to [m]$, $\epsilon/2$, and $\delta = 1/6$, and then returns $\tilde{s} = X - \epsilon n/2$.

Let M be the maximal matching defined by the ordering induced by π and $s = |M|$. Then, we have:
$$|X - s| \le \frac{\epsilon n}{2},$$
with probability at least 5/6. When this happens, by the fact $\text{mm}(G)/2 \le s \le \text{mm}(G)$, we have:

$$\tilde{s} = X - \frac{\epsilon n}{2} \ge s - \epsilon n \ge \frac{\text{mm}(G)}{2} - \epsilon n,$$
$$\tilde{s} = X - \frac{\epsilon n}{2} \le s \le \text{mm}(G),$$

which means that our algorithm is an $(1/2, \epsilon n)$-approximation algorithm to the maximum size of a matching.

Since the number of queries to $\mathcal{O}_G^{\text{mat}}$ is $O(\epsilon^{-2})$, by Lemma 5.15, the expected number of queries to G is $\epsilon^{-2} 2^{O(d)}$. By Markov's inequality, with probability at least 5/6, the query complexity is bounded by $\epsilon^{-2} 2^{O(d)}$.

By the union bound, we get the desired result. □

An *augmenting path* with respect to a matching $M \subseteq E$ is a path $P = (e_1, \ldots, e_{2k+1})$ for $k \ge 0$ such that $e_{2i-1} \notin E$ for every $i \in [k+1]$ and $e_{2i} \in E$ for every $i \in [k]$. By applying an augmenting path P to M, that is, adding e_{2i-1} for each $i \in [k+1]$ to M and removing e_{2i} from M for each $i \in [k]$, we can get a larger matching M' with $|M'| = |M| + 1$.

We have considered a greedy algorithm that outputs a maximal set of disjoint edges. Instead, consider an algorithm that iteratively applies a maximal set of disjoint augmenting paths of length $2i-1$ for each $i \in [k+1]$. Then, it is known that the size of the resulting matching is an $1 - O(1/k)$-approximation to the maximum size of a matching. By extending Algorithm 5.11, we can simulate this iterative algorithm with $k = \Theta(\epsilon^{-1})$, and we can obtain a $(1, \epsilon n)$-approximation algorithm to the maximum size of a matching with query complexity $2^{d^{O(\epsilon^{-1})}}$.

augmenting path

Exercise 5.5. Design a constant-query approximation algorithm for the minimum size of a vertex cover using Theorem 5.15.

5.8.2 Improved Simulation of the Greedy Algorithm

In this section, we briefly describe a more efficient implementation of $\mathcal{O}_G^{\mathrm{mat}}$, whose expected query complexity is $\mathrm{poly}(d)$.

A key observation to improve the query complexity is that an edge e cannot be contained in a matching M when another edge f incident to e already appears in M. Furthermore, an edge with a lower rank (with respect to the ordering π) is likely to be in M since it is checked earlier by the greedy algorithm. Thus, to determine the value of $\mathcal{O}_G^{\mathrm{mat}}(\pi, e)$, it will be effective to access $\mathcal{O}_G^{\mathrm{mat}}(\pi, f)$ from edges f with lower ranks and immediately return **false** once we have found $\mathcal{O}_G^{\mathrm{mat}}(\pi, f) = $ **true**. From this intuition, we get Algorithm 5.12.

Algorithm 5.12 Improved query access $\mathcal{O}_G^{\mathrm{mat}}$ to a maximal matching

---

Input: A permutation $\pi\colon E \to [m]$ and an edge $e \in E$.
1: Collect edges incident to e by using $\mathcal{O}_G$.
2: Let $e_1, \ldots, e_k$ be those edges increasingly sorted by their ranks.
3: **for** $i \in [k]$ **do**
4:     **if** the rank of e_i is lower than that of e **then**
5:         **if** $\mathcal{O}_G^{\mathrm{mat}}(\pi, e_i) = $ **true then**
6:             **return false.**
7:         **end if**
8:     **end if**
9: **end for**
10: **return true.**

Let $T(\pi, e)$ be the number of (recursive) accesses to $\mathcal{O}_G^{\mathrm{mat}}$ during the evaluation of $\mathcal{O}_G^{\mathrm{mat}}(\pi, e)$ (including the access to $\mathcal{O}_G^{\mathrm{mat}}(\pi, e)$ at the top level). We have the following theorem:

Lemma 5.16. *For any graph $G = (V, E)$ with m edges, we have:*

$$\mathop{\mathbf{E}}_{\pi\colon E \to [m]} \mathop{\mathbf{E}}_{e \in E} [T(\pi, e)] \le 1 + \frac{\ell}{m},$$

where $\ell = \left| \left\{ \{e, f\} \in \binom{E}{2} : e, f \in E, e \text{ is incident to } f \right\} \right|$.

We omit the proof as it is quite involved. A subtle difference from Lemma 5.15 is that we take the expectation over permutations and edges, not just over permutations. Indeed, $\mathbf{E}_{\pi:\,E\to[m]}[T(\pi,e)]$ can be larger than $1+\ell/m$ for some $v \in V$ in general.

We get the following as an immediate corollary:

Corollary 5.4. *The expected query complexity of $\mathcal{O}_G^{\mathrm{mat}}(\pi,e)$ over permutations $\pi\colon E \to [m]$ and edges $e \in E$ is $O(d^2)$.*

Proof. For each access to $\mathcal{O}_G^{\mathrm{mat}}(\pi,e)$, we enumerate all the edges incident to e, which requires $2d$ queries to G. As ℓ is at most $2(d-1)m$, by Lemma 5.16, the expected query complexity is at most $2d \cdot (1 + \ell/m) = O(d^2)$. $\qquad\square$

Comparing with the bound of $2^{O(d)}$ shown in Lemma 5.15, Corollary 5.4 claims that the simple pruning exponentially decreases the query complexity.

Now, we have the following:

Theorem 5.16. *There is a $(1/2,\epsilon n)$-approximation algorithm to the maximum size of a matching with query complexity $O(\epsilon^{-2}d^4)$.*

Proof. For a permutation $\pi\colon E \to [m]$, we define $f_\pi\colon V \times [d] \to \{0,1\}$ as follows:

$$f_\pi(u,i) = \begin{cases} 1 & \text{if } \mathcal{O}_G(u,i) = v \in V \text{ and } \mathcal{O}_G^{\mathrm{mat}}(\pi,\{u,v\}) = \textbf{true}, \\ 0 & \text{if } \mathcal{O}_G(u,i) = v \in V \text{ and } \mathcal{O}_G^{\mathrm{mat}}(\pi,\{u,v\}) = \textbf{false}, \\ 0 & \text{if } \mathcal{O}_G(u,i) = \perp. \end{cases}$$

For a uniformly sampled $\pi\colon E \to [m]$, let X be the output obtained by applying Lemma 2.2 on f_π, $\frac{\epsilon}{2d}$, and $1/6$. Then, we return $X - \epsilon n/2$.

Using the same argument as in the proof of Theorem 5.15, we can show that the output is an $(1/2,\epsilon n)$-approximation to the maximum size of a matching with probability at least $5/6$.

Now, we analyze the query complexity. Note that the algorithm in Lemma 2.2 uniformly samples tuples from $V \times [d]$, which causes accesses to $\mathcal{O}_G^{\mathrm{mat}}(\pi,e)$ for uniformly sampled edges $e \in E$. As we uniformly sample $\pi\colon E \to [m]$, by Corollary 5.4, the expected number of queries to G performed by each access of $\mathcal{O}_G^{\mathrm{mat}}$ is $O(d^2)$. As the number of accesses to f_π is $O(\epsilon^{-2}d^2)$, the expected query complexity is $O(\epsilon^{-2}d^4)$. By Markov's inequality, with probability at least $5/6$, the query complexity is bounded by $O(\epsilon^{-2}d^4)$.

By the union bound, we get the desired result. $\qquad\square$

Combining the idea described in the end of Section 5.8.1 with Algorithm 5.12, we obtain a $(1,\epsilon n)$-approximation algorithm to the maximum size of a matching with query complexity $d^{O(\epsilon^{-2})}$.

Theorem 5.17. *There exists a $(1,\epsilon n)$-approximation algorithm to the maximum size of a matching with query complexity $d^{O(1/\epsilon^2)}(1/\epsilon)^{O(1/\epsilon)}$.*

5.9 Additional Topics

Expansion Properties

expander

We say that a graph $G = (V, E)$ on n vertices is a (γ, α)-*expander* if for every subset $S \subseteq V$ such that $|S| \geq \gamma n$, we have $|\Gamma_G(S)| \geq \alpha |S|$. When γ is not explicitly specified, we assume it to be $1/2$. Expanders have numerous applications in theoretical computer science (see [257] for a survey), and we actually use it in Section 7.3. Thus it is natural to consider testing expansion properties of graphs.

For any reasonable choice of γ and α, we have a trivial lower bound of $\Omega(\sqrt{n})$. To see this, recall that, in Section 5.5.2, we have seen that we cannot distinguish a random 3-regular graph, which is a good expander with high probability, from a graph that consists of several such disjoint subgraphs, which is far from being an expander, with $o(\sqrt{n})$ queries. Goldreich and Ron [217] conjectured that there is an almost matching upper bound in terms of the dependence on n. They proposed a random-walks based algorithm, which performs $\sqrt{n} \cdot \text{poly}(\epsilon^{-1})$ random walks of length $\text{poly}(\epsilon^{-1} \log n)$ and counts the number of collisions, that is, the number of times that the same vertex appears as an endpoint of the walks. Then, the algorithm accepts only if this number is below a certain threshold. The underlying idea of this algorithm is that, if a graph is a good expander, then the distribution induced by the endpoints of random walks is close to uniform. Later, it is shown that this algorithm can actually distinguish with high probability between an α-expander and a graph that is ϵ-far from being an α'-expander for $\alpha' = c\alpha^2/d^2$ for some constant c [144, 273, 325]. It is still open whether we can improve α' to be linear in α.

conductance

conductance
clusterability

Czumaj, Peng, and Sohler [141] considered testing clusterability, which can be seen as a generalization of the expansion property. The *conductance* of a set $\emptyset \subsetneq S \subsetneq V$ in a graph $G = (V, E)$ is $\phi_G(S) := |E_G(S, V \setminus S)| / \sum_{v \in S} \deg_G(v)$ and the *conductance* of the graph G is $\phi(G) := \min_{\emptyset \subsetneq S \subsetneq V} \phi_G(S)$. Then, we say that a graph is (k, α, ϵ)-*clusterable* if it can be partitioned into $S_1, \ldots, S_{k'}$ with $k' \in [k]$ so that so that $\phi(G[S_i]) \geq \alpha$ for each $i \in [k']$ and $\phi_G(G[S_i]) \leq c_{d,k} \epsilon^4 \alpha^2$ for each $i \in [k']$, where $c_{d,k}$ depends only on d and k. They showed a tester with query complexity $\widetilde{O}(\sqrt{n} \cdot \text{poly}(\alpha, k, \epsilon^{-1}))$ that distinguishes (k, α, ϵ)-clusterable graphs from graphs that are ϵ-far from (k, α^*, ϵ)-clusterability for $\alpha^* = c'_{d,k} \alpha^2 \epsilon^4 / \log n$, where $c'_{d,k}$ depends only on d and k. Later Chiplunkar, Kapralov, Khanna, Mousavifar, and Peres [131] shaved off the $\log n$ factor in α^*.

Digraphs

There are two major variations of the bounded-degree model for digraphs. In both variations, the model has an integer parameter $d \in \mathbb{Z}_{>0}$, and we assume that both the in-degree and the out-degree of a vertex is bounded by d. Then, in the first model, called the *bidirectional model*, one allows queries on both incoming and outgoing edges, and in the second model, called the *unidirectional model*, one allows queries only on outgoing edges.

bidirectional model

unidirectional model
strong connectivity

A digraph is called *strongly connected* if, for any two vertices u and v, there are directed paths from u to v and from v to u. The query complexity for testing strong connectivity drastically changes by choice of the model: In the bidirectional model, the strong connectivity can be tested with $\widetilde{O}(\epsilon^{-1})$ queries [71]. In the unidirectional model, however, testing strong connectivity requires $\Omega(\sqrt{n})$ queries and the best known upper bound is $O(n^{1-\epsilon/(3+\alpha)})$ for any $\alpha > 0$ [255].

In both models, testing acyclicity requires $\Omega(n^{1/3})$ queries [71] and the best known upper bound is merely $O(n)$. A lower bound of $\Omega(n^{5/9})$ for one-sided error testers is also known [124]. Using an approach similar to that in 5.3, k-edge-connectivity and k-vertex-connectivity were shown to be constant-query testable [341, 404] in the bidirectional model.

General Graph Model

A motivation of studying bounded-degree model is to make testing sensitive and sparse properties meaningful. The reason that we have bounded the maximum degree of a graph is that a graph $G = (V, E)$ of the maximum degree at most d can be conveniently expressed as a function $f : V \times [d] \to V$. However, it cannot express sparse graphs whose maximum degree is unbounded. A typical example of such graphs is *planar graphs*, which can be embedded into a plane in a way that edges intersect only at their endpoints: Although the number of edges in a planar graph on n vertices is bounded by $3n - 6$ (see, e.g., [148]), it can have a vertex of degree $n - 1$.

planar graph

To deal with such graphs, the *general graph model* has been introduced by Parnas and Ron [344]. In the general graph model, given a number of vertices $n \in \mathbb{Z}_{>0}$, we can use the following three kinds of queries to get information of the input graph $G = (V, E)$:

general graph model

- Degree query: On a vertex $v \in V$, we get the degree $\deg_G(v)$.
- Neighbor query: On a vertex $v \in V$ and an integer $i \in [\deg_G(v)]$, we get the i-th neighbor of v.
- Adjacency query: On two vertices $u, v \in V$, we get 1 if u and v are adjacent in G and 0 otherwise.

Typically, neighbor queries are useful when the graph is sparse (as in the bounded-degree model), and adjacency queries are useful when the graph is dense (as in the adjacency matrix model). The query complexity of a tester is the total number of degree, neighbor, and adjacency queries.

The distance $d(G, G')$ between two graphs $G = (V, E)$ and $G' = (V, E')$ on the same vertex set V is defined as:

$$d(G, G') = \frac{|E \triangle E'|}{\max\{|E|, |E'|\}},$$

where $E \triangle E' = (E \setminus E') \cup (E' \setminus E)$ denotes the symmetric difference between E and E'. For $\epsilon \in (0, 1)$, we say that a graph G on n vertices is ϵ-far from a property $\mathcal{P}$ if $d(G, G') > \epsilon \max\{|E|, |E'|\}$ for every graph G' on n vertices satisfying $\mathcal{P}$. In order to avoid technical trivialities, we often assume that $|E| = \Omega(n)$.

When $|E| = \Omega(n^2)$, the general graph model is more or less the same as the adjacency matrix model augmented with degree and neighbor queries (although the definition of ϵ-farness differs by a constant factor). However, the general graph model with $|E| = O(dn)$ does not match the bounded-degree model with a degree bound d because it allows vertices of degree more than d.

There are only a few studies on the general graph model compared to the adjacency matrix model and the bounded-degree model. We can modify the testers for connectivity properties given in Section 5.3 so that they work in the general graph model. By reduction it is known that bipartiteness can be tested with $\widetilde{O}(\sqrt{n}) \cdot \operatorname{poly}(\epsilon^{-1})$ queries in the general graph model [276]. We have seen in Section 4.5.2 that triangle-freeness is constant-query testable in the adjacency matrix model. This also implies it is constant-query testable in the general graph model when the average degree is $\Omega(n)$. However, when the average degree drops down to $n^{1-o(1)}$, we need $\Omega(n^{1/3})$ queries [14]. A general upper bound of $O(n^{6/7})$ is known [14], but the gap is still significant.

Assuming that we can sample edges in the input graph uniformly at random, for constant k, we can also test whether there is a vertex cover of size k, whether there is a feedback vertex set of size k, and whether there is a path of length k, with a constant number of queries [263]. A natural generalization to CSPs has also been studied [121].

Sublinear-query algorithms for estimating parameters of a graph in the general graph model have also been studied. All the algorithm described below estimates a parameter to within a factor of $1 \pm \epsilon$ for a given error parameter $\epsilon \in (0, 1)$. We do not explicitly mention the dependence of the query complexity on ϵ as the primary interest is the dependence on the number of vertices n. Goldreich and Ron [214] showed that the average degree can be estimated with $\widetilde{O}(\sqrt{n})$ queries. Gonen, Ron, and Shavitt [223] and Eden, Levi, Ron, and Seshadhri [165, 166] gave sublinear-time algorithms for estimating the number of stars and cliques, respectively, in a graph for any constant k.

Assadi, Kapralov, and Khanna [34], assuming we can sample edges uniformly
at random, gave an algorithm for estimating the number of copies of a graph
H in the input graph in $O(m^{\rho(H)}/\#H)$ time, where $\rho(H)$ is the *fractional*   fractional edge cover
edge cover number of H, the optimal value of a natural LP relaxation of the   number
edge cover problem, and $\#H$ is the number of copies of H in the input graph.
This bound is known to be tight for cycles.

In network science, we analyze networks through various parameters such
as average degree and the number of cliques. It is desirable if we can quickly
approximate those parameters as real networks such as the Web graph and
social networks could be very large. The results mentioned in the last paragraph have direct applications here. A related work by Gonen, Ron, Weinsberg, and Wool [224] considered sublinear-time algorithms for finding dense
cores in router networks. Eden, Jain, Pinar, Ron, Seshadhri [164] considered
approximating the entire (cumulative) degree distribution and gave an algorithm that runs in sublinear time when a fatness measure called the h-index
of the distribution is large. Cohen-Steiner, Kong, Sohler, and Valiant [134]
considered approximating the entire (cumulative) distribution of the eigen-
values of the normalized Laplacian. Here, the normalized Laplacian $\mathcal{L}_G$ of a
graph G is defined as $\mathcal{L}_G = I - D_G^{-1/2} A_G D_G^{-1/2}$, where A_G is the adjacency
matrix and D_G is the diagonal degree matrix.

Relations to Other Computational Models

Property testing in the bounded-degree model has proved related to some
other computational models such as distributed computing and streaming.

In distributed computing for graph problems, we have a processor for each
vertex, and they communicate with each other through edges. In the **LO-
CAL** model, every vertex can send messages to all of its neighbors in each
round of communication, and there is no restriction on the lengths of the mes-
sages. Parnas and Ron [345] observed that a *distributed algorithm* for a graph   distributed algorithm
optimization problem can be used to solve the same problem in the bounded-
degree model. The reduction is merely selecting a small number of vertices at
random and emulating the distributed algorithm only for them. If the number
of rounds of the distributed algorithm is k and the number of selected vertices
is s, the resulting query complexity is $O(sd^k)$. As an application of this reduction, Marko and Ron [311] showed a $(2, \epsilon n)$-approximation algorithm for
the minimum vertex cover problem with $d^{O(\log(\epsilon^{-1}d))}$ queries. Although this
reduction typically does not give tight bounds (e.g., an $\widetilde{O}(d \cdot \mathrm{poly}(\epsilon^{-1}))$-query
algorithm is known for $(2, \epsilon n)$-approximation to the minimum vertex cover
problem.), its virtue is its simplicity.

In the streaming model for graph problems, edges of a graph arrive one
by one, and an algorithm should output a solution when all the edges have
arrived. If algorithms can store all the edges, there is no difference from the

standard setting. Hence, we are interested in the trade-off between the space complexity and the solution quality. Monemizadeh, Muthukrishnan, Peng, and Sohler [318] showed that, if the input graph is of bounded degree and edges arrive in a random order, then we can transform any constant-time algorithm in the bounded-degree model to a constant-space streaming algorithm. Peng and Sohler [348] extended this result to general graphs for a number of problems including estimating the number of connected components and the minimum weight of a spanning tree.

5.10 Bibliographic Notes

The study of the bounded-degree model is initiated by Goldreich and Ron [213]. The algorithms and analysis for H-freeness, connectivity, and cycle-freeness introduced in Sections 5.2, 5.3, and 5.4 are based on [213].

We refer the reader to [315] for Menger's theorem used in Section 5.3.3. The idea of using the Watanabe-Nakamura theorem [392] to test k-edge-connectivity is due to [341], and the idea of applying Karger's analysis [274] to improve the query complexity is due to [213]. Forster, Nanongkai, Saranurak, Yang, and Yingchareonthaworncha [188] considered another local algorithm for detecting violating sets, and gave a one-sided error tester with query complexity $\widetilde{O}(\epsilon^{-1}k)$. A constant-query tester for k-vertex connectivity was given in [402], and is simplified by using Jordan-Jackson theorem [264] by [340]. The local algorithm given in [188] can be generalized to vertex connectivity and they obtained a one-sided error tester for k-vertex connectivity with $\widetilde{O}(\epsilon^{-1}k\epsilon)$ queries. Those results were extended to digraphs [341, 404].

The one-sided error lower bound of $\Omega(\sqrt{n})$ for cycle-freeness mentioned at the end of Section 5.4 is due to Goldreich and Ron [213]. It is known that there is a one-sided error tester for cycle-freeness with query complexity $\widetilde{O}(\sqrt{n})$ [139].

All the constant-query testers studied here is adaptive. Indeed, adaptivity is essential in the bounded-degree model because non-adaptive constant-query testers can only test properties that only depend on the degree distribution [352].

The tester and the lower bound for bipartiteness explained in Section 5.5 is due to Goldreich and Ron [212, 213]. The tester was further extended for the general graph model [276]. The ideas in the analysis of the bipartiteness tester has been used in the context of testing expansions of a graph [144, 217, 273, 325], testing cluster structures [141], and testing minor-freeness with one-sided error [139, 288].

The linear lower bound for 3-colorability explained in Section 5.6 was shown by Bogdanov and Trevisan [97]. In particular, Lemma 5.12 is shown in [97]. Using gap-preserving local reductions from 3-SAT, several other NP-complete problems such as 3-edge-colorability, having a Hamilton path, and

3-dimensional matching have been shown to have linear lower bounds in the bounded-degree model [403].

The approximation algorithm to the minimum weight of a spanning tree explained in Section 5.7 is due to Chazelle, Rubinfeld, and Trevisan [119], though we used a weaker analysis than theirs for simplicity. We can get an approximation algorithm with $O(\epsilon^{-2}dW \log dW)$ queries using a more sophisticated analysis and it is known that we need $\Omega(\epsilon^{-2}dW\epsilon^2)$ queries to estimate $\mathrm{mst}(G)$ to within ϵn [119]. A directed graph is called a *branching* if it is acyclic and each vertex has at most one incoming edge. A $(1, \epsilon n)$-approximation algorithm to the minimum weight of a branching with $O(\epsilon^{-3}d)$ queries was shown in [294].

branching

The $(1/2, \epsilon n)$-approximation algorithm to the maximum size of a matching explained in Section 5.8.1 is due to Nguyen and Onak [334], and the improved one in Section 5.8.2 is due to Yoshida, Yamamoto, and Ito [407]. The current best query complexity in terms of d is $\widetilde{O}(d \cdot \mathrm{poly}(\epsilon^{-1}))$ [337]. Nguyen and Onak [334] obtained a $(1, \epsilon n)$-approximation algorithm for the maximum size of a matching with query complexity $2^{d^{O(\epsilon^{-1})}}$ based on their $(1/2, \epsilon n)$-approximation algorithm. The query complexity was improved to $d^{O(\epsilon^{-2})}$ by [407]. The observation that the size of any maximal matching is at least half the maximum size of a matching can be found in [29, 162].

A vertex cover of a graph $G = (V, E)$ is a vertex set $S \subseteq V$ such that every edge is incident to a vertex in S. Computing the minimum size of a vertex cover is NP-Hard, but it is known that the vertex set consisting of endpoints of an arbitrary maximal matching is a 2-approximation. Hence, we can obtain a $(2, \epsilon n)$-approximation algorithm to the minimum size of a vertex cover by using a $(1/2, \epsilon n)$-approximation algorithm to the maximum size of a matching, because the latter gives an $(1, \epsilon n)$-approximation to the size of some maximal matching. Approximating the minimum size of a vertex cover (with an approximation factor of 2) has been intensively studied [345, 312, 407, 337], and the current best query complexity in terms of d is $\widetilde{O}(d \cdot \mathrm{poly}(\epsilon^{-1}))$ [337], which almost matches the lower bound of $\Omega(d)$ [345].

Problems

5.1. Show that the property of being a regular graph is testable with $O(\epsilon^{-1})$ queries.

5.2. An undirected graph is called an *Eulerian* if there exists a path that passes through all the edges in the graph. Show that Eulerianity is constant-query testable.

Eulerianity

5.3. Show that triangle-freeness is non-adaptively testable with $O(\sqrt{n})$ queries in the bounded-degree model.

5.4. Show that any non-adaptive tester for triangle-freeness requires $\Omega(\sqrt{n})$ queries in the bounded-degree model.

For positive integers d, n with dn being even, a d-regular random graph $G = (V, E)$ with n vertices is a graph sampled uniformly at random from the family of all d-regular graphs on n vertices.

5.5. Let G be a 3-regular random graph with n vertices for even n. For a vertex $v \in V$, let $p(v)$ be the probability that a random walk starting at a fixed arbitrary vertex reaches v after $\ell = \mathrm{poly}\log(n)$ steps. Show that G satisfies:

$$\frac{1}{2n} < p(v) < \frac{2}{n},$$

for any $v \in V$ with high probability.

5.6. Show that cycle-freeness is testable with one-sided error with $\sqrt{n} \cdot \mathrm{poly}(\epsilon^{-1} \log n)$ queries using Theorem 5.9.

5.7. Show that any algorithm that approximates the number of connected components to within $O(\epsilon dn)$ requires $\Omega(\epsilon^{-2})$ queries. (**Hint**: Use the result in Problem 2.4.)

5.8. Show that testing 4-colorability requires $\Omega(n)$ queries in the general graph model.

source/sink

5.9. A *source* (resp., *sink*) component in a digraph is a strongly connected component that has no in-coming (resp., out-going) arcs. Show that a directed graph ϵ-far from being strongly connected has $\Omega(\epsilon dn)$ source or sink components. Based on this result, show that strong connectivity is testable with $O(\epsilon^{-2}/d)$ queries in the bidirectional model.

5.10. In this problem, you are asked to design an algorithm that estimates the average degree $\bar{d}$ of a graph $G = (V = [n], E)$ in the general graph model.

(a) Let $\prec$ be the ordering on V such that $u < v$ if and only if either $\deg(u) < \deg(v)$ or $\deg(u) = \deg(v)$ and $u < v$. (We can compare vertices because they are integers) Define $\deg^+(u)$ as the number of neighbors v of u such that $u \prec v$. Let H be the set of largest $\sqrt{m}$ vertices according to $\prec$. Show the following:

   (i) $\sum_{v \in V} \deg^+(v) = m$, where $m = |E|$.
   (ii) $\deg^+(v) \le \sqrt{m}$ for every $v \in H$.
   (iii) $\deg(v) \le \sqrt{m}$ for every $v \in L$.

(b) Design a random variable X that can be computed with $O(1)$ queries to G such that $\mathbf{E}[X] = \bar{d}$ and $\mathbf{Var}[X] = O(\sqrt{m} \cdot \bar{d})$. (**Hint**: Sample a random vertex $u \in V$ and a random neighbor $v \in V$, and then use the degree of u only when $u \prec v$.)

(c) Show that we can estimate $\bar{d}$ to within a factor of $1 \pm \epsilon$ with probability at least $2/3$ making $O(\sqrt{n}/\epsilon^2)$ queries to G.

Chapter 6
Functions over Hypercubes

In this chapter, we look at the task of testing properties of functions. Throughout, we will discuss functions over hypercubes, that is, $f\colon \{0,1\}^n \to R$, where $n \in \mathbb{Z}_{>0}$ and $R \subseteq \mathbb{R}$ is a set. Our primary focus is *Boolean functions*, that is, the case that $R = \{0,1\}$.

Boolean function

For functions over hypercubes, it makes sense to use the *Hamming distance* as a distance metric. For two functions $f, g\colon \{0,1\}^n \to R$, we define:

Hamming distance

$$d_{\mathrm{H}}(f,g) = |\{x \in \{0,1\}^n : f(x) \neq g(x)\}|.$$

Let $\mathcal{P}$ denote a function property, that is, a family $\{\mathcal{P}_n : n \in \mathbb{Z}_{>0}\}$, where each $\mathcal{P}_n$ is a subset of functions mapping $\{0,1\}^n$ to R. As usual, we say that a function $f\colon \{0,1\}^n \to R$ is ϵ-*far* from $\mathcal{P}$ if for every $g \in \mathcal{P}_n$, $d_{\mathrm{H}}(f,g) > \epsilon 2^n$. An algorithm is said to be a *tester* for $\mathcal{P}$ if given a positive integer n, an error parameter $\epsilon \in (0,1)$ and query access to a function $f\colon \{0,1\}^n \to R$, it accepts with probability at least $2/3$ if f satisfies $\mathcal{P}$ and rejects with probability at least $2/3$ if f is ϵ-far from $\mathcal{P}$.

The study of property testing originated with testing properties of functions in works by Blum, Luby and Rubinfeld [94] and by Rubinfeld and Sudan [368]. Over the years, many connections have emerged between testing function properties and other topics in theoretical computer science, such as coding theory, hardness of approximation, and program checking. Also, a variety of mathematical tools are intimately connected to questions in the area, making it a very rich field of study.

In this chapter, we will give an overview of some of the fundamental problems in testing function properties. Just as a course on standard algorithms often starts with a discussion of sorting, we begin in Section 6.1 with algorithms for testing monotonicity (of Boolean functions). Next, in Section 6.2 we develop some basic results in Fourier analysis for Boolean functions which are useful for many problems in the area. In Section 6.3, we analyze the so-called Blum-Luby-Rubinfeld (BLR) tester for linearity, both using Fourier analysis as well as a "self-correcting" approach. In Section 6.4, we study another classic problem in the area: junta testing. Then, in Section 6.5, we move on to showing lower bounds for the query complexity of these testing problems. In this context, we also look at a simple and powerful connection to *communication complexity*.

6.1 Testing Monotonicity of Boolean Functions

In this section, we discuss testing monotonicity of Boolean functions. Although we will discuss testing monotonicity over general directed acyclic subgraphs (DAGs), we defer it to Section 7.2, as the model is very different from the one we study in this chapter.

monotonicity

For $x, y \in \{0,1\}^n$, we write $x \preceq y$ if $x_i \leq y_i$ for any $i \in [n]$. We say that a Boolean function $f\colon \{0,1\}^n \to \{0,1\}$ is *monotone* if $f(x) \leq f(y)$ for any $x \preceq y$. In this section, we prove the following.

Theorem 6.1. *Monotonicity of Boolean functions* $f\colon \{0,1\}^n \to \{0,1\}$ *can be tested using* $O(\epsilon^{-1}n)$ *queries, non-adaptively with one-sided error.*

edge

First, we modify the tester discussed in Section 1.6.2 for Boolean functions. We view the set $\{0,1\}^n$ as vertices of the n-dimensional hypercube graph. We say that a pair $(x, y) \in \{0,1\}^n \times \{0,1\}^n$ an *edge* if $x \prec y$ and the Hamming distance between x and y is exactly one. For a function $f\colon \{0,1\}^n \to \{0,1\}$,

violating edge

we say that an edge (x, y) is *f-violating* if $f(x) > f(y)$. Then, the edge tester uniformly chooses an edge (x, y) and accept if and only if it is not violating. Note that the edge tester is a non-adaptive one-sided error tester. Now, let us define the following two quantities:

$$\epsilon_{\mathrm{mon}}(f) := \min_{g:\, \mathrm{monotone}} \frac{d_{\mathrm{H}}(f, g)}{2^n}$$

$$\rho_{\mathrm{mon}}(f) := \Pr_{e:\, \mathrm{edge}}\left[e \text{ violated by } f\right].$$

To prove Theorem 6.1, it suffices to show the following.

Lemma 6.1. *For any* $f\colon \{0,1\}^n \to \{0,1\}$,

$$\rho_{\mathrm{mon}}(f) \geq \frac{2\epsilon_{\mathrm{mon}}(f)}{n}.$$

Then, repeating the edge tester $\Theta(\epsilon^{-1}n)$ times, we can reject functions ϵ-far from being monotone.

Proof. Let $f\colon \{0,1\}^n \to \{0,1\}$ be a function with at most $\epsilon 2^n$ violating edges. We show how to obtain a monotone function by modifying the value of f at only $\epsilon 2^n$ many vertices of the hypercube. Then, by the contrapositive, we will have that $\rho_{\mathrm{mon}}(f) \geq \frac{\epsilon_{\mathrm{mon}}(f)2^n}{n2^{n-1}} = 2\epsilon_{\mathrm{mon}}(f)/n$.

The modification of f proceeds in n stages, where at each stage i, we repair the violating edges that lie in the direction i. That is, we define a sequence of Boolean functions $g_0 = f, g_1, \ldots, g_n$ such that all violating edges of each g_i lie in directions greater than i. So, the last function g_n, must be monotone.

Let us define g_i, given g_{i-1}, for some $i \in \{1, \ldots, n\}$. We assume inductively that g_{i-1} does not have any violating edges in directions $< i$. Let $H_i^0 = \{x : x_i = 0\}$ and let $H_i^1 = \{x : x_i = 1\}$. The edges $\{(x, x^{\oplus i}) : x \in H_i^0\}$ form a perfect matching between H_i^0 and H_i^1, where $x^{\oplus i}$ is the string $(x_1, \ldots, x_{i-1}, \overline{x_i}, x_{i+1}, \ldots, x_n)$. Let M_i be the subset of the edges of this matching which are g_{i-1}-violating. That is, if $(x, y) \in M_i$, then $x_i = 0$ and $y_i = 1$ but $g_{i-1}(x) = 1$ and $g_{i-1}(y) = 0$. Additionally, we define the following sets of edges which are g_{i-1}-violating:

$$L_i = \{(x, y) : (x, y) \text{ violating w.r.t. } g_{i-1}, x, y \in H_i^0\},$$
$$L_i^1 = \{(x, y) \in L_i : (x, x^{\oplus i}) \in M_i\},$$
$$L_i^2 = L_i \setminus L_i^1,$$
$$R_i = \{(x, y) : (x, y) \text{ violating w.r.t. } g_{i-1}, x, y \in H_i^1\},$$
$$R_i^1 = \{(x, y) \in R_i : (y^{\oplus i}, y) \in M_i\},$$
$$R_i^2 = R_i \setminus R_i^1.$$

Now, g_i is defined as follows. If $|L_i^1| \leq |R_i^1|$, then:

$$g_i(x) = \begin{cases} 1 & \text{if } (x^{\oplus i}, x) \in M_i, \\ g_{i-1}(x) & \text{otherwise.} \end{cases} \qquad (6.1)$$

Otherwise, if $|L_i^1| > |R_i^1|$, then:

$$g_i(x) = \begin{cases} 0 & \text{if } (x, x^{\oplus i}) \in M_i, \\ g_{i-1}(x) & \text{otherwise.} \end{cases}$$

So, g_i repairs g_{i-1} in the i-th direction by changing g_{i-1} so that either all the edges in M_i have both endpoints labeled 1 or all the edges in M_i have both endpoints labeled 0. Furthermore, we will show that g_i does not introduce any new violating edges in directions less than i. Formally, we show the following:

Claim 6.1. *For any $g \colon \{0,1\}^n \to \{0,1\}$ and any $i \in [n]$, let $\Delta_i(g)$ be the number of g-violating edges lying in the i-th direction. Then:*

- *For all $k \in [i]$, $\Delta_k(g_i) = 0$.*
- $\sum_{k=i+1}^n \Delta_k(g_i) \leq \sum_{k=i+1}^n \Delta_k(g_{i-1})$
- $\sum_x |g_i(x) - g_{i-1}(x)| = \Delta_i(g_{i-1})$

Proof. Suppose $|L_i^1| \leq |R_i^1|$ so that g_i is defined by equation (6.1); a symmetric argument works for the other case.

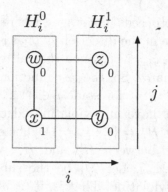

Fig. 6.1: Values of g_{i-1}

Clearly, property (iii) is true, since $|M_i| = \Delta_i(g_{i-1})$ and g_i differs from g_{i-1} in only $|M_i|$ many vertices.

To see properties (i) and (ii), observe the following. Any edge between two vertices in H_i^0 is g_i-violating if and only if it is g_{i-1}-violating; so the edges in L_i remain violated. Also, all the edges in R_i^2 are still g_i-violating because their endpoints are not incident to edges in M_i. However, the edges in R_i^1 are now not g_i-violating. This is so, because for any $(x, y) \in R_i^1$, it must have been that $g_{i-1}(x) = 1$ and $g_{i-1}(y) = 0$ but since $g_i(y) = 1$ and $g_i(x)$ remains 1, the edge is now non-violating. Finally, there are some g_i-violating edges that were not g_{i-1}-violating. Let N_i be this set of newly violating edges. We will show that any edge in N_i must lie in a direction greater than i and that $|N_i| \leq |L_i^1|$. This proves properties (i) and (ii): Property (i) holds because clearly $\Delta_i(g_i) = 0$ and none of N_i lie in directions $k \leq i$. Property (ii) holds because:

$$\sum_{k=i+1}^{n} \Delta_k(g_i) = |L_i| + |R_i^2| + |N_i| \leq |L_i| + |R_i^2| + |L_i^1|$$

$$\leq |L_i| + |R_i^2| + |R_i^1| = |L_i| + |R_i| = \sum_{k=i+1}^{n} \Delta_k(g_{i-1}),$$

where the inequality in the last line is from the assumption that $|L_i^1| \leq |R_i^1|$.

To see that any edge in N_i must lie in a direction greater than i and that $|N_i| \leq |L_i^1|$, refer to Figure 6.1. Consider two edges $(x, y) \in M_i$ and $(y, z) \in N_i$. Let (y, z) lie in direction j. It must have been the case that $g_{i-1}(x) = 1$ and $g_{i-1}(y) = g_{i-1}(z) = 0$. For (y, z) to become violated, it must also be the case that z is not incident to an edge in M_i so that $g_i(z)$ is still 0. But this implies that $g_{i-1}(w) = 0$, where $w = x^{\oplus j}$. Therefore, $(x, w) \in L_i^1$. Since g_{i-1} does not violate any edges in directions less than i and (x, w) lies in direction j, we see that $j > i$. Also, we have shown an injective mapping from edges in N_i to edges in L_i^1, namely the one that takes (y, z) to (x, w); so, $|N_i| \leq |L_i^1|$, completing our proof.   □

Now we get back to proving Lemma 6.1. By property (i), g_n is monotone, as desired. The number of modifications needed to transform f to g_n is $\sum_x |g_n(x) - g_0(x)| \leq \sum_{i=1}^n \sum_x |g_i(x) - g_{i-1}(x)| \leq \sum_{i=1}^n \Delta_i(g_{i-1})$ by property (iii). But by repeated application of property (ii), it follows that $\sum_{i=1}^n \Delta_i(g_{i-1}) \leq \sum_{i=1}^n \Delta_i(g_0) \leq \epsilon 2^n$. So, f can be converted to a monotone function by changing its value at $\epsilon 2^n$ vertices at most. $\square$

6.2 Fourier Analysis on Boolean Hypercubes

The goal of this section is to introduce some concepts from Fourier analysis that are extremely useful in many areas of theoretical computer science, including of course property testing. Although we restrict ourselves to functions on Boolean hypercubes, the definitions and results here can be extended without much change to functions on any finite abelian group, and using representation theory, to any finite group. The power of Fourier analysis will be clear in the next section when we use it to give a quick analysis of the BLR linearity test. For further details and applications of Fourier analysis, we refer to a book by O'Donnell [335].

Let $f: \{0,1\}^n \to \mathbb{R}$. When f is Boolean, its range is the 2-element set $\{0,1\}$. We identify $\{0,1\}^n$ with $\mathbb{F}_2^n$, where $\mathbb{F}_2$ is the finite field on 2 elements. So, for $x, y \in \{0,1\}^n$, $x + y = ((x_i + y_i) \pmod 2 : i \in [n])$.

We can view the set of functions $\{\{0,1\}^n \to \mathbb{R}\}$ as a 2^n-dimensional vector space over the reals. We endow this space with the following inner product:

$$\langle f, g \rangle = \mathop{\mathbf{E}}_{x \in \{0,1\}^n} [f(x) \cdot g(x)].$$

We also have $\|f\| = \sqrt{\langle f, f \rangle}$.

The Fourier transform of a function $f: \{0,1\}^n \to \mathbb{R}$ is simply a basis transformation of this space. Specifically, consider the set of functions $\chi_\alpha: \mathbb{F}_2^n \to \mathbb{R}$ where $\alpha \in \{0,1\}^n$ and:

$$\chi_\alpha(x) = (-1)^{\sum_{i=1}^n \alpha_i x_i}. \tag{6.2}$$

These functions are called the *Fourier characters*.

Fourier character

Lemma 6.2. *The Fourier characters* $\{\chi_\alpha : \alpha \in \{0,1\}^n\}$ *form an orthonormal basis for* $\{\{0,1\}^n \to \mathbb{R}\}$.

Proof. The proof of orthogonality depends upon the following fact:

Exercise 6.1. If $\ell \in \{0,1\}^n$ is not the zero vector, then:

$$\left| \Pr_{x \sim \{0,1\}^n} \left[\sum_{i \in [n]} \ell_i \cdot x_i = 0 \right] = \frac{1}{2}. \right.$$

For $\alpha \neq \beta$, this fact implies:

$$\langle \chi_\alpha, \chi_\beta \rangle = \mathbf{E}_x \left[(-1)^{\sum_{i \in [n]} (\alpha_i + \beta_i) x_i} \right] = 0.$$

Additionally, $\|\chi_\alpha\| = \sqrt{\langle \chi_\alpha, \chi_\alpha \rangle} = 1$, so the Fourier characters are an orthonormal set of vectors. That they span the whole space is immediate from the fact that the dimension of the space of functions $\{\{0,1\}^n \to \mathbb{R}\}$ is at most 2^n and there are 2^n many Fourier characters. $\qquad \square$

Fourier coefficient

For $f \colon \{0,1\}^n \to \mathbb{R}$ and $\alpha \in \{0,1\}^n$, we can now define the *Fourier coefficient of f at α*:

$$\hat{f}(\alpha) = \langle f, \chi_\alpha \rangle = \mathbf{E}_x \left[f(x) \cdot (-1)^{\sum_{i=1}^n \alpha_i x_i} \right].$$

The Fourier coefficients now define the basis expansion of f in terms of the Fourier characters:

$$f(x) = \sum_{\alpha \in \{0,1\}^n} \hat{f}(\alpha) \cdot \chi_\alpha(x).$$

Exercise 6.2. Compute the Fourier coefficients of the majority function on 3 Boolean variables.

Note that for any $\alpha \in \{0,1\}^n$, $|\hat{f}(\alpha)| \leq \mathbf{E}_x[|f(x)|]$, so that in particular for Boolean functions, $|\hat{f}(\alpha)| \leq 1$. Also, if f is Boolean:

$$\hat{f}(0) = \mathbf{E}_x[f(x)] = \frac{|f^{-1}(1)|}{2^n},$$

where 0 is the zero vector.

Orthonormality of the Fourier characters implies the following results.

Plancherel's theorem

Theorem 6.2 (Plancherel's Theorem). *For any $f, g \colon \{0,1\}^n \to \mathbb{R}$:*

$$\langle f, g \rangle = \mathbf{E}_{x \sim \{0,1\}^n} [f(x)g(x)] = \sum_{\alpha \in \{0,1\}^n} \hat{f}(\alpha) \cdot \hat{g}(\alpha).$$

Parseval's theorem

Corollary 6.1 (Parseval's Theorem). *For any $f \colon \{0,1\}^n \to \mathbb{R}$:*

$$\langle f, f \rangle = \mathbf{E}_{x \sim \{0,1\}^n} \left[f(x)^2 \right] = \sum_{\alpha \in \{0,1\}^n} \hat{f}(\alpha)^2.$$

> **Exercise 6.3.** Prove Theorem 6.2 and Corollary 6.1.

> **Exercise 6.4.** For $\epsilon > 0$ and $f: \{0,1\}^n \to [-1,1]$, let $\text{Spec}_\epsilon(f) = \{\alpha \in \{0,1\}^n : |\hat{f}(\alpha)| > \epsilon\}$. Show that $|\text{Spec}_\epsilon(f)| < \epsilon^{-2}$.

6.3 Linearity

A Boolean function $f: \{0,1\}^n \to \{0,1\}$ is *linear* if f can be written as: linearity

$$f(x) = \sum_{i=1}^n a_i x_i \pmod 2,$$

where $a_1, \ldots, a_n \in \{0,1\}$ are the coefficients[1]. We identify the set $\{0,1\}$ with the field $\mathbb{F}_2$, and henceforth, we will omit saying $\mod 2$ as all arithmetic over Boolean functions in this section is over $\mathbb{F}_2$.

A function is ϵ-*far from linearity* if for every linear $g: \{0,1\}^n \to \{0,1\}$, its ϵ-farness
Hamming distance from f, that is, $|\{x : f(x) \neq g(x)\}|$, is more than $\epsilon \cdot 2^n$.

The question of testing linearity was originally motivated by *program checking*. The problem is to verify whether a program whose output is claimed to be linear in its inputs is indeed so. A tester for linearity can be immediately used to solve this problem; moreover, the tester would only query the program as a black box and never examine its internals. Motivated by this application, Blum, Luby, and Rubinfeld (BLR) [94] proposed the following tester:

Algorithm 6.1 BLR Linearity Tester

Input: An integer n, $\epsilon \in (0,1)$, and query access to a function $f: \{0,1\}^n \to \{0,1\}$.
  1: **for** $q := \Theta(\epsilon^{-1})$ times **do**
  2:     Sample x, y from $\{0,1\}^n$ independently and uniformly at random.
  3:     Reject if $f(x) + f(y) \neq f(x + y)$.
  4: **end for**
  5: Accept.

Theorem 6.3. *The BLR Linearity tester is a non-adaptive, one-sided error tester for linearity using $O(\epsilon^{-1})$ queries.*

The only non-trivial part of Theorem 6.3 is that it rejects functions ϵ-far from being linear with probability 2/3. This is implied by the following lemma:

---
[1] If there was an additive constant term, we would call the function *affine*.

Lemma 6.3. *If f is ϵ-far from linearity,*

$$\Pr_{x,y}[f(x) + f(y) = f(x + y)] < 1 - \epsilon.$$

6.3.1 A Fourier-analytic Proof

Here, we present a proof of Lemma 6.3 using Fourier analysis. The main idea of the proof is to re-express the acceptance probability of the tester using Fourier coefficients. (Re-expressing the acceptance probability in a more analytic way is a technique we will come back to repeatedly!) Just this one idea makes the whole analysis a straightforward calculation.

It will be very convenient to work with $g \colon \{0, 1\}^n \to \{-1, +1\}$ defined as $g(x) = (-1)^{f(x)}$. We can now compute:

$$
\begin{aligned}
&\Pr_{x,y}[f(x) + f(y) = f(x + y)] \\
&= \Pr_{x,y}[g(x) \cdot g(y) \cdot g(x + y) = 1] \\
&= \frac{1}{2} + \frac{1}{2} \mathop{\mathbf{E}}_{x,y}[g(x) \cdot g(y) \cdot g(x + y)] \\
&= \frac{1}{2} + \frac{1}{2} \mathop{\mathbf{E}}_{x,y}\left[\sum_\alpha \hat{g}(\alpha)\chi_\alpha(x) \cdot \sum_\beta \hat{g}(\beta)\chi_\beta(x) \cdot \sum_\gamma \hat{g}(\gamma)\chi_\gamma(x + y)\right] \\
&= \frac{1}{2} + \frac{1}{2} \sum_{\alpha,\beta,\gamma} \mathop{\mathbf{E}}_{x,y}[\hat{g}(\alpha)\chi_\alpha(x) \cdot \hat{g}(\beta)\chi_\beta(y) \cdot \hat{g}(\gamma)\chi_\gamma(x)\chi_\gamma(y)] \\
&= \frac{1}{2} + \frac{1}{2} \sum_{\alpha,\beta,\gamma} \hat{g}(\alpha)\hat{g}(\beta)\hat{g}(\gamma) \cdot \langle \chi_\alpha, \chi_\gamma \rangle \cdot \langle \chi_\beta, \chi_\gamma \rangle \\
&= \frac{1}{2} + \frac{1}{2} \sum_\alpha \hat{g}(\alpha)^3,
\end{aligned}
\tag{6.3}
$$

where the fourth line uses the basis expansion of g in terms of its Fourier coefficients and the last line uses the orthogonality of the Fourier characters.

We next observe that $\hat{g}(\alpha)$ exactly measures the correlation of f with the linear function $\sum_i \alpha_i x_i$:

$$\hat{g}(\alpha) = \mathop{\mathbf{E}}_x\left[(-1)^{f(x)} \cdot (-1)^{\sum_i \alpha_i x_i}\right] = 1 - 2 \cdot \Pr_x\left[f(x) \neq \sum_i \alpha_i x_i\right].$$

Therefore, because f is ϵ-far from being linear, $\hat{g}(\alpha) < 1 - 2\epsilon$ for every $\alpha \in \{0, 1\}^n$. Hence, plugging into (6.3):

$$\Pr_{x,y}[f(x) + f(y) = f(x + y)] \leq \frac{1}{2} + \frac{1}{2} \cdot \max_{\alpha} \hat{g}(\alpha) \cdot \sum_{\alpha} \hat{g}(\alpha)^2$$

$$< \frac{1}{2} + \frac{1}{2} \cdot (1 - 2\epsilon) \cdot 1 = 1 - \epsilon,$$

where we used Parseval's Theorem (Corollary 6.1) to compute $\sum_{\alpha} \hat{g}(\alpha)^2 = \langle g, g \rangle = 1$.

6.3.2 Self-correction-based proof

In this section, we prove a slightly weaker version of Lemma 6.3 using more combinatorial techniques. Although the argument is more complicated and the result is weaker, the benefit of this approach is that it applies to the more general problem of *homomorphism testing*. Given two finite groups G and H endowed with additions $+_G$ and $+_H$, respectively, a function $f: G \to H$ is said to be a *homomorphism* if $f(x +_G y) = f(x) +_H f(y)$ for any $x, y \in G$. The BLR test can be used as-is for this problem, and the analysis in this section shows that the lower bound on the rejection probability is independent of the groups G and H. Specifically, we show:

homomorphism

> **Lemma 6.4.** *For finite abelian[a] groups G and H, if $f: G \to H$ is ϵ-far from homomorphisms, then[b]:*
>
> $$\Pr_{x,y}[f(x) + f(y) \neq f(x + y)] \geq \frac{\epsilon}{12}.$$
>
> ---
>
> [a] The abelian assumption is only for simplicity of presentation. See Problem 6.2 for the analysis for general groups.
> [b] Below and later, we do not specify which group each $+$ sign is for, as this is clear from the context.

In the rest of this section, we prove Lemma 6.4.

Let $\rho_f = \Pr_{x,y}[f(x) + f(y) \neq f(x + y)]$. We will show that if $\rho_f < 1/6$, then f can be "self-corrected" to a homomorphism $v: G \to H$ that is close to f. More precisely, $d_H(f, v) \leq 2\rho_f |G|$. Thus, $\rho_f \geq \min(\epsilon/2, 1/6) \geq \epsilon/12$.

The self-corrected function v is constructed by a very natural voting procedure. For $x, y \in G$, define:

$$v_y(x) = f(x + y) - f(y).$$

Note that if f was in fact a homomorphism, $v_y(x) = f(x)$ for every $y \in G$. So, $v_y(x)$ can be regarded as y's vote for the value of $f(x)$. We define $v(x)$ to be the plurality winner among these votes[2]:

---

[2] Ties can be broken arbitrarily.

$$v(x) = \arg\max_{v \in H} |\{y : v_y(x) = v\}|.$$

The following claim holds because the majority winner also wins the plurality vote.

Claim 6.2. *If for some* $x \in G, v \in H$, $\Pr_{y \in G}[v_y(x) = v] > 1/2$, *then* $v(x) = v$.

We can use this to bound $d_{\mathrm{H}}(f, v)$.

Lemma 6.5.

$$d_{\mathrm{H}}(f, v) \leq 2\rho_f |G|.$$

Proof. Note that:

$$\rho_f = \Pr_{x,y}[f(x+y) \neq f(x) + f(y)] = \Pr_{x,y}[f(x) \neq v_y(x)].$$

But for every $x \in G$:

$$\mathbf{1}[f(x) \neq v(x)] \leq 2 \cdot \Pr_y[f(x) \neq v_y(x)], \tag{6.4}$$

where $\mathbf{1}[\cdot]$ is the indicator function. This is so because if $\Pr_y[f(x) \neq v_y(x)] < 1/2$, then $\mathbf{1}[f(x) \neq v(x)] = 0$ by the above claim, whereas if $\Pr_y[f(x) \neq v_y(x)] \geq 1/2$, (6.4) is trivial. Taking expectation over x on both sides of (6.4):

$$\frac{d_{\mathrm{H}}(f, v)}{|G|} = \Pr_x[f(x) \neq v(x)] \leq 2 \cdot \Pr_{x,y}[f(x) \neq v_y(x)] = 2 \cdot \rho_f. \qquad \square$$

What remains is to show that v is a homomorphism. This is the more challenging part of the proof. Our strategy will be to show that if $\rho_f < 1/6$, then actually for every x, more than $2/3$ of the votes $v_y(x)$ are for $v(x)$. This is equivalent to saying that $\Pr_y[v(x) = f(x+y) - f(y)] > 2/3$. This will be enough to imply that v is a homomorphism.

Lemma 6.6. *If* $\rho_f < \frac{1}{6}$, *then* $\Pr_{y \in G}[v_y(x) = v(x)] > 2/3$ *for every* $x \in G$.

Proof. Fix $x \in G$. Consider the random variable Φ which equals $v_y(x)$ for a random $y \in G$. We would like to show that Φ is biased towards a particular value.

min-entropy

In general, to show that a random variable is far from uniform, a useful idea is to show an upper bound on its entropy. Indeed, the *min-entropy* of a random variable Z is defined as $H_\infty(Z) = -\log\max_z \Pr[Z = z]$; so, small min-entropy means that $\Pr[Z = z]$ is large at some z. But the min-entropy can be hard to compute. It is sometimes easier to study the *Rényi entropy*:

Rényi entropy

$H_2(Z) = -\log \Pr[Z_1 = Z_2]$ where Z_1 and Z_2 are two i.i.d. samples of Z.

Exercise 6.5. Show that $H_\infty(Z) \leq H_2(Z) \leq 2H_\infty(Z)$.

Now we get back to the proof. We have:

$$\Pr_{y_1, y_2}[v_{y_1}(x) = v_{y_2}(x)] = \Pr_{y_1, y_2}[f(x + y_1) - f(y_1) = f(x + y_2) - f(y_2)]$$
$$= \Pr_{y_1, y_2}[f(x + y_1) - f(x + y_2) = f(y_1) - f(y_2)].$$

Note that $f(x + y_1) - f(x + y_2) = f(y_1 - y_2)$ with probability $1 - \rho_f$ (since $y_1 - y_2$ and $x + y_2$ are distributed independently and uniformly). Similarly, $f(y_1) - f(y_2) = f(y_1 - y_2)$ with probability $1 - \rho_f$. Thus, by the union bound:

$$\Pr_{y_1, y_2}[f(x + y_1) - f(x + y_2) = f(y_1) - f(y_2)]$$
$$\geq \Pr_{y_1, y_2}[f(x + y_1) - f(x + y_2) = f(y_1 - y_2) = f(y_1) - f(y_2)]$$
$$\geq 1 - 2\rho_f > \frac{2}{3}.$$

The lemma follows because $H_\infty(\Phi) \leq H_2(\Phi)$ by Exercise 6.5. $\square$

Lemma 6.7. If $\Pr_{y \in G}[v_y(x) = v(x)] > 2/3$ for every $x \in G$, then v is a homomorphism.

Proof. The proof is short but tricky! Fix $x, y \in G$. We want to show that $v(x + y) = v(x) + v(y)$. We claim that there exists $z \in G$ which makes all three of the following hold:

$$v(x) = f(x + z) - f(z) = v_z(x)$$
$$v(y) = f(z) - f(z - y) = v_{z-y}(y)$$
$$v(x + y) = f(x + z) - f(z - y) = v_{z-y}(x + y).$$

Each of the three equalities individually holds with probability $> 2/3$ for randomly chosen z. So, by the union bound, all three simultaneously hold with probability > 0, meaning there exists a z satisfying all three. Then, it follows that $v(x) + v(y) = v(x + y)$. $\square$

Combining the three lemmas, we get that either $\rho_f \geq 1/6$ or v is a homomorphism, so that $\rho_f \geq \frac{d_H(f, v)}{2|G|} \geq \epsilon/2$.

6.4 Juntas

A *k-junta* is a Boolean function that depends on a subset of at most k variables. More precisely, $f \colon \{0, 1\}^n \to \{0, 1\}$ is a k-junta if there exists a set

junta

$J \subseteq [n]$ of size at most k such that for any $x, y \in \{0,1\}^n$ satisfying $x_J = y_J$, we have $f(x) = f(y)$. (Throughout this section, x_J denotes x restricted to the coordinate set J.)

The name arises from the English word which refers to a government run dictatorially by a small number of military officials; in this case, any decision is a function only of the people in the ruling council. Junta functions arise also in many other, less tense, situations. For example, in machine learning and its applications to computational biology, econometrics and other areas, the objective is often to learn a sparse classifier (another term for a junta function), having a particular structure[3]. k-juntas are a clear abstraction of such situations, in which the function is not restricted in any way except for the fact that it depends on an unknown subset of k variables.

Our focus is naturally on the problem of testing k-juntas. We note that 1-juntas $f \colon \{0,1\}^n \to \{0,1\}$ of the form $f(x) = x_i$ for some $i \in [n]$ are also called *dictators*, and testing dictatorship is an interesting problem in its own right[4]. Although the tester we study here for k-juntas also applies for $k = 1$, Problem 6.4 leads you through a simpler dictatorship test by leveraging the BLR tester for linearity.

For technical reasons, we will make a notational change to describe Boolean functions. Throughout this section, a Boolean function will refer to a function $f \colon \{0,1\}^n \to \{-1,+1\}$ where the "-1" can be interpreted as the "true" value and the "$+1$" as the "false" value. If $f \colon \{0,1\}^n \to \{0,1\}$, then its corresponding $\{-1,+1\}$-valued function is $\tilde{f} = (-1)^f = 1 - 2 \cdot f$.

Exercise 6.6. Write the Fourier coefficients of $\tilde{f}$ in terms of the Fourier coefficients of f.

6.4.1 The Junta Tester

The most obvious approach for testing juntas is to learn each relevant variable and reject if their number becomes more than k. Suppose at some point, a subset R of variables has been identified as relevant for an input function $f \colon \{0,1\}^n \to \{-1,1\}$, and we ask: is there a variable outside R that is also relevant? A natural way to proceed is to pick random $x, y \in \{0,1\}^n$ that agree on R and query $f(x)$ and $f(y)$. If $f(x) \neq f(y)$, there must be a relevant variable $i^* \in [n]$ among those $i \notin R$ where $x_i \neq y_i$. We can identify i^* using an additional $O(\log n)$ queries by a binary-search-like process on the coordinates i where $x_i \neq y_i$.

---

[3] Learning algorithms that are efficient with respect to k, the number of relevant variables, are called *attribute efficient* [93].

[4] Dictatorship tests (or conceptually similar variants thereof) form an important component of many probabilistically checkable proofs and hardness of approximation results. See Chapter 7 of [335].

Exercise 6.7. Given $x, y \in \{0, 1\}^n$ such that $f(x) \neq f(y)$, find a variable i^* on which f depends, using $O(\log n)$ queries to f. (**Hint**: At the i-th step, flip the values of a block of $n/2^i$ variables.)

After identifying i^*; we add i^* to R and repeat. In this way, if we find more than k relevant variables, we reject, and otherwise, accept. The resulting tester makes $O(k \log n)$ queries (ignoring the dependence on ϵ).

Can we make the query complexity independent of n? Notice that we have been trying to learn the relevant variables, and this may be much more demanding than property testing. Suppose we partition the n variables into s parts $T_1, T_2, \ldots, T_s$. If f is a k-junta, then there can be at most k parts which contain relevant variables. And if f is far from being a k-junta, and s is sufficiently large as a function of k, then it should be true that the relevant variables fall in more than k parts. Therefore, we can design a similar tester to the one sketched above, except that the new tester would find a relevant part at each iteration instead of a relevant variable. The query complexity would now be $O(k \log s)$ without any dependence on n!

For a subset $R \subseteq [n]$, and strings $x, y \in \{0, 1\}^n$, let $x_R y_{\bar{R}}$ be the string which agrees with x on R and with y on $\bar{R} = [n] \setminus R$. The junta testing algorithm is formally described as Algorithm 6.2 and has the following guarantee:

Algorithm 6.2 Junta Tester

Input: Integers n and k, $\epsilon \in (0, 1)$, and query access to $f: \{0, 1\}^n \to \{-1, 1\}$.
1: Initialize $R \leftarrow \emptyset, p = 0, s = O(\epsilon^{-5} k^9), r = O(\epsilon^{-1} k)$.
2: Randomly partition $[n]$ into s parts: $T_1, T_2, \ldots, T_s$.
3: **for** $i := 1, \ldots, r$ **do**
4:     Sample x, y from $\{0, 1\}^n$ independently and uniformly at random.
5:     **if** $f(x) \neq f(x_R y_{\bar{R}})$ **then**
6:         Find a part T_j that contains a relevant variable (see Exercise 6.7).
7:         $R \leftarrow R \cup T_j, p \leftarrow p + 1$.
8:         **if** $p > k$ **then**
9:             Reject.
10:         **end if**
11:     **end if**
12: **end for**
13: Accept.

Theorem 6.4. *Algorithm 6.2 is a one-sided error tester for k-juntas using $O(k \log k + \epsilon^{-1} k)$ queries.*

We will show that if f is ϵ-far from k-juntas, then Algorithm 6.2 rejects with probability at least $2/3$. More specifically:

Lemma 6.8. *Let $f \colon \{0,1\}^n \to \{-1,+1\}$ be ϵ-far from k-juntas. Then, with probability $5/6$ over the choice of the random partition $T_1, \ldots, T_s$, for any union $R \subseteq [n]$ of at most k parts of the partition,*

$$\Pr_{x,y}[f(x) \neq f(x_R y_{\bar{R}})] \geq \epsilon/4.$$

Theorem 6.4 follows straightforwardly from the lemma.

Proof of Theorem 6.4. The query complexity is immediate because there are $O(\epsilon^{-1}k)$ iterations of the for loop, and Line 6 is entered at most $k + 1$ times. Also, the algorithm clearly accepts any k-junta.

Suppose f is ϵ-far from k-juntas. Condition on the random partition satisfying the conclusion of Lemma 6.8. Then, as long as R is a union of at most k parts, in each iteration of the for loop, the algorithm finds a new relevant variable in $\bar{R}$ with probability at least $\epsilon/4$.

Exercise 6.8. The expected number of iterations before $k + 1$ relevant variables are found is at most $4\epsilon^{-1}(k + 1) \leq 5\epsilon^{-1}k$.

By the claim of the exercise, with probability at least $5/6$, $k + 1$ relevant variables are found before $30\epsilon^{-1}k$ iterations, causing the algorithm to reject.

$\square$

influence

To prove Lemma 6.8, we need to develop some techniques for analyzing the *influence* of variables on a function.

6.4.2 Influence and Fourier Coefficients

Intuitively speaking, the influence of a variable $i \in [n]$ on a Boolean function $f \colon \{0,1\}^n \to \{-1,+1\}$ measures whether i is relevant for computing $f(x)$ for a random x.

Definition 6.1. Given $f \colon \{0,1\}^n \to \{-1,+1\}$ and an index $i \in [n]$, then:

$$\mathrm{Inf}_f(i) = 2 \cdot \Pr_{x,y \sim \{0,1\}^n}\left[f(x) \neq f(x_{[n] \setminus \{i\}} y_i)\right].$$

Exercise 6.9. Show that equivalently:

$$\mathrm{Inf}_f(i) = \Pr_{x \sim \{0,1\}^n}[f(x) \neq f(x^{\oplus i})],$$

where $x^{\oplus i}$ is the string $(x_1, \ldots, x_{i-1}, \overline{x_i}, x_{i+1}, \ldots, x_n)$ that differs from x on the i-th coordinate and nowhere else.

The influence of a subset S of variables on a function f can be defined similarly.

Definition 6.2. Given $f \colon \{0,1\}^n \to \{-1,+1\}$ and a subset $S \subseteq [n]$, then:

$$\mathrm{Inf}_f(S) = 2 \cdot \Pr_{x,y \sim \{0,1\}^n}[f(x) \neq f(x_{\bar{S}} y_S)].$$

Exercise 6.10. If f is a parity on more than k variables, and S is a subset of k variables, what is $\mathrm{Inf}_f(\bar{S})$?

Exercise 6.11. Check that Lemma 6.8 is equivalent to:

$$\Pr_{T_1,\ldots,T_s}\left[\forall i_1, i_2, \ldots, i_k \in [s], \mathrm{Inf}_f\left(\overline{\bigcup_{j \in [k]} T_{i_j}}\right) \geq \frac{\epsilon}{2}\right] \geq \frac{5}{6}.$$

It turns out to be amazingly powerful to reexpress influence in terms of the function's Fourier coefficients.

Lemma 6.9. *For any $S \subseteq [n]$ and $f \colon \{0,1\}^n \to \{-1,+1\}$:*

$$\mathrm{Inf}_f(S) = \sum_{\alpha \in \{0,1\}^n : \alpha_S \neq 0} \hat{f}(\alpha)^2,$$

where $\alpha_S \neq 0$ means that the vector obtained by restricting α to S is not the all-zero vector, that is, α has at least one non-zero coordinate in S. In particular, for any $i \in [n]$, $\mathrm{Inf}_f(i) = \sum_{\alpha \in \{0,1\}^n : \alpha_i = 1} \hat{f}(\alpha)^2$.

It immediately implies the following fact that is intuitive but not so easy to prove directly.

Corollary 6.2. *For all $S, T \subseteq [n]$:*

$$\mathrm{Inf}_f(S) \leq \mathrm{Inf}_f(S \cup T) \leq \mathrm{Inf}_f(S) + \mathrm{Inf}_f(T).$$

You will be asked to prove Lemma 6.9 in Problem 6.8.

6.4.3 Proof of Lemma 6.8

Fix $f \colon \{0,1\}^n \to \{-1,1\}$ that is ϵ-far from k-juntas. To start off, let us rephrase ϵ-farness from juntas in the language of the last section.

Lemma 6.10. *For any set $R \subseteq [n]$ of size at most k, $\mathrm{Inf}_f(\bar{R}) > \epsilon$.*

Proof. Suppose there exists a set R of size at most k such that $\mathrm{Inf}_f(\overline{R}) \leq \epsilon$ or:

$$\Pr_{x,y \sim \{0,1\}^n}[f(x) \neq f(x_R y_{\overline{R}})] \leq \frac{\epsilon}{2}.$$

So, there can be at most $\epsilon \cdot 2^n$ x's such that $\Pr_y[f(x) \neq f(x_R y_{\overline{R}})] > 1/2$.

Therefore, if we define $g \colon \{0,1\}^n \to \{-1,+1\}$ as $g(x) = \mathsf{Maj}(\{x_R y_{\overline{R}} : y \in \{0,1\}^n\})$, where $\mathsf{Maj}(S)$ denotes the majority of the elements in the multiset S, then g is clearly a k-junta, and $\Pr_x[f(x) \neq g(x)] \leq \epsilon$.   □

Using Lemma 6.9, it follows that if f is ϵ-far from k-juntas, for any set $R \subseteq [n]$ of size at most k:

$$\sum_{A \cap \overline{R} \neq \emptyset} \hat{f}(A)^2 > \epsilon.$$

Note that here we made a change of notation, using the set A to denote the corresponding vector $\alpha = (\mathbf{1}_{i \in A} : i \in [n])$. Using Parseval's theorem (Corollary 6.1):

$$\sum_{A \subseteq R} \hat{f}(A)^2 < 1 - \epsilon \tag{6.5}$$

for any set $R \subseteq [n]$ of size at most k.

Our goal will be to show that:

$$\Pr_{T_1,\ldots,T_s}\left[\max_{i_1,\ldots,i_k \in [s]} \sum_{A \subseteq T_{i_1} \cup \cdots \cup T_{i_k}} \hat{f}(A)^2 \leq 1 - \frac{\epsilon}{2} \right] \geq \frac{5}{6}. \tag{6.6}$$

This is equivalent to showing Lemma 6.8, by Exercise 6.11 and the same use of Parseval's theorem as above.

The idea of the proof is to separate the sum $\sum_{A \subseteq T_{i_1} \cup \cdots \cup T_{i_k}} \hat{f}(A)^2$ into three pieces. The first piece consists of sets A whose size is "large." The second piece consists of small sets containing only "important" variables. The third piece contains the remaining sets.

Large Sets

Lemma 6.11. *We have:*

$$\Pr_{T_1,\ldots,T_s}\left[\max_{i_1,\ldots,i_k \in [s]} \sum_{\substack{A \subseteq \cup_{j \in [k]} T_{i_j}, \\ |A| > 2k}} \hat{f}(A)^2 > \frac{\epsilon}{4} \right] \leq \frac{1}{18}$$

if $s > 600\epsilon^{-1}k$.

Proof. The idea behind the proof is that if A is large, then A very likely does not belong to the union of only k parts. So, the expected contribution of such A's to the sum is small. Formally:

$$
\mathop{\mathbf{E}}_{T_1,\ldots,T_s} \left[\max_{i_1,\ldots,i_k \in [s]} \sum_{\substack{A \subseteq \cup_{j \in [k]} T_{i_j}, \\ |A| > 2k}} \hat{f}(A)^2 \right]
$$

$$
\leq \sum_{A : |A| > 2k} \hat{f}(A)^2 \mathop{\mathbf{E}}_{T_1,\ldots,T_s} \left[\mathbf{1} \left[\exists i_1,\ldots,i_k \in [s], A \subseteq \bigcup_{j \in [k]} T_{i_j} \right] \right]
$$

$$
= \sum_{A : |A| > 2k} \hat{f}(A)^2 \mathop{\Pr}_{T_1,\ldots,T_s} \left[\exists i_1,\ldots,i_k \in [s], A \subseteq \bigcup_{j \in [k]} T_{i_j} \right]
$$

$$
\leq \sum_{A : |A| > 2k} \hat{f}(A)^2 \cdot \binom{s}{k} \left(\frac{k}{s} \right)^{|A|}
$$

$$
\leq \left(\frac{es}{k} \right)^k \left(\frac{k}{s} \right)^{2k} \sum_A \hat{f}(A)^2
$$

$$
\leq \frac{\epsilon}{200} \cdot 1,
$$

where the penultimate inequality is by $\binom{s}{k} \leq \left(\frac{es}{k} \right)^k$ and the last inequality is by Parseval's theorem and $s \gg \epsilon^{-1} k$. The lemma follows by Markov's inequality. $\square$

Important Sets

Next, we define a notion of "important" variables. Intuitively, these are the variables contained in the sets whose Fourier coefficients are large.

Definition 6.3. $i \in [n]$ is an (ℓ, θ)-*important variable* if: important variable

$$
\sum_{B \ni i, |B| \leq \ell} \hat{f}(B)^2 > \theta.
$$

We say a set $A \subseteq [n]$ is (ℓ, θ)-*important* if all $i \in A$ are (ℓ, θ)-important variables.

The first observation is that there cannot be too many important variables.

Lemma 6.12. *The number of (ℓ, θ)-important variables is at most ℓ/θ.*

Proof. Note that:

$$\sum_{i\in[n]}\sum_{B:|B|\leq\ell}\hat{f}(B)^2\cdot\mathbf{1}[i\in B]=\sum_{B:|B|\leq\ell}\hat{f}(B)^2\cdot\sum_{i\in[n]}\mathbf{1}[i\in B]\leq\ell\qquad(6.7)$$

using Parseval's theorem. So, if there are more than ℓ/θ (ℓ,θ)-important variables, there is a contradiction to the above. $\qquad\square$

We next argue that a union of k parts in the random partition most likely contains at most k important variables.

Lemma 6.13. *We have:*

$$\Pr_{T_1,\ldots,T_s}\Big[\exists i_1,\ldots,i_k,$$

$$\bigcup_{j\in[k]}T_{i_j}\ \text{contains more than}\ k\ (2k,\theta)\text{-important variables}\Big]<\frac{1}{18}$$

if $s>72\theta^{-2}k^2.$

Proof. Let I denote the set of $(2k,\theta)$-important variables. By Lemma 6.12, $|I|\leq2\theta^{-1}k$. Then, by the "birthday paradox" argument:

$$\Pr_{T_1,\ldots,T_s}\Big[\exists j\in[s],|I\cap T_j|\geq2\Big]\leq\binom{|I|}{2}\cdot\frac{1}{s}\leq\frac{4k^2}{s\theta^2}<\frac{1}{18}.$$

So, with probability $>17/18$, each part in the random partition contains at most 1 important variable, and therefore, the union of k parts contains at most k important variables. $\qquad\square$

We can now bound the contribution to the sum in (6.6) coming from important sets.

Lemma 6.14. *If* $s>72\theta^{-2}k^2$, *then:*

$$\Pr_{T_1,\ldots,T_s}\left[\max_{i_1,\ldots,i_k\in[s]}\sum_{\substack{A\subseteq T_{i_1}\cup\cdots\cup T_{i_k},\\A\ (2k,\theta)\text{-}important}}\hat{f}(A)^2\geq1-\epsilon\right]<\frac{1}{18}.$$

Proof. By the preceding lemma, with probability at least $17/18$, for any choice of $i_1,\ldots,i_k$, the number of $(2k,\theta)$-important variables contained in $T_{i_1}\cup\cdots\cup T_{i_k}$ is at most k. Conditioned on this event:

$$\max_{i_1,\ldots,i_k\in[s]}\sum_{\substack{A\subseteq T_{i_1}\cup\cdots\cup T_{i_k},\\A\ (2k,\theta)\text{-}important}}\hat{f}(A)^2\leq\max_{R\subseteq[n],|R|\leq k}\sum_{A\subseteq R}\hat{f}(A)^2<1-\epsilon,$$

where the last inequality follows from (6.5) that uses the ϵ-farness of f from k-juntas.   □

Small, Unimportant Sets

The remaining contribution to the sum in (6.6) comes from sets that are of size at most $2k$ and contain at least one variable not $(2k, \theta)$-important. Let I be the set of $(2k, \theta)$-important variables. Note that:

$$\sum_{A:|A| \leq 2k} \hat{f}(A)^2 \cdot \mathbf{1}\left[A \subseteq \bigcup_{j \in [k]} T_{i_j}, A \cap \overline{I} \neq \emptyset\right]$$

$$\leq \sum_{A:|A| \leq 2k} \hat{f}(A)^2 \cdot \mathbf{1}\left[A \cap \left(\bigcup_{j \in [k]} T_{i_j} \cap \overline{I}\right) \neq \emptyset\right]$$

$$\leq \sum_{j \in [k]} \sum_{A:|A| \leq 2k} \hat{f}(A)^2 \cdot \mathbf{1}\left[A \cap (T_{i_j} \setminus I) \neq \emptyset\right]$$

$$\leq \sum_{j \in [k]} \sum_{\ell \in [n]} \mathbf{1}[\ell \in T_{i_j} \setminus I] \sum_{A \ni \ell, |A| \leq 2k} \hat{f}(A)^2. \tag{6.8}$$

Let $X_{j,\ell}$ denote the random variable:

$$X_{j,\ell} = \mathbf{1}[\ell \in T_{i_j} \setminus I] \cdot \sum_{A \ni \ell, |A| \leq 2k} \hat{f}(A)^2.$$

Note that the only source of randomness in $X_{j,\ell}$ is in the choice of T_{i_j}. So, $X_{j,\ell}$ and $X_{j,\ell'}$ are independent for $\ell \neq \ell'$ since $\mathbf{1}[\ell \in T_{i_j} \setminus I]$ and $\mathbf{1}[\ell' \in T_{i_j} \setminus I]$ are independent.

Lemma 6.15. *We have:*

$$\Pr_{T_{i_j}}\left[\sum_{\ell \in [n]} X_{j,\ell} > \frac{\epsilon}{4k}\right] < \frac{1}{18s}$$

if $s > 16\epsilon^{-1}k$ and $\theta \leq \epsilon^2/(64k^3 \log(18s))$.

Proof. Since $\sum_\ell X_{j,\ell}$ is a sum of independent random variables, we can use standard concentration bounds. Firstly, see that:

$$\mathop{\mathbf{E}}_{T_{i_j}}\left[\sum_\ell X_{j,\ell}\right] = \frac{1}{s} \sum_\ell \sum_{A \ni \ell, |A| \leq 2k} \hat{f}(A)^2 \leq \frac{2k}{s},$$

where the last inequality uses (6.7). Next, we argue concentration. Using the Chernoff-Hoeffding bound:

$$\Pr_{T_{i_j}}\left[\sum_\ell X_{j,\ell} - \frac{2k}{s} > t\right] \leq \exp\left(-\frac{2t^2}{\sum_\ell b_\ell^2}\right),$$

where b_ℓ is an upper bound on $X_{j,\ell}$. Note that $b_\ell = 0$ if $\ell \in I$ and otherwise, $b_\ell \leq \sum_{A\ni\ell,|A|\leq 2k} \hat{f}(A)^2$. So:

$$\sum_\ell b_\ell^2 \leq \sum_{\ell\notin I}\left(\sum_{A\ni\ell,|A|\leq 2k} \hat{f}(A)^2\right)^2 \leq \theta \cdot \sum_{\ell\notin I}\sum_{A\ni\ell,|A|\leq 2k} \hat{f}(A)^2 \leq 2k\theta,$$

where for the second inequality, we used the definition of $(2k,\theta)$-important variables, and for the third inequality, we again used (6.7).

Therefore:

$$\Pr_{T_{i_j}}\left[\sum_\ell X_{j,\ell} - \frac{2k}{s} > \frac{\epsilon}{8k}\right] \leq \exp\left(-\frac{\epsilon^2}{64k^3\theta}\right).$$

The lemma follows by our choice of parameters.   □

By the union bound, it follows that with probability 17/18, for every $j \in [s]$, $\sum_\ell X_{j,\ell} \leq \epsilon/(4k)$. Plugging into (6.8), we get:

Corollary 6.3. *Let $s > 16\epsilon^{-1}k$ and $\theta \leq \epsilon^2/(64k^3 \log(18s))$. With probability at least 17/18 over choice of $T_1,\ldots,T_s$, for any $i_1,\ldots,i_k \in [s]$:*

$$\sum_{A:|A|\leq 2k} \hat{f}(A)^2 \cdot \mathbf{1}\left[A \subseteq \bigcup_{j\in[k]} T_{i_j}, A\cap\overline{I} \neq \emptyset\right] \leq \frac{\epsilon}{4}.$$

Finishing up

We view the collection of $A \subseteq \bigcup_{j\in[k]} T_{i_j}$ as the union of three collections: A such that $|A| > 2k$, A that are $(2k,\theta)$-important, and A that are neither. Lemma 6.11, Lemma 6.14 and Corollary 6.3 bound the contribution of A's from each collection to the sum in (6.6). Therefore, using the union bound, setting $\theta = O(\epsilon^{-2}k^2)$ and $s = O(\epsilon^{-5}k^9)$, we obtain:

$$\Pr_{T_1,\ldots,T_s}\left[\max_{i_1,\ldots,i_k\in[s]}\sum_{A\subseteq T_{i_1}\cup\cdots\cup T_{i_k}} \hat{f}(A)^2 > \frac{\epsilon}{4} + 1 - \epsilon + \frac{\epsilon}{4}\right] \leq \frac{1}{18} + \frac{1}{18} + \frac{1}{18},$$

proving Lemma 6.8.

6.5 Lower Bounds

In this section, we turn to proving lower bounds for the query complexity of testing function properties functions. Our main tool so far for this task has been Yao's minimax principle (Theorem 2.4), whereby we create two distributions, one concentrated on positive instances and other on negative instances, and show that they cannot be distinguished from each other by any deterministic algorithm making a small number of queries. For instance, this method can be immediately used to show that the $O(\epsilon^{-1})$ query complexity of the BLR test for linearity is optimal; see Problem 6.7.

Although the minimax principle will still be our main tool for proving lower bounds in future chapters, here we introduce another general technique which gives dramatically simple and powerful results for several interesting function properties. In Section 6.5.1, we formulate the communication complexity methodology for proving query complexity lower bounds. In Sections 6.5.2 and 6.5.3, we use it to analyze the query complexity of testing k-juntas and testing monotonicity respectively.

6.5.1 The Communication Complexity Methodology

Property testers for many function properties can be used to design protocols for well-studied 2-party communication problems. Thus, lower bounds for the communication complexity of these problems imply lower bounds on the query complexity of corresponding testing problems.

Background

A communication problem is defined by a function $f: \{0,1\}^n \times \{0,1\}^n \to \{0,1\}$. Two parties, traditionally named Alice and Bob, are each handed an input, $x \in \{0,1\}^n$ and $y \in \{0,1\}^n$ respectively, and the goal is to design a protocol between Alice and Bob such that they can jointly compute $f(x,y)$. We focus on the *shared randomness* model where Alice and Bob have free access to a common random string r. During the course of the protocol, Alice and Bob can communicate by sending bits to each other; in a *one-way protocol*, Alice can send bits to Bob but not the other way around[5].

---

[5] For one-way protocols, only Bob is required to compute the output.

communication
complexity

The *communication complexity* of a particular protocol is the maximum number of bits exchanged between the two parties, over all choices of the inputs x, y and the random string r. The *communication complexity of f*, denoted $\mathsf{CC}(f)$, is the minimum communication complexity of all protocols in which f is computed correctly with probability at least $2/3$ for all inputs x and y. The *one-way communication complexity of f*, denoted $\mathsf{CC}^{\rightarrow}(f)$, is the same notion but restricted to one-way protocols.

Communication complexity has a rich history of study, as we describe in the bibliographic notes section of this chapter, with many connections to fundamental problems in computer science. The communication problems below are of basic importance as they appear repeatedly in many applications:

set disjointness

- The *set disjointness* problem is to jointly compute:

$$\mathrm{DISJ}_n(x,y) = \bigvee_{i=1}^{n} (x_i \wedge y_i)$$

In other words, if x and y are indicator vectors of sets $S \subseteq [n]$ and $T \subseteq [n]$, then $\mathrm{DISJ}_n(x,y)$ is 1 if and only if $S \cap T \neq \emptyset$.

We also define the problem, $\mathrm{DISJ}_{n,k}$, where the function is the same but the inputs x, y are additionally promised to satisfy $|x| = |y| = k$ and $|\{i : x_i \wedge y_i = 1\}| \leq 1$. In other words, the inputs correspond to sets of size k, and they are either disjoint or they intersect at exactly one element.

The trivial protocol for DISJ_n, where Alice sends her input x to Bob, has communication complexity $O(n)$. This is tight.

> **Theorem 6.5.**
> $$\mathsf{CC}(\mathrm{DISJ}_n) = \Theta(n).$$

For $\mathrm{DISJ}_{n,k}$, the trivial protocol has communication complexity $O(\log \binom{n}{k})$, which is the number of bits needed by Alice to describe her input to Bob. Although this is tight for deterministic protocols, there is a non-trivial randomized protocol with communication complexity $O(k)$. The current best lower bound is:

> **Theorem 6.6.** *For any $1 \leq k < n/2 - 1$:*
> $$\mathsf{CC}(\mathrm{DISJ}_{n,k}) = \Omega(\min(2k, n - 2k)).$$

index

- The most widely studied problem in the one-way model is the *index* problem. Here, Alice is given a string $x \in \{0,1\}^n$ and Bob is given an index $i \in [n]$, and the goal is to compute:

$$\mathrm{INDEX}_n(x,i) = x_i.$$

Note that Alice has no information about i, so it seems intuitive that she will need to send all n bits to Bob. This can be proven formally:

Theorem 6.7.
$$CC^{\rightarrow}(\text{INDEX}_n) = \Theta(n).$$

For technical reasons, it is sometimes convenient to work with a variant, the *augmented index* problem, where Alice is given the string $x \in \{0,1\}^n$ and Bob is given not only an index $i \in [n]$ but also an additional $i-1$ bits which are promised to be $x_1, \ldots, x_{i-1}$, and:

$$\text{AUGINDEX}_n(x, \langle i, x_1, \ldots, x_{i-1} \rangle) = x_i.$$

augmented index

Intuitively, it does not seem that the extra information possessed by Bob can be used to reduce the communication, and indeed this can be proved.

Theorem 6.8.
$$CC^{\rightarrow}(\text{AUGINDEX}_n) = \Theta(n).$$

Reduction to Property Testing

Let us start with an example to illustrate the communication complexity methodology to proving lower bounds for property testing. We sketch how to reduce the $\text{DISJ}_{n,k}$ communication problem to the problem of testing $(2k-2)$-juntas; the formal proof appears in Section 6.5.2.

Let the inputs for Alice and Bob be $x, y \in \{0,1\}^n$ respectively (with the promise that $|x|, |y| = k$ and $|x \cap y| \le 1$). For any $z \in \{0,1\}^n$, define the function $f_z \colon \{0,1\}^n \to \{0,1\}$ as:

$$f_z(w) = \sum_{i : z_i = 1} w_i \pmod 2.$$

Then, Alice can view her input as f_x, and Bob can view his as f_y. Note that f_x and f_y are each a linear function over $\mathbb{F}_2$ on k variables.

Define $h = f_x + f_y \pmod 2$. Note that if $|x \cap y| = 1$, then h is linear (over $\mathbb{F}_2$) on $2k - 2$ variables, whereas if $|x \cap y| = 0$, h is linear on $2k$ variables. Hence, in the first case, h is a $(2k - 2)$-junta, whereas in the second case, it can be shown that h is $\frac{1}{2}$-far from a $(2k-2)$-junta. Let A be a tester for $1/2$-testing $(2k - 2)$-juntas. Alice and Bob both invoke the tester A on h, using the shared randomness. Whenever A calls for $h(w)$, Alice and Bob exchange $f_x(w)$ and $f_y(w)$ with each other, so that they can each individually compute $h(w)$. Alice and Bob return 1 if the tester accepts and 0 if it rejects.

It should be clear that the resulting protocol computes $\text{DISJ}_{n,k}$ correctly with probability 2/3, and its communication complexity is at most two times the query complexity of A. Invoking Theorem 6.6, we get an $\Omega(\min(k, n-2k))$ lower bound on the query complexity of testing $(2k - 2)$-juntas.

Now, we formulate the above methodology more systematically.

Definition 6.4. A *simple combining operator* ψ is an operator that takes two functions $f\colon \{0,1\}^n \to Z_1, g\colon \{0,1\}^n \to Z_2$ and returns another function $h\colon \{0,1\}^n \to R$, denoted $h = \psi[f,g]$, such that for any $w \in \{0,1\}^n$, $h(w)$ can be computed only from w, $f(w)$, and $g(w)$. Here, Z_1, Z_2, and R are arbitrary finite sets.

For example, in the above sketch, we used $\psi[f,g](w) = f(w) + g(w) \pmod 2$ which is therefore simple combining. If on the other hand, $\psi[f,g](w)$ depended on the value of f or g at points other than w, then ψ would not be a simple combining operator[6].

A simple combining operator ψ and a property $\mathcal{P} \subseteq \{\{0,1\}^n \to R\}$ defines the communication problem $C_\psi^\mathcal{P}$. In $C_\psi^\mathcal{P}$, Alice and Bob get as input functions f and g respectively, and the goal is for them to compute[7]:

$$C_\psi^\mathcal{P}(f,g) = \begin{cases} 1 & \text{if } \psi[f,g] \in \mathcal{P} \\ 0 & \text{if } \psi[f,g] \text{ is } \frac{1}{40}\text{-far from } \mathcal{P} \end{cases}$$

Note that the function $C_\psi^\mathcal{P}(f,g)$ is not specified if neither of the cases are met. The communication complexity of $C_\psi^\mathcal{P}$ can be bounded in terms of the query complexity of $\mathcal{P}$, using exactly the same approach we saw earlier for juntas.

Lemma 6.16. *For any simple combining function* $\psi\colon \{\{0,1\}^n \to Z_1\} \times \{\{0,1\}^n \to Z_2\} \to \{\{0,1\}^n \to R\}$ *and any property* $\mathcal{P} \subseteq \{\{0,1\}^n \to R\}$:

(i) $\mathsf{CC}(C_\psi^\mathcal{P}) \leq (\lceil \log |Z_1| \rceil + \lceil \log |Z_2| \rceil) \cdot \mathsf{Q}(\mathcal{P})$

(ii) $\mathsf{CC}^\rightarrow(C_\psi^\mathcal{P}) \leq \lceil \log |Z_1| \rceil \cdot \mathsf{Q}^{\mathsf{na}}(\mathcal{P})$

where $\mathsf{Q}(\mathcal{P})$ *is the minimum query complexity of a tester that accepts functions in* $\mathcal{P}$ *with probability 2/3 and rejects functions 1/40-far from* $\mathcal{P}$ *with probability 2/3 and* $\mathsf{Q}^{\mathsf{na}}(\mathcal{P})$ *is defined similarly but restricted to non-adaptive testers.*

Proof. Suppose A is a (possibly adaptive, two-sided) tester for $\mathcal{P}$ with the optimal query complexity $\mathsf{Q}(\mathcal{P})$. Let $h = \psi[f,g]$. Alice and Bob both invoke A on h using the shared randomness. Each time the tester calls for the query $h(x)$, Alice and Bob exchange $f(x)$ and $g(x)$ with each other, requiring $(\lceil \log |Z_1| \rceil + \lceil \log |Z_2| \rceil)$ bits of communication. Since ψ is a simple combining operator, Alice and Bob can each evaluate $h(x)$ and feed it to A. Note that since the tester may be adaptive, the next query could depend on the outcome of the previous queries, but because both Alice and Bob have the

---

[6] Even if ψ is not a simple combining operator, the overall methodology may still apply. See Problem 6.11. On the other hand, Goldreich [206] has shown that restricting to simple combining functions does not make the method significantly weaker.

[7] The distance threshold 1/40 is not particularly important, but we fix some constant since our main concern will be dependence on n.

same record of previous queries and use the same random source, adaptivity is not an issue. The inequality in part (i) follows. We leave part (ii) as an exercise. □

Exercise 6.12. Show part (ii) of Lemma 6.16. (**Hint**: In a non-adaptive tester, the sequence of queries can be fixed beforehand. Use this fact to design a one-way protocol for $C_\psi^\mathcal{P}$.)

Thus, to prove a lower bound on $\mathsf{Q}(\mathcal{P})$, it suffices to prove a lower bound on $\mathsf{CC}(C_\psi^\mathcal{P})$. Although just a simple change of perspective, the new viewpoint allows us to deploy non-trivial results in communication complexity. In particular, the goal now becomes to design a simple combining operator ψ so that there is a reduction from a basic communication problem (such as the set disjointness or index problems) to $C_\psi^\mathcal{P}$.

6.5.2 k-juntas

We formally prove the theorem sketched earlier.

Theorem 6.9. *For any $1 \leq k < 0.9n$, testing k-juntas requires $\Omega(k)$ queries.*

We note that Theorem 6.9 is slightly weaker than the best known lower bound of $\Omega(k \log k)$ [370].

Proof of Theorem 6.9. Assume k is even. Problem 6.12 asks you to complete the proof for odd k.

Let $\ell = k/2 + 1$. Due to Theorem 6.6 and Lemma 6.16, we will be done if we can show $\mathsf{CC}(\mathrm{DISJ}_{n,\ell}) \leq \mathsf{CC}(C_\psi^{k\text{-junta}})$ for some simple combining operator $\psi \colon \{\{0,1\}^n \to \{0,1\}\}^2 \to \{\{0,1\}^n \to \{0,1\}\}$.

Identifying the set $\{0,1\}$ with the field $\mathbb{F}_2$, let $\psi[f,g] = f + g$. We show a reduction from $\mathrm{DISJ}_{n,\ell}$ to $C_\psi^{k\text{-junta}}$. Suppose for the problem $\mathrm{DISJ}_{n,\ell}$, Alice and Bob have inputs $x, y \in \{0,1\}^n$ with the promise that $|x| = |y| = \ell$ and $|x \cap y| \leq 1$. Define the functions:

$$f_x(w) = \sum_{i:x_i=1} w_i \qquad \text{and} \qquad f_y(w) = \sum_{i:y_i=1} w_i.$$

Obviously, Alice and Bob can compute f_x and f_y respectively, given their inputs of x and y. We now claim that if Alice and Bob run a protocol for $C_\psi^{k\text{-junta}}$ on inputs f_x and f_y, then they solve the $\mathrm{DISJ}_{n,\ell}$ problem.

If x and y satisfy $\mathrm{DISJ}_{n,\ell}(x,y) = 1$, then f_x and f_y have one relevant variable in common. So, $\psi[f_x, f_y] = f_x + f_y$ is a linear form on $2\ell - 2 = k$

variables, and therefore, the protocol for $C_\psi^{k\text{-junta}}$ outputs 1 with probability at least $2/3$.

On the other hand, if x and y have disjoint supports, then we claim that $h = f_x + f_y$ is $1/2$-far from a k-junta. Note that by construction, h is a linear form on $2\ell = k + 2$ variables.

> **Claim 6.3.** *Any linear form h on $k + 2$ variables is $1/2$-far from a k-junta.*

Proof. Without loss of generality, say $h(x) = x_1 + \cdots + x_{k+2}$. As in Section 6.4, it is convenient to think of Boolean functions as mapping to $\{-1, 1\}$. Let $H(x) = (-1)^{h(x)}$, and let $G \colon \{0, 1\}^n \to \{-1, 1\}$ be a k-junta. Note that because h is a linear form on the first k variables, $\hat{H}(\alpha)$ is zero for all α except $1^{k+2}0^{n-k-2}$. Since G is a k-junta, we have the following.

> **Exercise 6.13.** Show that $\hat{G}(\alpha) = 0$ for all α such that $|\alpha| > k$.

Then, we have:

$$\Pr_x[H(x) \neq G(x)] = \frac{1}{2} + \frac{1}{2} \mathop{\mathbf{E}}_x[H(x) \cdot G(x)]$$
$$= \frac{1}{2} + \frac{1}{2} \sum_\alpha \hat{H}(\alpha) \cdot \hat{G}(\alpha) = \frac{1}{2},$$

where the last equality uses the fact that $\hat{G}(1^{k+2}0^{n-k-2}) = 0$. $\square$

Therefore, if $|x \cap y| = 0$, a protocol for $C_\psi^{k\text{-junta}}$ will return 0. $\square$

6.5.3 Monotonicity over Hypercubes

As we mentioned in Section 6.1, it is known that monotonicity of functions $f \colon \{0, 1\}^n \to \mathbb{R}$ can be tested with $O(\epsilon^{-1} n)$ queries. In this section, we show an $\Omega(n)$ lower bound for constant ϵ, again using the communication complexity methodology.

> **Theorem 6.10.** *Testing monotonicity of functions $f \colon \{0, 1\}^n \to \mathbb{R}$ requires $\Omega(n)$ queries.*

Proof. Let mon denote the monotonicity property of functions $f \colon \{0, 1\}^n \to \mathbb{R}$. Due to Theorem 6.5 and Lemma 6.16, we will be done if we can show $\mathsf{CC}(\mathrm{Disj}_n) \leq \mathsf{CC}(C_\psi^{\mathrm{mon}})$ for a simple combining operator $\psi \colon \{\{0, 1\}^n \to \{-1, 1\}\}^2 \to \{\{0, 1\}^n \to \mathbb{R}\}$. Define ψ as:

$$\psi[f, g](x) = 2|x| + f(x) + g(x).$$

We now give a reduction from DISJ_n to C_ψ^{mon}. Suppose for the problem DISJ_n, Alice and Bob have inputs $\alpha, \beta \in \{0, 1\}^n$ respectively. We claim that if Alice and Bob run a protocol for C_ψ^{mon} on inputs χ_α and χ_β, then they can solve the DISJ_n problem. Recall that $\chi_\alpha(x) = (-1)^{\sum_i \alpha_i x_i}$ is the Fourier character (as defined in (6.2)).

Claim 6.4. *If* $\text{DISJ}_n(\alpha, \beta) = 0$, *then* $C_\psi^{mon}(\chi_\alpha, \chi_\beta) = 1$.

Proof. The claim is that if $|\alpha \cap \beta| = 0$, then the function:

$$h(x) = 2|x| + \chi_\alpha(x) + \chi_\beta(x)$$

is monotone. We check that for any $i \in [n]$, if x and x' satisfy $x_i = 0, x'_i = 1$ and $x_j = x'_j$ for all $j \neq i$, then $h(x) \leq h(x')$.

Because α and β have disjoint supports, it cannot be that $\alpha_i = \beta_i = 1$. Suppose without loss of generality that $\beta_i = 0$, and so $\chi_\beta(x) = \chi_\beta(x')$. Then:

$$
\begin{aligned}
h(x') &= 2|x'| + \chi_\alpha(x') + \chi_\beta(x') \\
&= 2|x| + 2 + \chi_\alpha(x') + \chi_\beta(x) \\
&\geq 2|x| + \chi_\alpha(x) + \chi_\beta(x) = h(x),
\end{aligned}
$$

where the last inequality is there for the case: $\chi_\alpha(x') = -\chi_\alpha(x) = -1$. $\square$

Claim 6.5. *If* $\text{DISJ}_n(\alpha, \beta) = 1$, *then* $\psi[\chi_\alpha, \chi_\beta]$ *is 1/8-far from being monotone, and so,* $C_\psi^{mon}(\chi_\alpha, \chi_\beta) = 0$.

Proof. Again, let $h(x) = 2|x| + \chi_\alpha(x) + \chi_\beta(x)$. Fix $i^* \in [n]$ such that $\alpha_{i^*} = \beta_{i^*} = 1$. Consider any x which satisfies the following three constraints:

$$x_{i^*} = 0,$$

$$\sum_j \alpha_j x_j = 0 \pmod 2,$$

$$\sum_j \beta_j x_j = 0 \pmod 2.$$

For any such x, note that $h(x) > h(x')$ where x' equals x everywhere except at i^*. This is because $h(x) = 2|x| + 1 + 1 = 2|x| + 2$ whereas $h(x') = 2(|x| + 1) - 1 - 1 = 2|x|$. Moreover, all such pairs (x, x') are disjoint, and so in order to make h monotone, it must be modified once for every such pair. Therefore:

$$\frac{d_\text{H}(h, \text{mon})}{2^n} \geq \Pr_x \left[x_{i^*} = 0, \sum_j \alpha_j x_j = 0, \sum_j \beta_j x_j = 0 \right]$$

> **Exercise 6.14.** Show that the RHS of the above inequality is at least $1/8$.

The lemma follows from the claim of the exercise.   □

Therefore, Alice and Bob can run the protocol for C_ψ^{mon} on χ_α and χ_β and flip the output in order to compute $\mathrm{DISJ}_n(\alpha, \beta)$.   □

We note that the functions $\psi[\chi_\alpha, \chi_\beta]$ shown to be hard to test in the above proof have range $[0, 2n + 2]$. The range size is decreased to $O(\sqrt{n})$ in Problem 6.13.

6.5.4 Monotonicity over the Line

In Section 3.5, we saw that monotonicity of functions $f: [n] \to \mathbb{R}$ can be tested non-adaptively using $O(\log n)$ queries. In this section, we will use the communication complexity methodology to argue that there are no non-adaptive testers for this problem using $o(\log n)$ queries.

> **Theorem 6.11.** *Non-adaptively testing monotonicity of functions $f: [n] \to \mathbb{R}$ requires $\Omega(\log n)$ queries.*

We will not cover the stronger theorem due to Fischer [178] that $\Omega(\log n)$ queries are necessary even for adaptive testers. We mention that Belovs [50] further showed that $\Omega(\frac{\log r}{\log \log r})$ queries are necessary even for adaptive testers when the range of f is restricted to $[r]$.

Proof of Theorem 6.11. For ease of presentation, assume n is a power of 2.

Let mon denote the monotonicity property of functions $f: [n] \to \mathbb{R}$. Due to Theorem 6.8 and Lemma 6.16, we will be done if we can show $\mathsf{CC}^{\to}(\mathrm{AUGINDEX}_{\log n}) \leq \mathsf{CC}^{\to}(C_\psi^{\mathrm{mon}})$ for a simple combining operator $\psi \colon \{[n] \to \{-1, 1\}\} \times \{[n] \to \mathbb{R} \times \{-1, 1\}\} \to \{[n] \to \mathbb{R}\}$. Define ψ as:

$$\psi[f, g](w) = 2 \cdot g_1(w) + f(w) \cdot g_2(w)$$

where we view $g = (g_1, g_2)$ with $g_1 \colon [n] \to \mathbb{R}$ and $g_2 \colon [n] \to \{-1, 1\}$.

For convenience, we will index $(\log n)$-bit strings from 0 to $\log n - 1$. We now give a reduction from $\mathrm{AUGINDEX}_{\log n}$ to C_ψ^{mon}. For the problem $\mathrm{AUGINDEX}_{\log n}$, suppose Alice is given as input $\alpha \in \{0, 1\}^{\log n}$ and Bob is given $i \in \{0, \ldots, \log n - 1\}$ as well as $\alpha_0, \ldots, \alpha_{i-1} \in \{0, 1\}$. Recall that the goal is for Bob to output α_i using a protocol that only sends bits from Alice to Bob.

Given $x \in [n]$, let $\bar{x} \in \{0, 1\}^{\log n}$ be the binary expansion of $x - 1$. For $x \in [n]$, we use the convention that $\bar{x}_0$ is the least significant bit of $x - 1$ and $\bar{x}_{\log n - 1}$ the most significant bit. Now, define:

$$f(x) = (-1)^{\sum_{j=0}^{\log n - 1} \alpha_j \bar{x}_j}$$

$$g_1(x) = \left\lfloor \frac{x-1}{2^{i+1}} \right\rfloor$$

$$g_2(x) = (-1)^{\sum_{j=0}^{i-1} \alpha_j \bar{x}_j}.$$

It is clear that Alice can compute f while Bob can compute g_1 and g_2. We claim that if Alice and Bob solve C_ψ^{mon} on inputs f and (g_1, g_2), then they can solve the AUGINDEX$_{\log n}$ problem. Let:

$$h(x) = \psi[f, (g_1, g_2)](x) = 2 \cdot \left\lfloor \frac{x-1}{2^{i+1}} \right\rfloor + (-1)^{\sum_{j=i}^{\log n - 1} \alpha_j \bar{x}_j}.$$

Claim 6.6. *If $\alpha_i = 0$, then $h = 2 \cdot g_1 + f \cdot g_2$ is monotone.*

Proof. Since $\alpha_i = 0$, $h(x) = 2 \cdot \left\lfloor \frac{x-1}{2^{i+1}} \right\rfloor + (-1)^{\sum_{j=i+1}^{\log n - 1} \alpha_j \bar{x}_j}$. We show $h(x+1) \geq h(x)$ for all $x \in [n-1]$. There are two cases.

- x **is a multiple of** 2^{i+1}: In this case, it is clear that:

$$\left\lfloor \frac{(x+1)-1}{2^{i+1}} \right\rfloor = 1 + \left\lfloor \frac{x-1}{2^{i+1}} \right\rfloor.$$

So, even if $(-1)^{\sum_{j=i+1}^{\log n - 1} \alpha_j \bar{x}_j}$ is 1 while $(-1)^{\sum_{j=i+1}^{\log n - 1} \alpha_j \overline{x+1}_j}$ is -1, overall, $h(x+1) - h(x) \geq 2 \cdot 1 - 2 = 0$.

- x **is not a multiple of** 2^{i+1}: In this case, $\left\lfloor \frac{(x+1)-1}{2^{i+1}} \right\rfloor = \left\lfloor \frac{x-1}{2^{i+1}} \right\rfloor$. Also, $\overline{x+1}$, the binary expansion of x, must have a 1 among coordinates $0, \ldots, i$. Since $x - 1 < x$, $\bar{x}$ must differ from $\overline{x+1}$ only in coordinates $0, \ldots, i$, and hence, $(-1)^{\sum_{j=i+1}^{\log n - 1} \alpha_j \overline{x+1}_j} = (-1)^{\sum_{j=i+1}^{\log n - 1} \alpha_j \bar{x}_j}$. So, $h(x+1) = h(x)$.

$\square$

Claim 6.7. *If $\alpha_i = 1$, then $h = 2 \cdot g_1 + f \cdot g_2$ is 1/4-far from being monotone.*

Proof. We show that:

$$\Pr_{0 \leq \ell < 2^{\log n - i - 1}} \left[\forall t \in [2^i], h(\ell \cdot 2^{i+1} + t) > h(\ell \cdot 2^{i+1} + 2^i + t) \right] \geq \frac{1}{2}. \quad (6.9)$$

This implies that there are at least $\frac{1}{2} \cdot 2^{\log n - i - 1} \cdot 2^i = n/4$ disjoint pairs of monotonicity violations, proving the claim.

For some fixed ℓ and t, let $x = \ell \cdot 2^{i+1} + t$ and $x' = \ell \cdot 2^{i+1} + 2^i + t$. Note that $\left\lceil \frac{x-1}{2^{i+1}} \right\rceil = \left\lceil \frac{x'-1}{2^{i+1}} \right\rceil = \ell$. Also, $\bar{x}$ and $\bar{x}'$ differ only at the i'th coordinate, where $\bar{x}_i = 0$ and $\bar{x}'_i = 1$. Thus:

Table 6.1: Examples of the function h for $n = 16$ and $i = 0$. Here, the functions h_{yes} and h_{no} àre constructed from $\alpha = (0,0,1,1)$ and $\alpha = (1,0,1,1)$, respectively. As $\alpha_i = 0$ for h_{yes}, h_{yes} is monotone. On the other hand, As $\alpha_i = 1$ for h_{no}, h_{no} is 1/4-far from being monotone.

x	1	2	3	4	5	6	7	8	9	10	11	12	13	14	15	16
$h_{\text{yes}}(x)$	1	1	3	3	3	3	5	5	7	7	9	9	13	13	15	15
$h_{\text{no}}(x)$	1	-1	3	1	3	5	5	7	7	9	9	11	13	11	15	13

$$(-1)^{\sum_{j \geq i} \alpha_j \overline{x}_j} = 1 \cdot (-1)^{\sum_{j > i} \alpha_j \overline{x}_j} = (-1)^{\langle \alpha_{>i}, \ell \rangle}$$

while

$$(-1)^{\sum_{j \geq i} \alpha_j \overline{x'}_j} = -1 \cdot (-1)^{\sum_{j > i} \alpha_j \overline{x'}_j} = -(-1)^{\langle \alpha_{>i}, \ell \rangle}$$

where $\alpha_{>i}$ is the restriction of α to the coordinates $\{i + 1, \ldots, \log n - 1\}$ and we have interpreted ℓ as the string given by its binary expansion. Then:

$$\Pr_{0 \leq \ell < 2^{\log n - i - 1}} \left[\forall j \in [2^i], h(\ell \cdot 2^{i+1} + j) > h(\ell \cdot 2^{i+1} + 2^i + j) \right]$$

$$= \Pr_{\ell \in \{0,1\}^{\log n - i - 1}} \left[(-1)^{\langle \alpha_{>i}, \ell \rangle} = 1 \right]$$

$$= \frac{1}{2} + \frac{1}{2} \mathbf{E}_{\ell} \left[(-1)^{\langle \alpha_{>i}, \ell \rangle} \right] \geq \frac{1}{2}$$

because $\mathbf{E}_{\ell} \left[(-1)^{\langle \alpha_{>i}, \ell \rangle} \right] = 0$ if $\alpha_{>i} \neq 0$ and is 1 if $\alpha_{>i} = 0$. $\qquad \square$

Table 6.1 depicts what h looks like when $\alpha_i = 1$ and when $\alpha_i = 0$.

Given these claims, a one-way protocol for C_ψ^{mon} implies a one-way protocol for $\text{AUGIND}_{\log n}$. $\qquad \square$

6.6 Additional Topics

Unateness

unateness

A function $f \colon [n]^d \to \mathbb{R}$ is *unate* if for every $i \in [d]$, the function is either non-increasing or non-decreasing in the i-th coordinate.

First we review results for testing unateness of Boolean functions on a hypercube $f \colon \{0,1\}^d \to \{0,1\}$. Goldreich, Goldwasser, Lehman, Ron, and Samorodnitsky [208] showed a non-adaptive one-sided error tester with query complexity $O(\epsilon^{-1} d^{3/2})$. Khot and Shinkar [281] improved the query complexity to $O(\epsilon^{-1} d \log d)$, albeit with an adaptive tester. Later, Chen, Waingarten,

Table 6.2: Testing unateness of a function $f: \{0,1\}^d \to \{0,1\}$

	Non-adaptive	Adaptive
One-sided error	$O\left(\epsilon^{-1}d^{3/2}\right)$ [208], $\widetilde{\Omega}(d)$ [128]	$\widetilde{O}\left(\epsilon^{-2}d^{3/4}\right)$ [129]
Two-sided error		$\widetilde{O}\left(\epsilon^{-2}d^{2/3}\right)$ [127], $\widetilde{\Omega}(d^{2/3})$ [128]

and Xie [129] gave an adaptive one-sided error tester with query complexity $\widetilde{O}(\epsilon^{-2}d^{3/4})$, and then Chen and Waingarten improved it to $\widetilde{O}(\epsilon^{-2}d^{2/3})$ [127]. As for lower bounds, it is known that we need $\widetilde{\Omega}(d^{2/3})$ queries in general and $\widetilde{\Omega}(d)$ queries for non-adaptive one-sided error testers [128]. The former almost settles the query complexity of testing unateness on a hypercube, and the latter shows that the adaptivity helps by a polynomial factor for testing unateness with one-sided error. These bounds are summarized in Table 6.2.

For testing unateness of functions $f: [n]^d \to \mathbb{R}$, Baleshzar, Chakrabarty, Pallavoor, Raskhodnikova, and Seshadhri [41] showed a non-adaptive tester with query complexity $O(\epsilon^{-1}d \cdot (\log(\epsilon^{-1}d) + \log n))$ and an adaptive tester with query complexity $O(\epsilon^{-1}d \log n)$, both one-sided. For the non-adaptive case, almost matching lower bound of $\Omega(d(\log d + \log n))$ was obtained [41].

Submodularity

A function $f: \{0,1\}^n \to \mathbb{R}$ is *submodular* if $f(\mathbf{1}_S) + f(\mathbf{1}_T) \geq f(\mathbf{1}_{S \cup T}) + f(\mathbf{1}_{S \cap T})$ for every $S, T \subseteq [n]$. Seshadhri and Vondrák studied testing submodularity and showed a non-adaptive one-sided error tester with query complexity $(1/\epsilon)^{O(\sqrt{n}\log n)}$ [372]. To improve the query complexity, several special cases have been studied. Raskhodnikova and Yaroslavtsev [353] showed that when the range is $\{0, 1, \ldots, k\}$ instead of $\mathbb{R}$, submodularity can be tested with $k^{O(\epsilon^{-1}k\log k)}$ queries. A function $f: \{0,1\}^n \to \mathbb{R}$ is called a *coverage function* if there exists an universe U and sets $A_1, \ldots, A_m \subseteq U$ such that $f(\mathbf{1}_S) = |\bigcup_{i \in S} A_i|$.

submodularity

coverage function

> **Exercise 6.15.** Show that any coverage function is submodular.

Chakrabarty and Huang [114] showed that the property of being a coverage function is testable with $O(n|U|)$ queries.

Fourier Sparsity

For a Boolean function $f\colon \mathbb{F}_2^n \to \{-1,1\}$, let $\mathrm{spec}(f)$ be the *Fourier spectrum* of f, that is, the set $\{\alpha \in \mathbb{F}_2^n : \hat{f}(\alpha) \neq 0\}$. (We write $\mathbb{F}_2$ rather than $\{0,1\}$ in this subsection for convenience.) A function $f\colon \mathbb{F}_2^n \to \{-1,1\}$ is said to be *k-dimensional* if $\mathrm{spec}(f)$ lies in a k-dimensional subspace of $\mathbb{F}_2^n$. A function f is said to be *s-sparse* if $|\mathrm{spec}(f)| \leq s$. Both notions represent sparsity in the Fourier domain. Note that k-dimensionality and s-sparsity are linear-invariant, that is, if $f\colon \mathbb{F}_2^n \to \{-1,1\}$ satisfies those properties then $f \circ A\colon x \mapsto f(Ax)$ also satisfies the properties, where $A \in \mathbb{F}_2^{n \times n}$ is any matrix. Gopalan, O'Donnell, Servedio, Shpilka, and Wimmer [225] showed that k-dimensionality is non-adaptively testable with $O(\epsilon^{-1} k 2^{2k})$ queries and that any (even adaptive) tester requires $\Omega(2^k/2)$ queries for $\epsilon = 0.49$. They also showed that s-sparsity is non-adaptively testable with $\mathrm{poly}(s, \epsilon^{-1})$ queries and that any (even adaptive) tester requires $\Omega(s)$ queries for $\epsilon = 0.49$.

For a Boolean function $f\colon \mathbb{F}_2^n \to \{-1,1\}$, denote by $\|\hat{f}\|_1$ the *spectral norm* of f, that is, $\sum_\alpha |\hat{f}(\alpha)|$.

Exercise 6.16. Show that an s-sparse function has spectral norm at most $\sqrt{s}$ and that a k-dimensional function has spectral norm at most $2^{k/2}$.

Wimmer and Yoshida [395] showed that the property of having spectral norm at most s is testable with $\mathrm{poly}(s, \epsilon^{-1})$ queries.

Isomorphism

For Boolean functions, we can consider two types of isomorphisms. The first one is isomorphism with respect to relabeling of variables and the second one is isomorphism with respect to linear transformations.

We first discuss isomorphism with respect to relabeling of variables. Here, we say that two functions $f, g\colon \{0,1\}^n \to \{0,1\}$ are *isomorphic* if for some permutation π over $[n]$, we have $f(x) = g(x_{\pi_1}, \ldots, x_{\pi_n})$ for every $x \in \{0,1\}^n$. We call the property of being isomorphic to g *g-isomorphism*.

Exercise 6.17. Show that, for any symmetric function $g\colon \{0,1\}^n \to \{0,1\}$, that is, $g(x) = g(x_{\pi_1}, \ldots, x_{\pi_n})$ for every permutation π over $[n]$, g-isomorphism is testable with $O(\epsilon^{-1})$ queries.

Fischer, Kindler, Ron, Safra, and Samorodnitsky [179] initiated the study of testing isomorphism with respect to relabeling of variables, and showed that if a function $g\colon \{0,1\}^n \to \{0,1\}$ is a k-junta, then we can non-adaptively test g-isomorphism with $\mathrm{poly}(\epsilon^{-1} k)$ queries. Alon, Blais, Chakraborty, García-

Soriano, and Matsliah [7] improved the query complexity to $O(k \log k)$. For a subset $S \subseteq [n]$, a function $f: \{0,1\}^n \to \{0,1\}$ is called *S-symmetric* if permuting the labels of the variables of S does not change the function. Moreover, f is called *k-symmetric* if there exists $S \subseteq [n]$ of size at least k such that f is S-symmetric. Note that $(n-k)$-symmetric functions encompass k-juntas and symmetric functions. The result for k-juntas [179] was extended to $(n-k)$-symmetric functions by Chakraborty, Fischer, García-Soriano, and Matsliah [117] and Blais, Weinstein, and Yoshida [91].

As for lower bounds, Alon, Blais, Chakraborty, García-Soriano, and Matsliah [7] showed that testing g-isomorphism for most k-juntas $g: \{0,1\}^n \to \{0,1\}$ requires $\Omega(k)$ queries, improving upon [179, 89]. They also considered general bounds regardless g. More specifically, they showed that the query complexity of testing isomorphism is $\widetilde{\Theta}(n)$.

We next discuss isomorphism with respect to linear transformations. Here, we say that two functions $f, g: \mathbb{F}_2^n \to \mathbb{F}_2$ are *isomorphic* if for some matrix $A \in \mathbb{F}_2^{n \times n}$, we have $f(x) = g(Ax)$ for every $x \in \mathbb{F}_2^n$. Wimmer and Yoshida [395] showed that, for any function $g: \mathbb{F}_2^n \to \{-1, 1\}$ with a spectral norm s, g-isomorphism is testable with $\text{poly}(s, \epsilon^{-1})$ queries. They also showed that if g is ϵ-far from having spectral norm at most s, then, testing g-isomorphism requires $\Omega(\log s)$ queries.

L_p-testing

When the range of a function is (a subset of) $\mathbb{R}$, it is natural to consider L_p norm for $p \geq 1$ as a distance measure. Specifically, we say that a function $f: [n]^d \to [0, 1]$ is ϵ-far from a property $\mathcal{P}$ if $\min_{g \in \mathcal{P}} \|f - g\|_p > \epsilon$, where $\|f\|_p = \left(\sum_{x \in [n]^d} f(x)^p \right)^{1/p}$ is the L_p norm of f. Berman, Raskhodnikova, and Yaroslavtsev [73] initiated the study of testing properties of functions with respect to the L_p norm. They showed that, for $p = 1, 2$, there is a non-adaptive one-sided error tester for the monotonicity of a function $f: [n] \to \mathbb{R}$ with query complexity $O(\epsilon^{-p})$ and that this query complexity is tight even for adaptive two-sided error testers. Note that the query complexity is constant as opposed to the Hamming distance case, which requires $\Omega(\epsilon^{-1} \log n)$ queries. Similarly, for functions over the hypergrid $[n]^d$, they showed a non-adaptive one-sided error tester with query complexity $O(\epsilon^{-p} d \log(\epsilon^{-p} d))$ and that this query complexity is tight for non-adaptive one-sided error testers.

Although the best query complexity for testing submodularity known to date is $(1/\epsilon)^{O(\sqrt{n} \log n)}$ [372], we can test submodularity with respect to L_p norm for $p \geq 1$ with $2^{\widetilde{O}(1/\epsilon^{\max\{2,p\}})}$ queries [87].

Table 6.3: Testing monotonicity of a function $f\colon \{0,1\}^n \to \{0,1\}$

	Non-adaptive	Adaptive
One-sided error	$\widetilde{O}(\epsilon^{-2}\sqrt{n})$ [280], $\Omega(\sqrt{n})$ [182]	$\Omega(n^{1/2-\delta})$ [123]
Two-sided error		$\widetilde{\Omega}(n^{1/3})$ [128]

6.7 Bibliographic Notes

As we already mentioned, the study of property testing originated with testing properties of functions in works by Blum, Luby and Rubinfeld [94] and by Rubinfeld and Sudan [368]. Below, we show references for each topic discussed in this chapter in order.

Monotonicity of Boolean functions

Testing monotonicity of Boolean functions $f\colon \{0,1\}^n \to \{0,1\}$ has a rich history. Goldreich, Goldwasser, Lehman, Ron, and Samorodnitsky [208] proposed the edge tester and showed that it is an $O(\epsilon^{-1}n)$ non-adaptive one-sided error tester. The analysis of the edge tester described in Section 6.1 is due to a note by Bhattacharyya [75]. Then, Fischer, Lehman, Newman, Raskhodnikova, Rubinfeld, and Samorodnitsky [182] showed that non-adaptive monotonicity testing with two-sided error and one-sided error require $\Omega(\log n)$ and $\Omega(\sqrt{n})$ queries, respectively. Chakrabarty and Seshadhri [116] improved the linear upper bound of [208] to $\widetilde{O}(\epsilon^{-3/2}n^{7/8})$ using a "pair tester", which looks for a pair (x,y) satisfying $x < y$ and $f(x) > f(y)$. Chen, Servedio, Tan [125] refined the analysis to obtain an $\widetilde{O}(\epsilon^{-4}n^{5/6})$ upper bound. They also gave an $\widetilde{\Omega}(n^{1/5})$ lower bound for non-adaptive testers. The lower bounds was improved by Chen, De, Servedio, and Tan [123] to $\Omega(n^{1/2-\delta})$ for any $\delta > 0$. Later Khot, Minzer, and Safra [280] obtained an upper bound of $\widetilde{O}(\epsilon^{-2}n^{1/2})$ via a deep analysis of the pair tester based on a new isoperimetric-type theorem. These results almost settled the query complexity of non-adaptive monotonicity testing over Boolean functions. For adaptive testers, Belovs and Blais [51] gave an $\widetilde{\Omega}(n^{1/4})$ lower bound, and then Chen, Waingarten, and Xie [128] gave an $\widetilde{\Omega}(n^{1/3})$ lower bound. The best results known to date are summarized in Table 6.3.

Monotonicity over hypercubes and hypergrids

Now, we review results on testing monotonicity of a function $f\colon [n]^d \to \mathbb{R}$. Dodis, Goldreich, Lehman, Raskhodnikova, Ron, and Samorodnitsky [159] generalized the analysis for Boolean functions [208] to show that $O(\epsilon^{-1}d^2 \log n)$ queries are sufficient. The upper bound was improved to $O(\epsilon^{-1}d \log n)$ by Chakrabarty and Seshadhri [115], which matches the lower bound of $\Omega(d \log n)$ due to Blais, Raskhodnikova, and Yaroslavtsev [90]. When the range is $\{0, 1\}$, Black, Chakrabarty, and Seshadhri [84] obtained a $\widetilde{O}(d^{5/6}) \cdot$ poly(ϵ^{-1})-query tester, which is sublinear in d and independent of n.

Linearity and Homomorphisms

The BLR tester explained in Section 6.3 was proposed by Blum, Luby, and Rubinfeld [94], which was originally designed for testing whether a function $f \colon G \to H$ is a homomorphism for finite groups G and H. The number of queries depends on the number of generators of G, which may depend on the size of G in general. Ben-Or, Coppersmith, Luby, and Rubinfeld [57] gave another algorithm without such a dependency. Bellare, Coppersmith, Håstad, Kiwi, and Sudan [46] gave a Fourier-analytic proof of the BLR tester, which is described in Section 6.3.1, when the domain and the range are $\mathbb{F}_2^n$ and $\mathbb{F}_2$, respectively. Oono and Yoshida [339] generalize the analysis to functions over finite groups using representation theory. Rubinfeld [366] studied properties of a function on a finite group defined by functional equations, which are generalizations of being homomorphic, and gave a sufficient condition of constant-query testability.

There has been an interest in improving parameters of homomorphism testing, due to their applications in the construction of probabilistically checkable proof (PCP) [31]. Bellare, Coppersmith, Håstad, Kiwi, and Sudan [46] gave an almost tight connection between the distance to homomorphism and the rejection probability of the BLR tester. Ben-Sasson, Sudan, Vadhan, and Wigderson [68] and Shpilka and Wigderson [373] reduced the number of random bits required by the test as it affects the efficiency of the proof system and in turn the hardness of approximation results that one can achieve using the proof system.

Fleming and Yoshida [187] studied distribution-free testing of linearity of functions on $\mathbb{R}^n$. For a distribution $\mathcal{D}$ over $\mathbb{R}^n$, we define the distance between two (measurable) functions $f, g \colon \mathbb{R}^n \to \mathbb{R}$ as $\Pr_{x \sim \mathcal{D}}[f(x) \neq g(x)]$. Then, we want to design an algorithm that, given query access to the input function $f \colon \mathbb{R}^n \to \mathbb{R}$, sampling access to a distribution $\mathcal{D}$ over $\mathbb{R}^n$, and $\epsilon > 0$, accepts with high probability if f is linear, and rejects with high probability if f is ϵ-far from being linear, that is, the distance to any linear function with respect to $\mathcal{D}$ is more than ϵ. They showed that the linearity can be tested with $\widetilde{O}(\epsilon^{-1})$ queries for any distribution $\mathcal{D}$.

Juntas

The problem of testing k-juntas was introduced by Fischer, Kindler, Ron, Safra, and Samorodnitsky [179] and they showed an $\epsilon^{-1}\mathrm{poly}(k)$-query tester. Blais [85] gave a non-adaptive tester with query complexity $O(\epsilon^{-1}k^{3/2})$ and he gave an adaptive $O(k\log k + \epsilon^{-1}k)$-query tester [86]. The argument in Section 6.4 is based on the analysis of the latter tester. On the hardness side, Fischer, Kindler, Ron, Safra, and Samorodnitsky [179] initially gave an $\Omega(\sqrt{k})$ lower bound for non-adaptive testing, which also implies an $\Omega(\log k)$ lower bound for adaptive testing. The adaptive lower bound was improved to $\Omega(k)$ by Chockler and Gutfreund [132] and then to $\Omega(k\log k)$ by Sağlam [370], and the non-adaptive lower bound was improved to $\widetilde{\Omega}(\epsilon^{-1}k^{3/2})$ by Chen, Servedio, Tan, Waingarten, Xie [126]. Thus in both the adaptive and non-adaptive cases, the query complexity has been settled to within logarithmic factors.

Liu, Chen, Servedio, Sheng, and Xie [303] studied testing k-juntas in the distribution-free setting, and showed that k-juntas are adaptively testable with $O(\epsilon^{-1}k^2)$ queries whereas any non-adaptive tester requires $\Omega(2^{k/3})$ queries. Bshouty [106] improved the query complexity to $\widetilde{O}(\epsilon^{-1}k)$.

Blais, Weinstein, and Yoshida [91] showed that $(n-k)$-symmetric functions (see the isomorphism section in Additional Topics for the definition) are testable with $O((\epsilon^{-1}k) \cdot \log(\epsilon^{-1}k))$ queries, improving the bound given in [117].

Lower bounds

Since the notion of communication complexity was introduced by Yao [396], it has been applied to many other areas, including circuit and formula complexity, VLSI design, proof complexity, and streaming algorithms. See the excellent book of Kushilevitz and Nisan [292] for more details on these applications and communication complexity in general.

The argument in Section 6.5 is based on the work by Blais, Brody, and Matulef [88]. Since they showed connections between property testing and communication complexity, lower bounds for many properties are shown via communication complexity, including Lipschitzness [269], approximating the number of relevant variables [362], and testing codes [206, 236]. By using a variant of the argument in Section 6.5.3, Brody and Hatami [104] have improved the lower bound for monotonicity over hypercubes to $\Omega(\epsilon^{-1}n)$, which is tight both in its dependence on n and ϵ. A general frame

Problems

6.1. Show that we can test whether a function $f\colon \{0,1\}^n \to \{0,1\}$ is affine with $O(\epsilon^{-1})$ queries.

6.2. Extend the proof of Lemma 6.4 to the case that G and H are non-abelian.

6.3. Show that linearity of functions $f\colon \{0,1\}^n \to \{0,1\}$ is testable with $O(\epsilon^{-1})$ queries in the distribution-free setting (See Definition 1.5). (**Hint:** Provide query access to a linear function close to f by applying the self-correction technique.)

6.4. In this problem, you are asked to design a constant-query tester for dictatorship of functions $f\colon \{0,1\}^n \to \{0,1\}$. The function f is a dictator if $f(x) = x_i$ for some $i \in [n]$.

1. Show that a function $f\colon \{0,1\}^n \to \{0,1\}$ is a dictator if and only if (i) $\Pr_x[f(x) = 1] = 1/2$ and (ii) $f(x \wedge y) = f(x) \wedge f(y)$ for every $x, y \in \{0,1\}^n \to \{0,1\}$, where $x \wedge y$ is a coordinate-wise AND operation.
2. Suppose $f\colon \{0,1\}^n \to \{0,1\}$ is a linear function of the form $f(x) = \sum_{i \in S} x_i \pmod 2$ for $S \subseteq [n]$. Then show that, if $|S|$ is even, then

$$\Pr[f(x \wedge y) = f(x) \wedge f(y)] = \frac{1}{2} + \frac{1}{2^{|S|+1}},$$

and if $|S|$ is odd, then

$$\Pr[f(x \wedge y) = f(x) \wedge f(y)] = \frac{1}{2} + \frac{1}{2^{|S|}}.$$

3. Show that dictatorship is testable with $O(\epsilon^{-1})$ queries by first testing linearity and then using the self-corrected function (see Section 6.3.2) to test for dictatorship.

6.5. Consider the following "Not-All-Equal (NAE)" test: Given query access to $f\colon \{-1,1\}^n \to \{-1,1\}$, sample $x,y,z \in \{-1,1\}^n$ so that each (x_i, y_i, z_i) $(i \in [n])$ is uniformly and independently distributed over $\{-1,1\}^3 \setminus \{(-1,-1,-1),(1,1,1)\}$, and then accept if and only if $(f(x), f(y), f(z)) \in \{-1,1\}^3 \setminus \{(-1,-1,-1),(1,1,1)\}$.

1. Show that

$$\Pr[\text{the NAE test accepts}] = \frac{3}{4} - \frac{3}{4} \sum_{S \subseteq [n]} \left(-\frac{1}{3}\right)^{|S|} \hat{f}(S)^2.$$

2. Show that, if the NAE test accepts with probability at least $1 - \epsilon$ for $\epsilon \geq 0$, then we have $\sum_{|S|=1} \hat{f}(S)^2 \geq 1 - \frac{9}{2}\epsilon$.

3. Design an $O(\epsilon^{-1})$-query tester for dictatorship based on the BLR tester and the NAE test.

6.6. Consider the following 'dictatorship test' for functions $f\colon \{\pm 1\}^n \to \{\pm 1\}$. It is not a standard property tester, but nevertheless, it plays a key role in the theory of probabilistically checkable proofs.

Choose $x, y \in \{\pm 1\}^n$ uniformly at random. Choose $\eta \in \{\pm 1\}^n$ such that for each i, $\eta_i = 1$ with probability $1 - \epsilon/2$ and $\eta_i = -1$ with probability $\epsilon/2$. Accept if $f(x) \cdot f(y) \cdot f(xy\eta) = 1$ where $xy\eta$ is the component-wise product of the three vectors.

Argue that if the tester accepts with probability $\frac{1}{2} + \delta$, there exists a set $S \subseteq [n]$ such that $|S| = O(\epsilon^{-1} \log \delta^{-1})$ and $|\hat{f}(S)| \geq \Omega(\delta)$.

6.7. Show $\Omega(\epsilon^{-1})$ lower bound for testing linearity of functions $f\colon \{0,1\}^n \to \{0,1\}$. (**Hint**: Use the fact that two linear functions have distance 2^{n-1} and the idea behind Theorem 2.6.)

6.8. Prove Lemma 6.9 by directly using the definition of Fourier coefficients.

6.9. Show that, if a function $f\colon \{0,1\}^n \to \{0,1\}$ is ϵ-close to a k-junta on a subset S, then the influence of $\overline{S}$ is at most ϵ.

6.10. For a function $h\colon \{0,1\}^n \to \{0,1\}^2$, consider the property that the two functions $h_1, h_2 \colon \{0,1\}^n \to \{0,1\}$ are boolean functions sharing no common relevant variables. Show that testing this property requires $\Omega(n)$ queries.

6.11. Show that Lemma 6.16 holds even when ψ is of the form $\psi[f,g](w) = \sum_{u \in A_w} f(u) + \sum_{v \in B_w} g(v)$ for sets $A_w, B_w \subseteq \{0,1\}^n$.

6.12. Complete the proof of Theorem 6.9 by extending it to odd k.

6.13. In this problem, you are asked to show that the hardness shown in Section 6.5.3 holds even when the functions are restricted to have range $[-R, R]$ where $R = \sqrt{n}$. Taking $\psi[f,g](x) = 2|x| + f(x) + g(x)$ as in the text, let:

$$\psi'[f,g](x) = \begin{cases} -\sqrt{n}, & \text{if } |x| \leq \frac{n}{2} - \frac{\sqrt{n}}{2} \\ \sqrt{n}, & \text{if } |x| \geq \frac{n}{2} + \frac{\sqrt{n}}{2} \\ \psi[f,g](x) - n, & \text{otherwise} \end{cases}$$

Argue that the reduction from the set disjointness problem holds for the ψ' combining operator also.

6.14. Suppose $\mathbb{F}$ is a finite field of order q. A function $f : \mathbb{F}^n \to \mathbb{F}$ is said to be in the *Reed-Muller code* of degree d on n variables over $\mathbb{F}$, denoted $\mathsf{RM}_{q,d,n}$, if it is a a polynomial of degree[8] at most d.

Reed-Muller code

---

[8] More precisely, total degree, meaning the maximum sum of the degrees of the variables in any monomial.

We study the problem of testing $RM_{q,d,n}$ in detail later in Chapter 12, but here, you will see a different self-correction-based analysis, in the same spirit as the result for linearity in Section 6.3.2. You will need the following result which we state below without proof.

Theorem 6.12. *Suppose $q > 2d$. A function $f : \mathbb{F}^n \to \mathbb{F}$ is in $RM_{q,d,n}$ if and only if for all $x, h \in \mathbb{F}^n$:*

$$\sum_{i=0}^{d+1}(-1)^{i+1}\binom{d+1}{i} \cdot f(x+ih) = 0 \tag{6.10}$$

Theorem 6.12 suggests a natural test: pick x, h uniformly at random from $\mathbb{F}_q^n$ and check if it satisfies (6.10). Clearly, the test accepts when f is in the property. The parts below guide you through the test of the analysis. Let ρ_f be the probability that the tester rejects.

(a) For $x, h \in \mathbb{F}^n$, define:

$$v_h(x) = \sum_{i=1}^{d+1}(-1)^{i+1}\binom{d+1}{i}f(x+ih); \qquad v(x) = \arg\max_{v\in\mathbb{F}}|\{h : v_h(x) = v\}|$$

Argue that $\Pr_x[f(x) \neq h(x)] \leq 2\rho_f$.

(b) Prove the claim that for any $x \in \mathbb{F}^n$:

$$\Pr_h[v(x) = v_h(x)] \geq 1 - 2(d+1)\rho_f$$

Analogously to the proof of Lemma 6.6, obtain this by showing the lower bound for $\Pr_{h_1,h_2}[v_{h_1}(x) = v_{h_2}(x)]$. Towards this end, argue first that if:

$$u_{h_1,h_2}(x) = \sum_{i=1}^{d+1}\sum_{j=1}^{d+1}(-1)^{i+j}\binom{d+1}{i}\binom{d+1}{j}f(x+ih_1+jh_2),$$

then both $\Pr_{h_1,h_2}[v_{h_1}(x) = u_{h_1,h_2}(x)]$ and $\Pr_{h_1,h_2}[v_{h_2}(x) = u_{h_1,h_2}(x)]$ are at least $1 - (d+1)\rho_f$.

(c) Analogously to the proof of Lemma 6.7, you can use part (b) above to show that v satisfies the criterion in (6.10) and hence is in $RM_{q,d,n}$.
Fix $x, h \in \mathbb{F}^n$. Let h_1, h_2 be uniformly drawn from $\mathbb{F}^n$. Observe that for every $i \in [d+1]$,

$$v(x+ih) = v_{h_1+ih_2}(x+ih)$$

holds with probability at least $1 - 2(d+1)\rho_f$ from part (b).
Also, prove for any j:

$$\Pr\left[\sum_{i=0}^{d+1}(-1)^{i+1}\binom{d+1}{i}f(x+ih+j(h_1+ih_2)) = 0\right] = 1 - \rho_f$$

Put these pieces together to show that

$$\Pr_{h_1, h_2}\left[\sum_{i=0}^{d+1}(-1)^{i+1}\binom{d+1}{i}v(x+ih) = 0\right]$$

is at least $1 - O(d^2 \rho)$. Hence, conclude that that if f is ϵ-far from $\mathsf{RM}_{q,d,n}$, then the rejection probability ρ_f is at least[9] $\Omega(\epsilon)$.

---

[9] Where the constant in the $\Omega(\cdot)$ depends on d.

Chapter 7
Massively Parameterized Model

In this chapter, we study *massively parameterized models*. A crucial difference of massively parameterized models from the models we have seen so far is that, even after fixing the input size n, we need a large number of parameters, that is, a function of n, to determine the property to be tested.

massively
parameterized models

As a simple example, let us consider the problem of testing whether a vertex labeling $f\colon V \to \{0,1\}$ on a bipartite graph $G = (V, E)$ is a (proper) 2-coloring, that is, $f(u) \neq f(v)$ for every $\{u, v\} \in E$. The property to be tested consists of 2-colorings on G and is determined by $\Theta(n^2)$ parameters, that is, whether an edge exists between each pair of vertices in V. We assume that an algorithm is given the whole bipartite graph G, an error parameter $\epsilon \in (0, 1)$, and query access to a labeling $f\colon V \to \{0,1\}$, which might not be a 2-coloring. Then, the goal is to test whether f is a 2-coloring or far from being so. We will see in Section 7.1 that there is a constant-query tester for 2-coloring.

The example above can be seen as a problem such that an induced subgraph of a fixed graph is given through query access and the goal is to test whether the induced subgraph is 2-colorable. This problem can be motivated in a circumstance where the fixed graph represents an existing network, and the subgraph represents the nodes that are actually in operation. Then naturally, we want to minimize the number of checks to see the nodes are in operation.

In Section 7.2, we study testing whether a labeling $f\colon V \to \{0,1\}$ on a directed acyclic subgraph (DAG) $G = (V, E)$ is monotone. Here, f is said to be *monotone* if $f(u) \leq f(v)$ holds for every arc $(u, v) \in E$. Again, the property to be tested consists of monotone labelings on G and is determined by $\Theta(n^2)$ parameters. This problem can be seen as a generalization of testing monotonicity of a function studied in Sections 3.5 and 6.1. We will see that monotonicity of a labeling is testable with $O(\sqrt{n})$ queries and is not testable with $o\left(\frac{\log n}{\log \log n}\right)$ queries.

monotonicity

As an example of a massively parameterized property that is not testable with a sublinear number of queries, in Section 7.3, we see that testing whether a vector $x \in \mathbb{F}_2^n$ given as query access belongs to an explicitly specified subspace $V \subseteq \mathbb{F}_2^n$ requires $\Omega(n)$ queries. Here, V determines the property to be tested.

All these problems can be seen as a problem of testing whether an assignment to an instance of a (Boolean) constraint satisfaction problem (CSP) is a satisfying assignment. In Section 7.4, we formally introduce testing assignments to constraint satisfaction problems, and see that 2-SAT is testable with $O(\sqrt{n})$ queries whereas 3-SAT requires $\Omega(n)$ queries. Later in Chapter 13, we will classify all the Boolean CSPs in terms of query complexity using a mathematical theory called universal algebra.

7.1 2-Coloring

2-colorability

Let $G = (V, E)$ be a graph and $f \colon V \to \{0, 1\}$ be a vertex labeling with two labels. We say that f is a (proper) 2-*coloring* of G if $f(u) \neq f(v)$ for every $\{u, v\} \in E$. In this section, we consider testing whether a vertex labeling on a graph is a 2-coloring or is far from being so, and show that there is a tester for this problem that queries f a constant number of times. Note that, if the input graph is not bipartite, then the problem is uninteresting because no 2-coloring exists. Henceforth, we assume that the input graph is bipartite.

Let us formally define the problem. Let $G = (V, E)$ be a bipartite graph on n vertices. Then, we define $\mathcal{P}_{G,2\mathrm{col}}$ as the set of 2-colorings of G. Note that $\mathcal{P}_{G,2\mathrm{col}}$ is non-empty because G is bipartite. For $\epsilon \in (0, 1)$, we say that a vertex

ϵ-farness

tester for 2-coloring

labeling $f \colon V \to \{0, 1\}$ is ϵ-*far from being a 2-coloring* if $d_{\mathrm{H}}(f, \mathcal{P}_{G,2\mathrm{col}}) > \epsilon n$. Then, we say that an algorithm is a *tester for 2-coloring* if, given a bipartite graph $G = (V, E)$, an error parameter $\epsilon \in (0, 1)$, and query access to a vertex labeling $f \colon V \to \{0, 1\}$, it accepts with probability at least $2/3$ when f is a 2-coloring of G, and rejects with probability at least $2/3$ when f is ϵ-far from being a 2-coloring.

In order to get the idea of the tester, suppose that the bipartite input graph $G = (V, E)$ on n vertices is connected. Then, for the unique bipartition (L, R) of V, we only have the following two 2-colorings:

$$f_1(u) = \begin{cases} 0 & u \in L, \\ 1 & u \in R, \end{cases} \quad \text{and} \quad f_2(u) = \begin{cases} 1 & u \in L, \\ 0 & u \in R. \end{cases}$$

Suppose that the vertex labeling $f \colon V \to \{0, 1\}$ is ϵ-far from being a 2-coloring. Then, we have $d_{\mathrm{H}}(f, f_1) > \epsilon n$ and $d_{\mathrm{H}}(f, f_2) > \epsilon n$. This implies we can reject with high probability because we can find a vertex $u_1 \in V$ with $f(u_1) \neq f_1(u_1)$ and a vertex $u_2 \in V$ with $f(u_2) \neq f_2(u_2)$ by sampling a constant number of vertices.

In the general case that we may have several connected components, we need a more delicate argument. For a vertex labeling $f \colon V \to \{0, 1\}$ and a set of vertices $S \subseteq V$, we define $f|_S \colon S \to \{0,1\}$ as the function whose domain is restricted to S. For a vertex $v \in V$, let C_v be the connected component containing v. Then, the following proposition states that if a vertex labeling $f \colon V \to \{0,1\}$ is ϵ-far from being a 2-coloring, then the expected farness of a randomly sampled connected component is more than ϵ:

Proposition 7.1. *Let $G = (V, E)$ be a bipartite graph on n vertices and $f \colon V \to \{0,1\}$ be a vertex labeling. If f is ϵ-far from being a 2-coloring, then we have:*
$$\mathop{\mathbf{E}}_{v \in V} \left[\delta_{\mathrm{H}}(f|_{C_v}, \mathcal{P}_{G[C_v], 2\mathrm{col}}) \right] > \epsilon.$$

Exercise 7.1. Prove Proposition 7.1.

We also need the following simple proposition on a random variable.

Proposition 7.2. *Let X be a random variable taking values in $[0,1]$ such that $\mathbf{E}[X] > \epsilon$ for $\epsilon \in (0,1)$. Then, $\Pr[X > \epsilon/2] > \epsilon/2$ holds.*

Exercise 7.2. Prove Proposition 7.2.

Now, we show that we can reduce the original problem to the problem in which the bipartite input graph is connected:

Lemma 7.1. *Suppose that there exists a tester $\mathcal{T}$ for 2-coloring with query complexity $q(\epsilon)$, provided that the bipartite input graph is connected. Then, there exists a tester $\mathcal{T}'$ for 2-coloring with query complexity $O(\epsilon^{-1} q(\epsilon/2))$ for any input graph. Moreover, the reduction preserves one-sided error testability.*

Proof. The tester $\mathcal{T}'$ for 2-coloring is as follows: Given a bipartite graph $G = (V, E)$, an error parameter $\epsilon \in (0,1)$, and query access to f, we first sample a set S of $\Theta(\epsilon^{-1})$ vertices uniformly at random. For each vertex $v \in S$, we run $\mathcal{T}$ with an error parameter $\epsilon/2$ on the input whose domain is restricted to C_v. We reject if $\mathcal{T}$ rejects for some $v \in S$, and we accept otherwise.

The algorithm above always accepts when f is a 2-coloring, and the query complexity is at most $O(\epsilon^{-1} q(\epsilon/2))$.

We show that the tester $\mathcal{T}'$ rejects with probability at least $2/3$ when G is ϵ-far. From Proposition 7.1, we have $\mathbf{E}_{v \in V}[\delta_{\mathrm{H}}(f|_{C_v}, \mathcal{P}_{G[C_v], 2\mathrm{col}})] > \epsilon$. Then, $\Pr[\delta_{\mathrm{H}}(f|_{C_v}, \mathcal{P}_{G[C_v], 2\mathrm{col}}) > \epsilon/2] > \epsilon/2$ holds from Proposition 7.2 since $\delta_{\mathrm{H}}(f|_{C_v}, \mathcal{P}_{G[C_v], 2\mathrm{col}}) \in [0,1]$ for any $v \in V$. For a vertex $v \in V$ with $\delta_{\mathrm{H}}(f|_{C_v}, \mathcal{P}_{G[C_v]}) > \epsilon/2$, the tester $\mathcal{T}$ rejects with probability at least $2/3$. Thus, $\mathcal{T}'$ rejects with probability at least $1 - (1 - 2/3 \cdot \epsilon/2)^{\Theta(\epsilon^{-1})} \geq 2/3$ by setting the hidden constant to be large enough. $\qquad\square$

The following lemma for the connected case formalizes the idea discussed at the beginning of this section.

Lemma 7.2. *Provided that the bipartite input graph is connected, there exists a one-sided error tester for 2-coloring with query complexity $O(\epsilon^{-1})$.*

Proof. Let $G = (V, E)$ be the input graph. As we have observed, there are only two (proper) 2-colorings $f_1, f_2 \colon V \to \{0, 1\}$ for G.

The tester is as follows: We sample $\Theta(\epsilon^{-1})$ vertices uniformly at random, and then check whether they are consistent with either of f_1 and f_2. More specifically, we reject if we have sampled two vertices u_1 and u_2 such that $f(u_1) \neq f_1(u_1)$ and $f(u_2) \neq f_2(u_2)$, and we accept otherwise.

The tester always accepts when f is a 2-coloring, and the query complexity is $O(\epsilon^{-1})$.

Suppose that f is ϵ-far from being a 2-coloring. Then, we have $\Pr_{u \in V}[f(u) \neq f_i(u)] > \epsilon$ for each $i \in \{1, 2\}$. By the union bound, the probability that we do not sample two vertices u_1 and u_2 with $f(u_1) \neq f_1(u_1)$ and $f(u_2) \neq f_2(u_2)$ is bounded from above by:

$$2(1 - \epsilon)^{O(\epsilon^{-1})} \leq \frac{1}{3}$$

by setting the hidden constant in the query complexity to be large enough. $\square$

Combining Lemmas 7.1 and 7.2, we get the following:

Theorem 7.1. *There exists a one-sided error tester for 2-coloring with query complexity $O(\epsilon^{-2})$.*

You will be asked to improve the query complexity to $\tilde{O}(\epsilon^{-1})$ (Problem 7.1).

The reason that we succeeded to obtain a constant-query tester is that, if the bipartite graph is connected, then the number of 2-colorings is constant no matter how large the graph is. In the subsequent sections, we study properties whose labelings exhibit a more complicated structure.

7.2 Monotonicity

monotonicity

Let $G = (V, E)$ be a directed acyclic graph (DAG). Then, a labeling $f \colon V \to \{0, 1\}$ on vertices is called *monotone* if $f(u) \leq f(v)$ for every arc $(u, v) \in E$. In this section, we consider testing monotonicity on a given DAG G. The reason that we only consider DAGs is that otherwise no monotone labeling exists.

We formally define the problem. For a DAG $G = (V, E)$, let $\mathcal{P}_{G,\mathrm{mon}}$ be the set of monotone labelings. Note that $\mathcal{P}_{G,\mathrm{mon}}$ is non-empty because G

is a DAG. For $\epsilon \in (0,1)$, we say that $f\colon V \to \{0,1\}$ is ϵ-*far from being monotone* if $d_{\mathrm{H}}(f, \mathcal{P}_{G,\mathrm{mon}}) > \epsilon n$. Then, we say that an algorithm is a *tester for monotonicity* if, given a DAG $G = (V, E)$, an error parameter $\epsilon \in (0,1)$, and query access to a labeling $f\colon V \to \{0,1\}$, it accepts with probability at least $2/3$ when f is monotone, and rejects with probability at least $2/3$ when f is ϵ-far from being monotone.

ϵ-farness
tester for
monotonicity

Apparently, monotonicity is a more complicated property than 2-colorings because, even when the input graph is connected, there could be an exponential number of monotone labelings. (To see this, think of a star graph whose all edges are directed toward the center.) Indeed, monotonicity is not testable with a constant number of queries, and we see in Section 7.2.1 that every non-adaptive tester requires $n^{\Omega(\frac{\log n}{\log\log n})}$ queries (and hence every adaptive tester requires $\Omega(\frac{\log n}{\log\log n})$ queries). The proof requires a tool from graph theory called Ruzsa-Szemerédi graphs. On the other hand, as we will see in Section 7.2.2, it is testable with $O(\sqrt{n})$ queries, which is sublinear in n.

Testing monotonicity over DAGs studied in this section is a natural generalization of testing monotonicity of Boolean-valued functions over the line and hypercubes studied in Sections 1.6.2 and 6.1, respectively. We note that the non-adaptive lower bound of $n^{\Omega(\frac{\log n}{\log\log n})}$ mentioned above implies testing monotonicity over DAGs is harder than testing monotonicity over lines and hypercubes because they can be non-adaptively solved with $O(1)$ and $O(\log n)$ queries, respectively (here n is the number of vertices in the hypercube, not the dimension).

7.2.1 Super-Constant Lower Bounds

In this section, we show that there is no constant-query tester for monotonicity on DAGs.

To this end, we first introduce Ruzsa-Szemerédi graphs. We then show that monotonicity over such graphs (with suitable parameters) is hard to test non-adaptively with a constant number of queries. This will also imply that monotonicity is hard to test adaptively with a constant number of queries.

Let $U = (V, E)$ be an undirected graph and let $M \subseteq E$ be a matching in U. Let $V(M)$ be the set of the endpoints of edges in M. A matching M in U is called *induced* if the induced graph $U[V(M)]$ contains only the edges of M. Namely, for any $u, v \in V(M)$, $\{u, v\} \in E$ holds if and only if $\{u, v\} \in M$ holds. A (bipartite) graph $U = (X, Y; E)$ is called (s,t)-*Ruzsa-Szemerédi* if its edge set can be partitioned into at least s induced matchings $M_1, \ldots, M_s$, each of size at least t.

induced matching

Ruzsa-Szemerédi
graph

A construction of a Ruzsa-Szemerédi graph with the following parameter is known:

Lemma 7.3. *For infinitely many n, there exists an $(n^{\Omega(1/\log\log n)}, n/3 - o(1))$-Ruzsa-Szemerédi graph $U = (L, R; E)$ with $|L| = |R| = n$.*

violating arc

We say that an arc (u, v) in a DAG $G = (V, E)$ is *violating* with respect to a labeling $f \colon V \to \{0, 1\}$ if $f(u) > f(v)$. If we have found a violating arc, we can immediately reject. However, the following lemma states that it is hard to find violating arcs in a DAG constructed from a Ruzsa-Szemerédi graphs.

Lemma 7.4. *Let $U = (L, R; E)$ be an $(s, \epsilon n)$-Ruzsa-Szemerédi graph with $|L| = |R| = n$. Direct all edges of U from L to R to obtain a bipartite DAG G. Then, any non-adaptive tester for monotonicity on G requires $\Omega(\sqrt{s})$ queries.*

Proof. By Yao's minimax principle (Corollary 2.1), it suffices present two input distributions $\mathcal{D}_Y$ and $\mathcal{D}_N$ such that $\mathcal{D}_Y$ consists of monotone labelings and $\mathcal{D}_N$ (almost) consists of labelings far from being monotone and any deterministic tester with query complexity $q := o(\sqrt{s})$ cannot distinguish them with high probability.

Now, we define the distributions $\mathcal{D}_Y$ and $\mathcal{D}_N$. For both distributions, we first choose a random $i \in [s]$ uniformly at random. Set $f(u) = 0$ for every $u \in L \setminus V(M_i)$, and set $f(v) = 1$ for every $v \in R \setminus V(M_i)$. For $\mathcal{D}_Y$, uniformly choose $f(u) = f(v) = 0$ or $f(u) = f(v) = 1$ independently for each edge $\{u, v\} \in M_i$. For $\mathcal{D}_N$, uniformly choose $(f(u), f(v)) = (0, 1)$ or $(f(u), f(v)) = (1, 0)$ independently for each edge $\{u, v\} \in M_i$.

Note that $\mathcal{D}_Y$ is supported only on monotone labelings. Although $\mathcal{D}_N$ is not supported only on negative labelings, for n large enough, with probability more than 0.99 at least $1/3$ of the arcs made from M_i are violating when the input is chosen according to $\mathcal{D}_N$, making it $\epsilon/6$-far from being monotone. Since the matchings are induced, for $\mathcal{D}_N$, an arc is violating only if it belongs to M_i.

Let us consider a deterministic non-adaptive tester A that makes a set S of q queries. The probability that one or more of M_i's arcs have both endpoints in S is at most $q^2/(4s)$ for both $\mathcal{D}_Y$ and $\mathcal{D}_N$. This is because the matchings are disjoint, and the vertex set S induces at most $q^2/4$ arcs of G. For the choice of q, with probability more than 0.99, no arc of M_i has both endpoints in S. Conditioned on any choice of i for which M_i has no such arc, the distribution of $f|_S$ is identical for both $\mathcal{D}_Y$ and $\mathcal{D}_N$: every vertex outside of M_i has value 0 if it is in L and 1 if it is in R, and the value of every other vertex is uniform and independent over $\{0, 1\}$. Then for any partial labeling $\phi \colon S \to \{0, 1\}$, we have

$$\Pr_{f \sim \mathcal{D}_Y}[f|_S = \phi \mid E(G[S]) \cap M_i = \emptyset] = \Pr_{f \sim \mathcal{D}_N}[f|_S = \phi \mid E(G[S]) \cap M_i = \emptyset],$$

and hence we have

$$\left| \Pr_{f \sim \mathcal{D}_Y} [A \text{ accepts on } f] - \Pr_{f \sim \mathcal{D}_N} [A \text{ accepts on } f] \right| \leq 0.01,$$

which gives the desired lower bound. $\square$

> **Theorem 7.2.** *For infinitely many n, there exists a DAG G on n vertices such that*
>
> - *Every non-adaptive tester for monotonicity on G requires $n^{\Omega(1/\log \log n)}$ queries;*
> - *Every (adaptive) tester for monotonicity on G requires $\Omega\left(\frac{\log n}{\log \log n}\right)$ queries.*

Proof. The first claim is obtained by combining Lemmas 7.3 and 7.4.

To show the second claim, note that any deterministic adaptive tester with q queries can be simulated by a non-adaptive tester with 2^q queries because the input labeling $f \colon V \to \{0,1\}$ is Boolean, that is, we simply query all the vertices that are possibly queried by the adaptive tester. Hence, we get a lower bound of $\log\left(n^{\Omega(1/\log \log n)}\right) = \Omega\left(\frac{\log n}{\log \log n}\right)$ for deterministic adaptive testers. We can get the same lower bound for randomized adaptive testers because, by flipping the internal coin before querying, we can reduce the argument to the one for deterministic testers. $\square$

7.2.2 Sublinear Upper Bounds

In this section, we show that monotonicity is testable with $O(\sqrt{n})$ queries.

To understand the difficulty in testing monotonicity on a general DAG, consider the following natural algorithm: Sample q arcs uniformly and independently for sufficiently large q, and then reject if and only if some sampled arc is violating.

Unfortunately, in order to make this algorithm a valid tester for monotonicity, we need to set q to be linear in the graph size. To see this, suppose that the input DAG $G = (\{v_1, \ldots, v_n\}, E)$ is a directed path of length $n - 1$, that is, $E = \{(v_i, v_{i+1}) : i \in [n-1]\}$. Then, we set $f(v_i) = 1$ if $i \leq n/2$ and $f(v_i) = 0$ otherwise. It is clear that f is roughly $(1/2)$-far from monotone labelings because we need to have $f(v_i) \leq f(v_j)$ for every $i < j$ in a monotone labeling. However, the probability that the algorithm samples the unique violating arc is $O(1/n)$, which means that we need to set $q = \Omega(n)$.

To obtain a tester with a sublinear number of queries, we need to consider consistency in a longer range. To this end, we introduce several notions. For a digraph $G = (V, E)$, we say that a vertex $v \in V$ is *reachable* from a vertex $u \in V$ if there is a directed path from u to v in G. We denote it by $u \leq_G v$ because it imposes a constraint $f(u) \leq f(v)$. Then, the *transitive closure* $\mathrm{TC}(G)$ of a digraph $G = (V, E)$ is a digraph on the vertex set V and the arc

reachability

transitive closure

set $\{(u,v) \in V^2 : u \leq_G v\}$. Note that the transitive closure of a DAG is again a DAG.

violating pair

We say that a pair (u,v) of vertices in a DAG $G = (V, E)$ is a *violating pair* with respect to a labeling $f \colon V \to \{0,1\}$ if $f(u) > f(v)$ and v is reachable from u. This is equivalent to being a violating arc in $\mathrm{TC}(G)$. Note that, if there exists a violating pair (u,v), then there exists a violating arc in G. Hence, if we have found a violating pair, then we can immediately reject.

For an undirected graph, let $\mathrm{VC}(G)$ denote the minimum size of a vertex cover. Then, we have the following characterization:

Lemma 7.5. *Let $G = (V, E)$ be a DAG and $f \colon V \to \{0,1\}$ be a labeling. Let G' be an undirected graph on the vertex set V and the edge set consisting of violating pairs in G (disregarding the direction). Then, we have $d_{\mathrm{H}}(f, \mathcal{P}_{G,\mathrm{mon}}) = \mathrm{VC}(G')$.*

Proof. For each violating pair $(u,v) \in V^2$, we need to modify at least one of $f(u)$ and $f(v)$ to make f monotone. Hence, we have $d_{\mathrm{H}}(f, \mathcal{P}_{G,\mathrm{mon}}) \geq \mathrm{VC}(G')$.

Now, we show $d_{\mathrm{H}}(f, \mathcal{P}_{G,\mathrm{mon}}) \leq \mathrm{VC}(G')$. Let S be any vertex cover of G'. We show that we can obtain a monotone labeling by modifying the value of f only on vertices in S.

Let $T = V \setminus S$. By the definition of S, there is no violating pair between any pair of vertices in T. Consider the following iterative process, where in each step, we modify the value of f on an arbitrary $v \in S$, remove v from S, and add it to T. We maintain the property that there is no violating pair between vertices in T. The process ends when $S = \emptyset$ and $T = V$, so that the final labeling is monotone. To redefine the value of f on v, we consider the following two subsets of T:

$$T_1 = \{u \in T : (u,v) \text{ is a violating pair with respect to the current } f\}.$$
$$T_2 = \{w \in T : (v,w) \text{ is a violating pair with respect to the current } f\}.$$

If T_1 is non-empty, then $f(v) = 0$ and hence T_2 is empty. Similarly, if T_2 is non-empty, then $f(v) = 1$ and hence T_1 is empty. This means that at most one of T_1 and T_2 is non-empty.

If T_1 is non-empty, then we let $f(v) = 1$. If T_2 is non-empty, then we let $f(v) = 0$. In case both are empty, the value of v may remain unchanged. We can easily see that these modifications do not create any violating pair within $T \cup \{v\}$. $\qquad\square$

Our strategy of testing monotonicity is applying the abovementioned edge-sampling algorithm on $\mathrm{TC}(G)$. The details are given in Algorithm 7.1. To make the analysis easier, we sample two sets S_1 and S_2.

When showing a super-constant lower bound in Section 7.2.1, we make use of a graph for which the maximum size of a matching consisting of violating arcs is small. Here, in order to show the correctness of Algorithm 7.1, we use the property that the maximum size of a matching consisting of violating

---

Algorithm 7.1 Monotonicity Testing for DAGs

Input: A DAG $G = (V, E)$, $\epsilon \in (0, 1)$, and query access to $f \colon V \to \{0, 1\}$.

1: $q \leftarrow \Theta(\sqrt{\epsilon^{-1} n})$.
2: Let S be the set obtained by sampling each vertex with probability q/n
3: **if** $|S| > 10q$ **then**
4:     Accept.
5: **end if**
6: Query $f(v)$ for each vertex $v \in S$.
7: **if** there exists a violating pair $(u, v) \in S \times S$ with respect to f **then**
8:     Reject.
9: **else**
10:     Accept.
11: **end if**

---

arcs in an ϵ-far graph is somewhat large. The following is immediate from Lemma 7.5 by the fact that the maximum size of a matching is at least half the minimum size of a vertex cover.

Corollary 7.1. *Let $G = (V, E)$ be a DAG on n vertices and $f \colon V \to \{0, 1\}$ be a labeling that is ϵ-far from being monotone. Then, there is a matching consisting of violating pairs of size at least $\epsilon n/2$.*

Theorem 7.3. *Algorithm 7.1 is a one-sided error tester for monotonicity with query complexity $O(\sqrt{\epsilon^{-1} n})$.*

Proof. Algorithm 7.1 accepts all monotone functions and the query complexity is clearly $O(\sqrt{\epsilon^{-1} n})$.

Suppose that $f \colon V \to \{0, 1\}$ is ϵ-far from being monotone. From Markov's inequality, the query complexity is at most $10q$ with probability at least $1/10$.

Then by Corollary 7.1, there is a matching M consisting of $\epsilon n/2$ violating pairs. Note that for each violating pair, the probability that we do not find it is $1 - q^2/n^2$. Thus, the probability that we do not find any violating pair is at most:

$$\left(1 - \frac{q^2}{n^2}\right)^{|M|} \leq \exp\left(-\frac{q^2 |M|}{n^2}\right) = \exp\left(-\frac{\epsilon q^2}{2n}\right).$$

If we set the constant hidden in q to be large enough, the probability above is bounded by $1/10$. Thus, by the union bound, we reject the instance with probability at least $1 - 2/10 \geq 2/3$. $\square$

The crucial property that leads to the sublinear-query testability of monotonicity is Lemma 7.5, which essentially states that, for any labeling $f \colon V \to \{0, 1\}$ and a vertex set $S \subseteq V$ such that there exists no violating pair between vertices in $V \setminus S$, we can extend $f|_S$ to a monotone labeling. Because of this property, we can show that there are a super-constant number of violating pairs (Corollary 7.1), and we can detect a violating pair with a sublinear number of queries. A similar property will be used to design testers for 2-SAT in Section 7.4.1.

7.3 Subspace Membership

Let $\mathbb{F}_2$ be the finite field of order two and let $V \subseteq \mathbb{F}_2^n$ be a subspace. In this section, we consider testing whether a vector $x \in \mathbb{F}_2^n$, given as query access, belongs to V. Whether x belongs to V is a *global* property in the sense that we always need to look at whole x to determine x does not belong to V, which intuitively implies that this problem is hard. In what follows, we see that this problem indeed requires $\Omega(n)$ queries to test. We note that 2-coloring and monotonicity studied in Sections 7.1 and 7.2, respectively, are more *local* in the sense that, if a labeling does not satisfy either of them, then we can confirm it just by looking at the values of some two vertices.

First, we formally define the problem. For $\epsilon > 0$ and a subspace $V \subseteq \mathbb{F}_2^n$, we say that a vector $x \in \mathbb{F}_2^n$ is *ϵ-far from (belonging to) V* if $d_{\mathrm{H}}(x, V) > \epsilon n$. Then, we say that an algorithm is a *tester for subspace membership* if, given a subspace $V \subseteq \mathbb{F}_2^n$, an error parameter $\epsilon \in (0, 1)$, and query access to a vector $x \in \mathbb{F}_2^n$, it accepts with probability at least 2/3 when x belongs to V, and rejects with probability at least 2/3 when x is ϵ-far from V. Then, using the query access to x, we can obtain the value of x_i by specifying an index $i \in [n]$. We call this problem *testing subspace membership*. We note that the notion of a tester for subspace membership has been studied in the context of *locally testable codes*, which we will discuss in Chapter 12. The goal of this section is to show that there is some subspace $V \subseteq \mathbb{F}_2^n$ for which testing the membership in V is hard whereas the primary interest of locally testable codes is to design a subspace $V \subseteq \mathbb{F}_2^n$ with some nice properties including the existence of an efficient tester for the membership in V.

ϵ-farness

tester for subspace membership

testing subspace membership

locally testable code

For our analysis, it is convenient to introduce more parameters. For $\epsilon \in (0, 1)$, $0 \le \delta_- < 1 - \delta_+ \le 1$, and an integer q, we say that an algorithm is an *$(\epsilon, \delta_+, \delta_-, q)$-tester for a subspace V* if, given query access to a vector $x \in \mathbb{F}_2^n$, by querying q coordinates of x, it accepts with probability at least $1 - \delta_+$ if x belongs to V, and accepts with probability at most δ_- if x is ϵ-far from V. A standard tester corresponds to the case that V and ϵ are also given as a part of the input and $\delta_- = \delta_+ = 1/3$. When we are not concerned with the query complexity, we call it an *$(\epsilon, \delta_+, \delta_-)$-tester* for V.

$(\epsilon, \delta_+, \delta_-, q)$-tester for a subspace V

$(\epsilon, \delta_+, \delta_-)$-tester

For a linear subspace $V \subseteq \mathbb{F}_2^n$, the *dual space* $V^\perp$ is the set of all vectors orthogonal to V, that is, $V^\perp := \{v \in \mathbb{F}_2^n : v \perp V\}$. Note that $V^{\perp\perp} = V$ holds. For $I \subseteq [n]$, let $V_I^\perp$ be the subset of $V^\perp$ consisting of all vectors with support in I, that is, $v \in V_I^\perp$ if and only if $v \in V^\perp$ and the indices of non-zero entries of v lie in I. For two vectors $x, y \in \mathbb{F}_2^n$, let $\langle x, y\rangle = \sum_{i \in [n]} x_i y_i \bmod 2$ be their inner product in $\mathbb{F}_2$.

dual space

7.3.1 Proof Outline

In order to show lower bounds for testing subspace membership, it is convenient if we can restrict the form of testers. Here, we consider the following form of a tester.

Definition 7.1 (Linear tester). A tester for a subspace $V \subseteq \mathbb{F}_2^n$ is called a *linear tester* if it selects a set $I \subseteq [n]$ of indices (according to some distribution), queries the input $x \in \mathbb{F}_2^n$ at coordinates in I, and accepts if and only if $x \perp V_I^\perp$.

linear tester

Linear testers are by definition non-adaptive and have only a one-sided error, that is, members of V are always accepted.

The following shows that we can restrict our attention to linear testers to show lower bounds for testing subspace membership.

Lemma 7.6. *If there is a (two-sided error) adaptive $(\epsilon, \delta_+, \delta_-, q)$-tester for a subspace $V \subseteq \mathbb{F}_2^n$, then there is a linear $(\epsilon, 0, \delta_+ + \delta_-, q)$-tester for V.*

The reduction to linear testers does not increase the sum of failure probabilities $\delta_+ + \delta_-$ but shifts it from the positive instances to the negative instances. Lemma 7.6 shows an exceptional feature of testing subspace membership. In general, simulating an adaptive tester with a non-adaptive tester exponentially blows up the query complexity. However, Lemma 7.6 shows that we do not need such a loss for testing subspace membership. Also, two-sided error testers are often much more potent than one-sided error testers. Recall that, for testing cycle-freeness in the bounded-degree model, there is a constant-query two-sided error tester but any one-sided error tester requires $\Omega(\sqrt{n})$ queries (see Section 5.4). However, Lemma 7.6 shows that there is no substantial difference between two-sided error testers and one-sided error testers for testing subspace membership. We give the proof of Lemma 7.6 in Section 7.3.2.

Consider a subspace $V \subseteq \mathbb{F}_2^n$ and let $\mathcal{B} = (b_1, \ldots, b_m)$ be a basis of the dual space $V^\perp$. We can view each vector $b_i \in \mathcal{B}$ as a linear constraint on Boolean variables $x_i, \ldots, x_n$ of the form $\langle x, b_i \rangle = 0$. Hence, we can see a subspace as a set of vectors satisfying all constraints in the dual space: $V = \{x \in \mathbb{F}_2^n : \langle x, b_i \rangle = 0 \; \forall i \in [m]\}$.

We will employ Yao's minimax principle to show a linear lower bound for testing subspace membership. Hence, we want to design a distribution on the inputs on which any deterministic linear tester with a sublinear number of queries fails. More specifically, we need a subspace $V \subseteq \mathbb{F}_2^n$ and a distribution on vectors that are far from V but are orthogonal with high probability to any fixed set of linear constraints having a support of a sublinear size. We now present conditions for a subspace that are sufficient to make such a distribution.

Definition 7.2 (Hard subspace). Let $V \subseteq \mathbb{F}_2^n$ be a subspace and let $\mathcal{B} = \{b_1, \ldots, b_m\}$ be a basis of $V^\perp$.

- For $\epsilon \in (0, 1)$, we say that $\mathcal{B}$ is ϵ-*separating* if every $x \in \mathbb{F}_2^n$ that falsifies exactly one constraint in $\mathcal{B}$ satisfies $|\mathrm{supp}(x)| > \epsilon n$.
- For $q \in \mathbb{Z}_{>0}$ and $\mu \in (0, 1)$, we say $\mathcal{B}$ is (q, μ)-*local* if every $\alpha \in \mathbb{F}_2^n$ that is a sum of at least μm vectors in $\mathcal{B}$ has $|\alpha| \geq q$.

We will consider the distribution over vectors that falsifies exactly one constraint in $\mathcal{B}$ and the first condition will be used to show that such vectors are ϵ-far from V. Indeed, if such a vector $x \in \mathbb{F}_2^n$ is ϵ-close to a vector $y \in V$, then $x + y$ falsifies exactly one constraint in $\mathcal{B}$ and $|\mathrm{supp}(x + y)| \leq \epsilon n$, which contradicts the first condition.

The second condition is used to show that the distribution is hard to test. Assume for simplicity that a linear tester selects some vector $u \in V^\perp$ with $|u| \leq q$ and then checks $\langle x, u \rangle = 0$. (In general, a linear tester may check several vectors in $V^\perp$, whose total support size is at most q.) Then, we can write $u = \sum_{j \in J} b_j$ for some $J \subseteq [m]$. Let $b_k \in \mathcal{B}$ be the random constraint falsified by a vector x in our hard distribution. Clearly, the linear tester rejects x if and only if $k \in J$. The second condition implies that the latter occurs with probability at most μ.

Formally, we show the following. The proof will be given in Section 7.3.3.

Lemma 7.7. *Let $V \subseteq \mathbb{F}_2^n$ be a subspace such that $V^\perp$ has an ϵ-separating (q, μ)-local basis $\mathcal{B} = \{b_1, \ldots, b_m\}$ for some $\epsilon \in (0, 1)$, $\mu \in (0, 1/2)$, and $q \in \mathbb{Z}_{>0}$. Then, there exists no linear $(\epsilon, \delta_+, \delta_-)$-tester for V with $\delta_+, \delta_- \leq 1 - 2\mu$ and query complexity at most q.*

The following lemma shows that a hard subspace satisfying the conditions in Definition 7.2 exists:

Lemma 7.8 (Hard subspace exists). *There exist constants $\epsilon, \gamma, \mu \in (0, 1/2)$ such that, for infinitely many $n \in \mathbb{Z}_{>0}$, there exists a subspace $V \subseteq \mathbb{F}_2^n$ for which the basis $\mathcal{B}$ of the dual subspace $V^\perp$ is ϵ-separating and $(\gamma n, \mu)$-local.*

As an immediate corollary, we conclude that testing subspace membership requires a linear number of queries:

Theorem 7.4. *There exist constants $\epsilon, \gamma, \mu \in (0, 1/2)$ such that, for infinitely many $n \in \mathbb{Z}_{>0}$, any $(\epsilon, \delta_+, \delta_-)$-tester for subspace membership in $\mathbb{F}_2^n$ with $\delta_+, \delta_- \leq 1 - 2\mu$ requires γn queries.*

Proof. Directly follows from Lemmas 7.6, 7.7, and 7.8. $\square$

In subsequent sections, we prove Lemmas 7.6, 7.7, and 7.8.

7.3.2 Proof of Lemma 7.6

We perform the reduction in two stages: we first reduce an adaptive tester
with two-sided error to an adaptive linear tester (Lemma 7.9), and then
remove the adaptivity (Lemma 7.11).

We start with an observation that any randomized tester can be viewed
as a distribution over deterministic testers, and each deterministic tester can
be represented by a decision tree (see Figure 2.2 in Chapter 2). Thus, any
tester $\mathcal{T}$ can be represented by a pair $(\Upsilon_{\mathcal{T}}, \mathcal{D}_{\mathcal{T}})$, where $\Upsilon_{\mathcal{T}} = \{\Gamma_1, \Gamma_2, \ldots\}$
is a set of decision trees and $\mathcal{D}_{\mathcal{T}}$ is a distribution on this set. Then, given a
vector $x \in \mathbb{F}_2^n$, $\mathcal{T}$ chooses a decision tree Γ with probability $\mathcal{D}_{\mathcal{T}}(\Gamma)$ and then
answers according to Γ applied on x.

Let V be a vector space. For any leaf ℓ of a decision tree Γ, let $V_\ell \subseteq V$
be the subset of vectors consistent with the answers along the path to ℓ.
Similarly, for any vector $x \in \mathbb{F}_2^n$, let $V_\ell^x \subseteq x + V$ be the subset of vectors that
are consistent with the answers along the path to ℓ. Note that V_ℓ and V_ℓ^x are
linear and affine subspaces, respectively. We will frequently use the following
observation.

> **Proposition 7.3.** *Let $V \subseteq \mathbb{F}_2^n$ be a subspace and $x \in \mathbb{F}_2^n$ be a vector. For
> any decision tree Γ and a leaf ℓ in Γ, if both V_ℓ and V_ℓ^x are nonempty,
> then $|V_\ell| = |V_\ell^x|$.*

Proof. Let U be the set of all vectors in V that have zeros in all the positions
queried along the path to ℓ. Since $0^n \in U$, we have that U is nonempty.
Observe that if $u \in U$ and $v \in V_\ell$, then $u + v \in V_\ell$. In fact, $V_\ell = v + U$ holds
for any $v \in V_\ell$. Hence, we have $|V_\ell| = |U|$. Similarly, $V_\ell^x = v + U$ holds for
any $v \in V_\ell^x$. Hence, we have $|V_\ell^x| = |U|$ and the lemma follows. $\square$

7.3.2.1 Reduction from two-sided error adaptive testers to adaptive linear testers

We first formally define an adaptive linear tester, which is of one-sided error.

> **Definition 7.3** (Adaptive linear tester). A tester for a subspace $V \subseteq \mathbb{F}_2^n$
> is called an *adaptive linear tester* if it adaptively make queries $I \subseteq [n]$ adaptive linear tester
> (according to some distribution) to the input $x \in \mathbb{F}_2^n$ and accepts if and
> only if $x \perp V_I^\perp$.

Let $\mathcal{T} = (\Upsilon_{\mathcal{T}}, \mathcal{D}_{\mathcal{T}})$ be a two-sided error (adaptive) $(\epsilon, \delta_+, \delta_-, q)$-tester for
V. We say that a leaf ℓ is labeled *optimally* if its label is **reject** when the   optimally
answers on the path to ℓ falsify some constraint in $V^\perp$, and its label is **accept**
otherwise. Then, we relabel the leaves of each tree Γ in $\Upsilon_{\mathcal{T}}$ optimally to obtain
the tree Γ_{opt}. This process produces a one-sided error tester $\mathcal{T}_{\text{opt}}$ with the

same query complexity. However, the new tester $\mathcal{T}_{\mathrm{opt}}$ performs well only on average over the choice of the input vector. To get good performance on every vector, we randomize the input vector x by sampling a vector v from V uniformly and performing the tester on $x + v$ instead of x. Now, we formally define the reduction.

Definition 7.4. Given a two-sided error (adaptive) tester $\mathcal{T}$ for V, define the tester $\mathcal{T}'$ as follows: Given an input vector $x \in \mathbb{F}_2^n$, choose $v \in V$ uniformly at random, and then answer according to $\mathcal{T}_{\mathrm{opt}}$ applied on $x+v$.

Lemma 7.9. *Let $\mathcal{T}$ be an adaptive $(\epsilon, \delta_+, \delta_-, q)$-tester for a subspace $V \subseteq \mathbb{F}_2^n$. Then, the tester $\mathcal{T}'$ as in Definition 7.4 is a (one-sided error) adaptive linear $(\epsilon, 0, \delta_+ + \delta_-, q)$-tester for V.*

Proof. Clearly, $\mathcal{T}'$ is adaptive linear and has the same query complexity as $\mathcal{T}$. It remains to check that $\mathcal{T}'$ has failure probability $\delta_+ + \delta_-$ on ϵ-far instances.

For any $x \in \mathbb{F}_2^n$ and any tester $\mathcal{T}$, let $\rho_x^{\mathcal{T}}$ be the average acceptance probability of $\mathcal{T}$ over all vectors in $x + V$, that is, $\rho_x^{\mathcal{T}} = \mathbf{E}_{y \in x+V} \Pr[\mathcal{T} \text{ accepts } y]$. For notational brevity, we denote $\rho_{0^n}^{\mathcal{T}}$, the average acceptance probability of vectors in V, by $\rho^{\mathcal{T}}$. Observe that the probability that the new tester $\mathcal{T}'$ accepts x is equal to $\rho_x^{\mathcal{T}_{\mathrm{opt}}}$.

Lemma 7.10 below shows that the transformation from $\mathcal{T}$ to $\mathcal{T}_{\mathrm{opt}}$ increases the acceptance probability of any vector not in V by at most $\rho^{\mathcal{T}_{\mathrm{opt}}} - \rho^{\mathcal{T}}$. As all vectors in $x + V$ have the same distance to V, if x is ϵ-far from V, then $\rho_x^{\mathcal{T}} \leq \delta_-$. Together with Lemma 7.10, it implies that for any vector x that is ϵ-far from V, the failure probability is low:

$$\Pr[\mathcal{T}' \text{ accepts } x] = \rho_x^{\mathcal{T}_{\mathrm{opt}}} \leq \rho^{\mathcal{T}_{\mathrm{opt}}} - \rho^{\mathcal{T}} + \rho_x^{\mathcal{T}} \leq 1 - (1 - \delta_+) + \delta_- = \delta_+ + \delta_-.$$

This completes the proof. $\square$

Lemma 7.10. $\rho^{\mathcal{T}} - \rho_x^{\mathcal{T}} \leq \rho^{\mathcal{T}_{\mathrm{opt}}} - \rho_x^{\mathcal{T}_{\mathrm{opt}}}$ *for any vector $x \in \mathbb{F}_2^n$.*

Proof. Let $x \in \mathbb{F}_2^n$. It suffices to show that relabeling one leaf ℓ of a decision tree Γ in $\Upsilon_{\mathcal{T}}$ optimally does not decrease $\rho^{\mathcal{T}} - \rho_x^{\mathcal{T}}$. Then we obtain the claim by iteratively relabeling leaves to get $\mathcal{T}_{\mathrm{opt}}$ from $\mathcal{T}$. There are two cases to consider:

- The path to ℓ falsifies some constraint in $V^{\perp}$.
  In this case, ℓ is relabeled from **accept** to **reject**. This change preserves $\rho^{\mathcal{T}}$ because it can only decrease the acceptance probability for vectors that falsify some constraint. Therefore, $\rho_x^{\mathcal{T}}$ does not increase. Hence, $\rho^{\mathcal{T}} - \rho_x^{\mathcal{T}}$ does not decrease.
- The path to ℓ does not falsify any constraint in $V^{\perp}$.
  In this case, ℓ is relabeled from **reject** to **accept**. Thus, every vector in

$V_\ell \cup V_\ell^x$ was rejected before relabeling but is accepted now. The output of the algorithm on the remaining vectors in V and $x + V$ is unaltered. Hence, the probability ρ^T increases by $\mathcal{D}_T(\Gamma) \cdot |V_\ell|/|V|$. Similarly, ρ_x^T increases by $\mathcal{D}_T(\Gamma) \cdot |V_\ell^x|/|V|$.

It suffices to show that $|V_\ell| \geq |V_\ell^x|$. Since the path to ℓ does not falsify any constraint, V_ℓ is nonempty. If V_ℓ^x is empty, we are done. Otherwise, both V_ℓ and V_ℓ^x are nonempty, and by Proposition 7.3, $|V_\ell| = |V_\ell^x|$.

Now, we obtain the claim.   □

7.3.2.2 Reduction to non-adaptive linear testers

In this section, we show that we can remove the adaptivity from the linear testers. The intuition behind this reduction is as follows: To check whether a linear constraint is satisfied, a tester needs to query all the variables that appear in that constraint. Any adaptive decision based on a partial view involving some of the variables does not help because the tester cannot guess if the constraint will be satisfied until it reads the final variable. Now, we formally define the reduction:

Definition 7.5. Given an adaptive linear tester T for V, define the tester T' as follows: On input $x \in \mathbb{F}_2^n$, choose a random $v \in V$, query x on all variables that T queries on input v, and reject if and only if some constraint is violated.

We note that a similar idea was used to remove adaptivity in the adjacency matrix model for graphs (see Section 4.4).

Lemma 7.11. *If there is an adaptive linear $(\epsilon, 0, \delta, q)$-tester for a subspace $V \subseteq \mathbb{F}_2^n$, the tester T' is a (non-adaptive) linear $(\epsilon, 0, \delta, q)$-tester for V.*

Proof. T' makes the same number of queries as T. As the queries depend only on the random vector $v \in V$ and not on the input x, the tester T' is non-adaptive.

The following claim shows a relation between the acceptance probability of T' and the average acceptance probability of T.

Claim 7.1. *For any vector $x \in \mathbb{F}_2^n$, we have:*

$$\Pr[T' \text{ accepts } x] = \mathop{\mathbf{E}}_{v \in V}\Big[\Pr[T \text{ accepts } x + v]\Big].$$

Proof. For a decision tree Γ, let $L_{\mathbf{acc}}(\Gamma)$ denote the set of leaves in Γ that are labeled **accept**. For a leaf ℓ in a decision tree Γ, let $\mathrm{var}(\ell)$ denote the set of variables queried along the path to ℓ. Let V_ℓ and V_ℓ^x be the set of all vectors in V and $x + V$, respectively, consistent with the answers along the path to ℓ. Also, let I_ℓ^x be the indicator variable for the event that x does not violate any constraint in $V^\perp$ involving only the variables in $\mathrm{var}(\ell)$. Observe that if the tester $\mathcal{T}'$ chooses a decision tree $\Gamma \in \Upsilon_\mathcal{T}$ and a vector $v \in V$ such that $v \in V_\ell$ for some leaf ℓ labeled **accept** in the tree Γ, then $I_\ell^x = 1$ if and only if $\mathcal{T}'$ accepts x.

We can obtain $\mathbf{E}_{v \in V}[\Pr[\mathcal{T} \text{ accepts } x+v]]$ as follows: First, choose a decision tree $\Gamma \in \Upsilon_\mathcal{T}$ according to the distribution $\mathcal{D}_\mathcal{T}$. Then for each leaf ℓ labeled **accept** in Γ, find the fraction of vectors in $x + V$ that follow the path to ℓ. The weighted sum of these fractions is $\mathbf{E}_{v \in V}[\Pr[\mathcal{T} \text{ accepts } x + v]]$. Thus:

$$\mathop{\mathbf{E}}_{v \in V}\left[\Pr[\mathcal{T} \text{ accepts } x + v]\right] = \sum_{\Gamma \in \Upsilon_\mathcal{T}} \mathcal{D}_\mathcal{T}(\Gamma) \sum_{\ell \in L_{\mathbf{acc}}(\Gamma)} \frac{|V_\ell^x|}{|V|}. \qquad (7.1)$$

Now consider the probability that $\mathcal{T}'$ accepts x. The tester $\mathcal{T}'$ can be viewed as follows: On input $x \in \mathbb{F}_2^n$, $\mathcal{T}'$ chooses a decision tree $\Gamma \in \Upsilon_\mathcal{T}$ according to the distribution $\mathcal{D}_\mathcal{T}$. It then chooses a leaf ℓ labeled **accept** in Γ with probability proportional to the fraction of vectors $v \in V$ that are accepted along the path to ℓ (that is, $|V_\ell|/|V|$), queries x on all variables in $\mathrm{var}(\ell)$, accepts if $I_\ell^x = 1$ and rejects otherwise. This gives us the following expression for the probability that $\mathcal{T}'$ accepts x:

$$\Pr[\mathcal{T}' \text{ accepts } x] = \sum_{\Gamma \in \Upsilon_\mathcal{T}} \mathcal{D}_\mathcal{T}(\Gamma) \sum_{\ell \in L_{\mathbf{acc}}(\Gamma)} \frac{|V_\ell|}{|V|} I_\ell^x. \qquad (7.2)$$

From (7.1) and (7.2), it suffices to show that $|V_\ell^x| = I_\ell^x |V_\ell|$ for all leaves ℓ labeled **accept** to achieve the claim.

Observe that $|V_\ell|$ is nonempty since ℓ is labeled **accept**. Hence, by Proposition 7.3, we have $|V_\ell| = |V_\ell^x|$ if V_ℓ^x is also nonempty. It now suffices to show that V_ℓ^x is nonempty if and only if $I_\ell^x = 1$.

Suppose V_ℓ^x is nonempty. Then, there exists $y \in x + V$ that does not violate any constraint involving only the variables $\mathrm{var}(\ell)$. However, as y and x satisfy the same set of constraints, x also does not violate any constraint involving only the variables $\mathrm{var}(\ell)$. Thus, $I_\ell^x = 1$.

Now, for the other direction, suppose $I_\ell^x = 1$. Then the values of the variables in $\mathrm{var}(\ell)$ of x do not violate any constraint in $V^\perp$. Hence, there exists $u \in V$ that has the same values as x for the variables in $\mathrm{var}(\ell)$. Let $v \in V_\ell$. Then, the vector $x - u + v \in x + V$ has the same values for the variables $\mathrm{var}(\ell)$ as v. Hence, V_ℓ^x is nonempty. This concludes the proof of the claim. $\qquad \square$

The above claim proves that $\mathcal{T}'$ inherits its acceptance probability from $\mathcal{T}$. As mentioned earlier, $\mathcal{T}'$ inherits its query complexity from $\mathcal{T}$. Hence, $\mathcal{T}'$ is a linear $(\epsilon, 0, \delta, q)$-tester for V. $\qquad \square$

7.3.3 Proof of Lemma 7.7

Let us restate Lemma 7.7 and prove it.

Lemma 7.7. *Let $V \subseteq \mathbb{F}_2^n$ be a subspace such that $V^\perp$ has an ϵ-separating (q, μ)-local basis $\mathcal{B} = \{b_1, \ldots, b_m\}$ for some $\epsilon \in (0, 1)$, $\mu \in (0, 1/2)$, and $q \in \mathbb{Z}_{>0}$. Then, there exists no linear $(\epsilon, \delta_+, \delta_-)$-tester for V with $\delta_+, \delta_- \leq 1 - 2\mu$ and query complexity at most q.*

Proof. We employ Yao's minimax principle. It states that to prove that every q-query randomized linear test fails with probability more than δ, it is enough to exhibit a distribution $\mathcal{D}$ on the inputs for which every q-query deterministic linear test fails with probability more than δ.

For $i \in [m]$, let $\mathcal{D}_i$ be the uniform distribution over vectors in $\mathbb{F}_2^n$ that falsify constraint b_i and satisfy the rest. The distribution $\mathcal{D}$ is the uniform distribution over the $\mathcal{D}_i$'s.

The ϵ-separability ensures that the distribution $\mathcal{D}$ is over vectors which are ϵ-far from the subspace. Indeed, if the distance of $x \in \mathrm{supp}(\mathcal{D})$ from $y \in V$ is at most ϵn, then $|\mathrm{supp}(x + y)| \leq \epsilon n$ and $x + y$ falsifies exactly one constraint, which is a contradiction.

A deterministic linear tester $\mathcal{T}$ with query complexity q is identified by a subset $I \subseteq [n]$ with $|I| = q$ and rejects the input x only if x is not orthogonal to $V_I^\perp$. For a vector $u \in V^\perp$, let $\alpha_u \in \mathbb{F}_2^m$ denote the unique vector with $\sum_{i \in [m]} \alpha_u(i) b_i = u$. Also, let $J = \bigcup_{u \in V_I^\perp} \mathrm{supp}(\alpha_u)$. We claim that $\mathcal{T}$ rejects x distributed according to $\mathcal{D}$ if and only if the index of the unique constraint falsified by x belongs to J. This is because x is orthogonal to all but one $b_i \in \mathcal{B}$, so the subspace of $V^\perp$ that is orthogonal to x is precisely the span of $\mathcal{B} \setminus \{b_i\}$. Summing up, the probability that $\mathcal{T}$ rejects x is precisely $|J|/m$.

We now give an upper bound on $|J|$. Notice that $V_I^\perp$ is a vector space, and so is the set $A := \{\alpha_u : u \in V_I^\perp\}$. Since $\mathcal{B}$ is (q, μ)-local, we have $|\alpha_u| \leq \mu m$ for every $u \in V_I^\perp$. Thus, A is a vector space over $\mathbb{F}_2^m$ in which each element has support size at most μm. We claim that $|J| = |\bigcup_{\alpha \in A} \mathrm{supp}(\alpha)| \leq 2\mu m$. To show this, we note that:

$$\mathop{\mathbf{E}}_{\alpha \in A} |\alpha| = \frac{\left|\bigcup_{\alpha \in A} \mathrm{supp}(\alpha)\right|}{2},$$

which follows from the linearity of expectation and the fact that the projection of A onto any $i \in \bigcup_{\alpha \in A} \mathrm{supp}(\alpha)$ is a linear function, and hence the expected value of $\alpha(i)$ is $1/2$. Since $\mathcal{B}$ is (q, μ)-local, we know $\mathbf{E}_{\alpha \in A} |\alpha| \leq \mu m$, which means that $|J| \leq 2\mu m$. This implies that our deterministic test will detect a violation with probability at most $|J|/m \leq 2\mu$. $\qquad\square$

7.3.4 Proof of Lemma 7.8

We construct a hard subspace from a graph. The construction is known as low density parity check (LDPC) codes in coding theory:

Definition 7.6 (LDPC Code). Let $G = ([n], [m]; E)$ be a bipartite multigraph. For each $j \in [m]$, let $b_j \in \mathbb{F}_2^n$ be a vector, where the i-th coordinate of b_j is $|\{(i, j) \in E\}|$ mod 2. Then, the subspace $V_G \subseteq \mathbb{F}_2^n$ is defined as:

$$V_G = \{x \in \{0,1\}^n : \forall j \in [m], \langle x, b_j \rangle = 0\}.$$

We will show that, if G is an expander in a certain sense, then the subspace V_G satisfies the conditions in Definition 7.2. To formally state the relation, we need to introduce several definitions.

Definition 7.7. Let $G = (V, E)$ be a multigraph. For a subset $S \subseteq V$, let

- $N(S)$ be the set of neighbors of S.
- $N^1(S)$ be the set of unique neighbors of S, that is, vertices with exactly one neighbor in S.
- $N^{\text{odd}}(S)$ be the set of neighbors of S with an odd number of neighbors in S. (Notice that $N^1(S) \subseteq N^{\text{odd}}(S)$.)

Definition 7.8. Let $G = (L, R; E)$ be a bipartite multigraph with $|L| = n$ and $|R| = m$

expander

- G is called a (γ, μ)-*right expander* if, for any $S \subseteq R$ with $|S| \leq \mu m$, we have $|N(S)| > \gamma|S|$.

unique neighbor expander

- G is called a (γ, μ)-*right unique neighbor expander* if, for any $S \subseteq R, |S| \leq \mu m$, we have $|N^1(S)| > \gamma|S|$.

odd expander

- G is called a (γ, μ)-*right odd expander* if, for any $S \subseteq R$ with $|S| \geq \mu m$, we have $|N^{\text{odd}}(S)| > \gamma|S|$.

Note that an expander and a unique neighbor expander are concenred with subsets of size at most μn, whereas an odd expander is concerned with subsets of size at least μn. Left expanders are defined analogously by taking $S \subseteq L$ with $|S| \leq \mu n$ in Definition 7.8.

The following construction of an expander is known (see [62]). We say

(c, d)-regular

that a bipartite graph $G = (L, R; E)$ is (c, d)-*regular* if every vertex in L has degree c and every vertex in R has degree d.

Lemma 7.12. *There exist constants $c, d \in \mathbb{Z}_{>0}$ and $\gamma, \mu \in (0, 1/2)$ such that, for infinitely many $n \in \mathbb{Z}_{>0}$, there exists a (c, d)-regular multigraph $G = (L, R; E)$ with the following property:*

- *$|L| = n$;*
- *G is a $(1, \mu)$-left unique neighbor expander;*
- *G is a $(1, \mu)$-right unique neighbor expander;*
- *G is a (γ, μ)-right odd expander.*

We show that the subspace V_G constructed from the expander G given by Lemma 7.12 is a hard subspace. Let us restate Lemma 7.8 and prove it.

Lemma 7.8 (Hard subspace exists). *There exist constants $\epsilon, \gamma, \mu \in (0, 1/2)$ such that, for infinitely many $n \in \mathbb{Z}_{>0}$, there exists a subspace $V \subseteq \mathbb{F}_2^n$ for which the basis $\mathcal{B}$ of the dual subspace $V^\perp$ is ϵ-separating and $(\gamma n, \mu)$-local.*

Proof. Let $G = (L, R; E)$ be the (c, d)-regular graph with $|L| = n$ and $|R| = m$ given by Lemma 7.12. Let $\gamma', \mu \in (0, 1/2)$ be the constants given by Lemma 7.12.

Let $\mathcal{B}$ be the basis of $V_G^\perp$ given by Definition 7.6. We prove that $\mathcal{B}$ is (i) linearly independent, (ii) $(\gamma n, \mu)$-local, and (iii) ϵ-separating.

(i) We need to show that adding up vectors in any subset of $\mathcal{B}$ cannot yield $0 \in \mathbb{F}_2^n$. This is equivalent to proving that, for any $T \subseteq R$, we have $N^{\mathrm{odd}}(T) \neq \emptyset$. We use unique neighbor expansion for small T, and we use odd neighbor expansion for large T.

Recall that G is a $(1, \mu)$-right unique neighbor expander. This implies that, if $|T| \leq \mu m$, then $N^{\mathrm{odd}}(T) \neq \emptyset$ because $N^{\mathrm{odd}}(T) \supseteq N^1(T)$ and $N^1(T) \neq \emptyset$.

Recall that G is a (γ', μ)-right odd neighbor expander. This means that, if $|T| \geq \mu m$, then $N^{\mathrm{odd}}(T) \geq \gamma' m > 0$.

(ii) Notice that if $T \subseteq R$, then $N^{\mathrm{odd}}(T)$ is exactly the support of $\sum_{j \in T} b_j$. Thus, it suffices to show that $|N^{\mathrm{odd}}(T)| \geq \gamma n$ for subsets $T \subseteq R$ with $|T| \geq \mu m$. This follows from the fact that G is a (γ', μ)-right odd expander and by setting $\gamma = \gamma' m / n$.

(iii) Let $G - j$ be the graph obtained from G by removing the vertex $j \in R$ and all edges incident to it. Since $\mathcal{B}$ is linearly independent, it suffices to show that V_{G-j} has no non-zero vector of Hamming weight at most ϵn. Let $x \in V_{G-j}$ be a non-zero vector and let $S_x \subseteq L$ be the set of coordinates at which x is 1. In the graph $G - j$, the set of unique neighbors of S_x is empty because $x \in V_{G-j}$ (otherwise, some $j' \in N^1(S_x)$, so $\langle b_{j'}, x \rangle = 1$, a contradiction). Thus:

$$N^1(S_x) \subseteq \{j\}, \tag{7.3}$$

where $N^1(S_x)$ is the set of unique neighbors of S_x in G. Clearly, $|S_x| > 1$ because the degree of a vertex in L is $c > 1$. But if $|S_x| \leq \mu n$, then we have

$|N^1(S_x)| \geq |S_x| > 1$, which contradicts (7.3). We conclude that $|\text{supp}(x)| \geq \mu n$ holds for any $x \in V_{G-j}$, and hence $\mathcal{B}$ is ϵ-separating with $\epsilon = \mu$.   □

7.4 Constraint Satisfaction Problems

constraint satisfaction problem

satisfying assignment

In *constraint satisfaction problems* (CSPs), we are given a set of variables on a finite domain and a set of constraints imposed on variables, and the objective is to find an assignment that satisfies all the constraints. Such an assignment is called a *satisfying assignment*. Depending on the constraints we use, CSPs can represent many fundamental problems. Let us give several examples:

Example 7.1 (2-Coloring). 2-COL is the problem of finding a 2-coloring, or bipartition, in a graph. This problem can be restated as a CSP. Given a graph $G = (V, E)$ on n vertices, consider a CSP instance on a set $X = \{x_1, \ldots, x_n\}$ of Boolean variables with a constraint $x_i \neq x_j$ for each edge $\{i, j\} \in E$. Then, G admits 2-coloring if and only if this CSP instance has a satisfying assignment.

Example 7.2 (Monotonicity). Finding a monotone labeling on a digraph can be restated as a CSP. Given a directed graph $G = (V, E)$, consider a CSP instance on a set $X = \{x_1, \ldots, x_n\}$ of $\{0, 1\}$-valued variables with a constraint $x_i \leq x_j$ for each edge $(i, j) \in E$. Then, G admits a monotone labeling if and only if this CSP instance has a satisfying assignment.

---

conjunctive normal form

literal

k-CNF

Example 7.3 (SAT). A Boolean formula is said to be in *conjunctive normal form* (CNF) if it consists of clauses joined by $\land$'s, where each clause is an $\lor$ of literals. Here, a *literal* is a Boolean variable or a negated Boolean variable. If all clauses have exactly k literals, the formula is said to be a *k-CNF*. The following is an example of a 3-CNF on a variable set $\{x, y, z, w\}$:

$$(x \lor y \lor z) \land (\bar{x} \lor y \lor w) \land (x \lor \bar{z} \lor \bar{w}) \land (\bar{y} \lor z \lor w),$$

where, say, $\bar{x}$, is the negated variable of x. k-SAT is the problem of finding a satisfying assignment to a given k-CNF.

Horn CNF

Example 7.4 (Horn SAT). A CNF is called *Horn* if each clause has at most one positive literal. The following CNF is an example of Horn SAT on a variable set $\{x, y, z, w\}$:

$$(x) \wedge (\bar{y}) \wedge (\bar{y} \vee w) \wedge (\bar{x} \vee \bar{y} \vee z) \wedge (\bar{x} \vee \bar{y} \vee \bar{w}).$$

Equivalently, this CNF can be rewritten as:

$$(x) \wedge (y \to \textbf{false}) \wedge (y \to w) \wedge (x \wedge y \to z) \wedge (x \wedge y \wedge w \to \textbf{false}),$$

where $A \to B$ means "if A is true, then B is true".

If all clauses in a Horn CNF have at most k literals, it is said to be a *Horn k-CNF*. Horn k-SAT is the problem of finding a satisfying assignment to a given Horn k-CNF. The reason that each clause can have less than k literals is that, for $k \geq 2$, a Horn CNF with each clause having exactly k literals is always satisfiable and the problem is uninteresting.

Horn k-CNF

Example 7.5 (System of linear equations). k-LIN is the problem of finding a solution to a system of linear equations on $\mathbb{F}_2$ for which each equation involves exactly k variables. The following is an example of an instance of k-LIN on a variable set $\{x, y, z, w\}$:

$$x + y + z = 0 \bmod 2,$$
$$x + y + w = 1 \bmod 2,$$
$$y + z + w = 1 \bmod 2.$$

A CSP instance is said to be *satisfiable* if it admits a satisfying assignment. For each CSP, we can think of a corresponding testing problem: Given an instance of the CSP, and query access to an assignment for the instance, test whether the assignment is a satisfying assignment or far from being so. We assume that the given instance is satisfiable as otherwise we have nothing to test. We simply call the problem *testing (assignments to) the CSP*.

satisfiability

The problems studied in Sections 7.1 and 7.2 correspond to testing 2-coloring and monotonicity, respectively. Also, the problem studied in 7.3 can be seen as testing k-LIN for some large k. To see this, recall that the vector space V considered there can be represented as $V = \{x \in \mathbb{F}_2^n : \forall i \in [m], \langle x, b_i \rangle = 0\}$ for some $b_1, \ldots, b_m \in \mathbb{F}_2^n$ and each b_i has only a constant number, say, k, of non-zero coordinates.

As k-SAT is one of the most fundamental CSPs, it is natural to ask whether there is a tester for assignments to k-SAT with a sublinear number of queries, and how the hardness of the problem changes as k increases. In Section 7.4.1, we show that assignments to 2-SAT can be tested with $O(\sqrt{n})$ queries, and in Section 7.4.2, we briefly see that testing assignments to 3-SAT requires $\Omega(n)$ queries. Recalling that 2-SAT can be solved in polynomial time whereas 3-SAT is NP-complete, these facts seem related to the computational complexity of k-SAT. Indeed, there is a strong connection between the computational complexity of a CSP and the query complexity of the testing counterpart. We will investigate this issue more in Chapter 13.

7.4.1 2-SAT

In this section, we consider testing 2-**SAT** and show that we can test 2-SAT with $O(\sqrt{n})$ queries.

Let ϕ be a satisfiable 2-CNF on a set X of n variables, and $f\colon X \to \{0,1\}$ be an assignment to ϕ. Our idea is reducing the problem to testing monotonicity on a DAG, which was studied in Section 7.2. From ϕ and f, we construct a DAG G_ϕ and an assignment f_G as follows: For each variable $x \in X$, associate two vertices v_x and $v_{\bar{x}}$ that represent literals corresponding to x and $\bar{x}$, respectively. We use the convention $v_x = \bar{v}_{\bar{x}}$ and $v_{\bar{x}} = \bar{v}_x$. Define the *implication graph* G_ϕ on the set of the corresponding vertices as follows: for each clause $x \vee y$ in ϕ, where x and y are literals, add edges $(\bar{v}_y, v_x)$ and $(\bar{v}_x, v_y)$, whose intended meanings are $\bar{y} \to x$ (if y is false, then x is true) and $\bar{x} \to y$ (if x is false, then y is true), respectively. For any edge (u,v) in G_ϕ, call the edge $(\bar{v}, \bar{u})$ its *dual arc*. Note that dual arcs appear in the implication graph in pairs, except for edges of the form $(u, \bar{u})$, which are dual to themselves. Define the associated assignment f_G of G_ϕ by $f_G(v_x) = f(x)$ and $f_G(v_{\bar{x}}) = 1 - f(x)$ for every variable $x \in X$.

We have the following relations between $\mathcal{P}_\phi$ and $\mathcal{P}_{G_\phi,\mathrm{mon}}$, that is, the set of monotone labelings on G_ϕ:

> **Lemma 7.13.** *The following hold:*
>
> - *If f satisfies ϕ, then the assignment f_G is monotone on G_ϕ.*
> - *We have*
> $$\frac{\delta_{\mathrm{H}}(f, \mathcal{P}_\phi)}{2} \leq \delta_{\mathrm{H}}(f_G, \mathcal{P}_{G_\phi,\mathrm{mon}}).$$

Proof. The first claim is clear.

To show the second claim, we transform f into a satisfying assignment for ϕ by changing assignments to at most $d_{\mathrm{H}}(f_G, \mathcal{P}_{G_\phi,\mathrm{mon}})$ variables. To this end, an assignment of an implication graph is called *negation-compliant* if v_x and $\bar{v}_x$ have different assignments for all literals. Note that every negation-compliant assignment of G_ϕ has a corresponding assignment to ϕ. Furthermore, if f'_G is monotone and negation-compliant for G_ϕ, then the corresponding assignment f' for ϕ, given by $f'(x) = f'(v_x)$ for every variable $x \in X$, is a satisfying assignment for ϕ.

We say that two vertices in G_ϕ are *equivalent* if they belong to the same strongly connected component. Note that for every literal x, v_x and $\bar{v}_x$ are never equivalent because ϕ is satisfiable. Also, if v_x is equivalent to v_y in G_ϕ, then $\bar{v}_x$ is equivalent to $\bar{v}_y$.

(margin notes) implication graph · dual arc · negation-compliant · equivalence

The following algorithm transforms f_G into a monotone, negation-compliant assignment.

Algorithm 7.2

1: Convert f_G to a closest monotone assignment f_G^* on G_ϕ.
2: $\tilde{f}_G \leftarrow f_G^*$.   ▷ $\tilde{f}_G$ may not be negation-compliant.
3: **while** G_ϕ has a vertex v_x with $\tilde{f}_G(v_x) = \tilde{f}_G(\bar{v}_x) = 0$ **do**
4:     Let v_x be the maximal one with respect to $\leq_{G_\phi}$.
5:     Change $\tilde{f}_G(v_y)$ to 1 for all v_y equivalent to v_x (including v_x itself).
6: **end while**
7: **while** G_ϕ has a vertex v_x with $\tilde{f}_G(v_x) = \tilde{f}_G(\bar{v}_x) = 1$ **do**
8:     Let v_x be the minimal one with respect to $\leq_{G_\phi}$.
9:     Change $\tilde{f}_G(v_y)$ to 0 for all v_y equivalent to v_x (including v_x itself).
10: **end while**

First, we show that the resulting assignment $\tilde{f}_G$ is monotone on G_ϕ. Indeed, $\tilde{f}_G$ is monotone from the definition. Since it is monotone, vertices in the same strongly connected component (that is, equivalent vertices with respect to G_ϕ) have the same labels. Hence, after each change in the loop from Line 3, equivalent vertices remain to have the same labels. Suppose $\tilde{f}_G$ is monotone before some iteration of the loop from Line 3 and is not monotone after it. Then, some edge (v_x, v_y) is violated by changing $\tilde{f}_G(v_x)$ to 1. Then $\tilde{f}_G(v_y) = 0$ both before and after this iteration, and v_y is not equivalent to v_x. Since $v_y \geq_G v_x$, it must be that $\tilde{f}_G(\bar{v}_y) = 1$ (otherwise, v_y would have changed before v_x). But then the dual arc $(\bar{v}_y, \bar{v}_x)$ is violated before the iteration, giving a contradiction.

Similarly, if $\tilde{f}_G$ is monotone before some iteration of the loop from Line 7, then it is monotone after it.

Secondly, the resulting assignment $\tilde{f}_G$ is negation-compliant because the loop from Line 3 relabels all vertices v_x with $\tilde{f}(v_x) = \tilde{f}(\bar{v}_x) = 0$, and the loop from Line 7 relabels all vertices with $\tilde{f}(v_x) = \tilde{f}(\bar{v}_x) = 1$.

Finally, let $\tilde{f} \colon X \to \{0, 1\}$ be the assignment with $\tilde{f}(x) = \tilde{f}_G(v_x)$ for every variable $x \in X$. By the argument above, $\tilde{f}$ is a satisfying assignment for ϕ.

Note that $f(x) \neq \tilde{f}(x)$ only when $f_G(x) \neq f_G^*(x)$ at Line 1. Hence, we have $d_H(f, \tilde{f}) \leq d_H(f_G, f_G^*) = d_H(f_G, \mathcal{P}_{G_\phi, \mathrm{mon}})$, and it follows that:

$$
\delta_H(f, \mathcal{P}_\phi) \leq \delta_H(f, \tilde{f}) \leq \frac{d_H(f_G, \mathcal{P}_{G_\phi, \mathrm{mon}})}{|V|}
$$

$$
= \frac{2 d_H(f_G, \mathcal{P}_{G_\phi, \mathrm{mon}})}{|V(G_\phi)|}
$$

$$
= 2 \delta_H(f_G, \mathcal{P}_{G_\phi, \mathrm{mon}}). \qquad \square
$$

The proof of Lemma 7.13 is somewhat similar to that of Lemma 7.5. We will generalize these arguments for CSPs having a certain property in Section 13.2.

Now, we get the following reduction to monotonicity testing.

Lemma 7.14. *Suppose that the monotonicity on a graph on n vertices is testable with $q(n, \epsilon)$ queries. Then, there is a tester for 2-SAT with query complexity $q(2n, \epsilon/2)$. Moreover, the reduction preserves one-sided error testability.*

Proof. Let ϕ be a 2-CNF on a set X of n variables and $f \colon X \to \{0,1\}$ be an assignment to ϕ. Let G_ϕ and $f_G \colon V(G) \to \{0,1\}$ be the graph and its labeling as defined above.

If f is a satisfying assignment, then f_G is monotone from the first claim of Lemma 7.13. Also, if f is ϵ-far from satisfying assignments, then f_G is $\epsilon/2$-far from being monotonicity on G_ϕ from the second claim of Lemma 7.13. Hence, by running a tester for monotonicity on G and f_G with the error parameter $\epsilon/2$, we can test the assignment f to ϕ. The query complexity is clearly $q(2n, \epsilon/2)$ because the number of vertices in G is $2n$. $\square$

Combining Theorem 7.3 and Lemma 7.14, we get the following.

Theorem 7.5. *There is a one-sided error tester for 2-SAT with $O(\sqrt{\epsilon^{-1}n})$ queries.*

Exercise 7.3. Show a gap-preserving local reduction from testing monotonicity to 2-SAT, which yields lower bounds for 2-SAT.

ϵ-far

Exercise 7.4. Let $G = (V, E)$ be a graph on n vertices and $f \colon V \to \{0,1\}$ be a vertex labeling. We say that f is ϵ-*far* from being an independent set if we must modify more than ϵn values of f to make $f^{-1}(1) \subseteq V$ an independent set. Show that the property of being an independent set is testable with $O(\sqrt{\epsilon^{-1}n})$ queries.

7.4.2 3-SAT

In this section, we see that testing 3-SAT requires a linear number of queries by reduction from testing k-LIN.

Recall that the construction from Section 7.3 produces instances of k-LIN for some constant k that are hard to test. First, we show that we can assume that k is 3. To this end, we consider a reduction from an instance of k-LIN to an instance of $(\lceil k/2 \rceil + 1)$-LIN. Let φ be an instance of k-LIN on a set of variables $X = \{x_1, \ldots, x_n\}$ and m constraints. The reduction maps φ to an instance of $(\lceil k/2 \rceil + 1)$-LIN on variables $X \cup Z$, where $Z = \{z_1, \ldots, z_m\}$ is another set of variables. Then, for each constraint in φ of the form $x_1 + \cdots +$

$x_k = 0 \pmod 2$, we add two constraints $x_1 + \cdots + x_{\lceil k/2 \rceil} + z_i = 0 \pmod 2$ and $x_{\lceil k/2 \rceil + 1} + \cdots + x_k + z_i = 0 \pmod 2$. Also, for each constraint in φ of the form $x_1 + \cdots + x_k = 1 \pmod 2$, we add two constraints $x_1 + \cdots + x_{\lceil k/2 \rceil} + z_i = 1 \pmod 2$ and $x_{\lceil k/2 \rceil + 1} + \cdots + x_k + z_i = 0 \pmod 2$. Let φ' be the resulting instance of $(\lceil k/2 \rceil + 1)$-LIN. Let $V_\phi \subseteq \mathbb{F}_2^n$ and $V_{\phi'} \subseteq \mathbb{F}_2^{n+m}$ be the subspaces of vectors satisfying constraints in ϕ and ϕ', respectively. Then, we can show that, if V_ϕ is a hard subspace in the sense of Definition 7.2, then $V_{\phi'}$ is also a hard subspace. Although the parameters slightly deteriorate, they are sufficient to show that testing $(\lceil k \rceil + 1)$-LIN also requires $\Omega(n)$ queries. By applying this reduction $O(\log k)$ times to the original instance of k-LIN, we get the following:

Theorem 7.6. *Testing assignments to 3-LIN requires $\Omega(n)$ queries.*

Given an instance of 3-LIN on a variable set X and an assignment $f : X \to \{0, 1\}$, we can apply a canonical reduction from 3-LIN to 3-SAT, described in Section 5.6. As the variable set is the same, we use f as the assignment to the instance of 3-SAT. Then, the lower bound for 3-LIN carries over to 3-SAT, and we get the following:

Corollary 7.2. *Testing assignments to 3-SAT requires $\Omega(n)$ queries.*

7.5 Bibliographic Notes

The upper bound for testing 2-coloring presented in Section 7.1 is folklore. The sublinear upper bound and the super-constant lower bound for testing monotonicity presented in Section 7.2, including Lemma 7.3, were given in [182]. The proof of Lemma 7.5 is due to [208]. The linear lower bound for subspace membership problem presented in Section 7.3 was given in [62]. The $O(\sqrt{n})$ upper bound for testing 2-SAT is given in [182] and the $\Omega(n)$ lower bound for 3-SAT is given in [62]. By reduction to testing 3-SAT, it is shown that testing Horn 3-SAT, that is, Horn SAT with each clause having size at most 3, requires $\Omega(n)$ queries in [81]. As mentioned at the beginning of this chapter, all the results studied in this chapter can be seen as testing whether an assignment is a satisfying assignment to a specified instance of a CSP. We will elaborate on this aspect in Chapter 13.

Another well studied massively parameterized model is the *orientation model* of a graph. In this model, we are given an explicit representation of an undirected graph $G = (V, E)$ and query access to an assignment to edges $\alpha \in \{0, 1\}^E$. The interpretation of α is an orientation of the edges relative to a fixed orientation. E.g., one can interpret α as the digraph $G_\alpha = (V, E_\alpha)$, where

$$E_\alpha = \{(i, j) : \alpha(\{i, j\}) = 0\} \cup \{(j, i) : \alpha(\{i, j\}) = 1\}.$$

orientation model

source/sink

source/sink-freeness

We illustrate several known results for the orientation model. A *source* in a digraph is a vertex v for which $d^-(v) = 0$, namely, has no incoming edges. Similarly v is a *sink* if $d^+(v) = 0$. A graph is *source-free* (resp., *sink-free*) if it contains no source (resp., sink). Let H be a fixed digraph that is either source-free or sink-free. Then, if the input graph $G = (V, E)$ has a bounded-degree, then there is a one-sided error tester for H-freeness with $\mathrm{poly}(\epsilon^{-1})$ queries [243]. It was shown in [118] that, when two vertices $s, t \in V$ are given as a part of the input, there is a one-sided error tester for the s-t connectivity with query complexity at most:

$$\left(\frac{2}{\epsilon}\right)^{2^{O\left((1/\epsilon)^{1/\epsilon}\right)}}.$$

Testing Eulerianity with one-sided error requires $\Omega(|E|)$ queries [180]. See a survey [330] for more details.

subgraph model

Goldreich and Ron [219] considered the *subgraph model*. As with the orientation model, we are explicitly given an undirected graph $G = (V, E)$ and query access to an assignment to edges $\alpha \in \{0, 1\}^E$. Then, we want to test whether the subgraph $G' = (V, \alpha^{-1}(1))$ of G satisfies some predetermined property. Note that the adjacency matrix model studied in Chapter 4 is a special case of the subgraph model in which the complete graph is given as the original graph.

read-k-times formula

Another interesting massively parameterized model is testing membership in Boolean formulas. More specifically, we are explicitly given a Boolean formula, consisting of $\vee$ (OR), $\wedge$ (AND), and $\neg$ (NOT) gates, and query access to a Boolean assignment, and then we want to test whether the evaluation of the formula with the assignment is true. A *read-k-times formula* is a formula in which every variable appears at most k times. By exploiting Theorem 7.4, we can show a linear lower bound even when the Boolean formula is restricted to read-three times formulas. On the other hand, read-once formulas are known to be one-sided error testable with $(1/\epsilon)^{O(\epsilon^{-1})}$ queries (see [330] for the proof). If the form of a formula is restricted to CNF, then read-twice formulas are known to be one-sided error testable with a constant number of queries [330]. However, a general upper bound on read-twice formulas is unknown.

Problems

In the following problems, we always consider the massively parameterized model, that is, a graph $G = (V, E)$ or a CSP instance is explicitly given and query access to a function is given as oracle. We use symbols n and m to denote the number of vertices and edges, respectively, in G.

7.1. Design a one-sided error tester for 2-coloring with query complexity $\tilde{O}(\epsilon^{-1})$.

7.2. Show that the monotonicity of a function $f\colon V \to \{0,1\}$ on a directed graph $G = (V, E)$ is testable with a constant number of queries when G is an *arborescence*, that is, a directed tree with a root $r \in V$ such that there is exactly one path from r to each vertex $v \in V$.

arborescence

7.3. We say that $f\colon V \to \{0,1\}$ is a *vertex cover* in a graph $G = (V, E)$ if the corresponding set $f^{-1}(1) := \{v \in V : f(v) = 1\}$ is a vertex cover of G. Show that the property of being a vertex cover is testable with $O(\sqrt{\epsilon^{-1}n})$ queries.

vertex cover

In the following problems, we say that $f\colon E \to \{0,1\}$ is *triangle-free*, a *matching*, and a *global minimum cut* if the corresponding edge set $f^{-1}(1) := \{e \in E : f(e) = 1\}$ satisfies the corresponding property.

triangle-freeness
matching
global minimum cut

7.4. Show the following.

1. Triangle-freeness is testable with $O(\epsilon^{-1/3}m^{2/3})$ queries.
2. Triangle-freeness is testable with $O(\epsilon^{-1}\sqrt{m})$ queries using the fact that there are at most $O(m^{3/2})$ many triangle in an m-edge graph.

7.5. Show that the property of being a matching is testable with $O(\sqrt{\epsilon^{-1}m})$ queries.

7.6. Show that the property of being a global minimum cut is testable with $O(\log n)$ queries, using the fact that there are at most $O(n^2)$ global minimum cuts.

7.7. The distance of a linear code $\mathcal{C} \subseteq \{0,1\}^n$ is the minimum Hamming weight of a non-zero codeword. Prove that the LDPC code constructed in the proof of Lemma 7.8 (in Section 7.3.4) has distance $\Omega(n)$.

7.8. Let $M \in \mathbb{F}_2^{n \times k}$ be a matrix whose column space equals a subspace in $\mathbb{F}_2^n$ of dimension k. Define the property Π_M as:

$$\Pi_M = \{Mx \circ My : x, y \in \mathbb{F}_2^k \text{ disjoint}\}$$

where $x, y \in \mathbb{F}_2^n$ are said to be disjoint if there does not exist $i \in [n]$ for which $x_i = y_i = 1$. Show that there exists M such that testing membership in Π_M requires $\Omega(n)$ queries (for a constant distance parameter). Use the communication complexity methodology introduced in Chapter 6.

Chapter 8
Vectors and Matrices over the Reals

In previous chapters, we studied testing problems on discrete objects such as strings, graphs, functions over finite fields, and CSPs. In this chapter, we shift our focus on objects with a slightly more continuous nature, or more specifically, vectors and matrices over $\mathbb{R}$.

In Section 8.1, we consider testing one of the most important properties of a matrix, that is, having a low rank. In Section 8.2, we consider testing whether a given vector belongs to a fixed low-dimensional subspace. This problem is different from the one we studied in Section 7.3 in that the underlying field is $\mathbb{R}$ instead of $\mathbb{F}_2$ and that the fixed subspace is low-dimensional. We will see that linear algebraic tools are useful to solve these problems.

8.1 Low Rank Matrices

In this section, we consider the problem of testing whether a given matrix $A \in \mathbb{R}^{m \times n}$ has rank at most d for a fixed integer $d \in \mathbb{Z}_{>0}$. Our model is similar to the dense graph model studied in Chapter 4. We say that a matrix $A \in \mathbb{R}^{m \times n}$ is ϵ-far from having rank at most d for a positive integer d if we need to modify more than ϵmn elements in A to make it have rank at most d. The input matrix $A \in \mathbb{R}^{m \times n}$ is given through query access: If we specify a pair $(i, j) \in [m] \times [n]$, then it returns the element A_{ij}. We say that an algorithm is a *tester* for the property of having rank at most d if, given $m, n \in \mathbb{Z}_{>0}$, $\epsilon \in (0, 1)$, and query access to a matrix $A \in \mathbb{R}^{m \times n}$, it accepts with probability at least $2/3$ if the rank of A is at most d and rejects with probability at least $2/3$ if A is ϵ-far from having rank at most d.

ε-farness

tester

Our goal is to show the following:

Theorem 8.1. *There is a one-sided error tester for the property of having rank at most d with $O(\epsilon^{-2}d^2)$ queries.*

© The Author(s), under exclusive license to Springer Nature Singapore Pte Ltd 2022
A. Bhattacharyya and Y. Yoshida, *Property Testing*,
https://doi.org/10.1007/978-981-16-8622-1_8

For a set of rows R and a set of columns C, let $A|_{R \times C}$ denote the submatrix of A induced by R and C. Our tester for having a low rank is given in Algorithm 8.1.

Algorithm 8.1 One-sided error tester for having a low rank

Input: $m, n, d \in \mathbb{Z}_{>0}$, $\epsilon \in (0, 1)$, and query access to a matrix $A \in \mathbb{R}^{m \times n}$.
1: $\ell \leftarrow \Theta(\epsilon^{-1} d)$.
2: Let $R \subseteq [m]$ be a set obtained by sampling ℓ rows independently and uniformly.
3: Let $C \subseteq [n]$ be a set obtained by sampling ℓ columns independently and uniformly.
4: **if** $\text{rank}(A|_{R \times C}) \leq d$ **then**
5:     Accept.
6: **else**
7:     Reject.
8: **end if**

It is evident that the algorithm accepts any matrix with rank at most d and the query complexity is $O(\epsilon^{-2} d^2)$. Hence, it suffices to show that Algorithm 8.1 rejects ϵ-far matrix $A \in \mathbb{R}^{m \times n}$ with probability at least $2/3$.

For the sake of analysis, we think of Algorithm 8.1 as if it starts with an empty submatrix, and then iteratively augments the current submatrix by one random row and by one random column. For an integer $t \geq 0$, let B_t be the submatrix of A obtained after t iterations. Note that $A|_{R \times C}$ is equal to B_ℓ.

The lemma below shows the probability that the rank increases in one iteration.

Lemma 8.1. *Suppose $A \in \mathbb{R}^{m \times n}$ is ϵ-far from having rank at most d. Then for any $t \geq 1$, we have*

$$\Pr[\text{rank}(B_t) > \text{rank}(B_{t-1}) \mid \text{rank}(B_{t-1}) \leq d] \geq \epsilon/3. \qquad (8.1)$$

augmenting row
consistent row

Proof. Suppose $\text{rank}(B_{t-1}) \leq d$. We say that a row is *augmenting* B_{t-1} if the row is not included in B_{t-1}. We say that a row augmenting B_{t-1} is *consistent* with B_{t-1} if augmenting B_{t-1} with this row does not increase its rank. If at least $\epsilon m/3$ augmenting rows are inconsistent with B_{t-1}, then (8.1) holds.

Using analogous definitions for the columns, we have that if at least $\epsilon n/3$ augmenting columns are inconsistent with B_{t-1}, then (8.1) holds.

strongly augmenting
element

consistent element

We say that the element A_{ij} is *strongly augmenting* B_{t-1} if each of the i-th row and the j-th column (separately) is both augmenting and consistent with respect to B_{t-1}. We say that a strongly augmenting element A_{ij} is *consistent* with B_{t-1} if the augmentation of the submatrix B_{t-1} with the i-th row and the j-th column (simultaneously) does not increase its rank. If the number of strongly augmenting elements inconsistent with B_{t-1} is at least $\epsilon nm/3$, then (8.1) holds.

We now show that at least one of the three cases mentioned above must hold. Assume to the contrary that (i) less than $\epsilon m/3$ augmenting rows are inconsistent with B_t, (ii) less than $\epsilon n/3$ augmenting columns are inconsistent with B_t, and (iii) less than $\epsilon nm/3$ strongly augmenting elements are inconsistent with B_t. Suppose that we modify all the elements in augmenting rows and columns inconsistent with B_t to zeros and that we modify the value of every strongly augmenting element A_{ij} inconsistent with B_t to a value consistent with B_t. (Such a value always exists, because augmenting B_t with the i-th row adds a row that is a linear combination of the rows already in B_t, so we can take the same linear combination also in the j-th column.) The rank of the resulting matrix is at most $\mathrm{rank}(B_t) \le d$, while the total number of modified elements is at most ϵnm, which contradicts the assumption that A is ϵ-far from having rank at most d. □

The following lemma completes the proof of Theorem 8.1.

Lemma 8.2. *Suppose $A \in \mathbb{R}^{m \times n}$ is ϵ-far from having rank at most d. Then Algorithm 8.1 rejects with probability at least $2/3$.*

Proof. For $t \in [\ell]$, we say that the t-th iteration is *successful* if $\mathrm{rank}(B_t) = \mathrm{rank}(B_{t-1}) + 1$. By Lemma 8.1 the probability that the t-th iteration is successful is at least $\epsilon/3$, and we want to analyze the probability that more than d iterations have succeeded at the end of the algorithm, that is, the rank of B_ℓ exceeds d. Although we do not know any lower bound on the probability that the t-th iteration succeeds when $\mathrm{rank}(B_t) > d$, for our purpose, it suffices to analyze the probability that more than d iterations succeed assuming that every iteration succeeds with probability at least $\epsilon/3$.

By applying Lemma 2.3 with $\eta := \epsilon/3$, the number of successful iterations after ℓ steps is at least $\eta\ell - 2\sqrt{\ell}$ with probability at least $2/3$. By choosing the hidden constant in ℓ to be large enough, we have $d+1$ successful iterations with probability at least $2/3$. □

successful iteration

Exercise 8.1. Check that Algorithm 8.1 can be used as a tester for low-rank matrices also when the underlying field is $\mathbb{F}_2$.

8.2 Subspace Membership

In this section, we consider the problem of testing whether a given vector $v \in \mathbb{R}^n$ belongs to a given low-dimensional subspace. For a matrix $A \in \mathbb{R}^{n \times d}$, let $\mathrm{span}(A)$ be the subspace spanned by the column vectors of A. Note that a vector $v \in \mathbb{R}^n$ belongs to $\mathrm{span}(A)$ if and only if there exists a vector $x \in \mathbb{R}^d$ such that $v = Ax$. Then, for a vector $v \in \mathbb{R}^n$ and $\epsilon \in (0,1)$, we say that v is *ϵ-far from (belonging to)* $\mathrm{span}(A)$ if we must modify more than ϵn elements of

ϵ-farness

v to make it belong to span(A). In other words, v is ϵ-far when $\|v - Ax\|_0 > \epsilon n$ for every $x \in \mathbb{R}^d$, where $\|\cdot\|_0$ denotes the number of non-zero coordinates. A vector $v \in \mathbb{R}^n$ is given through query access: If we specify an index $i \in [n]$, then we can obtain the i-th coordinate of v.

tester for subspace
membership
We say that an algorithm is a *tester for subspace membership* if, given $n, d \in \mathbb{Z}_{>0}$, $\epsilon \in (0, 1)$, a matrix $A \in \mathbb{R}^{n \times d}$, and query access to $v \in \mathbb{R}^n$, it accepts with probability at least $2/3$ if v belongs to span(A) and rejects with probability at least $2/3$ if v is ϵ-far from span(A). Our primary interest is the regime $d \ll n$. Throughout this section, we assume without loss of generality that A has rank exactly d; otherwise, we can just remove redundant columns from A.

In this section, we show that subspace membership is testable with $O(d + \epsilon^{-1})$ queries with one-sided error (Section 8.2.1) and that any one-sided error tester requires $\Omega(d + \epsilon^{-1})$ queries (Section 8.2.2) whereas any non-adaptive (possibly two-sided error) tester requires roughly $\Omega(d^{1/2})$ queries (Section 8.2.3).

For simplicity, we assume that the matrix A is explicitly given. We note that, however, our algorithm can be modified to work even when A is given as query access with which we can get the i-th row of A by querying an index $i \in [n]$.

8.2.1 Upper Bounds

We give a tester for subspace membership in Algorithm 8.2. It first determines $x \in \mathbb{R}^d$ with $v = Ax$ by querying d coordinates, where the corresponding rows of A form a full-rank submatrix, and then it checks that other coordinates of v are consistent with Ax.

Algorithm 8.2 One-sided error tester for subspace membership

Input: $n, d \in \mathbb{Z}_{>0}$, $\epsilon \in (0, 1)$, a matrix $A \in \mathbb{R}^{n \times d}$, and query access to $v \in \mathbb{R}^n$.
1: $S \leftarrow$ a subset of $[n]$ with size d such that $A|_S$ is a full-rank matrix.
2: Solve $A|_S x = v|_S$.
3: **if** the linear equation above has no solution **then**
4:     Reject.
5: **end if**
6: **for** $q := \Theta(\epsilon^{-1})$ times **do**
7:     Sample $i \in [n]$ uniformly at random.
8:     **if** $v_i \neq (Ax)_i$ **then**
9:         Reject.
10:     **end if**
11: **end for**
12: Accept.

Theorem 8.2. *Algorithm 8.2 is a one-sided error tester with $O(d + \epsilon^{-1})$ queries.*

Proof. Suppose that $v \in \mathbb{R}^n$ belongs to $\text{span}(A)$. Then, the system of linear equations at Line 2 must have a solution $x \in \mathbb{R}^d$. We never reject in the loop as $v = Ax$ holds.

Suppose that $v \in \mathbb{R}^n$ is ϵ-far from $\text{span}(A)$. Also, suppose the system of linear equations in Line 2 has a solution $x \in \mathbb{R}^d$. Then, $\|v - Ax\|_0 > \epsilon n$ holds from the assumption. Hence, the probability that we reject is at least $1 - (1 - \epsilon)^q$, which is at least $2/3$ by choosing the hidden constant in q to be large enough.

The analysis of the query complexity is trivial.   □

8.2.2 Lower bounds for One-Sided Error Testers

In this section, we show a lower bound of $\Omega(d + \epsilon^{-1})$ for one-sided error testers, which shows the tightness of Theorem 8.2. The main ingredient in our argument is the notion of matrix spark. The *spark* of a matrix $X \in \mathbb{R}^{d \times n}$ is the smallest number q such that there exists a linearly dependent set of q columns in X. Formally,   spark

$$\text{spark}(X) = \min_{v \in \mathbb{R}^n \setminus \{0\}} \|v\|_0 \text{ such that } Xv = 0.$$

> **Exercise 8.2.** Check that the spark of the following matrix is 3:
>
> $$\begin{pmatrix} 1 & 2 & 0 & 1 \\ 1 & 2 & 0 & 2 \\ 1 & 0 & 3 & 3 \\ 1 & 0 & 3 & 4 \end{pmatrix}$$

We note that the spark of a matrix $X \in \mathbb{R}^{d \times n}$ is at most $d + 1$, and when $d < n$, a matrix with spark $d + 1$ is said to have a *full spark*. It is easy to see   full spark
that the random Gaussian matrix $X \in \mathbb{R}^{d \times n}$ has a full spark with probability one because any $d \times d$ submatrix of X is invertible with probability one.

Theorem 8.3. *Any one-sided error tester for subspace membership requires $\Omega(d + \epsilon^{-1})$ queries.*

Proof. Let $X \in \mathbb{R}^{d \times n}$ be a matrix with full spark, and set $A = X^{\top}$.

First, we show a lower bound of $\Omega(d)$. Let $v \in \mathbb{R}^n$ be an arbitrary vector that is ϵ-far from $\mathrm{span}(A)$. Suppose that we have queried $v|_S$, where $S \subseteq [n]$ is a subset of size at most d. Then, no matter what $v|_S$ is, the system $A|_S x = v|_S$ has a solution because $A|_S$ has rank $|S|$. Then, the vector $w := Ax$ belongs to $\mathrm{span}(A)$, and $w|_S = v|_S$. This means that we cannot reject with d queries because the tester is of one-sided error.

Next, we show a lower bound of $\Omega(\epsilon^{-1})$. Here we use Yao's minimax principle. Let $x \in \mathbb{R}^d$ be an arbitrary vector. Let $\mathcal{D}_Y$ be the distribution that always generates Ax, and let $\mathcal{D}_N$ be the distribution obtained by replacing random $2\epsilon n$ coordinates of Ax with Gaussian values. We call those replaced coordinates *dirty*. With probability one, the vector sampled from $\mathcal{D}_N$ is ϵ-far from $\mathrm{span}(A)$.

Let $\mathcal{A}$ be a deterministic algorithm with query complexity q. Since $\mathcal{A}$ is deterministic, as long as $\mathcal{A}$ does not query a dirty coordinate, the behavior of $\mathcal{A}$ on $v \sim \mathcal{D}_Y$ and that on $v \sim \mathcal{D}_N$ are exactly the same. The probability that $\mathcal{A}$ hits some dirty coordinate is $1 - (1 - \epsilon)^q$. To make this probability at least $2/3$, we need to have $q = \Omega(\epsilon^{-1})$. $\qquad\square$

8.2.3 Lower Bounds for Non-Adaptive Testers

The goal of this section is to show the following:

> **Theorem 8.4.** *For any $\delta > 0$, any non-adaptive tester for subspace membership requires $\Omega(d^{1/2-\delta})$ queries.*

The idea behind the proof of Theorem 8.4 is as follows: Let $A \in \mathbb{R}^{n \times d}$ be a matrix with $A^\top$ being *incoherent*, that is, any two rows of A are almost orthogonal. Then, we consider two distributions $\mathcal{D}_Y$ and $\mathcal{D}_N$, where $\mathcal{D}_Y$ generates Ax for a d-dimensional Gaussian vector x, and $\mathcal{D}_N$ generates an n-dimensional Gaussian vector. We will see that $\mathcal{D}_Y$ generates vectors belonging to $\mathrm{span}(A)$ whereas $\mathcal{D}_N$ generates vectors far from $\mathrm{span}(A)$ with high probability. Furthermore, we will show that $\mathcal{D}_Y$ and $\mathcal{D}_N$ cannot be distinguished with a small number of queries. By Yao's minimax principle, this turns out to be a lower bound for testing subspace membership.

In Section 8.2.3.1, we examine properties of incoherent matrices. Then, we prove Theorem 8.4 in Section 8.2.3.2.

8.2.3.1 Matrix construction

Here, we construct matrices whose submatrices satisfy the following property:

Lemma 8.3. *Let $n, k \in \mathbb{Z}_{>0}$ and $\epsilon > 0$. Then, there exists a matrix $X \in \mathbb{R}^{d \times n}$ with $d = O(\log^{2k+1} n)$ such that any matrix $Y \in \mathbb{R}^{d \times q}$ obtained by collecting $q = O(\epsilon d^{k/(2k+1)})$ columns from X satisfies $\det(Y^\top Y) \geq \frac{1}{1+\epsilon}$ and $\operatorname{trace}(Y^\top Y) \leq q + \epsilon$.*

The main tool used to show Lemma 8.3 is coherence. Let $X \in \mathbb{R}^{d \times n}$ be a matrix whose columns $a^1, \ldots, a^n$ are ℓ_2-normalized; that is, $\|a^i\| = 1$ holds for every $i \in [n]$. The *coherence* $\mu(X)$ of X is defined as:

$$\mu(X) = \max_{i,j \in [n] : i \neq j} |\langle a^i, a^j \rangle|.$$

coherence

A construction of matrices with a small coherence is known:

Lemma 8.4. *For any (sufficiently large) $n \in \mathbb{Z}_{>0}$ and $\epsilon > 0$, there exists a matrix $X \in \mathbb{R}^{d \times n}$ with $d = O(\epsilon^{-2} \log n)$ and $\mu(X) \leq \epsilon$.*

The following fact is also known:

Lemma 8.5. *Let $A \in \mathbb{R}^{n \times n}$ be a matrix of the form $I + E$, where each element of E has absolute value at most ϵ and E has zeros in its diagonal. Then, we have $\det A \geq \frac{1}{1+n\epsilon}$.*

Proof of Lemma 8.3. Let $\delta = 1/\log^k n$ and let $X \in \mathbb{R}^{d \times n}$ be a matrix with $d = O(\log^{2k+1} n)$ and $\mu(X) \leq \delta$, whose existence is guaranteed by Lemma 8.4. Then, $Y^\top Y \in \mathbb{R}^{q \times q}$ can be represented as $I + E$, where each element of E has absolute value at most δ and E has zeros in its diagonal. By Lemma 8.5, we have $\det(Y^\top Y) \geq \frac{1}{1+q\delta}$. Also, we have $\operatorname{trace}(Y^\top Y) = \operatorname{trace}(I) + \operatorname{trace}(E) \leq q + q\delta$. Hence, we have $\det(Y^\top Y) \geq \frac{1}{1+\epsilon}$ and $\operatorname{trace}(Y^\top Y) \leq q + \epsilon$ when $q = O(\epsilon d^{k/(2k+1)})$. $\square$

8.2.3.2 Lower bounds

In order to show Theorem 8.4, we use a variant of Yao's minimax principle. Fix $n, k \in \mathbb{Z}_{>0}$ and let $X \in \mathbb{R}^{d \times n}$ be the matrix given by Lemma 8.3 for sufficiently small $\epsilon > 0$. Then, we set $A = X^\top$. Let $\mathcal{N}(\mu, \Sigma)$ be the Gaussian distribution with mean vector μ and covariance matrix Σ. Then, we define two distributions $\mathcal{D}_Y$ and $\mathcal{D}_N$ so that the distribution $\mathcal{D}_Y$ generates $x \sim \mathcal{N}(0_m, I_m)$ and then outputs $v = Ax$, and the distribution $\mathcal{D}_N$ simply outputs $v \sim \mathcal{N}(0_n, I_n)$, where $0_m \in \mathbb{R}^m$ and $0_n \in \mathbb{R}^n$ are all-zero vectors.

Lemma 8.6. *The following hold:*

- *Every $v \in \mathbb{R}^n$ in the support of $\mathcal{D}_Y$ belongs to $\operatorname{span}(A)$.*
- *With probability one, $v \in \mathbb{R}^n$ sampled from $\mathcal{D}_N$ is $1/2$-far from $\operatorname{span}(A)$.*

Proof. For the first claim, as v can be represented as Ax for some $x \in \mathbb{R}^d$, v must belong to span(A).

Now, we show the second claim. Let $S = \{1, \ldots, d\}$, and let x be the solution to $A|_S x = v|_S$. Then, the probability that $(Ax)_i = v_i$ is zero for each $i \in [n] \setminus S$. Hence, v is (at least) 1/2-far from span(A). □

Now, to show the lower bound of q for non-adaptive testers, it suffices to show that:

$$d_{\mathrm{TV}}(\mathcal{D}_Y|_S, \mathcal{D}_N|_S) < \frac{1}{10}$$

for every set $S \subseteq [n]$ of size q, where $\mathcal{D}_Y|_S$ and $\mathcal{D}_N|_S$ are the distributions of $v|_S$ for $v \sim \mathcal{D}_Y$ and $v \sim \mathcal{D}_N$, respectively. To this end, we need the following fact.

Lemma 8.7. *Let $n \in \mathbb{Z}_{>0}$ and $\Sigma, \Sigma' \in \mathbb{R}^{n \times n}$ be invertible covariance matrices. For n-variate Gaussian distributions $\mathcal{D} = \mathcal{N}(0_n, \Sigma)$ and $\mathcal{D}' = \mathcal{N}(0_n, \Sigma')$, we have:*

$$d_{\mathrm{KL}}(\mathcal{D} \| \mathcal{D}') = \frac{1}{2}\left(\log \frac{\det \Sigma'}{\det \Sigma} + \mathrm{trace}(\Sigma'^{-1}\Sigma) - n\right).$$

Now, we have the following:

Lemma 8.8. *For any $S \subseteq [n]$ of size $q = O(d^{k/(2k+1)})$, we have $d_{\mathrm{TV}}(\mathcal{D}_Y|_S, \mathcal{D}_N|_S) \leq 1/10$.*

Proof. Let $v \sim \mathcal{D}_Y$ and $w \sim \mathcal{D}_N$. Note that $v|_S$ and $w|_S$ can be regarded as sampled from $\mathcal{N}(0_q, A|_S(A|_S)^\top)$ and $\mathcal{N}(0_q, I_q)$, respectively. From the choice of the matrix A, we have:

$$\det\left(A|_S(A|_S)^\top\right) \geq \frac{1}{1+\epsilon} \quad \text{and} \quad \mathrm{trace}\left(A|_S(A|_S)^\top\right) \leq q + \epsilon.$$

By Lemma 8.7 and the choice of the matrix A, we have:

$$d_{\mathrm{KL}}(\mathcal{D}_Y|_S, \mathcal{D}_N|_S) = \frac{1}{2}\left(\log \frac{1}{\det(A|_S(A|_S)^\top)} + \mathrm{trace}\left(A|_S(A|_S)^\top\right) - q\right)$$

$$\leq \frac{1}{2}\left(\log(1+\epsilon) + \epsilon\right) \leq \frac{1}{50},$$

by choosing ϵ to be small enough. By Pinsker's inequality (Theorem 2.9), we have $d_{\mathrm{TV}}(\mathcal{D}_Y|_S, \mathcal{D}_N|_S) \leq 1/10$. □

Proof of Theorem 8.4. Lemmas 8.6 and 8.8 combined with Yao's minimax principle imply that testing subspace membership on a matrix $A \in \mathbb{R}^{n \times d}$ requires $\Omega(d^{k/(2k+1)})$ queries, where $d = O(\log^{2k+1}(n))$.

In order to remove the dependency between n and d, we duplicate each row of A arbitrarily many times and let $A' \in \mathbb{R}^{n' \times d}$ be the resulting matrix. Since an algorithm cannot obtain any further information from A', testing subspace membership on A' requires $\Omega(d^{k/(2k+1)})$ queries. By choosing k large enough, we get a lower bound of $\Omega(d^{1/2-\delta})$. □

8.3 Additional Topics

Testing Sparsity

Barman, Bhattacharyya, and Ghoshal [42] considered testing algorithms for sparsity that observe a low-dimensional projection of the input. They considered two settings. The first setting is testing sparsity with respect to an unknown basis: Given some oracle access to vectors $y_1, \ldots, y_p \in \mathbb{R}^d$ whose concatenation as columns forms $Y \in \mathbb{R}^{d \times p}$, we want to distinguish the case that there exist matrices $A \in \mathbb{R}^{d \times m}$ and $X \in \mathbb{R}^{m \times p}$ such that $Y = AX$ and each column of X is k-sparse, that is, having at most k non-zero entries, from the case that Y is far from having such a decomposition. The second setting is testing sparsity with respect to a known basis: For a fixed design matrix $A \in \mathbb{R}^{d \times m}$, given some oracle access to a vector $y \in \mathbb{R}^d$, we want to distinguish the case that $y = Ax$ for some k-sparse vector $x \in \mathbb{R}^m$, from the case that y is far from having such a decomposition. These settings can be seen as testing versions of dictionary learning and sparse recovery, respectively, which are both intensively studied in the machine learning community. See [161, 189] for books on these topics. Assuming the existence of a linear measurement oracle, which returns inner products with Gaussian vectors, Barman, Bhattacharyya, and Ghoshal gave efficient testers such that the numbers of measurements are independent of d.

Chen, De, and Servedio [122] studied another setting for testing k-sparsity of $x \in \mathbb{R}^m$. Namely, they assumed oracle that returns $x^\top w + \eta$, where $w \in \mathbb{R}^m$ is sampled from some (known) product distribution that is not Gaussian and $\eta \in \mathbb{R}$ is some Gaussian noise. Under a suitably defined notion of farness, they showed a tester for k-sparsity such that the number of accesses to the oracle is independent of m.

k-sparsity

Polynomial Optimization

Yoshida and Hayashi [251] considered the *quadratic function minimization problem*, where the goal is to minimize a quadratic function $x^\top A x + b^\top x + c$ over $x \in \mathbb{R}^n$, where $A \in \mathbb{R}^{n \times n}$, $b \in \mathbb{R}^n$ and $c \in \mathbb{R}^n$. This problem appears

quadratic function minimization problem

in various machine learning problems such as linear regression. Assuming that the elements in A, b, and c have bounded absolute values, they gave a constant-time algorithm that approximates the optimal value to within an additive error of ϵn^2 by exploiting Szemerédi's regularity lemma for graphons (see Chapter 9). Levi and Yoshida [299] gave a different guarantee by exploiting a spectral version of Szemerédi's regularity lemma.

tensor

A *tensor of order k* (over $\mathbb{R}$) is a k-dimensional array of real numbers. A vector and a matrix can be seen as tensors of order one and two, respectively.

Tucker decomposition

Tucker decomposition [256, 384] is a popular method for decomposing a tensor into a small tensor and matrices, and has many applications in machine learning. Let us focus on the case $k = 3$ for simplicity. Then, the Tucker decomposition of a tensor $T \in \mathbb{R}^{n \times n \times n}$ is decomposing it as $T(i, j, k) = \sum_{p,q,r \in [R]} \lambda_{pqr} x_{pi} y_{qj} z_{rk}$, where $R \in \mathbb{Z}_{>0}$, $\lambda_{pqr} \in \mathbb{R}$, and $x_{pi}, y_{qj}, z_{rk} \in \mathbb{R}^n$.

Tucker rank

The smallest R for which such a decomposition exists is called the *Tucker rank* of T. Hayashi and Yoshida [252] gave a constant-time algorithm that, given query access to a tensor $T \in \mathbb{R}^{n \times n \times n}$ and a parameter R, approximates the minimum residual error caused by approximating T by another tensor of Tucker rank R.

Ising model

An *Ising model* is specified by a probability distribution on the discrete cube $\{-1, 1\}^n$ of the form:

$$\Pr[X = x] := \frac{1}{Z} \exp\left(\sum_{i,j} J_{ij} x_i x_j\right),$$

where the matrix $J \in \mathbb{R}^{n \times n}$ is an arbitrary real, symmetric matrix with zeros on the diagonal. The normalizing constant $Z = \sum_{x \in \{-1,1\}^n} \exp\left(\sum_{i,j} J_{ij} x_i x_j\right)$

partition function
free energy

is called the *partition function* of the Ising model and the quantity $F := \log Z$ is known as the *free energy*. The free energy is a crucial quantity of Ising models, with which we can compute many fundamental quantities associated with Ising models including magnetization and the location of various phase transitions. Jain, Koehler, and Mossel [265] gave a constant-time algorithm that approximates the free energy within an additive error of (roughly) $\epsilon n \|J\|_F$,

Frobenius norm

where $\|J\|_F := \sqrt{\sum_{i,j \in [n]} J_{ij}^2}$ is the *Frobenius norm* of J.

Density Estimation

density estimation
problem

One of the most fundamental problems in statistics is the *density estimation problem* In this problem, given samples from a distribution, we want to reconstruct the probability density function of the distribution. Imaizumi, Maehara, and Yoshida [259] designed the first density estimation algorithm that has a provable guarantee for non-smooth probability density functions.

Their algorithm buildes on Szemerédi's regularity lemma: It partitions the whole domain into a constant number of blocks and estimates the average density of each block. For the true probability density function $f^*\colon \mathbb{R}^d \to \mathbb{R}$ and the output of the algorithm $f\colon \mathbb{R}^d \to \mathbb{R}$, the error $\|f - f^*\|_1$ decreases as $O(1/\sqrt{\log n})$, where n is the number of samples. They showed that this bound is tight.

Testing Properties of Functions on $\mathbb{R}^n$

As an extension of testing properties of functions over hypercubes, which we studied in Chapter 6, it is natural to study testing properties of functions over $\mathbb{R}^n$. As the uniform distribution over $\mathbb{R}^n$ is not well defined, we first fix a distribution $\mathcal{D}$ over $\mathbb{R}^n$, and then define ϵ-farness according to the distribution. Namely, the *distance* $d_{\mathcal{D}}(f, g)$ between two (measurable) functions $f, g\colon \mathbb{R}^n \to \mathbb{R}$ with respect to $\mathcal{D}$ is defined to be $\Pr_{x \sim \mathcal{D}}[f(x) \neq g(x)]$. Then, we say that a function $f\colon \mathbb{R}^n \to \mathbb{R}$ is ϵ-*far* from a property $\mathcal{P}$ with respect to $\mathcal{D}$ if we have $d_{\mathcal{D}}(f, g) > \epsilon$ for any function $g\colon \mathbb{R}^n \to \mathbb{R}$ satisfying $\mathcal{P}$. Besides query access to the input function $f\colon \mathbb{R}^n \to \mathbb{R}$, we assume that we can sample points from $\mathcal{D}$.

distance

ϵ-farness

Fleming and Yoshida [187] showed that the linearity of a function $f\colon \mathbb{R}^n \to \mathbb{R}$ is testable with $\widetilde{O}(\epsilon^{-1})$ queries and samples for any distribution $\mathcal{D}$. Their algorithm is a modification of the self-correction approach discussed in Section 6.3.2. Black Chakrabarty, and Seshadhri [84] showed that the monotonicity of a function $f\colon \mathbb{R}^n \to \{0, 1\}$ is testable with $\widetilde{O}(n^{5/6})$ queries for any product distribution $\mathcal{D}$. Their algorithm first reduces the domain from $\mathbb{R}^n$ to a finite domain by sampling points, then argue that, if the original function is ϵ-far, then the resulting functions is also far from monotonicity with high probability.

Historically, testing algebraic properties of functions has been developed in the context of program checking, and in this context testing properties of $\mathbb{R}$-valued functions over a finite domain, such as $\{i/s : |i| \leq n, i \in \mathbb{Z}\}$ for some $n, s \in \mathbb{Z}_{>0}$, has been already studied in the early 90's [302, 367]. Because it is unrealistic to assume that programs can perform exact computations on real values, *approximate testing* has been studied, where the answers of the query access to the input function have some small error [28, 172]. See [282] for a survey about this direction.

approximate testing

8.4 Bibliographic Notes

The argument in Section 8.1 is based on [287]. The query complexity was later improved to $\widetilde{O}(\epsilon^{-1}d^2)$ in [40, 301] and an almost matching lower bound was obtained [40]. As related questions, Balcan, Li, Woodruff, and Zhang [40] studied testing stable rank and Schatten p-norm. Here, the *stable rank* of a matrix $A \in \mathbb{R}^{m \times n}$ is $\|A\|_F^2 / \|A\|_2^2 = \sum_{1 \le i \le \min\{m,n\}} \sigma_i^2 / \sigma_1^2$, where σ_i is the i-th largest singular value of A. Stable rank is always upper bounded by the usual rank, and is less sensitive to perturbation on the matrix. The *Schatten p-norm* of a matrix $A \in \mathbb{R}^{n \times n}$ is $\left(\sum_{1 \le i \le \min\{m,n\}} \sigma_i^p\right)^{1/p}$, which is the ℓ_p norm of the vector consisting of the singular values. They obtained testers for testing low stable rank and Schatten p-norm with polylogarithmic numbers of queries.

The argument in Section 8.2 is due to Hayashi and Yoshida [253]. Indeed, they studied a more general problem called the *subspace proximity problem*, in which a parameter $\Delta \in \mathbb{R}$ is additionally given and the goal is to test whether there exists $x \in \mathbb{R}^d$ such that $\|v - Ax\|_\infty \le \Delta$. They gave a one-sided error tester with query complexity $O(\epsilon^{-1} d \log(\epsilon^{-1} d))$ and a two-sided error tester with query complexity $O(\epsilon^{-1} d)$. Lemmas 8.4 and 8.5 are due to [1] and [342], respectively.

Problems

8.1. Consider the property $\mathcal{P}$ of Boolean matrices such that $A \in \{0,1\}^{m \times n}$ satisfies $\mathcal{P}$ if there exist subsets $S \subseteq [m]$ and $T \subseteq [n]$ such that $A_{ij} = 1$ if and only if $i \in S$ or $j \in T$. Show that $\mathcal{P}$ is testable with $O(\epsilon^{-2})$ queries.

8.2. Let $\mathcal{M} = (E, \mathcal{I})$ be a matroid (see Appendix B for the definition and properties of a matroid). For $\epsilon \in (0, 1)$ and an integer $r \in \mathbb{Z}_{>0}$, we say that $\mathcal{M}$ is ϵ-*far from having rank at most r* if any matroid obtained from $\mathcal{M}$ by removing at most $\epsilon |E|$ elements of E has rank more than r. Suppose we have query access to $\mathcal{I}$, that is, it returns whether S belongs to $\mathcal{I}$ if we specify a set $S \subseteq E$. Show that we can test the property of having rank at most r with $O(\epsilon^{-2})$ queries.

8.3. Let $A \in \mathbb{R}^{d \times n}$ and $b \in \mathbb{R}^d$. Suppose that a solution $x \in \mathbb{R}^n$ to a linear equation $Ax = b$ satisfies $\|x\|_0 < \text{spark}(A)/2$. Then, show that x is the unique sparsest possible solution to the linear equation.

8.4. Let $A \in \mathbb{R}^{d \times n}$. Show that $\text{spark}(A) \ge 1 + \mu(A)^{-1}$, where $\mu(A)$ is the coherence of A. You can use the fact that if a matrix $B \in \mathbb{R}^{k \times k}$ is *strictly diagonally dominant*, that is, $B_{ii} > \sum_{j \ne i} B_{ij}$ for every $i \in [k]$, then B is positive definite and hence is of full rank.

In the following two problems, we regard an integer $d \in \mathbb{Z}_{>0}$ is constant and assume query access to an input matrix $A \in \mathbb{R}^{d \times n}$, and we say that A is ϵ-*far* from a property $\mathcal{P}$ if modifying at most $\epsilon d n$ entries of A does not make A satisfy $\mathcal{P}$.

8.5. Let $0 \leq k \leq d$. Show that the property of having spark more than k is testable with $q := O(n^{(k-1)/k} \cdot \epsilon^{-1/k})$ queries (ignoring the dependency on d). (**Hint**: Call a set $S \subseteq [n]$ of columns of size at most k a *violating set* if there exists $v \in \mathbb{R}^n$ supported on S such that $Av = 0$. Show that the set of q randomly sampled columns contains a violating set with high probability.)

8.6. Let $0 \leq k \leq d$. Show that the property of being k-sparse is testable with $O(\epsilon^{-1})$ queries (ignoring the dependency on d).

violating set

Part III

Chapter 9
Graphs in the Adjacency Matrix Model: Characterizations via Regularity Lemmas

In this chapter, we explain general results on testing graph properties in the adjacency matrix model. In Section 9.1, we show that monotone properties, that is, properties closed under taking subgraphs, are constant-query testable with one-sided error. In Section 9.2, we extend the argument to show that hereditary properties, that is, properties closed under taking induced subgraphs, are constant-query testable with one-sided error. Note that a hereditary property is also a monotone property. In Section 9.3, we introduce the notion of an oblivious tester. Ignoring uninteresting technical properties, a property is constant-query testable if and only if it is constant-query testable by an oblivious tester. Then, we show that a graph property is constant-query testable with one-sided error (by an oblivious tester) if and only if it is essentially a hereditary property. In Section 9.4, we show a characterization of properties that a property is constant-query testable (by an oblivious tester) if and only if whether a graph satisfies the property is determined by densities among parts in a regular partition of the graph.

The underlying theme of this chapter is Szemerédi's regularity lemma, introduced earlier in Chapter 4. We introduce a stronger version of Szemerédi's regularity lemma that will be needed to show that monotone and hereditary properties are constant-query testable. Also, the characterization of constant-query testable properties is, roughly speaking, that the property can be well approximated by a finite number of regular partitions.

9.1 Monotone Properties

A graph property is called *monotone* if it is closed under taking subgraphs. In this section, we show the following:

monotone property

> **Theorem 9.1.** *Every monotone property is constant-query testable with one-sided error.*

© The Author(s), under exclusive license to Springer Nature Singapore Pte Ltd 2022
A. Bhattacharyya and Y. Yoshida, *Property Testing*,
https://doi.org/10.1007/978-981-16-8622-1_9

Monotone properties include bipartiteness, H-freeness for any connected graph H and k-colorability for any integer $k \geq 2$, all of which are studied in Chapter 4. Another interesting monotone property is defined via homomorphism. First, let us recall the definition of homomorphism.

homomorphism

Definition 9.1 (Homomorphism). A *homomorphism* from a graph G to a graph H is mapping $\varphi \colon V(G) \to V(H)$, which maps edges to edges, namely $\{u, v\} \in E(G)$ implies $\{\varphi(u), \varphi(v)\} \in E(H)$.

We say that a graph G is *homomorphic* to H, denoted by $G \mapsto H$, if there exists a homomorphism from G to H.

Exercise 9.1. Show that a graph G is k-colorable if and only if it is homomorphic to a k-vertex complete graph.

We note that the property of being homomorphic to a fixed graph H is closed under taking subgraphs, that is, a monotone property, because the requirement of homomorphism imposes constraints only on existing edges.

Theorem 9.1 automatically shows that all the monotone properties mentioned above are constant-query testable with one-sided error. However, the theorem guarantees are of no practical impact because the obtained query complexity will be a Wowzer-type[1] function of ϵ^{-1}.

$\mathcal{F}$-freeness

For a (possibly infinite) family of forbidden graphs $\mathcal{F}$, we say that a graph G is $\mathcal{F}$-free if G is F-free for any $F \in \mathcal{F}$. For a monotone property $\mathcal{P}$, let $\mathcal{F}_{\mathcal{P}}$ be a family of graphs consisting of minimal graphs (with respect to taking subgraphs) that do not satisfy $\mathcal{P}$. Then, we can characterize $\mathcal{P}$ using $\mathcal{F}_{\mathcal{P}}$ as follows:

Proposition 9.1. *Let $\mathcal{P}$ be a monotone property. Then, a graph G satisfies $\mathcal{P}$ if and only if G is $\mathcal{F}_{\mathcal{P}}$-free.*

Proof. Suppose that G satisfies $\mathcal{P}$. Then, G cannot contain any $F \in \mathcal{F}_{\mathcal{P}}$ as its subgraph because any subgraph of G must satisfy $\mathcal{P}$ from the monotonicity of $\mathcal{P}$.

Conversely, suppose that G does not satisfy $\mathcal{P}$. Let F be a minimal subgraph of G that does not satisfy $\mathcal{P}$. Then, F must be a member of $\mathcal{F}_{\mathcal{P}}$.   □

As the triangle removal lemma (Lemma 4.5) was the main technical step for showing the constant-query testability of triangle-freeness, the main technical step in the proof of Theorem 9.1 is the following lemma:

---

[1] A wowzer function $W(k)$ is defined as k nested tower functions $T(T(\cdots T(2) \cdots))$ where $T(u)$ is a tower of exponentials of 2 of height u.

Lemma 9.1 ($\mathcal{F}$-removal lemma). *For every (possibly infinite) family of graphs $\mathcal{F}$, there are functions $n_\mathcal{F}(\epsilon)$, $f_\mathcal{F}(\epsilon)$, and $\delta_\mathcal{F}(\epsilon)$ with the following properties: If G is a graph on $n \geq n_\mathcal{F}(\epsilon)$ vertices that is ϵ-far from being $\mathcal{F}$-free for $\epsilon > 0$, then there exists a graph $F \in \mathcal{F}$ with $f \leq f_\mathcal{F}(\epsilon)$ vertices such that G contains $\delta_\mathcal{F}(\epsilon)n^f$ copies of F.*

Theorem 9.1 is immediate from Lemma 9.1: We sample a random subgraph of $f_{\mathcal{F}_\mathcal{P}}(\epsilon)$ vertices $\Theta(\delta_{\mathcal{F}_\mathcal{P}}(\epsilon)^{-1})$ times, and we accept if all the subgraphs satisfy $\mathcal{P}$ and reject otherwise. If G satisfies $\mathcal{P}$, then we always accept because any subgraph of G satisfies $\mathcal{P}$. If G is ϵ-far from $\mathcal{P}$, then from Lemma 9.1, with probability at least $2/3$, we find a copy of $F \in \mathcal{F}_\mathcal{P}$ in the subgraphs and hence we reject.

9.1.1 Functional Regularity Lemma

In order to understand the difficulty in proving Lemma 9.1, let us consider a natural extension of the proof of the triangle removal lemma. Extending the proof of Lemma 4.7, we can show the following:

Lemma 9.2. *For every $\eta \in (0,1)$ and $k, f \in \mathbb{Z}_{>0}$, there exist $\gamma = \gamma_{9.2}(\eta, k, f)$ and $\delta = \delta_{9.2}(\eta, k, f)$ with the following property: Let F be any graph on f vertices, and let $U_1, \ldots, U_k$ be k pairwise disjoint vertex sets in a graph G. Suppose that there is a mapping $\varphi \colon V(F) \to [k]$ such that the following holds: If a pair $\{i, j\}$ is an edge of F then $\{U_{\varphi(i)}, U_{\varphi(j)}\}$ is γ-regular with density at least η. Then, the sets $U_1, \ldots, U_k$ span at least $\delta \prod_{i=1}^{f} |U_i|$ copies of F.*

Using Lemma 9.2, we can show Lemma 9.1 for any *finite* family of graphs $\mathcal{F}$ as follows. We first use Lemma 9.2 by setting k and f to be the size of the largest graph in $\mathcal{F}$ and letting $\eta = \epsilon$. Lemma 9.2 gives $\gamma = \gamma_{9.2}(\eta, k, f)$, which tells us how regular an equipartition should be in order to find many copies of a member of $\mathcal{F}$ in G, assuming that the input graph is ϵ-far from being $\mathcal{F}$-free. We then apply Szemerédi's regularity lemma (Lemma 4.6) with γ.

The main difficulty in applying this strategy when $\mathcal{F}$ is infinite is that we do not know a priori the size of the subgraph in $\mathcal{F}$ that we will eventually find in the equipartition that the regularity lemma returns. Let G be a graph that is ϵ-far from being $\mathcal{F}$-free and $\mathcal{A}$ be the equipartition obtained by applying the regularity lemma to G with a parameter γ. By choosing γ small enough as a function of ϵ, we can guarantee that there exists a copy of $F \in \mathcal{F}$ in $\mathcal{A}$. Note that the size of F depends on γ. In order to guarantee that many copies of F exist in G, we need to choose γ small enough as a function of the size of F. This leads to circular dependencies between γ and the size of F.

To break the circular dependencies, we use the following functional regularity lemma, where one can use a function that controls regularity as a function of the size of the partition, rather than using a fixed γ as in the standard regularity lemma.

Lemma 9.3 (Functional regularity lemma). *Let* $m \in \mathbb{Z}_{>0}$ *and* $\mathcal{E} \colon \mathbb{Z}_{\geq 0} \to (0, 1)$ *be a monotone non-increasing function. Then, there exists* $T = T_{9.3}(m, \mathcal{E})$ *such that, for any graph* $G = (V, E)$ *on* $n \geq T$ *vertices, there exist an equipartition* $\mathcal{A} = \{A_i\}_{i \in [k]}$ *of* V, *and an induced subgraph* $G[B]$ *of* G *with an equipartition* $\mathcal{B} = \{B_i\}_{i \in [k]}$ *of* B *with the following properties:*

(1) $m \leq k \leq T$.
(2) $B_i \subseteq A_i$ *for all* $i \in [k]$, *and* $|B_i| \geq n/T$.
(3) In the equipartition $\mathcal{B}$, *all pairs are* $\mathcal{E}(k)$-*regular.*
(4) All but at most $\mathcal{E}(0)\binom{k}{2}$ *of the pairs* $\{i, j\} \in \binom{[k]}{2}$ *satisfy* $|d(A_i, A_j) - d(B_i, B_j)| < \mathcal{E}(0)$.

We note that the regularity of the equipartition $\mathcal{B}$ can be made sufficiently small as a function of k. Also, the size of each part in $\mathcal{B}$ is bounded from below as a function of $\mathcal{E}$, but not a function of k. Hence, we can apply Lemma 9.2 on the equipartition $\mathcal{B}$. A formal proof of Lemma 9.1 is given in Section 9.1.2.

We also note that, even for a moderate function $\mathcal{E}$, the integer T is a tower of towers of exponents of height polynomial in m and $\mathcal{E}(0)$.

9.1.2 Proof of Lemma 9.1

In this section, we prove Lemma 9.1. At a high level, the proof will be structured as follows. Let G be a graph ϵ-far from being $\mathcal{F}$-free. First, we apply Lemma 9.1.1 to G, and get equipartitions $\mathcal{A}$ and $\mathcal{B}$ of size k. Then, we "cleanse" the graph G by removing less than ϵn^2 edges and let $\tilde{G}$ be the obtained graph. In particular, every pair of parts in $\mathcal{B}$ has density zero or at least $\epsilon/6$. Since $\tilde{G}$ is obtained from G by removing less than ϵn^2 edges, there is a copy of $F \in \mathcal{F}$ in $\tilde{G}$. Then, we show that we can assume that the size of F is bounded as a function of ϵ. Finally, from the fact that every pair of parts in $\mathcal{B}$ has regularity $\mathcal{E}(k)$ and density zero or $\epsilon/6$, by Lemma 9.2, we can show that $\tilde{G}$ has many copies of F.

Given this technical overview, we now describe the proof in detail.

9.1.2.1 Graph cleansing

Let $\mathcal{E} : \mathbb{Z}_{>0} \to (0, 1)$ be an error function determined later, which will depend only on ϵ. We set $T = T_{9.3}(6\epsilon^{-1}, \mathcal{E})$ and $n_{\mathcal{F}}(\epsilon) = T$.

Let G be a graph that is ϵ-far from being $\mathcal{F}$-free. We apply Lemma 9.3 to G with $m = 6\epsilon^{-1}$ and $\mathcal{E}$, in order to obtain an equipartition $\mathcal{A} = (A_1, \ldots, A_k)$

of V and an induced subgraph $G[B]$ with an equipartition $\mathcal{B} = (B_1, \ldots, B_k)$ of B, where $6\epsilon^{-1} \leq k \leq T$ (by item (1) in Lemma 9.3). We remove from G the edges according to the following order:

- Any edge $\{u, v\}$ for which both u and v belong to the same part A_i. As each of the parts contains at most $n/k + 1$ vertices, the total number of edges removed is at most $k(n/k)^2$. As $k \geq 6\epsilon^{-1}$ we have $k(n/k)^2 < \epsilon n^2/6$.
- If we have $|d(A_i, A_j) - d(B_i, B_j)| > \epsilon/6 = \mathcal{E}(0)$ for some $\{i, j\} \in \binom{[k]}{2}$, then remove all the edges between A_i and A_j. By item (4) of Lemma 9.3, there are at most $\epsilon/6 \cdot \binom{k}{2}$ such pairs $\{i, j\}$. As A_i and A_j contain at most $\frac{n}{k} + 1$ vertices, we remove at most $\epsilon/6 \cdot \binom{k}{2}(n/k + 1)^2 \leq \epsilon n^2/6$ edges in this step.
- If we have $d(B_i, B_j) < \epsilon/6$ for some $\{i, j\} \in \binom{[k]}{2}$, then remove all the edges between A_i and A_j. As we have already removed all the edges between pairs (A_i, A_j) for which $|d(A_i, A_j) - d(B_i, B_j)| > \epsilon$ in the previous step, we may conclude that, if $d(B_i, B_j) < \epsilon/6$, then we also have $d(A_i, A_j) < \epsilon/6 + \mathcal{E}(0) = \epsilon/3$. As A_i and A_j contain at most $n/k + 1$ vertices, we remove at most $\binom{k}{2} \cdot \epsilon/3(n/k + 1)^2 \leq \epsilon n^2/6$ edges.

Call the graph obtained after removing the above edges $\tilde{G}$, and observe that $\tilde{G}$ is obtained from G by removing less than ϵn^2 edges. For ease of future reference, we summarize properties of $\tilde{G}$:

Proposition 9.2. *The following hold:*

- $d_{\tilde{G}}(A_i) = 0$ *for every* $i \in [k]$.
- *Either* $d_{\tilde{G}}(A_i, A_j) = 0$ *or* $d_{\tilde{G}}(B_i, B_j) \geq \epsilon/6$ *for every* $\{i, j\} \in \binom{[k]}{2}$.
- *Every pair* $\{B_i, B_j\}$ *is* $\mathcal{E}(k)$-*regular*.

9.1.2.2 Bounding the size of a member of $\mathcal{F}$ in $\tilde{G}$

As G is by assumption ϵ-far from being $\mathcal{F}$-free, and $\tilde{G}$ is obtained from G by removing less than ϵn^2 edges, $\tilde{G}$ must contain a copy of a graph $F' \in \mathcal{F}$. Here, we show that $\tilde{G}$ contains a copy of $F \in \mathcal{F}$ whose size is bounded by a function of ϵ.

To this end, we first define the following:

Definition 9.2 (The family $\mathcal{F}_r$). For any (possibly infinite) family of graphs $\mathcal{F}$, and any $r \in \mathbb{Z}_{>0}$, let $\mathcal{F}_r$ be the set of graphs R such that R has at most r vertices and there is some $F \in \mathcal{F}$ such that $F \mapsto R$.

Exercise 9.2. Show that, if $\mathcal{F}$ is the family of odd cycles, then $\mathcal{F}_r$ is precisely the family of non-bipartite graphs of size at most r.

Consider the following graph R on k vertices $r_1, \ldots, r_k$, where vertices r_i and r_j are connected if and only if (B_i, B_j) is an $\mathcal{E}(k)$-regular pair in G with density at least $\epsilon/6$. We show that R belongs to $\mathcal{F}_k$ by checking $F' \mapsto R$. Let R_i contain all the vertices of F' that belong to the part A_i. By Proposition 9.2, if there is an edge between A_i and A_j in $\tilde{G}$, then there is an edge between r_i and r_j in R. Hence, there is a natural homomorphism $\varphi \colon V(F') \to V(R)$ which maps all the vertices of $R_i \subseteq V(F')$ to r_i.

In order to show that $\tilde{G}$ contains a copy of $F \in \mathcal{F}$ whose size is bounded by a function of ϵ, we consider the following function:

> **Definition 9.3** (The function $\Psi_{\mathcal{F}}$). For any family of graphs $\mathcal{F}$ and $r \in \mathbb{Z}_{>0}$ for which $\mathcal{F}_r \neq \emptyset$, define:
>
> $$\Psi_{\mathcal{F}}(r) = \max_{R \in \mathcal{F}_r} \min_{\{F \in \mathcal{F} : F \mapsto R\}} |V(F)|.$$
>
> Define $\Psi_{\mathcal{F}}(r) = 0$ if $\mathcal{F}_r = \emptyset$. Therefore, $\Psi_{\mathcal{F}}(r)$ is monotone non-decreasing in r.

> **Exercise 9.3.** Show that, if $\mathcal{F}$ is the family of odd cycles, then $\Psi_{\mathcal{F}}(r) = r$ when r is odd (the maximizer is an odd cycle of length r), and $\Psi_{\mathcal{F}}(r) = r - 1$ when r is even (the maximizer is an odd cycle of length $r - 1$).

By definition, there is a graph $F \in \mathcal{F}$ of size at most $\Psi_{\mathcal{F}}(k)$ such that $F \mapsto R$. Since k is a function of ϵ, the size of F is also a function of ϵ.

9.1.2.3 Bounding the number of copies of F in $\tilde{G}$: Proof of Lemma 9.1

Let F and R be graphs as in the previous section. Let $\varphi \colon V(F) \to V(R)$ be the homomorphism mapping the vertices of F to the vertices of R. By definition, whenever $\{i, j\}$ is an edge of F, its image $\{\varphi(i), \varphi(j)\}$ is an edge of R. Furthermore, by definition of R, we know that if $\{\varphi(i), \varphi(j)\}$ is an edge of R then $\{B_{\varphi(i)}, B_{\varphi(j)}\}$ is an $\mathcal{E}(k)$-regular pair with density at least $\epsilon/6$.

We have thus arrived at the following situation: We have k parts of vertices $B_1, \ldots, B_k$ of the same size. We also have a graph F of size at most $\Psi_{\mathcal{F}}(k)$, and a mapping $\varphi \colon V(F) \to [k]$ that satisfies the condition; if $\{i, j\} \in E(F)$ then $\{B_{\varphi(i)}, B_{\varphi(j)}\}$ is an $\mathcal{E}(k)$-regular pair with density $\epsilon/6$. Now we define:

$$\mathcal{E}(r) = \begin{cases} \dfrac{\epsilon}{6} & r = 0 \\ \gamma_{9.2}\left(\dfrac{\epsilon}{6}, r, \Psi_{\mathcal{F}}(r)\right) & r \geq 1. \end{cases}$$

Now we apply Lemma 9.2 on the graph $\tilde{G}[B]$, where $B = B_1 \cup \cdots \cup B_k$. Let $f \leq \Psi_{\mathcal{F}}(k)$ denote the size of F. Item (4) in Lemma 9.3 states that each B_i contains at least n/T vertices. Therefore, we apply Lemma 9.2 on the sets $B_1, \ldots, B_k$ to conclude that B spans at least:

$$\delta \prod_{i=1}^{f} |B_i| \geq \delta \left(\frac{n}{T}\right)^f \geq \frac{\delta n^f}{T^{\Psi_{\mathcal{F}}(k)}} \geq \frac{\delta n^f}{T^{\Psi_{\mathcal{F}}(T)}}$$

copies of F, where $\delta = \delta_{9.2}(\epsilon/6, k, \Psi_{\mathcal{F}}(k))$, which is at least $\delta_{9.2}(\epsilon/6, T, \Psi_{\mathcal{F}}(T))$ from the monotonicity properties of $\delta_{9.2}$ and $\Psi_{\mathcal{F}}$. As $G[B]$ is a subgraph of G, we may conclude that G contains at least as many copies of F. Thus, we can set:

$$f_{\mathcal{F}}(\epsilon) = T$$

$$\delta_{\mathcal{F}}(\epsilon) = \frac{\delta_{9.2}(\epsilon/6, T, \Psi_{\mathcal{F}}(T))}{T^{\Psi_{\mathcal{F}}(T)}}.$$

This concludes the proof of Lemma 9.1.

Remark 9.1. A tester is *non-uniform* if it knows ϵ in advance and it can precompute any quantity that depends on ϵ. A tester is *uniform* if it accepts ϵ as a part of the input. We note that the proof above of Theorem 9.1 only showed that every monotone property is non-uniformly testable with a constant number of queries with one-sided error. This is because a uniform tester must computes $n_{\mathcal{F}}(\epsilon)$, $f_{\mathcal{F}}(\epsilon)$, and $\delta_{\mathcal{F}}(\epsilon)$, which depends on the value $\Psi_{\mathcal{F}}(k)$, and the function $\Psi_{\mathcal{F}}$ may not be *recursive*, that is, incomputable in finite time. Indeed, it is known that recursiveness is necessary in the sense that, if the function $\Psi_{\mathcal{F}_{\mathcal{P}}}$ is not recursive, then $\mathcal{P}$ is not uniformly testable with a constant number of queries (even with two-sided error) [24]. This is surprising because the function $\Psi_{\mathcal{F}}$ has little to do with property testing. Having said that, for any reasonable monotone property $\mathcal{P}$, the function $\Psi_{\mathcal{F}_{\mathcal{P}}}$ is recursive, and hence there is a uniform tester for it.

non-uniform tester
uniform tester

In this section, we have seen that every monotone property is constant-query testable with one-sided error. However, the query complexity we need to test a monotone property varies from a polynomial in ϵ^{-1} (bipartiteness) to a tower-type function of ϵ^{-1} depending on the property. Gishboliner and Shapira [202] showed that, for every decreasing function $f: (0,1) \to \mathbb{Z}_{>0}$ satisfying $f(x) \geq 1/x$, there is a monotone property $\mathcal{P}$ such that testing $\mathcal{P}$ with one-sided error requires at least $\sqrt{f(\epsilon)}$ queries and at most $\epsilon^{-14} f(\epsilon/c)$ queries for some constant c. The property $\mathcal{P}$ used here is just the property of not containing cycles of certain (carefully chosen) lengths.

It is an interesting question whether two-sided error testers can be stronger than one-sided error testers. Gishboliner and Shapira [202] showed that it is the case even for monotone properties. More specifically, they showed that, for every decreasing function $f: (0,1) \to \mathbb{Z}_{>0}$ satisfying $f(x) \geq 1/x$, there is a monotone graph property $\mathcal{P}$ such that testing $\mathcal{P}$ with one-sided error requires at least $f(\epsilon)$ queries whereas testing $\mathcal{P}$ with two-sided error can be done with $\text{poly}(\epsilon^{-1})$ queries.

9.2 Hereditary Properties

hereditary property

A graph property $\mathcal{P}$ is called *hereditary* if it is closed under taking induced subgraphs. We note that a hereditary property is also a monotone property. The main goal of this section is proving the following result, which extends Theorem 9.1.

> **Theorem 9.2.** *Every hereditary property is constant-query testable with one-sided error.*

We list examples of hereditary properties that are not monotone:

induced H-freeness

perfect graph

chordal graph

interval graph

circular-arc graph

comparability graph

permutation graph

asteroidal triple-freeness

split graph

- Induced H-freeness: Let H be a connected graph. Then a graph is said to be *induced H-free* if it has no copy of H as its induced subgraph.
- Perfect graphs: A graph G is *perfect* if, for every induced subgraph H of G, the chromatic number of H equals the size of the largest clique in H.
- Chordal graphs: A graph G is *chordal* if it contains no induced cycle of length at least 4.
- Interval graphs: A graph $G = (V, E)$ is an *interval graph* if there are closed intervals $\{I_u\}_{u \in V}$ on the real line such that $\{u, v\} \in E$ if and only if $I_u \cap I_v \neq \emptyset$.
- Circular-arc graphs: A graph $G = (V, E)$ is a *circular-arc graph* if there are closed intervals $\{I_u\}_{u \in V}$ on a circle, that is, $\{(x, y) \in \mathbb{R}^2 : x^2 + y^2 = 1\}$, such that $\{u, v\} \in E$ if and only if $I_u \cap I_v \neq \emptyset$.
- Comparability graphs: A graph G is a *comparability graph* if its edges can be oriented so that, if there is a directed edge from u to v and from v to w, then there is one from u to w.
- Permutation graphs: A graph $G = ([n], E)$ is a *permutation graph* if there is a permutation σ of $[n]$ such that $\{i, j\} \in E$ if and only if $i < j$ and $\sigma(i) > \sigma(j)$.
- Asteroidal triple-free graphs: A graph G is *asteroidal triple-free* if it contains no independent set of 3 vertices such that each pair has a path that avoids the neighborhood of the third.
- Split graphs: A graph G is a *split graph* if $V(G)$ can be split into a clique and an independent set.

induced $\mathcal{F}$-freeness

For a (possibly infinite) family of forbidden graphs $\mathcal{F}$, a graph G is said to be *induced $\mathcal{F}$-free* if it contains no induced copy of any graph $F \in \mathcal{F}$. For a hereditary graph property $\mathcal{P}$, let $\mathcal{F}_\mathcal{P}$ be a family of minimal graphs (with respect to taking induced subgraphs) consisting of graphs that do not satisfy $\mathcal{P}$.

> **Exercise 9.4.** Show that, if $\mathcal{P}$ is the property of being chordal, then $\mathcal{F}_\mathcal{P}$ is the set of all cycles of length more than 3.

> **Exercise 9.5.** Show that, if $\mathcal{P}$ is the property of being bipartite, then $\mathcal{F}_\mathcal{P}$ is *not* the family of odd cycles.

Then, as monotone properties can be characterized by using forbidden subgraphs, hereditary properties can also be characterized by forbidden induced subgraphs.

> **Proposition 9.3.** *Let $\mathcal{P}$ be a hereditary property. Then, a graph G satisfies $\mathcal{P}$ if and only if G is induced $\mathcal{F}_\mathcal{P}$-free.*

As with the monotone case, the following lemma is the main technical step in the proof of Theorem 9.2.

> **Lemma 9.4.** *For every (possibly infinite) family of graphs $\mathcal{F}$, there are functions $n_\mathcal{F}(\epsilon)$, $f_\mathcal{F}(\epsilon)$ and $\delta_\mathcal{F}(\epsilon)$ with the following properties: If a graph G on $n \geq n_\mathcal{F}(\epsilon)$ vertices is ϵ-far from being induced $\mathcal{F}$-free for $\epsilon > 0$, then there exists a graph $F \in \mathcal{F}$ with $f \leq f_\mathcal{F}(\epsilon)$ vertices such that G contains $\delta_\mathcal{F}(\epsilon)n^f$ induced copies of F.*

Theorem 9.2 is immediate from Lemma 9.4: We sample a random (induced) subgraph of $f_{\mathcal{F}_\mathcal{P}}(\epsilon)$ vertices $\Theta(\delta_{\mathcal{F}_\mathcal{P}(\epsilon)}^{-1})$ times, and we accept if all the induced subgraphs satisfy $\mathcal{P}$ and reject otherwise. If G satisfies $\mathcal{P}$, then we always accept because any induced subgraph of G satisfies $\mathcal{P}$. If G is ϵ-far from $\mathcal{P}$, then from Lemma 9.4, we find an induced copy of $F \in \mathcal{F}_\mathcal{P}$ in the induced subgraphs with probability at least $2/3$, and hence we reject with probability at least $2/3$.

9.2.1 Preparation

The main idea behind the proof of Lemma 9.4 is similar to that of Lemma 9.1. However, we need several notions and lemmas that are suitable to analyze induced subgraphs.

The first one is an extension of Lemma 9.2 for induced subgraphs.

> **Lemma 9.5.** *For every $\eta \in (0,1)$ and $k, f \in \mathbb{Z}_{>0}$, there exist $\gamma = \gamma_{9.5}(\eta, k, f)$ and $\delta = \delta_{9.5}(\eta, k, f)$ with the following property. Let F be any graph on f vertices, and let $U_1, \ldots, U_k$ be k pairwise disjoint vertex sets in a graph G such that every pair $\{U_i, U_j\}$ is γ-regular. Moreover, suppose that there is a mapping $\varphi : V(F) \to [k]$ such that the following holds: If a pair $\{i, j\}$ is an edge of F, then the pair $\{U_{\varphi(i)}, U_{\varphi(j)}\}$ has density at least η, and if $\{i, j\}$ is an non-edge of F, then the pair $\{U_{\varphi(i)}, U_{\varphi(j)}\}$ has density at most $1 - \eta$. Then, the sets $U_1, \ldots, U_k$ span at least $\delta \prod_{i=1}^{f} |U_i|$ induced copies of F.*

Later, we use the following variant of the regularity lemma.

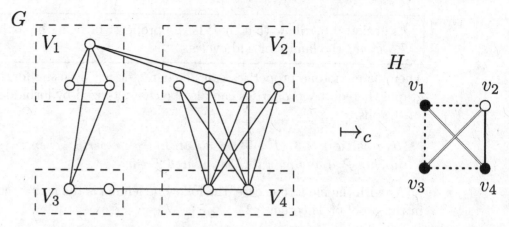

Fig. 9.1: Colored-homomorphism from a graph G to another graph H. The vertex set V_i ($i = 1, 2, 3, 4$) is mapped to the vertex v_i. Gray edges in H are drawn as dashed edges.

Lemma 9.6. *For every $\ell \in \mathbb{Z}_{>0}$ and $\gamma \in (0, 1)$ there exists $\delta = \delta_{9.6}(\ell, \gamma)$ such that for every graph G with $n \geq \delta^{-1}$ vertices there exist disjoint vertex sets $W_1, \ldots, W_\ell$ satisfying:*

- $|W_i| \geq \delta n$ *for every $i \in [\ell]$*
- *All pairs are γ-regular.*
- *Either all pairs are with densities at least $1/2$, or all pairs are with densities less than $1/2$.*

Now we extend the notion of $\mathcal{F}_r$ and $\Psi_{\mathcal{F}}$ for hereditary properties. The standard notion of homomorphism is insufficient because it has no requirement about non-existing edges. Instead, we use the following notion of colored-homomorphism:

colored-homomorphism

Definition 9.4 (Colored-Homomorphism). Let H be a complete graph whose vertices are colored black or white, and whose edges are colored black, white, or gray (neither the vertex coloring nor the edge coloring is assumed to be proper in the standard sense). A *colored-homomorphism* from a graph G to a graph H is a mapping $\varphi\colon V(G) \to V(H)$, which satisfies the following:

- If $\{u, v\} \in E(G)$ then either $\varphi(u) = \varphi(v) = t$ and t is colored black, or $\varphi(u) \neq \varphi(v)$ and $\{\varphi(u), \varphi(v)\}$ is colored black or gray.
- If $\{u, v\} \notin E(G)$ then either $\varphi(u) = \varphi(v) = t$ and t is colored white, or $\varphi(u) \neq \varphi(v)$ and $\{\varphi(u), \varphi(v)\}$ is colored white or gray.

We write $G \mapsto_c H$ if there is a colored-homomorphism from a graph G to a colored complete graph H.

Now we explain the meaning of colors in the definition above and differences from homomorphisms. The fact that $G \mapsto H$ for a graph H on a vertex set $[h]$ means that we can partition the vertex set of G into h subsets $V_1, \ldots, V_h$ such that each V_i is empty, and if $\{i, j\} \notin E(H)$, then there is no edge between V_i and V_j in G.

Returning to the colored-homomorphism, suppose we interpret the colors of H as follows: White, black, and gray edges of H represent non-existing, existing, and "don't care" edges, respectively. Then, black and white vertices represent complete and empty graphs, respectively. Thus, the fact that $G \mapsto_c H$ for a colored complete graph H on a vertex set $[h]$ can be understood as follows: There is a partition of $V(G)$ into h subsets $V_1, \ldots, V_h$ such that:

- If $i \in [h]$ is black, then V_i is complete.
- If $i \in [h]$ is white, then V_i is empty.
- If a pair $\{i, j\} \in \binom{[h]}{2}$ is colored white, then there is no edge between V_i and V_j in G.
- If a pair $\{i, j\} \in \binom{[h]}{2}$ is colored black, then the pair V_i and V_j induces a complete bipartite graph.
- If a pair $\{i, j\} \in \binom{[h]}{2}$ is colored gray then, there is no restriction on pairs $(u, v) \in V_i \times V_j$.

See Figure 9.1 for a schematic.

As with the monotone case, the following functions are important ingredients in the proof of Lemma 9.4.

Definition 9.5 (The family $\mathcal{F}_r$). For any (possibly infinite) family of graphs $\mathcal{F}$, and any $r \in \mathbb{Z}_{>0}$, let $\mathcal{F}_r$ be the set of colored complete graphs R on at most r vertices such that there is $F \in \mathcal{F}$ with $F \mapsto_c R$.

Definition 9.6 (The function $\Psi_{\mathcal{F}}$). For any family of graphs $\mathcal{F}$ and $r \in \mathbb{Z}_{>0}$ for which $\mathcal{F}_r \neq \emptyset$, let:

$$\Psi_{\mathcal{F}}(r) = \max_{R \in \mathcal{F}_r} \min_{\{F \in \mathcal{F} : F \mapsto_c R\}} |V(F)|.$$

Define $\Psi_{\mathcal{F}}(r) = 0$ if $\mathcal{F}_r = \emptyset$. Therefore, $\Psi_{\mathcal{F}}(r)$ is monotone non-decreasing in r.

9.2.2 Proof of Lemma 9.4

In this section, we prove Lemma 9.4. The proof consists of several steps. Let G be a graph ϵ-far from being $\mathcal{F}$-free. First, we apply Lemma 9.1.1 to G, and get equipartitions $\mathcal{A} = (A_1, \ldots, A_k)$ and $\mathcal{B} = (B_1, \ldots, B_k)$ of size k. Then, we "cleanse" the graph G by modifying less than ϵn^2 edges and let $\tilde{G}$ be the obtained graph. Since $\tilde{G}$ is obtained from G by modifying ϵn^2 edges, there is an induced copy of $F \in \mathcal{F}$ in $\tilde{G}$. Then, we show that we can assume that the size of F is bounded as a function of ϵ. A subtlety here is that, even if there are many induced copies of F in $\tilde{G}$, it does not mean there are many induced copies of F in G. In order to guarantee that we have many induced copies of F in G, we further partition each of B_i into $W_{i,1}, \ldots, W_{i,\ell}$ for large ℓ (as a function of k) so that we can relate the densities between $d_{\tilde{G}}(A_i, A_j)$ and $d_G(W_{i,i'}, W_{j,j'})$. Then, we can apply Lemma 9.5 to show that G has many induced copies of F.

9.2.2.1 Graph cleansing

We first define several functions:

$$\alpha(r) = \delta_{9.6}\left(\Psi_{\mathcal{F}}(r), \gamma_{9.5}\left(\frac{\epsilon}{6}, r, \Psi_{\mathcal{F}}(r)\right)\right),$$

$$\beta(r) = \alpha(r) \cdot \gamma_{9.5}\left(\frac{\epsilon}{6}, r, \Psi_{\mathcal{F}}(r)\right),$$

$$\mathcal{E}(r) = \begin{cases} \dfrac{\epsilon}{6} & r = 0 \\ \min\left\{\beta(r), \dfrac{\epsilon}{6}\right\} & r \geq 1. \end{cases}$$

We set $T = T_{9.3}(6\epsilon^{-1}, \mathcal{E})$. Let G be a graph that is ϵ-far from being induced $\mathcal{F}$-free. We apply Lemma 9.3 to G with $m = 6\epsilon^{-1}$ and $\mathcal{E}$, in order to obtain an equipartition $\mathcal{A} = (A_1, \ldots, A_k)$ of $V(G)$ and an induced subgraph $G[B]$ with an equipartition $\mathcal{B} = (B_1, \ldots, B_k)$, where $6\epsilon^{-1} \leq k \leq T$ (by item (1) in Lemma 9.3). For each $i \in [k]$, apply Lemma 9.6 on the subgraph induced by G on each B_i with $\ell = \Psi_{\mathcal{F}}(k)$ and $\gamma = \gamma_{9.5}(\epsilon/6, k, \Psi_{\mathcal{F}}(k))$ in order to obtain the appropriate sets $W_{i,1}, \ldots, W_{i,\Psi_{\mathcal{F}}(k)} \subseteq B_i$, all of size at least $\alpha(k)|B_i|$. The following observation is useful for the rest of the proof:

Proposition 9.4. *Every pair $(W_{i,i'}, W_{j,j'})$ is $\gamma_{9.5}(\epsilon/6, k, \Psi_{\mathcal{F}}(k))$-regular. Also, if $i \neq j$, then we also have $|d(W_{i,i'}, W_{j,j'}) - d(B_i, B_j)| \leq \epsilon/6$.*

Proof. First, consider pairs that belong to the same set B_i. In this case, we immediately have that any pair $\{W_{i,i'}, W_{i,j'}\}$ is $\gamma_{9.5}(\epsilon/6, k, \Psi_{\mathcal{F}}(k))$-regular, as we applied Lemma 9.6 on each set B_i with $\gamma = \gamma_{9.5}(\epsilon/6, k, \Psi_{\mathcal{F}}(k))$.

Now consider pairs that belong to different sets B_i and B_j with $i \neq j$. Note that (B_i, B_j) is $\beta(k)$-regular. As each set $W_{i,j}$ satisfies $|W_{i,j}| \geq \alpha(k)|B_i|$, we get that any pair $(W_{i,i'}, W_{j,j'})$ is at least $\frac{\beta(k)}{\alpha(k)} = \gamma_{9.5}(\epsilon/6, k, \Psi_{\mathcal{F}}(k))$-regular.

Finally, as each of the sets $W_{i,j}$ satisfies $|W_{i,j}| \geq \alpha(k)|B_i| \geq \beta(k)|B_i| \geq \mathcal{E}(k)|B_i|$, we get from the fact that each pair $\{B_i, B_j\}$ is $\mathcal{E}(k)$-regular that $|d(W_{i,i'}, W_{j,j'}) - d(B_i, B_j)| \leq \mathcal{E}(k) \leq \epsilon/6$, thus completing the proof. $\quad\square$

Our goal is to apply Lemma 9.5 on some appropriately chosen subset of the sets $W_{i,j}$ defined above. As by Proposition 9.4, all the pairs are regular, we just have to find sets whose densities will correspond to the edge set of a graph $F \in \mathcal{F}$ (recall the statement of Lemma 9.5). To this end, we define a graph $\tilde{G}$ that will help us in choosing the sets $W_{i,j}$. The graph $\tilde{G}$ is obtained from G by adding and removing the following edges, in the following order:

- For every pair $\{i, j\} \in \binom{[k]}{2}$ such that $|d(A_i, A_j) - d(B_i, B_j)| > \epsilon/6$, for all $u \in A_i$ and $v \in A_j$ the pair $\{u, v\}$ becomes an edge if $d(B_i, B_j) \geq 1/2$ and becomes a non-edge if $d(B_i, B_j) < 1/2$.
- For every pair $\{i, j\} \in \binom{[k]}{2}$ such that $d(B_i, B_j) < 2\epsilon/6$, all edges between A_i and A_j are removed. For every pair $\{i, j\} \in \binom{[k]}{2}$ such that $d(B_i, B_j) > 1 - 2\epsilon/6$, all non-edges between A_i and A_j become edges.
- If, for a fixed $i \in [k]$, all densities of pairs from $W_{i,1}, \ldots, W_{i,\ell}$ are less than $1/2$, all edges within the vertices of A_i are removed. Otherwise, all the above densities are at least $1/2$ (by the choice of $W_{i,1}, \ldots, W_{i,\ell}$ through Lemma 9.6), in which case all non-edges within A_i become edges.

By a simple counting, we can show that the graphs G and $\tilde{G}$ differ by less than ϵn^2 edges. For ease of future reference we state the following relations between G and $\tilde{G}$.

Proposition 9.5. *For any $i \in [k]$, one of the following holds:*

- $d_{\tilde{G}}(W_{i,i'}, W_{i,j'}) = 1$ *and* $d_G(W_{i,i'}, W_{i,j'}) \geq \frac{1}{2}$ *for every* $\{i', j'\} \in \binom{[\ell]}{2}$: *Indeed $\tilde{G}[A_i]$ is a complete graph.*
- $d_{\tilde{G}}(W_{i,i'}, W_{i,j'}) = 0$ *and* $d_G(W_{i,i'}, W_{i,j'}) < \frac{1}{2}$ *for every* $\{i', j'\} \in \binom{[\ell]}{2}$. *Indeed, $\tilde{G}[A_i]$ is an empty graph.*

Also, for any $\{i, j\} \in \binom{[k]}{2}$ and any $i', j' \in [k]$ one of the following holds:

- $d_{\tilde{G}}(A_i, A_j) = 1$ *and* $d_G(W_{i,i'}, W_{j,j'}) \geq \epsilon/6$.
- $d_{\tilde{G}}(A_i, A_j) = 0$ *and* $d_G(W_{i,i'}, W_{j,j'}) \leq 1 - \epsilon/6$.
- $\epsilon/6 \leq d_{\tilde{G}}(A_i, A_j) \leq 1 - \epsilon/6$ *and* $\epsilon/6 \leq d_G(W_{i,i'}, W_{j,j'}) \leq 1 - \epsilon/6$.

The proof is straightforward and we omit.

9.2.2.2 Bounding the size of a member of $\mathcal{F}$ in $\tilde{G}$

As G is ϵ-far from being induced $\mathcal{F}$-free by assumption, and $\tilde{G}$ is obtained from G by making less than ϵn^2 modifications (of adding and removing edges) $\tilde{G}$ spans an induced copy of a graph $F' \in \mathcal{F}$. Here, we show that $\tilde{G}$ contains an induced copy of $F \in \mathcal{F}$ whose size is bounded by a function of ϵ.

We define a colored complete graph R on the vertex set $[k]$ as follows. We color $i \in [k]$ white if A_i is empty in $\tilde{G}$ and color it black otherwise (that is, A_i is a complete graph in $\tilde{G}$). We color $\{i, j\} \in \binom{[k]}{2}$ white if $d_{\tilde{G}}(A_i, A_j) = 0$, color it black if $d_{\tilde{G}}(i, j) = 1$, and color it gray otherwise (that is, $\epsilon/6 \leq d(A_i, A_j) \leq 1 - \epsilon/6$ by Proposition 9.5).

Lemma 9.7. *We have $F' \mapsto_c R$.*

Proof. Consider a mapping $\varphi \colon V(F') \to V(R)$ that maps all the vertices of F' in A_i to the vertex i of R. We claim that this mapping is a colored-homomorphism from F' to R.

Suppose first that $\{u, v\}$ is an edge of F'. If u and v are in the same vertex set A_i, then A_i must be complete in $\tilde{G}$. They are both mapped to $i \in V(R)$ by definition of φ, the vertex i is colored black by our coloring of R. If $u \in A_i$ and $v \in A_j$ for $i \neq j$, then it cannot be the case that $d_{\tilde{G}}(A_i, A_j) = 0$, hence $\{i, j\} \in E(R)$ was not colored white.

Suppose that $\{u, v\}$ is not an edge of F'. If both u and v belong to the same vertex set A_i, then A_i must be empty. Hence, vertex i is colored white. If $u \in A_i$ and $v \in A_j$ for $i \neq j$, then it cannot be the case that $d_{\tilde{G}}(A_i, A_j) = 1$, hence $(i, j) \in E(R)$ was not colored black.

We thus get that φ satisfies the definition of a colored-homomorphism. □

Lemma 9.8. *There is a graph $F \in \mathcal{F}$ of size $f \leq \Psi_{\mathcal{F}}(k)$ for which $F \mapsto_c R$.*

Proof. By Lemma 9.7, we have $F' \mapsto_c R$. Therefore, R belongs to $\mathcal{F}_k$. It thus follows from the definition of $\Psi_{\mathcal{F}}$ that $\mathcal{F}$ contains a graph of size at most $\Psi_{\mathcal{F}}(k)$ such that $F \mapsto_c R$. □

9.2.2.3 Bounding the number of induced copies of F in $\tilde{G}$: Proof of Lemma 9.4

Let F and R be graphs as in the previous section. The number f of vertices in F satisfies $f \leq \Psi_{\mathcal{F}}(k)$. Let $\varphi \colon V(F) \to V(R)$ be the colored-homomorphism from F to R. By the way we colored R and by the definition of a colored-homomorphism, we get the following: If $\{u, v\} \in E(F)$ then either $\varphi(u) = \varphi(v) = i$ and A_i is a complete graph in $\tilde{G}$ or $\varphi(u) = i \neq j = \varphi(v)$ and $\tilde{d}(A_i, A_j) \geq \epsilon/6$. If $\{u, v\} \notin E(F)$ then either $\varphi(u) = \varphi(v) = i$ and A_i is an empty graph in $\tilde{G}$ or $\varphi(u) = i \neq j = \varphi(v)$ and $\tilde{d}(A_i, A_j) \leq 1 - \epsilon/6$. By Proposition 9.5 this implies the following:

Proposition 9.6. *Let $\varphi \colon V(F) \to V(R)$ be a colored-homomorphism and put $t_i = \varphi(v_i)$ for every $i \in V(F)$. We have the following:*

- *If $\{i, j\} \in E(F)$ then $d(W_{t_i, i}, W_{t_j, j}) \geq \epsilon/6$.*
- *If $\{i, j\} \notin E(F)$ then $d(W_{t_i, i}, W_{t_j, j}) \leq 1 - \epsilon/6$.*

The proof now follows quickly from the above proposition. Consider the sets $W_{t_1, 1}, \ldots, W_{t_f, f}$ as in Proposition 9.6. Note that we choose the sets as $W_{t_i, i}$ in order to make sure that we do not choose the same $W_{i, i'}$ twice, because we may need to use several sets $W_{i,j}$ from the same set B_i. Also, observe that as $f \leq \Psi_{\mathcal{F}}(k)$ and we obtained $\ell = \Psi_{\mathcal{F}}(k)$ sets $W_{i,j}$ from each B_i through Lemma 9.6, we can indeed choose the sets as above, even if all the chosen sets $W_{i,j}$ belong to the same B_i. By Proposition 9.4, any pair of these sets is at least $\gamma_{9.5}(\epsilon/6, k, \Psi_{\mathcal{F}}(k))$-regular in G. Moreover, by Proposition 9.6, these $f \leq \Psi_{\mathcal{F}}(k)$ sets satisfy in G (not in $\tilde{G}$) the edge requirements of Lemma 9.5, which are needed to guarantee that they span many induced copies of F. Lemma 9.5 ensures that $W_{t_1,1}, \ldots, W_{t_f,f}$ span in G (not in $\tilde{G}$) at least:

$$\delta_{9.5}\left(\frac{\epsilon}{6}, k, \Psi_{\mathcal{F}}(k)\right) \cdot \prod_{i=1}^{f} |W_{t_i,i}|$$

induced copies of F.

We next show that we can take a graph F as in the statement of the lemma. To this end, we define the functions $f_{\mathcal{F}}(\epsilon)$ and $\delta_{\mathcal{F}}(\epsilon)$. As $|B_i| \geq n/T$ and $|W_{t_i,i}| \geq \alpha(k)|B_i|$, we conclude G contains at least:

$$\delta_{9.5}\left(\frac{\epsilon}{6}, k, \Psi_{\mathcal{F}}(k)\right) \cdot \left(\frac{\alpha(k)}{T}\right)^{f} \cdot n^{f}$$

induced copies of F. Thus, as $f \leq \Psi_{\mathcal{F}}(k)$, $k \leq T$, and by the monotonicity of all the functions considered in the proof, we can set:

$$f_{\mathcal{F}}(\epsilon) = \Psi_{\mathcal{F}}(T)$$

$$\delta_{\mathcal{F}}(\epsilon) = \delta_{9.5}\left(\frac{\epsilon}{6}, T, \Psi_{\mathcal{F}}(T)\right) \cdot \left(\frac{\alpha(T)}{T}\right)^{\Psi_{\mathcal{F}}(T)} .$$

This completes the proof of Lemma 9.4.

> **Remark 9.2.** As in Remark 9.1, we have the issue of recursiveness of $\Psi_{\mathcal{F}}$. The proof above only guarantees that a hereditary property $\mathcal{P}$ is non-uniformly testable and is uniformly testable if the function $\Psi_{\mathcal{F}_{\mathcal{P}}}$ is recursive.

9.3 Characterization of Constant-Query Testable Properties with One-Sided Error

In this section, we give a characterization of properties that are constant-query testable with one-sided error. We only consider "natural" properties that are constant-query testable in the sense that we do not need to use the information of the number of vertices. In Section 9.3.1, we observe that any such a property is constant-query testable by an oblivious tester, which is a slightly restricted version of a canonical tester (Definition 4.5). Then in Section 9.3.2, we show that a (natural) property that is constant-query testable is essentially a hereditary property.

9.3.1 Oblivious Tester

Before introducing an oblivious tester, let us recall the definition of a canonical tester from Section 4.4:

canonical tester

> **Definition 4.5.** A tester is *canonical* if there exists a function $s\colon \mathbb{Z}_{>0} \times (0, 1) \to \mathbb{Z}_{>0}$ such that, given $n \in \mathbb{Z}_{>0}$, $\epsilon \in (0, 1)$, and query access to a graph G on n vertices, it uniformly selects a set of $s(n, \epsilon)$ vertices and accepts if and only if the induced subgraph obtained through the query access has some fixed property $\mathcal{P}$.

Recall that any tester can be canonicalized by blowing up its query complexity quadratically (Theorem 4.4). Hence, in order to characterize properties that are constant-query testable, we only have to look at canonical testers.

Indeed, we further restrict our attention to oblivious testers, defined below.

oblivious tester

> **Definition 9.7** (Oblivious Tester). A tester is *oblivious* if it is canonical and it accepts or rejects according to ϵ and the obtained induced subgraph.

The only difference between an oblivious tester and a canonical tester is that the former does not use the input size to determine its output.

Because oblivious testers do not use the input size to determine its output, one can easily construct graph properties that cannot be tested by an oblivious tester. One example is a property consisting of bipartite graphs on an even number of vertices and triangle-free graphs on an odd number of vertices. Clearly, this property is constant-query testable by using a non-oblivious tester by combining results from Section 4.3.2 and 4.5.2. However, such properties are unnatural and inadequate for understanding the reasons that make properties constant-query testable. Hence, we are interested in characterizing properties that are constant-query testable by an oblivious tester.

9.3.2 Semi-Hereditary Property

In Section 9.2, we have seen that hereditary properties are constant-query testable with one-sided error. Using this result, we can characterize graph properties that are constant-query testable with one-sided error by an oblivious tester. To state the characterization, we need the following definition, which adds a technical condition to a hereditary property:

Definition 9.8 (Semi-hereditary). A graph property P is *semi-hereditary* if there exists a hereditary graph property $\mathcal{H}$ such that the following holds:

(1) Any graph satisfying P also satisfies $\mathcal{H}$.
(2) For any $\epsilon > 0$, there is an $n(\epsilon)$ such that any graph on at least $n(\epsilon)$ vertices that is ϵ-far from satisfying P does not satisfy $\mathcal{H}$.

semi-hereditary
property

Any hereditary property P is also semi-hereditary because we can take $\mathcal{H}$ in the definition above to be P itself. The first item says that P is contained in $\mathcal{H}$. The second item says that, for any $\epsilon > 0$, there will be only finitely many graphs that are ϵ-far from satisfying P but satisfies $\mathcal{H}$.

Now, we are ready to state the characterization of constant-query testable properties with one-sided error by an oblivious tester.

Theorem 9.3. *A graph property P has an oblivious one-sided error tester if and only if P is semi-hereditary.*

Proof. ($\Leftarrow$) Let P be a semi-hereditary property, and let $\mathcal{H}$ and $n(\cdot)$ be the hereditary graph property and the function as in Definition 9.8. We show that P has an oblivious one-sided error tester. We first note that the tester used in Theorem 9.2 was an oblivious tester. Hence, as $\mathcal{H}$ is hereditary, we can obliviously test $\mathcal{H}$ with one-sided error that samples a set of $s_{\mathcal{H}}(\epsilon)$ vertices uniformly at random for some function $s_{\mathcal{H}} : (0, 1) \to \mathbb{Z}_{>0}$. The tester $\mathcal{T}$ for P works as follows: First, given a graph $G = (V, E)$, it samples a set $S \subseteq V$ of $s = \max\{n(\epsilon/2), q_{\mathcal{H}}(\epsilon/2)\}$ vertices uniformly at random (if $|V| < s$, then $\mathcal{T}$ obtains V), and obtain the induced subgraph $G[S]$ by querying. Then, the tester $\mathcal{T}$ proceeds as follows: If $|S| < s$, then the algorithm accepts if and only if $G[S]$ satisfies P. If $|S| \geq s$, then the algorithm accepts if and only if $G[S]$ satisfies $\mathcal{H}$.

We turn to show that $\mathcal{T}$ is indeed an oblivious one-sided error tester for P. We first observe that $\mathcal{T}$ satisfies the definition of an oblivious tester. Also, if $|V| < s$, then we accept if and only if G satisfies P because $G[S]$ is equal to the whole graph G.

Let us now consider the case that $|V| \geq s$. Recall that $q \geq n(\epsilon/2)$. If G satisfies P, then by item (1) of Definition 9.8 it also satisfies $\mathcal{H}$. Hence, $G[S]$ also satisfies $\mathcal{H}$, and hence $\mathcal{T}$ accepts. This means that $\mathcal{T}$ has one-sided error.

Suppose now that G is ϵ-far from satisfying P. This means that after adding and deleting $\epsilon n^2/2$ edges in total, G is still $(\epsilon/2)$-far from satisfying P. By item (2) of Definition 9.8 and $|V| \geq n(\epsilon/2)$, after adding and deleting $\epsilon n^2/2$ edges, G still contains an induced subgraph not satisfying $\mathcal{H}$. In other words, this means that G is at least $(\epsilon/2)$-far from satisfying $\mathcal{H}$. As

$s \geq s_{\mathcal{H}}(\epsilon/2)$, we infer that the graph $G[S]$ spans an induced subgraph not satisfying $\mathcal{H}$, and therefore $G[S]$ does not satisfy $\mathcal{H}$ with probability at least $2/3$. This means that $\mathcal{T}$ rejects with probability at least $2/3$.

($\Rightarrow$) Assume now that property $\mathcal{P}$ has a one-sided error oblivious tester $\mathcal{T}$. Let $s : (0, 1) \to \mathbb{Z}_{>0}$ be the functions such that, given $\epsilon \in (0, 1)$, $\mathcal{T}$ samples a set of $s(\epsilon)$ vertices (recall that the query complexity of $\mathcal{T}$ is a function of ϵ only).

We now show that a hereditary property $\mathcal{H}$ as in Definition 9.8 exists. Let $\mathcal{F}$ be the following family of graphs: a graph F belongs to $\mathcal{F}$ if the following conditions hold:

1. For some $\epsilon > 0$, we have $s(\epsilon) = |V(F)|$.
2. For this ϵ, if $\mathcal{T}$ obtains an induced subgraph isomorphic to F, then $\mathcal{T}$ rejects with a positive probability.

We claim that we can take $\mathcal{H}$ to be induced $\mathcal{F}$-freeness.

To establish the first item of Definition 9.8, it is enough to show that there is no graph G satisfying $\mathcal{P}$, which spans an induced subgraph isomorphic to some $F \in \mathcal{F}$. Suppose such G exists, and consider the execution of $\mathcal{T}$ on G with an ϵ with $s(\epsilon) = |V(F)|$. By definition of $\mathcal{F}$, $\mathcal{T}$ rejects G with a positive probability. As we assume that G has an induced subgraph isomorphic to F, $\mathcal{T}$ rejects G with a positive probability, which contradicts our assumption that $\mathcal{T}$ has a one-sided error.

To establish the second item of Definition 9.8, we claim that we can take $n(\epsilon) = s(\epsilon)$. Consider a graph G on at least $s(\epsilon)$ vertices that is ϵ-far from satisfying $\mathcal{P}$. As $\mathcal{T}$ is a tester for $\mathcal{P}$, it should reject G with a positive probability. By definition of an oblivious tester and as G has at least $s(\epsilon)$ vertices, G must contain an induced subgraph F, of size precisely $s(\epsilon)$, such that $\mathcal{T}$ rejects G when it gets F from the oracle. By definition of F, this means that $F \in \mathcal{F}$. Hence, we can take F itself as the graph not satisfying $\mathcal{F}$.   □

Although Theorem 9.3 is impressive, as it relies on the functional regularity lemma (Lemma 9.3), the query complexity of testers provided by Theorem 9.3 is prohibitively large, that is, a tower of towers of exponents of height polynomial in ϵ^{-1}. Having observed this, the following two questions naturally arise:

- Is it possible to characterize properties that are (one-sided error) testable with a reasonable number of queries, say, polynomial or exponential in ϵ^{-1}?
- Is there any specific constant-query testable property (with one-sided error) that requires an exponential number of queries in ϵ^{-1}? The current best lower bound is $(1/\epsilon)^{\Omega(\log \epsilon^{-1})}$, which is explained in Section 4.5.3.

There is some progress in this direction and we will discuss it in Section 9.5.

9.4 Characterization of Constant-Query Testable Properties with Two-sided Error

In this section, we give a characterization of constant-query testable properties.

Recall that, by the regularity lemma, for any $\gamma \in (0, 1)$ and a graph $G = (V, E)$, there is a partition $(V_1, \ldots, V_k)$ of V, where k is bounded by a function of γ, such that, for all but at most $\gamma\binom{k}{2}$ of the pairs $\{i, j\} \in \binom{[k]}{2}$, the pair $\{V_i, V_j\}$ is γ-regular. Let $\eta_{ij} = d(V_i, V_j)$ be the density between V_i and V_j, and let $\bar{R} \subseteq \binom{[k]}{2}$ be the exception set of at most $\gamma\binom{k}{2}$ pairs in $\binom{[k]}{2}$ whose corresponding vertex pairs are not γ-regular. Then, for many applications in property testing, including testing monotone and hereditary properties, we only need the information about the densities $\{\eta_{ij}\}_{\{i,j\} \in \binom{[k]}{2}}$ and the exception set $\bar{R}$ to determine whether the graph G satisfies the property of interest. Hence, it is meaningful to define a property that represents the property of having specific densities and an exception set:

> **Definition 9.9** (Regularity-instance). A *regularity-instance* R is given by an error-parameter $\gamma \in (0, 1)$, an integer k, a set of $\binom{k}{2}$ densities $\eta_{ij} \in [0, 1]$ indexed by $\{i, j\} \in \binom{[k]}{2}$, and a set $\bar{R} \subseteq \binom{[k]}{2}$ of pairs $\{i, j\}$ of size at most $\gamma\binom{k}{2}$. A graph is said to *satisfy* R if it has an equipartition $\{V_i\}_{i \in [k]}$ such that for all $\{i, j\} \notin \bar{R}$ the pair $\{V_i, V_j\}$ is γ-regular and satisfies $d(V_i, V_j) = \eta_{ij}$.[a] The *complexity* of the regularity-instance is $\max(k, 1/\gamma)$.
>
> ---
> [a] By $d(V_i, V_j) = \eta_{ij}$, we mean that the number of edges between V_i and V_j is between $\lfloor \eta_{ij}|V_i||V_j| \rfloor$ and $\lceil \eta_{ij}|V_i||V_j| \rceil$.

regularity-instance

By the regularity lemma, for any $\gamma \in (0, 1)$ any graph satisfies some regularity instance with an error parameter γ and with a complexity bounded by a function of γ.

Then, we have the following:

> **Theorem 9.4.** *For any regularity-instance R, the property of satisfying R is constant-query testable.*

The proof of Theorem 9.4 is quite technical, and we omit it.

Previous applications of regularity lemmas used regular partitions in an *implicit* way. For example, when testing triangle-freeness, the main observation is that, if the regular partition has three sets V_i, V_j, V_k, each pair of which is regular and dense, then the graph contains many triangles. In particular, we do not need to know the regular partition itself, and what we only have to do is finding a triangle in the graph.

Since Theorem 9.4 states that we can check whether a graph satisfies a specific regular partition, it is natural to try and test properties by explicitly checking whether the input graph admits a regular partition with a desired property. The following definition captures the graph properties that can be tested via testing a certain set of regularity instances.

regular-reducibility

Definition 9.10 (Regular-reducible). A graph property $\mathcal{P}$ is *regular-reducible* if for any $\delta \in (0, 1)$, there exists an $r = r_{\mathcal{P}}(\delta)$ such that for any $n \in \mathbb{Z}_{>0}$, there is a family $\mathcal{R}$ of at most r regularity-instances each of complexity at most r, such that the following holds for every $\epsilon \in (0, 1)$ and every graph G on n vertices:

1. If G satisfies $\mathcal{P}$, then for some $R \in \mathcal{R}$, G is δ-close to satisfying R.
2. If G is ϵ-far from satisfying $\mathcal{P}$, then for any $R \in \mathcal{R}$, G is $(\epsilon - \delta)$-far from satisfying R.

Note that we can take δ arbitrarily close to 0. If we think of $\delta = 0$, then a graph satisfies $\mathcal{P}$ if and only if it satisfies one of the regularity instances in $\mathcal{R}$. We also note that the number of regularity-instances in $\mathcal{R}$ is constant (as long as $\delta > 0$). Hence, we have reduced the testing of $\mathcal{P}$ to the testing of regularity-instances. Then, the characterization of constant-query testable properties can be stated as follows:

Theorem 9.5. *A graph property is testable with a constant number of queries if and only if it is regular-reducible.*

Proof sketch. ($\Leftarrow$) Let $\epsilon > 0$ be the error parameter. By setting $\delta = \epsilon/3$, we obtain a family $\mathcal{R}$ of regularity-instances such that

- if G satisfies $\mathcal{P}$, then G is $\epsilon/3$-close to satisfying some $R \in \mathcal{R}$.
- if G is ϵ-far from $\mathcal{P}$, then G is $2\epsilon/3$-far from any $R \in \mathcal{R}$.

This means that we can test $\mathcal{P}$ if we can estimate the distance to each regularity-instance. Indeed, this is possible using a general result that converts constant-query testability of a property to constant-query estimability of the distance to the property, which will be explained in Section 9.5.

($\Rightarrow$) Let $\mathcal{T}$ be a constant-query tester for a property $\mathcal{P}$. The behavior of $\mathcal{T}$ depends only on the distribution of induced subgraphs sampled from the input graph G, and this distribution is determined by regularity-instances that G satisfies. Hence, for each regularity-instance R (of a sufficiently large complexity), we add it to the family $\mathcal{R}$ if there exists a graph G satisfying $\mathcal{P}$ as well as R. As $\mathcal{T}$ is a valid tester, any graph G that is ϵ-far from $\mathcal{P}$ will not satisfy any regularity-instance in $\mathcal{R}$; otherwise, $\mathcal{T}$ will accept G with high probability. Finally, in order to keep the size of $\mathcal{R}$ constant, we discretize the densities of regularity-instances in $\mathcal{R}$. $\qquad\qquad\square$

It says that a graph property $\mathcal{P}$ is testable if and only if knowing a regular partition of the input graph G is sufficient for telling whether G is far or close to satisfying $\mathcal{P}$. In other words, there is a short "proof" that G is either close or far from satisfying $\mathcal{P}$.

Unfortunately, Theorem 9.5 is not a quick recipe for inferring whether a particular property is constant-query testable. Nevertheless, we can recover constant-query testability of some properties, including triangle-freeness and k-colorability, using Theorem 9.5 (See Problem 9.5).

9.5 Additional Topics

Testability with Polynomially Many Queries

Having obtained a characterization of constant-query testable properties, a natural question is characterizing properties that are *easily testable*, that is, testable with $\text{poly}(\epsilon^{-1})$ queries for the error parameter ϵ. Although the full characterization is out of reach, much progress has been made to characterize induced subgraph-freeness that are easily testable.

easy testability

Let P_k and C_k denote the path and cycle, respectively, on k vertices. In [20], it was shown that for any F other than P_2, P_3, P_4, C_4, and their complements, the induced F-freeness is not easily testable (indeed, $(1/\epsilon)^{\Omega(\log \epsilon^{-1})}$ queries are needed). On the other hand, when F is P_2, P_3, P_4, or their complements, the induced F-freeness is easily testable [12, 20], and the induced C_4-freeness is testable with $2^{\text{poly}(\epsilon^{-1})}$ queries [201] (and is conjectured to be testable with $\text{poly}(\epsilon^{-1})$ queries).

> **Exercise 9.6.** Show that a graph is induced P_3-free if and only if it is the disjoint union of cliques.

We now discuss the easy testability of the induced $\mathcal{F}$-freeness for a finite family of forbidden graphs $\mathcal{F}$. We say that a graph F is *co-bipartite* if $V(F)$ can be partitioned into two cliques.

co-bipartiteness

> **Theorem 9.6** ([200]). *The following hold:*
>
> - *If $\mathcal{F}$ is a finite family of graphs that contains a bipartite graph, a co-bipartite graph and a split graph then the induced $\mathcal{F}$-freeness is easily testable.*
> - *Let $\mathcal{F}$ be a finite family for which the induced $\mathcal{F}$-freeness is easily testable. Then $\mathcal{F}$ contains a bipartite graph and a co-bipartite graph.*

Note that P_2, P_3, and P_4 are bipartite, co-bipartite, and split. Hence when F is one of those, Theorem 9.6 immediately gives the easy testability of the induced F-freeness. It is also known that neither of the condition in Theorem 9.6 characterizes easy testability of the induced $\mathcal{F}$-freeness.

We move on to the case when $\mathcal{F}$ is an infinite family of forbidden graphs. We start by introducing an important feature of a hereditary graph property.

Definition 9.11. Let F be a graph with vertex set $V(F) = \{1, \ldots, p\}$ and let $g: V(F) \to \{0, 1\}$. We say that a graph G is a *g-blowup* of F if G admits a vertex partition $V(G) = P_1 \cup \cdots \cup P_p$ with the following properties:

- For every $1 \le i < j \le p$, if $\{i, j\} \in E(F)$ then (P_i, P_j) is a complete bipartite graph, and if $\{i, j\} \notin E(F)$ then (P_i, P_j) is an empty bipartite graph.
- For every $1 \le i \le p$, if $g(i) = 1$ then P_i is a clique, and if $g(i) = 0$ then P_i is an independent set.

Exercise 9.7. Show that there is a colored-homomorphism from any g-blowup of a graph F to a colored complete graph H on the vertex set $\{1, \ldots, p\}$ such that a vertex v is colored white (resp., black) if $g(v) = 0$ (resp., $g(v) = 1$), and an edge $\{u, v\} \in E(H)$ is colored white (resp., black) if $\{i, j\} \notin E(F)$ (resp., $\{i, j\} \in E(F)$).

Definition 9.12. We say that a graph property $\mathcal{P}$ has the *blowup quality* if for every graph F which satisfies $\mathcal{P}$ there is a function $g: V(F) \to \{0, 1\}$ such that every g-blowup of F satisfies $\mathcal{P}$.

Then, the following general result is known:

Theorem 9.7 ([200]). *Let $\mathcal{F}$ be a graph family such that:*

- *$\mathcal{F}$ contains a bipartite graph, a co-bipartite graph and a split graph.*
- *The induced $\mathcal{F}$-freeness has the blowup quality.*

Then the induced $\mathcal{F}$-freeness is easily testable.

The first item only is not sufficient to guarantee easy testability [200].

Theorem 9.7 can be used to the derive easy testability of semi-algebraic graph properties. Here, a *semi-algebraic graph property* $\mathcal{P}$ is given by an integer $k \ge 1$, a set of real $2k$-variate polynomials $f_1, \ldots, f_t \in \mathbb{R}[x_1, \ldots, x_{2k}]$ and a Boolean function $\Phi: \{\textbf{true}, \textbf{false}\}^t \to \{\textbf{true}, \textbf{false}\}$. A graph $G = (V, E)$ satisfies the property $\mathcal{P}$ if one can assign a point $\boldsymbol{p}_v \in \mathbb{R}^k$ to each vertex $v \in V$ in such a way that two vertices u, v are adjacent if and only if:

$$\Phi\left(f_1(\boldsymbol{p}_u, \boldsymbol{p}_v) \ge 0; \ldots; f_t(\boldsymbol{p}_u, \boldsymbol{p}_v) \ge 0\right) = \textbf{true}.$$

In the expression $f_i(\boldsymbol{p}_u, \boldsymbol{p}_v)$, we substitute $\boldsymbol{p}_u$ into the first k variables of f_i and $\boldsymbol{p}_v$ into the last k variables of f_i.

Some examples of semi-algebraic graph properties are being an intersection graph of certain semi-algebraic sets in $\mathbb{R}^k$. For example, a graph is an *interval graph* if one can assign an interval in $\mathbb{R}$ to each vertex so that u, v are adjacent if and only if their intervals intersect. Similarly, a graph is a *unit disc graph* if it is the intersection graph of unit discs in $\mathbb{R}^2$.

semi-algebraic graph property

interval graph

unit disc graph

Theorem 9.8 ([200]). *Every semi-algebraic graph property is easily testable.*

Tolerant Testing

A *tolerant tester* for a graph property $\mathcal{P}$ (in the adjacency matrix model) is an algorithm that, given a number of vertices $n \in \mathbb{Z}_{>0}$, $\epsilon, \delta \in (0, 1)$ with $\delta \leq \epsilon$, and query access to a graph G on n vertices, distinguishes the case that G is $(\epsilon - \delta)$-close to satisfying $\mathcal{P}$ from the case that G is ϵ-far from $\mathcal{P}$. When $\delta = \epsilon$, it coincides with the standard testing. We say that a tolerant tester has a constant query complexity when its query complexity only depends on δ (not ϵ). Note that, if a property $\mathcal{P}$ is tolerantly testable with a constant number of queries, then it is also testable with a constant number of queries. The following theorem states that actually the converse also holds:

tolerant tester

Theorem 9.9 ([185]). *Every property that is testable with a constant number of queries is also tolerantly testable with a constant number of queries.*

As we have seen, Theorem 9.9 plays an important role in establishing Theorem 9.5: Recall that, in the definition of regular-reducibility, we need to distinguish the case that the input graph G is close to satisfying someone in a family of regularity-instances from the case that G is far from any of them. That is, we need to test the property of satisfying a regularity-instance tolerantly. In order to lift Theorem 9.4 to tolerant testing, we use Theorem 9.9.

Nondeterministic Testing

We call a complete graph whose vertices are colored with $[k]$ and edges are colored with $[\ell]$ briefly a (k, ℓ)-*colored graph*. For $m \leq \ell$, a (k, ℓ, m)-*coloring* of a graph $G = (V, E)$ is a coloring of vertices with $[k]$ and of pairs of vertices with $[\ell]$ so that edges are colored with one of $\{1, \ldots, m\}$ and non-edges are colored with one of $\{m + 1, \ldots, \ell\}$. Then, we say that a property $\mathcal{P}$ is *nondeterministically testable with* $q(n, \epsilon)$ *queries* if there is a property $\mathcal{Q}$ of (k, ℓ)-colored graphs such that:

nondeterministic tester

1. A graph G satisfies $\mathcal{P}$ if and only if G has a (k, ℓ, m)-coloring satisfying $\mathcal{Q}$.
2. $\mathcal{Q}$ is testable with $q(n, \epsilon)$ queries.

When testing colored graphs, we assume query access to a (k, ℓ)-colored graph with which we can obtain the color of any vertex or vertex pair by one query.

The reason that we use the term "nondeterministic" is that we should guess the (k, ℓ, m)-coloring of the input graph in order to test whether it satisfies $\mathcal{Q}$.

Clearly, every constant-query testable property is nondeterministically constant-query testable (choosing $k = 1$, $\ell = 2$, $m = 1$, and $\mathcal{Q} = \mathcal{P}$). Indeed, the converse holds:

Theorem 9.10 ([307, 199]). *A graph property is constant-query testable if and only if it is non-deterministically constant-query testable.*

Theorem 9.10 is a very handy theorem for showing constant-query testability of properties. For example, it is easy to see the following:

Proposition 9.7. *k-colorability (of vertices) is nondeterministically constant-query testable.*

Proof. We set $\mathcal{Q}$ as the property of $(k, 2, 1)$-colored graphs such that no adjacent vertices have the same color. Then, a graph is k-colorable if and only if there is a $(k, 2, 1)$-coloring that satisfies $\mathcal{Q}$. Moreover, it is easy to show that $\mathcal{Q}$ is constant-query testable.   □

By Theorem 9.10 and Proposition 9.7, we can show that k-colorability is constant-query testable. Similarly, we can show that other coloring properties such as k-edge-colorability and the property of being a split graph are testable.

Other applications of Theorem 9.10 can be found in Problems 9.6 and 9.7.

Graph Limit Theory

testable graph parameter

We say that a graph parameter f is *testable*, if for every $\epsilon > 0$, there is an integer $k \in \mathbb{Z}_{>0}$ such that if G is a graph with at least k nodes and we select a set S of k independent uniform random nodes of G, then from the induced subgraph $G[S]$ we can compute an estimate $\widetilde{f}(G[S])$ of f such that $\Pr(|f(G) - \widetilde{f}(G[S])| > \epsilon) < \epsilon$.

Exercise 9.8. Show that a graph property is testable if and only if the distance to the property as a graph parameter is testable. (**Hint**: Use Theorem 9.9.)

A characterization of testable graph parameters was obtained by [101] using the graph limit theory, which was developed by Lovász and Szegedy [306] and Borgs, Chayes, Lovász, Sós, and Vesztergombi [100, 102]. In the graph limit theory, we consider convergence of graph sequences via subgraph frequency. More specifically, for two graphs H and G with $|V(H)| \leq |V(G)|$, let $t(H, G)$ be the probability that a random $|H|$-vertex induced subgraph of G

is isomorphic to H. Then, we say that a sequence of graphs $(G_n)_{n \in \mathbb{Z}_{>0}}$ with $|V(G_n)| \to \infty$ is *convergent* if $t(H, G_n)$ converges for every graph H.

convergent graph
sequence

> **Exercise 9.9.** Show that:
>
> - the sequence $(K_n)_n$, where K_n is the complete graph on n vertices, is convergent;
> - any sequence of bounded-degree graphs is convergent;

Borgs, Chayes, Lovász, Sós, Szegedy, and Vesztergombi [101] showed that a graph parameter f is testable if and only if $f(G_n)$ is convergent when G_n is convergent.

As the limit object of a convergent graph sequence, the notion of a *graphon* naturally arises. Here, a *graphon* is a symmetric measurable function $W : [0, 1]^2 \to [0, 1]$. Then, a *W-random graph* of n vertices is constructed from W as follows: Sample n random points $x_i \in [0, 1]$ and regard them as vertices, and then connect each pair of vertices (x_i, x_j) by an edge with probability $W(x_i, x_j)$. For a graph H, let $t(H, W)$ be the probability that a W-random graph of $|H|$ vertices is isomorphic to H. Then, every convergent sequence $(G_n)_n$ has a limit graphon W such that $t(H, W) = \lim_{n \to \infty} t(H, G_n)$ for every graph H.

Besides parameter testing, the graph limit theory has been applied to many other areas such as extremal graph theory and network analysis. See a book [305] for extensive explanations on the graph limit theory.

Characterization of Graph Properties Having a Proximity Oblivious Tester

A *proximity-oblivious tester (POT)* for a property $\mathcal{P}$ is required to have a detection probability that only depends on the distance of the input graph from $\mathcal{P}$. Formally, it is defined as follows:

proximity oblivious
tester

> **Definition 9.13** (Proximity oblivious tester (POT)). An algorithm is said to be a *proximity oblivious tester* for a property $\mathcal{P}$ if, given $n \in \mathbb{Z}_{>0}$ and query access to a graph G on n vertices:
>
> - it accepts with probability one when G satisfies $\mathcal{P}$, and
> - there exists a monotone non-decreasing function $\rho : (0, 1) \to (0, 1)$ such that it rejects any graph that is ϵ-far from $\mathcal{P}$ with probability at least $\rho(\epsilon)$.
>
> The function ρ is called the detection probability.

Notably, a POT does not take the error parameter ϵ as a part of the input.

We have seen that induced $\mathcal{F}$-freeness is proximity oblivious testable if $\mathcal{F}$ is of finite size (Section 9.2). The following theorem states that this is indeed the best possible:

> **Theorem 9.11** ([216]). *Let $\mathcal{P} = \{\mathcal{P}_n\}_{n \in \mathbb{Z}_{>0}}$ be a graph property. Then, $\mathcal{P}$ has a constant-query POT if and only if there exist a constant f and a sequence $\mathcal{F} = \{\mathcal{F}_n\}_{n \in N}$ of sets of graphs with the following properties:*
>
> - *Each $\mathcal{F}_n$ contains graphs of size at most f, and*
> - *$\mathcal{P}_n$ equals induced $\mathcal{F}_n$-freeness.*

Proof. We already have seen in Section 9.2 that the conditions imply the existence of a constant-query POT. Hence, in what follows, we focus on the other direction.

Suppose that $\mathcal{P} = \{\mathcal{P}_n\}_{n \in \mathbb{Z}_{>0}}$ has a constant-query POT. By Lemma 4.4, every one-sided error tester of query complexity q for $\mathcal{P}_n$ can be converted into a one-sided error canonical tester of query complexity $O(q^2)$, where for some $\mathcal{G}_n$ (which depends only on $\mathcal{P}_n$ and q), the canonical tester uniformly selects a random set of cq vertices and accepts the input graph if and only if the induced subgraph is in $\mathcal{G}_n$. Here, c is some fixed constant. Thus, if $\mathcal{P}$ has a q-query POT, then for every n, there exists a set of cq-vertex graphs $\mathcal{G}_n$ such that a graph is in $\mathcal{P}_n$ if and only if each of its cq-vertex induced subgraphs is in $\mathcal{G}_n$. Defining $\mathcal{F}_n$ as the set of all cq-vertex graphs that are not in $\mathcal{G}_n$, we conclude that $\mathcal{P}_n$ equals the set of n-vertex graphs that are $\mathcal{F}_n$-free. $\qquad\square$

Hence for example, bipartiteness does not admit constant-query POTs (Problem 9.8).

Vertex-Distribution-Free Model

In the model we have investigated, we assumed that the number of vertices n is given and the vertices in the input graph are numbered from 1 to n. As the existence of the canonical tester (Section 4.4) suggests, if we only care about constant-query testability, it is equivalent to assuming that we can obtain uniformly distributed vertices.

As a generalization of this standard model, Goldreich [205] introduced the *vertex-distribution-free (VDF) model* in which we can obtain vertices drawn from an arbitrary and unknown distribution. The distance between graphs are defined with respect to the distribution. He showed that if a property is constant-query testable in the VDF model then it is testable in the standard model with one-sided error, that is, it is semi-hereditary (Section 9.3.2).

Gishboliner and Shapira [203] gave a characterization of constant-query testable properties in the VDF model. We say that a graph property P is *extendable* if for every graph G satisfying P there is a graph G' on $|V(G)| + 1$ vertices which satisfies P and contains G as an induced subgraph. Then, they showed that a graph property is constant-query testable in the VDF model if and only if it is hereditary and extendable.

Query Hierarchy Theorem

The famous time hierarchy theorem [247] states that if $t \colon \mathbb{Z}_{>0} \to \mathbb{Z}_{>0}$ is a time-constructible function[2], then there exists a decision problem which cannot be solved in $o(\frac{t(n)}{\log t(n)})$ time but can be solved in $O(t(n))$ time by a deterministic Turing machine. A similar result can be shown for property testing in the dense graph model:

> **Theorem 9.12** ([210]). *For every function $q \colon \mathbb{Z}_{>0} \to \mathbb{Z}_{>0}$ that is at most quadratic, there exists a graph property $\mathcal{P}$ such that testing it can be done with $q(n)$ queries and requires $\Omega(q(n))$ queries.*

Hence, testers with $q(n)$ queries are strictly more powerful than testers with $o(q(n))$ queries.

As we already mentioned, Gishboliner and Shapira [202] showed a hierarchy theorem for one-sided error testers with respect to the error parameter is ϵ instead of n. That is, for every decreasing function $f \colon (0, 1) \to \mathbb{Z}_{>0}$ satisfying $f(x) \geq 1/x$, there is a monotone property $\mathcal{P}$ such that testing $\mathcal{P}$ with one-sided error requires at least $f(\epsilon)$ queries and at most $\epsilon^{-14} f(\epsilon/c)$ queries for some constant c.

Ordered Graphs

In graph theory, we usually identify a graph G and another graph G' obtained from G by applying some isomorphism. Following this convention, in the dense graph model (and other models on graphs), we assumed that a graph property is invariant under isomorphism. However, it is also interesting to consider the situation that we have a total order among the vertices and we cannot identify G and G'. We use integers to denote vertices so that they can represent a total order naturally. An *ordered graph property* is just a collection of graphs, which may not be invariant under isomorphism.

ordered graph property

Note that induced subgraphs exhibit a natural total order: For a graph $G = ([n], E)$ and $U \subseteq [n]$, where the elements of U are $u_1 < \cdots < u_k$, the subgraph of G induced by U is $([k], \{\{i, j\} \in \binom{[k]}{2} : \{u_i, u_j\} \in E\})$, whose vertices are

---

[2] t is *time-constructible* if $t(n)$ can be computed from n by a Turing machine in the time of order $t(n)$

time-constructibility

ordered. Then, we say that an ordered graph property is *hereditary* if it is closed under taking induced subgraphs. Alon, Ben-Eliezer, and Fischer [6] established a removal lemma for hereditary ordered graph properties and showed that any hereditary ordered graph property is constant-query testable with a one-sided error. The proof relies on the machinery explained in this chapter but is more involved. Ben-Eliezer and Fischer [54] introduced the notion of the *earth-mover resilience* of a property, which roughly means that a small change in the order of vertices does not significantly change the distance to the property. Then, they showed that for earth-mover resilient properties, constant-query testability by a canonical tester, constant-query estimability of a distance to the property, and constant-query tolerant testability, and regular-reducibility (with an appropriate definition) are all equivalent. Hence, the situations for graph properties and earth-mover resilient properties are almost the same. Those results have been extended to properties on matrices (or images) $M : U \times V \to \Sigma$, where U and V are totally ordered and Σ is a finite set.

An analogue of graphons for ordered graphs has also been investigated [55].

Permutations

permutation

A *permutation* π of length $n \in \mathbb{Z}_{>0}$ is a bijection from $[n]$ to itself. Testing properties of permutations have been intensively studied as a branch of property testing. Here, we assume that an algorithm is given $n \in \mathbb{Z}_{>0}$ and query access to a permutation π with which we can get the value of $\pi(i)$ by specifying $i \in [n]$. Although permutations seem nothing to do with graphs, the techniques developed to test graph properties has been used to test permutation properties, and hence we discuss some results on permutation property testing here.

subpermutation-freeness

subpermutation

σ-freeness

hereditary property

Aparently, *subpermutation-freeness* is the property of permutations that has attracted the most attention. First, we say that a permutation σ of length k is a *subpermutation* of another permutation π of length n if there are $1 \le i_1 < i_2 < \cdots < i_k \le n$ such that $\pi(i_j) < \pi(i_\ell)$ if and only if $\sigma(j) < \sigma(\ell)$. If π does not contain σ as a subpermutation, then we say that π is σ-*free*. A property of permutations is called *hereditary* if it is closed under taking subpermutations. For a (possibly infinite) set $\mathcal{F}$ of permutations, we say that a permutation π is $\mathcal{F}$-free if π is σ-free for every $\sigma \in \mathcal{F}$. As with the graph case, any hereditary property can be represented as $\mathcal{F}$-freeness for some $\mathcal{F}$.

To define testing properties of permutations, we need distance notion of permutations. Here, we describe two major distance notions: rectangular (cut) distance and Kendall's tau distance.

rectangular distance

To consider rectangular distance, it is convenient to view a permutation π as n points in the plane with the coordinates of the i-th point being $(i, \pi(i))$. Then, the *rectangular distance* between two permutations π_1, π_2 of length n

is defined as:

$$\delta_\square(\pi_1, \pi_2) = \frac{1}{n} \max_{S,T} \Big| |\pi_1(S) \cap T| - |\pi_2(S) \cap T| \Big|,$$

where the maximum is over all sub-intervals S, T of $[n]$. Thus, the rectangular distance is the normalized maximum discrepancy in rectangles between the number of points of the form $(i, \pi_1(i))$ and the number of points of the form $(i, \pi_2(i))$.

Kendall's tau distance for two permutations π_1, π_2 of length n is defined as: Kendall's tau distance

$$\delta_{\mathrm{KT}}(\pi_1, \pi_2) = \frac{1}{\binom{n}{2}} \Big| \big\{ (i, j) \in [n]^2 : \pi_1(i) < \pi_1(j), \pi_2(i) > \pi_2(j) \big\} \Big|.$$

Alternatively, Kendall's tau distance between π_1, π_2 can be defined as the minimum number of adjacent transpositions required to turn π_1 into π_2, and normalized by dividing by $\binom{n}{2}$. The rectangular distance is small if Kendall's tau distance is small, but the converse is not true.

Using these distance notions, we can define a *tester* for a permutation property $\mathcal{P}$ as usual: Given an integer $n \in \mathbb{Z}_{>0}$, $\epsilon \in (0, 1)$, and query access to a permutation π of length n, it accepts with probability at least $2/3$ if π satisfies $\mathcal{P}$ and rejects with probability at least $2/3$ if π is ϵ-far from satisfying $\mathcal{P}$, that is, the (rectangular or Kendall's tau) distance from π to any permutation satisfying $\mathcal{P}$ is more than ϵ. tester

Hoppen, Kohayakawa, de A Moreira, and Sampaio [258] proved that every hereditary permutation property is one-sided error testable with respect to the rectangular distance. However, their proof uses a compactness argument and does not give any bound on the query complexity. Klimošová and Král' [283] showed that any hereditary property is one-sided error testable with respect to the Kendall's tau distance. Although their argument gives an explicit query complexity, it is of Ackermann type even for σ-freeness for fixed permutation σ. Fox and Wei [193] improved it to polynomial in ϵ^{-1} for testing σ-freeness with respect to Kendall's tau distance and to almost quadratic in ϵ^{-1} for any hereditary property with respect to rectangular distance.

9.6 Bibliographic Notes

Alon, Fischer, Krivelevich, and Szegedy [10] studied testing first-order graph properties, that is, expressions that contain quantifiers (over vertices), conjunctions, disjunctions, equality and adjacency. For example, the graph properties describable by a first-order expression with one existential quantifier and no universal quantifiers are exactly those of containing a member of some fixed family of graphs as an induced subgraph. Then, the functional regularity lemma was shown and used to prove that first-order graph properties of the form:

$$\exists x_1, \ldots, x_t \forall y_1, \ldots, y_s \phi(x_1, \ldots, x_t, y_1, \ldots, y_s),$$

where s and t are constants and ϕ is a quantifier-free first-order expression, are constant-query testable. Those properties can be seen as a certain generalization of coloring properties. On the other hand, there exists a first order graph property of the form:

$$\forall x_1, \ldots, x_t \exists y_1, \ldots, y_s \phi(x_1, \ldots, x_t, y_1, \ldots, y_s)$$

that is not constant-query testable. Other properties defined by logical expressions are studied in [22, 271].

Constant-query testability of monotone properties discussed in Section 9.1 was shown by Alon and Shapira [23]. What they exactly showed is that, for very monotone property $\mathcal{P}$, there is a function $q_{\mathcal{P}}(\epsilon)$ such that $\mathcal{P}$ can be tested with query complexity $q_{\mathcal{P}}(\epsilon)$. They also show a "converse", that is, for any function $q \colon (0, 1) \to \mathbb{Z}_{>0}$, there is a monotone graph property $\mathcal{P}$, which has no one-sided error property-tester with query-complexity $o(q(\epsilon))$.

Constant-query testability of hereditary properties discussed in Section 9.3 and the characterization of one-sided error testable properties discussed in 9.3 were obtained by Alon and Shapira [22]. Extensions of the removal graph lemma to (directed) hypergraphs are also known [35, 360]. Refer to an excellent survey [21] for the connections between homomorphism, removal lemmas, and property testing.

The characterization of constant-query testable properties discussed in Section 9.4 was obtained by Alon, Fischer, Newman, and Shapira [11]. It was then generalized to k-uniform hypergraphs [36, 270, 284, 358, 360]. Although the characterization was obtained, there are many interesting problems yet to be solved such as the characteriztaion of properties that are testabie with $\mathrm{poly}(\epsilon^{-1})$ queries. Refer to an article by Goldreich [207] for more open problems.

Problems

blowup

9.1. For an integer $s \geq 1$, an *s-blowup* of a graph K is the graph obtained from K by replacing every vertex $v_i \in V(K)$ with an independent set I_i, of size s, and replacing every edge $(v_i, v_j) \in E(K)$ with a complete bipartite graph whose partition classes are I_i and I_j. Let F be a graph on f vertices with at least one edge, let K be a graph on k vertices, and suppose $F \to K$ (thus, $k \geq 2$). Show that, for every sufficiently large n, an (n/k)-blowup of K is $\Omega(1/k^2)$-far from being F-free.

9.2. For $\epsilon \in (0, 1)$ and an integer $d \in \mathbb{Z}_{\geq 0}$, we say that a matrix $A \in \mathbb{F}_2^{n \times n}$ is ϵ-far from having rank d if we need to change more than ϵn^2 entries of A to make it to have rank at most d. Assume that we have query access to the input matrix A, that is, we can get the entry A_{ij} by specifying i and j, and that A is symmetric. Show that the property of having rank d is testable with a constant number of queries, for any constant $d \in \mathbb{Z}_{\geq 0}$.

9.3. Show that, for any (possibly infinite) set of monotone graph properties $\mathcal{P} = \{\mathcal{P}_1, \mathcal{P}_2, \ldots\}$, there exists a function $\delta_{\mathcal{P}} \colon (0, 1) \to (0, 1)$ with the following property: If a graph G is ϵ-far from satisfying all the properties of $\mathcal{P}$, then G is $\delta_{\mathcal{P}}(\epsilon)$-far from satisfying $\mathcal{P}_i$ for some i.

9.4. We call a pair $G = (V, f)$ with a symmetric function $f \colon V \times V \to \{1, 2, \ldots, k\}$, that is, $f(u, v) = f(v, u)$ for every $u, v \in V$, a k-*valued graph*. Note that an ordinary graph $G = (V, E)$ can be represented as a two-valued graph by setting $f(u, v) = 1$ if $\{u, v\} \in E$ and $f(u, v) = 0$ otherwise. We can naturally extend the adjacency matrix model for graphs to k-valued graphs, where we measure the distance between $G_1 = (V, f_1)$ and $G_2 = (V, f_2)$ as

$$d(G_1, G_2) := \left| \left\{ \{u, v\} \in \binom{V}{2} : f(u, v) \neq f'(u, v) \right\} \right|.$$

We say that a property $\mathcal{P}$ of k-valued graphs is *monotone* if for any $G = (V, f)$ satisfying $\mathcal{P}$ and a symmetric function $f' \colon V \times V \to [k]$ with $f'(u, v) \leq f(u, v)$ for every $u, v \in V$, the k-valued graph $G' = (V, f')$ satisfies $\mathcal{P}$. Show that monotone properties of k-valued graphs are testable with a constant number of queries.

9.5. In this problem, you will show that triangle-freeness is constant-query testable using Theorem 9.5. Fix $\delta > 0$, and set γ to be sufficiently small as a function of δ. Let $\mathcal{R}$ be the family of all the regularity-instances R satisfying the following:

- They have error parameter γ.
- They have order at least $1/\gamma$ and at most $T_{4.6}(1/\gamma, \gamma)$.
- Their densities η_{ij} are taken from the set $\{0, \gamma, 2\gamma, \ldots, 1\}$.
- They do not contain three parts V_i, V_j, V_k such that $\eta_{ij}, \eta_{jk}, \eta_{ik}$ are all positive.

To show that triangle-freeness is regular-reducible, check the following two properties.

1. If G is ϵ-far from being triangle-free, then for any $R \in \mathcal{R}$, G is $(\epsilon - \delta)$-far from satisfying R. (**Hint**: Show that we can make a graph satisfying a regularity-instance $R \in \mathcal{R}$ triangle-free by removing less than δn^2 edges.)
2. If G is triangle-free, then for some $R \in \mathcal{R}$, G is δ-close to satisfying R. (**Hint**: Apply Szemerédi's regularity lemma on G to get a partition $V_1, \ldots, V_\ell$, and then argue that there is no $i, j, k \in [\ell]$ such that

$(V_i, V_j), (V_j, V_k), (V_i, V_k)$ are γ-regular and $d(V_i, V_j), d(V_j, V_k), d(V_i, V_k) \geq \delta$. Using this fact, find a way to transform G to a graph satisfying some $R \in \mathcal{R}$ by removing a small number of edges.)

9.6. Let $\rho \in (0, 1)$. Show that ρ-cut, that is, the property of having a cut at least ρn^2, is constant-query testable, using Theorem 9.10.

9.7. Prove Theorem 9.9 using Theorem 9.10.

9.8. Prove that bipartiteness has no proximity oblivious tester with a constant number of queries, without relying on the characterization (Theorem 9.11).

Chapter 10
Graphs in the Bounded-Degree Model: General Testability Results via Matroid Theory and Graph Minor Theory

In this chapter, we turn back to graph properties in the bound-degree model. In contrast to the adjacency matrix model, we do not know the complete characterizations of constant-query testable properties (even with one-sided error). Hence, the primary goal of this chapter is deriving general conditions that make graph properties constant-query testable.

The properties that were shown to be constant-query testable in Chapter 5 can be naturally classified into two categories:

(1) Closed under edge additions: k-edge-connectivity and k-vertex-connectivity (Section 5.3).
(2) Closed under edge removals (monotone): H-freeness (Section 5.2) and cycle-freeness (Section 5.4).

However, these two closedness conditions are not sufficient to make a property constant-query testable. For (1), recall that testing the property of having a Hamiltonian path requires $\Omega(n)$ queries (Section 5.6), and for (2), recall that testing bipartiteness requires $\Omega(\sqrt{n})$ queries (Section 5.5).

As an example of general properties closed under edge additions, we consider (k, ℓ)-fullness in Section 10.1. By changing the parameters k and ℓ, (k, ℓ)-fullness coincides with many interesting properties such as connectivity, the property of having k edge-disjoint spanning trees, and a notion from structural rigidity theory. We will show that using tools from matroid theory, (k, ℓ)-fullness is constant-query testable with two-sided error. We briefly mention other constant-query testable properties closed under edges additions in Section 10.2.

An important feature of cycle-freeness is that it is minor-closed, that is, closed under taking subgraphs and edge contractions. Minor-closed properties is a restricted class of monotone properties, but it still contains many important properties such as planarity. In Section 10.3, we see that any minor-closed property is constant-query testable with two-sided error. Furthermore, we show that, if the input graph is restricted to satisfy a minor-closed property, then every graph property is constant-query testable.

A. Bhattacharyya and Y. Yoshida, *Property Testing*,
https://doi.org/10.1007/978-981-16-8622-1_10

Although these results are general and interesting, it seems we are still far from reaching the complete characterizations, and further study should be conducted.

10.1 (k, ℓ)-Fullness

In this section, we show that (k, ℓ)-fullness is constant-query testable with two-sided error:

We start by introducing related notions. A graph $G = (V, E)$ is called (k, ℓ)-*sparse* if $|F| \leq k|V(F)| - \ell$ for any $F \subseteq E$ with $F \neq \emptyset$, where $V(F)$ denotes the set of vertices incident to edges in F. Note that (k, ℓ)-sparsity is meaningful only when $2k - \ell \geq 1$; otherwise, any non-empty graph cannot be (k, ℓ)-sparse since just an edge violates the condition. Hence, we assume $k \geq 1, \ell \geq 0$ and $2k - \ell \geq 1$ throughout this section. A graph G is called (k, ℓ)-*tight* if G is (k, ℓ)-sparse and $|E| = k|V| - \ell$. A graph G is called (k, ℓ)-*full* if G contains a (k, ℓ)-tight spanning subgraph.

Before describing testers for (k, ℓ)-fullness, let us see several concrete properties that are related to (k, ℓ)-fullness:

- A graph is a forest/tree/connected graph if and only if it is $(1, 1)$-sparse/-tight/-full.
- A graph is called a *pseudoforest* if each connected component contains at most one cycle, and is called a *pseudotree* if it is a connected pseudoforest. A graph is a pseudoforest and a pseudotree if and only if it is $(1, 0)$-sparse and $(1, 0)$-tight, respectively.
- Nash-Williams's theorem [329] states that a graph contains k edge-disjoint spanning trees if and only if it is (k, k)-full.
- When $k > \ell$, a graph is (k, ℓ)-full if and only if it has ℓ edge-disjoint spanning trees and $k - \ell$ spanning pseudotrees [238, 393].
- Another application of (k, ℓ)-fullness is rigidity of graphs. In structural rigid theory, we regard a graph as a structure formed by rigid rods (edges) connected by flexible hinges (vertices). We say that a graph in a Euclidean space is *flexible* if there is a continuous motion of the graph in the Euclidean space that preserves the distances between adjacent vertices whereas the distances between some non-adjacent vertices are altered. The latter condition rules out translation and rotation. We say that a graph in a Euclidean space is *rigid* if it is not flexible. A classical theorem by Laman [298] states that a graph in a plane is rigid if and only if it is a $(2, 3)$-full.

(k, ℓ)-sparse graph

(k, ℓ)-tight graph
(k, ℓ)-full graph

pseudoforest
pseudotree

flexibility

rigidity

Exercise 10.1. Show that a graph is a forest (resp., a tree) if and only if it is $(1, 1)$-sparse (resp., $(1, 1)$-tight).

Exercise 10.2. Show that a graph is a pseudoforest (resp., pseudotree) if and only if it is $(1, 0)$-sparse (resp., $(1, 0)$-tight).

The goal of this section is to show the following.

Theorem 10.1. Let $k \geq 1, \ell \geq 0$ be integers with $2k - \ell \geq 1$. Then, there is a testing algorithm for the (k, ℓ)-fullness with query complexity $(k + d)^{O(1/\tilde{\epsilon}^2)}(1/\tilde{\epsilon})^{O(1/\tilde{\epsilon})}$, where $\tilde{\epsilon} = \frac{\epsilon}{k + d\ell}$.

10.1.1 Proof Overview

As the tester for (k, ℓ)-fullness consists of several components, we provide a proof overview. We use several notions from matroid theory, and those who are unfamiliar with matroid theory are referred to Appendix B.

For a graph $G = (V, E)$ on n vertices and integers $k \geq 1, \ell \geq 0$, we define a function $f_{k,\ell} \colon 2^E \to \mathbb{Z}$ by $f_{k,\ell}(F) = k|V(F)| - \ell$. Consider the pair $(E, \mathcal{I})$ with $\mathcal{I} \subseteq 2^E$, where $F \in \mathcal{I}$ if and only if $|I| \leq f_{k,\ell}(I)$ holds for any non-empty $I \subseteq F$. The pair forms a matroid and called the (k, ℓ)-*sparsity matroid* (k, ℓ)-sparsity matroid $\mathcal{M}_{k,\ell}(G)$ (See Exercise 10.3).

Exercise 10.3. Show that the sparsity matroid $\mathcal{M}_{k,\ell}(G)$ is indeed a matroid for $k \geq 1$ and $\ell \geq 0$ with $2k - \ell \geq 0$.

The rank function and the closure operator of the matroid are denoted by $\rho_{k,\ell}$ and $\mathrm{cl}_{k,\ell}$, respectively. We note that $\rho_{k,\ell}(F)$ equals the size of the largest (k, ℓ)-sparse edge set contained in F. This implies that G is (k, ℓ)-tight if and only if $\rho_{k,\ell}(E)$, that is, the rank of $\mathcal{M}_{k,\ell}(G)$, is $kn - \ell$.

We develop a constant-query algorithm that outputs $(1, \epsilon n)$-approximation to $\rho_{k,\ell}(E)$, that is, a value ν with $\rho_{k,\ell}(E) - \epsilon n \leq \nu \leq \rho_{k,\ell}(E)$ (Theorem 10.3). This immediately gives a constant-query tester for (k, ℓ)-fullness since a (k, ℓ)-full graph has rank $kn - \ell$, and a graph that is ϵ-far from (k, ℓ)-fullness has rank less than $kn - \ell - \epsilon n$ (note that we can increase the rank by one by adding one edge).

As with the constant-query approximation algorithm to the maximum size of a matching given in Section 10.1.3, in order to estimate the rank of $\mathcal{M}_{k,\ell}(G)$, we want to simulate the following greedy algorithm efficiently: We try to add edges one by one while we discard it if a newly added edge forms a circuit with respect to $\mathcal{M}_{k,\ell}(G)$, and count the number of added edges in the end.

An issue here is that the number of edges in a circuit can be huge and we cannot detect it with a constant number of queries. For example, a circuit in $\mathcal{M}_{1,1}(G)$ corresponds to a cycle in G. However a random 3-regular graph has no cycle of length $o(\log n)$ (with high probability), and $\Omega(\log n)$ queries are required to detect a cycle. Thus, we should estimate the rank without using large circuits. We note that, for the special case of $k = \ell = 1$, we have $\rho_{1,1}(E) = n - c$, where c is the number of connected components, and we can estimate the rank with a constant number of queries (This fact was implicitly used in Section 5.4). However, there is no such closed formula for general k and ℓ.

To resolve this issue, we first remove edges so that constant-size circuits with respect to $\mathcal{M}_{k,\ell}(G)$ are destructed, and let $G' = (V, E')$ be the resulting graph. We can show that $\rho_{k,\ell}(E) = \rho_{k,\ell}(E')$. Also, we can provide query access to G' in a way that any query to G' can be answered by querying G a constant number of times. A crucial fact of G' is that $\rho_{k,\ell}(E')$ is close to $\rho_{k,0}(E')$, and it suffices to estimate the latter with a constant number of queries to G'. The rank $\rho_{k,0}(G')$ equals the maximum size of matching of an auxiliary graph, and we can compute it using a constant-query approximation algorithm for the maximum size of a matching given in Section 5.8.

10.1.2 Basic Facts on Sparsity Matroids

Before starting the proof, we observe several basic facts.

A set $F \subseteq E$ is called (k, ℓ)-*connected* if, for any pair $e, e' \in F$, F has a circuit of $\mathcal{M}_{k,\ell}(G)$ that contains both e and e'. For simplicity of exposition, a singleton $\{e\}$ is also considered as (k, ℓ)-connected. A maximal (k, ℓ)-connected

set with respect to edge inclusion is called a (k, ℓ)-*connected component*. The following property of (k, ℓ)-connected sets is just a restatement of a general fact on matroid-connectivity in our case.

> **Proposition 10.1.** $\mathcal{M}_{k,\ell}(G)$ *has the following properties:*
>
> (i)   *For two (k, ℓ)-connected sets F_1 and F_2 with $F_1 \cap F_2 \neq \emptyset$, $F_1 \cup F_2$ is also (k, ℓ)-connected.*
>
> (ii) *We can uniquely partition E into (k, ℓ)-connected components $\{C_1, \ldots, C_s\}$, and*
>
> $$\rho_{k,\ell}(E) = \sum_{i=1}^{s} \rho_{k,\ell}(C_i).$$

A (k, ℓ)-connected set (or component) is called *trivial* if it is singleton and *non-trivial* otherwise. We remark that a singleton $\{e\}$ is a trivial (k, ℓ)-connected component if and only if e is a *coloop* in $\mathcal{M}_{k,\ell}(G)$, that is, every base contains e, since $\mathcal{M}_{k,\ell}(G)$ has no loop (in the matroid sense) if $2k - \ell \geq 1$. Hence, denoting the family of non-trivial (k, ℓ)-connected components in $\mathcal{M}_{k,\ell}(G)$ by $\{C_1, \ldots, C_s\}$, Proposition 10.1(ii) implies

$$\rho_{k,\ell}(E) = |E \setminus \bigcup_{i=1}^{s} C_i| + \sum_{i=1}^{s} \rho_{k,\ell}(C_i). \tag{10.1}$$

We need the following properties of $\mathcal{M}_{k,\ell}(G)$.

Lemma 10.1. $\mathcal{M}_{k,\ell}(G)$ *satisfies the following:*

(i)   For any circuit C of $\mathcal{M}_{k,\ell}(G)$, we have $\rho_{k,\ell}(C) = f_{k,\ell}(C)$.

(ii)   For any non-trivial (k,ℓ)-connected set $F \subseteq E$, we have $\rho_{k,\ell}(F) = f_{k,\ell}(F)$. Namely, F is (k,ℓ)-full.

Proof. (i) Since C is a minimal dependent set, we have $|C| > f_{k,\ell}(C)$ and $|C| - 1 = |C - e| \le f_{k,\ell}(C - e) \le f_{k,\ell}(C)$ for any $e \in C$. This implies $|C| = f_{k,\ell}(C) + 1$. Thus, $\rho_{k,\ell}(C) = |C| - 1 = f_{k,\ell}(C)$.

(ii) Suppose $\rho_{k,\ell}(F) < f_{k,\ell}(F)$. Then, there is an edge $\{u,v\} \notin F$ with $u,v \in V(F)$ such that $\rho_{k,\ell}(F + \{u,v\}) = \rho_{k,\ell}(F) + 1$. Let e and e' be two distinct edges of F incident to u and v, respectively. Note that such two edges always exist since F is (k,ℓ)-connected. From the definition of (k,ℓ)-connectivity, there is a circuit $C \subseteq F$ that contains e and e'. Then, by (i) and by $f_{k,\ell}(C + \{u,v\}) = f_{k,\ell}(C)$, we obtain $\rho_{k,\ell}(C + \{u,v\}) \le f_{k,\ell}(C + \{u,v\}) = f_{k,\ell}(C) = \rho_{k,\ell}(C)$, implying $\rho_{k,\ell}(C + \{u,v\}) = \rho_{k,\ell}(C)$. In other words, $\{u,v\}$ is contained in the closure of C. This contradicts $\rho_{k,\ell}(F + \{u,v\}) = \rho_{k,\ell}(F) + 1$. $\square$

We also note the following relation between $\mathcal{M}_{k,\ell}(G)$ and $\mathcal{M}_{k,\ell'}(G)$ for distinct ℓ and ℓ':

Lemma 10.2. *Any (k,ℓ)-sparse set $F \subseteq E$ is (k,ℓ')-sparse for every $\ell' \le \ell$.*

Proof. For any nonempty $F' \subseteq F$, we have $|F'| \le k|V(F')| - \ell \le k|V(F')| - \ell'$. $\square$

10.1.3 Approximating the Rank of $\mathcal{M}_{k,0}(G)$

In this section, we present a constant-query approximation algorithm to the rank $\rho_{k,0}(E)$ of $\mathcal{M}_{k,0}(G)$ for a graph $G = (V,E)$. A crucial fact is that computing $\rho_{k,0}(E)$ can be reduced to computing the maximum size of a matching in an auxiliary bipartite graph G_k obtained from G: The vertex set of G_k is $E \cup (V \times [k])$ where E and $V \times [k]$ form the bipartition, and G_k has an edge between $e \in E$ and $(v,i) \in V \times [k]$ if and only if e is incident to v in the original graph G (no matter what i is). From the celebrated Hall's marriage theorem (Recall Theorem 3.4), the following result follows:

Proposition 10.2. *Let $G = (V,E)$ be a graph and k be an integer. Then, G_k contains a matching covering $F \subseteq E$ if and only if F is $(k,0)$-sparse.*

Proof. From Hall's theorem, there exists a matching covering $F \subseteq E$ if and only if $|F'| \leq |\Gamma_{G_k}(F')|$ holds for every $F' \subseteq F$. From the construction of G_k, this means that $|F'| \leq k|V(F')|$ for every $F' \subseteq F$, that is, F is $(k, 0)$-sparse.   □

Proposition 10.2 implies that the rank of $\mathcal{M}_{k,0}(G)$ is equal to the maximum size of a matching in G_k. Let us recall the constant-query approximation algorithm for the maximum matching from Section 5.8.2:

> **Theorem 5.17.** *There exists a $(1, \epsilon n)$-approximation algorithm to the maximum size of a matching with query complexity $d^{O(1/\epsilon^2)}(1/\epsilon)^{O(1/\epsilon)}$.*

By applying Theorem 5.17 on the graph G_k with $\tilde{\epsilon} = \epsilon/(k + d)$, we obtain the following:

> **Lemma 10.3.** *Let G be a graph on n vertices. Then, there exists a $(1, \epsilon n)$-approximation algorithm to the rank of $\mathcal{M}_{k,0}(G)$ with query complexity $(k + d)^{O(1/\tilde{\epsilon}^2)}(1/\tilde{\epsilon})^{O(1/\tilde{\epsilon})}$ where $\tilde{\epsilon} = \epsilon/(k + d)$.*

Note that the additive error is at most ϵn because $\tilde{\epsilon}|V(G_k)| \leq \tilde{\epsilon}(k+d)n = \epsilon n$. The reason that $k + d$ appears instead of d in the query complexity is that the maximum degree of G_k is $O(k + d)$.

A subtle issue we ignored here is that we cannot provide query access to G_k because we do not have a method to access members of E in a random access fashion. Nevertheless, by considering an auxiliary graph slightly different from G_k, we can get Lemma 10.3 (Problem 10.2). We omit the details here as it is technical.

10.1.4 Approximating the Rank of $\mathcal{M}_{k,\ell}(G)$

In this section, we describe a constant-query approximation algorithm to the rank of $\mathcal{M}_{k,\ell}(G)$ for a graph $G = (V, E)$. Let $t \in \mathbb{Z}_{>0}$ be a parameter depending on ϵ, which will be determined later. We say that a subset $S \subseteq E$ is *large* if $|S| \geq t$ and *small* otherwise.

large
small

For an edge $e = \{u, v\}$ and an integer $r \in \mathbb{Z}_{>0}$, let $G_r(e)$ be the graph induced by the set of vertices whose distance to u or that to v is at most r, and let $E_r(e)$ be the set of edges in $G_r(e)$. The core of the approximation algorithm is an efficient implementation of an algorithm COMPONENT, which (approximately) decides whether a given edge $e \in E$ belongs to a large (k, ℓ)-connected set. As a subroutine, we first consider an algorithm called SMALLCIRCUITS (Algorithm 10.1), which returns the union of small circuits containing a specified edge, and then show COMPONENT (Algorithm 10.2).

In the following sequence of lemmas, we show structural properties of outputs of SMALLCIRCUITS(e) and COMPONENT(e).

Algorithm 10.1

```
1: procedure SMALLCIRCUITS(e)
2:     S = {e}.
3:     while there is an unmarked small circuit C ⊆ Eₜ(e) containing e do
4:         Mark C.
5:         S = S ∪ C.
6:         if |S| ≥ t then
7:             return large (a special symbol).
8:         end if
9:     end while
10:     return S.
11: end procedure
```

Algorithm 10.2

```
1: procedure COMPONENT(e)
2:     S = {e}.
3:     while there is an unmarked element f in S do
4:         Mark f.
5:         if SMALLCIRCUITS(f) = large then
6:             return large.
7:         end if
8:         S = S ∪ SMALLCIRCUITS(f).
9:         if |S| ≥ t then
10:             return large.
11:         end if
12:     end while
13:     return S.
14: end procedure
```

Lemma 10.4. *For any $e \in E$, the outputs of* SMALLCIRCUITS*(e) and* COMPONENT*(e) are small (k, ℓ)-connected sets unless they return* large.

Proof. Let $S =$ SMALLCIRCUITS(e) be an edge set. If $S = \{e\}$, then S is a trivial (k, ℓ)-connected set. If $|S| > 1$, then S is the union of circuits including e. By the first item of Proposition 10.1, S is (k, ℓ)-connected.

Let $S =$ COMPONENT(e) be an edge set. The latter claim similarly follows from the first item of Proposition 10.1 since COMPONENT(e) coincides with the union of SMALLCIRCUIT(e') for all $e' \in$ COMPONENT(e). □

We define a relation $\sim$ on E such that $e \sim f$ if and only if $\mathcal{M}_{k,\ell}(G)$ has a small circuit that contains both e and f.

Lemma 10.5. *Suppose that* COMPONENT*(e) returns* large. *Then, there is a large (k, ℓ)-connected set S containing e such that, for each $f \in S$:*

- *$e \sim f$, or*
- *$e \sim f' \sim f$ for some $f' \in S$.*

Proof. If SMALLCIRCUITS(e) returns **large**, then the union of small circuits containing e forms a large (k, ℓ)-connected set. This set satisfies the desired properties.

Thus, assume SMALLCIRCUITS(e) $\neq$ **large**. Since COMPONENT(e) returns **large**, we encounter either one of the following two situations at the end of COMPONENT: a small (k, ℓ)-connected set S with $e \in S$ contains an edge f such that (i) SMALLCIRCUITS(f) returns **large** or (ii) SMALLCIRCUITS(f) is small but $S \cup$ SMALLCIRCUITS(f) is large. In both cases, let S_f be the union of all small circuits containing f. Then, $S \cup S_f$ is the desired large (k, ℓ)-connected set.   □

Lemma 10.6. *Let $e \in E$. Suppose that COMPONENT(e) does not return* **large**. *Then, every small (k, ℓ)-connected set intersecting COMPONENT(e) is contained in COMPONENT(e).*

Proof. Let $S =$ COMPONENT(e). Suppose that $\mathcal{M}_{k,\ell}(G)$ has a small (k, ℓ)-connected set S' such that $S \cap S' \neq \emptyset$ and $S' \setminus S \neq \emptyset$. Take $f \in S \cap S'$ and $f' \in S' \setminus S$. Since $f \sim f'$; we have $f' \in$ SMALLCIRCUITS(f). By Line 8 of COMPONENT, we obtain $f' \in$ COMPONENT(e) $= S$, a contradiction.   □

Lemma 10.7. *For any $e \in E$ with COMPONENT(e) $\neq$* **large** *and $f \in$ COMPONENT(e), we have COMPONENT(e) $=$ COMPONENT(f).*

Proof. Let $S =$ COMPONENT(e). Suppose that COMPONENT(f) $=$ **large**. Then, by Lemma 10.5, there exists a large (k, ℓ)-connected set S_f containing f such that, for each $f' \in S_f$, $f \sim f'$ or $f \sim f'' \sim f'$ holds for some $f'' \in S_f$. In particular, S contains every element of S_f since $e \sim f$ and COMPONENT(e) never returns **large** during the process of COMPONENT. This contradicts that S is small.

Thus, COMPONENT(f) is a small (k, ℓ)-connected set by Lemma 10.4. Lemma 10.6 now implies COMPONENT(f) $\subseteq S$ and $S \subseteq$ COMPONENT(f).   □

Let $L = \{e \in E : $ COMPONENT(e) $=$ **large**$\}$, and let $\{S_1, S_2, \ldots, S_m\}$ be the family of subsets of E such that $S_i =$ COMPONENT(e) for some $e \in E$. Then, by Lemma 10.7, $\{L, S_1, \ldots, S_m\}$ forms a partition of E. The following theorem shows the correctness of our algorithm.

Theorem 10.2. *Let $\{L, S_1, \ldots, S_m\}$ be the partition of E defined as above. For each $i \in [m]$, let B_i be a base of S_i in $\mathcal{M}_{k,\ell}(G)$, and let $E' = L \cup \bigcup_{i=1}^{t} B_i$. Then, $\rho_{k,0}(E') - \frac{\ell d n}{t} \leq \rho_{k,\ell}(E) \leq \rho_{k,0}(E')$.*

Proof. Since B_i is a base of S_i in $\mathcal{M}_{k,\ell}(G)$, we have $S_i \subseteq \mathrm{cl}_{k,\ell}(B_i) \subseteq \mathrm{cl}_{k,\ell}(E')$ for each i. This implies $\rho_{k,\ell}(E') = \rho_{k,\ell}(E)$. Also, by Lemma 10.2, we have $\rho_{k,\ell}(E') \leq \rho_{k,0}(E')$.

To see $\rho_{k,0}(E') - \ell dn/t \leq \rho_{k,\ell}(E')$, recall that (k, ℓ)-connected components of $\mathcal{M}_{k,\ell}(G)|_{E'}$ partitions E' by the second item of Proposition 10.1, where $\mathcal{M}_{k,\ell}(G)|_{E'}$ denotes the restriction of $\mathcal{M}_{k,\ell}(G)$ to E'. We have the following properties:

Claim 10.1. *Any $e \in L$ is contained in a large (k, ℓ)-connected component in $\mathcal{M}_{k,\ell}(G)|_{E'}$.*

Proof. Let us take a large (k, ℓ)-connected set S_e of $\mathcal{M}_{k,\ell}(G)$ satisfying the property of Lemma 10.5 for e. Suppose, for a contradiction, that COMPONENT(f) returns a small (k, ℓ)-connected set S_f for some $f \in S_e$. Note that for every $f' \in S_e$ we have $f \sim f_1 \sim e \sim f_2 \sim f'$ for some $f_1, f_2 \in S_e$. As COMPONENT(f) never returns **large**, we have $S_e \subseteq S_f$ according to Algorithm 10.2, contradicting that S_f is small. Thus, each element of S_e is added to L, and hence S_e remains in E'. It follows that S_e exists as a large (k, ℓ)-connected set even in $\mathcal{M}_{k,\ell}(G)|_{E'}$, and e is contained in a large (k, ℓ)-connected component in $\mathcal{M}_{k,\ell}(G)|_{E'}$. $\square$

Claim 10.2. *Every non-trivial (k, ℓ)-connected component in $\mathcal{M}_{k,\ell}(G)|_{E'}$ is large.*

Proof. To see this, suppose that there is a non-trivial small (k, ℓ)-connected component C in $\mathcal{M}_{k,\ell}(G)|_{E'}$. By the previous claim, each element of L belongs to a large (k, ℓ)-connected component in $\mathcal{M}_{k,\ell}(G)|_{E'}$. This implies $C \subseteq \bigcup_{i=1}^{m} B_i$. Also, since B_i is independent in $\mathcal{M}_{k,\ell}(G)$, C must intersect at least two sets among $\{B_1, \ldots, B_m\}$. It follows that C intersects at least two sets among $\{S_1, \ldots, S_m\}$. Since C is a small (k, ℓ)-connected set in $\mathcal{M}_{k,\ell}(G)$, this contradicts Lemma 10.6. $\square$

Let $\{C_1, C_2, \ldots, C_s\}$ be the family of non-trivial (k, ℓ)-connected components in $\mathcal{M}_{k,\ell}(G)|_{E'}$. Note that $s \leq dn/t$ holds by the second claim. Therefore:

$$\rho_{k,\ell}(E') = |E' \setminus \bigcup_{i=1}^{s} C_i| + \sum_{i=1}^{s} \rho_{k,\ell}(C_i) \quad \text{(by (10.1))}$$

$$= |E' \setminus \bigcup_{i=1}^{s} C_i| + \sum_{i=1}^{s} (k|V(C_i)| - \ell) \quad \text{(by Lemma 10.1(ii))}$$

$$\geq |E' \setminus \bigcup_{i=1}^{s} C_i| + \sum_{i=1}^{s} k|V(C_i)| - \frac{\ell dn}{t} \quad \text{(by } s \leq \frac{dn}{t} \text{).}$$

On the other hand:

$$\rho_{k,0}(E') \leq |E' \setminus \bigcup_{i=1}^{s} C_i| + \sum_{i=1}^{s} \rho_{k,0}(C_i) \quad \text{(by the submodularity of } \rho_{k,0})$$

$$\leq |E' \setminus \bigcup_{i=1}^{s} C_i| + \sum_{i=1}^{s} k|V(C_i)|.$$

This completes the proof. □

Theorem 10.3. *Let $G = (V, E)$ be a graph on n vertices, and let $k \geq 1, \ell \geq 0$ be integers with $2k - \ell \geq 1$. Then, there exists a $(1, \epsilon n)$-approximation algorithm for the rank of $\mathcal{M}_{k,\ell}(G)$ with query complexity $(k + d)^{O(1/\tilde{\epsilon}^2)}(1/\tilde{\epsilon})^{O(1/\tilde{\epsilon})}$ where $\tilde{\epsilon} = \frac{\epsilon}{k+d\ell}$.*

Proof. Let $G' = (V, E')$, where E' is as given in Theorem 10.2. Set $t = \epsilon^{-1}\ell d$. Our algorithm computes $\rho_{k,0}(E')$ based on the algorithm given in Lemma 10.3 for the error threshold ϵ and just returns this value. By Lemma 10.3 and Theorem 10.2, this value approximates $\rho_{k,\ell}(E)$ with additive error ϵn. Therefore, if we can make query access $\mathcal{O}_{G'}$ to the graph G', we are done.

For a query $\mathcal{O}_{G'}(v, i)$, we return a value as follows. If $\mathcal{O}_G(v, i) = \bot$, we return $\bot$. Suppose that $\mathcal{O}_G(v, i) = e$. Then, we invoke COMPONENT(e). If COMPONENT(e) returns **large**, we return e. Otherwise, we take an arbitrary base B of the returned set of COMPONENT(e) by an existing algorithm. We return e if $e \in B$ and return $\bot$ if otherwise. Note that for another edge $f \in S$, we use the same base B.

Next we analyze the query complexity. During COMPONENT(e), we perform queries $\mathcal{O}_G(v, i)$ only for vertices v in $G_{3t}(e)$. So, to perform COMPONENT(e), we need $d^{3t} = d^{3\epsilon^{-1}\ell d}$ queries to $\mathcal{O}_G$. In total, we need:

$$d^{3\epsilon^{-1}\ell d}(k + d)^{O(\tilde{\epsilon}^{-2})}\left(\frac{1}{\tilde{\epsilon}}\right)^{O(\tilde{\epsilon}^{-1})} = (k + d)^{O(\tilde{\epsilon}^{-2})}\left(\frac{1}{\tilde{\epsilon}}\right)^{O(\tilde{\epsilon}^{-1})}$$

queries, where $\tilde{\epsilon} = \frac{\epsilon}{k+d\ell}$. □

Theorem 10.1 directly follows form Theorem 10.3.

10.2 Other Properties Closed under Edge Additions

We briefly mention other properties closed under edge additions that are known to be testable with a constant number of queries.

(k, ℓ)-Edge-Connected Orientability

A digraph $G = (V, E)$ is called (k, l)-edge-connected with a root $r \in V$ if, for each $v \in V \setminus \{r\}$, G has k arc-disjoint directed paths from r to v and l arc-disjoint dipaths from v to r. An undirected graph $G = (V, E)$ is called (k, l)-edge-connected-orientable ((k, l)-ec-orientable, in short) if one can assign an orientation to each edge so that the resulting digraph is (k, l)-edge-connected with some root $r \in V$. It is not hard to show that the choice of r is actually not important, and we may specify any vertex as r.

(k, ℓ)-edge-connectivity

(k, ℓ)-edge-connected-orientability

Then, we have the following:

> **Theorem 10.4.** *There is a two-sided error tester for (k, ℓ)-ec-orientability with query complexity $(k + d)^{O(1/\tilde{\epsilon}^2)}(1/\tilde{\epsilon})^{O(1/\tilde{\epsilon})}$ queries, where:*
> $$\tilde{\epsilon} = \min\left\{\frac{\epsilon}{dk}, d\epsilon/\ell\right\}.$$

Nash-Williams' graph-orientation theorem [328] implies that a graph G admits an orientation such that the resulting digraph is k-edge-connected if and only if G is $2k$-edge-connected. This implies that (k, k)-ec-orientability is equivalent to $2k$-edge-connectivity. In another work, Nash-Williams [329] showed that an undirected graph G contains k edge-disjoint spanning trees if and only if G is (k, k)-full. Combined with Edmonds' arc-disjoint branching theorem [167], we have that G is $(k, 0)$-ec-orientable if and only if G is (k, k)-full. From these results, we can regard (k, l)-ec-orientability as a unified concept of sparsity and edge-connectivity.

Supermodular-Cut Condition

Let V be a finite set. A pair $X, Y \subseteq V$ is said to be *crossing* if $X \cap Y \neq \emptyset$, $X \setminus Y \neq \emptyset$, $Y \setminus X \neq \emptyset$ and $X \cup Y \neq V$. Let $f: 2^V \to \mathbb{R}$ be a set function on V. f is called *submodular* if:

crossing pair

submodularity

$$f(X) + f(Y) \geq f(X \cup Y) + f(X \cap Y) \tag{10.2}$$

holds for any $X, Y \subseteq V$. f is called *crossing submodular* if the submodular inequality (10.2) is satisfied for any crossing pair $X, Y \subseteq V$. Hence, the crossing submodularity is a weaker property than submodularity. f is called *supermodular* (resp., *crossing supermodular*) if $-f$ is submodular (resp., crossing submodular).

crossing submodularity

supermodularity

Let $f: 2^V \to \mathbb{Z}_{\geq 0}$ be a set function on V. A graph G is called *f-connected* if it satisfies the following *f-cut condition*: $d_G(X) \geq f(X)$ for any $X \subseteq V$. Then, we have the following:

f-connectivity

f-cut condition

Theorem 10.5. *Let $f: 2^V \to \mathbb{Z}_+$ be a crossing supermodular function with $f(\emptyset) = f(V) = 0$. Then, there is a one-sided error tester for f-connectivity with query complexity $(\epsilon^{-1}d)^{O(\epsilon^{-3})}$.*

Theorem 10.5 implies the testability of k-edge-connectivity. To see this, set $f(X) = k$ if $0 < |X| < |V|$ and $f(\emptyset) = f(V) = 0$. Then, f is indeed crossing supermodular, and a graph is f-connected if and only if it is k-edge-connected.

Although we will not discuss the details here, (k, ℓ)-fullness, (k, ℓ)-edge-connected orientability, and f-connectivity can be seen within a unified framework by using the result of Fujishige [197] on crossing submodular function polyhedrons. From this viewpoint, testing those properties are special cases of the following general problem: For a crossing supermodular function $f: 2^V \to \mathbb{R}$, test whether $\sum_{X \in \mathcal{P}}(f(V) - f(V \setminus X)) \leq f(V) \leq \sum_{X \in \mathcal{P}} f(X)$ for any partition $\mathcal{P}$ of V.

10.3 Minor-Closed Properties

In this section, we study minor-closed properties. A graph property $\mathcal{P}$ is called *minor-closed* if it is closed under taking subgraphs and contracting edges. Here, *contracting* an edge $e = \{u, v\}$ means removing e and merging u and v into a new vertex w, where the edges incident to w each correspond to an edge incident to either u or v.

Let us see several concrete minor-closed properties:

- The property of being a forest, or cycle-freeness, is minor-closed.
- The property of being a pseudoforest is minor-closed (see Section 10.1 for the definition).
- Planarity is minor-closed. Here, a graph G is *planar* if it can be embedded into a plane in a way that edges intersect only at their endpoints.
- Outerplanarity is minor-closed. Here, a graph G is *outerplanar* if it can be embedded into a plane in a way that edges intersect only at their endpoints and there exists a unique face to which every vertex belong.
- For any $k \in \mathbb{Z}_{\geq 0}$, the property of having a vertex cover of size at most k is minor-closed.
- For any $k \in \mathbb{Z}_{\geq 0}$, the property of having a feedback vertex set of size at most k is minor-closed. Here, a vertex set S in a graph a *feedback vertex set* if the resulting graph obtained by removing S is cycle-free.
- The property of knotlessly embeddable in 3-dimensional Euclidean space is minor-closed.
- The *treewidth* of a graph measures how much the graph is tree-like. When the treewidth is bounded, many NP-hard problems become polynomial-time tractable (see [138, Chapter 7] for example). For any $k \in \mathbb{Z}_{\geq 0}$, the property of having treewidth at most k is minor-closed.

An example of properties that are *not* minor-closed properties is bipartiteness because it is not close under edge contractions. For example, although a 4-cycle is bipartite, a 3-cycle, which is obtained from a 4-cycle by contracting an edge, is not bipartite.

In this section, we see that any minor-closed property is constant-query testable with two-sided error. Furthermore, we show that, if the input graph is restricted to satisfy a minor-closed property, then every graph property is constant-query testable.

Before going into details, let us mention that we cannot test minor-closed properties with one-sided error using a constant number of queries: We can show an $\Omega(\sqrt{n})$ lower bound for testing cycle-freeness with one-sided error by considering detecting a cycle in a random graph and by using an argument similar to that in Section 5.5.2. On the other hand, it is known that we can test cycle-freeness with $\widetilde{O}(\sqrt{n})$ queries using a random-walk-based algorithm [139] and it is shown that every minor-closed property is one-sided error testable with $\widetilde{O}(n^{1/2+\delta})$ queries for arbitrarily small $\delta > 0$ [176, 288].

10.3.1 Basic Facts on Minor-Closed Properties

We say that a graph H is a *minor* of a graph G if H is isomorphic to a graph that can be obtained by contracting (possibly zero) edges of a subgraph of G. A graph G is H-*minor-free* if H is not a minor of G. Note that H-minor-freeness is a minor-closed property.

minor

H-minor-freeness

The following theorem is a cornerstone of the graph minor theory.

> **Theorem 10.6** ([356]). *Let $\mathcal{P}$ be a minor-closed property. Then, there exists a finite set of graphs $\mathcal{H} = \{H_1, \ldots, H_t\}$ such that a graph G satisfies $\mathcal{P}$ if and only if G is H_i-minor free for every $i \in [t]$.*

An important feature of Theorem 10.6 is that the set $\mathcal{H}$ is finite. For example, by Kuratowski's theorem [291], a graph is planar if and only if it is K_5-minor-free and $K_{3,3}$-minor-free, where K_5 is the complete graph on 5 vertices and $K_{3,3}$ is the complete bipartite graph with 3 vertices in both sides. This does not hold for a monotone property, that is, a property closed under taking subgraphs. For example, bipartiteness is a monotone property and can be characterized by odd-cycle freeness. However, the length of those odd cycles can be arbitrarily long.

Because $\mathcal{H}$ is a finite set, we can reduce the problem of testing a minor-closed property to a sequence of problems of testing H-minor-freeness.

> **Corollary 10.1.** *If we can test H-minor-freeness with a constant number of queries for any fixed H, then we can test any minor-closed property with a constant number of queries.*

Proof. Let $\mathcal{P}$ be a minor-closed property and let $\mathcal{H} = \{H_1, \ldots, H_t\}$ be the finite set of graphs that characterizes $\mathcal{P}$, whose existence is guaranteed by Theorem 10.6.

If a graph $G = (V, E)$ satisfies $\mathcal{P}$, then G is H_i-minor free for every $i \in [t]$. On the other hand, if a graph $G = (V, E)$ is ϵ-far from satisfying $\mathcal{P}$, then there exists $i \in [t]$ such that G is (ϵ/t)-far from H_i-minor freeness. To see this, suppose that G is (ϵ/t)-close to H_i-minor freeness for every $i \in [t]$, and let E_i be the set of edges such that $(V, E \setminus E_i)$ satisfies H_i-minor freeness and $|E_i| \leq \epsilon dn/t$. Then, the graph $(V, E \setminus \bigcup_{i \in [t]} E_i)$ is H_i-minor free for every $i \in [t]$ and hence satisfies $\mathcal{P}$. However, the number of removed edges is at most ϵdn, which contradicts the fact that G is ϵ-far from satisfying $\mathcal{P}$.

Hence, in order to test $\mathcal{P}$ with an error parameter ϵ, it suffices to test H_i-minor freeness with an error parameter (ϵ/t), and accept if and only if all of those tests accept. The resulting query complexity is constant because the query complexity to test each H_i-minor freeness is constant, and t only depends on the property $\mathcal{P}$.   □

Corollary 10.1 motivates us to look at properties of H-minor-free graphs. First, any H-minor-free graph should be sparse as shown in the next lemma.

Lemma 10.8 ([310, 329]). *For any graph H, there exists a constant c_H such that every H-minor-free graph $G = (V, E)$ satisfies $|E| \leq c_H|V|$. Furthermore, E can be partitioned into at most c_H forests.*

Next, we see that an H-minor-free graph of bounded degree can be partitioned into small connected subgraphs by removing a small number of edges. We formally define such a partition.

(ϵ, k)-partition

Definition 10.1. For $\epsilon \in (0, 1]$, $k \geq 1$ and a graph $G = (V, E)$ of n vertices, we say that a partition $\mathcal{S} = (S_1, \ldots, S_t)$ of V is an (ϵ, k)-*partition* (with respect to G), if the following conditions hold:

- $|S_i| \leq k$ for every $i \in [t]$.
- The subgraph induced by S_i in G is connected for every $i \in [t]$.
- The total number of edges whose endpoints belong to different parts of the partition is at most ϵn. That is,

$$|\{\{u, v\} \in E : u \in S_i, v \in S_j, i \neq j\}| \leq \epsilon n.$$

separator theorem

The following theorem, called the *separator theorem*, states that every H-minor-free graph has a small vertex cut that separates the graph into small pieces.

Theorem 10.7 ([17]). *Let H be a graph on h vertices and let $G = (V, E)$ be an H-minor-free graph with n vertices and m edges, where the vertices of G are associated with nonnegative weights that sum up to 1. Then, for any $\beta \in (0, 1]$, there is a set $S \subseteq V$ of $O(h^{3/2}\sqrt{n/\beta})$ vertices such that $G - S$ has no connected component with weight greater than β. Moreover, such a set S can be found in $O(\sqrt{hn} \cdot m)$ time.*

As a corollary we get that H-minor-free graph has a good partition.

Corollary 10.2. *Let H be a graph on h vertices and $\epsilon \in (0, 1]$. Then, any H-minor-free graph $G = (V, E)$ with a degree bound d has an $(\epsilon d, O(\epsilon^{-2}h^3))$-partition.*

Proof. Let n be the number of vertices in G. We apply Theorem 10.7 with equal weights $1/n$ to all vertices and with $\beta = \Theta(\frac{h^3}{\epsilon^2 n})$. Then, we obtain a set S of vertices such that $|S| = O(\epsilon n)$ and each connected component of $G - S$ has size at most $O(\epsilon^{-2}h^3)$. Consider the partition $\mathcal{S}$ of V consisting of a singleton for each vertex in S and a subset for each connected component (containing vertices in the connected component). Since the number of edges incident to S is $O(\epsilon dn)$, the partition $\mathcal{S}$ is an $(O(\epsilon d), O(\epsilon^{-2}h^3))$-partition. Multiplying ϵ by a constant adequately, we get an $(\epsilon d, O(\epsilon^{-2}h^3))$-partition. $\square$

10.3.2 Partition Oracle

By Corollary 10.1, if we want to test minor-closed properties, it suffices to design constant-query testers for H-minor-freeness.

Let us fix a graph H. In order to test whether a graph $G = (V, E)$ is H-minor-free, suppose first that we know a partition $\mathcal{S}$ of the vertex set V with the following conditions for some $k = k(\epsilon)$ and we can freely ask whether two distinct vertices are in the same part of $\mathcal{S}$:

- $\mathcal{S}$ is a partition into connected subgraph of size at most k.
- Moreover, if G is H-minor-free, then $\mathcal{S}$ is an $(\epsilon d/2, k)$-partition.

Then, we can test H-minor-freeness (in polynomial time) as follows. First, we check whether the partition is indeed an $(\epsilon d/2, k)$-partition. This can be done by counting the number of edges connecting different connected subgraphs in the partition, and checking each connected subgraph in $\mathcal{S}$ has size at most k. Second, we check each connected subgraph in $\mathcal{S}$ is H-minor-free. This is easy because the size of each connected subgraph is at most k.

If G is H-minor-free, then the first test passes because $\mathcal{S}$ is an $(\epsilon d/2, k)$-partition, and the second test passes because each connected subgraph is indeed H-minor-free. On the other hand, if G is ϵ-far from satisfying H-minor-freeness and the first test passes, then the second test must fail. The reason is that the graph consisting of the connected subgraphs in $\mathcal{S}$ is at least $\epsilon/2$-far from H-minor-freeness because $\mathcal{S}$ cuts at most $\epsilon dn/2$ edges.

Assuming that the partition $\mathcal{S}$ is at hand, that is, we can freely ask whether two distinct vertices are in the same part of $\mathcal{S}$, it is not hard to convert the algorithm above to a constant-query tester that correctly distinguishes H-minor-free graphs from graphs ϵ-far from being H-minor-free with high probability.

The remaining issue is how to obtain the partition $\mathcal{S}$. Of course, we cannot obtain the full knowledge of $\mathcal{S}$ in constant time because the partition is a global object. Instead, we design query access to the partition, called partition oracle, that returns the part of $\mathcal{S}$ that a specified vertex belongs to if it is of constant size, just by looking around a local neighborhood of the vertex.

Let $G = (V, E)$ be a graph and let $\mathcal{S} = (S_1, \ldots, S_t)$ be a partition of V. For a vertex $v \in V$, let $\mathcal{S}[v]$ denote the vertex set S_i that v belongs to. Then, we define partition oracle as follows:

partition oracle

> **Definition 10.2** (Partition oracle). An oracle $\mathcal{O}$ is a *partition oracle* if, given query access to $G = (V, E)$ (in the bounded-degree model), the oracle $\mathcal{O}$ provides query access to a partition $\mathcal{S} = (S_1, \ldots, S_t)$ of V, where $\mathcal{S}$ is determined by G and the internal randomness of the oracle. Namely, on input $v \in V$, the oracle returns $\mathcal{S}[v]$ and for any sequence of queries, $\mathcal{O}$ answers consistently with the same $\mathcal{S}$.
>
> (γ, k)-partition oracle with respect to a graph property $\mathcal{P}$
>
> Moreover, an oracle $\mathcal{O}$ is a (γ, k)-*partition oracle with respect to a graph property* $\mathcal{P}$ if the partition $\mathcal{S}$ has the following properties.
>
> - For every $S_i \in \mathcal{S}$, $|S_i| \leq k$, the induced subgraph $G[S_i]$ is connected.
> - If G satisfies $\mathcal{P}$, then the number of edges cut by $\mathcal{S}$, that is:
>
> $$|\{(u, v) \in E : \mathcal{S}[u] \neq \mathcal{S}[v]\}|$$
>
> is at most γn with probability at least $9/10$, where the probability is taken over the internal randomness of $\mathcal{O}$.

By the above definition, if $G \in \mathcal{P}$, then the partition $\mathcal{S}$ is a (γ, k)-partition with probability at least $9/10$. On the other hand, if $G \notin \mathcal{P}$, then we only require that each part of the partition is connected and has size at most k.

10.3.3 Testing H-Minor-Freeness

Before describing how to implement a partition oracle, we first formalize the idea in the beginning of Section 10.3.2 and present a constant-query tester for H-minor-freeness assuming the existence of a partition oracle.

For a partition $\mathcal{S}$ of a vertex set V, we define $f_{\mathcal{S}} \colon V \times [d] \to \{0, 1\}$ as:

$$f_{\mathcal{S}}(u, i) = \begin{cases} 1 & \text{if } \mathcal{S}[u] \neq \mathcal{S}[v], \text{ where } v \text{ is the } i\text{-th neighbor of } u. \\ 0 & \text{otherwise.} \end{cases}$$

Then, $\sum_{u \in V, i \in [d]} f(u, i)$ equals the number of edges cut by $\mathcal{S}$. Hence, we can estimate the number of edges cut by $\mathcal{S}$ by applying Lemma 2.2 on f. Now, the detailed description of our tester is given in Algorithm 10.3. We assume that there is an $(\epsilon d/4, k)$-partition oracle.

Algorithm 10.3 Tester for H-minor-freeness

Input: $n \in \mathbb{Z}_{>0}$, $\epsilon > 0$, and query access to a graph G.
1: Let $\mathcal{S}$ be the partition given through an $(\epsilon d/4, k)$-partition oracle for H-minor-free graphs.
2: Let $\tilde{c}$ be the value obtained by applying Lemma 2.2 on $f_{\mathcal{S}}$, $\epsilon dn/8$, and $1/10$.
3: **if** $\tilde{c} \geq 3\epsilon dn/8$ **then**
4:     Reject.
5: **end if**
6: **for** $\Theta(\epsilon^{-1}k)$ times **do**
7:     $v \leftarrow$ a vertex uniformly sampled from V.
8:     **if** the graph induced by $\mathcal{S}[v]$ is not H-minor-free **then**
9:         Reject.
10:     **else**
11:         Accept.
12:     **end if**
13: **end for**

Theorem 10.8. *Let H be a graph. Suppose that we have an $(\epsilon d/4, k)$-partition oracle for H-minor-free graphs such that a query to the oracle results in at most q queries to the input graph. Then, H-minor-freeness is testable with query complexity $O(\epsilon^{-1}qk + \epsilon^{-2}q)$.*

Proof. If G is H-minor-free, then the number of edges cut by $\mathcal{S}$ is at most $\epsilon dn/4$ with probability at least $9/10$. If this is the case, the estimate on the number of broken edges that is computed by the tester is at most $3\epsilon dn/8$ with probability $9/10$. Moreover, every induced subgraph of G is also H-minor-free, so G cannot be rejected in the loop from Line 6. By the union bound, we accept with probability at least $8/10 > 2/3$.

Suppose now that G is ϵ-far from being H-minor-free. If the partition $\mathcal{S}$ cuts more than $\epsilon dn/2$ edges, then we reject with probability at least $9/10$. We, therefore, assume $\mathcal{S}$ cuts less than $\epsilon dn/2$ edges.

Let G' be the graph obtained by the partition $\mathcal{S}$. G' remains $\epsilon/2$-far from H-minor-freeness, and there are at least $\epsilon dn/2$ edges that must be removed to get an H-minor-free graph. As each connected subgraph in G' has size at most k, the number of connected subgraphs that are not H-minor-free is at least:

$$\frac{\epsilon dn/2}{kd} = \frac{\epsilon n}{2k} = O\left(\frac{\epsilon n}{k}\right).$$

Hence, with probability at least $9/10$, we hit a vertex in such a connected subgraph and reject in the loop from Line 6, we reject.

The analysis of the query complexity is obvious. □

10.3.4 Implementation of Partition Oracle

Because we are designing a constant-query tester for H-minor-freeness, we are interested in a local partition oracle in the sense that it queries the input graph only a constant number of times. However, in Section 10.3.4.1, we first consider a global partition oracle that accesses the whole graph because it is easier to think of. Then in Section 10.3.4.2, we will obtain a local partition oracle by locally simulating the global partition oracle described in this section.

10.3.4.1 Global Partition Oracle

We start with defining operations on partitions.

> **Definition 10.3** (Contraction by partition). Let $G = (V, E, w)$ be an edge-weighted graph and let $\mathcal{S} = (S_1, \ldots, S_t)$ be a partition of V such that $G[S_i]$ is connected for every $i \in [t]$. Define the *contraction $G/\mathcal{S}$ of G with respect to the partition $\mathcal{S}$* to be the edge-weighted graph $G' = (V', E', w')$, where:
>
> - $V' = \{S_1, \ldots, S_t\}$, that is, there is a vertex in V' for each subset of the partition $\mathcal{S}$;
> - There is an edge $\{S_i, S_j\} \in E'$ if and only if $i \neq j$ and there exists $u \in S_i$ and $v \in S_j$ such that $\{u, v\} \in E$;
> - The weight $w'(\{S_i, S_j\})$ is equal to $\sum_{\{u,v\} \in E(S_i, S_j)} w(\{u, v\})$.

contraction $G/\mathcal{S}$ of G with respect to the partition $\mathcal{S}$

If $\{u, v\}$ is an edge of G, and $\mathcal{S}$ is the partition of V into $\{u, v\}$ and singletons $\{w\}$ for every $w \in V \setminus \{u, v\}$, then $G/\mathcal{S}$ is the graph obtained from G by contracting the edge $\{u, v\}$.

Now we describe the global partition algorithm. The algorithm proceeds in ℓ iterations, where $\ell := \Theta(\log \frac{1}{\epsilon d})$. Initially, we have a trivial partition $\mathcal{S}^0 := \{\{v\} : v \in V\}$ and a graph $G^0 := G/\mathcal{S}^0 = G$. We regard each edge of G has weight 1. In the i-th iteration, we create a new partition $\mathcal{S}^i$ by coarsening $\mathcal{S}^{i-1}$, and then we obtain $G^i := G/\mathcal{S}^i$. At the end of the algorithm, we output the final partition $\mathcal{S}^\ell$.

In the i-th iteration, we make a graph G^i by contracting some edges of G^{i-1}, or in other words, merging some connected subgraphs in $\mathcal{S}^{i-1}$. We want to contract edges so that total weight of the edges in G^i is smaller than that for G^{i-1} by a certain constant factor. Note that contracting an edge in G^{i-1}

corresponds to coarsening the partition $\mathcal{S}^{i-1}$ by merging subsets containing the endpoints of the edge. Then after ℓ iterations, the total weight of the edges in G^ℓ is at most ϵdn (by choosing the hidden constant in ℓ to be large enough), which implies that the number of edges cut by $\mathcal{S}^\ell$ is at most ϵdn. Meanwhile, we want to make sure that the diameter of each connected subgraph increases only by constant in each iteration so that the connected subgraphs in $\mathcal{S}^\ell$ are of constant size.

We exploit Lemma 10.8 to guarantee that the total weight of edges decreases by a certain factor. Observe that if the graph G is H-minor-free for some fixed graph H, then every G^i is H-minor-free as well. Hence, we can partition the edge set of G^{i-1} into at most c_H forests, and one of them has at least $\frac{1}{c_H}$-fraction of the weight. Let F be such a forest. Then, we can partition the edge set of F into two edges sets F_{odd} and F_{even}, which consists of the edges in the odd and even, respectively, layers in terms of an arbitrarily chosen root for each tree in F. Note that F_{odd} and F_{even} consist of vertex-disjoint stars and one of F_{odd} and F_{even} has at least $\frac{1}{2c_H}$-fraction of the weight. By contracting edges in it, we can decrease the total weight by at least $\frac{1}{2c_H}$-factor whereas the diameter of each subgraph in $\mathcal{S}^{i-1}$ by at most one.

Having said that, using the forest F is not a good idea for designing constant-query algorithms because we need the whole graph to compute F and provide query access to it. Instead, we proceed as follows: Each vertex in G^{i-1} selects an incident edge with the maximum weight and tosses a fair coin. Here, we assume that each vertex in G^{i-1} has an ID, and when there are two or more incident edges with the maximum weight, we break ties by adopting the one whose other endpoint has the maximum ID. Each selected edge is contracted if and only if it is selected by a heads vertex and its other endpoint is a tails vertex. Note that the contracted edges form a set of vertex-disjoint stars. The detailed procedure is provided in Algorithm 10.4.

Theorem 10.9. *If G is H-minor-free (and has a degree bound d), then Algorithm 10.4 outputs an $(\epsilon d, d^{O(\log(1/\epsilon d))})$-partition of G with probability at least $9/10$.*

Proof. We first claim that in each iteration, when making $\mathcal{S}^i$ from $\mathcal{S}^{i-1}$, the total weight of the edges decreases by a factor of $1 - \frac{1}{8c_H}$ with probability at least $\frac{1}{8c_H - 1}$, where the probability is taken over the coin tosses.

Fix $i \in [\ell]$. By Lemma 10.8, the edge set of G^{i-1} can be partitioned into at most c_H forests. Hence, for one of these forests, the total weight of edges is at least $w(G^{i-1})/c_H$, where $w(G^{i-1})$ denotes the total weight of the edges in G^{i-1}. Then, we orient the edges of the forest from the root to leaves, so that each vertex has in-degree at most 1. This way, we can associate a unique edge in G^{i-1} in the forest with each vertex u (except the root) and let $e_F(u)$ denote this edge. For each vertex u, let $e_A(u)$ be the edge selected by u in the algorithm. Recall that $e_A(u)$ has the largest weight

---

Algorithm 10.4 Global partition oracle

Input: Graphs G and H, $d \in \mathbb{Z}_{>0}$, and $\epsilon \in (0,1)$.
Output: A partition.
1: $G^0 \leftarrow G$ and $\mathcal{S}^0 \leftarrow \{\{v\} : v \in V\}$.
2: **for** $i = 1$ to $\ell = \Theta(\log \frac{1}{\epsilon d})$ **do**
3:     $\mathcal{S}^i \leftarrow \mathcal{S}^{i-1}$.
4:     Toss a fair coin for every vertex in G^{i-1}.
5:     **for** each vertex u in G^{i-1} **do**
6:         $\{u,v\} \leftarrow$ an edge with the maximum weight that is incident to u.
7:         **if** The coin tosses of u and v are heads and tails, respectively **then**
8:             $S \leftarrow$ the connected subgraph in $\mathcal{S}^i$ that u belongs to.
9:             $T \leftarrow$ the connected subgraph in $\mathcal{S}^i$ that v belongs to.
10:            Merge S and T in $\mathcal{S}^i$.
11:        **end if**
12:    **end for**
13:    $G^i \leftarrow G/\mathcal{S}^i$.
14: **end for**
15: **return** $\mathcal{S}^\ell$.

---

among edges incident to u. Hence, we have $w^{i-1}(e_A(u)) \geq w^{i-1}(e_F(u))$, where we regarded $w^{i-1}(e_F(u)) = 0$ when u is the root of the tree and $e_F(u)$ is not defined. Therefore, the total weight of selected edges, that is, $\sum_{u \in V(G^{i-1})} w^{i-1}(e_A(u))$, is at least the weight of the forest. We stress that if an edge $\{u,v\}$ is selected both by u and by v, that is, $e_A(u) = e_A(v)$, then we add both $w^{i-1}(e_A(u))$ and $w^{i-1}(e_A(v))$ to the total weight of the selected edges. It follows that:

$$\sum_{v \in V(G^{i-1})} w^{i-1}(e_A(v)) \geq \frac{w(G^{i-1})}{c_H}.$$

As each selected edge is contracted with probability $1/4$, the expected total weight of edges contracted when making $\mathcal{S}^i$ from $\mathcal{S}^{i-1}$ is at least $\frac{w(G^{i-1})}{4c_H}$. Thus, the expected total weight of non-contracted edges is at most $w(G^{i-1}) - \frac{w(G^{i-1})}{4c_H} = \left(1 - \frac{1}{4c_H}\right) w(G^{i-1})$. By Markov's inequality, the probability that the total weight of non-contracted edges is at least $\left(1 - \frac{1}{8c_H}\right) w(G^{i-1})$ is at most:

$$\frac{\left(1 - \frac{1}{4c_H}\right) w(G^{i-1})}{\left(1 - \frac{1}{8c_H}\right) w(G^{i-1})} = 1 - \frac{1}{8c_H - 1}. \tag{10.3}$$

successful interation   We say that the i-th iteration is *successful* if $w(G^i) \leq \left(1 - \frac{1}{8c_H}\right) w(G^{i-1})$. Applying Lemma 2.3 with $\eta := \frac{1}{8c_H - 1}$, with probability at least $9/10$, there are at least $\eta\ell - 3\sqrt{\ell} \geq \frac{\ell}{16c_H - 2}$ successful iterations. This implies that, after the ℓ-th iteration, with probability at least $9/10$, the weight of the edges in G_ℓ is at most:

$$c_H n \left(1 - \frac{1}{8c_H}\right)^{\ell/(16c_H - 2)} \leq \epsilon dn.$$

As the diameter of each connected subgraph increases by one in each iteration, the size of each connected subgraph is bounded by $d^\ell = d^{O(\log(1/\epsilon d))}$.

□

10.3.4.2 Local Partition Oracle

Next, we show that we can locally simulate the global partitioning oracle (Algorithm 10.4) by only looking at a constant-size local neighborhood of the queried vertex.

Recall that the partition $\mathcal{S}$ is determined randomly based on the coin tosses of the vertices in each iteration. To make the oracle efficient, we toss coins on the fly only when they are required, as we did in Section 5.3.4. Moreover, we also assign IDs to vertices in each of G^{i-1} on the fly by using random values in $[0, 1]$. A similar technique was also used in testing k-edge-connectivity (Section 5.3.4) and approximating the size of a maximal matching (Section 5.8.2).

Theorem 10.10. *For any graph H, there exists an $(\epsilon d, d^{O(\log(1/\epsilon d))})$-partition-oracle for H-minor free graphs that makes $(1/\epsilon)^{O(\log^2(1/\epsilon d))}$ queries to the graph for each query to the oracle.*

Proof. Recall that Algorithm 10.4 constructs a sequence of graphs $G^0 = G, G^1, \ldots, G^\ell$ as well as the partition $\mathcal{S}^0, \ldots, \mathcal{S}^\ell$. For a vertex $v \in V$, let $\mathcal{S}^i[v]$ denote the connected subgraph that v belongs to in $\mathcal{S}^i$. Let $k := d^{\Theta(\log \epsilon^{-1})}$ be the upper bound on the sizes of subgraphs in $\mathcal{S}^\ell$.

The query access to $\mathcal{S}^i$ is built upon the query access to $\mathcal{S}^{i-1}$. The query access to $\mathcal{S}^0$ is trivial: Given a vertex $q \in V$, it simply returns the set $\{q\}$.

Suppose that we have query access to $\mathcal{S}^{i-1}$. Then, in order to implement query access to $\mathcal{S}^i$, we need to consider the following two cases. Let $q \in V$ be the queried vertex.

- Case 1: $\mathcal{S}^{i-1}[q]$ is a tails vertex for the i-th iteration. In this case, we query all edges incident to vertices in $\mathcal{S}^{i-1}[q]$, which amounts to at most $d \cdot k$ edges. For each endpoint v of such an edge, we find $\mathcal{S}^{i-1}[v]$. For each $\mathcal{S}^{i-1}[v]$ that is heads, we determine whether its heaviest incident edge connects to $\mathcal{S}^{i-1}[q]$, and if so the edge is contracted (so that $\mathcal{S}^{i-1}[v] \subseteq \mathcal{S}^i[q]$). To do so, we need to query all the edges incident to vertices in $\mathcal{S}^{i-1}[v]$, and for each endpoint y of such an edge we need to find $\mathcal{S}^{i-1}[y]$. The weight of each edge $(\mathcal{S}^{i-1}[v], \mathcal{S}^{i-1}[y])$ is $|\{(a,b) : a \in \mathcal{S}^{i-1}[v], b \in \mathcal{S}^{i-1}[y]\}|$ (and since all edges incident to vertices in $\mathcal{S}^{i-1}[y]$ have been queried, this weight can be calculated). The total number of vertices x for which we need to compute $\mathcal{S}^{i-1}[x]$ is upper bounded by $d^2 k^2$, and this is also an upper bound on the number of queries performed to $\mathcal{S}^{i-1}$.

- Case 2: $\mathcal{S}^{i-1}[q]$ is a heads vertex in the i-th iteration. In this case, we find its heaviest edge incident to vertices in $\mathcal{S}^{i-1}[q]$, as previously described for $\mathcal{S}^{i-1}[v]$. Let C' denote the other endpoint in G^{i-1}. If C' is a tails vertex, then we apply the same procedure to C' as described in Case 1 for $\mathcal{S}^{i-1}[q]$ (that is, in the case that $\mathcal{S}^{i-1}[q]$ is a tails vertex in G^{i-1}). The number of queries performed to $\mathcal{S}^{i-1}$ can be analyzed as with Case 1.

Let $Q^i(v)$ denote the number of queries to G that are performed in order to determine $\mathcal{S}^i[v]$, and let Q^i denote an upper bound on $Q^i(v)$ that holds for any vertex v. We first observe that $Q^0 = 0$. We thus get the following recurrence for Q^i: $Q^i = d^2 \cdot k^2 + d^2 \cdot k^2 \cdot Q^{i-1}$. Since $k = d^{O(\log(1/\epsilon d))}$, we get that:

$$Q^\ell \leq d^{O(\log(1/\epsilon d)) \cdot 2\ell} = d^{O(\log^2(1/\epsilon d))},$$

as claimed.   □

Combined with Theorem 10.8, we get the following:

Corollary 10.3. *Let H be a graph. Then, H-minor-freeness is testable with query complexity $(1/\epsilon)^{O(\log^2(1/\epsilon d))}$.*

It is known that we can obtain an $(\epsilon d, O(\epsilon^{-2}))$-partition oracle whose query complexity is $(1/\epsilon)^{O(\log(1/\epsilon d))}$ by, in each iteration, breaking connected subgraphs of size $\omega(\epsilon^{-2})$ into smaller ones using the separator theorem (Theorem 10.7) [300]. This leads to a two-sided error tester for H-minor-freeness with query complexity $(1/\epsilon)^{O(\log(1/\epsilon d))}$, which is slightly better than Corollary 10.3.

10.3.5 Testing Properties in H-Minor-Free Graphs

As an application of partition oracle, we see that *every* graph property is testable with a constant number of queries if the input graph is H-minor-free. Recall that, a graph property is a property on graphs closed under isomorphism (Definition 4.1).

learner

Definition 10.4. We say that an algorithm is an ϵ-*learner* if, given query access to the input graph G, it outputs a graph G' with $d(G, G') \leq \epsilon d n$ with probability at least $2/3$.

Proposition 10.3. *Let $\mathcal{D}$ be a distribution on a support of size n. Let $\mathcal{D}'$ be an empirical distribution resulting from $\Theta(\epsilon^{-2}n)$ independent samples from $\mathcal{D}$. With probability $9/10$, we have $d_{\mathrm{TV}}(\mathcal{D}, \mathcal{D}') \leq \epsilon$.*

Theorem 10.11. *If there is an $(\epsilon d/2, k)$-partitioning oracle $\mathcal{O}$ for a class $\mathcal{C}$ of graphs, then there is an ϵ-learner for $\mathcal{C}$. The algorithm makes $O(\epsilon^{-2} 2^{k^2})$ queries to $\mathcal{O}$ and additionally $O(\epsilon^{-2} k^2 2^{k^2})$ queries to the input graph.*

Proof. The oracle $\mathcal{O}$ provides query access to a partition $\mathcal{S}$ of the input graph. Every connected subgraph in $\mathcal{S}$ has at most k vertices. Let $\mathcal{G}_k$ be the set of unlabeled connected graphs on at most k vertices. It is easy to show that $|\mathcal{G}_k| \le 2^{k^2}$. Each vertex v in $\mathcal{S}$ belongs to a connected subgraph isomorphic to one of $\mathcal{G}_k$. Let $\mathcal{D}$ be the distribution over $\mathcal{G}_k$, where the probability we sample $H \in \mathcal{G}_k$ is proportional to the number of vertices v in $\mathcal{S}$ for which v belongs to a connected graph isomorphic to H. It follows from Proposition 10.3 that with probability $9/10$, we can learn a distribution $\mathcal{D}'$ such that $d_{\text{TV}}(\mathcal{D}, \mathcal{D}') \le \epsilon/4$ by sampling $O(\epsilon^{-2} |\mathcal{G}_k|)$ vertices. The exploration of each connected subgraph takes at most $O(k^2)$ queries, so the total number of queries necessary to learn $\mathcal{D}'$ is bounded by $O(\epsilon^{-2} k^2 2^{k^2})$.

Let n be the number of vertices in the input graph. Next the algorithm searches for a graph G^* on n vertices with the corresponding distribution $\mathcal{D}^*$ over $\mathcal{G}_k$ such that $d_{\text{TV}}(\mathcal{D}^*, \mathcal{D}') \le \epsilon/4$. If $\mathcal{D}'$ has been computed correctly, such a distribution $\mathcal{D}^*$ exists and moreover, $d_{\text{TV}}(\mathcal{D}^*, \mathcal{D}) \le \epsilon/2$. We now bound the distance between the partition provided by $\mathcal{O}$ and G^*. The total number of vertices which have to be moved to connected subgraphs of a different type is bounded by $\epsilon n/4$. Their neighbor lists are the only ones that have to be modified to turn one of the graphs into the other. The total number of edge insertions and deletions is bounded by $\epsilon dn/2$, which bounds the distance between the graphs by $\epsilon dn/2$.

Now observe that the oracle $\mathcal{O}$ removes at most $\epsilon dn/2$ edges with probability $9/10$. In this case, the distance between the partition and the original graph is bounded by $\epsilon dn/2$. By the triangle inequality, the distance between the input graph and G^* is bounded by ϵdn, provided that all the specified events hold. The probability that any of them does not hold is bounded by $1/10 + 1/10 \le 1/3$. To summarize, the algorithm is an ϵ-learner. □

Note that the time complexity of the algorithm provided in Theorem 10.11 is a large function in n though its query complexity is constant.

Once we have obtained G^* from the input graph G such that $d(G, G^*) \le \epsilon dn$, we can easily test any graph property.

Theorem 10.12. *Let H be a fixed graph. If the input graph is H-minor-free, then every graph property is constant-query testable.*

Proof. For the class of H-minor-free graphs, we know that there is an $(\epsilon d, k)$-partition oracle for $k = (1/\epsilon)^{O(\log^2(1/\epsilon d))}$ by Theorem 10.10. Then, we can learn a graph G^* from the input graph using Theorem 10.11 with the error parameter $\epsilon/4$. Now, we accept if and only if G^* is $\epsilon/4$-close to satisfying the property $\mathcal{P}$ we are concerned with.

The correctness is almost trivial. First note that $d(G, G^*) \leq \epsilon dn/2$ holds with high probability. If G satisfies $\mathcal{P}$, then G^* is $\epsilon/4$-close to satisfying $\mathcal{P}$ and we accept. If G is ϵ-far from satisfying $\mathcal{P}$, then G^* is $3\epsilon/4$-far from satisfying $\mathcal{P}$ and we reject. $\qquad\square$

10.3.6 Further Results

The following notion that abstracts the property of decomposability into small connected components was introduced by Elek [168]. Let $\epsilon \in (0, 1)$ and hyperfiniteness $k \in \mathbb{Z}_{>0}$. A graph G is called (ϵ, k)-*hyperfinite* if one can remove ϵn edges from G and obtain a graph whose connected components have size at most k. For a function $\rho\colon \mathbb{R}_{>0} \to \mathbb{R}_{>0}$, a graph G is ρ-*hyperfinite* if for every $\epsilon \in (0, 1)$, G is $(\epsilon, \rho(\epsilon))$-hyperfinite. A collection of graphs is ρ-*hyperfinite* if every graph in the collection is ρ-hyperfinite. A collection of graphs is called *hyperfinite* if there exists a function $\rho\colon \mathbb{R}_{>0} \to \mathbb{R}_{>0}$ such that the collection is ρ-hyperfinite.

Exercise 10.4. Show that any minor-freeness is a hyperfinite property.

We can design a partitioning oracle for any hyperfinite property, and hence any hyperfinite property is constant-query testable [248].

Hyperfiniteness is not the only reason that we can test properties closed subdivision under edge removals. A *subdivision* of a graph G is a graph resulting from the subdivision of edges in G. Here, the *subdivision* of some edge e with endpoints $\{u, v\}$ yields a graph containing one new vertex w, and with an edge set replacing e by two new edges, $\{u, w\}$ and $\{w, v\}$. For a graph H, we H-subdivision-freeness say that a graph G is H-*subdivision-free* if G does not contain a subdivision of H as a subgraph.

Exercise 10.5. Show that any H-minor-free graph it is H-subdivision-free.

As opposed to minor-freeness, subdivision-freeness does not exclude expanders. For example, a 3-regular graph is always K_5-subdivision-free but can be an expander. Kawarabayashi and Yoshida [279] showed that, for any graph H, H-subdivision-freeness is constant-query testable with two-sided error.

Nonetheless, hyperfiniteness plays a vital role in every constant-query testable property. Fichtenberger, Peng, and Sohler [177] showed that every constant-query testable infinite property (meaning that the property contains an infinite number of graphs) contains an infinite hyperfinite subproperty.

As a consequence, no infinite graph property that only consists of expander graphs is constant-query testable.

10.4 Additional Topics

Relation between the Unidirectional and Bidirectional Models for Digraphs

Czumaj, Peng, and Sohler [142] studied relation between the unidirectional and bidirectional models for digraphs (see Section 5.9 for definitions) and obtained the following general result:

Theorem 10.13 ([142]). *A graph property that can be tested with two-sided error and query complexity $O_{\epsilon,d}(1)$ in the bidirectional model can be tested with $n^{1-\Omega_{\epsilon,d}(1)}$ queries and two-sided error in the unidirectional model.*

Note that the two-sided feature is necessary as testing strong connectivity is one-sided error testable with a constant number of queries in the bidirectional model [71] whereas any one-sided error tester for strong connectivity requires $\Omega(n)$ in the unidirectional model [255].

Extending the result in Section 10.3.5 to digraphs and then combining it with Theorem 10.13, we get the following:

Theorem 10.14 ([142]). *Every graph property of in a digraph satisfying a minor-closed property is testable with query complexity $O_{\epsilon,d}(1)$ in the bidirectional model and with query complexity $n^{1-\Omega_{\epsilon,d}(1)}$ in the unidirectional model.*

General Graph Model

A few general results on the general graph model are known (See Section 5.9 for the definition). When the graph is restricted to be planar, bipartiteness is testable with a constant number of queries [140]. Note that, in general, testing bipartiteness requires $\Omega(\sqrt{n})$ queries even when the average degree is constant (Section 5.5.2). Czumaj and Sohler [145] showed that a graph property is testable with one-sided error for planar graphs if and only if testing the property can be reduced to testing for a finite family of forbidden subgraphs, which may depend on the proximity parameter ϵ.

Every graph property is testable with poly$(\log n)$ queries when the graph is restricted to be cycle-free [293] or outerplanar [38] (possibly with high-degree vertices), A slight variant of this results is that every graph property is constant-query testable in a class of graphs for which the degree distribution obeys power law [261].

10.5 Bibliographic Notes

Sparsity matroids were introduced in [304] and have been successfully used in structural rigidity theory [298, 275, 381, 394]. The algorithm and analysis for (k, ℓ)-sparsity presented here are due to Ito, Tanigawa, and Yoshida [262]. They also showed that testing (k, ℓ)-fullness with one-sided error requires $\Omega(n)$ queries. Theorems 10.4 and 10.5 are due to [262] and [379], respectively.

Benjamini, Schramm, and Shapira [72] gave the first constant-query tester for minor-closed properties. The query complexity of their algorithm is triply exponential in poly(ϵ^{-1}). Hassidim, Kelner, Nguyen, and Onak [248] introduced the notion of partition oracle and improved the query complexity to a single exponential in ϵ^{-1}. The partition oracle presented here is due to [300], which further improved the query complexity to quasi-polynomial in ϵ^{-1}, that is, $(1/\epsilon)^{O(\log 1/\epsilon d)}$. For bounded treewidth graphs, partitioning oracles with query complexity polynomial in ϵ^{-1} are known [163, 405].

Bypassing the construction of partitioning oracles, Kumar, Seshadhri, and Stolman [289] showed a random-walk-based tester for minor-closed properties with poly($\epsilon^{-1}d$) queries.

Czumaj, Goldreich, Ron, Seshadhri, Shapira, and Sohler [139] initiated the study of one-sided error testability of minor-freeness and showed that C_3-minor-freeness, that is, cycle-freeness, is one-sided error testable with $\widetilde{O}(\sqrt{n})$ queries, by reducing the problem to testing bipartiteness and applying the bipartiteness tester described in Section 5.5. Fichtenberger, Levi, Vasudev, and Wötzel [176] extended this result and showed that some other minor-closed properties including outerplanarity are one-sided error testable with $\widetilde{O}(\sqrt{n})$ queries. Finally, Kumar, Seshadhri, and Stolman [288] showed that every minor-closed property is one-sided error testable with $n^{1/2+o(1)}$ queries.

Newman and Sohler showed that every graph property is constant-query testable when the input graph is restricted to satisfy a minor-closed property [333]. The simplified proof presented here is due to Onak [336]. Note that, although their algorithms have constant query complexity, their time complexity is prohibitively large functions of the input size. Adler and Harwath [2] showed that, when the input graph is restricted to have bounded-treewidth, every property definable in monadic second-order logic with modulo counting is testable with a constant number of queries and polylogarithmic time.

It is interesting to pursue the trade-off between the restriction on the input graph and the extent to which properties are constant-query testable. Czumaj, Shapira, and Sohler [143] showed that every hereditary property is constant-query testable when the graph is *strongly non-expanding*, that is,

strongly
non-expanding

every induced subgraph of a certain size has a small cut. Elek [169] extended their results to optimization problems such as the size of the maximum independent set.

Despite general results we have seen in this chapter, it seems still far from obtaining a complete characterization of constant-query testable properties. One reason is that an analogue of Szemerédi's regularity lemma for bounded-degree graphs [170] is very complicated and it is not clear how to exploit it to design constant-query testers for non-trivial properties.

Problems

10.1. Show that $(1,0)$-fullness is one-sided error testable with a constant number of queries. (**Hint**: Modify the tester for $(1,1)$-fullness, that is, connectivity.)

10.2. Prove Lemma 10.3 formally by designing an auxiliary graph and query access to it.

10.3. Let $G = (V,E)$ be a (k,ℓ)-full graph. Let G' be a graph obtained from G by adding a new vertex and connecting it to distinct k vertices in G. Show that the grpah G' is (k,ℓ)-full.

10.4. In this problem, you are asked to show that any one-sided error tester for (k,ℓ)-fullness for $k \geq 3$ has query complexity $\Omega(n)$. You can use the fact that, for any sufficiently large n, there is a $(2k-1)$-regular graph $G = (V,E)$ on n vertices with the following property: for any vertex set $S \subseteq V$ with $|S| \leq \beta n$, where β is a universal constant, we have $|\Gamma(S)| \geq (2k-3)|S|$.

1. Show that G is $\Omega(1/k)$-far from (k,ℓ)-fullness.
2. Let $S \subseteq V$ be a set of at most βn vertices. Show that the induced subgraph $G[S]$ can be extended to a (k,ℓ)-full graph, that is, there exists a (k,ℓ)-sparse supergraph of $G[S]$. (Hint: Use Problem 10.3 and the fact that $k \geq 3$.)
3. Show that any one-sided error tester for (k,ℓ)-fullness has query complexity $\Omega(n)$.

10.5. Show that $K_{1,3}$-minor-freeness is one-sided error testable with $O(\epsilon^{-1})$ queries.

10.6. Show that testing P_k-minor-freeness is testable with $O(\epsilon^{-1}d^k)$ queries, where P_k is the path of length k.

10.7. The *arboricity* of an undirected graph is the minimum number of spanning forests needed to cover all the edges of the graph. Show that, for any integer $d \in \mathbb{Z}_{>0}$, the property of having arboricity at most d is testable with a constant number of queries.

arboricity

10.8. Show that any minor closed property is constant-query testable in the general graph model if the average degree of vertices in the input graph is bounded by a constant.

Chapter 11
Affine-Invariant Properties of Functions

In this chapter, we explain general results on testing properties of functions, defined on vector spaces over finite fields. The goal of these results is to characterize testability for a large class of natural properties of such functions, similar to how the results in Chapter 9 characterized testability for large classes of dense graph properties. In particular, we study *affine-invariant* properties of functions f taking values on $\mathbb{F}^n$ (for a finite field $\mathbb{F}$).

> **Definition 11.1.** Given a finite field $\mathbb{F}$ and an integer $R \geq 1$, a property[a] $\mathcal{P} \subseteq \{\mathbb{F}^n \to [R]\}$ is said to be *affine-invariant* if for any $f \in \mathcal{P}$ and any affine map $A: \mathbb{F}^n \to \mathbb{F}^n$, $f \circ A$ is also in $\mathcal{P}$.
>
> ───────────────
> [a] As usual, a property is really a family of properties defined for each natural number n. The dependence on n is suppressed for convenience.

affine-invariance

Informally, membership in $\mathcal{P}$ does not depend on the basis chosen to represent the underlying vector space or on affine shifts to the space. A prominent example of an affine-invariant property is having degree $\leq d$, but arguably, most interesting properties of multivariate functions on finite fields that one would classify as "algebraic" display affine-invariance.

Intriguingly, although the properties we consider are algebraic in flavor, the technical tools we wield to prove testability are often analytic in nature. In Section 11.2, we start by describing these techniques, which collectively go by the name of "higher-order Fourier analysis." Higher-order Fourier analysis has clear parallels to Szemerédi's regularity lemma and the associated apparatus described in Chapter 9. Again, just like the regularity lemma, it has many applications in several areas beyond property testing.

We apply higher-order Fourier analysis to study testability of *subspace-hereditary* affine-invariant properties.

© The Author(s), under exclusive license to Springer Nature Singapore Pte Ltd 2022
A. Bhattacharyya and Y. Yoshida, *Property Testing*,
https://doi.org/10.1007/978-981-16-8622-1_11

subspace-hereditary
property

Definition 11.2. Given a finite field $\mathbb{F}$ and an integer $R \geq 1$, an affine-invariant property $\mathcal{P} \subseteq \{\mathbb{F}^n \to [R]\}$ is said to be *subspace-hereditary* if for any $f \in \mathcal{P}$ and any affine subspace $H \leq \mathbb{F}^n$ of dimension $n-1$, the restriction of f to H, denoted $f|_H \colon \mathbb{F}^{n-1} \to [R]$, is also in $\mathcal{P}$.

This is a class of properties of functions that contains many natural algebraic and coding-theoretic properties, as we illustrate later in the chapter. In Section 11.3, we use higher-order Fourier analysis to show that all *locally characterized* subspace-hereditary affine-invariant properties are constant-query testable with a one-sided tester and argue that this is a near-characterization of testability in a certain sense. Although the results of higher-order Fourier analysis are very powerful and general, they yield extremely bad bounds for the query complexity. In Section 11.4, we see that the query complexity can be much improved for a specific property by bypassing higher-order Fourier analysis.

11.1 Testability and Affine-Invariance

This chapter focuses on one-sided testability of affine-invariant properties[1]. Unless mentioned otherwise, all properties in this chapter are for functions mapping $\mathbb{F}^n$ to a bounded range $[R]$, where $\mathbb{F}$ is the prime field of a fixed order p (e.g., 2).

Before discussing general one-sided testers, it will be useful to first consider *proximity oblivious testers*. Analogous to their definition for graph properties in Section 9.5, PO testers are defined in the current context as follows:

proximity oblivious
tester

Definition 11.3 (Proximity oblivious tester (POT)). An algorithm is said to be a *proximity oblivious tester* for a property $\mathcal{P} \subseteq \{\mathbb{F}^n \to [R]\}$ if, given $n \in \mathbb{Z}_{>0}$ and query access to a function $f \colon \mathbb{F}^n \to [R]$:

- it accepts with probability 1 when f satisfies $\mathcal{P}$, and
- there exists a monotone non-decreasing function $\rho \colon (0,1) \to (0,1)$ such that it rejects any function that is ϵ-far from $\mathcal{P}$ with probability at least $\rho(\epsilon)$.

Consider a function property $\mathcal{P}$ that admits a PO tester with fixed query complexity q. For any function $f \notin \mathcal{P}$, the tester rejects f with positive probability. Suppose $\alpha_1, \ldots, \alpha_q$ is a set of queries that makes the tester reject f. Let $\sigma = (f(\alpha_1), \ldots, f(\alpha_q))$. Since the tester always accepts functions in $\mathcal{P}$, $x_1, \ldots, x_q$ must be a witness for non-membership in $\mathcal{P}$. In other words, if for any function g, it holds that $(g(\alpha_1), \ldots, g(\alpha_q)) = \sigma$, it must

---

[1] We briefly discuss in Section 11.5 what is known for two-sided testability of affine-invariant properties.

be the case that $g \notin \mathcal{P}$. Moreover, if $\mathcal{P}$ is affine-invariant, $g \in \mathcal{P}$ implies $(g(\ell(\alpha_1)), \ldots, g(\ell(\alpha_q))) \neq \sigma$ for all affine maps ℓ.

It is useful to consider a 'dual' formulation of the above observation, which treats ℓ as a variable. We say that a vector $W = (w_1, w_2, \ldots, w_k) \in \mathbb{F}^k$ is an *affine form on k variables* if $w_1 = 1$ and the vector is interpreted as a a function from $(\mathbb{F}^n)^k \to \mathbb{F}^n$ via $(x_1, \ldots, x_k) \mapsto w_1 x_1 + w_2 x_2 + \cdots + w_k x_k$. For technical reasons, it is useful to specify a partial order among affine forms. We say $(w_1, \ldots, w_k) \preceq (w_1', \ldots, w_k')$ if $|w_i| \le |w_i'|$ for all $i \in [k]$, where $|\cdot|$ is the obvious map from $\mathbb{F}$ to $\{0, 1 \ldots, p-1\}$.

Definition 11.4 (Affine constraints). Let $m = p^{k-1}$. An *affine constraint on k variables* is a tuple $A = (W_1, \ldots, W_m)$ of m affine forms $W_1, \ldots, W_m$ over $\mathbb{F}$ on k variables, where:

(i) $W_1(x_1, \ldots, x_k) = x_1$;
(ii) If W belongs to A and $W' \preceq W$, then W' also belongs to A.

By the observation in the paragraph after Definition 11.3, it is straightforward to check that if an affine-invariant $\mathcal{P}$ has a PO tester, then corresponding to the queries made for a function $f \notin \mathcal{P}$, there exist k, an affine constraint $A = (W_1, \ldots, W_m)$ on k variables (where $m = p^{k-1}$) and $\sigma \in [R]^m$ such that if for a function $g \colon \mathbb{F}^n \to [R]$, there are $x_1, \ldots, x_k \in \mathbb{F}^n$ satisfying:

$$(g(W_1(x_1, \ldots, x_k)), \ldots, g(W_m(x_1, \ldots, x_k))) = \sigma,$$

then $g \notin \mathcal{P}$. The number of variables $k \le q$, the tester's query complexity.

We can also go in the reverse direction and define affine-invariant properties in terms of affine constraints.

Definition 11.5 (Properties defined by induced affine constraints).

- An *induced affine constraint on ℓ variables* is a pair (A, σ) where A is an affine constraint on ℓ variables and $\sigma \in [R]^m$.

- Given such an induced affine constraint (A, σ) where $A = (W_i)_i$, a function $f \colon \mathbb{F}^n \to [R]$ is said to be (A, σ)-*free* if there exist no $x_1, \ldots, x_\ell \in \mathbb{F}^n$ such that $f(W_i(x_1, \ldots, x_\ell)) = \sigma_i$ for all i. On the other hand, if such $x_1, \ldots, x_\ell$ exist, we say that f *induces* (A, σ) at $x_1, \ldots, x_\ell$.

- Given a (possibly infinite) collection

$$\mathcal{A} = \{(A^1, \sigma^1), (A^2, \sigma^2), \ldots, (A^i, \sigma^i), \ldots\}$$

of induced affine constraints, a function $f \colon \mathbb{F}^n \to [R]$ is said to be $\mathcal{A}$-*free* if it is (A^i, σ^i)-free for every $i \ge 1$.

- An affine-invariant property $\mathcal{P}$ is said to be *k-locally characterized* if it corresponds to $\mathcal{A}$-freeness for a collection $\mathcal{A}$ of induced affine constraints on at most k variables.

As an example consider the property of having degree at most 1 as a polynomial, for function $F\colon \mathbb{F}^n \to \mathbb{F}$. It is easy to see that F satisfies this property if and only if $F(x_1) - F(x_1 + x_2) - F(x_1 + x_3) + F(x_1 + x_2 + x_3) = 0$ for all $x_1, x_2, x_3 \in \mathbb{F}$. Consequently the property can be defined by the set of induced affine constraints that forbid any values for $F(x_1), F(x_1 + x_2), F(x_1 + x_3), F(x_1 + x_2 + x_3)$ that do not satisfy the identity $F(x_1) - F(x_1 + x_2) - F(x_1 + x_3) + F(x_1 + x_2 + x_3) = 0$. The property is 4-locally characterized.

One of the main results of this chapter is that analogously to Theorem 9.11, we can characterize PO testable affine invariant properties in terms of induced affine constraints.

Theorem 11.1. *An affine-invariant property $\mathcal{P} = \{\mathcal{P}_n\}_{n \in \mathbb{Z}_{\geq 0}}$ has a constant query PO tester if and only if there exist a constant k and a sequence $\mathcal{A} = \{\mathcal{A}_n\}_n$ of families of induced affine constraints with the following properties:*

- *Each $\mathcal{A}_n$ contains induced affine constraints on at most k variables;*
- *$\mathcal{P}_n$ equals $\mathcal{A}_n$-freeness.*

The "only if" part of the theorem follows from the previous discussion. The "if" part is shown in Section 11.3.

Exercise 11.1. Show that that $\mathcal{P}$ is a subspace-hereditary property if and only if it corresponds to $\mathcal{A}$-freeness for a collection $\mathcal{A}$ of induced affine constraints (not necessarily on a bounded number of variables).

To characterize general one-sided testable affine-invariant properties in terms of subspace-hereditary properties, the same technicalities arise as those for graph properties described in Section 9.3.2. Analogously, we define *semi-subspace-hereditary properties*.

semi-subspace-
hereditary property

Definition 11.6. An affine-invariant property $\mathcal{P}$ is said to be *semi-subspace-hereditary* if there exists a subspace-hereditary property $\mathcal{Q}$ such that the following holds:

(1) Any function satisfying $\mathcal{P}$ also satisfies $\mathcal{Q}$.
(2) For all $\epsilon > 0$, there is an $n(\epsilon)$ such that for any function $f\colon \mathbb{F}^n \to [R]$ with $n > n(\epsilon)$ that is ϵ-far from satisfying $\mathcal{P}$, $f \notin \mathcal{Q}$.

The following characterization of one-sided testable affine-invariant properties is known, generalizing the above Theorem 11.1.

Theorem 11.2. *An affine-invariant property $\mathcal{P} = \{\mathcal{P}_n\}_{n \in \mathbb{Z}_{\geq 0}}$ has a constant query one-sided tester if and only if $\mathcal{P}$ is semi-subspace-hereditary.*

The "only if" direction can shown using the same idea as in the proof of Theorem 9.3. In Section 11.3, the "if" direction is proved with an additional 'boundedness' assumption.

11.2 Higher-order Fourier Analysis

Higher-order Fourier analysis is a study of the connections between the algebraic and analytic properties of functions over finite fields. These connections have been an integral part of mathematics for a long time; the celebrated Weil bound for character sums is a striking example. The set of results covered here gives a fine-grained understanding of the algebraic structure of a polynomial and how it distributes over its image, which is then used to decompose arbitrary functions into "pseudo-random components", akin to how Szemerédi's regularity lemma partitions arbitrary graphs into pseudo-random subgraphs.

11.2.1 Derivatives and Polynomials

In the context of higher-order Fourier analysis, the concept of polynomials is best defined locally: a polynomial of degree $< d$ is a function which vanishes identically after d differentiations. The derivative operation is naturally defined additively.

> **Definition 11.7** (Additive Derivative). For any additive group G, given a function $P \colon \mathbb{F}^n \to G$ and an element $h \in \mathbb{F}^n$, define the *additive derivative in direction h* of P to be the function $D_h P \colon \mathbb{F}^n \to G$ satisfying $D_h P(x) = P(x+h) - P(x)$ for all $x \in \mathbb{F}^n$.

additive derivative

> **Definition 11.8** (Classical Polynomials). For an integer $d \geq 1$, a function $P \colon \mathbb{F}^n \to \mathbb{F}$ is a *classical polynomial of degree $\leq d$* if for all $h_1, \ldots, h_{d+1} \in \mathbb{F}^n$, $D_{h_1} D_{h_2} \cdots D_{h_{d+1}} P$ is identically zero.

classical polynomial

> **Example 11.1.** If $P(x) = x_1 x_2 + x_3 x_4$, $D_h P(x) = x_1 h_2 + x_2 h_1 + x_3 h_4 + x_4 h_3$, $D_k D_h P(x) = h_1 k_2 + h_2 k_1 + h_3 k_4 + h_4 k_3$, and $D_\ell D_k D_h P(x) = 0$ for any $h, k, \ell \in \mathbb{F}^n$. Hence, P is a classical polynomial of degree ≤ 2.

The local definition of classical polynomials is equivalent to the more standard global definition in terms of degrees of monomials.

Exercise 11.2. Prove that $P \colon \mathbb{F}^n \to \mathbb{F}$ is a classical polynomial of degree $\leq d$ if and only if one can write:

$$P(x_1, \ldots, x_n) = \sum_{0 \leq d_1, \ldots, d_n < p : d_1 + \cdots + d_n \leq d} c_{d_1, \ldots, d_n} x_1^{d_1} \cdots x_n^{d_n}$$

for coefficients $c_{d_1, \ldots, d_n} \in \mathbb{F}$.

Remark 11.1. The above correspondence holds because $p = |\mathbb{F}|$ is prime. One can check that over $\mathbb{F}_{2^2}$, the function x^2 is a classical polynomial of degree 1.

It turns out though that for developing the theory of higher-order Fourier analysis, we need to consider functions that are not $\mathbb{F}$-valued. Let us introduce some new notations. Let $\mathbb{T}$ denote the circle group $\mathbb{R}/\mathbb{Z}$. This is an additive group (abelian group with group operation denoted $+$). We use $\iota \colon \mathbb{F} \to \mathbb{T}$ to denote the isomorphism $x \mapsto |x|/p \mod 1$, where $|x|$ is the standard map from $\mathbb{F}$ to $\{0, 1, \ldots, p-1\}$.

non-classical
polynomial

Definition 11.9 (Non-classical polynomials). For an integer $d \geq 0$, a function $P \colon \mathbb{F}^n \to \mathbb{T}$ is said to be a *non-classical polynomial of degree* $\leq d$ (or simply a *polynomial of degree* $\leq d$) if for all $h_1, \ldots, h_{d+1} \in \mathbb{F}^n$, it holds that:

$$D_{h_1} \cdots D_{h_{d+1}} P \equiv 0. \tag{11.1}$$

Example 11.2. Suppose $P \colon \mathbb{F}_2 \to \mathbb{T}$ is defined as $P(0) = 0$ and $P(1) = 3/4$. Then, letting $P' = D_1 P$, we compute $P'(0) = 3/4$ and $P'(1) = 1/4$. Similarly, $P''(0) = P''(1) = 1/2$, while $P''' \equiv 0$. Hence, P is a non-classical polynomial of degree 2.

Example 11.3. If P is a classical polynomial, then $\iota(P)$ is a non-classical polynomial with the same degree.

Exercise 11.3. Show that $|x|/p^k$ is a non-classical polynomial of degree k.

The global structure of non-classical polynomials is somewhat more complicated than that of classical polynomials (Exercise 11.2).

Lemma 11.1 (Global Structure of Non-classical Polynomials). *For an integer $d \geq 1$, a function $P \colon \mathbb{F}^n \to \mathbb{T}$ is a polynomial of degree $\leq d$ if and only if P can be represented as:*

$$P(x_1, \ldots, x_n) = \alpha + \sum_{\substack{0 \leq d_1, \ldots, d_n < p; k \geq 0: \\ 0 < \sum_i d_i \leq d - k(p-1)}} \frac{c_{d_1, \ldots, d_n, k} |x_1|^{d_1} \cdots |x_n|^{d_n}}{p^{k+1}} \mod 1,$$

for a unique choice of $c_{d_1, \ldots, d_n, k} \in \{0, 1, \ldots, p-1\}$ and $\alpha \in \mathbb{T}$. The element α is called the shift *of P, and the largest integer k such that there exist $d_1, \ldots, d_n$ for which $c_{d_1, \ldots, d_n, k} \neq 0$ is called the* depth *of P.*

shift

depth

Example 11.4. The non-classical polynomial of degree 2 in Example 11.2 can be written as $P(x) = |x|/4 + |x|/2 \pmod 1$. Its depth is 1.

For an integer $k \geq 0$, let $\mathbb{U}_k$ denote $\frac{1}{p^k} \mathbb{Z}/\mathbb{Z}$, a subgroup of $\mathbb{T}$. Lemma 11.1 yields that polynomials of depth k take values in a coset of $\mathbb{U}_{k+1}$. In particular, polynomials of depth 0 take values in shifts of $\{0/p, 1/p, \ldots, (p-1)/p\}$ and correspond to shifts of classical polynomials. The following exercise makes the important observation that when $d < p$, non-classical polynomials are necessarily of depth 0.

Exercise 11.4. Suppose $p > d$. Show that there exists a one-to-one correspondence between classical polynomials of degree d and non-classical polynomials of degree d and shift 0.

11.2.2 The Gowers Norm and the Inverse Theorem

In order to use ideas from analysis, it will be convenient to consider *phase polynomials*. Let $\mathbf{e} \colon \mathbb{T} \to \mathbb{C}$ where $\mathbf{e}(x) = e^{2\pi i x}$.

Definition 11.10 (Phase Polynomial). A function $f \colon \mathbb{F}^n \to \mathbb{C}$ is a *phase polynomial* of *degree d and depth ℓ* if and only if $f = \mathbf{e}(P)$, where P is a non-classical polynomial of degree d and depth ℓ.

phase polynomial

To be more explicit, f is a phase polynomial of degree $\leq d$ if and only if:

$$\Delta_{h_1} \Delta_{h_2} \cdots \Delta_{h_{d+1}} f \equiv 1,$$

where the multiplicative derivative operator Δ is defined as follows:

multiplicative
derivative

Definition 11.11 (Multiplicative Derivative). Given a function $f\colon \mathbb{F}^n \to \mathbb{C}$ and an element $h \in \mathbb{F}^n$, define the *multiplicative derivative in direction* h of f to be the function $\Delta_h f\colon \mathbb{F}^n \to \mathbb{C}$ satisfying $\Delta_h f(x) = f(x+h)\overline{f(x)}$ for all $x \in \mathbb{F}^n$.

Given this formulation, it is natural to consider the following test for phase polynomials of degree $\leq d$: choose $x, h_1, h_2, \ldots, h_{d+1}$ uniformly at random from $\mathbb{F}^n$ and check whether $\Delta_{h_1} \ldots \Delta_{h_{d+1}} f(x) = 1$. Formally, we define the *Gowers norm*:

Gowers norm

Definition 11.12 (Gowers norm). Given a function $f\colon \mathbb{F}^n \to \mathbb{C}$ and an integer $d \geq 1$, the *Gowers norm of order* d for f is given by:

$$\|f\|_{U^d} = \left| \mathop{\mathbf{E}}_{h_1,\ldots,h_d, x \in \mathbb{F}^n} [(\Delta_{h_1} \Delta_{h_2} \cdots \Delta_{h_d} f)(x)] \right|^{1/2^d}.$$

The Gowers norm satisfies several useful properties.

Exercise 11.5. For any function $f\colon \mathbb{F}^n \to \mathbb{C}$, show that $\|f\|_{U^1} = |\mathbf{E}_x f(x)|$.

Exercise 11.6. For any function $f\colon \mathbb{F}^n \to \mathbb{C}$ and phase polynomial $p\colon \mathbb{F}^n \to \mathbb{C}$ of degree $< d$, show that $\|f\|_{U^d} = \|f \cdot p\|_{U^d}$.

Also, as you will prove in Problem 11.1, the Gowers norm is monotonically non-decreasing in d.

Lemma 11.2. *For any function* $f\colon \mathbb{F}^n \to \mathbb{C}$, $\|f\|_{U^d} \leq \|f\|_{U^{d+1}}$ *for all* $d \geq 1$.

We have already observed that if f is a phase polynomial of degree $\leq d$, then $\|f\|_{U^{d+1}} = 1$. We can strengthen this fact:

correlation with
polynomials

Lemma 11.3. *Given a function* $f\colon \mathbb{F}^n \to \mathbb{C}$, *suppose it is δ-correlated with degree-d polynomials for some $\delta > 0$, meaning there exists a degree-d polynomial $P\colon \mathbb{F}^n \to \mathbb{T}$ such that:*

$$\left| \mathop{\mathbf{E}}_x f(x)\mathbf{e}\left(-P(x)\right) \right| \geq \delta.$$

Then, $\|f\|_{U^{d+1}} \geq \delta$.

Proof. Our assumption is that $\|f \cdot \mathbf{e}\left(-P\right)\|_{U^1} \geq \delta$. By Lemma 11.2, $\|f \cdot \mathbf{e}\left(-P\right)\|_{U^{d+1}} \geq \delta$. The result of Exercise 11.6 then proves the claim. $\square$

In the other direction, we have the following result which states that the Gowers norm of order $d+1$ also provides a lower bound on the correlation with degree d polynomials.

Theorem 11.3 (Inverse Theorem for the Gowers Norm). *Suppose $\delta > 0$ and $d \geq 1$ is an integer. There exists an $\epsilon = \epsilon_{11.3}(\delta, d)$ such that the following holds. For every function $f \colon \mathbb{F}^n \to \mathbb{C}$ with $\|f\|_\infty \leq 1$ and $\|f\|_{U^{d+1}} \geq \delta$, there exists a polynomial $P \colon \mathbb{F}^n \to \mathbb{T}$ of degree $\leq d$ that is ϵ-correlated with f, meaning:*

$$\left| \mathop{\mathbf{E}}_{x \in \mathbb{F}^n} f(x) \mathbf{e}\left(-P(x)\right) \right| \geq \epsilon.$$

Inverse theorem for Gowers norm

We will not attempt to give a proof of Theorem 11.3, as all current proofs require a substantial number of ideas beyond the scope of this book. Note that the result holds even when δ is a small constant[2], although ϵ decreases as a function of δ extremely rapidly.

It is known that in the inverse theorem for Gowers norm, we cannot insist on P being a classical polynomial. Consider the function $S_4 \colon \mathbb{F}_2^n \to \mathbb{F}_2$ defined as:

$$S_4(x) = \sum_{S \subseteq [n], |S|=4} \prod_{i \in S} x_i.$$

On one hand, $\|S_4\|_{U^4} > \epsilon$ for a constant ϵ. On the other hand, for any *classical* degree-3 polynomial $P \colon \mathbb{F}_2^n \to \mathbb{F}_2$, it holds that:

$$\left| \mathop{\mathbf{E}}_{x \in \mathbb{F}_2^n} \mathbf{e}\left(S_4(x) - P(x)\right) \right| < \exp(-\Omega(n)).$$

11.2.3 Rank

In this section, we introduce an algebraic property of polynomials of degree d that is tightly connected to the Gowers norm of order d for the corresponding phase polynomial. This connection is the crucial component that will allow us to perform the "regular decompositions" in the next section.

---

[2] When δ is very close to 1 (the so-called "99% setting"), we have a tighter understanding. For example, over $\mathbb{F}_2$, it can be shown (see Problem 11.2) that for a function $F \colon \mathbb{F}_2^n \to \mathbb{F}_2$, the results of Section 12.4 imply: if $\|\mathbf{e}(F)\|_{U^{d+1}} = \gamma \geq 1 - \epsilon 2^{-d}$ for a sufficiently small ϵ, then F is $\Theta(1-\gamma)$-close to a degree-d *classical* polynomial $P \colon \mathbb{F}_2^n \to \mathbb{F}_2$ in Hamming distance.

rank

Definition 11.13 (Rank of a polynomial). Given a polynomial $P: \mathbb{F}^n \to \mathbb{T}$ and an integer $d > 1$, the *d-rank* of P, denoted $\mathrm{rank}_d(P)$, is defined to be the smallest integer r such that there exist polynomials $Q_1, \ldots, Q_r: \mathbb{F}^n \to \mathbb{T}$ of degree $\leq d - 1$ and a function $\Gamma: \mathbb{T}^r \to \mathbb{T}$ satisfying $P(x) = \Gamma(Q_1(x), \ldots, Q_r(x))$. If $d = 1$, then 1-rank is defined to be ∞ if P is non-constant and 0 otherwise.

The *rank* of a polynomial $P: \mathbb{F}^n \to \mathbb{T}$ is its $\deg(P)$-rank.

Exercise 11.7. Show that for integer $\lambda \in [1, p - 1]$, $\mathrm{rank}(P) = \mathrm{rank}(\lambda P)$.

Exercise 11.8. Suppose $P: \mathbb{F}^n \to \mathbb{F}$ is a quadratic defined by $P(x) = x^T A x$ for a symmetric n-by-n matrix A. Suppose $\mathbb{F}$ is a prime field of odd order p and r is the matrix rank of A. Show that:

(a) The rank of $\iota(P)$ is r.
(b) $\|\mathbf{e}(P)\|_{U^1} = p^{-r/2}$. (Hint: Expand $|\mathbf{E}\,\mathbf{e}(P)|^2$)

As Exercise 11.8 shows, for classical quadratics, there is a correspondence between rank and the bias (that is, the U^1 norm). In fact, this is an instance of a much more general phenomenon between the rank and Gowers norm of polynomials. One direction of this relationship is not hard to show.

Exercise 11.9. Suppose $P: \mathbb{F}^n \to \mathbb{T}$ is a polynomial of degree d and has rank $\leq r$.

(a) Use Fourier analysis to show that $\mathbf{e}(P) = \sum_{i=1}^{t} \gamma_i \cdot q_i$ where each q_i is a phase polynomial of degree $d - 1$, each $|\gamma_i| \leq 1$, and $t \leq p^{(1 + \lceil (d-1)/(p-1) \rceil)r}$.
(b) Argue that there exists a degree $d - 1$ phase polynomial q such that $\mathbf{e}(P)$ is $1/t$-correlated with q.
(c) Use Lemma 11.3 to conclude that $\|P\|_{U^d} \geq 1/t$.

The reverse direction is a serious result in additive combinatorics that we will not prove here. In fact, it forms the major component of the proof of the inverse theorem for the Gowers norm (Theorem 11.3).

inverse theorem

Theorem 11.4 (Inverse theorem for rank). *For any $\epsilon > 0$ and integer $d \geq 1$, there exists an integer $r = r_{11.4}(d, \epsilon)$ such that the following is true. For any polynomial $P: \mathbb{F}^n \to \mathbb{T}$ of degree $\leq d$, if $\|\mathbf{e}(P)\|_{U^d} \geq \epsilon$, then $\mathrm{rank}_d(P) \leq r$.*

> **Exercise 11.10.** Show that Theorem 11.4 implies Theorem 11.3 for phase polynomials f. (**Hint**: Use the same idea as in Exercise 11.9.)

Often, we will be satisfied with a weaker corollary which follows directly from Lemma 11.2.

> **Corollary 11.1** (Rank-versus-bias for polynomials). *For any $\epsilon > 0$ and integer $d \geq 1$, there exists an integer $r = r_{11.4}(d, \epsilon)$ such that the following is true. For any polynomial $P \colon \mathbb{F}^n \to \mathbb{T}$ of degree $\leq d$, if $\mathrm{rank}_d(P) \geq r$, then $|\mathbf{E}_x\, \mathbf{e}\, (P(x))| = \|P\|_{U^1} \leq \epsilon$.*

11.2.4 Regular Decompositions

We are now ready to apply the above results to decompose functions $f \colon \mathbb{F}^n \to \mathbb{C}$ into "pseudorandom" components. We will begin with phase polynomials f and then describe how to handle general functions.

11.2.4.1 Polynomial Decompositions

Instead of one polynomial, it will prove useful in what follows to consider a collection of polynomials at once. More precisely, we will consider *polynomial factors*. A polynomial factor $\mathcal{B}_{P_1,\dots,P_C}$ simply denotes a sequence of polynomials $P_1, \dots, P_C \colon \mathbb{F}^n \to \mathbb{T}$. The *complexity* of $\mathcal{B}$, denoted $|\mathcal{B}|$, is the number of defining polynomials C. The *degree* of $\mathcal{B}$ is the maximum degree among its defining polynomials $P_1, \dots, P_C$. If $P_1, \dots, P_C$ are of depths $k_1, \dots, k_C$, respectively, then $\|\mathcal{B}\| = \prod_{i=1}^{C} p^{k_i + 1}$ is called the *order* of $\mathcal{B}$. For a point $x \in \mathbb{F}^n$, we use $\mathcal{B}(x)$ to denote the atom of the induced partition that contains x:

$$\mathcal{B}(x) = \{y : P_i(x) = P_i(y)\ \forall i \in [C]\}.$$

The rank of a factor can now be defined as follows.

> **Definition 11.14** (Rank and Regularity). A polynomial factor $\mathcal{B}$ defined by a sequence of polynomials $P_1, \dots, P_C \colon \mathbb{F}^n \to \mathbb{T}$ with respective depths $k_1, \dots, k_C$ is said to have *rank* r if r is the least integer for which there exist $(\lambda_1, \dots, \lambda_C) \in \mathbb{Z}^C$ so that $(\lambda_1 \bmod p^{k_1+1}, \dots, \lambda_C \bmod p^{k_C+1}) \neq (0, \dots, 0)$ and the polynomial $Q = \sum_{i=1}^{C} \lambda_i P_i$ satisfies $\mathrm{rank}_d(Q) \leq r$ where $d = \max_i \deg(\lambda_i P_i)$.
>
> Given a polynomial factor $\mathcal{B}$ and a function $r \colon \mathbb{Z}_{>0} \to \mathbb{Z}_{>0}$, we say $\mathcal{B}$ is *r-regular* if $\mathcal{B}$ is of rank larger than $r(|\mathcal{B}|)$.

The decomposition theorem for polynomials we give in this section expresses any polynomial factor in terms of a high-rank polynomial factor of

complexity
degree

order

rank

regularity

bounded size. In particular, given any factor $\mathcal{B}$ that is not regular, we find a refinement $\mathcal{B}'$ of $\mathcal{B}$ that is regular up to our desires. We distinguish between two kinds of refinements:

syntactic refinement
semantic refinement

Definition 11.15 (Semantic and syntactic refinements). $\mathcal{B}'$ is called a *syntactic refinement* of $\mathcal{B}$, and denoted $\mathcal{B}' \succeq_{\text{syn}} \mathcal{B}$, if the sequence of polynomials defining $\mathcal{B}'$ extends that of $\mathcal{B}$. It is called a *semantic refinement*, and denoted $\mathcal{B}' \succeq_{\text{sem}} \mathcal{B}$ if the induced partition is a combinatorial refinement of the partition induced by $\mathcal{B}$. In other words, if for every $x, y \in \mathbb{F}^n$, $\mathcal{B}'(x) = \mathcal{B}'(y)$ implies $\mathcal{B}(x) = \mathcal{B}(y)$.

The following lemma gives the decomposition of an arbitrary polynomial factor into regular factors.

Lemma 11.4 (Polynomial Regularity Lemma). *Let $r\colon \mathbb{Z}_{>0} \to \mathbb{Z}_{>0}$ be a non-decreasing function and $d > 0$ be an integer. Then, there is a function $C_{11.4}^{(r,d)}\colon \mathbb{Z}_{>0} \to \mathbb{Z}_{>0}$ such that the following is true. Suppose $\mathcal{B}$ is a factor defined by polynomials $P_1, \ldots, P_C\colon \mathbb{F}^n \to \mathbb{T}$ of degree at most d. Then, there is an r-regular factor $\mathcal{B}'$ consisting of polynomials $Q_1, \ldots, Q_{C'}\colon \mathbb{F}^n \to \mathbb{T}$ of degree $\leq d$ such that $\mathcal{B}' \succeq_{\text{sem}} \mathcal{B}$ and $C' \leq C_{11.4}^{(r,d)}(C)$.*

Moreover, if $\mathcal{B}$ is itself a refinement of some $\hat{\mathcal{B}}$ that has rank $> (r(C') + C')$ and consists of polynomials, then additionally $\mathcal{B}'$ will be a syntactic refinement of $\hat{\mathcal{B}}$.

The proof of Lemma 11.4 is quite involved, and we skip it. For *classical* polynomials, the proof is much simpler and you will be asked to prove it in Problem 11.3.

11.2.4.2 General bounded functions

The above section shows that given a function $r\colon \mathbb{Z}_{>0} \to \mathbb{Z}_{>0}$, any phase polynomial $p\colon \mathbb{F}^n \to \mathbb{C}$ of degree d can be written as $\gamma(Q_1, \ldots, Q_C)$ where $Q_1, \ldots, Q_C$ are non-classical polynomials with degree bounded by d forming an r-regular factor, C is bounded as a function of r and d, and $\gamma\colon \mathbb{T}^C \to \mathbb{C}$ is a function. Next, instead of phase polynomials, we consider arbitrary bounded functions $f\colon \mathbb{F}^n \to \mathbb{C}$ such that $|f| \leq 1$.

We will show that any bounded function f admits a decomposition:

$$f = f_1 + f_2 + f_3,$$

where f_1 is a function of a high-rank polynomial factor, f_2 has small Gowers norm, and f_3 is an "error" term. This is analogous to the Szemerédi regularity lemma in the sense that f_1 corresponds to the regularity partition, f_2 corresponds to the pseudorandom edges among the regular pairs, and f_3 corresponds to the error contributed by the irregular pairs. (In fact, this analogy can be made entirely formal.)

As a starting point, we show the following coarser decomposition. Below, for a function $f\colon \mathbb{F}^n \to \mathbb{C}$, the notation $\mathbf{E}[f|\mathcal{B}]$ denotes the function:

$$\mathbf{E}[f|\mathcal{B}](x) = \mathbf{E}_{y \in \mathcal{B}(x)}[f(y)].$$

In particular, note that if f is Boolean (that is, maps to $\{0, 1\}$), then $\mathbf{E}[f|\mathcal{B}]$ maps to $[0, 1]$.

Lemma 11.5. *Suppose $\eta, d \geq 1$ are integers. Let $r\colon \mathbb{Z}_{>0} \to \mathbb{Z}_{>0}$ be an arbitrary non-decreasing function. Then, there exists $N = N_{11.5}(\eta, d, r, p)$ and $C = C_{11.5}(\eta, d, r, p)$ such that the following holds. For any function $f\colon \mathbb{F}^n \to \mathbb{C}$ for $n > N$ satisfying $|f| \leq 1$, we can write:*

$$f = f_1 + f_2,$$

where $f_1 = \mathbf{E}[f|\mathcal{B}]$ for an r-regular polynomial factor $\mathcal{B}$ of degree d and order at most C and $f_2\colon \mathbb{F}^n \to \mathbb{C}$ such that $|f_2| \leq 1$ and $\|f_2\|_{U^{d+1}} \leq 1/\eta$.

The proof of this Lemma is a good example of the *energy increment* method, an important proof technique for many such results. The basic idea is that if $f - f_1$ has large U^{d+1} norm, then it is correlated with a degree-d polynomial g by Theorem 11.3. We add g to the polynomial factor $\mathcal{B}$, regularize using Lemma 11.4, and repeat. If $f - f_1$ has small U^{d+1} norm, then we are already done. The fact that this process terminates can be shown by a transfinite induction. You will be asked to fill out the details in Problem 11.4.

Just as in Lemma 9.3 for the case of graphs, we need a functional regularity lemma so that η in the above lemma is controlled by a function of the size of the factor.

energy increment

Lemma 11.6. *Suppose $d \geq 1$ is an integer, $\epsilon > 0$, $\eta\colon \mathbb{Z}_{>0} \to (0, 1)$ is a non-increasing function and $r\colon \mathbb{Z}_{>0} \to \mathbb{Z}_{>0}$ is a non-decreasing function. Then, there exists $N = N_{11.6}(d, \epsilon, \eta, r, p)$ and $C = C_{11.6}(d, \epsilon, \eta, r, p)$ such that the following holds. For any function $f\colon \mathbb{F}^n \to \mathbb{C}$ for $n > N$ satisfying $|f| \leq 1$, we can write:*

$$f = f_1 + f_2 + f_3,$$

where $f_1 = \mathbf{E}[f|\mathcal{B}]$ for an r-regular polynomial factor $\mathcal{B}$ of degree d and order at most C, $f_2\colon \mathbb{F}^n \to \mathbb{C}$ such that $|f_2| \leq 2$ and $\|f_2\|_{U^{d+1}} \leq \eta(|\mathcal{B}|)$, and $f_3\colon \mathbb{F}^n \to \mathbb{C}$ such that $\|f_3\|_2 \leq \epsilon$.

The proof is again an application of the energy increment method; we repeatedly apply Lemma 11.5 so as to make $\|f_2\|_{U^{d+1}}$ small with respect to the current factor, stopping when $\|f_3\|_2$ becomes sufficiently small. You will be guided through the proof in Problem 11.5.

Remark 11.2.

(i) When f is Boolean, as is often the case for our applications, f_1 and $f_1 + f_3$ map to $[0, 1]$, and f_2 and f_3 map to $[-1, 1]$.

(ii) In Lemma 11.6 (as well as Lemma 11.5), we can insist that $\mathcal{B}$ be a syntactic refinement of a given factor $\mathcal{B}'$. This requires essentially no changes to the proofs: instead of starting the induction with an empty factor, we can start it with $\mathcal{B}'$ instead.

Lemma 9.3 for graphs has a feature that is missing in the Lemma 11.6 above. It constructs an equipartition $\mathcal{A}$ and an equipartition $\mathcal{B}$ of an induced subgraph such that for each part $A \in \mathcal{A}$, there exists a $B \in \mathcal{B}$ such that $B \subseteq A$, and moreover, the edge density between most parts in $\mathcal{A}$ are close to the density between the corresponding parts in $\mathcal{B}$. This feature was crucially used in the testing results for hereditary properties in Chapter 9. We will need an analogous version of the regularity lemma for the testing results in this chapter.

Lemma 11.7 (Two-level Functional Regularity Lemma). *Suppose $d \geq 1$ is an integer, $\zeta > 0$, $\epsilon, \eta \colon \mathbb{Z} \to (0, 1)$ are non-increasing functions, and $r \colon \mathbb{Z}_{>0} \to \mathbb{Z}_{>0}$ is a non-decreasing function. Then, there exists $N = N_{11.7}(d, \zeta, \epsilon, \eta, r, p)$ and $C = C_{11.7}(d, \zeta, \epsilon, \eta, r, p)$ such that the following holds.*

For any function $f \colon \mathbb{F}^n \to \{0, 1\}$, there exist r-regular polynomial factors $\mathcal{B}$ and $\mathcal{B}'$ of degree at most d and order at most C such that $\mathcal{B}'$ syntactically refines $\mathcal{B}$. They define a decomposition:

$$f = f_1 + f_2 + f_3,$$

where $f_1 = \mathbf{E}[f|\mathcal{B}']$, $\|f_2\|_{U^{d+1}} < \eta(|\mathcal{B}'|)$, and $\|f_3\|_2 < \epsilon(|\mathcal{B}|)$. Moreover, there exists an $s \in \mathbb{T}^{|\mathcal{B}'|-|\mathcal{B}|}$ such that[a]: (i) for every atom c of $\mathcal{B}$, the atom (c, s) of $\mathcal{B}'$ satisfies:

$$\|f_3|_{(c,s)}\|_2 < \epsilon(|\mathcal{B}|),$$

and (ii) for at least $1 - \zeta$ fraction of atoms in $\mathcal{B}$:

$$|\mathbf{E}[f|_{(c,s)}] - \mathbf{E}[f|_c]| < \zeta.$$

---

[a] We use the shorthand $g|_A$ to denote the restriction of a function g to a subset A of its domain.

In short, Lemma 11.7 provides a sub-atom corresponding to each atom of $\mathcal{B}$ such that on *each* sub-atom, f_3 is small and moreover for *most* atoms, the density of f on the corresponding sub-atom approximates the density on the whole atom.

11.2.5 Counting Lemmas

Recall that in Chapter 9, the reason why the regularity lemma was helpful was because we could use Lemma 9.2 and Lemma 9.5 to count the number of copies of a subgraph induced by regular pairs. The idea is similar in this chapter, but instead of counting subgraphs, we will count images of a system of affine forms.

> **Definition 11.16** (Linear and affine forms). A *linear form* on k variables is a vector $L = (w_1, w_2, \ldots, w_k) \in \mathbb{F}^k$ that is interpreted as a function from $(\mathbb{F}^n)^k$ to $\mathbb{F}^n$ via the map $(x_1, \ldots, x_k) \mapsto w_1 x_1 + w_2 x_2 + \cdots + w_k x_k$. A linear form $L = (w_1, \ldots, w_k)$ is said to be *affine* if $w_1 = 1$. A *system of affine forms* is a collection of such affine forms.

linear form

affine form
system of affine forms

Example 11.5. Consider the following system of affine forms

$$L_1(x_1, x_2, x_3) = x_1$$
$$L_2(x_1, x_2, x_3) = x_1 + x_2$$
$$L_3(x_1, x_2, x_3) = x_1 + x_3$$
$$L_4(x_1, x_2, x_3) = x_1 + x_2 + x_3$$

The image of L_1, L_2, L_3, L_4 forms an affine subspace of dimension 2.

For functions $f_1, \ldots, f_m \colon \mathbb{F}^n \to \mathbb{C}$, we will want to estimate:

$$\sum_{x_1, \ldots, x_k \in \mathbb{F}^n} f_1(L_1(x_1, \ldots, x_k)) \cdots f_m(L_m(x_1, \ldots, x_k)). \qquad (11.2)$$

When $f_1, \ldots, f_m$ are the indicator functions of subsets, this is exactly the count of the number of $(x_1, \ldots, x_k)$ such that each $L_i(x_1, \ldots, x_k)$ lies in the set supported by f_i.

The results in this section show that if one of the f_i's is pseudorandom, in the sense of having a small Gowers norm of the appropriate order, then (11.2) above is small. On the other hand, if each f_i is structured, in the sense that it is a function of a regular polynomial factor, then we can lower bound (11.2).

11.2.5.1 Pseudorandom Case

Observe that in the simplest instantiation of the problem, $m = k = 1$ with $L(x) = x$, then $|\mathbf{E}[f]|$ is precisely $\|f\|_{U^1}$. This provokes the question: can (11.2) be controlled by the Gowers norm of the f_i's?

> **Exercise 11.11.** Show that if $f\colon \mathbb{F}_2^n \to [-1,1]$ and $\|f\|_{U^2} \leq \epsilon$, then $|\mathbf{E}[f(x)f(y)f(x+y)]| \leq \epsilon$.

What about for more general systems?

> **Theorem 11.5** (Counting — Pseudorandom Case). *Let $L_1, \ldots, L_m$ be a system of linear forms over $\mathbb{F}$ in k variables. Suppose $d \geq 1$ is the smallest integer such that $L_1^{\otimes d+1}, \ldots, L_m^{\otimes d+1}$ are linearly independent (if it exists). Then, for any $\epsilon > 0$, there exists $\delta > 0$ such that if $f_1, \ldots, f_m\colon \mathbb{F}^n \to \mathbb{C}$ such that $\max_i \|f_i\|_\infty \leq 1$ and $\min_i \|f_i\|_{U^{d+1}} \leq \delta$, then:*
> $$\left| \mathop{\mathbf{E}}_{X \in (\mathbb{F}^n)^k} \left[\prod_{i=1}^m f_i(L_i(X)) \right] \right| \leq \epsilon.$$

Here, if $L = (w_1, \ldots, w_k)$ is a linear form, then $L^{\otimes d} = (\prod_{j=1}^d w_{i_j} : i_1, \ldots, i_d \in [k])$ is the tensor power of order d. The smallest d for which $L_1^{\otimes d+1}, \ldots, L_m^{\otimes d+1}$ are linearly independent is called the *true complexity* of the system.

true complexity

> **Exercise 11.12.** Verify that for the system in Exercise 11.11, its true complexity (over $\mathbb{F}_2$) is 1.

11.2.5.2 Structured Case

Consider the case when each $f_i = \mathbf{E}[f_i' | \mathcal{B}]$ for a regular polynomial factor $\mathcal{B}$ of order C. Then, our strategy to lower bound (11.2) is to find atoms $b_1, \ldots, b_m \in \mathbb{T}^C$ such that there are many $x_1, \ldots, x_k$ for which $\mathcal{B}(L_i(x_1, \ldots, x_k)) = b_i$ for all i and, moreover, $\mathbf{E}[f_i'|_{b_i}]$ is large for each i. In this section, we discuss how to guarantee the first of these two requirements, namely that:

$$\mathop{\Pr}_{x_1, \ldots, x_k} [\mathcal{B}(L_i(x_1, \ldots, x_k)) = b_i \; \forall i \in [m]]$$

is large, for some choice of $b_1, \ldots, b_m$.

Even when the system consists of a single form, the problem is already interesting.

> **Lemma 11.8** (Size of Atoms). *Let $\epsilon > 0$, and $\mathcal{B}$ be a polynomial factor of degree $d > 0$, order C, and rank $r > r_{11.4}(d, \epsilon)$, defined by a tuple of polynomials $P_1, \ldots, P_C\colon \mathbb{F}^n \to \mathbb{T}$ having respective depths $k_1, \ldots, k_C$. Suppose $b = (b_1, \ldots, b_C) \in \mathbb{U}_{k_1+1} \times \cdots \times \mathbb{U}_{k_C+1}$. Then:*
> $$\mathop{\Pr}_x[\mathcal{B}(x) = b] = \frac{1}{\|\mathcal{B}\|} \pm \epsilon.$$

Proof. We have:

$$
\Pr_x[\mathcal{B}(x) = b] = \mathbf{E}_x\left[\prod_i \frac{1}{p^{k_i+1}} \sum_{\lambda_i=0}^{p^{k_i+1}-1} \mathbf{e}\left(\lambda_i(P_i(x) - b_i)\right)\right]
$$

$$
= \prod_i p^{-(k_i+1)} \cdot \sum_{\substack{(\lambda_1,\ldots,\lambda_C) \\ \in \prod_i[0,p^{k_i+1}-1]}} \mathbf{E}_x\left[\mathbf{e}\left(\sum_i \lambda_i(P_i(x) - b_i)\right)\right]
$$

$$
= \prod_i p^{-(k_i+1)} \cdot \left(1 \pm \epsilon \prod_i p^{k_i+1}\right) = \frac{1}{\|\mathcal{B}\|} \pm \epsilon.
$$

The first equality uses the fact that $P_i(x) - b_i$ is in $\mathbb{U}_{k_i+1}$ and that for any nonzero $x \in \mathbb{U}_{k_i+1}$, $\sum_{\lambda=0}^{p^{k+1}-1} \mathbf{e}(\lambda x) = 0$. The third equality uses Corollary 11.1 and the fact that unless every $\lambda_i = 0$, the polynomial $\sum_i \lambda_i(P_i(x) - b_i)$ has rank at least $r_{11.4}(d, \epsilon)$. $\qquad\square$

When $\mathcal{B}$ consists of dependent linear forms, we cannot hope for a statement as strong as Lemma 11.8. Take for example the system of affine forms in Example 11.5. If a polynomial P in the factor $\mathcal{B}$ is of degree ≤ 1, then for any choice of $x_1, x_2, x_3 \in \mathbb{F}^n$, $P(x_1) - P(x_1+x_2) - P(x_1+x_3) + P(x_1+x_2+x_3) = 0$. This clearly implies that $\mathcal{B}(L_1(x_1, x, x_3))$, $\mathcal{B}(L_2(x_1, x, x_3))$, $\mathcal{B}(L_3(x_1, x, x_3))$, and $\mathcal{B}(L_4(x_1, x, x_3))$ are not distributed independently.

The good news though is that this is the only obstruction to equidistribution that can be present. The definition below captures the type of dependencies that arise just because of degree and depth bounds:

Definition 11.17. Given an affine constraint A with affine forms $L_1, \ldots, L_m \in \mathbb{F}^\ell$ and integers $d, k > 0$ such that $d > k(p-1)$, the (d, k)-*dependency set of A* is the set of tuples $(\lambda_1, \ldots, \lambda_m) \in [0, p^{k+1} - 1]$ such that $\sum_{i=1}^m \lambda_i \cdot (P \circ L_i) \equiv 0$ for all $n > 0$ and all polynomials $P: \mathbb{F}^n \to \mathbb{T}$ of degree d and depth k.

dependency set

Elements $b_1, \ldots, b_m \in \mathbb{T}$ are said to be (d, k)-*consistent with A* if for every $(\lambda_1, \ldots, \lambda_m)$ in the (d, k)-dependency set of A, $\sum_{i=1}^m \lambda_i b_i = 0$.

consistency

Exercise 11.13. Show that if $(\lambda_1, \ldots, \lambda_m)$ are in the (d, k)-dependency set of an affine constraint A, then it is also in A's $(d-1, k)$-dependency set and $(d, k-1)$-dependency set. (Assume $d > k(p-1) + 1$ so that the parameters are feasible.)

Theorem 11.6 (Counting — Structured Case). *Let $\epsilon > 0$, $\mathcal{B} = (P_1, \ldots, P_C)$ be a polynomial factor of degree $d > 0$ and rank $> r_{11.4}(d, \epsilon)$, $A = (L_1, \ldots, L_m)$ be a system of affine forms on ℓ variables, and Λ be a tuple of integers $(\lambda_{i,j})_{i \in [C], j \in [m]}$. Define:*

$$P_{A, \mathcal{B}, \Lambda}(x_1, \ldots, x_\ell) = \sum_{i \in [C], j \in [m]} \lambda_{i,j} P_i(L_j(x_1, \ldots, x_\ell)).$$

Then, one of the two statements below is true.

- *For every $i \in [C]$, $(\lambda_{i,1}, \ldots, \lambda_{i,m})$ belongs to the (d_i, k_i)-dependency set of A where $d_i = \deg(P_i)$ and $k_i = \mathrm{depth}(P_i)$. (Then, clearly, $P_{A, \mathcal{B}, \Lambda} \equiv 0$.)*
- *$P_{A, \mathcal{B}, \Lambda}$ has small bias:*

$$\left| \mathop{\mathbf{E}}_{x_1, \ldots, x_\ell} \left[\mathbf{e}\left(P_{A, \mathcal{B}, \Lambda}(x_1, \ldots, x_\ell) \right) \right] \right| < \epsilon.$$

The corollary below immediately follows using the same Fourier analysis as used in the proof of Lemma 11.8.

Corollary 11.2. *Given $\epsilon > 0$, suppose $\mathcal{B} = (P_1, \ldots, P_C)$ is a polynomial factor of degree $d > 0$ and rank $> r_{11.4}(d, \epsilon)$, $A = (L_1, \ldots, L_m)$ is a system of affine forms on ℓ variables. Let d_i and k_i be the degree and depth, respectively, of P_i.*

For each $j \in [m]$, suppose we have $b_j = (b_{i,j} : i \in [C]) \in \mathbb{T}^C$. They satisfy the following hypothesis: for every $i \in [C]$, $b_{i,1}, \ldots, b_{i,m}$ are (d_i, k_i)-consistent with A. Then:

$$\mathop{\mathrm{Pr}}_{x_1, \ldots, x_k} \left[\mathcal{B}(L_i(x_1, \ldots, x_k)) = b_i \ \forall i \in [m] \right]$$

$$= \prod_{\substack{i \in [C] \\ \lambda_{i,1}, \ldots, \lambda_{i,m} \\ \in [0, p^{k_i+1}]}} \mathop{\mathrm{Pr}} \left[\sum_{j \in [m]} (\lambda_{i,1}, \ldots, \lambda_{i,m}) \in (d_i, k_i)\text{-dependency set of } A \right]$$

$$\pm \epsilon.$$

Exercise 11.14. Prove Corollary 11.2.

11.3 Locally Characterized Properties

Let $\mathcal{A}$ be a collection of induced affine constraints such that the true complexity (as defined in Section 11.2.5.1) of any affine constraint appearing in $\mathcal{A}$ is bounded by a fixed constant d. In this section, we prove that under this condition, $\mathcal{A}$-freeness is testable. This establishes Theorem 11.1 and a restricted version of Theorem 11.2.

Suppose $f : \mathbb{F}^n \to [R]$ is ϵ-far from $\mathcal{A}$-free. For $i \in [R]$, define $f^{(i)}$: $\mathbb{F}^n \to \{0,1\}$ so that $f^{(i)}(x) = 1$ if $f(x) = i$ and 0 otherwise. We first apply Lemma 11.7 to the functions $f^{(1)}, f^{(2)}, \ldots, f^{(R)}$ simultaneously with the parameters $d, \zeta, \mathcal{E}, \eta, r_{11.4}(d, \alpha)$, and p where $\zeta, \mathcal{E}, \eta$ and α are yet to be specified[3]. This yields polynomial factors $\mathcal{B}$ and $\mathcal{B}'$ of order C and C' respectively such that:

- $\mathcal{B}'$ is a syntactic refinement of $\mathcal{B}$
- $\mathcal{B}$ and $\mathcal{B}'$ are each of degree at most d
- $\mathcal{B}$ and $\mathcal{B}'$ are each $r_{11.4}(d, \alpha)$-regular
- Both C and C' are bounded by $C_{11.7}(d, \zeta, \mathcal{E}, \eta, r_{11.4}(d, \alpha), p)$.

11.3.1 Function Cleansing

We now use the factors $\mathcal{B}$ and $\mathcal{B}'$ to modify the function f in the following order:

(i) For any atom c of $\mathcal{B}$, if there exists $i \in [R]$ such that:

$$\left| \Pr_{x:\mathcal{B}(x)=c}[f(x) = i] - \Pr_{x:\mathcal{B}'(x)=(c,s)}[f(x) = i] \right| > \zeta,$$

change f on the atom c to the most popular value of f on (c, s), that is:

$$f(x) \leftarrow \arg\max_{j \in [R]} \Pr_{y:\mathcal{B}'(y)=(c,s)}[f(x) = j] \quad \text{for all } x \in \mathcal{B}^{-1}(c)$$

(ii) For any atom c of $\mathcal{B}$, for any $i \in [R]$ such that:

$$\Pr_{x:\mathcal{B}'(x)=(c,s)}[f(x) = i] < \zeta$$

change f on $f^{-1}(i) \cap c$ to the most popular value of f on (c, s), that is:

$$f(x) \leftarrow \arg\max_{j \in [R]} \Pr_{y:\mathcal{B}'(y)=(c,s)}[f(y) = j] \quad \text{for all } \{x : \mathcal{B}(x) = c, f(x) = i\}$$

Call the modified function f_{mod}.

Claim 11.1. *f_{mod} is $3\zeta R$-far from f, assuming $\alpha(C) < p^{-dC}$.*

Proof. By Lemma 11.7, step (i) applies to only ζ fraction of the atoms of $\mathcal{B}$. The size of each atom of $\mathcal{B}$ is at most $1/\|\mathcal{B}\| + \alpha(|\mathcal{B}|)$ fraction of the entire

---

[3] Recall p is $|\mathbb{F}|$ and prime.

domain. So, the fraction of points whose values changed in the first step is at most $\zeta \left(1/\|\mathcal{B}\| + \alpha(|\mathcal{B}|)\right) < \zeta$ as long as $\alpha(C) < 1/p^{dC}$.

If step (ii) is applied to atom c, then step (i) has not been applied, and hence, $\Pr_{x:\mathcal{B}(x)=c}[f(x) = i] < 2\zeta$. Hence, in total, at most $2\zeta R$ fraction of the domain can be modified in step (ii).   □

Therefore, if we choose $\zeta < \frac{\epsilon}{3R}$, then f_{mod} is not $\mathcal{A}$-free.

11.3.2 The Size of a Witness

The goal of this section is to show that, with the right choice of parameters, not only is f_{mod} not $\mathcal{A}$-free but that f_{mod} induces an element of $\mathcal{A}$ whose size is bounded by a function of ϵ.

We first define a collection of functions that conceptually serves as a "net" for all functions that induce an element of $\mathcal{A}$.

Definition 11.18 (The family $\mathcal{G}_{C,R,\mathbf{d},\mathbf{k},\mathcal{A}}$). Suppose we are given positive integers C and R, tuples of non-negative integers $\mathbf{d} = (d_1, \ldots, d_C)$ and $\mathbf{k} = (k_1, \ldots, k_C)$, and a collection of affine constraints $\mathcal{A}$. Then, $\mathcal{G}_{C,R,\mathbf{d},\mathbf{k},\mathcal{A}}$ is the set of functions $g : \prod_{i=1}^{C} \mathbb{U}_{k_i+1} \to 2^{[R]}$ for which there exists an affine constraint $(A, \sigma) \in \mathcal{A}$ of size m on ℓ variables and elements $b_1, \ldots, b_m \in \prod_{i=1}^{C} \mathbb{U}_{k_i+1}$ such that:

1. For each $j \in [m]$, $\sigma_j \in g(b_j)$.
2. There exist $n \geq 1$, non-classical polynomials $P_1, \ldots, P_C : \mathbb{F}^n \to \mathbb{T}$, where each P_i is of degree d_i and depth k_i, and elements $x_1, \ldots, x_\ell \in \mathbb{F}^n$, such that for each $i \in [C]$ and $j \in [m]$:

$$P_i(L_j(x_1, \ldots, x_\ell)) = b_{j,i}$$

partial induction   In this case, we say that g *partially induces* (A, σ).

Think of $\prod_{i=1}^{C} \mathbb{U}_{k_i+1}$ as the indices for the atoms of a polynomial factor $\mathcal{B}$ given by C polynomials of degree d_i and depth k_i respectively. Then, any $g \in \mathcal{G}_{C,R,\mathbf{d},\mathbf{k},\mathcal{A}}$ associates a subset of $[R]$ to each atom of $\mathcal{B}$. Moreover, g "partially induces" a constraint in $\mathcal{A}$, in the sense that for some constraint $(A, \sigma) \in \mathcal{A}$ involving m affine forms, there are m atoms which each contains the corresponding component of σ and, moreover, the indices of these m atoms are consistent with them being the evaluations of C polynomials of degrees d_i and depths k_i respectively at the affine forms of A.

Now, we can are ready to define the function $\Psi_{\mathcal{A}}$.

Definition 11.19 (The function $\Psi_{\mathcal{A}}$). Let $\mathcal{A}$ be a collection of affine constraints. Given positive integers C and R and non-negative integers d and k, let:

$$\Psi_{\mathcal{A}}(C, R, d, k) = \max_{\mathbf{d} \in [d]^C, \mathbf{k} \in [k]^C} \; \max_{g \in \mathcal{G}_{C,R,\mathbf{d},\mathbf{k},\mathcal{A}}} \; \min_{\substack{(A,\sigma) \text{ partially} \\ \text{induced by } g}} \text{size}(A)$$

Note that if C, R, d, k are bounded, then $\Psi_{\mathcal{A}}$ is defined as an optimization problem over a finite domain, so that the optimum exists and is achieved. Also, $\Psi_{\mathcal{A}}$ can be taken to be non-decreasing in each of its parameters.

The main point of these definitions is the following observation.

Lemma 11.9. *The function f_{mod} induces a constraint in $\mathcal{A}$ of size at most $\Psi_{\mathcal{A}}(C, R, d, \frac{d}{p-1})$*

Exercise 11.15. Prove Lemma 11.9. (**Hint**: This should be nearly obvious: f_{mod} naturally gives a function in $\mathcal{G}_{C,R,\mathbf{d},\mathbf{k},\mathcal{A}}$.)

Going forwards, we fix (A, σ) to be the constraint in $\mathcal{A}$ induced by f_{mod} according to Lemma 11.9.

11.3.3 The Number of Copies of (A, σ) Induced by f

Let A consist of the affine forms $L_1, \ldots, L_m$ on ℓ variables each, where m is upper-bounded by Lemma 11.9. We will give a lower bound for:

$$\Pr_{x_1, \ldots, x_\ell \in \mathbb{F}^n} [f(L_1(x_1, \ldots, x_\ell)) = \sigma_1 \wedge \cdots f(L_m(x_1, \ldots, x_\ell)) = \sigma_m]. \quad (11.3)$$

Recall that for any $j \in [R]$, we defined $f^{(j)}$ to the Boolean function that is supported on $f^{-1}(j)$. Then, we can rewrite the above as:

$$\mathbb{E}_{x_1, \ldots, x_\ell \in \mathbb{F}^n} [f^{(\sigma_1)}(L_1(x_1, \ldots, x_\ell)) \cdots f^{(\sigma_m)}(L_m(x_1, \ldots, x_\ell))]$$

Now, we are in the setting of (11.2), and so we can apply the results from Section 11.2.5.

Recall that at the start of this Section 11.3, we applied Lemma 11.7 to the functions $f^{(1)}, \ldots, f^{(m)}$, which for each $j \in [m]$, yields the functions $f_1^{(j)}, f_2^{(j)}, f_3^{(j)}$ so that $f^{(j)} = f_1^{(j)} + f_2^{(j)} + f_3^{(j)}$. Applying this decomposition, the above expression is equivalent to:

$$\mathbb{E}_{x \in (\mathbb{F}^n)^\ell} \left[\left(f_1^{(\sigma_1)} + f_2^{(\sigma_1)} + f_3^{(\sigma_1)} \right) (L_1(x)) \cdots \left(f_1^{(\sigma_m)} + f_2^{(\sigma_m)} + f_3^{(\sigma_m)} \right) (L_m(x)) \right]$$

We can now expand the expression inside the expectation as a sum of 3^m terms. The expectation of any term which is a multiple of $f_2^{(\sigma_j)}$ for any $j \in [m]$ is at most $\|f_2^{(\sigma_j)}\|_{U^{d+1}} \leq \eta(|\mathcal{B}'|)$ because of Theorem 11.5 and the fact that complexity of A is bounded by d. Hence, we can lower bound the above expectation as at least:

$$\mathop{\mathbf{E}}_{x \in (\mathbb{F}^n)^\ell} [(f_1^{(\sigma_1)} + f_3^{(\sigma_1)})(L_1(x)) \cdots (f_1^{(\sigma_m)} + f_3^{(\sigma_m)})(L_m(x))] - 3^m \cdot \eta(|\mathcal{B}'|).$$

Now, we will leverage the results of Section 11.2.5.2 to lower bound the expectation in the above. We will only focus on the contribution coming from tuples in the sub-atoms corresponding to the atoms where A is induced by f_{mod}.

More precisely, let $b_1, \ldots, b_m \in \mathbb{T}^{|\mathcal{B}|}$ be the atoms of $\mathcal{B}$ where (A, σ) is induced by f_{mod}, that is, there exist $x_1^*, \ldots, x_\ell^*$ such that:

$$f_{\mathrm{mod}}(L_j(x_1^*, \ldots, x_\ell^*)) = \sigma_j$$

and:

$$\mathcal{B}(L_j(x_1^*, \ldots, x_\ell^*)) = b_j$$

for every $j \in [m]$. Also, let $b_1', \ldots, b_m' \in \mathbb{T}^{|\mathcal{B}'|}$ be the corresponding sub-atoms of $\mathcal{B}'$, that is, $b_j' = (b_j, s)$ for every $j \in [m]$ (where $s \in \mathbb{T}^{|\mathcal{B}'|-|\mathcal{B}|}$ is as in Lemma 11.7). For $x_1, \ldots, x_\ell \in \mathbb{F}^n$, let $\mathcal{I}(x_1, \ldots, x_\ell)$ be 1 if $\mathcal{B}'(L_j(x_1, \ldots, x_\ell)) = b_j'$ for every $j \in [m]$, and 0 otherwise.

We now analyze:

$$\mathop{\mathbf{E}}_{x \in (\mathbb{F}^n)^\ell} [(f_1^{(\sigma_1)} + f_3^{(\sigma_1)})(L_1(x)) \cdots (f_1^{(\sigma_m)} + f_3^{(\sigma_m)})(L_m(x)) \cdot \mathcal{I}(x)] \qquad (11.4)$$

Note that because $f_1^{(\sigma)} + f_3^{(\sigma)}$ is non-negative for any σ (see Remark 11.2), the above is a lower bound for:

$$\mathop{\mathbf{E}}_{x \in (\mathbb{F}^n)^\ell} [(f_1^{(\sigma_1)} + f_3^{(\sigma_1)})(L_1(x)) \cdots (f_1^{(\sigma_m)} + f_3^{(\sigma_m)})(L_m(x))].$$

and hence can be used to lower bound (11.3).

Expanding out the product inside the expectation in (11.4), we obtain 2^m terms. We argue next that the term consisting of a product of $f_1^{(\sigma_j)}$'s dominates all others. Before we prove this in the two lemmas below, let us define:

$$\beta = \prod_{i \in [C']} \mathop{\mathrm{Pr}}_{\substack{\lambda_{i,1}, \ldots, \lambda_{i,m} \\ \in [0, p^{k_i+1})}} [(\lambda_{i,1}, \ldots, \lambda_{i,m}) \in (d_i, k_i)\text{-dependency set of } A]$$

where d_i and k_i are the degree and depth respectively of the i'th polynomial in the sequence defining $\mathcal{B}'$.

Lemma 11.10.

$$\underset{x \in (\mathbb{F}^n)^\ell}{\mathbf{E}} \left[f_1^{(\sigma_1)}(L_1(x)) \cdots f_1^{(\sigma_m)}(L_m(x)) \cdot \mathcal{I}(x) \right] \geq (\beta - \alpha) \cdot \zeta^m.$$

Proof. Because of the second step in the cleansing procedure in Section 11.3.1, if f_{mod} induces (A, σ) at atoms $b_1, \ldots, b_m$, then for each $j \in [m]$, we have $\Pr_{x : \mathcal{B}'(x) = b'_j}[f(x) = i] > \min(\zeta, 1/R) = \zeta$ (as we have chosen $\zeta < \frac{\epsilon}{3R}$ in Section 11.3.1). So, each $f_1^{(\sigma_j)}$ is constant and at least ζ on the atom b'_j. Then:

$$\underset{x \in (\mathbb{F}^n)^\ell}{\mathbf{E}} \left[f_1^{(\sigma_1)}(L_1(x)) \cdots f_1^{(\sigma_m)}(L_m(x)) \cdot \mathcal{I}(x) \right]$$

$$\geq \Pr_x[\mathcal{B}'(L_1(x)) = b'_1, \ldots, \mathcal{B}'(L_m(x)) = b'_m] \cdot \zeta^m.$$

Now, applying Corollary 11.2 finishes the proof, provided the following holds.

> **Exercise 11.16.** Show that $b'_1, \ldots, b'_m$ satisfy the hypothesis in Corollary 11.2 applied to the factor $\mathcal{B}'$. (**Hint:** First argue that $b_1, \ldots, b_m$ satisfy the hypothesis applied to $\mathcal{B}$. Use Exercise 11.13 to argue for the rest of the coordinates.)

$\square$

It remains to show that any term in (11.4) that contains $f_3^{(\cdot)}$ is small.

> **Lemma 11.11.** *Suppose g is a function satisfying $\|g\|_\infty \leq 1$. Then, in the above notation:*
>
> $$\underset{x \in (\mathbb{F}^n)^\ell}{\mathbf{E}} [f_3^{(\sigma_1)}(L_1(x)) \cdot g(x) \cdot \mathcal{I}(x)] \leq \mathcal{E}(C) \cdot \sqrt{\frac{1}{\|\mathcal{B}'\|} + \alpha} \cdot \sqrt{\beta^2 \cdot \|\mathcal{B}'\| + \alpha}$$

Proof. The most direct way to proceed is to use Cauchy-Schwarz, so that the expectation is at most $\|f_3^{(\sigma_1)}\|_2 \leq \mathcal{E}(C)$. This however is not good enough because the lower bound from Lemma 11.10 is in terms of β which depends on C', not C.[4]

For ease of notation, assume without loss of generality that $L_1(x_1, \ldots, x_\ell) = x_1$. Then, Cauchy-Schwarz yields:

---

[4] One might be tempted to make $\mathcal{E}$ small in terms of the upper bound on C' provided in Lemma 11.7; however that bound itself depends on $\mathcal{E}$, leading to a circularity.

$$\mathop{\mathbf{E}}_{x\in(\mathbb{F}^n)^\ell}[f_3^{(\sigma_1)}(x_1)\cdot g(x)\cdot\mathcal{I}(x)]$$

$$\leq \mathop{\mathbf{E}}_{x\in(\mathbb{F}^n)^\ell}[|f_3^{(\sigma_1)}(x_1)\cdot\mathbf{1}[\mathcal{B}'(L_1(x))=b_1']|\cdot\mathcal{I}(x)]$$

$$\leq \mathcal{E}(C)\cdot\sqrt{\mathop{\mathrm{Pr}}_{x_1}[\mathcal{B}'(x_1)=b_1']}\cdot\sqrt{\mathop{\mathbf{E}}_{x_1\in\mathbb{F}^n}\left[\left(\mathop{\mathbf{E}}_{x_2,\ldots,x_\ell\in\mathbb{F}^n}[\mathcal{I}(x_1,\ldots,x_\ell)]\right)^2\right]}$$

$$\leq \mathcal{E}(C)\cdot\sqrt{\frac{1}{\|\mathcal{B}'\|}+\alpha}\cdot\sqrt{\mathop{\mathbf{E}}_{x_1\in\mathbb{F}^n}\left[\left(\mathop{\mathbf{E}}_{x_2,\ldots,x_\ell\in\mathbb{F}^n}[\mathcal{I}(x_1,\ldots,x_\ell)]\right)^2\right]} \qquad (11.5)$$

where the last inequality is using Lemma 11.8.

We next analyze the expectation inside the square root:

$$\mathop{\mathbf{E}}_{x_1\in\mathbb{F}^n}\left[\left(\mathop{\mathbf{E}}_{x_2,\ldots,x_\ell\in\mathbb{F}^n}[\mathcal{I}(x_1,\ldots,x_\ell)]\right)^2\right]$$

$$=\frac{1}{\|\mathcal{B}'\|^{2m}}\mathop{\mathbf{E}}_{x_1}\left(\sum_{\substack{\lambda_{i,j}\in[0,p^{k_i+1}):\\ i\in[C'],j\in[m]}}\mathop{\mathbf{E}}_{x_2,\ldots,x_\ell}\mathbf{e}\left(\sum_{\substack{i\in[C'],\\ j\in[m]}}\lambda_{i,j}(P_i(L_j(x_1,\ldots,x_\ell))-b_{i,j}')\right)\right)^2$$

$$\leq\frac{1}{\|\mathcal{B}'\|^{2m}}\cdot$$

$$\sum_{\substack{\lambda_{i,j}\in[0,p^{k_i+1}):\\ i\in[C'],j\in[2m]}}\left|\mathop{\mathbf{E}}_{\substack{x_1,\\ x_2,\ldots,x_m,\\ y_2,\ldots,y_m}}\left[\mathbf{e}\left(\sum_{\substack{i\in[C'],\\ j\in[2m]}}\lambda_{i,j}P_i(L_j'(x_1,x_2,\ldots,x_\ell,y_2,\ldots,y_\ell))\right)\right]\right|$$

$$\qquad\qquad\qquad\qquad\qquad\qquad\qquad\qquad\qquad (11.6)$$

where $L_j'=L_j(x_1,x_2,\ldots,x_\ell)$ for $j\in[m]\}$ and $L_j'=L_{j-m}(x_1,y_2,\ldots,y_\ell)$ for $j\in[m+1,2m]$. Let A' be the affine constraint given by the affine forms $(L_1',\ldots,L_{2m}')$.

Let:

$$\beta'=\prod_{i\in[C']}\mathop{\mathrm{Pr}}_{\substack{\lambda_{i,1},\ldots,\lambda_{i,2m}\\ \in[0,p^{k_i+1})}}[(\lambda_{i,1},\ldots,\lambda_{i,2m})\in(d_i,k_i)\text{-dependency set of }A'].$$

Applying Theorem 11.6 to (11.6), we get:

$$\mathop{\mathbf{E}}_{x_1\in\mathbb{F}^n}\left[\left(\mathop{\mathbf{E}}_{x_2,\ldots,x_\ell\in\mathbb{F}^n}[\mathcal{I}(x_1,\ldots,x_\ell)]\right)^2\right]\leq\beta'+\alpha \qquad (11.7)$$

Claim 11.2.

$$\beta' = \beta^2 \cdot \|\mathcal{B}'\|.$$

Proof. Recall that we have assumed $L_1(x_1, \ldots, x_\ell) = x_1$. Thus, $L_1' = L_{m+1}' = x_1$. So, if $(\lambda_{i,j})_{j \in [m]}$ and $(\tau_{i,j})_{j \in [m]}$ belong to the (d_i, k_i)-dependency set of A, then for any $c \in \mathbb{Z}/(p^{k_i+1}\mathbb{Z})$, $(\lambda_{i,1} + c, \lambda_{i,2}, \ldots, \lambda_{i,m}, \tau_{i,1} - c, \tau_{i,2}, \ldots, \tau_{i,m})$ belongs to the (d_i, k_i)-dependency set of A'. Hence, $\beta' \geq \beta^2 \prod_{i=1}^{C'} p^{k_i+1}$.

In the other direction, suppose $(\lambda_{i,1}, \ldots, \lambda_{i,m}, \tau_{i,1}, \ldots, \tau_{i,m})$ is in the (d_i, k_i)-dependency set of A'. Then for *any* polynomial Q of degree d_i and depth k_i:

$$\sum_{j=2}^{m} \lambda_{i,j} Q(L_j(x_1, x_2, \ldots, x_\ell)) = F_{i,Q}(x_1)$$

and:

$$\sum_{j=2}^{m} \tau_{i,j} Q(L_j(x_1, y_2, \ldots, y_\ell)) = G_{i,Q}(x_1)$$

for some functions $F_{i,Q}$ and $G_{i,Q}$, because if either of the two sums depended on a variable other than x_1, then that dependence cannot be canceled out by the other. In fact:

Exercise 11.17. Argue that each $F_{i,Q} = \alpha_i \cdot Q, G_{i,Q} = \beta_i \cdot Q$ for constants $\alpha_i, \beta_i \in \mathbb{U}_{k_i+1}$. (**Hint:** First, argue that for $Q(z) = z_1 \cdot z_2 \cdots z_{d_i}/p^{k_i+1}$, if $\sum_{j=2}^{m} \lambda_{i,j} Q(L_j(x_1, x_2, \ldots, x_\ell))$ needs to be independent of $x_2, \ldots, x_\ell$, $F_{i,Q}$ must be proportional to Q. Then, show that the same constant of proportionality holds for any other monomial Q of degree d_i and depth k_i.)

So, in the notation of the above exercise, $\lambda_{i,1} + \alpha_i + \tau_{i,1} + \beta_i = 0$.

Now, consider the map:

$$(\lambda_{i,1}, \ldots, \lambda_{i,m}, \tau_{i,1}, \ldots, \tau_{i,m}) \mapsto ((-\alpha_i, \lambda_{i,2}, \ldots, \lambda_{i,m}), (-\beta_i, \tau_{i,2}, \ldots, \tau_{i,m})).$$

This map takes an element in the (d_i, k_i)-dependency set of A' to a pair of elements in the (d_i, k_i)-dependency set of A. Moreover, it is p^{k_i+1}-to-1, because $\lambda_{i,1} + \tau_{i,1} = -\alpha_i - \beta_i$ is a constraint. The bound on β' follows. ∎

Plugging this into (11.7) and then into (11.5):

$$\mathop{\mathbf{E}}_{x_1 \in \mathbb{F}^n}\left[\left(\mathop{\mathbf{E}}_{x_2, \ldots, x_\ell \in \mathbb{F}^n}[\mathcal{I}(x_1, \ldots, x_\ell)]\right)^2\right] \leq \mathcal{E}(C) \cdot \sqrt{\frac{1}{\|\mathcal{B}'\|} + \alpha} \cdot \sqrt{\beta^2 \cdot \|\mathcal{B}'\| + \alpha}$$

∎

We now go back to our original problem of lower bounding (11.3):

$$\Pr_{x_1,\ldots,x_\ell\in\mathbb{F}^n}[f(L_1(x_1,\ldots,x_\ell))=\sigma_1\wedge\cdots f(L_m(x_1,\ldots,x_\ell))=\sigma_m]$$

$$=\mathop{\mathbf{E}}_{x\in(\mathbb{F}^n)^\ell}\left[\left(f_1^{(\sigma_1)}+f_2^{(\sigma_1)}+f_3^{(\sigma_1)}\right)(L_1(x))\cdots\left(f_1^{(\sigma_m)}+f_2^{(\sigma_m)}+f_3^{(\sigma_m)}\right)(L_m(x))\right]$$

$$\geq\mathop{\mathbf{E}}_{x\in(\mathbb{F}^n)^\ell}[(f_1^{(\sigma_1)}+f_3^{(\sigma_1)})(L_1(x))\cdots(f_1^{(\sigma_m)}+f_3^{(\sigma_m)})(L_m(x))\cdot\mathcal{I}(x)]-3^m\cdot\eta(C')$$

$$\geq(\beta(C')-\alpha(C'))\cdot\zeta^m-\mathcal{E}(C)\cdot\sqrt{\frac{1}{\|\mathcal{B}'\|}+\alpha(C')}\cdot\sqrt{\beta(C')^2\cdot\|\mathcal{B}'\|+\alpha(C')}$$

$$-3^m\cdot\eta(C')\quad(11.8)$$

where we used Lemmas 11.10 and 11.11 and put in all the dependencies on C and C'.

Set $\zeta=\epsilon/4R$. Recall that m is upper-bounded by $\Psi_\mathcal{A}(C,R,d,d/(p-1))$ from Lemma 11.9. Since $\beta\geq 1/\|\mathcal{B}'\|^m$, we can set:

- $$\alpha(C')=\frac{1}{2p^{\Psi_\mathcal{A}(C',R,d,d/(p-1))dC'}}<\beta/2.$$

- $$\mathcal{E}(C)=\frac{1}{10}\zeta^{\Psi_\mathcal{A}(C,R,d,d/(p-1))}<\zeta^m/10.$$

- $$\eta(C')=(\zeta/6p)^{\Psi_\mathcal{A}(C',R,d,d/(p-1))dC'}<\frac{\beta\cdot\zeta^m}{100}.$$

With these settings, (11.8) is at least $\rho=\Omega(\beta\zeta^m)\geq\Omega\left((\zeta/\|\mathcal{B}'\|)^m\right)$ which is a (tiny) positive constant independent of n, as $|\mathcal{B}'|$ and m are bounded by functions of C' and C, and $C\leq C'\leq C_{11.7}(d,\zeta,\mathcal{E},\eta,r_{11.4}(d,\alpha),p)$.

At this point, we have proved that if f is ϵ-far from being $\mathcal{A}$-free, and $x_1,\ldots,x_\ell$ are chosen uniformly at random from $\mathbb{F}_2^n$, where[5]:

$$\ell=\Psi_\mathcal{A}(C_{11.7}(d,\zeta,\mathcal{E},\eta,r_{11.4}(d,\alpha),p),R,d,d/(p-1)),$$

then the probability that f induces an affine constraint in $\mathcal{A}$ at $x_1,\ldots,x_\ell$ is at least ρ.

11.4 Fox-Lovász Analysis for Triangle-Freeness

So far, we have discussed how to use higher-order Fourier analysis to analyze testers for various affine-invariant properties. Although the results of higher-order Fourier analysis are very powerful and general, they yield extremely

---

[5] This was a bound on m, the number of forms in the constraint, which also bounds the number of variables without loss of generality (otherwise, we can do a basis change).

large bounds for the query complexity of testing simple properties. We are led to a natural question: what is the optimal number of queries for testing $\mathcal{A}$-freeness for a family $\mathcal{A}$ of linear/affine constraints?

Although this problem remains open (at the time of writing) for general $\mathcal{A}$, there has been dramatic progress recently in reducing the query complexity for the class[6] of *(arithmetic) cycle-freeness* properties. A function $f\colon \mathbb{F}^n \to \{0,1\}$ is said to be *k-cycle-free* (for some positive integer k) if there are no $x_1,\ldots,x_k \in \mathbb{F}^n$ such that $f(x_1) = \cdots = f(x_k) = 1$ and $x_1 + x_2 + \cdots + x_k = 0$. In this section, we examine the simplest of these properties: *triangle-freeness* or 3-cycle-freeness.

cycle-freeness

triangle-freeness

We can apply a stripped down version of the same machinery[7] as in Section 11.3 to analyze the tester which repeatedly samples random $(x,y) \in (\mathbb{F}^n)^2$ and rejects if and only if $f(x) = f(y) = f(-x-y) = 1$ for any of the samples (x,y). Redoing the proof while using the best known bounds for the decomposition theorems in Section 11.2.4 for the Gowers norm of order two, we see that if the tester has to reject functions ϵ-far from triangle-free with probability $2/3$, then the number of queries is a tower of twos of height polynomial in ϵ^{-1}! In contrast, here we show that the correct complexity is only polynomial in ϵ^{-1}.

Theorem 11.7. *Suppose $f\colon \mathbb{F}^n \to \{0,1\}$ is ϵ-far from triangle-freeness. Then, we have:*

$$\Pr_{x,y\in\mathbb{F}^n}[f(x) = f(y) = f(-x-y) = 1] \geq \left(\frac{\epsilon}{3}\right)^{C_p},$$

where C_p is a constant dependent on $p = |\mathbb{F}|$. For example, $C_2 \approx 13.239$ and $C_3 \approx 13.901$.

Consequently, the query complexity of testing triangle-freeness is $O(\epsilon^{-C_p})$. This bound is actually known to be tight up to constant factors (though we do not cover this here).

In the following, let's fix $\mathbb{F} = \mathbb{F}_2$; the proof for general p goes along the same lines. The main driver for the proof of Theorem 11.7 is a recent result on the extremal combinatorics of finite field vector spaces. A set of triples $\{(x_i, y_i, z_i) \in (\mathbb{F}_2^n)^3 : i \in [m]\}$ is said to be 3-*sum-free* if $x_i + y_j + z_k = 0$ holds exactly when $i = j = k$. We denote $X = \{x_i\}$, $Y = \{y_i\}$ and $Z = \{z_i\}$.

3-sum-freeness

Theorem 11.8. *The number of triples m in a 3-sum-free set of triples satisfies: $m \leq 2^{(1-c_2)n}$, where $c_2 = 5/3 - \log 3 \approx 0.0817$.*

Assuming Theorem 11.8, let us give some intuition for the proof of Theorem 11.7. Let A be the set $f^{-1}(1)$, and call a triple $(x, y, x+y) \in A^3$ a

---

[6] "Arithmetic" is used to distinguish from the more usual cycle-freeness in graphs, but because there's no chance of confusion in this chapter, we will omit it.

[7] See Problems 11.6 and 11.7 for details.

triangle in A. If f is ϵ-far from being triangle-free, then A must clearly have at least $\epsilon/3 \cdot 2^n$ many disjoint triangles.

Suppose that the *only* triangles were these $m \geq \epsilon/3 \cdot 2^n$ disjoint triangles, and let $m = \delta 2^{2n}$. We want to lower-bound δ to prove Theorem 11.7. Observe that the set of triangles forms a 3-sum-free collection (where $X = Y = Z = A$), and so, $m \leq 2^{(1-c_2)n}$ by Theorem 11.8. Hence:

$$m^{\frac{1}{c_2}} \leq 2^{\left(\frac{1}{c_2}-1\right)n} \implies m^{1+\frac{1}{c_2}} \leq m \cdot 2^{n\left(\frac{1}{c_2}-1\right)}$$

$$\implies \left(\frac{m}{2^n}\right)^{1+\frac{1}{c_2}} \leq \frac{m}{2^{2n}}$$

$$\implies \delta \geq (\epsilon/3)^{1+\frac{1}{c_2}} \geq \Omega(\epsilon^{13.239}).$$

For the full proof, we try to reduce to the case when the triangles form a large 3-sum-free collection. Suppose $f : \mathbb{F}_2^n \to \{0,1\}$ is ϵ-far from triangle-free and has $\delta 2^n$ many triangles. Let $A_1 = \{x \circ 01 : f(x) = 1\}$, $A_2 = \{x \circ 10 : f(x) = 1\}$, $A_3 = \{x \circ 11 : f(x) = 1\}$. Note that A_1, A_2, A_3 are disjoint. A *triangle in* (A_1, A_2, A_3) is a triple $(x, y, x+y) \in A_1 \times A_2 \times A_3$. Let $N = 2^{n+2}$. There are $\delta N^2/16$ triangles in total and at least $\epsilon N/12$ disjoint triangles in (A_1, A_2, A_3).

We first prove a lower bound on δ, assuming that each element of $A_1 \cup A_2 \cup A_3$ is contained in roughly the same number of triangles.

Lemma 11.12. *Suppose each element in $A_1 \cup A_2 \cup A_3$ is contained in at most $\epsilon^{-1} t \delta N$ triangles for some integer t. Then, $\delta = \Omega\left((\epsilon/t)^{1+1/c_2}\right)$.*

Proof. The proof idea is to choose a random subspace U in $\mathbb{F}_2^{n+2}$ of dimension $d = \log(\epsilon/20 t \delta)$ and to claim that there are many triangles in (A_1', A_2', A_3') where $A_1' = A_1 \cap U, A_2' = A_2 \cap U, A_3' = A_3 \cap U$ that together yield a 3-sum-free collection.

Claim 11.3. *A triangle (x, y, z) in (A_1, A_2, A_3) is also a triangle in (A_1', A_2', A_3') with probability $\Omega(2^{2d}/N^2)$.*

Proof. The probability that the 2-dimensional subspace spanned by x and y falls inside the random d-dimensional subspace U is exactly $\frac{(2^d-1)(2^{d-1}-1)}{(2^{n+2}-1)(2^{n+1}-1)} = \Omega(2^{2d}/N^2)$. $\qquad\square$

Claim 11.4. *Conditioned on (x, y, z) being a triangle in $A_1' \times A_2' \times A_3'$, the probability that (x, y, z) does not intersect any other triangle in $A_1' \times A_2' \times A_3'$ is at least $1/2$.*

Proof. Consider another triangle (x, y', z') in (A_1', A_2', A_3') intersecting (x, y, z) at x. The probability that y' belongs to U, conditioned on the subspace spanned by x and y is already in U, is exactly $\frac{2^{d-2}-1}{2^n-1} \le 5 \cdot 2^d/N$. Now, using the assumed bound on the number of triangles containing x, the probability that there exists some triangle in (A'_1, A'_2, A'_3) intersecting with (x, y, z) at either x or y or z is, by the union bound, at most:

$$3\frac{t\delta N}{\epsilon} \cdot \frac{5 \cdot 2^d}{N} \le \frac{1}{2}.$$

Combining the two lemmas, we get that in expectation, there are at least $\frac{\delta N^2}{16} \cdot \Omega(\frac{2^{2d}}{N^2}) \cdot \frac{1}{2} = \Omega(\delta \cdot 2^{2d}) = \Omega(\frac{\epsilon^2}{t^2\delta})$ disjoint triangles in (A'_1, A'_2, A'_3) with no other triangle in (A'_1, A'_2, A'_3) intersecting with them. These form a 3-sum-free collection of triples. Applying Theorem 11.8:

$$\frac{\epsilon^2}{t^2\delta} = O\left(2^{d(1-c_2)}\right) = O\left(\left(\frac{\epsilon}{t\delta}\right)^{1-c_2}\right),$$

which yields $\delta = \Omega\left((\epsilon/t)^{1+1/c_2}\right)$.

Next, we show that A_1, A_2, A_3 contain subsets which satisfy the hypothesis of Lemma 11.12.

Lemma 11.13. *There exist $B_1 \subseteq A_1, B_2 \subseteq A_2, B_3 \subseteq A_3$ such that there are $\epsilon N/24$ disjoint triangles and $\eta N^2/16$ triangles in total in (B_1, B_2, B_3), for some $\eta \le \delta$. Moreover, each element in $B_1 \cup B_2 \cup B_3$ is contained in $O(\log^2 \eta^{-1} \cdot \epsilon^{-1}\eta N)$ triangles in (B_1, B_2, B_3).*

Proof. We prove the lemma iteratively. Starting off, set $\eta = \delta$ and $B_i = A_i$ for $i \in [3]$. If there exists an element $x \in B_i$ that is contained in more than $100 \log^2 \eta^{-1} \cdot \epsilon^{-1}\eta N$ triangles, remove x from B_i and update η. Continue until no such elements remain.

We show that we remove at most $\epsilon N/24$ elements from $B_1 \cup B_2 \cup B_3$ through the course of this process, proving the lemma. When the number of triangles in (B_1, B_2, B_3) is between $2^{-i}N^2$ and $2^{-i+1}N^2$, the total number of elements removed from $B_1 \cup B_2 \cup B_3$ is at most: $2^{-i+1}N^2/(100\epsilon^{-1}i^2 2^{-i}N) = \frac{\epsilon N}{50} \cdot \frac{1}{i^2}$. Summing over all i shows that at most $\epsilon N/24$ elements are removed in total.

Applying Lemma 11.12 to B_1, B_2, B_3, we get that $\delta \ge \eta = \tilde{\Omega}(\epsilon^{1+1/c_2})$ where the $\tilde{\Omega}$ hides a polylog factor in ϵ. The polylog factor can be removed by a simple product trick that we defer to Problem 11.8.

11.5 Bibliographic Notes.

Additive combinatorics is an area of mathematics, which is concerned with linear patterns such as arithmetic progressions in subsets of integers. A seminal result in additive combinatorics is Szemerédi's theorem (do not confuse with Szemerédi's regularity lemma (Lemma 4.6)), which states that, for any positive integer k and $\delta > 0$, there exists a positive integer $N = N(k, \delta)$ such that every subset of the set $\{1, 2, \ldots, N\}$ of size at least δN contains an arithmetic progression of length k. Higher-order Fourier analysis was initiated by the seminal work of Gowers [228] on a new proof of Szemerédi's theorem and has been developed to study problems in additive combinatorics (see [376] and [380] and the references therein). The result mentioned at the end of Section 11.2.2 showing the necessity of non-classical polynomials in the inverse theorem is due to the independent works of Lovett, Meshulam and Samorodnitsky [309] and of Green and Tao [231]. More recently, improved bounds for the inverse theorem have been obtained by independent works of Janzer and Milićević [266, 316]. Besides property testing, higher-order Fourier analysis has been used in various areas in theoretical computer science including PCPs [369], coding theory [82, 250, 385], and computational complexity [83].

The first usage of higher-order Fourier analysis in property testing is due to Bhattacharyya, Grigorescu and Shapira [79] and Bhattacharyya, Fischer, and Lovett [77], who showed that a hereditary property is one-sided error testable if each affine constraint that determines the property has a Cauchy-Schwarz complexity lower than the order of the field p. Here, Cauchy-Schwarz complexity is an upper bound on the true complexity. Later, Bhattacharyya, Fischer, Hatami, Hatami, and Lovett [76] showed that a hereditary property is one-sided error testable if each affine constraint that determines the property has a bounded Cauchy-Schwarz complexity. As it is known that hereditariness is necessary for constant-query testability [79], this almost completes the characterization of properties that are constant-query testable with one-sided error. The argument in Section 11.1 follows [76]. Tidor and Zhao [383] later completed this line of work by removing the restriction of bounded Cauchy-Schwarz inequality, leading to a precise combinatorial characterization of testable affine-invariant properties. In fact, their work extends to the more general class of linear-invariant properties.

As with the dense graph case, it is shown that the constant-query testability of a property implies constant-query estimability of the distance to the property [249]. Building on those results, Yoshida [400] obtained a characterization of properties that are constant-query testable with two-sided error, which is a counterpart of Theorem 9.5 for affine invariant properties.

Section 11.4 describes the work of Fox and Lovász in [191]. Follow-up work by these authors and Sauermann [192] showed a polynomial bound on the query complexity for testing k-cycle-freeness for any constant k.

Problems

11.1. Show that, for any function $f : \mathbb{F}^n \to \mathbb{C}$, the Gowers norm $\|f\|_{U^d}$ is monotonically non-decreasing in d.

11.2. In this problem, we consider the property of a function $F : \mathbb{F}^n \to \mathbb{F}$ being a classical polynomial of degree at most d. Call the class of such functions $\mathsf{RM}_{p,d,n}$. Define:

$$\delta_d(F) = \min_{G \in \mathsf{RM}_{p,d,n}} \Pr_x[F(x) \neq G(x)]$$

(a) Argue that Lemma 11.3 implies:

$$\delta_d(F) \geq \frac{1 - \|\mathbf{e}\,(F)\,\|_{U^{d+1}}}{2}.$$

(b) Let $(d+1)$-span denote the following test for $\mathsf{RM}_{p,d,n}$. Given oracle access to a function $F : \mathbb{F}^n \to \mathbb{F}$, choose $x \in \mathbb{F}^n$ and directions $a_1, \ldots, a_{d+1} \in \mathbb{F}^n$ uniformly and independently, and accept iff $F|_A \in \mathsf{RM}_{p,d,d+1}$ where $A = \{x + \sum_{i=1}^{d+1} c_i a_i : c_1, \ldots, c_{d+1} \in \mathbb{F}\}$. Show that:

$$\|\mathbf{e}\,(F)\,\|_{U^{d+1}}^{2^{d+1}} = (\Pr[(d+1)\text{-span accepts } F] - \Pr[(d+1)\text{-span rejects } F])$$

(c) In Chapter 12, we study the $(d+1)$-flat test, which differs from the above $(d+1)$-span test in that $a_1, \ldots, a_{d+1}$ are chosen uniformly from all subsets of linearly independent $d+1$ vectors. Prove that for any $F : \mathbb{F}^n \to \mathbb{F}$:

$$\Pr[(d+1)\text{-span rejects } F] \geq \frac{1}{4} \cdot \Pr[(d+1)\text{-flat rejects } F].$$

(d) Suppose $\|\mathbf{e}\,(F)\,\|_{U^{d+1}} = 1 - \gamma$ where $\gamma < \alpha 2^{-d}$ for a sufficiently small constant α. Using the result of Theorem 12.4 that

$$\Pr[(d+1)\text{-flat rejects } F] \geq \min\left\{ 2^d \cdot \delta_d(F), \frac{1}{50} \right\}$$

and the above parts, show that:

$$\delta_d(f) = O(\gamma) = O(1 - \|\mathbf{e}\,(F)\,\|_{U^{d+1}}).$$

11.3. Consider a basic version of the polynomial regularity lemma. Suppose $d < p$ so that classical and non-classical polynomials coincide (recall Exercise 11.4, and so we omit their distinction here. If $P : \mathbb{F}^n \to \mathbb{F}$ is a polynomial of degree d, then its *classical d-rank*, $\mathsf{crank}_d(P)$, is defined to be the smallest r such that P is a function of $(d-1)$-degree polynomials $Q_1, \ldots, Q_r : \mathbb{F}^n \to \mathbb{F}$. Call a polynomial factor $\mathcal{B}$ defined by polynomials $P_1, \ldots, P_C : \mathbb{F}^n \to \mathbb{F}$ to have rank r if r is the least integer such that there exist $\lambda_1, \ldots, \lambda_C$ not all zero for which $\sum_i \lambda_i P_i$ has classical d'-rank at most r where $d' = \deg(\sum_i \lambda_i P_i)$.

(a) Let $\mathcal{B}$ be a polynomial factor. Show that for any r, there exists C and a polynomial factor $\mathcal{B}'$ of complexity C such that $\mathcal{B}' \succeq_{\text{sem}} \mathcal{B}$ and has classical rank at least r. (**Hint:** If the rank condition is violated, replace one of the polynomials supported by the violating linear combination by strictly lower degree polynomials.)

(b) Prove the claim in part (a) if $r : \mathbb{Z}_{>0} \to \mathbb{Z}_{>0}$ is a non-decreasing function and we require $\mathcal{B}'$ is r-regular in the sense of Definition 11.14.

11.4. This problem asks you to prove Lemma 11.5.

(a) For a function $f : \mathbb{F}^n \to \mathbb{C}$, suppose $\|f\|_{U^{d+1}} > \delta$. Use Theorem 11.3 to obtain $\epsilon > 0$ and a polynomial P of degree $\leq d$ such that if $f_1 = \mathbf{E}[f \mid P]$ and $f_2 = f - f_1$, then $\|f_1\|_2 \geq \epsilon$ and $\|f_2\|_2^2 \leq \|f\|_2^2 - \epsilon^2$.

(b) Repeatedly invoke part (a) to complete the proof of Lemma 11.5. Use Lemma 11.4 to ensure that the obtained factor is regular.

11.5. In this problem, you are asked to prove Lemma 11.6.

A mild variant of the argument in the above problem can be used to show that f_1 and f_2 can be taken to be orthogonal in Lemma 11.5. Define a sequence of functions $f_0, f_1, \ldots$ such that $f_0 = f$, and for each $i \geq 1$, $f_{i-1} = f_{i,1} + f_i$ where $f_{i,1} = \mathbf{E}[f_{i-1} \mid \mathcal{B}_i]$ for an r-regular polynomial factor $\mathcal{B}_i$ of degree d, f_i satisfies $\|f_i\|_{U^{d+1}} \leq \eta(|\mathcal{B}_i|)$, and f_i is orthogonal to $f_{i,1}$. Argue that there exists an $i \leq 1/\epsilon^2 + 1$ such that $\|f_{i,1}\|_2 \leq \epsilon$, and hence the lemma is obtained by setting $f_1 = f_{1,1} + \cdots + f_{i-1,1}$, $f_2 = f_i$, and $f_3 = f_{i,1}$.

11.6. Consider the triangle-freeness property, as defined in Section 11.4, for functions over $\mathbb{F}_2^n$.

(a) Show that for functions $f, g, h : \mathbb{F}_2^n \to \{0, 1\}$:

$$\Pr_{x,y}[f(x) = g(y) = h(x+y) = 1] = \sum_\alpha \widehat{f}(\alpha)\widehat{g}(\alpha)\widehat{h}(\alpha)$$

(b) Suppose $f, g, h : \mathbb{F}_2^n \to \{0, 1\}$ satisfy the following two conditions:

   (i) For all nonzero α, $|\widehat{f}(\alpha)|, |\widehat{g}(\alpha)|, |\widehat{h}(\alpha)| \leq \epsilon$.
   (ii) $\widehat{f}(0), \widehat{g}(0), \widehat{h}(0) \geq \eta$. Note that $\widehat{f}(0) = |f^{-1}(1)|$.

   Argue that:
   $$\Pr_{x,y}[f(x) = g(y) = h(x+y) = 1] \geq \eta^3 - \epsilon$$

(c) For a function $f : \mathbb{F}_2^n \to \{0, 1\}$, a subgroup $H \leq \mathbb{F}_2^n$, and a quotient group element $g \in \mathbb{F}_2^n/H$, define $f^{+g} : H \to \{0, 1\}$ as $f^{+g}(x) = f(x + g)$. Say that H is ϵ-regular for f if there are at most $\epsilon 2^n$ choices of $g \in \mathbb{F}_2^n/H$ such that: $\max_{\alpha \neq 0} |\widehat{f^{+g}}(\alpha)| > \epsilon$.

An energy increment argument similar to that for other regularity lemmas yields the following. For any $\epsilon \in (0, 1/2)$ and any $f : \mathbb{F}_2^n \to \{0, 1\}$, there exists a subgroup $H \leq G$ of codimension $C_{\text{Green}}(\epsilon)$ which is ϵ-regular for f. Here, C_{Green} grows as a tower of twos of height polynomial in ϵ^{-1} (and this dependence is known to be tight qualitatively).

Use this regularity lemma and the approach in Section 11.3 to show that there is a one-sided tester for triangle-freeness over $\mathbb{F}_2^n$ with query complexity only a function of ϵ.

11.7. As in the previous problem, consider the property of triangle-freeness for functions over $\mathbb{F}_2^n$. But here, we outline a graph-theoretic approach.

Given a function $f : \mathbb{F}_2^n \to \{0, 1\}$, define a tripartite graph G_f as follows. The vertex set of G_f consists of three parts, A, B and C. There is an edge between $a \in A$ and $b \in B$ iff $f(a + b) = 1$, between $b \in B$ and $c \in C$ iff $f(b + c) = 1$, and between $c \in C$ and $a \in A$ iff $f(c + a) = 1$.

(a) Show that there for every triple $x, y, z \in f^{-1}(1)$ such that $x + y + z = 0$, there are exactly 2^n many disjoint triangles in G_f.

(b) Argue that if f is ϵ-far from being a triangle-free function, then G_f is $\Omega(\epsilon)$-far from being a triangle-free graph.

   (**Hint**: Prove the contrapositive. If a set of edges E can be removed from G_f to make it triangle-free, consider removing from the support of f all elements x such that there are at least $2^n/3$ edges $(u, v) \in E$ satisfying $u + v = x$. Argue that the resulting function is triangle-free.)

(c) Combine with the results of Chapter 9 to show one-sided testability of triangle-freeness over $\mathbb{F}_2^n$.

11.8. Prove Theorem 11.7 by removing the polylog factors obtained in the bound at the end of Section 11.4. Argue this by first considering a function $f : \mathbb{F}_p^n \to \{0, 1\}$ where the theorem is not true, and then studying the function $f^k : \mathbb{F}_p^{nk} \to \{0, 1\}$ where $f^k(x_1, \dots, x_k) = f(x_1) \wedge \cdots \wedge f(x_k)$ where $k \to \infty$.

Chapter 12
Linear Properties of Functions

In the previous chapter, we considered affine-invariant properties of functions $f\colon \mathbb{F}^n \to [R]$, where $\mathbb{F}$ is a finite field of a fixed order, R is a fixed integer, and n is asymptotically growing. The main result there was an upper bound on the query complexity for a large class of such properties that is independent of n but a very rapidly growing function of $1/\epsilon$.

In this chapter, we discuss another natural class of properties of functions and give some very general criteria for testability. We study *linear* properties $\mathcal{P}$ of functions $f\colon D \to \mathbb{F}$ where D is a finite set and $\mathbb{F}$ is a finite field. $\mathcal{P}$ is said to be linear if for any $f, g \in \mathcal{P}$, $\alpha f + \beta g \in \mathcal{P}$ also for every $\alpha, \beta \in \mathbb{F}$. In contrast to the previous chapter, note that the emphasis here is on the algebraic structure of the functions' range, rather than their domain.

$\mathcal{P}$ can also be viewed as a vector space in $\mathbb{F}^D$. Therefore, testing membership of a function in $\mathcal{P}$ is equivalent to testing membership of a vector in a given vector space V. In this guise, we already studied the problem in Section 7.3 of Chapter 7. In particular, Lemma 7.6 shows that a tester for membership in a subspace can be assumed, without loss of generality, to be *non-adaptive* and with *one-sided* error. Formally, in the context of linear properties, we say:

> **Definition 12.1.** Let $V \subseteq \mathbb{F}^n$ be a vector space. V is said to be (q, δ, ϵ)-*locally testable* if there exists a tester that on input $w \in \mathbb{F}^n$, makes q non-adaptive queries to w, accepts with probability 1 if $w \in V$ and rejects with probability at least δ if w is ϵ-far from V.
>
> V is said to be (q, ρ)-*strongly locally testable* if there exists a tester that on input w, makes q non-adaptive queries to w and always accepts if $w \in V$, as above, but in addition, rejects w with probability at least $\rho \cdot \delta(w, V)$, where $\delta(w, V) := d_{\mathrm{H}}(w, V)/|\mathbb{F}|^n$.

Obviously, if V is (q, ρ)-strongly locally testable, then it is also $(q, \epsilon\rho, \epsilon)$-locally testable for any $\epsilon > 0$ [1]. Many natural classes of linear properties

---

[1] The converse is false; see 12.8 for further discussion.

© The Author(s), under exclusive license to Springer Nature Singapore Pte Ltd 2022
A. Bhattacharyya and Y. Yoshida, *Property Testing*,
https://doi.org/10.1007/978-981-16-8622-1_12

linearity

local testability

strong local testability

satisfy strong local testability. For instance, the analysis in Section 6.3 shows that the property of linear functions $f\colon \mathbb{F}_2^n \to \mathbb{F}_2$ (which itself is a linear property) is $(3,1)$-strongly locally testable.

linear code

Linear properties can also be viewed as *linear codes*. The elements in a vector space $V \subseteq \mathbb{F}^n$ correspond to codewords of a linear code having block length n over an alphabet $\mathbb{F}$. (See Section 12.1 for a detailed definition.) Viewed this way, linear properties which are (q, ϵ, δ)-locally testable are called

locally testable code

strong locally testable code

(q, ϵ, δ)-*locally testable codes (LTCs)*. Similarly, we define (q, ϵ)-*strong LTCs*. LTCs have played a very important role in complexity theory over the last two decades, because they underpin most constructions of probabilistically checkable proofs (PCPs) which are in turn used to prove hardness of approximation for optimization problems. For these applications, one needs to construct LTCs that have small query complexity in conjunction with other desirable features of codes, such as rate and distance. Note that here, the goal is to engineer new linear properties that admit efficient testers, whereas our goal so far in this book has been to understand the testability of given properties.

Section 12.1 opens the chapter by giving some basic preliminaries about coding theory. Section 12.2 lays out a general methodology for proving testability of linear codes. In Sections 12.3 and 12.4, we study the problem of testing whether a function $f\colon \mathbb{F}^n \to \mathbb{F}$ is a polynomial of degree $\leq d$ or far from being so. This problem has historically played a very significant role, both for its applications to PCP constructions as well as for the techniques that have been developed to analyze the problem. We study the problem both over large and small fields. In Section 12.5, we discuss the more general problem of testing membership in a tensor product code. Remarkably, we can show that for *any* linear code $\mathcal{C}$, the tensor product code $\mathcal{C}^{\otimes m}$ is strongly locally testable, if $m \geq 3$ is a constant.

In Section 12.6, we show that another 'automatic' way that a code can be strongly locally testable is if it belongs to particular classes of affine-invariant, linear properties. Note that in the previous chapter, we already obtained a near characterization of the testability of affine-invariant properties, even for non-linear properties. The differences in this chapter are that we do not need to restrict to constant field sizes and also that the query complexity bounds are much smaller. Both of these aspects are critical in certain applications. Finally, in Section 12.7, armed with the results of the previous sections, we discuss constructions of LTCs with good rate and distance.

12.1 Preliminaries on Coding Theory

Fix a finite field $\mathbb{F}$. A set $\mathcal{C}$ is said to be an $[n, k, d]_{\mathbb{F}}$-code[2] if $\mathcal{C}$ is a k-dimensional linear subspace of $\mathbb{F}^n$ and its *minimum distance*:

minimum distance

$$\Delta_{\mathcal{C}} := \min_{x,y \in \mathcal{C}: x \neq y} |\{i : x_i \neq y_i\}|$$

equals d. The vectors in $\mathcal{C}$ are called *codewords*.

codeword

> **Exercise 12.1.** Show that $\Delta_{\mathcal{C}} = \min_{\mathcal{C} \ni x \neq 0} |x|$, where $|x| = |\{i : x_i \neq 0\}|$.

The parameter n is called the code's *block length*, while k is called its *dimension*, $\dim(\mathcal{C})$. The *rate* of a code is the fraction $r_{\mathcal{C}} := \frac{k}{n}$. The *relative distance* of a code $\mathcal{C}$ is defined as: $\delta_{\mathcal{C}} := \frac{\Delta_{\mathcal{C}}}{n}$. A family of codes $\{\mathcal{C}_i : i \in \mathbb{Z}\}$ is said to be *asymptotically good* if the block length of $\mathcal{C}_i$ is i, $\lim_{i \to \infty} r_{\mathcal{C}_i} > 0$ and $\lim_{i \to \infty} \delta_{\mathcal{C}_i} > 0$. It is known that for any $\delta \in [0, 1 - 1/|\mathbb{F}|)$, there exists an asymptotically good family of codes with relative distance at least δ and rate at least the so-called *Gilbert-Varshamov (GV)* bound. See the references given at the end of this chapter for details.

block length
dimension
rate
relative distance
asymptotic goodness

Gilbert-Varshamov
bound

For any $x \in \mathbb{F}^n$, define the relative Hamming distance:

$$\delta_H(x, \mathcal{C}) = \min_{y \in \mathcal{C}} \frac{|\{i : x_i \neq y_i\}|}{n},$$

so that we say x is ϵ-*far from* $\mathcal{C}$ if $\delta_H(x, \mathcal{C}) > \epsilon$. In this chapter, we often omit the subscript H as it is always clear. It may be instructive for the reader to now review Definition 12.1 for LTCs, thinking of V as a code.

ϵ-farness

Often, we will analyze the following tester for a code $\mathcal{C}$: choose a subset $I \subseteq [n]$ of coordinates and accept if and only if the input restricted to I belongs to $\mathcal{C}|_I$. The code $\mathcal{C}|_I$ is the *restricted* or *punctured* code defined as:

restricted code
punctured code

$$\mathcal{C}|_I = \{(x_i)_{i \in I} : x \in \mathcal{C}\}.$$

For a string $x \in \mathbb{F}^n$, we also denote $(x_i)_{i \in I}$ as $x|_I$.

> **Exercise 12.2.** Show that $\mathcal{C}|_I$ is a linear code with block length $|I|$.

Tensor Product Codes.

The tensor product is a natural operation to perform on codes, and we will invoke it extensively through this chapter.

---

[2] We restrict ourselves to linear codes in this chapter.

tensor product code

Definition 12.2. Let $\mathcal{C}_1, \ldots, \mathcal{C}_m$ be $[n_i, k_i, d_i]_{\mathbb{F}}$ codes. The *tensor product code* $\mathcal{C}_1 \otimes \mathcal{C}_2 \otimes \cdots \otimes \mathcal{C}_m$ consists of functions $F : [n_1] \times [n_2] \times \cdots \times [n_m] \to \mathbb{F}$ such that for all $d \in [m]$ and for all $j_1 \in [n_1], \ldots, j_{d-1} \in [n_{d-1}], j_{d+1} \in [n_{d+1}], \ldots, j_m \in [n_m]$:

$$(F(j_1, \ldots, j_{d-1}, i, j_{d+1}, \ldots, j_m) : i \in [n_d]) \in \mathcal{C}_d.$$

For example, the tensor product $\mathcal{C}_1 \otimes \mathcal{C}_2$ of two codes $\mathcal{C}_1$ and $\mathcal{C}_2$ consists of matrices whose rows are individually codewords of $\mathcal{C}_1$ and columns are individually codewords of $\mathcal{C}_2$.

A more constructive way to define tensor product codes is as follows.

Proposition 12.1. *Let* $\mathcal{C}_1, \ldots, \mathcal{C}_m$ *be* $[n_i, k_i, d_i]_{\mathbb{F}}$ *codes. For any* $x^{(1)} \in \mathcal{C}_1, \ldots, x^{(m)} \in \mathcal{C}_m$, *define* $\hat{f}_{x^{(1)}, \ldots, x^{(m)}}(i_1, \ldots, i_m) = \prod_{d=1}^{m} x_{i_d}^{(d)}$. *Then,*

$$\mathcal{C}_1 \otimes \cdots \otimes \mathcal{C}_m = \mathrm{span}\left(\left\{\hat{f}_{x^{(1)}, \ldots, x^{(m)}} : x^{(1)} \in \mathcal{C}_1, \ldots, x^{(m)} \in \mathcal{C}_m\right\}\right).$$

We leave proving this proposition, as well as the following useful lemma, as instructive exercises for the reader.

Lemma 12.1. *For any two codes* $\mathcal{C}_1, \mathcal{C}_2$: *(a)* $r_{\mathcal{C}_1 \otimes \mathcal{C}_2} = r_{\mathcal{C}_1} \cdot r_{\mathcal{C}_2}$, *and (b)* $\delta_{\mathcal{C}_1 \otimes \mathcal{C}_2} \geq \delta_{\mathcal{C}_1} \cdot \delta_{\mathcal{C}_2}$.

For any $m \geq 1$ and a code $\mathcal{C}$, we define $\mathcal{C}^m = \mathcal{C}^{\otimes m-1} \otimes \mathcal{C}$. Clearly, if $\mathcal{C}$ has block length n, relative distance δ, and rate r, then $\mathcal{C}^m$ has block length n^m, relative distance at least δ^m, and rate r^m using Lemma 12.1.

Reed-Muller and Reed-Solomon Codes.

Reed-Muller code

Reed-Solomon code

Given a prime power q and positive integers d and n, the *Reed-Muller code of degree* d *on* n *variables over* $\mathbb{F}_q$, denoted $\mathsf{RM}_{q,d,n}$, is the set of evaluations $(P(x) : x \in \mathbb{F}_q^n)$ for every polynomial $P : \mathbb{F}_q^n \to \mathbb{F}_q$ of degree $\leq d$. The *Reed-Solomon code of degree* n *over* $\mathbb{F}_q$, denoted $\mathsf{RS}_{q,d}$, equals $\mathsf{RM}_{q,d,1}$, i.e., degree-d univariate polynomials over $\mathbb{F}_q$.

Exercise 12.3. Show that:

- $\mathsf{RM}_{q,d,n}$ is a linear subspace of $\mathbb{F}_q^{q^n}$
- The block length of $\mathsf{RM}_{q,d,n}$ is q^n.
- The dimension of $\mathsf{RM}_{q,d,n}$ is the number of monomials that can have non-zero coefficients in a polynomial of degree $\leq d$. This means:

$$\dim(\mathsf{RM}_{q,d,n}) = \binom{n+d}{d}.$$

The following fact gives the distance of $\mathsf{RM}_{q,d,n}$.

Fact 12.1. If $\mathcal{C}$ is the code $\mathrm{RM}_{q,d,n}$, then:

$$\delta_{\mathcal{C}} = \left(1 - \frac{t}{q}\right) \cdot q^{-r},$$

where t and r satisfy $r(q-1) + t = d$ and $0 \le t < q-1$. In particular, if $q = 2$, $\delta_{\mathcal{C}} = 2^{-d}$, and if $d < q$, $\delta_{\mathcal{C}} = 1 - \frac{d}{q}$.

Code Duality.

LTCs are intimately related to dual codewords. For a given code $\mathcal{C} \subseteq \mathbb{F}^n$, its *dual code* is:

dual code

$$\mathcal{C}^{\perp} := \left\{ y \in \mathbb{F}^n : \forall x \in \mathcal{C}, \langle x, y \rangle = \sum_{i \in [n]} x_i y_i = 0 \right\}.$$

By linear algebra, $\dim(\mathcal{C}^{\perp}) = n - \dim(\mathcal{C})$.

Let $\mathcal{C}^{\perp}_{\le q} = \{ y \in \mathcal{C}^{\perp} : |y| \le q \}$. We can give an alternate definition of locally testable codes in terms of $\mathcal{C}^{\perp}_{\le q}$.

Definition 12.3 (Alternate definition of LTCs). Let $\mathcal{C} \subseteq \mathbb{F}^n$ be a code. $\mathcal{C}$ is said to be a (q, δ, ϵ)-*LTC* if there exists a distribution Π on elements of $\mathcal{C}^{\perp}_{\le q}$ such that for any $x \in \mathbb{F}^n$:

locally testable code

(i) if $x \in \mathcal{C}$, then:

$$\Pr_{y \sim \Pi}[\langle x, y \rangle = 0] = 1;$$

(ii) if $\delta(x, \mathcal{C}) > \epsilon$, then:

$$\Pr_{y \sim \Pi}[\langle x, y \rangle = 1] \ge \delta.$$

If item (ii) above is replaced by "$\forall x \in \mathbb{F}^n, \Pr_{y \sim \Pi}[\langle x, y \rangle = 1] \ge \rho \cdot \delta(x, \mathcal{C})$", then $\mathcal{C}$ is said to be a (q, ρ)-*strong LTC*.

strong locally testable code

12.2 Robustness and the Conflict Graph Method

A standard approach to proving strong local testability is to establish a stronger condition: *robust testability*.

Definition 12.4. A code $\mathcal{C} \subseteq \mathbb{F}^n$ is said to be a (q, α)-*robust locally testable code* if there exists a tester that on input x, makes a set I of q random non-adaptive queries to x, always accepts if $x \in \mathcal{C}$ and satisfies:

$$\mathbf{E}_I[\delta(x|_I, \mathcal{C}|_I)] \geq \alpha \cdot \delta(x, \mathcal{C}).$$

In words, if x is ϵ-far from $\mathcal{C}$, the robust tester's view of x is itself $\geq \alpha\epsilon$-far from an acceptable view. A (q, α)-robust LTC is also an $(O(q/\alpha), 1/2)$-strong LTC; see Problem 12.1. By the way, we also use "robustness" informally to refer more broadly to conditions which are similar to Definition 12.4. For example, in Section 12.3, the error between $\mathbf{E}_I[\delta(x|_I, \mathcal{C}|_I)]$ and $\delta(x, \mathcal{C})$ is an additive factor instead of multiplicative, while in Section 12.4, we only assert the robustness condition for large $\delta(x, \mathcal{C})$.

Example 12.1 (Bivariate Low-Degree Testing). Consider the problem of testing whether a function $f \colon \mathbb{F}^2 \to \mathbb{F}$ belongs to the code $\mathsf{RM}_{q,d,2}$, for $q \gg d$. A natural test is the so-called *axis-parallel line test*: choose either x or y with probability $1/2$ each, fix that variable to a random constant from $\mathbb{F}$, and check whether the resulting univariate polynomial belongs to $\mathsf{RM}_{q,d,1}$. The test is (q, α)-robust if the following holds:

$$\frac{\mathbf{E}_{x_0 \in \mathbb{F}}[\delta(f(x_0, \cdot), \mathsf{RM}_{q,d,1})] + \mathbf{E}_{y_0 \in \mathbb{F}}[\delta(f(\cdot, y_0), \mathsf{RM}_{q,d,1})]}{2} \geq \alpha \cdot \delta(f, \mathsf{RM}_{q,d,2}).$$

Robustness is a convenient condition to study because it is often amenable to *composition*. Here is the general template. One introduces a sequence of distributions: $\mathcal{D}_0, \mathcal{D}_1, \ldots, \mathcal{D}_t$ where each $\mathcal{D}_i$ is a distribution on subsets of $[n]$ of size n_i, and $n_0 > n_1 > \cdots > n_t$. Here, $n_0 = n$, so clearly, $\mathbf{E}_{I \sim \mathcal{D}_0}[\delta(x|_I, \mathcal{C}|_I)] = \delta(x, \mathcal{C})$. The goal is to show via induction that for all $i \in [t]$:

$$\mathbf{E}_{I \sim \mathcal{D}_i}[\delta(x|_I, \mathcal{C}|_I)] \geq c \cdot \mathbf{E}_{I \sim \mathcal{D}_{i-1}}[\delta(x|_I, \mathcal{C}|_I)],$$

for some constant c. Chaining these approximations together, we obtain: $\mathbf{E}_{I \sim \mathcal{D}_t}[\delta(x|_I, \mathcal{C}|_I)] \geq c^t \delta(x, \mathcal{C})$. Therefore, if $\mathcal{D}_t$ is supported on subsets of size q, we obtain a robust LTC with query complexity q (assuming t is bounded).

The rest of this section lays out a particular methodology for carrying out the above analysis that we call the *conflict graph method*. Focus on a particular step of the analysis. Suppose $x \in \mathbb{F}^n$, $\mathcal{C} \subseteq \mathbb{F}^n$, and $\mathcal{D}$ is a distribution on m-sized subsets of n. The goal is to show that if $\delta(x, \mathcal{C})$ is large, then for non-negligibly many sets S in the support of $\mathcal{D}$, $\delta(x|_S, \mathcal{C}|_S)$ is large. To this end, the structure of the conflict graph of x is a useful object of study.

Definition 12.5 (Conflict Graph). For $x \in \mathbb{F}^n$ and a subset $S \subseteq [n]$ of size m, let $\hat{x}_S$ be an element of $\mathcal{C}|_S$ that is closest to $x|_S$ (ties can be broken arbitrarily). The *conflict graph of x*, denoted Conf_x, is a graph in which each vertex corresponds to a subset S in the support of $\mathcal{D}$, and two subsets S and S' are adjacent if $\hat{x}_S|_{S \cap S'} \neq \hat{x}_{S'}|_{S \cap S'}$.

conflict graph

In typical applications, $\mathcal{C}|_S$ corresponds to the same code for all S in the support of $\mathcal{D}$. For example, in the context of Example 12.1, it is easy to check that the restriction of degree-d bivariate polynomials to any line is exactly the set of degree-d univariate polynomials.

The conflict graph method[3] consists of completing the following program:

1. (**Many consistent tests**) Show that if for many sets S in the support of $\mathcal{D}$, $\delta(x|_S, \mathcal{C}|_S)$ is small, then there is a large independent set $\mathcal{I}$ in the conflict graph Conf_x.

2. (**Global decoding**) Show that if there is a sufficiently large independent set $\mathcal{I}$ in Conf_x, then there is a codeword $y \in \mathcal{C}$ such that:
$$y|_S = \hat{x}_S \qquad \forall S \in \mathcal{I}.$$

3. (**Distance analysis**) Show that if there exists $y \in \mathcal{C}$ that agrees with $\hat{x}_S$ on sufficiently many S in the support of $\mathcal{D}$, then $\delta(x, y)$ is small.

When the above program can be carried out, we can do a case analysis as follows. If $\delta(x|_S, \mathcal{C}|_S)$ has a good chance of being large, then it already follows that $\mathbf{E}_{S \sim \mathcal{D}}[\delta(x|_S, \mathcal{C}|_S)]$ is large. Otherwise, using the conflict graph method, we typically obtain an upper bound on $\delta(x, \mathcal{C})$ in terms of $\mathbf{E}_{S \sim \mathcal{D}}[\delta(x|_S, \mathcal{C}|_S)]$. Thus, robustness and, hence, strong local testability follows.

The conflict graph method is often more elegant and technically simpler than other approaches. It separates the parts of the analysis that are combinatorial from those that depend on the details of the code. The "distance analysis" step can be completed combinatorially by arguing that every $i \in [n]$ appears in roughly the same number of sets in the support of $\mathcal{D}$. In the "many consistent tests" step, one usually exploits the distance of $\mathcal{C}|_{S \cap S'}$ to argue that if there is an edge between S and S', then $\hat{x}_S$ and $\hat{x}_{S'}$ disagree on many points in $S \cap S'$, which implies that either $\delta(x|_S, \hat{x}_S)$ or $\delta(x|_{S'}, \hat{x}_{S'})$ is large by the triangle inequality, which leads to a contradiction if $\delta(x|_S, \hat{x}_S)$ and $\delta(x|_{S'}, \hat{x}_{S'})$ are small. The "global decoding" step typically involves the most detail as one needs to specify a construction that "stitches together" the codewords of the restricted code into a valid codeword of the original code.

---

[3] The term 'conflict graph method' and the general framework outlined here does not explicitly appear in the literature, although it is implicit in many works. The important notion of *agreement testing*, introduced in Problem 12.13, is also very closely related. See Section 12.8 for more specific pointers to the literature.

agreement testing

We next put the above ideas into action by analyzing the problem of testing the Reed-Muller code in two different parameter regimes. In Section 12.3, we analyze the case where the field size is large but $n = 3$. In Section 12.4, we analyze a different regime where the field $\mathbb{F} = \mathbb{F}_2$ but the parameter n is asymptotically growing.

12.3 Low-degree Testing over Large Fields

low-degree testing

The *low-degree testing* problem asks whether an input word $f \in \mathbb{F}_q^{q^n}$ belongs to $\mathsf{RM}_{q,d,n}$ or is ϵ-far from it. This is equivalent to testing whether a multivariate function $f : \mathbb{F}_q^n \to \mathbb{F}_q$ belongs to the set of low-degree (degree $\leq d$) polynomials. The problem has been extensively studied; see Section 12.8 for a brief account of its history and how it arises in various other contexts. Already, in Chapter 6, in Problem 6.14, we described the analysis of a tester for $\mathsf{RM}_{q,d,n}$ (for $q > 2d$) based on the idea of self-correction. The approach we follow here uses the conflict graph methodology from Section 12.2.

flat

k-flat low-degree test

For an integer $0 \leq k \leq n$, let a k-*flat* denote an affine subspace of $\mathbb{F}^n$ of dimension k. The k-*flat low-degree test* simply samples a random affine subspace A of dimension k and checks whether the restriction of f to A is a polynomial of degree $\leq d$. Formally:

Algorithm 12.1 k-flat low-degree tester

Input: Integer $d \geq 1$ and query access to a function $f : \mathbb{F}^n \to \mathbb{F}$ with $n \geq k$.
1: Choose a random k-flat A uniformly at random.
2: Query f on A.
3: Accept if and only if f restricted to A is of degree $\leq d$.

In this section, we look at the setting where $\mathbb{F}$ is asymptotically growing. In particular, suppose $q := |\mathbb{F}|$ is much larger than both d and n. Abbreviating $\delta(f, \mathsf{RM}_{q,d,n})$ for a function $f : \mathbb{F}^n \to \mathbb{F}$ by $\delta_d(f)$, the following result holds for the 2-flat low-degree test, also known as the *Raz-Safra test* or the *Plane vs. Point test* in this context.:

Raz-Safra test

Plane vs. Point test

> **Theorem 12.2** (Robustness for Raz-Safra). *There exists $\epsilon_0 = \mathrm{poly}(nd/q)$ such that the following holds. For any function $f : \mathbb{F}^n \to \mathbb{F}$:*
>
> $$\mathop{\mathbf{E}}_{P}[\delta_d(f|_P)] \geq \delta_d(f) - \epsilon_0,$$
>
> *where P is a random 2-flat.*

Hence, if f is ϵ-far from $\mathsf{RM}_{q,d,n}$, the Raz-Safra test rejects f with probability $\geq \epsilon - \epsilon_0$. So if $q \gg nd$, the Raz-Safra test is a $(q^2, 1 - o(1))$-strong LTC and an $(O(q^2/\epsilon), \frac{2}{3}, \epsilon)$-LTC for any fixed $\epsilon > 0$. In fact, we can easily reduce the query complexity by choosing $O(d^2)$ points on a randomly chosen 2-flat P, interpolating a degree-d bivariate polynomial through them and checking whether it matches f on a few randomly chosen points in P.

Exercise 12.4. For any fixed $\epsilon > 0$, design an $(O(d^2/\epsilon+1/\epsilon^2), \frac{2}{3}, \epsilon)$-LTC for the low-degree testing problem over $\mathbb{F}_q$ where $q \gg nd$.

One might wonder why we do not look at 1-flat tests, i.e., restrictions to random lines instead of random planes. Indeed, the 1-flat test (called the *Line vs. Point test* in this context) does work with similar guarantees, giving an $O(d)$-query tester; see Section 12.8. However, known proofs of correctness for it are heavily algebraic. In contrast, as we will see, the Raz-Safra test can be analyzed using elementary combinatorial techniques[4].

To illustrate the ideas that go into the proof of Theorem 12.2, we look at the case $n = 3$ and show the following weaker claim[5].

Line vs. Point test

Theorem 12.3 (Weaker robustness for Raz-Safra, $n = 3$). *Suppose* $1 < d < |\mathbb{F}|/3$. *For any* $f \colon \mathbb{F}^3 \to \mathbb{F}$, *letting P be a random 2-flat in $\mathbb{F}^3$:*

$$\mathbb{E}_P[\delta_d(f|_P)] \geq \frac{1}{100}\delta_d(f).$$

In the rest of this section, "flats" refer to 2-flats by default. The following facts will be useful in the proof of Theorem 12.3.

Exercise 12.5. Show the following:

(a) The number of flats passing through the origin in $\mathbb{F}^3$ is $q^2 + q + 1$.
(b) The number of flats in $\mathbb{F}^3$ is $q(q^2 + q + 1)$.
(c) A given flat in $\mathbb{F}^3$ does not intersect with $q - 1$ other flats and does intersect with $q^2(q + 1)$ other flats.
(d) Two distinct intersecting flats in $\mathbb{F}^3$ intersect in a line.
(e) Each point of $\mathbb{F}^3$ is contained in $q^2 + q + 1$ flats.

Our proof follows the conflict graph method described in Section 12.2. The conflict graph Conf_f has one vertex for each of the $q(q^2 + q + 1)$ flats in $\mathbb{F}^3$. For any flat P, fix $\hat{f}_P$ to be an element of $\mathsf{RM}_{d,2}$ that is closest to $f|_P$.

---

[4] The added complexity of analyzing the Line vs. Point test is justifiable in the following sense. As we discuss in Section 12.5, it is known that for arbitrary tensor product codes, the natural generalization of the Line vs. Point test is not robust while the natural generalization of the Raz-Safra test is. The Reed-Muller code $\mathsf{RM}_{d,q,n}$ is not exactly a tensor product code, but its block length-to-distance trade-off is very close to that of the tensor power $\mathsf{RM}_{q,d/n,1}^n$, so that we may expect similar behavior. This suggests that proving robustness of the Line vs. Point low-degree test should require properties of polynomials beyond their tensor product-like structure.

[5] We will sketch the additional ideas needed to prove Theorem 12.2 in Problem 12.2.

Two flats P and P' are adjacent in Conf_f if $\hat{f}_P|_{P \cap P'} \neq \hat{f}_{P'}|_{P \cap P'}$. Note that by Exercise 12.5, the degree of the conflict graph is bounded by $q^2(q+1)$.

highly conflicting flat

We say that a flat P is *highly conflicting* if its degree in Conf_f is at least $\frac{1}{2}\left(1 - \frac{d+1}{q}\right) \cdot q(q^2 + q + 1)$. Let $\mathcal{B}$ be the set of highly conflicting flats.

We now describe how we can execute the three steps of the conflict graph method. Proofs of the lemmas below are deferred to Sections 12.3.1, 12.3.2 and 12.3.3.

(i) (**Many consistent tests**) We need to argue that there is a large independent set in Conf_f when $\mathbf{E}_P[\delta_d(f|_P)]$ is small. Our first observation is that when flats P and P' conflict, the polynomials $\hat{f}_P$ and $\hat{f}_{P'}$ must be disagreeing on almost all of $P \cap P'$ by Fact 12.1. Hence, any other flat P'' intersecting $P \cap P'$ is likely to intersect at a conflicting point, so that $\hat{f}_{P''}$ is likely to disagree with either $\hat{f}_P$ and $\hat{f}_{P'}$. Thus, we can show:

Lemma 12.2. *The vertices in $\mathcal{B}$ form a vertex cover for Conf_f.*

On the other hand, we can use the triangle inequality and a simple counting argument to show that the expected distance of $f|_P$ to $\hat{f}_P$ is lower bounded by the size of $\mathcal{B}$.

Lemma 12.3.

$$\mathbf{E}_P[\delta_d(f|_P)] \geq \frac{|\mathcal{B}|}{4q^3}\left(1 - \frac{d+1}{q}\right)^2.$$

Combining the two above lemmas, it follows that there is an independent set $\mathcal{I}$ in Conf_f of size:

$$\left(1 - \frac{4}{(1-(d+1)/q)^2}\mathbf{E}_P[\delta_d(f|_P)]\right) \cdot q(q^2 + q + 1).$$

(ii) (**Global decoding**) Next, we show how to decode a polynomial $Q^* : \mathbb{F}^3 \to \mathbb{F}$ that is consistent with an independent set of sufficiently large size:

Lemma 12.4. *For any independent set $\mathcal{I}$ of size at least $(2d+1)(q^2 + q + 1)$, there exists $Q^* \in \mathsf{RM}_{d,3}$ such that for all $P \in \mathcal{I}$, $\hat{f}_P = Q^*|_P$.*

Our proof of this lemma is for the most part based only on Fact 12.1 and simple geometry. In fact, using only these tools, we decode a polynomial Q that has the same properties as the desired Q^* except that its degree bound is $2d$ instead of d. We can then argue that its degree is in fact $\leq d$ by inspecting the monomial structure of Q (this last bit will haunt us later in Section 12.6).

Note that the assumption $d < q/3$ implies: $\frac{1}{100} \leq \frac{1}{4}\left(1 - \frac{2d+1}{q}\right)\left(1 - \frac{d+1}{q}\right)^2$. Hence, if $\mathbf{E}_P[\delta_d(f|_P)] \leq 1/100$, then:

$$\mathop{\mathbf{E}}_{P}[\delta_d(f|_P)] \leq \frac{1}{4}\left(1 - \frac{2d+1}{q}\right)\left(1 - \frac{d+1}{q}\right)^2,$$

Thus, if $\mathbf{E}_P[\delta_d(f|_P)] \leq 1/100$, combining the conclusion of the "many consistent tests" step with Lemma 12.4, there exists a polynomial $Q^* \in \mathrm{RM}_{d,3}$ that agrees with the corrected polynomials on at least $\frac{2d+1}{q}$ fraction of the flats.

(iii) (**Distance estimation**) Assuming $\mathbf{E}_P[\delta_d(f|_P)] \leq 1/100$ so that we have a polynomial Q^* as above, we bound $\delta(f, Q^*)$.

$$\delta(f, Q^*) = \mathop{\mathbf{E}}_{P}\left[\mathop{\mathrm{Pr}}_{x \in P}[f(x) \neq Q^*(x)]\right]$$

$$\leq \mathop{\mathbf{E}}_{P}\left[\mathop{\mathrm{Pr}}_{x \in P}[f(x) \neq \hat{f}_P(x)] + \mathop{\mathrm{Pr}}_{x \in P}[\hat{f}_P(x) \neq Q^*(x)]\right]$$

$$\leq \mathop{\mathbf{E}}_{P}[\delta_d(f|_P)] + \frac{|\mathcal{B}|}{q(q^2+q+1)},$$

where the last inequality follows because Q^* equals $\hat{f}_P$ on all flats $P \notin \mathcal{B}$. Invoking Lemma 12.3:

$$\delta_d(f) \leq \mathop{\mathbf{E}}_{P}[\delta_d(f|_P)]\left(1 + \frac{4q^3}{q(q^2+q+1)}\frac{1}{\left(1 - \frac{d+1}{q}\right)^2}\right)$$

$$\leq 20 \cdot \mathop{\mathbf{E}}_{P}[\delta_d(f|_P)],$$

using the assumption $q > 3d$.

Putting the pieces together, we get that either $\mathbf{E}_P[\delta_d(f|_P)] > \frac{1}{100}$ or else, $\mathbf{E}_P[\delta_d(f|_P)] \geq \frac{1}{20}\delta_d(f)$, which proves Theorem 12.3. It remains to prove the Lemmas 12.2, 12.3, and 12.4.

12.3.1 Proof of Lemma 12.2

Denoting $E = E(\mathrm{Conf}_f)$, we will show that if $(P_1, P_2) \in E$, then:

$$\mathop{\mathrm{Pr}}_{P_3}[(P_1, P_3) \notin E \wedge (P_2, P_3) \notin E] \leq \frac{d+1}{q}.$$

Therefore, $\geq 1 - \frac{d+1}{q}$ fraction of the planes are neighbors of either P_1 or P_2, and so, either P_1 or P_2 neighbors $\geq \frac{1}{2}\left(1 - \frac{d+1}{q}\right)$ fraction of the planes, which implies that $\mathcal{B}$ is a vertex cover.

Consider an edge (P_1, P_2), and let $\ell = P_1 \cap P_2$. There are three cases:

(i) P_3 contains ℓ. In this case, $\hat{f}_{P_3}$ never agrees with both $\hat{f}_{P_1}$ and $\hat{f}_{P_2}$, since the latter two disagree on ℓ.

(ii) P_3 does not intersect ℓ. It is easy to check that this event happens with probability at most $\frac{1}{q}$.

(iii) P_3 intersects ℓ at a single point. This point of intersection is equally likely to be any point on ℓ. Observe by Fact 12.1, $\hat{f}_{P_1}$ and $\hat{f}_{P_2}$ agree on at most d/q fraction of the line $\ell = P_1 \cap P_2$. So, in this case, the probability that $\hat{f}_{P_3}$ agrees with both $\hat{f}_{P_1}$ and $\hat{f}_{P_2}$ is at most d/q.

Hence, the probability that $(P_1, P_3) \notin E$ and $(P_2, P_3) \notin E$ is at most $0 + \frac{1}{q} + \frac{d}{q}$.

12.3.2 Proof of Lemma 12.3

Let E be the edge set of Conf_f, and $N = q(q^2 + q + 1)$ the number of vertices. First, observe that the number of edges incident to the nodes in $\mathcal{B}$ is a lower bound on $|E|$, the total number of edges. Hence:

$$|E| \geq \frac{1}{2} \cdot \frac{1}{2} \left(1 - \frac{d+1}{q}\right) N \cdot |\mathcal{B}| = \frac{N|\mathcal{B}|}{4} \left(1 - \frac{d+1}{q}\right)$$

So, it will suffice to show that $\mathbf{E}_P[\delta_d(f|_P)] \geq \frac{|E|}{Nq^3} \left(1 - \frac{d+1}{q}\right)$. To do this, we re-express the left-hand side in terms of pairwise intersections of flats.

$$\mathbf{E}_P[\delta_d(f_P)] = \frac{1}{N} \sum_P \Pr_{x \in P}[f(x) \neq \hat{f}_P(x)]$$

$$= \frac{1}{N} \sum_P \sum_{P' : P \cap P' \neq \emptyset, P \neq P'} \frac{\Pr_{x \in P \cap P'}[f(x) \neq \hat{f}_P(x)]}{q(q^2 + q)}.$$

The last equality is true because for each $x \in P$, there are exactly $q^2 + q$ other flats P' also containing x (from part (e) of Exercise 12.5). There is also an extra factor of q because $P \cap P'$ is $1/q$ times the size of P. Continuing:

$$\mathop{\mathbf{E}}_{P}[\delta_d(f|_P)] \geq \frac{1}{q^3 N} \sum_{\substack{(P,P'): \\ P \cap P' \neq \emptyset, P \neq P'}} \left(\mathop{\Pr}_{x \in P \cap P'}[f(x) \neq \hat{f}_P(x)] + \mathop{\Pr}_{x \in P \cap P'}[f(x) \neq \hat{f}_{P'}(x)] \right)$$

$$\geq \frac{1}{q^3 N} \sum_{\substack{(P,P'): \\ P \cap P' \neq \emptyset, P \neq P'}} \mathop{\Pr}_{x \in P \cap P'}[\hat{f}_P(x) \neq \hat{f}_{P'}(x)]$$

$$\geq \frac{1}{q^3 N} \sum_{(P,P') \in E} \mathop{\Pr}_{x \in P \cap P'}[\hat{f}_P(x) \neq \hat{f}_{P'}(x)]$$

$$\geq \frac{|E|}{q^3 N} \left(1 - \frac{d}{N} \right),$$

where the second inequality uses the union bound and the last uses Fact 12.1.

12.3.3 Proof of Lemma 12.4

$\mathcal{I}$ contains at least $(2d+1)(q^2+q+1)$ flats. Using Exercise 12.5, there is a flat X passing through the origin such that there are at least $2d+1$ flats of $\mathcal{I}$ parallel to X. However, there cannot be more than q such flats, as there are only so many affine shifts of X. So, the number of remaining flats in $\mathcal{I}$ is at least $(2d+1)(q^2+q+1) - q \geq (d+1)(q^2+q)$. As a consequence, there is another flat Y passing through the origin such that $\mathcal{I}$ contains at least $d+1$ flats parallel to Y. By a linear transformation, we can assume without loss of generality that X is the plane $\{x = 0\}$ and Y is the plane $\{y = 0\}$. In summary, there exists $k \geq 2d+1$ such that $\mathcal{I}$ contains flats $P_1, \ldots, P_k$ where each $P_i = \{x = c_i\}$, and flats $P'_1, \ldots, P'_{d+1}$ where each $P'_i = \{y = c'_i\}$. Here, c_i and c'_i are constants in the field $\mathbb{F}$.

We first find a degree-$2d$ polynomial Q that agrees with $\hat{f}_{P'_i}$ for all $i \in [d+1]$. This is quite simple to achieve since $P'_1, \ldots, P'_{d+1}$ are parallel.

Exercise 12.6. Define degree-d polynomials $E_1, \ldots, E_{d+1} : \mathbb{F} \to \mathbb{F}$ such that for every $i \in [d+1]$, $E_i(c'_i) = 1$ but $E_i(c'_j) = 0$ for all $j \neq i$. It follows that $Q(x,y,z) = \sum_{i=1}^{d+1} E_i(y) \cdot \hat{f}_{P'_i}(x, c'_i, z)$ is a degree-$2d$ polynomial that agrees with $\hat{f}_{P'_i}$ for all $i \in [d+1]$

We now argue:

Proposition 12.2. *Q agrees with $\hat{f}_{P_i}$ for all $i \in [k]$.*

Proof. Consider the flat P_1. Since it does not neighbor $P'_1, \ldots, P'_{d+1}$ in Conf_f, $\hat{f}_{P_1}$ agrees with Q on the intersections $P_1 \cap P'_1, \ldots, P_1 \cap P'_{d+1}$. This is not quite enough to conclude $\hat{f}_{P_1} = Q$ using Fact 12.1 because Q is a degree-$2d$

polynomial while we have shown they agree on only $(d+1)/q$ fraction of P_1. However, the following claim directly follows from Exercise 12.6.

Claim 12.1. *For any $\alpha \in \mathbb{F}$, the polynomial Q restricted to $P_1 \cap \{z = \alpha\}$ has degree d.*

Let $\ell_\alpha = P_1 \cap \{z = \alpha\}$. Since $\hat{f}_{P_1}$ agrees with Q on $\ell_\alpha \cap P'_1, \ldots, \ell_\alpha \cap P'_{d+1}$, $\hat{f}_{P_1}$ agrees with the degree-d polynomial $Q|_{\ell_\alpha}$ on at least $(d+1)/q$ fraction of ℓ_α, implying that $\hat{f}_{P_1}$ is identical to Q on ℓ_α by Fact 12.1. Since this is true for any α, and P_1 is the disjoint union of the ℓ_α's, it follows that $\hat{f}_{P_1}$ equals Q on all of P_1. The same argument works for $P_2, \ldots, P_k$. $\qquad\square$

At this point, we can readily conclude:

Proposition 12.3. *Q agrees with $\hat{f}_P$ for all $P \in \mathcal{I}$.*

Proof. Consider any flat $P \in \mathcal{I}$ that is not one of $P_1, \ldots, P_k$. Because $\mathcal{I}$ is an independent set, $\hat{f}_P$ agrees with Q on $P \cap P_1, \ldots, P \cap P_k$, and so, $\hat{f}_P$ agrees with Q on $\geq (2d+1)/q$ fraction of P. The claims follows from Fact 12.1. $\quad\square$

The only remaining issue is that Q is a degree-$2d$ polynomial. However, note that Q restricted to any flat $P \in \mathcal{I}$ equals $\hat{f}_P$, a degree-d polynomial.

Proposition 12.4. *If $Q\colon \mathbb{F}^3 \to \mathbb{F}$ is a degree-$2d$ polynomial such that:*

$$\Pr_{P \text{ is a 2-flat in } \mathbb{F}^3}[\deg(Q|_P) \leq d] > \frac{2d}{q},$$

then $\deg(Q) \leq d$.

Proof. We can write Q as $Q^{=0} + Q^{=1} + \cdots + Q^{=2d}$ where $Q^{=i}$ contains only those monomials whose degrees are exactly i. Let r be the largest number such that $Q^{=r}$ is not identically 0. Suppose for contradiction $r > d$.

On a flat P, if $Q|_P$ has degree $< r$, $Q^{=r}|_P$ must be identically 0. A flat can be parameterized by two linearly independent vectors $u, v \in \mathbb{F}^3$ and an affine shift $w \in \mathbb{F}^3$; in particular, denote $P_{u,v,w} = \{t_1 u + t_2 v + w : t_1, t_2 \in \mathbb{F}\}$. If $Q^{=r}|_{P_{u,v,w}}$ is identically 0, all its coefficients are zero. Note that the coefficient for t_1^r in $Q^{=r}|_{P_{u,v,w}}$ is exactly $Q^{=r}(u)$. Hence, using Fact 12.1:

$$\Pr_{\substack{u,v,w: \\ u,v \text{ linearly independent}}}[Q^{=r}|_{P_{u,v,w}} = 0] \leq \Pr_{u \neq 0}[Q^{=r}(u) = 0] \leq \frac{rq^2 - 1}{q^3 - 1} \leq \frac{2d}{q},$$

since $r \leq 2d$. This is a contradiction. $\qquad\square$

12.4 Low-degree Testing over the Binary Field

We next turn to testing Reed-Muller codes over $\mathbb{F}_2$, the binary field. Fix an integer $d \geq 1$, and suppose n grows asymptotically. This regime is fundamentally different from that in Section 12.3 because the distance of $\mathsf{RM}_{2,d,n}$ is a fixed constant 2^{-d} while that of $\mathsf{RM}_{q,d,n}$ goes to 1 as q becomes large.

For a function $f: \mathbb{F}_2^n \to \mathbb{F}_2$, let $\delta_d(f) = \delta(f, \mathsf{RM}_{2,d,n})$. Let k-flat tests be defined in the same way as in the last section. Our main result for this section is the following.

Theorem 12.4. *For any integer $d > 0$, the $(d+1)$-flat low-degree tester on input $f: \mathbb{F}_2^n \to \mathbb{F}_2$ makes 2^{d+1} queries to f, accepts with probability 1 if $\deg(f) \leq d$, and rejects with probability at least $\min\{2^d \cdot \delta_d(f), \frac{1}{50}\}$.*

Exercise 12.7. Show that $\mathsf{RM}_{q,d,n}$ is a $(2^{d+1}, \frac{1}{25})$-strong LTC and an $(O(2^d + 1/\epsilon), \frac{2}{3}, \epsilon)$-LTC for any $\epsilon > 0$.

It is simpler to show the theorem for the $(d + 10)$-flat tester instead of the $(d+1)$-flat tester, and this is what we do in this section. Problem 12.5 shows how to extend the analysis to the $(d+1)$-flat tester. Problem 12.4 shows that if $k \leq d$, the k-flat tester cannot work. Also, Problem 12.6 shows that the query complexity $O(2^d + 1/\epsilon)$ is optimal for any tester which rejects inputs ϵ-far from $\mathsf{RM}_{q,d,n}$ with probability at least $2/3$.

As discussed in Section 12.2, our plan of attack will be to first show that the $(n-1)$-flat tester is robust and then use induction to argue that the $(d+10)$-flat tester is robust, thus establishing strong local testability. Let a *hyperplane* denote an $(n-1)$-flat. We will show:

hyperplane

Lemma 12.5 (Robustness Lemma for Low-Degree Testing over $\mathbb{F}_2$). *For $\alpha < \frac{1}{4} \cdot 2^{-d}$, $K > 4 \cdot 2^d$ and $f: \mathbb{F}_2^n \to \mathbb{F}_2$, suppose that there exist hyperplanes $H_1, \ldots, H_K$ such that for each $i \in [K]$, $\delta_d(f|_{H_i}) \leq \alpha$. Then, $\delta_d(f) \leq \frac{3}{2}\alpha + \frac{9}{K}$.*

Roughly speaking, the robustness lemma asserts that $\delta_d(f|_H)$ for a typical hyperplane H is at least $\frac{2}{3}\delta_d(f)$. This by itself is not enough for the induction, as we would need to apply the lemma $n - d - 10$ times and so, the distance would become exponentially small. Nevertheless, robustness forms the main part of the analysis, and we first describe how to prove it. After that, we complete the proof of Theorem 12.4.

We invoke the conflict graph methodology to prove Lemma 12.5. For a hyperplane, let $\hat{f}_H : H \to \mathbb{F}_2$ denote a degree-d polynomial that is closest to $f|_H$. The conflict graph Conf_f has a vertex for each of the $2(2^n - 1)$ hyperplanes, and there is an edge between H and H' if $\hat{f}_H|_{H \cap H'} \neq \hat{f}_{H'}|_{H \cap H'}$. Our arguments here critically use the geometry of hyperplanes over $\mathbb{F}_2$. Specifically, we need to use the following.

Exercise 12.8.

1. If H and H' are two hyperplanes, show that: $|H \cap H'|/|H| \in \{0, \frac{1}{2}, 1\}$.

2. The *linear part* of a hyperplane H is the vector $a \in \mathbb{F}_2^n$, where $H = \{x : \langle a, x \rangle = b\}$ for some $b \in \mathbb{F}_2$. Show that among any $2^\ell - 1$ distinct hyperplanes, there are at least ℓ whose linear parts are linearly independent.

3. There is an affine invertible transform that maps hyperplanes $H_1, \dots, H_\ell$ with linearly independent linear parts to the hyperplanes $\{x_1 = 0\}, \dots, \{x_\ell = 0\}$.

(i) (**Many consistent tests**) The following claim immediately implies that $H_1, \dots, H_K$ form an independent set in Conf_f.

Claim 12.2. *For two hyperplanes H and H', if $\delta(f|_H, \hat{f}_H) \leq \alpha$ and $\delta(f|_{H'}, \hat{f}_{H'}) \leq \alpha$ where $4\alpha < 2^{-d}$, then $\hat{f}_H|_{H \cap H'} = \hat{f}_{H'}|_{H \cap H'}$.*

Proof. If $H = H'$ or $H \cap H' = \emptyset$, we are done. Otherwise, by (1) of Exercise 12.8, $|H \cap H'| = \frac{1}{2}|H| = \frac{1}{2}|H'|$. Using the triangle inequality:

$$\delta(\hat{f}_H|_{H \cap H'}, \hat{f}_{H'}|_{H \cap H'}) \leq \delta(\hat{f}_H|_{H \cap H'}, f|_{H \cap H'}) + \delta(\hat{f}_{H'}|_{H \cap H'}, f|_{H \cap H'})$$
$$\leq 2\alpha + 2\alpha = 4\alpha < 2^{-d}.$$

Since $\hat{f}_H|_{H \cap H'}$ and $\hat{f}_{H'}|_{H \cap H'}$ are both degree-d polynomials on the flat $H \cap H'$, by Fact 12.1, $\hat{f}_H|_{H \cap H'} = \hat{f}_{H'}|_{H \cap H'}$. $\square$

(ii) (**Global decoding**) Next, we decode a polynomial $Q^* : \mathbb{F}_2^n \to \mathbb{F}_2$ that is consistent with an independent set of sufficiently large size.

Lemma 12.6. *For any independent set $\mathcal{I}$ of size $> 4 \cdot 2^d$, there exists $Q^* \in \mathsf{RM}_{2,d,n}$ such that for all $H \in \mathcal{I}$, $\hat{f}_H = Q^*|_H$.*

To prove this lemma, we first identify $\ell > d + 1$ hyperplanes in the independent set whose linear parts are linearly independent, using the lower bound on $|\mathcal{I}|$ and Exercise 12.8. Then, we define a degree-d polynomial Q that is consistent with the corrected polynomials on these hyperplanes. Finally, we show using the distance of $\mathsf{RM}_{2,d,n-1}$ that in fact, Q must be consistent with all the hyperplanes in $\mathcal{I}$. Details are in Section 12.4.1.

(iii) (**Distance estimation**) Assuming the hypothesis of Lemma 12.5, the above shows that there exists a degree-d polynomial Q^* that is consistent with $\hat{f}_{H_1}, \dots, \hat{f}_{H_K}$. We now bound $\delta(f, Q^*)$. To this end, call a point z *light* if z is contained in less than $K/3$ of the hyperplanes $H_1, \dots, H_K$, and *heavy* otherwise. Let τ be the fraction of points in $\mathbb{F}_2^n$ that are light.

Claim 12.3.

$$\delta(f, Q^*) \le \frac{3}{2}\alpha + \tau.$$

Proof.

$$\begin{aligned}
\delta(f, Q^*) &= \Pr_z[f(z) \ne Q^*(z)] \\
&= \Pr_z[f(z) \ne Q^*(z), z \text{ is heavy}] + \Pr_z[f(z) \ne Q^*(z), z \text{ is light}] \\
&\le \Pr_z[f(z) \ne Q^*(z), z \text{ is heavy}] + \tau.
\end{aligned}$$

Let us count the total number of pairs $(i, z) \in [K] \times \mathbb{F}_2^n$ such that $z \in H_i$ and $f(z) \ne Q^*(z)$. Call this number N. On one hand, $N \le K \cdot \alpha \cdot 2^{n-1}$ from Lemma 12.6 and the definition of α. On the other hand, $N \ge \frac{K}{3} \cdot \Pr_z[f(z) \ne Q^*(z), z \text{ is heavy}] \cdot 2^n$. Therefore:

$$\Pr_z[f(z) \ne Q^*(z), z \text{ is heavy}] \le \frac{3}{2}\alpha. \qquad \square$$

Together with the next exercise, we get: $\delta(f, Q^*) \le \frac{3}{2}\alpha + \frac{9}{K}$.

Exercise 12.9. For a point $z \in \mathbb{F}_2^n$ and $i \in [K]$, let $Y_i(z) = 1$ if $z \in H_i$ and -1 otherwise. Use Chebyshev's inequality to prove that:

$$\Pr_z\left[Y_1(z) + \cdots + Y_K(z) < -\frac{K}{3}\right] \le \frac{9}{K}.$$

Conclude that $\tau \le 9/K$.

The proof of the robustness lemma (Lemma 12.5) is now complete. We next turn to the proof of Theorem 12.4, i.e., showing strong local testability of the $(d+10)$-tester. As previously mentioned, an issue that arises in applying the robustness lemma repeatedly is that δ_d could keep decreasing by a constant factor after each restriction to a hyperplane. To avoid this problem, our strategy will be to apply the robustness lemma only when $\delta_d(f)$ exceeds a particular threshold, and when $\delta_d(f)$ does not, we show strong local testability directly.

Specifically, we invoke the robustness lemma when $\delta_d(f) > \frac{1}{4} \cdot 2^{-d}$, and we get the following:

Corollary 12.1. *For $f: \mathbb{F}_2^n \to \mathbb{F}_2$, suppose $\delta_d(f) > \frac{1}{4} \cdot 2^{-d}$. Then, there are at most $72 \cdot 2^d$ hyperplanes H such that $\delta_d(f|_H) \le \frac{1}{25} \cdot 2^{-d}$.*

When $\delta_d(f) \le \frac{1}{4} \cdot 2^{-d}$, the following guarantees strong local testability.

Lemma 12.7. *Let $k \geq d+1$. For $f \colon \mathbb{F}_2^n \to \mathbb{F}_2$, if $\delta_d(f) \leq \frac{1}{4} \cdot 2^{-d}$, then the k-flat test rejects with probability at least $\min\{\frac{1}{8}, 2^{k+1} \cdot \delta_d(f)\}$.*

In the proof (presented in Section 12.4.2), we argue that there is a good chance the restriction of f to a random k-flat differs from the closest polynomial to f on exactly one point, and hence, the restriction is not a polynomial since $2^{-k} < 2^{-d}$, the distance of $\mathsf{RM}_{2,d,k}$. We can now prove the main result.

Proof of Theorem 12.4 for $(d+10)$-flat tester. If $\delta_d(f) \leq \frac{1}{25} \cdot 2^{-d}$, we are already done by Lemma 12.7. So, suppose $\delta_d(f) > \frac{1}{25} \cdot 2^{-d}$.

Apply Lemma 12.1. Then, there are two cases:

(i) $\delta_d(f) \leq \frac{1}{4} \cdot 2^{-d}$. By Lemma 12.7, the $(d+10)$-flat test rejects f with probability at least $\min\{\frac{1}{8}, 2^{d+11} \cdot \frac{1}{25} 2^{-d}\} = \frac{1}{8}$.

(ii) $\delta_d(f) > \frac{1}{4} \cdot 2^{-d}$ and so, by Corollary 12.1, $\Pr_H\left[\delta_d(f|_H) \leq \frac{1}{25} \cdot 2^{-d}\right] \leq \frac{72 \cdot 2^d}{2^n} = 72 \cdot 2^{d-n}$.

In case (i), we are done. In case (ii), with probability at least $1 - 72 \cdot 2^{d-n}$, $\delta_d(f|_H) > \frac{1}{25} \cdot 2^{-d}$. Conditioning on such a choice of H, we recurse on $f|_H$. The probability that on some iteration while the dimension is $> d+10$, we hit case (ii) but choose an H such that $\delta_d(f|_H) \leq \frac{1}{25} \cdot 2^{-d}$ is at most $72 \cdot (2^{d-n} + 2^{d-(n-1)} + \cdots + 2^{d-(d+11)}) \leq 72 \cdot 2^{-10} \leq 0.08$. Thus, overall, the $(d+10)$-flat tester rejects with probability at least $\frac{1}{8} - 0.08 \geq \frac{1}{50}$ when $\delta_d(f) > \frac{1}{25} \cdot 2^{-d}$. $\qquad \square$

12.4.1 Proof of Lemma 12.6

We first invoke (2) and (3) of Exercise 12.8 with the assumption $K > 4 \cdot 2^d$ to get that after an affine invertible transformation, $\mathcal{I}$ contains without loss of generality the following hyperplanes: $H_1 = \{x_1 = 0\}, \ldots, H_\ell = \{x_\ell = 0\}$ for $\ell > d+1$. For $i \in [\ell]$, let P_i denote the degree-d polynomial $\hat{f}_{H_i}$.

Each $P_i \colon H_i \to \mathbb{F}_2$ for $i \in [\ell]$ extends to $Q_i \colon \mathbb{F}_2^n \to \mathbb{F}_2$ simply by:

$$Q_i(x_1, \ldots, x_n) = P_i(x_1, \ldots, x_{i-1}, x_i = 0, x_{i+1}, \ldots, x_n).$$

Because $\mathcal{I}$ is an independent set in Conf_f, these polynomials Q_i also share some common structure. To be precise, for each $i \in [\ell]$, let:

$$Q_i(x_1, \ldots, x_n) = \sum_{S \subseteq [\ell] \setminus \{i\}} \prod_{j \in S} x_j \cdot Q_{i,S}(x_{\ell+1}, \ldots, x_n).$$

Lemma 12.8. *For $i, j \in [\ell]$, if $S \subseteq [\ell] \setminus \{i, j\}$, then $Q_{i,S} = Q_{j,S}$.*

> **Exercise 12.10.** Show that Lemma 12.8 follows from the fact that $\mathcal{I}$ is an independent set.

Therefore, for each $S \subseteq [\ell]$, we can define the polynomial Q_S such that $Q_S = Q_{i,S}$ for any $i \in [\ell] \setminus S$. (Note that $Q_{[\ell]} = 0$.) Now, we are ready to define:

$$Q(x_1, \ldots, x_n) = \sum_{S \subseteq [\ell]} \prod_{i \in S} x_i \cdot Q_S(x_{\ell+1}, \ldots, x_n).$$

Clearly, $Q \colon \mathbb{F}_2^n \to \mathbb{F}_2$ is a degree-d polynomial. Moreover, as desired:

Lemma 12.9. *For all $H \in \mathcal{I}$, $Q|_H = \hat{f}_H$.*

Proof. It is easy to see that if $x \in H_j$ with $j \in [\ell]$, then $Q(x) = P_j(x) = \hat{f}_{H_j}(x)$. Therefore, for any $H \in \mathcal{I}$, Q and $\hat{f}_H$ agree on $H \cap (H_1 \cup \cdots \cup H_\ell)$. Note that:

$$\frac{|H_i \cap (H_1 \cup \cdots \cup H_\ell)|}{|H_i|} = 1 - \frac{|H_i \cap (\overline{H}_1 \cap \cdots \cap \overline{H}_\ell)|}{|H_i|} \geq 1 - 2^{-\ell+1}.$$

But since $\ell > d+1$, Q and $\hat{f}_H$ agree on $> 1 - 2^{-d}$ fraction of H, which implies that $Q|_H = \hat{f}_H$ using Fact 12.1. $\qquad\square$

12.4.2 Proof of Lemma 12.7

In this section, we prove:

Lemma 12.10. *For $f \colon \mathbb{F}_2^n \to \mathbb{F}_2$ with $\delta_d(f) = \delta$, if $\ell > d$, then the ℓ-flat test rejects f with probability at least $2^\ell \delta \cdot (1 - 2^\ell \delta)$.*

Let us see how Lemma 12.7 follows. Let $\delta = \delta_d(f)$. Set ℓ to be: (i) k if $\delta \leq \frac{1}{2} \cdot 2^{-k}$ and otherwise, (ii) an integer such that $\frac{1}{4} \cdot 2^{-\ell} < \delta \leq \frac{1}{2} \cdot 2^{-\ell}$. Apply Lemma 12.10 for each case.

(i) $\ell = k$ and so, the k-flat test rejects with probability at least $2^k \delta \cdot (1 - \frac{1}{2}) = 2^{k-1}\delta$.

(ii) Note that $\ell > d$ because $\delta \leq \frac{1}{4} \cdot 2^{-d}$. The above lemma yields that the ℓ-flat test rejects with probability at least $\frac{1}{4} \cdot (1 - \frac{1}{2}) = \frac{1}{8}$. Since $k \geq \ell$, the k-flat test rejects with at least the same probability as the ℓ-flat test.

Proof of Lemma 12.10. Fix a degree-d polynomial g such that $\delta(f, g) = \delta$.

A random ℓ-flat V is specified by a random full-rank matrix $M \in \mathbb{F}_2^{n \times \ell}$ and a random vector $b \in \mathbb{F}_2^n$, such that $V = \{Mx + b : x \in \mathbb{F}_2^\ell\}$. For any $x \in \mathbb{F}_2^\ell$, let F_x be the event that $f(Mx + b) \neq g(Mx + b)$ but for all $y \in \mathbb{F}_2^\ell \setminus \{x\}$, $f(My + b) = g(My + b)$. If F_x holds for some x, then the ℓ-flat test must reject, because then $0 < \delta(f|_V, g|_V) = 2^{-\ell} < 2^{-d}$ which means that $f|_V$ cannot be a degree-d polynomial (by Fact 12.1). For a fixed x,

$$\Pr_V[F_x]$$

$$\geq \Pr_V[f(Mx + b) \neq g(Mx + b)]$$

$$- \sum_{y \neq x} \Pr_V[f(Mx + b) \neq g(Mx + b), f(My + b) \neq g(My + b)]$$

$$\geq \delta - 2^\ell \delta^2.$$

Since the F_x's are mutually exclusive, $\Pr_V[\exists x, F_x] = \sum_x \Pr_V[F_x]$. □

12.5 Tensor Product Codes

A common and natural way to design new codes is to let them be tensor products of known ones. For example, polynomials in n variables where the degree of each variable *individually* is at most d form the n-fold tensor product of $\mathsf{RM}_{q,d,1}$. We have seen that the closely related Reed-Muller code is robustly testable and hence a strong LTC. Is this the case also for $\mathsf{RM}_{q,d,1}^{\otimes n}$? For all tensor product codes? The following gives an affirmative answer.

> **Theorem 12.5.** *Suppose $\mathcal{C} \subseteq \mathbb{F}^n$ is a linear code over a finite field $\mathbb{F}$, and let m be a constant at least 3. Then, $\mathcal{C}^{\otimes m}$ is an (n^2, α_m)-strong LTC where $\alpha_m > 0$ depends only on m and $\delta_\mathcal{C}$ (the relative distance of the code $\mathcal{C}$).*

On the other hand, as Problem 12.9 shows, robustness does not hold in general when $m = 2$.

If $N = n^m$ is the length of the code $\mathcal{C}^{\otimes m}$, Theorem 12.5 shows that the query complexity of testing $\mathcal{C}^{\otimes m}$ is only $N^{2/m}$. Hence, this yields a generic way to construct a strong LTC with N^ϵ query complexity for any constant $\epsilon > 0$. The tester we analyze is the natural analogue of the Raz-Safra tester described in Section 12.3 which restricts the input function to a random 2-dimensional affine subspace in $\mathbb{F}^n$. For tensor product codes, the *axis-parallel 2-flat tester* given below, randomly fixes all but two random coordinates.

axis-parallel 2-flat
tester

Algorithm 12.2 Axis-parallel 2-flat tester

Input: Query access to a tensor $F \colon [n]^m \to \mathbb{F}$ with $m \geq 3$.
  1: Choose random $d_1, d_2 \in [m]$ conditioned on $d_1 < d_2$.
  2: Choose random $i_j \in [n]$ for each $j \in [m] \setminus \{d_1, d_2\}$.
  3: Accept if and only if $F' \colon [n]^2 \to \mathbb{F}$ belongs to $\mathcal{C}^{\otimes 2}$, where $F'(i_{d_1}, i_{d_2}) = F(i_1, \ldots, i_m)$.

Over $[n]^m$, let an *axis-parallel k-flat* be defined by setting $m - k$ of the m coordinates to fixed values and varying over the remaining k coordinates. An axis parallel $(m - 1)$-flat will be called an *axis-parallel hyperplane*. For $d \in [m], i \in [n]$, the *axis-parallel hyperplane* H in $[n]^m$ *with direction* d *and level* i is:

$$H = \{(i_1, \ldots, i_m) \in [n]^m : i_d = i\}.$$

Any axis-parallel hyperplane in $[n]^m$ can naturally be identified with $[n]^{m-1}$. For a tensor $F : [n]^m \to \mathbb{F}$ and an axis-parallel hyperplane H, we let $F|_H : [n]^{m-1} \to \mathbb{F}$ be the restriction of F to the coordinates in H. The main component in the proof of Theorem 12.5 is the following robustness result.

Theorem 12.6 (Robustness). *Let $\mathcal{C} \subseteq \mathbb{F}^n$ be a linear code with relative distance $\delta_{\mathcal{C}}$. Suppose $F : [n]^m \to \mathbb{F}$ is ϵ-far from $\mathcal{C}^{\otimes m}$ for $m \geq 3$. Then:*

$$\mathbb{E}_H[d(F|_H, \mathcal{C}^{\otimes m-1})] \geq \frac{1}{24} \delta_{\mathcal{C}}^m \cdot \epsilon,$$

where the expectation is over a random axis-parallel hyperplane H.

Proof of Theorem 12.5. It is clear that the axis-parallel 2-flat test makes n^2 queries and accepts all codewords of $\mathcal{C}^{\otimes m}$. Suppose $F : [n]^m \to \mathbb{F}$ is ϵ-far from $\mathcal{C}^{\otimes m}$. Let $H_0 = [n]^m$ and $F_0 = F$. For $1 \leq j \leq m - 2$, choose a random $d_j \in [m] \setminus \{d_1, \ldots, d_{j-1}\}$, a random $i_j \in [n]$ and let $F_j : [n]^{m-j} \to \mathbb{F}$ be $F_j = F_{j-1}|_{H_j}$ where H_j is the axis-parallel hyperplane in H_{j-1} with direction d_j and level i_j. It is easy to see that F_{m-2} is the restriction of F to a random axis-parallel 2-flat. Invoking Theorem 12.6:

$$\mathbb{E}[d(F_{m-2}, \mathcal{C}^{\otimes 2})] \geq \left(\frac{1}{24} \delta_{\mathcal{C}}^m\right) \cdot \left(\frac{1}{24} \delta_{\mathcal{C}}^{m-1}\right) \cdots \left(\frac{1}{24} \delta_{\mathcal{C}}^3\right) \cdot \epsilon = \alpha_m \cdot \epsilon,$$

where α_m only depends on $\delta_{\mathcal{C}}$ and m. Thus, the rejection probability of the tester is also at least $\alpha_m \cdot \epsilon$. $\qquad \square$

We can prove Theorem 12.6 using the conflict graph method described in Section 12.2. Given a tensor $F : [n]^m \to \mathbb{F}$ and an axis-parallel hyperplane H in $[n]^m$, let $\hat{F}_H$ denote an element of $\mathcal{C}^{\otimes m-1}$ that is closest to $F|_H$. The conflict graph of F, denoted Conf_F, is a graph in which each vertex corresponds to an axis-parallel hyperplane in $[n]^m$ and two axis-parallel hyperplanes H and H' are adjacent if $\hat{F}_H|_{H \cap H'} \neq \hat{F}_{H'}|_{H \cap H'}$. We say that an axis-parallel hyperplane H is *highly conflicting* if its degree in Conf_F is at least $(m - 2)\delta_{\mathcal{C}} n / 2$. Let $\mathcal{B}$ be the set of highly conflicting axis-parallel hyperplanes.

We now show how to execute the steps of the conflict graph method. They are quite similar to how we analyzed the Raz-Safra test in Section 12.3. We will require the following facts about tensor product codes.

Exercise 12.11. Show the following using the property that no two elements of C can agree on more than $n - \delta_C n$ coordinates.

(a) Suppose $I \subseteq [n]$ is a set of size at least $n - \delta_C n + 1$. Then, for every tensor product codeword $T \in C^{\otimes m}$, there is a unique projection to the coordinates $I \times [n]^{m-1}$ that yields a codeword in $C|_I \otimes C^{\otimes m-1}$.

(b) Suppose $I_1, I_2, \ldots, I_m \subseteq [n]$ are each subsets of size at least $n - \delta_C n + 1$. Then, for every tensor product codeword $T \in C^{\otimes m}$, there is a unique projection to the coordinates $I_1 \times I_2 \times \cdots \times I_m$ that yields a codeword in $C|_{I_1} \otimes C|_{I_2} \otimes \cdots \otimes C|_{I_m}$.

(i) (**Many consistent tests**) The following two lemmas imply the existence of a large independent set in Conf_F.

Lemma 12.11. *The set $\mathcal{B}$ forms a vertex cover in the graph Conf_F.*

Lemma 12.12.

$$\mathbb{E}_H[\delta(F|_H, C^{\otimes m-1})] \geq \frac{\delta_C^{m-1}}{12} \frac{|\mathcal{B}|}{mn}.$$

Their proofs are very similar to that of Lemmas 12.2 and 12.3 in Section 12.3 and are left as an exercise for the reader in Problem 12.7. The above two lemmas imply that there exists an independent set $\mathcal{I}$ in Conf_F of size:

$$\left(1 - \frac{12}{\delta_C^{m-1}} \mathbb{E}_H[\delta(F|_H, C^{\otimes m-1})]\right) \cdot mn.$$

(ii) (**Global decoding**) The following lemma decodes a tensor product codeword that is consistent with a sufficiently large independent set in the conflict graph.

Lemma 12.13. *For any independent set $\mathcal{I}$ of size $> mn - (m-1)\delta_C n$, there exists $G^* \in C^{\otimes m}$ that is consistent with all the $\hat{F}_H$ for H in $\mathcal{I}$*

The proof, shown at the end of this section, repeatedly invokes the results in Exercise 12.11. Using the conclusion of the "many consistent tests" step, we obtain that if $\mathbb{E}_H[\delta(F|_H, C^{\otimes m-1})] \leq \frac{\delta_C^m}{24}$, then there exists a codeword $G^* \in C^{\otimes m}$ that is consistent with at least $mn - (m-1)\delta_C n$ axis-parallel hyperplanes.

(iii) (**Distance estimation**) Suppose $\mathbb{E}_H[\delta(F|_H, C^{\otimes m-1})] \leq \frac{\delta_C^m}{24}$. Then for the G^* from above:

$$\delta(F, G^*) = \mathop{\mathbf{E}}_{H}\left[\mathop{\Pr}_{x \in H}[F(x) \neq G^*(x)]\right]$$

$$\leq \mathop{\mathbf{E}}_{H}\left[\mathop{\Pr}_{x \in H}[F(x) \neq \hat{F}_H(x)] + \mathop{\Pr}_{x \in H}[\hat{F}_H(x) \neq G^*(x)]\right]$$

$$\leq \mathop{\mathbf{E}}_{H}[\delta(F|_H, \mathcal{C}^{\otimes m-1})] + \frac{|\mathcal{B}|}{mn},$$

since G^* equals $\hat{F}_H$ on all axis-parallel hyperplanes $H \notin \mathcal{B}$. By Lemma 12.12:

$$\delta(F, \mathcal{C}^{\otimes m}) \leq \delta(F, G^*)$$

$$\leq \mathop{\mathbf{E}}_{H}[\delta(F|_H, \mathcal{C}^{\otimes m-1})]\left(1 + \frac{12}{\delta_{\mathcal{C}}^{m-1}}\right)$$

$$\leq \mathop{\mathbf{E}}_{H}[\delta(F|_H, \mathcal{C}^{\otimes m-1})] \cdot \frac{24}{\delta_{\mathcal{C}}^m}.$$

Hence, either

$$\mathbb{E}_H[\delta(F|_H, \mathcal{C}^{\otimes m-1})] > \frac{\delta_{\mathcal{C}}^m}{24} \text{ or } \mathbb{E}_H[\delta(F|_H, \mathcal{C}^{\otimes m-1})] \geq \frac{\delta_{\mathcal{C}}^m}{24}\delta(F, \mathcal{C}^{\otimes m})$$

holds. Theorem 12.6 follows.

We end this section by giving the details of the global decoding step.

Proof of Lemma 12.13. For $d \in [m]$, let

$$I_d = \{i \in [n] : H \in \mathcal{I} \text{ has direction } d \text{ and level } i\}.$$

Since $\sum_d |I_d| > mn - (m-1)\delta_{\mathcal{C}}n$, there must be two distinct directions $d_1, d_2 \in [m]$ such that $|I_{d_1}|, |I_{d_2}| > n - \delta_{\mathcal{C}}n$, using a variant of the pigeonhole principle. Assume $d_1 = 1, d_2 = 2$ without loss of generality.

Let $\tilde{F} : I_1 \times I_2 \times [n]^{m-2} \to \mathbb{F}$ be defined as $\tilde{F}(x) = \hat{F}_H(x)$ where H is some hyperplane in $\mathcal{I}$ containing x. Note that $\tilde{F}$ is well-defined because $\mathcal{I}$ forms an independent set.

We claim that $\tilde{F}$ belongs to $\mathcal{C}|_{I_1} \otimes \mathcal{C}|_{I_2} \otimes \mathcal{C}^{\otimes m-2}$.

- Let ℓ be a line in $I_1 \times I_2 \times [n]^{m-1}$ that varies over I_1 along the first coordinate with the other coordinates fixed at $(i_2, \ldots, i_m)$ with $i_2 \in I_2$. Then, ℓ is contained in the hyperplane H with direction 2 and level i_2. Thus $\tilde{F}|_\ell$, being consistent with $\hat{F}_H$, must be in $\mathcal{C}|_{I_1}$.
- Similarly, if ℓ is a line that varies over I_2 in the second coordinate but keeps the other coordinates fixed, then $\tilde{F}|_\ell$ must be in $\mathcal{C}|_{I_2}$.
- Similarly, if ℓ is a line that varies over the jth coordinate for $j > 3$ but keeps the other coordinates fixed, then $\tilde{F}|_\ell$ must be in $\mathcal{C}$.

By Exercise 12.11(b), $\tilde{F}$ can be uniquely extended to a codeword G^* in $\mathcal{C}^{\otimes m}$.

It remains to check that $G^*|_H = \hat{F}_H$ for all $H \in \mathcal{I}$. Suppose H is in direction 1. Then, $G^*|_H \in \mathcal{C}^{\otimes m-1}$ and agrees with $\hat{F}_H \in \mathcal{C}^{\otimes m-1}$ on $I_2 \times [n]^{m-2}$. By part (a) of Exercise 12.11, $G^*|_H = \hat{f}_H$. The same argument (replacing I_2 with I_1) holds when H is in direction 2. Finally, suppose $H \in \mathcal{I}$ but is not in direction 1 or 2. Now, $G^*|_H$ agrees with $\hat{F}_H$ on $I_1 \times I_2 \times [n]^{m-3}$. Applying part (b) of Exercise 12.11, we again conclude that $G^*|_H = \hat{F}_H$. $\square$

12.6 Lifted Codes

Given a code $\mathcal{C} \subseteq \{\mathbb{F} \to \mathbb{F}\}$, we can think of the tensor product code $\mathcal{C}^m$ as the set of functions $f \colon \mathbb{F}^m \to \mathbb{F}$ such that for every *axis-parallel line* ℓ, the restriction $f|_\ell$ belongs to $\mathcal{C}$. However, when considering properties of functions from $\mathbb{F}^m$ to $\mathbb{F}$, the restriction to axis-parallel lines seems artificial. What if we require that the restriction to *every* line be a member of $\mathcal{C}$? The following formalizes this idea more generally[6].

m-dimensional lifted code

> **Definition 12.6.** Given a code $\mathcal{C} \subseteq \{\mathbb{F}^t \to \mathbb{F}\}$, and an integer $m \geq t$, the *m-dimensional lifted code* $\mathcal{C}^{t \nearrow m}$ is the set of functions $f \colon \mathbb{F}^m \to \mathbb{F}$ such that for any t-dimensional affine subspace A in $\mathbb{F}^m$, $f|_A$ (the restriction of f to A) belongs to $\mathcal{C}$. In this context, $\mathcal{C}$ is called the *base code*.

affine-invariant codes

The definition assumes that there is a canonical mapping between $\mathbb{F}^t$ and t-dimensional affine subspaces of $\mathbb{F}^m$. We will mainly work with *affine-invariant codes* $\mathcal{C}$ (see Chapter 11) so that the exact correspondence does not matter.

Let us give right away the most prominent example of lifted codes.

> **Example 12.2.** It is known that:
>
> $$\mathsf{RM}_{q,d,n} = \left(\mathsf{RM}_{q,d,\ell}\right)^{\ell \nearrow n},$$
>
> where:
>
> $$\ell = \left\lceil \frac{d+1}{q - q/p} \right\rceil$$
>
> and p is the characteristic of the field $\mathbb{F}_q$. In particular, if $d < q/2$, $\mathsf{RM}_{q,d,n}$ is the n-dimensional lift of the Reed-Solomon code $\mathsf{RS}_{q,d}$.

To give a different example of lifted codes, consider the 2-dimensional lift of $\mathsf{RS}_{8,5}$. This is the set of all bivariate polynomials over $\mathbb{F}_8$ such that their restriction to any one-dimensional line is a univariate degree-5 polynomial. One can show that $(\mathsf{RS}_{8,5})^{1 \nearrow 2}$ is not $\mathsf{RM}_{8,5,2}$ or any other Reed-Muller code!

---

[6] The definition below actually makes sense for any $\mathcal{C} \subseteq \{\mathbb{F}^t \to \mathbb{G}\}$ where $\mathbb{F}$ and $\mathbb{G}$ are potentially different finite fields. However, for simplicity, we stick to $\mathbb{F} = \mathbb{G}$.

Since their first systematic study in 2013, lifted codes have been shown to enjoy many interesting code-theoretic properties. It is easy to verify that $C^{t\nearrow m}$ is a linear code if C is. We can also observe that the distance of $C^{t\nearrow m}$ is not much less than that of C. Throughout this section, let $q = |\mathbb{F}|$.

Lemma 12.14.

$$\delta_{C^{t\nearrow m}} \geq \delta_C - q^{-t}.$$

Proof. Suppose $f \colon \mathbb{F}^m \to \mathbb{F}$ is a nonzero element of $C^{t\nearrow m}$ with minimum Hamming weight. Fix $x \in \mathbb{F}^m$ such that $f(x) \neq 0$. Suppose H is a random t-dimensional affine subspace containing x. Since H samples each point in $\mathbb{F}^m \setminus \{x\}$ uniformly at random, and since a random point $y \in \mathbb{F}^m \setminus \{x\}$ satisfies $f(y) \neq 0$ with probability $(\delta_{C^{t\nearrow m}} q^m - 1)/(q^m - 1)$, we get:

$$\mathop{\mathbf{E}}_{H}[|\{y \in H \setminus \{x\} : f(y) \neq 0\}|] = 1 + (q^t - 1) \cdot \frac{\delta_{C^{t\nearrow m}} q^m - 1}{q^m - 1} < 1 + \delta_{C^{t\nearrow m}}(q^t - 1).$$

So, there exists an H such that $f|_H \in C$ is nonzero on less than $q^{-t} + \delta_{C^{t\nearrow m}}$ fraction of it. Hence, $\delta_C < q^{-t} + \delta_{C^{t\nearrow m}}$. $\qquad \square$

The lifting operation can generate high-rate codes which are *locally correctable*. A code $C \subseteq \{\mathbb{F}^m \to \mathbb{F}\}$ is (c, δ)-locally correctable if for any $f \colon \mathbb{F}^m \to \mathbb{F}$ that is δ-close to a codeword $p \in C$, there is an algorithm that, given $x \in \mathbb{F}^m$, makes c queries to f and returns $p(x)$ with constant probability. In Problem 12.11, you are asked to show that lifted codes are naturally (c, δ)-locally correctable where c and δ depend only on the parameters of the base code. High rate can also be ensured simultaneously. For example, if q is a large power of 2, and $d = (1 - \epsilon)q$, the code $(\mathsf{RS}_{q,d})^{1\nearrow m}$ can be shown to have rate approaching 1 as ϵ goes to 0.

locally correctable code

We now turn to the testability of lifted codes. The definition of lifting suggests a test that is the analogue of the k-flat low degree test. Formally:

Algorithm 12.3 k-flat tester for $C^{t\nearrow m}$.

Input: Query access to a function $f \colon \mathbb{F}^m \to \mathbb{F}$.
1: Choose a random k-flat A uniformly at random.
2: Query f on A.
3: Accept if and only if f restricted to A belongs to $C^{t\nearrow k}$.

The most natural choice for k is $k = t$. In this case, it is possible to implement a self-correction based approach (similar to the BLR test analysis in Chapter 6) which shows the following weak robustness:

$$\mathop{\mathbf{E}}_{H:\dim(H)=t}[\delta(f|_H, C)] \geq \Omega(q^{-3t}) \cdot \delta(f, C^{t\nearrow m}), \tag{12.1}$$

when $\mathcal{C} \subseteq \{\mathbb{F}^t \to \mathbb{F}\}$ is a linear affine invariant code. The robustness parameter goes to 0 as q becomes large. It turns out that one can obtain a much stronger result by considering a larger value of k. This is very much akin to how the Raz-Safra tester for low-degree testing queries restrictions to planes instead of lines.

Theorem 12.7. *For any linear affine-invariant code* $\mathcal{C} \subseteq \{\mathbb{F}^t \to \mathbb{F}\}$ *satisfying* $\delta_{\mathcal{C}} = \delta$, *and for any function* $f \colon \mathbb{F}^m \to \mathbb{F}$,

$$\mathop{\mathbf{E}}_{H:\dim(H)=2t} [\delta(f|_H, \mathcal{C}^{t \nearrow 2t})] \geq \alpha \cdot \delta(f, \mathcal{C}^{t \nearrow m}),$$

where α *depends only on* δ.

Note that Theorem 12.7 strengthens even the results in Section 12.3 for low-degree testing, because unlike in Theorem 12.2 or 12.3, there is no assumption that q is much larger than d.

In the rest of this section, we will sketch the main ideas behind the proof of this result. For simplicity of exposition, we assume that $t = 1$ and $q \to \infty$. The ideas we describe to analyze this simpler setting can be extended to handle the general case as well. With the assumptions $t = 1$ and $q \to \infty$, we will first establish robustness for constant m.

Lemma 12.15. *For any* $m \geq 3$:

$$\mathop{\mathbf{E}}_{H:\dim(H)=m-1} [\delta(f|_H, \mathcal{C}^{1 \nearrow m-1})] \geq \frac{\delta^{3m}}{16m^2} \cdot \delta(f, \mathcal{C}^{1 \nearrow m}).$$

Exercise 12.12. Show that Lemma 12.15 implies that if $f \colon \mathbb{F}^4 \to \mathbb{F}$:

$$\mathop{\mathbf{E}}_{H:\dim(H)=2} [\delta(f|_H, \mathcal{C}^{1 \nearrow 2})] \geq \Omega(\delta^{21}) \cdot \delta(f, \mathcal{C}^{1 \nearrow 4}).$$

We will then show how to use Exercise 12.12 to argue robustness for large m.

12.6.1 Robustness for Fixed m

Lemma 12.15 is analogous to Theorem 12.3 for testing degree-d polynomials. So, can we implement that proof for general lifted codes? If we try to do this, we face a difficulty that seems fundamental. Recall that in the "global decoding" step of the proof of Theorem 12.3 (namely, Section 12.3.3), we decode a polynomial of degree $2d$ that agrees with the closest degree-d polynomials on many of the test hyperplanes. However, there is no analogous notion of "degree-$2d$ polynomials" for generic affine-invariant codes $\mathcal{C}$!

A more fruitful line of attack is to think of lifted codes as a stronger version of tensor product codes. To be more formal, we define a notion of *special tensor product codes*.

special tensor product codes

Definition 12.7. Let $\ell \in \mathbb{F}^m$ such that $\ell_i \neq 0$ for all $i \in [m]$. Given a linear affine-invariant code $\mathcal{C} \subseteq \{\mathbb{F} \to \mathbb{F}\}$, the *special tensor product code* $\mathcal{C}_\ell^{\otimes m}$ consists of all $f \in \mathcal{C}^{\otimes m}$ such that for all $x \in \mathbb{F}^m$, the function $f_{x,\ell}(t) = f(x + t\ell)$ belongs to $\mathcal{C}$.

In other words, if f is a special tensor product codeword, not only are the restrictions of f to all axis-parallel lines in $\mathcal{C}$ but also the restrictions to all lines in a special direction ℓ. For example, if $\mathcal{C} = \mathsf{RS}_{q,d}$, the tensor power $\mathcal{C}^{\otimes m}$ consists of polynomials where each variable individually has degree at most d. On the other hand, the special tensor power $\mathcal{C}_\ell^{\otimes m}$ excludes many of these polynomials because their restrictions to lines in direction ℓ may have degree $> d$. More generally, the following lemma shows that if $f \in \mathcal{C}^{\otimes m}$ but not in $\mathcal{C}^{1 \nearrow m}$, then there are many directions ℓ such that $f \notin \mathcal{C}_\ell^{\otimes m}$.

Lemma 12.16. *Let $\mathcal{C}$ be a linear affine-invariant code $\mathcal{C} \subseteq \{\mathbb{F} \to \mathbb{F}\}$ of distance δ. For any $f \in \mathcal{C}^{\otimes m} \setminus \mathcal{C}^{1 \nearrow m}$:*

$$\Pr_\ell[f \notin \mathcal{C}_\ell^{\otimes m}] \geq \delta^m - o(1).$$

We do not prove Lemma 12.16 as it requires development of the theory of linear affine-invariant codes. For intuition, again consider $\mathcal{C} = \mathsf{RS}_{q,d}$. Suppose $f \in \mathcal{C}^{\otimes m} \setminus \mathcal{C}^{1 \nearrow m}$. Treating x and ℓ as formal variables, we can write $f_{x,\ell}$ as a polynomial in t. Since $f_{x,\ell}$ is not a degree-d polynomial, there is a nonzero coefficient $C(x, \ell)$ of t^e where $e > d$. There must be a fixing of x for which $C(x, \ell)$ is still nonzero. Now, we can verify that $C(x, \ell)$ is itself a polynomial in $\mathcal{C}^{\otimes m}$. Hence, by the distance of the latter code, there must be many ℓ for which $C(x, \ell)$ is nonzero, which proves the claim. To prove Lemma 12.16 in full generality, a similar strategy can be followed since it can be shown that membership in any linear affine-invariant code corresponds to restricting the set of nonzero monomials (see Section 12.8).

The idea we now pursue is to reduce proving robustness of $\mathcal{C}^{1 \nearrow m}$ to proving robustness of $\mathcal{C}_\ell^{\otimes m}$. The overall plan is to construct a $g \in \mathcal{C}^{\otimes m}$ such that (i) g is close to f, and (ii) for less than $\delta^m - o(1)$ fraction of directions ℓ, $g \notin \mathcal{C}_\ell^{\otimes m}$. By Lemma 12.16, it follows that f is close to $\mathcal{C}^{1 \nearrow m}$.

Let

$$\rho = \mathop{\mathbf{E}}_{H : \dim(H) = m-1} [\delta(f|_H, \mathcal{C}^{1 \nearrow m-1})].$$

Henceforth, we assume $\rho < \frac{\delta^{3m}}{16m^2}$ because otherwise, we are already done.

Call a set of vectors $V \subseteq \mathbb{F}^m$ *proper* if any subset of n vectors from V are linearly independent. Note that a random affine subspace H of dimension $m - 1$ can be defined in the following way:

proper

(i)   Let V be a random proper subset of $\mathbb{F}^m$ of size $m+1$.
(ii) Let D be a random subset of V of size $m-1$.
(iii) Let $x \in \mathbb{F}^m$ be a random shift, and define $H = x + \mathsf{span}(D)$.

Given a proper subset $V \subseteq \mathbb{F}^m$, let $H(V)$ be the result of applying steps (ii) and (iii) above, i.e., choose a random subset of V of size $m-1$ and add a random shift to the space spanned by it. Therefore:

$$\rho = \mathop{\mathbf{E}}_{\substack{V=\{v_1,\ldots,v_m,\ell\} \\ \text{proper}}} [\delta(f|_{H(V)}, \mathcal{C}^{1\nearrow m-1})]$$

$$= \mathop{\mathbf{E}}_{\substack{V=\{v_1,\ldots,v_m\} \\ \text{lin. indep.}}} \left[\mathop{\mathbf{E}}_{\substack{\ell:W=V\cup\{\ell\} \\ \text{proper}}} [\delta(f|_{H(W)}, \mathcal{C}^{1\nearrow m-1})] \right].$$

So, there must exist a linearly independent set V such that the inner expectation above is at most ρ. Since $\mathcal{C}$ is affine invariant, V can be chosen to be the standard basis vectors $e_1, \ldots, e_m$ without loss of generality. Hence:

$$\rho \geq \mathop{\mathbf{E}}_{\ell \text{ proper}} [\delta(f|_{H(\ell)}, \mathcal{C}^{1\nearrow m-1})]$$

$$\geq \mathop{\mathbf{E}}_{\ell \text{ proper}} [\delta(f|_{H(\ell)}, \mathcal{C}^{\otimes m-1})],$$

where we used $\mathcal{C}^{1\nearrow m-1} \subseteq \mathcal{C}^{\otimes m-1}$. Above, we call ℓ proper if $\{e_1, \ldots, e_m, \ell\}$ is, and we use $H(\ell)$ to denote $H(\{e_1, \ldots, e_m, \ell\})$. By Markov's inequality:

$$\Pr_{\ell \text{ proper}} \left[\mathop{\mathbf{E}}_{H \sim H(\ell)} [\delta(f|_H, \mathcal{C}^{\otimes m-1})] \geq 2\delta^{-m}\rho \right] \leq \frac{1}{2}\delta^m. \tag{12.2}$$

Now, we invoke robustness of the special tensor product code $\mathcal{C}_\ell^{\otimes m}$.

Lemma 12.17. *Suppose $\ell \in \mathbb{F}^m$ is proper. Then, for any $f : \mathbb{F}^m \to \mathbb{F}$:*

$$\mathop{\mathbf{E}}_{H \sim H(\ell)} [\delta(f|_H, \mathcal{C}^{\otimes m-1})] \geq \frac{\delta^m}{4m^2} \cdot \delta(f, \mathcal{C}_\ell^{\otimes m}).$$

We omit the proof of this lemma, but it should be clear that it is similar in spirit to Theorem 12.6. Here, the test samples a random H from $H(\ell)$ instead of from the set of axis-parallel hyperplanes. Also, the guarantee is with respect to $\mathcal{C}_\ell^{\otimes m}$ instead of $\mathcal{C}^{\otimes m}$.

Returning to (12.2), we get that with probability at least $1 - \frac{1}{2}\delta^m$ over choice of proper ℓ, there exists a function $g^{(\ell)} \in \mathcal{C}_\ell^{\otimes m} \subseteq \mathcal{C}^{\otimes m}$ such that:

$$\delta(f, g^{(\ell)}) \leq 8m^2 \delta^{-2m} \cdot \rho < \frac{1}{2}\delta^m. \tag{12.3}$$

So, for all such ℓ, $g^{(\ell)} = g \in \mathcal{C}^{\otimes m}$, since by Lemma 12.1, the distance of the code $\mathcal{C}^{\otimes m}$ is δ^m. Since a random ℓ is proper with probability $1 - o(1)$:

$$\Pr_{\ell \in \mathbb{F}^m} [g \notin \mathcal{C}_\ell^{\otimes m}] \leq \frac{1}{2}\delta^m + o(1).$$

Lemma 12.16 then implies $g \in \mathcal{C}^{1 \nearrow m}$. We already have from (12.3) that $\delta(f, g) \leq 8m^2\delta^{-2m} \cdot \rho$.

12.6.2 Robustness for Large m

By Exercise 12.12, the 2-flat tester for $\mathcal{C}^{1 \nearrow 4}$ is robust. In this section, we show robustness of the 2-flat tester for $\mathcal{C}^{1 \nearrow m}$ where the robustness constant is independent of m. For simplicity, we assume the field size $q \to \infty$.

Departing from the general theme of this chapter, we sketch a self-correction based proof that (greatly) generalizes the analysis of the BLR linearity tester in Chapter 6. Let $f \colon \mathbb{F}^m \to \mathbb{F}$ be the input function. Let ρ be the robustness of the 2-flat tester:

$$\rho = \mathop{\mathbf{E}}_{H : \dim(H) = 2} [\delta(f|_H, \mathcal{C}^{1 \nearrow 2})].$$

Using this notation, we will show that

$$\rho \geq \Omega(\delta^{24}) \cdot \delta(f, \mathcal{C}^{1 \nearrow m})$$

where $\delta = \delta_{\mathcal{C}}$, the relative distance of the base code $\mathcal{C}$.

For any subspace H of $\mathbb{F}^m$, let $\hat{f}_H \colon H \to \mathbb{F}$ be the closest element of $\mathcal{C}^{1 \nearrow \dim(H)}$ to $f|_H$. The high-level proof strategy is to define a function $g \colon \mathbb{F}^m \to \mathbb{F}$ such that for any x, $g(x)$ is the majority of $\hat{f}_\ell(x)$ for all lines ℓ passing through x. We then need to argue: (i) g is well-defined, (ii) g is close to f, and (iii) $g \in \mathcal{C}^{1 \nearrow m}$. To argue (i), we follow the template of the BLR tester analysis, and, using the robustness for 4-dimensional functions, we prove that $\Pr_{\ell, \ell' \ni x}[\hat{f}_\ell(x) = \hat{f}_{\ell'}(x)]$ is close to 1. This allows us to conclude that for most ℓ's passing through x, the value $\hat{f}_\ell(x)$ is the same and hence, g is well-defined. For (ii), we argue that $\delta(f, g)$ is roughly at most the expected distance between $f|_\ell$ and $\hat{f}_\ell$ for a random ℓ (because of the proof for (i)), and the latter is at most ρ. Finally, for (iii), we show that $g|_\ell \in \mathcal{C}$ for all lines ℓ.

For a 4-dimensional subspace K, let

$$\rho_K = \mathop{\mathbf{E}}_{H \subset K : \dim(H) = 2} [\delta(f|_H, \mathcal{C}^{1 \nearrow 2})].$$

Below, we assume throughout that $\rho = O(\delta^{24})$, because otherwise we are done. We first show that g is well-defined:

Lemma 12.18. *For any $x \in \mathbb{F}^m$, if ℓ and ℓ' are random lines passing through x:*

$$\Pr_{\ell,\ell' \ni x}[\hat{f}_\ell(x) = \hat{f}_{\ell'}(x)] \geq 1 - \frac{\delta}{5}.$$

Proof Sketch. It is not hard to show that for very large q:

$$\Pr_{\ell,\ell' \ni x}[\hat{f}_\ell(x) = \hat{f}_{\ell'}(x)] \geq \mathop{\mathbf{E}}_{\substack{K \ni x: \\ \dim(K)=4}} \left[\Pr_{\substack{\ell,\ell' \subset K: \\ \ell,\ell' \ni x}}[\hat{f}_\ell(x) = \hat{f}_{\ell'}(x)] \right] - o(1). \quad (12.4)$$

nice   Let us call a 4-dimensional subspace K *nice* if $\rho_K \leq c\delta^{23}$ for a sufficiently small constant $c > 0$. We first argue that if K is nice, most lines ℓ though x lying in K have the same value $\hat{f}_\ell(x)$. Then, we claim that most K's containing x are nice. Plugging this information into (12.4) finishes the proof.

Proposition 12.5. *If K is nice, then for at least $1 - \delta/30$ fraction of lines $\ell \subseteq K$ containing x, $\hat{f}_\ell(x) = \hat{f}_K(x)$.*

Proof. Note that:

$$\mathop{\mathbf{E}}_{\substack{\ell:\ell \subset K \\ x \in \ell}}[\delta(f|_\ell, \hat{f}_K|_\ell)] = \mathop{\mathbf{E}}_{\substack{\ell:\ell \subset K \\ x \in \ell}} \Pr_{y \in \ell}[f(y) \neq \hat{f}_K(y)] \leq \Pr_{y \in K}[f(y) \neq \hat{f}_K(y)] + o(1),$$

where the last inequality comes from discarding the conditioning $x \in K$ and using the assumption of large q. Since K is nice, by Exercise 12.12,

$$\Pr_{y \in K}[f(y) \neq \hat{f}_K(y)] \leq \delta(f|_K, \mathcal{C}^{1 \nearrow 4}) \leq O(\delta^{-21}\rho_K) < \frac{\delta^2}{70}.$$

Hence, $\mathbf{E}_{\substack{\ell:\ell \subset K \\ x \in \ell}}[\delta(f|_\ell, \hat{f}_K|_\ell)] < \frac{\delta^2}{60}$. By Markov's inequality, with probability $> 1 - \delta/30$ over choice of ℓ containing x, $\delta(f|_\ell, \hat{f}_K|_\ell) < \delta/2$ and hence, $\hat{f}_\ell = \hat{f}_K|_\ell$. $\square$

Proposition 12.6. *For any line ℓ, $\mathbf{E}_K[\rho_K] \leq \rho + o(1)$, where the expectation is over 4-dimensional subspaces K containing ℓ.*

We omit a formal proof, but note that if K was a random 4-dimensional subspace, clearly $\mathbf{E}_K[\rho_K] = \rho$. We can remove the conditioning that $K \ni \ell$ with an extra $o(1)$ term, since $q \to \infty$.

    The last proposition implies, through Markov's inequality, that a random 4-dimensional subspace K containing x is nice with probability at least $1 - (\rho + o(1))/(c\delta^{23}) \geq 1 - \delta/10$, using our assumption on ρ. Then, from (12.4), we get:

$$\Pr_{\ell,\ell' \ni x}[\hat{f}_\ell(x) = \hat{f}_{\ell'}(x)] \geq \left(1 - \frac{\delta}{30}\right)^2 \left(1 - \frac{\delta}{10}\right) - o(1) \geq 1 - \frac{\delta}{5}. \qquad \square$$

We next analyze the distance between f and g.

Lemma 12.19. *Assuming $\rho = O(\delta^{24})$:*

$$\rho \geq \left(1 - \frac{\delta}{5}\right) \cdot \delta(f, g) \geq \frac{4}{5} \cdot \delta(f, g).$$

Exercise 12.13. Prove Lemma 12.19 using Lemma 12.18 and the fact that $\mathbf{E}_{H:\dim(H)=2}[\delta(f|_H, \hat{f}_H)] \geq \mathbf{E}_{\ell:\dim(\ell)=1}[\delta(f|_\ell, \hat{f}_\ell)]$.

It remains to show that $g \in \mathcal{C}^{1 \nearrow m}$.

Lemma 12.20. *For any line ℓ, $g|_\ell \in \mathcal{C}$.*

Proof Sketch. Fix a line ℓ. Let h be the closest codeword in $\mathcal{C}$ to $g|_\ell$. For all $x \in \ell$, we would like to show that $g(x) = h(x)$.

The proof we show is quite indirect and subtle, in the same spirit as Lemma 6.7 used for the BLR tester analysis in Chapter 6. We show that for any $x \in \ell$, there exists a 4-dimensional subspace $K(x)$ containing ℓ and a subset $S(x) \subseteq \ell$ containing x such that:

(i) $\hat{f}_{K(x)}(y) = g(y)$ for all $y \in S(x)$, and
(ii) $|S(x)| > (1 - \delta/2)q$.

Therefore, g differs from the codeword $\hat{f}_{K(x)}|_\ell$ on $< \delta/2$ fraction of ℓ, and hence, $\hat{f}_{K(x)}|_\ell = h$. Since $x \in S(x)$, $g(x) = \hat{f}_{K(x)}(x) = h(x)$, as desired.

We now show the existence of $K(x)$ and $S(x)$. Let us say that for a subspace K and a point $y \in K$, K *is consistent with g at y* if $\Pr_{\ell'}[\hat{f}_{\ell'}(y) = g(y)] > \frac{\delta}{20}$ where ℓ' is a random line passing through x and contained in K. Also, recall the definition of a nice K in the proof of Lemma 12.18. We claim that if S is a subset satisfying $x \in S \subseteq \ell$ and $|S| > (1 - \delta/2)q$ and K is a nice 4-dimensional subspace K such that K is consistent with g at all points in S, then we can take $K(x) = K$ and $S(x) = S$. We only need to verify condition (i) above. Since K is nice, we already know by Proposition 12.5, for all points $y \in S$,

$$\Pr_{\ell' \ni y, \ell \subset K}[\hat{f}_{\ell'} = \hat{f}_K] > 1 - \frac{\delta}{20}.$$

From the fact that K is consistent with g at $y \in S$, it follows that for any such y, there must exist an ℓ' such that $\hat{f}_K(y) = \hat{f}_{\ell'}(y) = g(y)$.

It turns out that a random choice of K now works! That is, it is nice and is consistent with g at points in a set $S \subseteq \ell$ satisfying our requirements. From

Proposition 12.6, a random K containing ℓ is nice with probability at least $1 - \delta/10$. To argue consistency with g, we first bound for any fixed $y \in \ell$:

$$\mathop{\mathbf{E}}_{K \supset \ell}\left[\mathop{\Pr}_{\ell' \subseteq K : y \in \ell'}[g(y) \neq \hat{f}_{\ell'}(y)]\right] \leq \mathop{\Pr}_{\ell' \ni y}[g(y) \neq \hat{f}_{\ell'}(y)] + o(1) \leq \frac{\delta}{4},$$

where the first inequality can be justified by $q \to \infty$ and the second follows from Lemma 12.18. Hence, with at most $(\delta/4)/(1-\delta/20) < 5\delta/19$ probability, K is not consistent with g at a fixed $y \in \ell$. In particular, this is true for x. Finally, by another application of Markov's inequality, the probability that K is not consistent with g at $\geq \delta/2$ fraction of y's in ℓ is $< (5\delta/19)/(\delta/2) = 10/19$. Applying a union bound demonstrates that K satisfies all the required conditions with nonzero probability. $\square$

12.7 Constructions of Locally Testable Codes

There is a fundamental tension between the rate, relative distance and query complexity of locally testable codes. On one hand, non-vanishing rate requires that the additional number of code symbols not be too large. On the other hand, non-vanishing distance and local testability require that codewords should be highly redundant. Can these constraints be met simultaneously? More precisely, the holy grail is to design *asymptotically good LTCs*, i.e., a family of linear codes $\mathcal{C}_n$ which are $[n, k, d]_{\mathbb{F}}$ codes satisfying:

asymptotically good locally testable code

- **Constant rate**: $n = O(k)$
- **Linear distance**: $d = \Omega(n)$
- **Constant locality**: $\mathcal{C}_n$ is (q, ρ)-strong locally testable where q and ρ are both constants independent of n.

Existence of asymptotically good LTCs (or non-existence thereof) is an outstanding open question in the area.

To explain the main motivation for constructing such codes, we need to delve a bit into the backstory. The notion of locally testable codes originally arose in the context of probabilistically checkable proofs (PCPs). A verifier for a PCP is a probabilistic algorithm that tests if the input string constitutes a proof of a solution to a computationally hard problem; the verifier's query complexity is the number of proof symbols inspected. Informally speaking, PCPs are stronger objects than LTCs, because testers for LTCs test closeness to a fixed set of codewords while verifiers for PCPs test closeness to the set of acceptable proofs (which are defined vis-à-vis the verifier). Indeed, in many PCP constructions, LTCs form the "combinatorial core" of the PCP verifier around which complexity-theoretic machinery is added. Hence, it seems that constructing good LTCs should be the stepping stone to producing short PCPs, which are desired in many applications, both theoretical and applied. A more detailed discussion is available in Section 12.8.

It should be emphasized, however, that the existence of good LTCs is a basic question, even ignoring the connection to PCPs. Rate and distance are the two most fundamental properties of error-correcting codes. In the context of local testability, it is only natural to ask how low query complexity can be achieved together with the requirements of asymptotically good codes.

At the time of this writing, there is no consensus in the community about whether asymptotically good LTCs exist. Observe that the results of Section 12.5 and 12.6 already give LTCs with constant rate and distance and polynomial query complexity.

> **Exercise 12.14.** Suppose $\mathcal{C} \subseteq \mathbb{F}^n$ is a code with rate r and relative distance δ. For any $\kappa > 0$, use the tensor product operation to construct a code $\mathcal{C}^\kappa \subseteq \mathbb{F}^N$ with block length $N = n^{O(1/\kappa)}$, rate $r^{O(1/\kappa)}$ and relative distance $\delta^{O(1/\kappa)}$ which is $(N^\kappa, \delta^{O(1/\kappa^2)})$-strongly locally testable. How do the parameters change if using lifting instead of tensoring?

Specifically, for any fixed $\kappa > 0$, starting from an asymptotically good family of codes $\mathcal{C} \subseteq \mathbb{F}^n$, one can obtain a family of codes $\mathcal{C}^\kappa \subseteq \mathbb{F}^N$ with constant rate r_κ and relative distance δ_κ that is an LTC with query complexity N^κ. In fact, it is known that sub-polynomial query complexity is possible while simultaneously achieving a near-optimal tradeoff between rate and distance.

> **Theorem 12.8.** *For every r in $(0, 1)$, there exists a family of $[n, k, d]_\mathbb{F}$ codes $\mathcal{C}_n$ satisfying:*
>
> - $r(\mathcal{C}_n) = k/n \geq r$;
> - $\delta(\mathcal{C}_n) = d/n \geq 1 - r - o(1)$;
> - $\mathcal{C}_n$ *is* $(n^{o(1)}, 1)$-*strongly locally testable*;
> - $|\mathbb{F}| \leq \exp\left(n^{o(1)}\right)$.

For general codes $\mathcal{C} \subseteq \mathbb{F}^n$, it is known that the parameters need to satisfy the *Singleton bound*: $\delta_{\mathcal{C}} \leq 1 - r_{\mathcal{C}} + 1/n$. The Singleton bound is achieved by the Reed-Solomon code, for example. Theorem 12.8 shows that the Singleton bound can be almost achieved even with sub-polynomial query complexity. Additionally, the code from Theorem 12.8 can be concatenated with a suitable binary code to yield a binary LTC with sub-polynomial query complexity and with a rate-distance tradeoff approaching the *Gilbert-Varshamov bound*.

The proof of Theorem 12.8 relies on a procedure to amplify the distance of a code while mildly affecting the rate. Specifically, this distance-amplification procedure uses a d-regular *expander* graph to convert a code with relative distance $\omega(1/d)$ to a code with relative distance δ while reducing the rate by a factor approximately $1 - \delta$. Additionally, it can be shown that if the procedure is applied on an LTC with query complexity q, the resulting code is also an LTC with query complexity $q \cdot \text{poly}(d)$. To prove Theorem 12.8, we can use the code constructed in Problem 12.12 that has constant rate, sub-constant relative distance and $n^{o(1)}$ query complexity, and then apply the

Singleton bound

Gilbert-Varshamov bound

expander

distance-amplification procedure using an expander of super-constant degree in order to obtain an asymptotically good code with $n^{o(1)}$ query complexity.

Theorem 12.8 is in the setting where the rate is kept fixed and the query complexity growing. In a different direction, it is known that the query complexity can be made constant but with polylogarithmically decreasing rate.

Theorem 12.9. *There exist constants $\delta, \rho > 0$ for which there is a family $\mathcal{C}_n$ of $[n, k, d]_{\mathbb{F}_2}$ codes satisfying:*

- $r(\mathcal{C}_n) = k/n \geq 1/\mathrm{polylog}(k)$;
- $\delta(\mathcal{C}_n) = d/n \geq \delta$;
- $\mathcal{C}_n$ *is* $(3, \rho)$-*strongly locally testable.*

Below, we sketch the proof of a weaker version of Theorem 12.9 which gives a weak $(\mathrm{polylog}(k), \tau, 1/\mathrm{polylog}(k))$-LTC with relative distance δ for constants $\delta, \tau > 0$. The query complexity of this weak LTC can be reduced to 3 using standard techniques (similar to the proof reducing k-LIN to 3-LIN in Section 7.4.2). Its rejection probability can also be made constant using standard "gap amplification" techniques from the PCP literature. Theorem 12.9 additionally posits that the LTC is strong; obtaining this property seems to require some additional ideas which we omit.

The main insight behind the LTC construction is to separate the codeword symbols responsible for maintaining relative distance from those responsible for local testability. Informally speaking, this allows for more efficient application of the tensor product operation that targets only the coordinates responsible for distance and thus leads to savings in the block length. To make these ideas rigorous, we define the notion of a *code with proof*.

code with proof

Definition 12.8. An $[n, k, d]_{\mathbb{F}}$ code $\mathcal{C}$ is said to be a (q, m, ρ)-*code with proof (CWP)* if there exists a tester T that:

(i) Gets access to two input strings $w \in \mathbb{F}^n$ and $\pi \in \mathbb{F}^m$.
(ii) Makes at most q non-adaptive queries to its input strings.
(iii) If $w \in \mathcal{C}$, there exists $\pi_w \in \mathbb{F}^m$ such that:

$$\Pr[T(w, \pi_w) \text{ accepts}] = 1.$$

(iv) For all $w \in \mathbb{F}^n, \pi \in \mathbb{F}^m$,

$$\Pr[T(w, \pi) \text{ rejects}] \geq \rho \cdot \delta(w, \mathcal{C}).$$

The *proof rate* of a CWP as above is defined to be k/m.

Clearly, a (q, ρ)-strong LTC is a $(q, 0, \rho)$-CWP. In the other direction, Problem 12.14 shows that if an $[n, k, d]_{\mathbb{F}}$ code $\mathcal{C}$ is a (q, m, ρ)-CWP, then for all small enough constant $\delta > 0$, there is an $[O(n+m), k, \Omega(d)]_\mathbb{F}$ code $\mathcal{C}'$ that is[7] a $(q, \delta, \Omega(\rho))$-LTC. The high-level idea here is to let $\mathcal{C}'$ be the concatenation of π_w with multiple copies of w, for each codeword $w \in \mathcal{C}$. Distance and testability of w are guaranteed by the CWP definition, and the repetitions of w ensure that their total length dominates the length of the proof string π_w.

We now describe an iterative construction of a sequence of CWP's $\mathcal{C}_0, \mathcal{C}_1, \ldots,$ with the final CWP having the desired parameters. Let $\mathcal{C}_0$ be a constant-length code with constant rate r and constant relative distance δ. $\mathcal{C}_0$ is trivially a CWP with constant query complexity and proof length 0. Each $\mathcal{C}_i$ is a $[n_i, k_i, d_i]_\mathbb{F}$ code that satisfies the (q_i, m_i, ρ_i)-CWP property. We maintain the rate $r = k_i/n_i$ and relative distance $\delta = d_i/n_i$ fixed for all the CWP's $\mathcal{C}_i$. For technical reasons, we ensure $m_i \geq n_i$ (by artificially padding the proof if necessary). The transition from $\mathcal{C}_i$ to $\mathcal{C}_{i+1}$ consists of three phases:

(i) **Tensor product**: Define $\mathcal{C}_i^{\mathrm{TP}}$ to be $\mathcal{C}_i^{\otimes 2}$. The rate $r(\mathcal{C}_i^{\mathrm{TP}}) = r^2$ and relative distance $\delta(\mathcal{C}_i^{\mathrm{TP}}) = \delta^2$. Although it is false (see Problem 12.9) that $\mathcal{C}_i^{\otimes 2}$ generally reduces to testing $\mathcal{C}_i$ on a random row or column, we assume so here for simplicity of exposition. Thus, $\mathcal{C}_i^{\mathrm{TP}}$ is a $(q_i, 2n_i m_i, \Omega(\rho_i))$-CWP, because the proof of a purported codeword in $\mathcal{C}_i^{\mathrm{TP}}$ would consist of proofs of membership in $\mathcal{C}_i$ for each of the $2n_i$ rows and columns.

(ii) **Random projection**: The next phase increases the rate back to r. Define $\mathcal{C}_i^{\mathrm{RP}}$ to be $\mathcal{C}_i^{\mathrm{TP}}|_I$ for a subset $I \subseteq [n_i^2]$ of size $k_i^2/r = n_i k_i$. It is easy to show via the Chernoff bound that there exists[8] a subset I for which the relative distance of $\mathcal{C}_i^{\mathrm{RP}}$ is at least $\frac{1}{2}\delta^2$.

To argue that $\mathcal{C}_i^{\mathrm{RP}}$ is a CWP, an immediate issue is that the tester for the unprojected string in $\mathcal{C}_i^{\mathrm{TP}}$ might query coordinates not in I. Here is a solution that seems far too easy to be of any value: for any $w \in \mathcal{C}_i^{\mathrm{TP}}$, if $w' = w|_I$, let $\pi_{w'}$ be the concatenation of π_w with $w|_{[n]\setminus I}$. The new tester simply invokes the tester for $\mathcal{C}_i^{\mathrm{TP}}$, using queries to the proof string for coordinates not in I. Clearly, the tester accepts all $w' \in \mathcal{C}_i^{\mathrm{RP}}$ with probability 1. On the other hand, for any w such that $w' = w|_I$, $\delta(w, \mathcal{C}_i^{\mathrm{TP}}) \geq \delta(w', \mathcal{C}_i^{\mathrm{RP}}) \cdot \frac{|I|}{n_i^2} = \frac{1}{r}\delta(w', \mathcal{C}_i^{\mathrm{RP}})$, and so, the new tester rejects w' (along with any π) with probability $\geq \Omega(\rho_i) \cdot \delta(w', \mathcal{C}_i^{\mathrm{RP}})$ as r is a constant. Hence, $\mathcal{C}_i^{\mathrm{RP}}$ is a $(q_i, 3n_i m_i, \Omega(\rho_i))$-CWP, since the proof string has length $2n_i m_i + n_i^2 - n_i k_i \leq 3n_i m_i$ if $m_i \geq n_i$.

(iii) **Distance Amplification**: The last phase increases the relative distance back to δ. There are standard constructions in the coding theory literature for this purpose, involving walks on *expander* graphs (see Section 12.8 for references), and it is straightforward to check that these affect the CWP parameters by constant factors.

expander

---

[7] Note that the LTC obtained is not necessarily strong.

[8] For this argument, $|I|$ needs to be $c_\delta k_i^2$ for a constant c_δ depending on δ, but if r is sufficiently small (which can be ensured by choosing $\mathcal{C}_0$ appropriately), then $|I| \leq k_i^2/r$.

We have: $k_{i+1} = k_i^2$, $n_{i+1} = O(k_{i+1})$, $q_{i+1} = O(q_i)$, $m_{i+1} = O(n_i m_i)$, and $\rho_{i+1} = \Omega(\rho_i)$. Note that the proof rate $P_{i+1} = k_{i+1}/m_{i+1} = \Omega(k_i^2/n_i m_i) = \Omega(P_i)$. Hence, if $t = O(\log\log k)$, C_t is a $[k/r, k, \delta k/r]_{\mathbb{F}}$ code with the $[\operatorname{polylog}(k), k \cdot \operatorname{polylog}(k), 1/\operatorname{polylog}(k)]$-CWP property. Invoking the above-mentioned transformation from CWP's to LTC's completes the construction.

Conceptually, the main reason that this construction does better than Exercise 12.14 is that the tensor product operation is not applied on the whole codeword. The portion responsible for local testability is isolated as the "proof" and is exempt from the powering. In each iteration, the code part of the CWP grows quadratically (while keeping the rate constant), but the proof part grows only linearly. The combinatorial nature of the above construction makes very clear the structural reason for this gain in efficiency.

We end this section by indicating how one can remove the assumption about the testability of tensor products. The idea is to always maintain that C_i equals $\tilde{C}_i^{\otimes 2}$ for some code[9] $\tilde{C}_i$. By Section 12.5, if C_i is a CWP, then $C_i^{\mathrm{TP}} = C_i^{\otimes 2} = \tilde{C}_i^{\otimes 4}$ is also a CWP; the proof string for a codeword of $\tilde{C}_i^{\otimes 4}$ consists of the proof strings for the codewords of $\tilde{C}_i^{\otimes 2}$ corresponding to every restriction on axis-parallel 2-flats. For the random projection and distance amplification steps, these operations are performed on the "square roots" of their inputs, and the result is then squared. For example, for the random projection step, if $C_i^{\mathrm{TP}} = (\tilde{C}_i^{\mathrm{TP}})^{\otimes 2}$, then $C_i^{RP} = (\tilde{C}_i^{\mathrm{TP}}|_I)^{\otimes 2}$ for a random subset I. One can show that with these modifications also, C_i^{RP} and C_{i+1} are CWP's with qualitatively similar parameters as those discussed above.

12.8 Bibliographic Notes

The notion of strong LTCs was introduced by Goldreich and Sudan [221]. Strong LTCs are a strict subset of weak LTCs, as demonstrated by a construction of Viderman [389]. The equivalence between Definitions 12.1 and 12.3 follows from the results of Section 7.3 and is explicitly argued in [61].

12.8.1 Probabilistically Checkable Proofs

The question of testing membership in codes was originally motivated by the problem of query-efficient verification of proofs.

Definition 12.9. For integer valued functions $m(\cdot)$ and $q(\cdot)$ defined on integers, a probabilistically checkable proof *(PCP) verifier* for a language

probabilistically
checkable proof

---

[9] $\tilde{C}_i$ need not be a code with proof.

L with *proof complexity* m and *query complexity* q is a probabilistic algorithm V for which the following hold:

(i) V receives as inputs two strings $x \in \{0,1\}^n$ and $\pi \in \{0,1\}^{m(n)}$;

(ii) V makes at most $q(n)$ queries to π;

(iii) If $x \in L$, then there exists a string π such that V accepts (x, π) with probability 1;

(iv) If $x \notin L$, then for any string π, V accepts (x, π) with probability at most $1/3$.

The probability of acceptance in case (iv) is called the *soundness* of the verifier.

Seminal work in the 1990s [31, 32, 48, 175, 49, 47, 349, 237] showed that the complexity class NP consists exactly of those languages for which there exist PCP verifiers with query complexity 3 and polynomial proof length. Later constructions [65, 151, 321] reduced the proof length to $n \cdot \text{polylog}(n)$ while keeping the query complexity constant. Historically, the main motivation for constructing PCP verifiers with low query complexity and proof length was their surprising connection to hardness of approximation for fundamental optimization problems (first observed by [174] for MAX-CLIQUE). More recently, PCPs have found applications in delegation of computation and decentralized cryptocurrencies (see [58] and references therein).

A PCP verifier is "morally" like a tester in the sense that it checks whether π is a correct proof for x. This idea was made precise in the following way. For $x \in \{0,1\}^n$ and a PCP verifier V, let $C_{V,x} = \{\pi \in \{0,1\}^{m(n)} : V(x, \pi) \text{ accepts with probability } 1\}$. Then, Goldreich and Sudan [221] constructed a PCP verifier V for an NP-hard language L that rejects with constant probability proof strings far from $C_{V,x}$ for *all* x, not just $x \notin L$ (in which case $C_{V,x} = \emptyset$)[10]. In this situation, for a fixed $x \in L$, the verifier V tests $C_{V,x}$ in the standard property testing sense.

12.8.2 Low-degree Testing

The construction of low-degree testers was originally identified by Friedl and Sudan [195], Rubinfeld and Sudan [368], Arora [30] and Spielman [375] as the centerpiece of contemporaneous PCP constructions. The standard approach towards constructing PCPs at the time was to encode the NP-witness of an $x \in L \in \text{NP}$ as a multivariate low-degree polynomial. The associated verifier tests: (i) whether a purported proof π indeed corresponds to a low-degree codeword, and (ii) whether π can be decoded to a standard NP-witness for the input x. Through this connection, the low-degree testing problem attracted

---

[10] Note that here, $C_{V,x}$ is itself defined in terms of V and for $x \in L$, $C_{V,x}$ need not correspond to the π's used in justifying part (iii) of Definition 12.9.

a huge amount of attention. Blum, Luby and Rubinfeld's work on linearity testing [94] was earlier in the same era and community, though motivated by the entirely different problem of program checking (see also [198]).

The early works on low-degree testing by Rubinfeld and Sudan [368], Arora and Safra [32], and Friedl and Sudan [195] analyzed the 1-flat low degree test (or the *Line vs. Point test*). They showed that there is a constant $\epsilon_0 > 0$ such that if a function f has relative distance $\epsilon \geq \epsilon_0$ from low-degree polynomials, then the test rejects with probability $\Omega(\epsilon)$. The remarkable work of Raz and Safra [354] showed that for the 2-flat test, ϵ_0 can be made sub-constant if the underlying field size is large enough. This is the result described in Section 12.3, although our proof there is for a weaker claim and inspired by the work of Chiesa, Manohar and Shinkar [130] for tensor product codes. Problem 12.2 outlining the proof of the full result for $n = 3$ uses material from lecture notes of Harsha [246] and Moshkovitz [319]. Arora and Sudan [33] showed that a similar guarantee for sub-constant ϵ_0 can also be made for the Line vs. Point test, although the analysis is considerably more algebraic. These works, as well as subsequent advances made by Dinur, Fischer, Kindler, Moshkovitz, Raz and Safra [152, 320, 322, 321] led to PCP verifiers with $o(1)$ soundness and improved hardness of approximation results.

A natural question to ask at this juncture is what is the smallest ϵ_0 achievable for a low-degree test? The best upper bound at the time of this writing is due to Bhangale, Dinur and Livni-Navon [74] who show $\epsilon_0 \leq O(1/\sqrt{q})$ for the 3-flat test (where the constant in the $O(\cdot)$ notation depends on the degree d). Their proof actually does not the use the inductive approach highlighted in this chapter and instead relies on the framework of *direct product testing*. Direct product testing, introduced by Goldreich and Safra [220], is yet another way to abstractify the low-degree testing problem. In this setting, the question is to understand the testability of the code which encodes a function $f: U \to V$ as $F: \mathcal{F} \to 2^V$ where $\mathcal{F}$ is a family of subsets of U and for any $S \in \mathcal{F}$, $F(S) = (f(x) : x \in S)$. The name 'direct product' comes from the frequently studied setting where $\mathcal{F}$ is simply the collection of all subsets of a fixed size. We omit further discussion of direct product testing, but the reader is encouraged to consult [147, 156, 157, 153, 260] for further study.

Section 12.4 describes the work of Bhattacharyya, Kopparty, Schoenebeck, Sudan and Zuckerman [80] over $\mathbb{F}_2$, which improves upon earlier approaches of Alon, Jutla, Kaufman, Krivelevich, Litsyn, Patthak, Ron, Rudra and Zuckerman [13, 272]. These previous works proved that the $(d+1)$-flat tester rejects with probability $\Omega(1/d2^d)$, whereas Section 12.4 shows that the rejection probability is lower bounded by a constant independent of d. This guarantee is called *absolutely sound testing*. Haramaty, Shpilka and Sudan [245] later showed that the Reed-Muller code over any prime field of constant size has an absolutely sound tester. For general fields, a tight bound on the query complexity remains open (see [363] for the current state-of-the-art).

Line vs. Point test

direct product testing

absolutely sound testing

12.8.3 Testing Tensor Products

An influential early work studying axis-parallel flat tests in the context of low-degree testing was that of Polishchuk and Spielman [349]. They considered testing bivariate polynomials by querying their restrictions on axis-parallel lines; this was motivated by their goal of constructing PCP verifiers using less randomness and, hence, proofs of shorter length. The systematic study of axis-parallel flat tests for tensor product codes began with a work by Ben-Sasson and Sudan [66]. It was also in this work they introduced the notion of robustness for LTCs, motivated by an analogous definition for PCPs in an earlier work [59]. They showed that $\mathcal{C}^m$ for $m \geq 3$ can be robustly tested, assuming a lower bound on the relative distance of $\mathcal{C}$ (which limits the applicability only to large fields). Viderman [390] later showed that the large relative distance requirement in [66] is not necessary, hence extending that work to any finite field; our proof of this result in Section 12.5 is based on the analysis of Chiesa, Manohar and Shinkar [130]. Incidentally, our general framework using the conflict graph is inspired by the "rectangle method" formalized by Meir [314] for capturing proofs of robustness of tensor products.

For a while after [66], it was believed that the $m = 2$ case was true and a proof would be eventually found. To the community's surprise, P. Valiant [387] proved that in fact, the tensor product of 2 codes may not be robustly testable! This result was refined by Coppersmith and Rudra [137] and Goldreich and Meir [211]; the latter work gives the argument sketched in Problem 12.9. Subsequently, Dinur, Sudan and Wigderson [158] showed that the situation is not all that bad: the tensor product of two codes *is* robustly testable if the codes have some additional properties (e.g., if one of the codes is an LTC itself); also see the subsequent works by Ben-Sasson and Viderman [69, 70] for more on this theme.

12.8.4 Affine Invariance and Lifted Codes

There are two 'generic' conditions for robust LTCs that have been identified so far. One is tensor product structure as described above. The other condition, first studied by Kaufman and Sudan [278], is symmetry with respect to group actions. In particular, for finite fields $\mathbb{K} \supseteq \mathbb{F}$, they looked at linear properties $\mathcal{P}$ of functions $f \colon \mathbb{K}^n \to \mathbb{F}$ that are $\mathbb{K}$-*affine-invariant*, in the sense that if $f \in \mathcal{P}$, then $f \circ L \in \mathcal{P}$ for every affine[11] map $L \colon \mathbb{K}^n \to \mathbb{K}^n$.

affine-invariance

Similar to Section 11.1, one can define local constraints and characterizations, but now with the additional restriction of linearity. A linear affine-

---

[11] Although strictly speaking, affine transformations form only a semi-group, not a group, Ben-Sasson, Grigorescu, Maatouk, Shpilka and Sudan [60] later showed that if $n = 1$ (a common setting), then any property invariant with respect to affine permutations is in fact invariant under all affine maps.

invariant property $\mathcal{P}$ is defined have a *k-single orbit characterization* if there exists a collection of points $u_1, \ldots, u_k : \mathbb{K}^n$ and a linear subspace $V \subset \mathbb{F}^k$ such that $f \in \mathcal{P}$ if and only if for all affine maps $A : \mathbb{K}^n \to \mathbb{K}^n$:

$$(f(A(u_1)), \ldots, f(A(u_k))) \in V.$$

As in Chapter 11, the natural test for k-locally characterized affine-invariant properties $\mathcal{P}$ is to choose A at random and check if $(f(A(u_1)), \ldots, f(A(u_k)))$ lies in V. Kaufman and Sudan proved that k-single-orbit characterized properties $\mathcal{P}$ are $(k, \Omega(1/k^2))$-strongly locally testable using this test. Note that this result is independent of $|\mathbb{F}|$, unlike the results of Chapter 11.

The surprising discovery at this point is that all known affine-invariant LTCs satisfy the k-single-orbit characterization for a bounded k. There are two 'basic' classes of affine-invariant LTCs known:

- **Reed-Muller codes**: It is obvious that as a property of multivariate functions from $\mathbb{F}_q^n \to \mathbb{F}_q$ (for a prime power q), Reed-Muller codes are $\mathbb{F}_q$-affine-invariant. But they can also be considered as a property of univariate polynomials from $\mathbb{F}_{q^n}$ to $\mathbb{F}_q$, and now, they are $\mathbb{F}_{q^n}$-affine-invariant. Reed-Muller codes are known to have the single-orbit characterization in both these guises; the latter is a non-trivial fact proved in [60].
- **Sparse codes**: A property $\mathcal{P}$ of functions $f : \mathbb{F}_{q^n} \to \mathbb{F}_q$ is said to be t-*size-sparse* if $|\mathcal{P}| \leq q^{nt}$. Ben-Sasson, Grigorescu, Kaufman, Lovett, Ron-Zewi and Sudan [232, 277, 64] showed that t-size-sparse $\mathbb{F}_{q^n}$-affine-invariant codes are k-single orbit characterized, where k is independent of n.

Furthermore, Ben-Sasson, Grigorescu, Guo, Maatouk, Shpilka and Sudan [60, 235] showed that if $\mathcal{P}_1$ and $\mathcal{P}_2$ are single-orbit characterized with a bounded k, so are $\mathcal{P}_1 \cap \mathcal{P}_2$ and $\mathcal{P}_1 + \mathcal{P}_2$. Moreover, if we make the stronger assumption that $\mathcal{P}_1$ and $\mathcal{P}_2$ are locally testable, we get local testability for $\mathcal{P}_1 \cap \mathcal{P}_2$ and $\mathcal{P}_1 + \mathcal{P}_2$. (It remains open whether all LTCs have single orbit characterizations.) These results are obtained by characterizing affine-invariant LTCs in terms of the degrees of monomials in the support of functions satisfying the property. A good overview of this theory is available in [60].

Reed-Muller and sparse codes suffer from poor rates; so, the above results do not seem to have any concrete applications. But this line of research was vindicated with the discovery by Guo, Kopparty and Sudan [234] of lifted codes. As discussed in Section 12.6, they have dramatically higher rates than Reed-Muller codes and also enjoy local decodability and correctibility properties. Lifts preserve bounded single-orbit characterization [63] and local testability [235]. The analysis in Section 12.6 showing robust testability of lifted codes is due to Guo, Haramaty and Sudan [233]. Dinur, Harsha, Ron-Zewi, and Kaufman [154] subsequently re-proved this result using more combinatorial techniques via a connection to *agreement testing* (see Problem 12.13 taken from this paper). They obtain a higher rejection probability but using a testing dimension of $6t$ instead of $2t$. Also, analogously to the result in Section 12.4, the t-flat test for the lifted code $\mathcal{C}^{t \nearrow m}$ is known to satisfy the

agreement testing

absolutely sound testing guarantee, a result due to Haramaty, Ron-Zewi and Sudan [244].

12.8.5 Construction of LTCs

The project of designing locally testable codes with constant rate, relative distance and locality was systematically initiated by the aforementioned work of Goldreich and Sudan [221] who constructed binary constant-query LTCs of constant relative distance, dimension k and length $k \cdot \exp(\tilde{O}(\sqrt{\log k}))$. The length was improved to $k \cdot \mathrm{polylog}(k)$ by Ben-Sasson and Sudan [67] and Dinur [151]. These constructions were made more combinatorial by the work of Meir [313] presented in the proof sketch of Theorem 12.9. Viderman [388, 389, 391] subsequently made Meir's result a strong LTC and fully algorithmic. Theorem 12.8 is due to the work of Kopparty, Meir, Ron-Zewi, and Saraf [286]. The comment below Theorem 12.8 about binary codes approaching the Gilbert-Varshamov bound was substantiated by the follow-up work of Gopi, Kopparty, Oliveira, Ron-Zewi and Saraf [226]. These results use previously known distance amplification techniques for codes [8, 9] that preserve local testability. Meir [313] also invokes Dinur's gap amplification technique [151].

What we did not discuss in this chapter is a currently ongoing attempt to design new LTCs through the framework of *high-dimensional expanders*. In particular, Dikstein, Dinur, Harsha and Ron-Zewi [150] show how one can construct asymptotically good LTCs if there exists a base code and a constant-degree high-dimensional expander that interact well with each other in a certain sense. We refer the reader to [155, 149, 150] for further details.

high-dimensional expanders

Problems

12.1. Show that if a code $\mathcal{C}$ is a (q, α)-robust LTC, then it is also an $(O(q/\alpha), 1/2)$-strong LTC.

12.2. In this problem, you are asked to fill in more details of the proof of Theorem 12.2 for the case $n = 3$

(a) With the following lemma, we can obtain more refined information about the structure of the conflict graph.

Proposition 12.7. *A graph $G = (V, E)$ is ϵ-transitive if for any pair of distinct vertices $(u, v) \notin E$:*

$$\Pr_{w \in V} [(u, w) \in E \wedge (v, w) \in E] \leq \epsilon.$$

If a graph G is ϵ-transitive, then one can remove $O(\sqrt{\epsilon} n^2)$ edges from G in order to make it a disjoint union of cliques.

This claim is purely graph-theoretic, and we skip its proof. Observe that $\overline{\mathrm{Conf}_f}$ is $\frac{d+1}{q}$-transitive from Section 12.3.1. Applying the above proposition and removing edges from the small cliques in the obtained decomposition, and letting V and E be the vertex and edge sets respectively of Conf_f, argue the following. There exists a partition of V as $\cup_i V_i$ where:

(i) Each V_i is either a singleton or an independent set of size $\Omega\left(\sqrt{\frac{d+1}{q}}\right)$.

(ii)

$$\Pr_{(P_1, P_2) \in V^2} [(P_1, P_2) \in E \vee \exists i : (P_1, P_2) \subseteq V_i] \geq 1 - O\left(\sqrt{\frac{d+1}{q}}\right).$$

(b) Combine part (a) with Lemma 12.4 to get that if $\delta = \Theta(\sqrt{d/q})$, there exists $t = O(1/\delta)$ polynomials $Q_1, \ldots, Q_t$ of degree $\leq d$ such that for random flats P_1, P_2:

$$\Pr_{P_1, P_2} [(P_1, P_2) \in E \vee \exists i : Q_i|_{P_1} = \hat{f}_{P_1}, Q_i|_{P_2} = \hat{f}_{P_2}] \geq 1 - \delta,$$

where E again denotes the edge set of Conf_f.

(c) For any line (1-flat), define the randomized function $g_\ell : \mathbb{F} \to \mathbb{F}$ as follows: choose two random 2-flats P_1 and P_2 that intersect at ℓ and if there exists Q_i that agrees with $\hat{f}_{P_1}$ on P_1 and $\hat{f}_{P_2}$ on P_2, then output Q_i restricted to ℓ; otherwise, output $\perp$. Observe that:

$$\Pr_\ell \Pr_{x \in \ell} [g_\ell(x) = f(x)]$$

$$= \Pr_{P_1, P_2, x} [\hat{f}_{P_1}(x) = \hat{f}_{P_2}(x) = f(x) \wedge \exists i : Q_i|_{P_1} = \hat{f}_{P_1}, Q_i|_{P_2} = \hat{f}_{P_2}]$$

where the probability on the LHS is also over the randomness of g_ℓ.

Let A be the event $\hat{f}_{P_1}(x) = \hat{f}_{P_2}(x) = f(x)$, let B be the event $\exists i : Q_i|_{P_1} = \hat{f}_{P_1}, Q_i|_{P_2} = \hat{f}_{P_2}$ and let C be the event that (P_1, P_2) do not form an edge in the conflict graph. Argue that:

(i) $\Pr[\neg A] \leq \mathbf{E}_P[\delta_d(f|_P)] + O(d/q)$. Use the argument in the proof of Lemma 12.3.

(ii) $\Pr[\neg B \wedge C] \leq O(\sqrt{d/q})$ from part (b).

(iii) $\Pr[A \mid \neg C] \leq O(d/q)$ using Fact 12.1.

Justify:

$$\Pr_{\ell}\Pr_{x \in \ell}[g_\ell(x) = f(x)] = \Pr[A \wedge B] \geq \Pr[A] - \Pr[\neg B \wedge C] - \Pr[A \mid \neg C]$$

$$\geq 1 - \mathbb{E}_{P}[\delta_d(f|_P)] - O(\sqrt{d/q}).$$

(d) You will show below that f agrees with one of the polynomials $Q_1, \ldots, Q_\ell$ on a large fraction of the domain. As a preliminary, show that if $A_i = \{x \in \mathbb{F}^3 : Q_i(x) = f(x)\}$, then by Chebyshev's inequality:

$$\Pr_{\ell}\left[\frac{|\ell \cap A_i|}{q} \geq \frac{|A_i|}{q^3} + \epsilon\right] \leq \frac{|A_i|}{\epsilon^2 q^4}.$$

Use the union bound and Fact 12.1 to prove:

$$\Pr_{\ell}\left[\exists i : \frac{|\ell \cap A_i|}{q} \geq \frac{|A_i|}{q^3} + \epsilon\right] \leq \frac{1}{\epsilon^2 q}\left(1 + \frac{d}{q}\right).$$

Set $\epsilon = \Theta(1/q^{1/3})$ so that the RHS becomes $< \epsilon$.

(e) Condition on ℓ satisfying $\forall i : \frac{|\ell \cap A_i|}{q} \leq \frac{|A_i|}{q^3} + \epsilon$; this happens with probability at least $1 - \epsilon$ for $\epsilon = \Theta(1/q^{1/3})$ as at the end of part (d). Justify the following lines:

$$\Pr_{\ell}\Pr_{x \in \ell}[g_\ell(x) = f(x)] = \Pr_{\ell}\Pr_{x \in \ell}[g_\ell(x) = f(x) \wedge \exists i : Q_i|_\ell = g_\ell]$$

$$\leq \Pr_{\ell}\Pr_{x \in \ell}[g_\ell(x) = f(x) \mid \exists i : Q_i|_\ell = g_\ell]$$

$$\leq \max_i \frac{|A_i|}{q^3} + \epsilon.$$

Combine with part (c) to deduce Theorem 12.2 for the case $n = 3$.

12.3. Analyze the 1-flat test (or Line vs. Point test) for linear functions, i.e., $d = 1$. Assume that $|\mathbb{F}|$ is sufficiently large, and show that if $f : \mathbb{F}^n \to \mathbb{F}$ is ϵ-far from linear, then the 1-flat test rejects with probability $1 - \Omega(\epsilon)$.

12.4. Argue that any function $f : \mathbb{F}_2^d \to \mathbb{F}_2$ is a degree-d polynomial, and hence, the d-flat tester cannot be used in Section 12.4.

12.5. In this problem, you are asked to complete the proof of Theorem 12.4. Recall that in the text, we only showed the correctness of the $(d + 10)$-flat tester instead of the $(d + 1)$-flat tester. Let $f : \mathbb{F}_2^n \to \mathbb{F}_2$.

(a) Suppose $n > d+1$ and the $(n-1)$-flat test rejects with probability less than $1/2$, but $\deg(f) > d$. Show that on one hand, there must exist two parallel hyperplanes such that the restriction to both are of degree at most d, and hence, $\deg(f) = d + 1$. On the other hand, argue that f must be divisible by at least $d + 2$ hyperplanes with linearly independent linear parts, so that $\deg(f) \geq d + 2$. Thus, conclude that if $\deg(f) > d$, the $(n-1)$-flat test rejects with probability at least $1/2$.

(b) Use part (a) to show that if $n \geq k \geq d+1$ and $\deg(f) > d$, then the k-flat test rejects with probability at least 2^{k-n}. Apply induction on n.

(c) Observe that the $(d+1)$-flat tester can be implemented by first sampling a random $(d+10)$-flat A of $\mathbb{F}_2^n$ and then sampling a random $(d+1)$-flat B of A. Conclude that if the $(d+10)$-flat tester rejects with probability δ, then the $(d+1)$-flat tester rejects with probability at least $\delta \cdot 2^{-9}$.

12.6. In this problem, you are asked to show a lower bound for testing $\mathsf{RM}_{2,d,n}$.

(a) Suppose $\epsilon < 2^{-d-1}$. Extend the idea in the proof of Theorem 2.6 to show that at least $\Omega(1/\epsilon)$ queries are necessary.

(b) Show that the dual code of $\mathsf{RM}_{2,d,n}$ has minimum distance 2^{d+1}.

(c) Suppose that for a binary linear code $\mathcal{C}$, the dual code $\mathcal{C}^{\perp}$ has minimum distance $d_{\perp}$. Argue that if x is uniformly drawn from $\mathcal{C}$ and I is any subset of size $< d_{\perp}$, then $x|_I$ is uniformly distributed in $\{0,1\}^{|I|}$. Combine with part (b) to show that testing $\mathsf{RM}_{2,d,n}$ requires $\Omega(2^{d+1})$ queries.

12.7. Prove Lemma 12.11.

12.8. Prove Lemma 12.12.

12.9. This problem sketches the construction of a tensor product code that is not robust. The proof described here uses a converse of the conflict graph method, as shown by Meir [314].

Let $\mathcal{C}_1 \subseteq \mathbb{F}^m, \mathcal{C}_2 \subseteq \mathbb{F}^n$ be two linear codes. The axis-parallel hyperplane test for $\mathcal{C}_1 \otimes \mathcal{C}_2$ simply consists of choosing with probability $1/2$ a uniform row and otherwise, a random column. In the first case, the tester checks membership in $\mathcal{C}_1$, and in the latter case, membership in $\mathcal{C}_2$. For $M \in \mathbb{F}^{m \times n}$, let

$$\rho(M) = \frac{\frac{1}{m}\sum_{i=1}^m \delta(M(i,\cdot),\mathcal{C}_1) + \frac{1}{n}\sum_{j=1}^n \delta(M(\cdot,j),\mathcal{C}_2)}{2}.$$

Hence, we say $\mathcal{C}_1 \otimes \mathcal{C}_2$ is α-robust if $\rho(M) \geq \alpha \cdot \delta(M, \mathcal{C}_1 \otimes \mathcal{C}_2)$ for all $M \in \mathbb{F}^{m \times n}$.

For a given M, let Conf_M denote the bipartite conflict graph on $m + n$ nodes. Section 12.5 describes why a large independent set in Conf_M implies robustness. The following result shows a partial converse:

Theorem 12.10. *Suppose $\mathcal{C}_1 \otimes \mathcal{C}_2 \subseteq \mathbb{F}^{m \times n}$ is α-robust. Then, for all M with $\rho(M) < \frac{1}{6}\delta_{\mathcal{C}_1}\delta_{\mathcal{C}_2} \cdot \alpha$, there exists an independent set in Conf_M with $> \left(1 - \frac{\delta_{\mathcal{C}_1}}{2}\right) m$ row vertices and $> \left(1 - \frac{\delta_{\mathcal{C}_2}}{2}\right) n$ column vertices.*

For linear two codes $\mathcal{C}, \mathcal{D} \subseteq \mathbb{F}^n$, let $G_{\mathcal{C}}$ and $G_{\mathcal{D}}$ be their respective generator matrices. Define the $n \times n$ matrix $H = G_{\mathcal{C}}^{\mathsf{T}} G_{\mathcal{D}}$. Let H' be the $n \times 10n$ matrix that is the concatenation of 10 consecutive copies of H and, similarly, I' be the $n \times 10n$ matrix that is the concatenation of 10 consecutive copies of the identity matrix I. Define $M = H' + I'$.

Let $\mathcal{C}_1$ be the space spanned by the rows of M, and let $\mathcal{C}_2 = \mathcal{C}$. Consider the problem of testing membership in $\mathcal{C}_1 \otimes \mathcal{C}_2 \subseteq \mathbb{F}^{n \times 10n}$.

(a) Show that $\rho(M) \leq \frac{1}{2n}$.

It is possible to construct $\mathcal{C}$ and $\mathcal{D}$ such that $\delta_{\mathcal{C}_1}$ and $\delta_{\mathcal{C}_2}$ are both at least $\frac{1}{100}$; we omit the details here. Assume this lower bound holds.

(b) Prove that $\mathcal{C}_1 \otimes \mathcal{C}_2$ is not α-robust for any constant α, by showing that M constructed above contradicts Theorem 12.10.

12.10. In this problem, you study the lifted code $\mathsf{RS}_{q,d}^{1\nearrow 2}$ where q is a power of 2 and $d < q$. Recall that over $\mathbb{F}_q$, the identity $x^q = x$ holds.

(a) Consider the code $\mathsf{RS}_{4,2}^{1\nearrow 2} \subseteq \mathbb{F}_{2^2}^2$. Argue that the monomial $X^3 Y$ does not belong to this code but $X^2 Y^2$ does.

(b) Consider the code $\mathsf{RS}_{8,5}^{1\nearrow 2} \subseteq \mathbb{F}_{2^3}^2$. Which of the monomials $\{X^i Y^j : 0 \leq i, j \leq 7\}$ belong to this code?

(c) Argue that $X^i Y^j$ belongs to $\mathsf{RS}_{q,d}^{1\nearrow 2}$ exactly when for all $i' \leq i, j' \leq j$ such that $\binom{i}{i'} \neq 0 \pmod 2$ and $\binom{j}{j'} \neq 0 \pmod 2$, it holds that $i' + j' \;(\mathrm{mod}^* q) \leq d$. Here $x \;\mathrm{mod}^* q$ equals 0 if $x = 0$ and else, equals $y \in \{1, \ldots, q-1\}$ satisfying $x \equiv y \pmod{q-1}$.

In fact, it turns out that the code consists exactly of the span of the monomials characterized in (c).

12.11. A code $\mathcal{C} \subseteq \{\mathbb{F}^n \to \mathbb{F}\}$ is said to be (q, δ)-*locally correctable* if there exists a probabilistic algorithm $\mathcal{A}$ that given $x \in \mathbb{F}^n$ and oracle access to a function $g : \mathbb{F} \to \mathbb{F}$ satisfying $\delta(f, g) \leq \delta$, $\mathcal{A}$ makes at most q queries to g and outputs $f(x)$ with probability at least $2/3$.

Let $\mathcal{C} \subseteq \{\mathbb{F}^t \to \mathbb{F}\}$ be a code with $\delta_{\mathcal{C}} > 2q^{-t}$ where $q = |\mathbb{F}|$. Prove that $\mathcal{C}^{t \nearrow m}$ is $(q^t - 1, q^{-t}/3)$-locally correctable. Use the natural corrector algorithm that chooses a random t-dimensional subspace containing the query point.

12.12. Design $q, d,$ and m so that $\mathsf{RS}_{q,d}^{\otimes m}$ has constant rate, $o(1)$ relative distance and $n^{o(1)}$ query complexity, where $n \leq q^m$ is the block length of the code.

12.13. In this problem, you are introduced to the notion of *agreement testing*. Let $\mathcal{C} \subseteq \{\mathbb{F}^\ell \to \mathbb{F}\}$ be an affine-invariant code, let $q = |\mathbb{F}|$, and suppose $m \geq s > t \geq \ell$. Let $\mathcal{F}$ denote a collection of functions $f_S \in \mathcal{C}^{\ell \nearrow s}$ for every s-dimensional affine subspace S. Define:

agreement testing

$$\delta_s(\mathcal{F}, \mathcal{C}^{\ell \nearrow m}) = \min\left\{ \Pr_{S:\dim(S)=s}[g|_S \neq f_S] : g \in \mathcal{C}^{\ell \nearrow m} \right\}$$

The lifted code $\mathcal{C}^{\ell \nearrow m}$ is said to be (s, t, α)-*agreement testable* if for every collection $\mathcal{F}$ of functions f_S on affine subspaces S of dimension s:

$$\Pr_{T, S \supseteq T, S' \supseteq T}[f_S|_T \neq f_{S'}|_T] \geq \alpha \cdot \delta_s(\mathcal{F}, \mathcal{C}^{\ell \nearrow m})$$

where the probability on the LHS is over a uniformly chosen t-dimensional affine subspace $T \subseteq \mathbb{F}^m$ and two uniformly, independently chosen s-dimensional affine subspaces S, S' containing T.

You are asked to show below that agreement testing implies robust testing. Suppose $f : \mathbb{F}^m \to \mathbb{F}$ satisfies $\mathbf{E}_S[\delta(f|_S, \mathcal{C}^{\ell \nearrow s})] = \epsilon$. The goal is to show that there exists $g \in \mathcal{C}^{\ell \nearrow m}$ satisfying $\delta(f, g) \leq \beta\epsilon$ for some β.

(a) For an s-dimensional affine subspace S, let $\hat{f}_S$ denote the closest codeword in $\mathcal{C}^{\ell \nearrow s}$ to $f|_S$. Argue that $\mathbf{E}_{S, T \subseteq S}[\delta(f|_T, \hat{f}_S|_T)] = \epsilon$.

(b) Apply the union bound and the Markov bound to get that for any $\delta > 0$:

$$\Pr_{T, S \supseteq T, S' \supseteq T}[\delta(\hat{f}_S|_T, \hat{f}_{S'}|_T) \geq \delta] \leq \frac{4\epsilon}{\delta}.$$

Let $\mu = \delta_{\mathcal{C}^{\ell \nearrow t}}$. Conclude that:

$$\Pr_{T, S \supseteq T, S' \supseteq T}[\hat{f}_S|_T \neq \hat{f}_{S'}|_T] \leq \frac{4\epsilon}{\mu}.$$

(c) Show that assuming $\mathcal{C}^{\ell \nearrow m}$ is (s, t, α)-agreement testable, there exists $g \in \mathcal{C}^{\ell \nearrow m}$ such that $\delta(f, g) \leq O(1/(\alpha\mu)) \cdot \epsilon$.

12.14. Let $\mathcal{C}$ be an $[n, k, d]_\mathbb{F}$ code that is a (q, m, ρ)-CWP, then for all small enough constant $\delta > 0$. Consider the code $\mathcal{C}'$ whose codewords consist of $\ell = O(1)$ repetitions of a codeword $c \in \mathcal{C}$ followed by one copy of its corresponding proof string π_c. Show that for large enough ℓ, $\mathcal{C}'$ is an $[O(n + m), k, \Omega(d)]_\mathbb{F}$ code $\mathcal{C}'$ that is a $(q, \delta, \Omega(\rho))$-LTC.

Chapter 13
Massively Parameterized Model: Classification of Boolean CSPs

Recall that all the testing problems studied in Section 7 can be understood as testing assignments to constraint satisfaction problems (CSPs), that is, given a (satisfiable) instance of a CSP and query access to an assignment to the instance, the goal is to test whether it is a satisfying assignment. In this chapter, we continue this line of study and classify all the Boolean CSPs in terms of query complexity. For a set of relations Γ over $\{0,1\}$, let CSP(Γ) be the CSP whose constraints are made by using relations in Γ (see Section 13.1.1 for more details). Then, the goal is to give characterizations of Γ for which CSP(Γ) is testable with a constant/sublinear number of queries.

The critical mathematical tool for studying CSPs is *universal algebra*. In universal algebra, instead of looking at constraints (or relations used to make constraints), we look at "polymorphisms," which map a tuple of satisfying assignments to another satisfying assignment. Then, we can associate a CSP with an algebra consisting of the set of all the polymorphisms of the CSP. It turns out that two CSPs having the same associated algebra have (almost) the same query complexity, and hence we can focus on algebras, instead of relations, to classify constraint languages in terms of query complexity.

universal algebra

In Section 13.1, we formally define CSPs, notions from universal algebra, and the testing problem studied in this chapter. In Section 13.2, we will see that CSPs having a specific polymorphism, called near-unanimity, admit sublinear-query testers. In Section 13.3, we see that CSPs having the same algebra can be reduced to each other, almost maintaining the query complexity. In Section 13.4, we give a complete classification of Boolean CSPs in terms of query complexity. Finally in Section 13.5, we briefly mention additional related topics.

13.1 Definitions

13.1.1 Constraint Satisfaction Problems

constraint satisfaction
problem

relation

constraint language

instance

satisfying assignment

In this section, we define *constraint satisfaction problems*. Let D be a finite domain. For an integer $k \geq 1$, a *k-ary relation* over D is a subset of D^k. A *constraint language* over D is a finite set of relations on D. For a constraint language Γ, we define the problem $\mathrm{CSP}(D, \Gamma)$ as follows. We often omit D if it is clear from the context. An *instance* $\mathcal{I} = (V, \mathcal{C})$ consists of a set of variables V and a set of constraints $\mathcal{C}$. Here, each constraint $C \in \mathcal{C}$ is of the form $(v_1, \ldots, v_k; R)$, where $v_1, \ldots, v_k \in V$ are variables, R is a relation in Γ and k is the arity of R. We say that an assignment $f : V \to D$ is a *satisfying assignment* if it satisfies all the constraints, that is $(f(v_1), \ldots, f(v_k)) \in R$ for every constraint $C = (v_1, \ldots, v_k; R) \in \mathcal{C}$. For a tuple $\mathbf{a} \in D^k$ and a set $S \subseteq [k]$, $\mathbf{a}|_S$ denotes the projection of $\mathbf{a}$ on S. Similarly for a relation $R \subseteq D^k$, $R|_S$ denotes the relation $\{\mathbf{a}|_S : \mathbf{a} \in R\}$.

We have already seen several CSPs in Chapter 7. They can be defined in terms of constraint languages:

SAT

Horn SAT

system of linear
equations

k-colorability

- *k-SAT* corresponds to $\mathrm{CSP}(\{0,1\}, \Gamma_{k\text{-SAT}})$, where $\Gamma_{k\text{-SAT}} = \{R_\phi : \phi \in \{0,1\}^k\}$ for $R_\phi = \{0,1\}^k \setminus \{\phi\}$.
- *Horn k-SAT* corresponds to $\mathrm{CSP}(\{0,1\}, \Gamma_{k\text{-Horn}})$, where $\Gamma_{k\text{-Horn}} = \{U\} \cup \{R_{1^\ell} : \ell \leq k\} \cup \{R_{1^{\ell-1}0} : \ell \leq k\}, U = \{1\}$ and $R_{1^k}, R_{1^{k-1}0}$ as above.
- *k-LIN* corresponds to $\mathrm{CSP}(\{0,1\}, \Gamma_{k\text{-LIN}})$, where $\Gamma_{k\text{-LIN}} = \{R_0, R_1\}, R_0 = \{(x_1, \ldots, x_k) : x_1 + \cdots + x_k = 0 \pmod 2\}$, and $R_1 = \{(x_1, \ldots, x_k) : x_1 + \cdots + x_k = 1 \pmod 2\}$.
- *k-COL* corresponds to $\mathrm{CSP}(\{1, 2, \ldots, k\}, \{\neq\})$, where $\neq$ is the relation $\{(a, b) \in \{1, 2, \ldots, k\}^2 : a \neq b\}$.

Hereafter, we mainly focus on the Boolean case, that is, $D = \{0, 1\}$. However, many of the definitions introduced in the subsequent sections can be easily generalized to arbitrary D.

13.1.2 Testing CSPs

Now, we formally define the problem of testing assignments to CSPs. For two assignments $f, g : V \to \{0, 1\}$ and a weight function $\boldsymbol{w} : V \to \mathbb{R}_{\geq 0}$ with $\sum_{v \in V} \boldsymbol{w}(v) = 1$, we define their *distance* with respect to $\boldsymbol{w}$ as:

distance

$$d_{\boldsymbol{w}}(f, g) = \sum_{v \in V : f(v) \neq g(v)} \boldsymbol{w}(v).$$

Let $\mathcal{I} = (V, \mathcal{C}, \boldsymbol{w})$ be a CSP instance on n variables, where $\boldsymbol{w} : V \to \mathbb{R}_{\geq 0}$ is a weight function on variables with $\sum_{v \in V} \boldsymbol{w}(v) = 1$. Then for an assignment $f : V \to \{0, 1\}$, we define $d(f, \mathcal{I})$ as the distance of f from satisfying assignments of $\mathcal{I}$ with respect to $\boldsymbol{w}$, that is $d(f,\mathcal{I}) = \min_{f'} d_{\boldsymbol{w}}(f,f')$, where $f'\colon V \to \{0,1\}$ is over satisfying assignments of $\mathcal{I}$. We say that f is ϵ-*far* *from satisfying* $\mathcal{I}$ if $d(f,\mathcal{I}) > \epsilon$.

ϵ-farness

For a constraint language Γ, an algorithm is called a *tester for* CSP(Γ) if, given an instance $\mathcal{I} = (V,\mathcal{C},\boldsymbol{w})$ of CSP(Γ), $\epsilon \in (0,1)$, and query access to an assignment $f\colon V \to \{0,1\}$, it accepts with probability at least $2/3$ if f is a satisfying assignment of $\mathcal{I}$ and rejects with probability at least $2/3$ if f is ϵ-far from satisfying $\mathcal{I}$. We say that CSP(Γ) is *testable* with query complexity $q(n,m,\epsilon)$ if there is a tester for CSP(Γ) with query complexity $q(n,m,\epsilon)$, where $n = |V|$ and $m = |\mathcal{C}|$.

tester

testability

13.1.3 Universal Algebra

An *n-ary operation* on a set $\{0,1\}$ is a map from $\{0,1\}^n$ to $\{0,1\}$. An n-ary operation f on $\{0,1\}$ *preserves* a k-ary relation R on $\{0,1\}$ (equivalently, we say that R is *invariant* under f) if the following holds: given any matrix M of size $k \times n$ whose columns are in R, applying f to the rows of M will produce a k-tuple in R. A *polymorphism* of a constraint language Γ is an operation that preserves all relations in Γ. An operation $f\colon \{0,1\}^k \to \{0,1\}$ of the form $f(x_1,\dots,x_k) = x_i$ for some $i \in [k]$ is called a *projection*. Note that projections are polymorphisms of any constraint language. Let Pol(Γ) denote the set of all polymorphisms of Γ. For any Γ, Pol(Γ) forms a *clone*, that is, a set of operations closed under compositions and containing all the projections. Also, in fact, the converse is true: every clone can be characterized as Pol(Γ) for some set of relations Γ. An *algebra* associated with a constraint language Γ is the pair $(\{0,1\}, \mathrm{Pol}(\Gamma))$.

operation

preservation

invariance

polymorphism

projection

clone

algebra

An operation $f\colon \{0,1\}^k \to \{0,1\}$ is called *essentially unary* if we have $f(a_1,\dots,a_k) = g(a_i)$ for some $g\colon \{0,1\} \to \{0,1\}$ and $i \in [k]$. An operation $f\colon \{0,1\}^k \to \{0,1\}$ is *idempotent* if $f(0,\dots,0) = 0$ and $f(1,\dots,1) = 1$. Note that an essentially unary operation is idempotent if and only if it is a projection. Also, we note that a projection and an essentially unary operation were called a dictator and a 1-junta in Chapter 6.

essentially unary operation

idempotence

Below, we show polymorphisms for CSPs introduced in Section 7.4.

Example 13.1. Let $\oplus$ be the binary addition modulo 2. Then, 2-COL admits $\oplus$ as its polymorphism.

Example 13.2. The ternary majority operation $f\colon \{0,1\}^3 \to \{0,1\}$ is an operation such that $f(a,b,c)$ equals the majority element of the multiset $\{a,b,c\}$. Note that the majority is uniquely determined as $a,b,c \in \{0,1\}$. Then, 2-SAT admits the ternary majority operation as its polymorphism.

Example 13.3. The binary minimum operation $f\colon \{0,1\}^2 \to \{0,1\}$ is defined as $f(a,b) = \min\{a,b\}$. Then, **Horn SAT** admits the binary minimum operation as its polymorphism.

Example 13.4. The ternary minority operation $f\colon \{0,1\}^3 \to \{0,1\}$ is an operation such that $f(a,b,c)$ equals the minority element (the other element of the majority element) of the multiset $\{a,b,c\}$. Then, k-**LIN** for any $k \in \mathbb{Z}_{>0}$ admits the ternary minority operation.

near-unanimity

Example 13.5. A k-ary operation $f\colon \{0,1\}^k \to \{0,1\}$ is called a *(k-)near-unanimity* if:

$$f(b,a,\ldots,a) = f(a,b,a,\ldots,a) = \cdots = f(a,\ldots,a,b) = a$$

for every $a,b \in \{0,1\}$. Note that the ternary majority operation is a near-unanimity operation. Let $\Gamma = \{R, =, 0, 1\}$ be a constraint language, where R is a k-ary relation consisting of all the tuples having more than or equal to $k-1$ ones, $=$ is the binary equality relation, 0 is the unary constant zero relation, and 1 is the unary constant one relation. Then, Γ admits a k-near-unanimity as its polymorphism.

Some CSPs have only simple polymorphisms that depend on only one argument.

Example 13.6. 3-**SAT** admits only projections as its polymorphism.

Remarkably, although there are countably many idempotent Boolean algebras, an explicit description of them is known. When ordered by inclusion, they form a lattice known as *Post's lattice*, shown in Figure 13.1 and Table 13.1 with standard notations for relevant operations. Here, BF is the algebra consisting of all Boolean operations, and I_2 is the algebra consisting of only projections.

Post's lattice

As we mentioned, two CSPs having the same algebra have almost the same query complexity. Hence, our goal is to settle the query complexity of the CSPs associated with each algebra in Post's lattice.

Before going into details, we briefly mention the connection between the universal algebra and the polynomial-time tractability of CSPs. It is known that two CSPs having the same algebra have log-space reductions to each other, and hence to characterize polynomial-time tractable CSPs, we only have to look at algebras. Then using the machinery of universal algebra, it has been shown that a CSP is polynomial-time tractable if its associated algebra has a non-trivial operation, that is, an operation that is not essentially unary, and is NP-Complete otherwise.

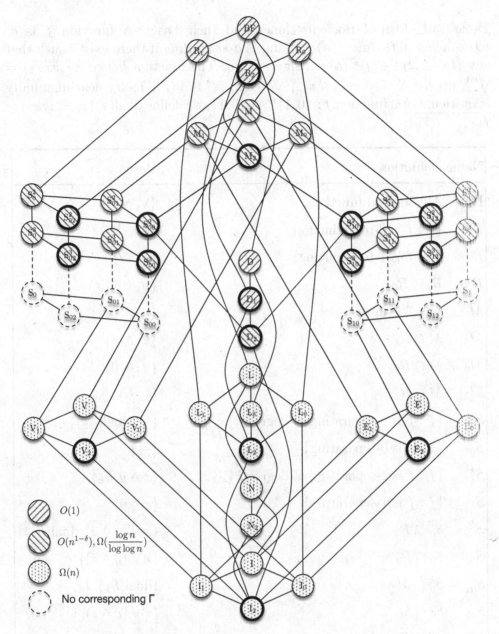

Fig. 13.1: Post's Lattice and query complexity. Here, $\delta > 0$ is a constant determined by the algebra. Algebras consisting of idempotent operations are circled in bold. No finite constraint language Γ can generate dashed clones.

Table 13.1: List of Boolean clones and their bases. A function f is a-*reproducing* if $f(a, a, \ldots, a) = a$ and is a-*separating* if there exist i such that any $(t_1, \ldots, t_k) \in f^{-1}(a)$ satisfies $t_i = a$. The function $h_k(x_1, \ldots, x_{k+1}) = \bigvee_{i=1}^{k+1}(x_1 \wedge x_2 \wedge \cdots \wedge x_{i-1} \wedge x_{i+1} \wedge \cdots \wedge x_{k+1})$ is a $(k+1)$-ary near-unanimity operation. For a function $f \colon \{0, 1\}^k \to \{0, 1\}$, we define $\mathrm{dual}(f)(x_1, \ldots, x_1) = \overline{f(\overline{x_1}, \ldots, \overline{x_k})}$.

Name	Definition	Base
BF	All Boolean functions	$\{\vee, \wedge, \neg\}$
R_0	$\{f : f \text{ is 0-reproducing}\}$	$\{\wedge, \oplus\}$
R_1	$\{f : f \text{ is 1-reproducing}\}$	$\{\vee, \leftrightarrow\}$
R_2	$R_1 \cap R_0$	$\{\vee, x \wedge (y \leftrightarrow z)\}$
M	$\{f : f \text{ is monotone}\}$	$\{\vee, \wedge, 0, 1\}$
M_1	$M \cap R_1$	$\{\vee, \wedge, 1\}$
M_0	$M \cap R_0$	$\{\vee, \wedge, 0\}$
M_2	$M \cap R_2$	$\{\vee, \wedge\}$
S_0^k	$\{f : f \text{ is 0-separating of degree } k\}$	$\{\to, \mathrm{dual}(h_k)\}$
S_0	$\{f : f \text{ is 0-separating}\}$	$\{\to\}$
S_1^k	$\{f : f \text{ is 1-separating of degree } k\}$	$\{x \wedge \overline{y}, h_k\}$
S_1	$\{f : f \text{ is 1-separating}\}$	$\{x \wedge \overline{y}\}$
S_{02}^k	$S_0^k \cap R_2$	$\{x \vee (y \wedge \overline{z}), \mathrm{dual}(h_k)\}$
S_{02}	$S_0 \cap R_2$	$\{x \vee (y \wedge \overline{z})\}$
S_{01}^k	$S_0^k \cap M$	$\{\mathrm{dual}(h_k), 1\}$
S_{01}	$S_0 \cap M$	$\{x \vee (y \wedge z), 1\}$
S_{00}^k	$S_0^k \cap R_2 \cap M$	$\{x \vee (y \wedge z), \mathrm{dual}(h_k)\}$
S_{00}	$S_0 \cap R_2 \cap M$	$\{x \vee (y \wedge z)\}$
S_{12}^k	$S_1^k \cap R_2$	$\{x \wedge (y \vee \overline{z}), h_k\}$
S_{12}	$S_1 \cap R_2$	$\{x \wedge (y \vee \overline{z})\}$
S_{11}^k	$S_1^k \cap M$	$\{h_k, 0\}$
S_{11}	$S_1 \cap M$	$\{x \wedge (y \vee z), 0\}$
S_{10}^k	$S_1^k \cap R_2 \cap M$	$\{x \wedge (y \vee z), h_k\}$

Name	Definition	Base
S_{10}	$S_1 \cap R_2 \cap M$	$\{x \wedge (y \vee z)\}$
D	$\{f : f \text{ is self-dual}\}$	$\{x\overline{y} \vee x\overline{z} \vee \overline{yz}\}$
D_1	$D \cap R_2$	$\{xy \vee x\overline{z} \vee y\overline{z}\}$
D_2	$D \cap M$	$\{xy \vee yz \vee xz\}$
L	$\{f : f \text{ is linear}\}$	$\{\oplus, 1\}$
L_0	$L \cap R_0$	$\{\oplus\}$
L_1	$L \cap R_1$	$\{\leftrightarrow\}$
L_2	$L \cap R_2$	$\{x \oplus y \oplus z\}$
L_3	$L \cap D$	$\{x \oplus y \oplus z \oplus 1\}$
V	$\{f : f \text{ is constant or a } k\text{-ary OR function}\}$	$\{\vee, 0, 1\}$
V_0	$[\{\vee\}] \cup [\{0\}]$	$\{\vee, 0\}$
V_1	$[\{\vee\}] \cup [\{1\}]$	$\{\vee, 1\}$
V_2	$[\{\vee\}]$	$\{\vee\}$
E	$\{f : f \text{ is constant or a } k\text{-ary AND function}\}$	$\{\wedge, 0, 1\}$
E_0	$[\{\wedge\}] \cup [\{0\}]$	$\{\wedge, 0\}$
E_1	$[\{\wedge\}] \cup [\{1\}]$	$\{\wedge, 1\}$
E_2	$[\{\wedge\}]$	$\{\wedge\}$
N	$[\{\neg\}] \cup [\{0\}] \cup [\{1\}]$	$\{\neg, 1\}$
N_2	$[\{\neg\}]$	$\{\neg\}$
I	$[\{\text{id}\}] \cup [\{0\}] \cup [\{1\}]$	$\{\text{id}, 0, 1\}$
I_0	$[\{\text{id}\}] \cup [\{0\}]$	$\{\text{id}, 0\}$
I_1	$[\{\text{id}\}] \cup [\{1\}]$	$\{\text{id}, 1\}$
I_2	$[\{\text{id}\}]$	$\{\text{id}\}$

Exercise 13.1. Show that $\text{dual}(h_k)$ is a near-unanimity operation.

13.2 CSPs Closed under $(k+1)$-Near-Unanimity

Before showing that the algebra associated with a CSP determines its constant-query and sublinear-query testability, we look that the existence of a certain polymorphism is helpful to design a sublinear-query tester. In this section, we show that if a CSP has a $(k+1)$-ary near-unanimity as its polymorphism, then it can be tested with $O(n^{1-1/k})$ queries.

We first review properties of $(k+1)$-ary near-unanimity operations. First, if a relation R is preserved by a $(k+1)$-ary near-unanimity operation, then R can be made k-ary by projecting R into every k-sized subset. More specifically, the following holds:

Lemma 13.1 ([173, 268]). *Let R be a relation preserved by a $(k+1)$-ary near-unanimity operation. Then, a tuple $\mathbf{a}$ belongs to R if and only if $\mathbf{a}|_U$ belongs to $R|_U$ for every subset U with $|U| = k$.*

Hence, when testing a CSP closed under a $(k+1)$-ary near-unanimity operation, we can assume that $\mathcal{I}$ consists of constraints of arity at most k.

Example 13.7. Let $R \subseteq \{0,1\}^3$ be a relation consisting of the following five tuples:

$$R = \left\{ \begin{array}{l} (1\ 1\ 0), \\ (0\ 0\ 1), \\ (0\ 1\ 1), \\ (1\ 0\ 1), \\ (1\ 1\ 1) \end{array} \right\}$$

We can easily verify R is preserved by the majority operation, which is 3-near-unanimity. Then, we can decompose R into the following three relations

$$R_{12} = \left\{ \begin{array}{l} (0\ 0), \\ (0\ 1), \\ (1\ 0), \\ (1\ 1) \end{array} \right\}, \quad R_{13} = \left\{ \begin{array}{l} (0\ 1), \\ (1\ 0), \\ (1\ 1) \end{array} \right\}, \quad R_{23} = \left\{ \begin{array}{l} (0\ 1), \\ (1\ 0), \\ (1\ 1) \end{array} \right\},$$

where R_{ij} is the projection of R onto the set $\{i, j\}$. We can check (by brute force) that a tuple $(a, b, c) \in R$ if and only if $(a, b) \in R_{12}$, $(a, c) \in R_{13}$, and $(a, c) \in R_{13}$.

Now, we introduce a propagation-type algorithm called (k, ℓ)-**Minimality** for deciding the satisfiability of a CSP instance. Let k, ℓ be positive integers with $k \leq \ell$. Let $\mathcal{U} = \{U \subseteq V : |U| = \ell\}$ be the family of sets of ℓ variables. For each $U \in \mathcal{U}$, we keep track of a set of partial assignments $\mathcal{S}_U \subseteq \{0,1\}^{|U|}$. Here, $\mathcal{S}_U$ maintains assignments on U that can be potentially extended to satisfying assignments on the whole domain. We initialize $\mathcal{S}_U$ as all partial assignments satisfying constraints whose domain is contained in U. Let $U, U' \in \mathcal{U}$ be sets of variables with $|U \cap U'| \leq k$. Then, we eliminate tuples $\mathbf{a}$ from $\mathcal{S}_U$ if $\mathbf{a}|_{U \cap U'}$ is not contained in $\mathcal{S}_{U'}|_{U \cap U'}$. We continue this process until no update occurs. For a set $W \subseteq V$ of less than ℓ variables, we define $\mathcal{S}_W$ as the projection of $\mathcal{S}_U$ on W, where U is any superset of W with ℓ variables. If $\mathcal{S}_U$ becomes empty for some set U of k variables, we can safely conclude that there is no satisfying assignment. Even if no $\mathcal{S}_U$ is empty when propagation stops, there may not exist a satisfying assignment in general. However, the following holds for CSPs with a near-unanimity operation as its polymorphism.

Lemma 13.2. *Let Γ be a constraint language preserved by a $(k+1)$-ary near-unanimity operation. Then, $(k, k+1)$-Minimality correctly decides the satisfiability of an instance of $\mathrm{CSP}(\Gamma)$.*

Also, the following k-Helly property is known.

Lemma 13.3 (k-Helly property). *Let Γ be a constraint language preserved by a $(k+1)$-ary near-unanimity operation. Let $\mathcal{I}$ be an instance of $\mathrm{CSP}(\Gamma)$ on a variable set V and let $\{\mathcal{S}_U : U \subseteq V, |U| = k\}$ be the family of sets of partial assignments obtained by running $(k, k+1)$-Minimality on $\mathcal{I}$. Then, any partial assignment $\mathbf{a} \in \{0,1\}^S$ for $S \subseteq V$ such that $\mathbf{a}|_U \in \mathcal{S}_U$ for every $U \subseteq S$ with $|U| \leq k$ can be extended to a satisfying assignment for $\mathcal{I}$.*

We say that a subset of variables $U \subseteq V$ of size at most k is *violating* with respect to an assignment $f : V \to \{0,1\}$ if $f|_U \notin \mathcal{S}_U$. The following is an extension of Corollary 7.1:

Lemma 13.4. *Let Γ be a constraint language preserved by a $(k+1)$-ary near-unanimity operation and let $\mathcal{I} = (V, \mathcal{C}, \mathbf{w})$ be an instance of $\mathrm{CSP}(\Gamma)$ on n variables. If an assignment $f : V \to A$ is ϵ-far from satisfying $\mathcal{I}$, then there is a family $\mathcal{S}$ of disjoint violating sets such that:*

$$\sum_{S \in \mathcal{S}} \prod_{v \in S} \mathbf{w}(v) \geq \frac{\epsilon^k}{k 2^k n^{k-1}}.$$

Proof. Let V' be the set of variables v such that $\mathbf{w}(v) \geq \epsilon/(2n)$ and let $\mathcal{U}$ be the family of violating sets $S \subseteq V'$ of size k. We say that a subset $H \subseteq V'$ is a *hitting set* of $\mathcal{U}$ if H intersects with all the sets in $\mathcal{U}$. We first observe that for any hitting set $H \subseteq V'$ of $\mathcal{U}$, the partial assignment $f|_{V' \setminus H}$ can be extended to a satisfying assignment for $\mathcal{I}$. Indeed, if $f|_{V' \setminus H}$ cannot not be extended, then there must be a variable set $S \subseteq V' \setminus H$ with $|S| = k$ and

$f|_S \notin R_S$ from the Helly property. However, such a set S must be a member of $\mathcal{U}$, contradicting the fact that H is a hitting set.

Since f is ϵ-far and every variable in $V \setminus V'$ has a weight at most $\epsilon/(2n)$, we have $\sum_{v \in H} \boldsymbol{w}(v) \geq \epsilon - \epsilon/(2n) \cdot n = \epsilon/2$. Then, we can take a family $\mathcal{S}$ of disjoint violating sets such that $\sum_{S \in \mathcal{S}} \sum_{v \in S} \boldsymbol{w}(v) \geq \epsilon/2$. In particular, this means that:

$$\sum_{S \in \mathcal{S}} \prod_{v \in S} \boldsymbol{w}(v) \geq \left(\frac{\epsilon}{2n}\right)^{k-1} \sum_{S \in \mathcal{S}} \max_{v \in S} \boldsymbol{w}(v) \geq \frac{1}{k}\left(\frac{\epsilon}{2n}\right)^{k-1} \sum_{S \in \mathcal{S}} \sum_{v \in S} \boldsymbol{w}(v)$$

$$\geq \frac{\epsilon}{2k}\left(\frac{\epsilon}{2n}\right)^{k-1} = \frac{\epsilon^k}{k2^k n^{k-1}}. \qquad \square$$

The tester, given in Algorithm 13.1, simply samples $\Theta(n^{k-1})$ variables (in expectation) and checks whether there is a violating set within the variables.

Algorithm 13.1 Testing CSPs closed under a near-unanimity operation

---

Input: An instance $\mathcal{I} = (V, \mathcal{C})$, $\epsilon \in (0, 1)$, and query access to $f : V \to \{0, 1\}$.
1: Run $(k, k+1)$-minimality and obtain a family of sets $\{\mathcal{S}_U : U \subseteq V, |U| \leq k\}$.
2: $q \leftarrow \Theta(\epsilon^{-1} k^{1/k} n^{1-1/k})$.
3: Let S be the set obtained by sampling each variable v with probability $q \cdot \boldsymbol{w}(v)$.
4: **if** $|S| > 10q$ **then**
5:      Accept.
6: **end if**
7: Query $f(v)$ for each variable in S.
8: **if** there exists a violating set $U \subseteq S$ (of size at most k) with respect to f **then**
9:      Reject.
10: **else**
11:      Accept.
12: **end if**

Lemma 13.5. *Let Γ be a constraint language such that $\mathrm{Pol}(\Gamma)$ contains a $(k+1)$-ary near-unanimity operation. Algorithm 13.1 is a one-sided error tester for $\mathrm{CSP}(\Gamma)$ with query complexity $O\left(\epsilon^{-1} n^{1-1/k}\right)$.*

Proof. It is easy to see that the algorithm always accepts if f is a satisfying assignment (no matter whether we stopped the process due to $|S|$ being large).

Now, we see that the algorithm rejects with high probability when the input is ϵ-far. From Markov's inequality, the probability that the number of queries exceeds $10q$ is at most $1/10$.

From Lemma 13.4, there is a family $\mathcal{S}$ of disjoint violating sets such that $\sum_{S \in \mathcal{S}} \prod_{v \in S} \boldsymbol{w}(v) \geq \frac{\epsilon^k}{k2^k n^{k-1}}$. Note that for each violating set $S \in \mathcal{S}$, the probability that we do not detect S is $1 - \prod_{v \in S}(q \cdot \boldsymbol{w}(v)) = 1 - q^k \prod_{x \in S} \boldsymbol{w}(v)$. Thus, because violating sets in $\mathcal{S}$ are disjoint, the probability that we do not detect any violating set is at most:

$$\prod_{S \in \mathcal{S}} \left(1 - q^k \prod_{x \in S} \boldsymbol{w}(x) \right) \leq \prod_{S \in \mathcal{S}} \exp \left(-q^k \prod_{x \in S} \boldsymbol{w}(x) \right)$$

$$= \exp \left(-q^k \sum_{S \in \mathcal{S}} \prod_{x \in S} \boldsymbol{w}(x) \right) \leq \exp \left(-q^k \frac{\epsilon^k}{k 2^k n^{k-1}} \right).$$

If we choose the constant hidden in q to be large enough, the probability above is bounded by $1/10$. Thus by the union bound, we reject with probability at least $1 - 2/10 \geq 2/3$. $\qquad\square$

13.3 Reductions between CSPs

In this section, we show that, if two constraint languages Γ and Γ' have the same algebra, then testing $\mathrm{CSP}(\Gamma)$ and $\mathrm{CSP}(\Gamma')$ have almost the same query complexity. We will also show that we can restrict our attention to CSPs with idempotent polymorphisms only without much loss of generality.

The results in this section are obtained through a sequence of reductions. First, we rephrase the definition of the gap-preserving local reduction (Definition 2.1) for testing CSPs.

gap-preserving local reduction

Definition 13.1 (Gap-preserving local reductions). Given constraint languages Γ, Γ', a *gap-preserving local reduction from* $\mathrm{CSP}(\Gamma')$ *to* $\mathrm{CSP}(\Gamma)$ exists if there are functions $t_1(n,m), t_2(n,m)$ and constants c_1, c_2 satisfying the following: given an instance $\mathcal{I}' = (V', \mathcal{C}', \boldsymbol{w}')$ of $\mathrm{CSP}(\Gamma')$, $\epsilon' \in (0,1)$, and an assignment $f' : V' \to \{0,1\}$ for $\mathcal{I}'$, there exist an instance $\mathcal{I} = (V, \mathcal{C}, \boldsymbol{w})$ of $\mathrm{CSP}(\Gamma)$, $\epsilon \in (0,1)$, and an assignment $f : V \to \{0,1\}$ for $\mathcal{I}$ such that:

(i) $|V| \leq t_1(|V'|, |\mathcal{C}'|)$.
(ii) $|\mathcal{C}| \leq t_2(|V'|, |\mathcal{C}'|)$.
(iii) If f' satisfies $\mathcal{I}'$, then f also satisfies $\mathcal{I}$.
(iv) If f' is ϵ'-far from satisfying $\mathcal{I}$, then f is $(c_1 \epsilon)$-far from satisfying $\mathcal{I}$.
(v) We can compute $f(v)$ for any $v \in V$ by querying f' at most c_2 times.

Lemma 13.6. *For constraint languages* Γ, Γ', *if there exists a tester for* $\mathrm{CSP}(\Gamma)$ *with query complexity* $q(n, m, \epsilon)$ *and a gap-preserving local reduction from* $\mathrm{CSP}(\Gamma')$ *to* $\mathrm{CSP}(\Gamma)$, *then there exists a tester for* $\mathrm{CSP}(\Gamma')$ *with query complexity* $O(q(t_1(n,m), t_2(n,m), O(\epsilon)))$.

Proof. Let $(\mathcal{I}', \epsilon', f')$ be an input of $\mathrm{CSP}(\Gamma')$ and let $(\mathcal{I}, \epsilon, f)$ be the input of $\mathrm{CSP}(\Gamma)$ given by the reduction. We run a tester $\mathcal{T}$ with an error parameter $c_1 \epsilon$. If f' is a satisfying assignment, then $\mathcal{T}$ accepts with probability at least $2/3$. If f' is ϵ-far from satisfying assignments, then $\mathcal{T}$ rejects with probability at least 2/3. In both cases, Since we can compute the value of $f(v)$ by querying f' at most c_2 times, the number of queries to f' is at most $c_2 q(t_1(n, m), t_2(n, m), c_1 \epsilon) = O(q(t_1(n, m), t_2(n, m), O(\epsilon)))$. □

We say that a k-ary relation R is *redundant* if there exist $i, j \in [k]$ such that for any $(a_1, \ldots, a_k) \in R$, we have $a_i = a_j$. Then we have:

Lemma 13.7. *For a constraint language* Γ, *suppose that* $\mathrm{CSP}(\Gamma)$ *is testable with* $q(n, m, \epsilon)$ *queries. If* Γ' *is a constraint language with no redundant relation and* $\mathrm{Pol}(\Gamma') \supseteq \mathrm{Pol}(\Gamma)$, *then* $\mathrm{CSP}(\Gamma')$ *is testable with* $q(O(n + m), O(m), O(\epsilon))$ *queries.*

Proof. It is known that any relation in Γ' can be obtained from relations in Γ by a finite sequence of the following steps:

1. Removing a relation;
2. Adding a relation obtained by permuting the variables of a relation;
3. Adding the intersection of two relations of the same arity;
4. Adding the product of two relations. (For two relations R and R', their *product* is $\{\mathbf{a} \circ \mathbf{a}' : \mathbf{a} \in R, \mathbf{a}' \in R'\}$, where $\circ$ is the concatenation.);
5. Adding a relation obtained by projecting an k-ary relation to its first $k-1$ variables.

(We note that, if Γ' has a redundant relation, then we also need another step of adding the equality relation.)

We now show that $\mathrm{CSP}(\Gamma')$ is testable with query complexity $q(O(n + m), O(m), O(\epsilon))$. To this end, assuming that Γ' is obtained by any of the five constructions from Γ, we will give a gap-preserving local reduction from $\mathrm{CSP}(\Gamma')$ to $\mathrm{CSP}(\Gamma)$ with $t_1(n, m) \leq n + m, t_2(n, m) \leq 2m, c_1 = c_2 = O(1)$. Then, the lemma follows by iteratively applying Lemma 13.6.

We use the following approach to show a gap-preserving local reduction from Γ' to Γ. Let $(\mathcal{I}' = (V', \mathcal{C}', \boldsymbol{w}'), f')$ be an input of $\mathrm{CSP}(\Gamma')$. Then, we construct another input $(\mathcal{I} = (V, \mathcal{C}, \boldsymbol{w}), f)$ of $\mathrm{CSP}(\Gamma)$ so that the construction satisfies conditions of gap-preserving local reductions. We omit to verify conditions (i), (ii), (iii) and (v) as they are straightforward. We will also omit to verify condition (iv) for the first four cases, because it is easy noting that the variable set and the set of satisfying assignments stay the same. In each of the five steps, V is a superset of V' and we set $\boldsymbol{w}(v) = \boldsymbol{w}'(v)$ for every $v \in V'$.

1. Let us suppose first that Γ' is obtained from Γ by removing a relation of Γ. Then, we simply set $\mathcal{I} = \mathcal{I}'$ and $f = f'$ because $\mathcal{I}'$ is also an instance of $\mathrm{CSP}(\Gamma)$.

2. Let us suppose that Γ' is obtained from Γ by adding a relation S obtained from a relation R of Γ by permuting the variables according to a permutation π. Then, we set $\mathcal{I}$ to be the instance obtained from $\mathcal{I}'$ by

(marginal notes) redundant relation

product

replacing each constraint of the form $(v_1, \ldots, v_r; S)$ with the constraint $(v_{\pi(1)}, \ldots, v_{\pi(r)}, R)$. We then set $f = f'$.

3. Let R and S be two relations of the same arity of Γ. Let T denote the intersection of R and S. Let us suppose that Γ' is obtained from Γ by adding the relation T. Then, we set $\mathcal{I}$ to be the instance obtained from $\mathcal{I}'$ by replacing each constraint of the form $(v_1, \ldots, v_r; T)$ with the constraints $(v_1, \ldots, v_r; R)$ and $(v_1, \ldots, v_r; S)$. We then set $f = f'$.

4. Let R and S be two relations of Γ. Let T denote the product of R and S and Γ' be obtained from Γ by adding the relation T. Then, we set $\mathcal{I}$ to be the instance obtained from $\mathcal{I}'$ by replacing each constraint of the form $(v_1, \ldots, v_r, v_{r+1}, \ldots, v_{r+s}; T)$, where r and s are arities of R and S, respectively, with the constraints $(v_1, \ldots, v_r; R)$ and $(v_{r+1}, \ldots, v_{r+s}; S)$. We then set $f = f'$.

5. Let us suppose that Γ' is obtained from Γ by adding the projection S of an r-ary relation R of Γ to its first $r - 1$ variables. Then, we set $\mathcal{I}$ to be the instance obtained from $\mathcal{I}'$ by replacing each constraint of the form $C = (v_1, \ldots, v_{r-1}; S)$ with $(v_1, \ldots, v_{r-1}, v_C; R)$, where v_C is a newly introduced vertex, and then set $\boldsymbol{w}(v_C) = 0$.

   We define $f \colon V \to \{0, 1\}$ as follows: For each $v \in V'$, we set $f(v) = f'(v)$. For each variable v_C corresponding to a constraint of the form $C = (v_1, \ldots, v_{r-1}; S)$, we define $f(v_C)$ as follows. If there exists some $a \in \{0, 1\}$ such that $(f(v_1), \ldots, f(v_{r-1}), a) \in R$, then we set $f(v_C) = a$. Otherwise, we set an arbitrary value to $f(v_C)$.

   Now, we check the condition (iv). Let $f^* \colon V \to \{0, 1\}$ be an arbitrary satisfying assignment for $\mathcal{I}$ closest to f. Then, we define an assignment $\widetilde{f}' \colon V' \to \{0, 1\}$ for $\mathcal{I}'$ as $\widetilde{f}'(v) = f^*(v)$. It is easy to check that $\widetilde{f}'$ is a satisfying assignment for $\mathcal{I}'$ and $d_{\boldsymbol{w}}(f, f^*) = d_{\boldsymbol{w}'}(f', \widetilde{f}') > \epsilon$ from the ϵ-farness of $\mathcal{I}'$. $\qquad\square$

Next, we show that Γ' can be assumed to only have idempotent polymorphisms without much loss of generality. Given a constraint language Γ, define the *singleton-expansion of* Γ to be $\Gamma' = \Gamma \cup \{\{0\}, \{1\}\}$. $\mathrm{Pol}(\Gamma')$ consists of exactly the idempotent polymorphisms of Γ since any polymorphism that preserves the relations $\{0\}$ and $\{1\}$ must be idempotent. We show a gap-preserving local reduction from $\mathrm{CSP}(\Gamma')$ to $\mathrm{CSP}(\Gamma)$.

singleton-expansion

> **Lemma 13.8.** *For a constraint language Γ, let Γ' be its singleton-expansion. Assume that $\epsilon \ll 1/2$. If $\mathrm{CSP}(\Gamma)$ is testable with $q(n, m, \epsilon)$ queries, then $\mathrm{CSP}(\Gamma')$ is testable with $q(O(n), O(m), O(\epsilon))$ queries.*

Proof. Suppose that $\mathrm{CSP}(\Gamma)$ is testable with $q(n, m, \epsilon)$ queries. Now, given an instance $\mathcal{I}' = (V', \mathcal{C}', \boldsymbol{w}')$ of $\mathrm{CSP}(\Gamma')$, we want to test whether f' is a satisfying assignment or is ϵ-far from satisfying $\mathcal{I}'$. For $i \in \{0, 1\}$, define

$V_i' \subseteq V'$ to be the set of all variables v for which there is a constraint $v = i$ in $\mathcal{C}'$. We say that f' is ϵ-far from singleton-consistency if

$$\sum_{v \in V_0', f(v)=1} \boldsymbol{w}'(v) + \sum_{v \in V_1', f(v)=0} \boldsymbol{w}'(v) > \epsilon.$$

By applying Lemma 2.1, we can $\epsilon/2$-test singleton-consistency with $O(\epsilon^{-1})$ queries and success probability at least $5/6$.

In what follows, we assume that this singleton-consistency test has succeeded. Let $\mathcal{C}$ be a set of constraints obtained from $\mathcal{C}'$ by removing all constraints using relations $\{0\}$ or $\{1\}$. Then, we run the tester for CSP(Γ) on the instance $\mathcal{I} := (V, \mathcal{C}, \boldsymbol{w})$, where $V = V'$ and $\boldsymbol{w} = \boldsymbol{w}'$, and the assignment f with a parameter $\epsilon/2$ and a success probability $5/6$.

If f' satisfies $\mathcal{I}'$, then f also satisfies $\mathcal{I}$, and the test accepts with probability at least $5/6$. If f' is ϵ-far from satisfying $\mathcal{I}$, then as the singleton-consistency test has passed, f must be still $\epsilon/2$-far from satisfying $\mathcal{I}$. Hence, the test rejects with probability at least $5/6$.

By the union bound, in both cases, we correctly answer with probability at least $2/3$.   □

13.4 Classification of Structures

We prove the classification shown in Figure 13.1 in this section. See Figure 13.1 and Table 13.1 for the definitions of the algebras used in this section.

First, we focus on constraint languages Γ for which all polymorphisms are idempotent.

Theorem 13.1. *Let Γ be a constraint language such that all its polymorphisms are idempotent. Then, the following hold:*

- *If $\mathrm{Pol}(\Gamma) \in \{D_1, R_2\}$, then CSP($\Gamma$) is testable with $O(1)$ queries.*
- *If $S_{00} \subseteq \mathrm{Pol}(\Gamma) \subseteq S_{02}^2, S_{10} \subseteq \mathrm{Pol}(\Gamma) \subseteq S_{12}^2$ or $\mathrm{Pol}(\Gamma) \in \{D_2, M_2\}$, then testing CSP($\Gamma$) requires $\Omega(\frac{\log n}{\log\log n})$ queries and is testable with $o(n)$ queries. The lower bound holds even when $m = n^{1+O(\frac{1}{\log\log n})}$.*
- *If $\mathrm{Pol}(\Gamma) \in \{I_2, E_2, V_2, L_2\}$, then testing CSP($\Gamma$) requires $\Omega(n)$ queries. The lower bound holds even when $m = O(n)$.*

Proof. Propositions 13.1, 13.2, 13.3 and 13.4 below imply the claim.   □

Proposition 13.1. *If $\mathrm{Pol}(\Gamma) \in \{D_1, R_2\}$, then CSP($\Gamma$) is testable with $O(1)$ queries.*

Proof. For $R = x \wedge (y \oplus z)$, we have $\mathrm{Pol}(\{R\}) = D_1$. Thus from Lemma 13.7, it suffices to show that $\mathrm{CSP}(\{R\})$ is testable with $O(1)$ queries. However, the problem is just **2-COL** plus constant relations, which is testable with $O(1)$ queries by Theorem 7.1. As $D_1 \subseteq R_2$, we have that $CSP(\Gamma)$ with $\mathrm{Pol}(\Gamma) = R_2$ is also testable with $O(1)$ queries. $\square$

Proposition 13.2. *If* $S_{00} \subseteq \mathrm{Pol}(\Gamma) \subseteq S_{02}^2, S_{10} \subseteq \mathrm{Pol}(\Gamma) \subseteq S_{12}^2$ *or* $\mathrm{Pol}(\Gamma) \in \{D_2, M_2\}$, *then we can test* $\mathrm{CSP}(\Gamma)$ *with* $o(n)$ *queries.*

Proof. If $\mathrm{Pol}(\Gamma) \in \{D_2, M_2\}$, then the algebra contains a majority operation, and hence $\mathrm{CSP}(\Gamma)$ is testable with $O(\sqrt{n})$ queries by Lemma 13.5. Otherwise, $\mathrm{Pol}(\Gamma) \in \{S_{00}^k, S_{10}^k, S_{02}^k, S_{12}^k\}$ for some finite $k \geq 2$ since we assume that each relation in Γ has finite arity. In any case, $\mathrm{Pol}(\Gamma)$ contains the $(k+1)$-ary near-unanimity operation h_k or $\mathrm{dual}(h_k)$. Thus, we can test $\mathrm{CSP}(\Gamma)$ with $O(n^{1-1/k})$ queries from Lemma 13.5. $\square$

Proposition 13.3. *If* $S_{00} \subseteq \mathrm{Pol}(\Gamma) \subseteq S_{02}^2, S_{10} \subseteq \mathrm{Pol}(\Gamma) \subseteq S_{12}^2$ *or* $\mathrm{Pol}(\Gamma) \in \{D_2, M_2\}$, *then testing* $\mathrm{CSP}(\Gamma)$ *requires* $\Omega(\frac{\log n}{\log \log n})$ *queries.*

Proof. It suffices to consider maximal algebras, that is, M_2, S_{02}^2, and S_{12}^2.

Suppose $\mathrm{Pol}(\Gamma) = M_2$, and assume that we can test $\mathrm{CSP}(\Gamma)$ with $o(\frac{\log n}{\log \log n})$ queries. Since the relation $(\rightarrow)$ is not redundant and is invariant under M_2, we have a tester for $\mathrm{CSP}(\{\rightarrow\})$ with $o(\frac{\log(n+m)}{\log \log n})$ queries from Lemma 13.7. However, we have a lower bound of $\Omega(\frac{\log n}{\log \log n})$ even when $m = n^{1+O(\frac{1}{\log \log n})}$ from Lemma 7.5, contradiction.

Similarly, we can show lower bounds for the cases $\mathrm{Pol}(\Gamma) = S_{02}^2$ and $\mathrm{Pol}(\Gamma) = S_{12}^2$ using relations $(\vee)$ and $(\wedge)$, respectively. $\square$

Proposition 13.4. *If* $\mathrm{Pol}(\Gamma) \in \{I_2, E_2, V_2, L_2\}$, *then testing* $\mathrm{CSP}(\Gamma)$ *requires* $\Omega(n)$ *queries.*

Proof. It suffices to consider maximal algebras, that is, L_2, E_2, and V_2.

Suppose that $\mathrm{Pol}(\Gamma) = L_2$, and we can test $\mathrm{CSP}(\Gamma)$ with $o(n)$ queries. We note that $R = \{(x, y, z) : x + y + z = 0 \ (\mathrm{mod}\ 2)\}$ in Theorem 5.12 satisfies $\mathrm{Pol}(\{R\}) = L_2$. Then, since R is not redundant, from Lemma 13.7, we have a tester for $\mathrm{CSP}(\{R\})$ with $o(n+m)$ queries. However, we have a lower bound of $\Omega(n)$ even when $m = O(n)$ from Theorem 7.6, contradiction.

Note that algebras corresponding to **Horn 3-SAT** and **Dual Horn 3-SAT** are E_2 and V_2, respectively. By reduction to **3-LIN**, one can show an $\Omega(n)$ lower bound for these CSPs even when $m = O(n)$ (Problem 13.7). Hence, we have the desired lower bound for E_2 and V_2. $\square$

In Figure 13.1, the clones handled in Theorem 13.1 are circled in bold. We can classify the remaining clones using Lemma 13.8, but we omit the straightforward details.

13.5 Additional Topics

In this chapter, we have considered testing whether an assignment to an instance of a constraint satisfaction problem (CSP) is a satisfying assignment. Because the object to be tested is the assignment, the assignment is given through query access and the instance is explicitly given as a part of the input. Another natural testing problem on CSPs is testing whether a CSP instance is satisfiable or not. In this case, because the object to be tested is the instance, it should be given through query access. As with graph property testing, depending on the instance is dense or not, we can think of two different models, that is, an extension of the adjacency matrix model (Chapter 4) and that of the bounded-degree model (Chapter 5). In this section, we briefly explain known results on those models.

Dense Model

dense model

The *dense model* is an extension of the adjacency matrix model for graphs. The dense model is parameterized by a domain D, an integer $k \in \mathbb{Z}_{>0}$, and a constraint language Γ consisting of k-ary relations, where we regard $|D|$ and k as constants. In this model, we assume for the instance $\mathcal{I} = (V, \mathcal{C})$ of $\mathrm{CSP}(D, \Gamma)$ to have at most one constraint for each tuple $(v_1, \ldots, v_k) \in V^k$. Let $R_\emptyset = D^k$ be a trivial relation. Then, we identify $\mathcal{I}$ with a function $f_{\mathcal{I}} \colon V^k \to \Gamma \cup \{R_\emptyset\}$ such that $f_{\mathcal{I}}(v_1, \ldots, v_k) = R$ if there is a constraint of the form $(v_1, \ldots, v_k; R)$ spanning $v_1, \ldots, v_k$, and $f_{\mathcal{I}}(v_1, \ldots, v_k) = R_\emptyset$ otherwise. Then, we access $\mathcal{I}$ through query access to $f_{\mathcal{I}}$. To avoid receiving the whole variable set V as a part of the input we assume $V = [n]$ for an integer $n \in \mathbb{Z}_>$ as in the graph case.

ϵ-farness

tester

For $\epsilon \in (0, 1)$, we say that an instance $\mathcal{I}$ on n variables is *ϵ-far from being satisfiable* if we need to remove more than ϵn^k constraints to make it satisfiable. An algorithm is said to be a *tester* for $\mathrm{CSP}(D, \Gamma)$ if, given an integer $n \in \mathbb{Z}_{>0}$, an error parameter $\epsilon \in (0, 1)$, and query access to an instance $\mathcal{I}$ of $\mathrm{CSP}(D, \Gamma)$ on n variables, it accepts with probability at least $2/3$ if $\mathcal{I}$ is satisfiable, and rejects with probability at least $2/3$ if $\mathcal{I}$ is ϵ-far from being satisfiable.

Frieze and Kannan [196] showed that, for any Γ over the Boolean domain $\{0, 1\}$ consisting of k-ary relations, one can approximate the maximum number of satisfiable constraints in an $\mathrm{CSP}(\{0, 1\}, \Gamma)$ to within ϵn^k with $\exp(\mathrm{poly}(\epsilon^{-1}))$ queries. This immediately gives a tester for $\mathrm{CSP}(\{0, 1\}, \Gamma)$

with $\exp(\text{poly}(\epsilon^{-1}))$ queries. In particular, their result implies that Γ does not affect the query complexity.

The focus of most of the existing works on testing CSPs in the dense model is the sample complexity of the *canonical tester*, which samples a constant number of variables, queries all the k-tuples consisting of sampled variables, and decide its output. Note that the canonical tester with a sample complexity s has a query complexity at most s^k. Andersson and Engebretsen [27] developed a two-sided error tester with a sample complexity $O(\epsilon^{-5})$. Alon, de la Vega, Kannan, and Karpinski [26] showed that one can approximate the maximum number of satisfiable constraints up to ϵn^k with sample complexity $O(\epsilon^{-12})$. Alon and Shapira [18] gave a one-sided error tester with a sample complexity $O(\epsilon^{-2})$. Finally, Sohler [374] improved the sample complexity to $\widetilde{O}(\epsilon^{-1})$, which almost matches a trivial lower bound of $\Omega(\epsilon^{-1})$.

Bounded-Degree Model

Next, we proceed to the *bounded-degree model*. The bounded-degree model is parameterized by a domain D, an integer $k \in \mathbb{Z}_{>0}$, a constraint language Γ consisting of relations of arity at most k, and a degree bound $d \in \mathbb{Z}_{>0}$. The *degree* of a variable $v \in V$ in a CSP instance is the number of constraints in which it appears. In this model, we assume for every variable of the input instance $\mathcal{I} = (V, \mathcal{C})$ of $\mathrm{CSP}(D, \Gamma)$ to have degree at most d. Such an instance $\mathcal{I}$ is provided through query access $\mathcal{O}_\mathcal{I} : V \times [d] \to \mathcal{C} \cup \{\bot\}$, where, for each variable $u \in V$, the set:

$$\{\mathcal{O}_\mathcal{I}(u, i) : i \in [d]\}$$

contains each constraint in which u appears exactly once and $d - \deg(u)$ many $\bot$'s, where $\deg(u)$ is the degree of u.

In the bounded-degree graph model with a degree bound $d \in \mathbb{Z}_{>0}$, we say that an instance $\mathcal{I} = (V, \mathcal{C})$ on n variables with a degree bound d is ϵ-*far* from being satisfiable if we must remove more than $\epsilon d n$ constraints in order to make it satisfiable. An algorithm is said to be a *tester* for $\mathrm{CSP}(D, \Gamma)$ if, given an integer $n \in \mathbb{Z}_{>0}$, an error parameter $\epsilon \in (0, 1)$, and query access to an instance $\mathcal{I}$ of $\mathrm{CSP}(D, \Gamma)$ on n variables with degree bound d, it accepts with probability at least $2/3$ if $\mathcal{I}$ is satisfiable, and rejects with probability at least $2/3$ if $\mathcal{I}$ is ϵ-far from being satisfiable.

In contrast to the dense model, the query complexity for testing $\mathrm{CSP}(D, \Gamma)$ significantly varies depending on the constraint language Γ. For example, Horn k-SAT is constant-query testable [406] whereas testing 2-COL requires $\Omega(\sqrt{n})$ queries as we have seen in Section 5.5.2. Moreover, testing 3-COL and 3-SAT requires $\Omega(n)$ queries as we have seen in Section 5.6. Yoshida [399] characterized constant-query testable CSPs in the bounded-degree model using a linear programming relaxation called a *basic LP* [290]. Intuitively, this LP makes up a local distribution over assignments for each constraint that are consistent at each variable so that the sum of probabilities that constraints are satisfied by the local distributions is maximized. As the basic LP is a relaxation, there are local distributions that satisfy all the constraints with probability one if the instance is truly satisfiable, but the converse may not hold in general. We say that the basic LP *refutes* an unsatisfiable CSP instance if the converse holds, that is, there are no local distributions that satisfy all the constraints with probability one, and that it *refutes* $\mathrm{CSP}(D, \Gamma)$ if it refutes all unsatisfiable instances of $\mathrm{CSP}(D, \Gamma)$. A concrete example of CSPs refuted by the basic LP is Horn-SAT, and see [290] for more examples. Yoshida [399] showed that one can test $\mathrm{CSP}(D, \Gamma)$ with a constant number of queries if it is refutable by the basic LP, and that we need $\Omega(\sqrt{n})$ queries otherwise.

13.6 Bibliographic Notes

The fact that every clone can be characterized as $\mathrm{Pol}(\Gamma)$ for some set of relations Γ was shown in [350]. Post's lattice in Figure 13.1 was obtained in [351]. Lemmas 13.2 and 13.3 are due to [173]. Refer to [95, 96, 112] for the five steps in the construction of Γ' from Γ described in the proof of Lemma 13.7.

We first review works on the decision version of CSPs, where the goal is to decide the satisfiability of the given instance. In the seminal work by Schaefer [371], it was shown that every Boolean CSP is either polynomial-time tractable or is NP-complete (assuming $\mathsf{P} \neq \mathsf{NP}$). The *dichotomy conjecture* by Feder and Vardi [173] claims that every CSP over a finite domain is either polynomial-time tractable or is NP-complete. The conjecture has been shown to be true for several special cases [109, 110, 43, 254] and was finally resolved [107, 408]. This conjecture is particularly interesting because an intermediate class between P and NP is known to exist if $\mathsf{P} \neq \mathsf{NP}$ [297]. Universal algebra has been introduced to study CSPs by Jeavons [267] and the dichotomy conjecture was restated in terms of polymorphisms in [108]. Refer to [44, 111] for more extensive surveys.

Yoshida [401] brought the algebraic approach to study testing list H-homomorphism, which is a special case of testing assignments to CSPs. Let G and H be graphs and let $L_v \subseteq V(H)$ $(v \in V(G))$ be lists. Then, we say that a mapping $f \colon V(G) \to V(H)$ is a *list homomorphism* if $f(v) \in L_v$ for every $v \in V(G)$ and $\{f(u), f(v)\} \in E(H)$ whenever $\{u, v\} \in V(G)$. Then for a graph H, testing list H-homomorphism is the problem in which, given a graph G, L_v $(v \in V(G))$, and query access to $f \colon V(G) \to V(H)$, the goal is to test whether f is a list homomorphism from G to H or is far from being so. Yoshida obtained a trichotomy result, that is, equivalent conditions of H such that testing list H-homomorphism is constant-query and sublinear-query testable. The trichotomy for testing assignments to Boolean CSPs, which is presented in this chapter, was obtained by Bhattacharyya and Yoshida [81]. Recently, a characterization of constant-query testable CSPs over general finite domains was obtained by Chen, Valeriote, and Yoshida [120].

Problems

13.1. The *discriminator* operation $d\colon \{0,1\}^3 \to \{0,1\}$ is the operation such   discriminator
that

$$d(x,y,z) = \begin{cases} z & \text{if } x = y, \\ x & \text{otherwise.} \end{cases}$$

Compose a ternary majority operation from d.

13.2. The *dual discriminator* operation $d\colon D \to D$ is the operation such that   dual discriminator

$$d(x,y,z) = \begin{cases} x & \text{if } y \neq z, \\ y & \text{otherwise.} \end{cases}$$

Show that a binary relation $R \subseteq D^2$ preserved by d has one of the following forms:

(i) $(x = a) \vee (y = b)$ for $a, b \in D$,
(ii) $x = \pi(y)$ where π is a permutation on D,
(iii) $A \times B$ where A and B are subsets of D,
(iv) intersection of a relation of type (i) or (ii) with a relation of type (iii).

(**Hint:** Use the fact that, for any $a, a', b, b', c \in D$ with $b \neq b'$, we have $d(a', a, a) = a$ and $d(c, b, b') = c$.)

13.3. Suppose that a relation $R \subseteq \{0,1\}^k$ is preserved by the ternary majority operation. Then, show that R can be written as a conjunction of binary and unary relations.

13.4. Suppose that a relation $R \subseteq \{0,1\}^k$ is preserved by the binary minimum function. Then, show that R can be written as a Horn CNF.

13.5. The *unique label cover* problem is a CSP over a finite domain $[q]$ for   unique label cover
an integer $q \in \mathbb{Z}_{>0}$ such that each relation R in the constraint language is binary and is of the form $R = \{(i, \pi(i)) : i \in [q]\}$, where $\pi\colon [q] \to [q]$ is a permutation. Show that the unique label cover problem is one-sided error testable with $O(\epsilon^{-2} \log q)$ queries.

13.6. Consider a CSP over a domain $\{0, 1, \ldots, 29\}$ with constraints of the form $x \equiv y \pmod 2$, $x \equiv y \pmod 3$, and $x \equiv y \pmod 5$. Show that this CSP is one-sided error testable with $O(\epsilon^{-2})$ queries.

13.7. In this problem, you are asked to show that testing **Horn** 3-**SAT** requires $\Omega(n)$ queries, as mentioned in the proof of Proposition 13.4. You can use the fact that testing 3-**LIN** requires $\Omega(n)$ queries even when the instance is restricted to satisfy the *unique neighbor property*, that is, for any subset of variables S with $|S| \leq \beta n$ for some universal constant $\beta > 0$, there exists a constraint which involves exactly one variable of S. (**Hint:** Replace each constraint of the form $x_i + x_j + x_k = 0 \pmod 2$ with the following 12 Horn constraints:

$$
\begin{array}{lll}
v_i \wedge v_j \to v_k', & v_i \wedge v_k \to v_j', & v_j \wedge v_k \to v_i', \\
v_i' \wedge v_j \to v_k, & v_i' \wedge v_k \to v_j, & v_j' \wedge v_k \to v_i, \\
v_i \wedge v_j' \to v_k, & v_i \wedge v_k' \to v_j, & v_j \wedge v_k' \to v_i, \\
v_i' \wedge v_j' \to v_k', & v_i' \wedge v_k' \to v_j', & v_j' \wedge v_k' \to v_i'
\end{array}
$$

for variables $v_i, v_i', v_j, v_j', v_k$, and v_k'.)

Appendix A
Concentration Inequalities

In this section, we review basic concentration inequalities that are frequently used throughout this book. For basic background on probability theory and other concentration inequalities, refer to textbooks on randomized algorithms and probabilistic methods such as [25, 317, 324].

We start with the following inequality:

Theorem A.1 (Markov's inequality). *Let X be a non-negative random variable. Then for any $a > 0$:*

$$\Pr[X \geq a] \leq \frac{\mathbf{E}[X]}{a}.$$

Proof. The expectation of X can be written as follows:

$$\mathbf{E}[X] = \int_0^\infty \Pr[X \geq x]\mathrm{d}x.$$

Since $\Pr[X \geq x]$ is monotonically non-increasing, we obtain for all $a > 0$:

$$\mathbf{E}[X] \geq \int_0^a \Pr[X \geq x]\mathrm{d}x \geq \int_0^a \Pr[X \geq a]\mathrm{d}x = a\Pr[X \geq a].$$

Rearranging the inequality, we get the inequality. $\square$

If we have a bound on the variance, we can use the following inequality:

Theorem A.2 (Chebyshev's inequality). *Let X be a random variable. Then for $a > 0$:*

$$\Pr\big[|X - \mathbf{E}[X]| \geq a\big] \leq \frac{\mathbf{Var}[X]}{a^2}.$$

© The Editor(s) (if applicable) and The Author(s), under exclusive license
to Springer Nature Singapore Pte Ltd 2022
A. Bhattacharyya and Y. Yoshida, *Property Testing*,
https://doi.org/10.1007/978-981-16-8622-1

Proof. Applying Markov's inequality on the random variable $(X - \mathbf{E}[X])^2$, we obtain for any $a > 0$:

$$\Pr\big[|X - \mathbf{E}[X]| \geq a\big] = \Pr\big[(X - \mathbf{E}[X])^2 \geq a^2\big] \leq \frac{\mathrm{Var}[X]}{a^2}. \qquad \square$$

Note that X does not have to be non-negative because we apply Markov's inequality on $(X - \mathbf{E}[X])^2$. Also Chebyshev's inequality is stronger than Markov's inequality in the following sense. Let X be a non-negative random variable with $\mathbf{E}[X] \leq a$. Then by Chebyshev's inequality, we have:

$$\Pr[X \geq a] \leq \Pr[X - \mathbf{E}[X] \geq a] \leq \Pr\big[|X - \mathbf{E}[X]| \geq a\big] \leq \frac{\mathrm{Var}[X]}{a^2} \leq \left(\frac{\mathbf{E}[X]}{a}\right)^2.$$

If the random variable X is a sum of independent Bernoulli random variables, we can show that the probability that X deviates from its expectation $\mathbf{E}[X]$ decays exponentially.

Chernoff's bound

Theorem A.3 (Chernoff's bound). *Let $X_1, \ldots, X_n$ be independent Bernoulli random variables, where $\Pr[X_i = 1] = p_i$ and $\Pr[X_i = 0] = 1 - p_i$ for every $i \in [n]$. Let $p = \sum_{i \in [n]} p_i$ and let $X = \sum_{i \in [n]} X_i$. Then, for any $\delta > 0$:*

$$\Pr[X > (1+\delta)p] \leq \exp(-h(\delta)p) \quad and \quad \Pr[X < (1-\delta)p] \leq \exp(-h(\delta)p),$$

where:

$$h(\delta) = (1+\delta)\log(1+\delta) - \delta.$$

Proof. Using the monotonicity of the exponent function and Markov's inequality, we have for any $t > 0$:

$$\Pr[X > (1+\delta)p] = \Pr\left[e^{tX} > e^{t(1+\delta)p}\right] \leq \frac{\mathbf{E}[e^{tX}]}{e^{(1+\delta)tp}}. \qquad (\text{A.1})$$

Note that:

$$\mathbf{E}\left[e^{tX}\right] = \mathbf{E}\left[e^{t\sum_{i \in [n]} X_i}\right] = \prod_{i \in [n]} \mathbf{E}\left[e^{tX_i}\right] \qquad (\text{by independence})$$

$$= \prod_{i \in [n]} (p_i e^t + (1 - p_i)e^0) = \prod_{i \in [n]} (1 + p_i(e^t - 1))$$

$$\leq \prod_{i \in [n]} e^{p_i(e^t - 1)} = e^{\sum_{i \in [n]} p_i(e^t - 1)} = e^{(e^t - 1)p}.$$

Combining the above with (A.1) and choosing $t = \log(1 + \delta)$ yields the first inequality.

The other direction can be obtained similarly by considering the probability that $-X > -(1-\delta)p$. $\qquad\qquad$ □

Using the fact that $h(\delta) > \delta^2/3$, we get the following handy bound:

Corollary A.1. Let $X_1, \ldots, X_n$ be independent Bernoulli random variables, where $\Pr[X_i = 1] = p_i$ and $\Pr[X_i = 0] = 1 - p_i$ for every $i \in [n]$. Let $p = \sum_{i \in [n]} p_i$ and let $X = \sum_{i \in [n]} X_i$. Then, for any $\delta > 0$:

$$\Pr[X > (1+\delta)p] \leq \exp(-\delta^2 p/3) \quad and \quad \Pr[X < (1-\delta)p] \leq \exp(-\delta^2 p/3).$$

We can further generalize Chernoff's bound for non-Bernoulli random variables:

Theorem A.4 (Hoeffding's inequality). *Let $X_1, \ldots, X_n$ be independent random variables with $a \leq X_i \leq b$ for each $i \in [n]$. We define:*

$$\bar{X} = \frac{1}{n} \sum_{i \in [n]} X_i.$$

Then, we have:

$$\Pr\left[|\bar{X} - \mathbf{E}[\bar{X}]| \geq t\right] \leq 2 \exp\left(-\frac{2nt^2}{(b-a)^2}\right).$$

Hoeffding's inequality

Proof. Let $Y_i = X_i - \mathbf{E}[X_i]$ and $\bar{Y} = \frac{1}{n} \sum_{i \in [n]} Y_i$. Using the monotonicity of the exponential function and Markov's inequality, we have that for every $\lambda > 0$ and $t > 0$:

$$\Pr\left[\bar{Y} \geq t\right] = \Pr\left[e^{\lambda \bar{Y}} \geq e^{\lambda t}\right] \leq e^{-\lambda t} \mathbf{E}\left[e^{\lambda \bar{Y}}\right].$$

By the independence of $X_1, \ldots, X_n$, we have:

$$\mathbf{E}\left[e^{\lambda \bar{Y}}\right] = \mathbf{E}\left[e^{\sum_{i \in [n]} \lambda Y_i/n}\right] = \prod_{i \in [n]} \mathbf{E}\left[e^{\lambda Y_i/n}\right].$$

By Hoeffding's lemma below (Lemma A.1), for every $i \in [n]$, we have:

$$\mathbf{E}\left[e^{\lambda Y_i/n}\right] \leq e^{\frac{\lambda^2(b-a)^2}{8n^2}}.$$

Therefore:

$$\Pr\left[\bar{Y} \geq t\right] \leq e^{-\lambda t} \prod_{i \in [n]} e^{\frac{\lambda^2(b-a)^2}{8n^2}} = e^{-\lambda t + \frac{\lambda^2(b-a)^2}{8n}}.$$

By choosing $\lambda = 4nt/(b-a)^2$, we obtain:

$$\Pr\left[\bar{Y} \geq t\right] \leq e^{-\frac{2nt^2}{(b-a)^2}}.$$

Applying the same argument on the variable $-\hat{Y}$, we obtain that $\Pr[\hat{Y} \leq -t] \leq e^{-\frac{2nt^2}{(b-a)^2}}$. The theorem follows by applying the union bound on the two cases. $\square$

Hoeffding's lemma

Lemma A.1 (Hoeffding's lemma). *Let X be a random variable with $\mathbf{E}[X] = 0$ that takes values in $[a, b]$. Then, for every $\lambda > 0$, we have:*

$$\mathbf{E}\left[e^{\lambda X}\right] \leq e^{\frac{\lambda^2 (b-a)^2}{8}}.$$

Proof. Since $f(x) = e^{\lambda x}$ is a convex function, we have:

$$f(x) \leq \alpha f(a) + (1 - \alpha) f(b)$$

for every $\alpha \in (0, 1)$ and $x \in [a, b]$. Setting $\alpha = \frac{b-x}{b-a} \in [0, 1]$ yields:

$$e^{\lambda x} \leq \frac{b - x}{b - a} e^{\lambda a} + \frac{x - a}{b - a} e^{\lambda b}.$$

Substituting the random variable X for x and taking the expectation, we obtain that:

$$\mathbf{E}\left[e^{\lambda X}\right] \leq \frac{b - \mathbf{E}[X]}{b - a} e^{\lambda a} + \frac{\mathbf{E}[X] - a}{b - a} e^{\lambda b} = \frac{b}{b - a} e^{\lambda a} - \frac{a}{b - a} e^{\lambda b}, \quad (A.2)$$

where we used the fact that $\mathbf{E}[X] = 0$.

Let $h = \lambda(b-a)$, $p = -\frac{a}{b-a}$, and $L(h) = -hp + \log(1 - p + pe^h)$. Then, (A.2) can be rewritten as $e^{L(h)}$. Therefore, it suffices to show that $L(h) \leq h^2/8$. This follows from $L(0) = L'(0) = 0$ and $L''(h) \leq 1/4$ for all h. $\square$

The following notion is useful to discuss the concentration of an iterative sequence of random variables.

martingale

Definition A.1 (Martingales). We say that a sequence of random variables $X_0, X_1, \ldots, X_n$ is a *martingale* if it satisfies:

$$\mathbf{E}[X_{i+1} \mid X_0, \ldots, X_i] = X_i$$

for all $i = 0, 1, \ldots, n - 1$.

Lemma A.2 (Azuma's inequality). *Let $X_0, X_1, \ldots, X_n$ be a martingale of random variables with $|X_i - X_{i-1}| < c_i$ for each $i \in [n]$. Then, we have:*

$$\Pr[X_n - X_0 \geq t] \leq \exp\left(-\frac{t^2}{2c^2 n}\right).$$

Proof. First, using Markov's inequality, we have:

$$\Pr[X_n - X_0 \geq t] = \Pr\left[e^{\lambda(X_n - X_0)} \geq e^{\lambda t}\right] \leq e^{-\lambda t}\, \mathbf{E}\left[e^{\lambda(X_n - X_0)}\right]$$

$$= e^{-\lambda t}\, \mathbf{E}\left[e^{\lambda \sum_{i \in [n]}(X_i - X_{i-1})}\right] = e^{-\lambda t}\, \mathbf{E}\left[\prod_{i \in [n]} e^{\lambda(X_i - X_{i-1})}\right].$$

We can always include additional conditional expectation and we obtain:

$$\Pr[X_n - X_0 \geq t]$$

$$\leq e^{-\lambda t} \underset{X_0, \ldots, X_{n-1}}{\mathbf{E}} \left[\underset{X_n}{\mathbf{E}} \left[\prod_{i \in [n]} e^{\lambda(X_i - X_{i-1})} \mid X_0, X_1, \ldots, X_{n-1} \right] \right].$$

Since $\prod_{i \in [n-1]} e^{\lambda(X_i - X_{i-1})}$ is constant once we condition on $X_0, \ldots, X_{n-1}$, we can take it out of the expectation and we obtain:

$$\Pr[X_n - X_0 \geq t]$$

$$\leq e^{-\lambda t} \underset{X_0, \ldots, X_{n-1}}{\mathbf{E}} \left[\prod_{i \in [n-1]} e^{\lambda(X_i - X_{i-1})} \underset{X_n}{\mathbf{E}} \left[e^{\lambda(X_n - X_{n-1})} \mid X_0, X_1, \ldots, X_{n-1} \right] \right].$$

Since $X_0, \ldots, X_n$ is a martingale, we know that $\mathbf{E}[X_n - X_{n-1} \mid X_0, \ldots, X_{n-1}] = 0$. Using Hoeffding's lemma and that $|X_n - X_{n-1}| \leq c$, we have:

$$\Pr[X_n - X_0 \geq t] \leq e^{-\lambda t} e^{\frac{\lambda^2 c^2}{2}} \underset{X_0, \ldots, X_{n-1}}{\mathbf{E}} \left[\prod_{i \in [n-1]} e^{\lambda(X_i - X_{i-1})} \right].$$

By induction, we obtain:

$$\Pr[X_n - X_0 \geq t] \leq e^{\frac{\lambda^2 c^2 n}{2} - \lambda t}.$$

By letting $\lambda = \frac{t}{c^2 n}$, we obtain:

$$\Pr[X_n - X_0 \geq t] \leq e^{-\frac{t^2}{2c^2 n}}. \qquad \square$$

Appendix B
Matroids

Here, we review basic notions from matroid theory. See, e.g., [343] for more details.

Let E be a finite set and $\mathcal{I} \subseteq 2^E$ be a family of subsets of E. For a set $S \subseteq E$, we call S *independent* if $S \in \mathcal{I}$ and *dependent* otherwise. The pair $(E, \mathcal{I})$ is called a *matroid* if the following three axioms hold:

- $\emptyset \in \mathcal{I}$.
- For any $S \subseteq T \in \mathcal{I}$, $S \in \mathcal{I}$ holds.
- For any $S, T \in \mathcal{I}$ with $|S| < |T|$, there exists $e \in T \setminus S$ such that $S \cup \{e\} \in \mathcal{I}$ holds.

The set E is called the *ground set* of the matroid.

> **Example B.1.** Let $G = (V, E)$ be a graph. Let $\mathcal{I} \subseteq 2^E$ be the set of all spanning forests. Then, the pair $(E, \mathcal{I})$ is a matroid. This matroid is called a *graphic matroid* associated with G.

Let $\mathcal{M} = (E, \mathcal{I})$ be a matroid. A maximal independent set is called a *base* of $\mathcal{M}$, and a minimal dependent set is called a *circuit* of $\mathcal{M}$. It is easy to check that any two bases of $\mathcal{M}$ have the same size. This number is called the *rank* of $\mathcal{M}$. The *rank* of a set $S \subseteq E$ is the maximum size of an independent subset of S. The *rank function* $\rho_{\mathcal{M}} : 2^E \to \mathbb{Z}_{\geq 0}$ associated with $\mathcal{M}$ is the function that returns the rank of the given set. The rank function $\rho_{\mathcal{M}}$ satisfies the following properties:

- $\rho_{\mathcal{M}}$ is non-negative.
- For any subset $S \subseteq E$, $\rho_{\mathcal{M}}(S) \leq |E|$.
- For any two subsets $S, T \subseteq E$, it holds that $\rho_{\mathcal{M}}(S) + \rho_{\mathcal{M}}(T) \geq \rho_{\mathcal{M}}(S \cap T) + \rho_{\mathcal{M}}(S \cup T)$, that is, $\rho_{\mathcal{M}}$ is *submodular*.
- For any set $S \subseteq E$ and an element $e \in E$, we have $\rho_{\mathcal{M}}(S) \leq \rho_{\mathcal{M}}(S \cup \{e\}) \leq \rho_{\mathcal{M}}(S) + 1$.

> **Example B.2.** Let $G = (V, E)$ be a graph and $\mathcal{M}$ be the graphic matroid associated with G. Then, an edge set $F \subseteq E$ is a base of $\mathcal{M}$ if and only if F forms a spanning tree. Also, an edge set $F \subseteq E$ is a circuit of $\mathcal{M}$ if and only if F forms a cycle. The rank of an edge set $F \subseteq E$ is the maximum number of edges in a forest in F. The rank of $\mathcal{M}$ is $n - c$, where c is the number of connected components in G.

closure

Let $\mathcal{M} = (E, \mathcal{I})$ be a matroid with rank function $\rho_{\mathcal{M}}$. The *closure* cl(S) of a set $S \subseteq E$ is the set:

$$\mathrm{cl}(S) = \{e \in E : \rho_{\mathcal{M}}(S \cup \{e\}) = \rho_{\mathcal{M}}(S)\}.$$

closure operator

This defines a *closure operator* cl: $2^E \to 2^E$ with the following properties:

- For any set $S \subseteq E$, $S \subseteq \mathrm{cl}(S)$.
- For any set $S \subseteq E$, $\mathrm{cl}(S) = \mathrm{cl}(\mathrm{cl}(S))$.
- For any sets $S, T \subseteq E$, $\mathrm{cl}(S) \subseteq \mathrm{cl}(T)$.

> **Example B.3.** Let $G = (V, E)$ be a graph and $\mathcal{M}$ be the graphic matroid associated with G. Then, for an edge set $F \subseteq E$, its closure cl(F) is the set of edges in the subgraph induced by $V(F)$, where $V(F)$ is the set of edges incident to F.

Index

References

[1] Achlioptas, D.: Database-friendly random projections: Johnson-Lindenstrauss with binary coins. Journal of Computer and System Sciences **66**(4), 671–687 (2003)

[2] Adler, I., Harwath, F.: Property testing for bounded degree databases. In: Proceedings of the 35th International Symposium on Theoretical Aspects of Computer Science (STACS), pp. 6:1–6:14 (2018)

[3] Ailon, N., Chazelle, B.: Information theory in property testing and monotonicity testing in higher dimension. Information and Computation **204**(11), 1704–1717 (2006)

[4] Alon, N.: The algorithmic aspects of the regularity lemma. In: Proceedings of the 33rd Annual IEEE Symposium on Foundations of Computer Science (FOCS), pp. 473–481 (1992)

[5] Alon, N.: Testing subgraphs in large graphs. Random Structures & Algorithms **21**(3-4), 359–370 (2002)

[6] Alon, N., Ben-Eliezer, O., Fischer, E.: Testing hereditary properties of ordered graphs and matrices. In: Proceedings of the 58th Annual IEEE Symposium on Foundations of Computer Science (FOCS), pp. 848–858 (2017)

[7] Alon, N., Blais, E., Chakraborty, S., García-Soriano, D., Matsliah, A.: Nearly tight bounds for testing function isomorphism. SIAM Journal on Computing **42**(2), 459–493 (2013)

[8] Alon, N., Bruck, J., Naor, J., Naor, M., Roth, R.M.: Construction of asymptotically good low-rate error-correcting codes through pseudorandom graphs. IEEE Transactions on information theory **38**(2), 509–516 (1992)

[9] Alon, N., Edmonds, J., Luby, M.: Linear time erasure codes with nearly optimal recovery. In: Proceedings of IEEE 36th Annual Symposium on Foundations of Computer Science (FOCS), pp. 512–519 (1995)

[10] Alon, N., Fischer, E., Krivelevich, M., Szegedy, M.: Efficient testing of large graphs. Combinatorica **20**(4), 451–476 (2000)

A. Bhattacharyya and Y. Yoshida, *Property Testing*, https://doi.org/10.1007/978-981-16-8622-1

[11] Alon, N., Fischer, E., Newman, I., Shapira, A.: A combinatorial characterization of the testable graph properties: It's all about regularity. SIAM Journal on Computing **39**(1), 143–167 (2009)

[12] Alon, N., Fox, J.: Easily testable graph properties. Combinatorics, Probability and Computing **24**(4), 646–657 (2015)

[13] Alon, N., Kaufman, T., Krivelevich, M., Litsyn, S., Ron, D.: Testing low-degree polynomials over $GF(2)$. In: Approximation, Randomization, and Combinatorial Optimization. Algorithms and Techniques (APPROX/RANDOM), pp. 188–199. Springer (2003)

[14] Alon, N., Kaufman, T., Krivelevich, M., Ron, D.: Testing triangle-freeness in general graphs. SIAM Journal on Discrete Mathematics **22**(2), 786–819 (2008)

[15] Alon, N., Krivelevich, M.: Testing k-colorability. SIAM Journal on Discrete Mathematics **15**(2), 211–227 (2006)

[16] Alon, N., Krivelevich, M., Newman, I., Szegedy, M.: Regular languages are testable with a constant number of queries. SIAM Journal on Computing **30**(6), 1842–1862 (2006)

[17] Alon, N., Seymour, P.D., Thomas, R.: A separator theorem for graphs with an excluded minor and its applications. In: Proceedings of the 22nd Annual ACM Symposium on Theory of Computing (STOC), pp. 293–299 (1990)

[18] Alon, N., Shapira, A.: Testing satisfiability. In: Proceedings of the 13th Annual ACM-SIAM Symposium on Discrete Algorithms (SODA), pp. 645–654 (2002)

[19] Alon, N., Shapira, A.: Testing subgraphs in directed graphs. In: Proceedings of the 35th Annual ACM Symposium on Theory of Computing (STOC), pp. 700–709 (2003)

[20] Alon, N., Shapira, A.: A characterization of easily testable induced subgraphs. Combinatorics, Probability and Computing **15**(6), 791–805 (2006)

[21] Alon, N., Shapira, A.: Homomorphisms in graph property testing. In: Topics in Discrete Mathematics, pp. 281–313. Springer Berlin Heidelberg, Berlin, Heidelberg (2006)

[22] Alon, N., Shapira, A.: A characterization of the (natural) graph properties testable with one-sided error. SIAM Journal on Computing **37**(6), 1703–1727 (2008)

[23] Alon, N., Shapira, A.: Every monotone graph property is testable. SIAM Journal on Computing **38**(2), 505–522 (2008)

[24] Alon, N., Shapira, A.: A separation theorem in property testing. Combinatorica **28**(3), 261–281 (2008)

[25] Alon, N., Spencer, J.H.: The Probabilistic Method, 4 edn. Wiley (2016)

[26] Alon, N., de la Vega, W.F., Kannan, R., Karpinski, M.: Random sampling and approximation of max-CSPs. Journal of Computer and System Sciences **67**(2), 212–243 (2003)

[27] Andersson, G., Engebretsen, L.: Property testers for dense constraint satisfaction programs on finite domains. Random Structures & Algorithms **21**(1), 14–32 (2002)

[28] Ar, S., Blum, M., Codenotti, B., Gemmell, P.: Checking approximate computations over the reals. In: Proceedings of the 25th Annual ACM Symposium on Theory of Computing (STOC), pp. 786–795 (1993)

[29] Aronson, J., Dyer, M., Frieze, A., Suen, S.: Randomized greedy matching. ii. Random Structures & Algorithms **6**(1), 55–73 (2006)

[30] Arora, S.: Probabilistic checking of proofs and the hardness of approximation problems. Ph.D. thesis, University of California, Berkeley (1994)

[31] Arora, S., Lund, C., Motwani, R., Sudan, M., Szegedy, M.: Proof verification and the hardness of approximation problems. Journal of the ACM **45**(3), 501–555 (1998)

[32] Arora, S., Safra, S.: Probabilistic checking of proofs: a new characterization of NP. Journal of the ACM **45**(1) (1998)

[33] Arora, S., Sudan, M.: Improved low-degree testing and its applications. Combinatorica **23**(3), 365–426 (2003)

[34] Assadi, S., Kapralov, M., Khanna, S.: A simple sublinear-time algorithm for counting arbitrary subgraphs via edge sampling. In: Proceedings of the 10th Innovations in Theoretical Computer Science Conference (ITCS), pp. 6:1–6:20 (2018)

[35] Austin, T., Tao, T.: Testability and repair of hereditary hypergraph properties. Random Structures & Algorithms **36**(4), 373–463 (2010)

[36] Avart, C., Rödl, V., Schacht, M.: Every monotone 3-graph property is testable. SIAM Journal on Discrete Mathematics **21**(1), 73–92 (2007)

[37] Babai, L.: Graph isomorphism in quasipolynomial time. In: Proceedings of the 48th Annual ACM SIGACT Symposium on Theory of Computing (STOC), pp. 684–697 (2016)

[38] Babu, J., Khoury, A., Newman, I.: Every property of outerplanar graphs is testable. In: Proceedings of the 20th International Workshop on Randomization and Computation (RANDOM), pp. 21:1–21:19 (2016)

[39] Balcan, M.F., Blais, E., Blum, A., Yang, L.: Active property testing. In: Proceedings of the IEEE 53rd Annual Symposium on Foundations of Computer Science (FOCS), pp. 21–30 (2012)

[40] Balcan, M.F., Li, Y., Woodruff, D.P., Zhang, H.: Testing matrix rank, optimally. In: Proceedings of the 30th Annual ACM-SIAM Symposium on Discrete Algorithms (SODA), pp. 727–746 (2019)

[41] Baleshzar, R., Chakrabarty, D., Pallavoor, R.K.S., Raskhodnikova, S., Seshadhri, C.: Optimal unateness testers for real-valued functions: Adaptivity helps. In: Proceedings of the 44th International Colloquium on Automata, Languages, and Programming (ICALP), pp. 5:1–5:14 (2017)

[42] Barman, S., Bhattacharyya, A., Ghoshal, S.: Testing sparsity over known and unknown bases. In: Proceedings of the 35th Annual International Conference on Machine Learning (ICML), pp. 500–509 (2018)

[43] Barto, L.: The dichotomy for conservative constraint satisfaction problems revisited. In: Proceedings of the 26th Annual IEEE Symposium on Logic in Computer Science (LICS), pp. 301–310 (2011)

[44] Barto, L.: Constraint satisfaction problem and universal algebra. ACM SIGLOG News **1**(2), 14–24 (2014)

[45] Behrend, F.A.: On sets of integers which contain no three terms in arithmetical progression. Proceedings of the National Academy of Sciences **32**, 331–332 (1946)

[46] Bellare, M., Coppersmith, D., Håstad, J., Kiwi, M., Sudan, M.: Linearity testing in characteristic two. IEEE Transactions on Information Theory **42**(6), 1781–1795 (1996)

[47] Bellare, M., Goldreich, O., Sudan, M.: Free bits, pcps, and nonapproximability—towards tight results. SIAM Journal on Computing **27**(3), 804–915 (1998)

[48] Bellare, M., Goldwasser, S., Lund, C., Russell, A.: Efficient probabilistically checkable proofs and applications to approximations. In: Proceedings of the 25th Annual ACM symposium on Theory of Computing (STOC), pp. 294–304 (1993)

[49] Bellare, M., Sudan, M.: Improved non-approximability results. In: Proceedings of the 26th Annual ACM symposium on Theory of Computing (STOC), pp. 184–193 (1994)

[50] Belovs, A.: Adaptive lower bound for testing monotonicity on the line. In: Approximation, Randomization, and Combinatorial Optimization. Algorithms and Techniques (APPROX/RANDOM), pp. 31:1–31:10 (2018)

[51] Belovs, A., Blais, E.: A polynomial lower bound for testing monotonicity. In: Proceedings of the 48th Annual ACM symposium on Theory of Computing (STOC), pp. 1021–1032 (2016)

[52] Ben-Eliezer, O., Canonne, C.L.: Improved bounds for testing forbidden order patterns. In: Proceedings of the 29th Annual ACM-SIAM Symposium on Discrete Algorithms (SODA), pp. 2093–2112 (2018)

[53] Ben-Eliezer, O., Canonne, C.L., Letzter, S., Waingarten, E.: Finding monotone patterns in sublinear time. In: Proceedings of the IEEE 60th Annual Symposium on Foundations of Computer Science (FOCS), pp. 1457–1482 (2019)

[54] Ben-Eliezer, O., Fischer, E.: Earthmover resilience and testing in ordered structures. In: Proceedings of the 33rd Conference on Computational Complexity, pp. 18:1–18:35 (2018)

[55] Ben-Eliezer, O., Fischer, E., Levi, A., Yoshida, Y.: Ordered graph limits and their applications. In: 12th Innovations in Theoretical Computer Science Conference (ITCS), vol. 185, pp. 42:1–42:20 (2021)

[56] Ben-Eliezer, O., Letzter, S., Waingarten, E.: Optimal adaptive detection of monotone patterns. arXiv.org (2019)

[57] Ben Or, M., Coppersmith, D., Luby, M., Rubinfeld, R.: Non-abelian homomorphism testing, and distributions close to their self-convolutions. Random Structures & Algorithms **32**(1), 49–70 (2007)

[58] Ben-Sasson, E., Bentov, I., Horesh, Y., Riabzev, M.: Scalable, transparent, and post-quantum secure computational integrity. IACR Cryptology ePrint Archive **2018**, 46 (2018)

[59] Ben-Sasson, E., Goldreich, O., Harsha, P., Sudan, M., Vadhan, S.: Robust pcps of proximity, shorter pcps, and applications to coding. SIAM Journal on Computing **36**(4), 889–974 (2006)

[60] Ben-Sasson, E., Grigorescu, E., Maatouk, G., Shpilka, A., Sudan, M.: On sums of locally testable affine invariant properties. In: Approximation, Randomization, and Combinatorial Optimization. Algorithms and Techniques (APPROX/RANDOM), pp. 400–411 (2011)

[61] Ben-Sasson, E., Guruswami, V., Kaufman, T., Sudan, M., Viderman, M.: Locally testable codes require redundant testers. SIAM Journal on Computing **39**(7), 3230–3247 (2010)

[62] Ben-Sasson, E., Harsha, P., Raskhodnikova, S.: Some 3CNF properties are hard to test. SIAM Journal on Computing **35**(1) (2005)

[63] Ben-Sasson, E., Maatouk, G., Shpilka, A., Sudan, M.: Symmetric LDPC codes are not necessarily locally testable. In: Proceedings of the 26th Annual Conference on Computational Complexity (CCC), pp. 55–65 (2011)

[64] Ben-Sasson, E., Ron-Zewi, N., Sudan, M.: Sparse affine-invariant linear codes are locally testable. Computational Complexity **26**(1), 37–77 (2017)

[65] Ben-Sasson, E., Sudan, M.: Simple pcps with poly-log rate and query complexity. In: Proceedings of the 37th Annual ACM symposium on Theory of Computing (STOC), pp. 266–275 (2005)

[66] Ben-Sasson, E., Sudan, M.: Robust locally testable codes and products of codes. Random Structures & Algorithms **28**(4), 387–402 (2006)

[67] Ben-Sasson, E., Sudan, M.: Short pcps with polylog query complexity. SIAM Journal on Computing **38**(2), 551–607 (2008)

[68] Ben-Sasson, E., Sudan, M., Vadhan, S., Wigderson, A.: Randomness-efficient low degree tests and short ppcps via epsilon-biased sets. In: Proceedings of the 35th Annual ACM Symposium on Theory of Computing (STOC), pp. 612–621 (2003)

[69] Ben-Sasson, E., Viderman, M.: Tensor products of weakly smooth codes are robust. Theory of Computing **5**(1), 239–255 (2009)

[70] Ben-Sasson, E., Viderman, M.: Composition of semi-ltcs by two-wise tensor products. Computational Complexity **24**(3), 601–643 (2015)

[71] Bender, M.A., Ron, D.: Testing properties of directed graphs: acyclicity and connectivity. Random Structures & Algorithms **20**(2), 184–205 (2002)

[72] Benjamini, I., Schramm, O., Shapira, A.: Every minor-closed property of sparse graphs is testable. Advances in Mathematics **223**(6), 2200–2218 (2010)

[73] Berman, P., Raskhodnikova, S., Yaroslavtsev, G.: l_p-testing. In: Proceedings of the 46th Annual ACM Symposium on Theory of Computing (STOC), pp. 164–173 (2014)

[74] Bhangale, A., Dinur, I., Livni Navon, I.: Cube vs. cube low degree test. In: Proceedings of the 8th Innovations in Theoretical Computer Science Conference (ITCS) (2017)

[75] Bhattacharyya, A.: A note on the distance to monotonicity of boolean functions. Electronic Colloquium on Computational Complexity (ECCC) **15** (2008)

[76] Bhattacharyya, A., Fischer, E., Hatami, H., Hatami, P., Lovett, S.: Every locally characterized affine-invariant property is testable. In: Proceedings of the 45th Annual ACM symposium on Theory of Computing (STOC), pp. 429–436 (2013)

[77] Bhattacharyya, A., Fischer, E., Lovett, S.: Testing low complexity affine-invariant properties. In: Proceedings of the 24th Annual ACM-SIAM Symposium on Discrete Algorithms (SODA), pp. 1337–1355 (2013)

[78] Bhattacharyya, A., Grigorescu, E., Jung, K., Raskhodnikova, S., Woodruff, D.P.: Transitive-closure spanners. SIAM Journal on Computing **41**(6), 1380–1425 (2012)

[79] Bhattacharyya, A., Grigorescu, E., Shapira, A.: A unified framework for testing linear-invariant properties. Random Structures & Algorithms **46**(2), 232–260 (2015)

[80] Bhattacharyya, A., Kopparty, S., Schoenebeck, G., Sudan, M., Zuckerman, D.: Optimal testing of Reed-Muller codes. In: 2010 IEEE 51st Annual Symposium on Foundations of Computer Science, pp. 488–497 (2010)

[81] Bhattacharyya, A., Yoshida, Y.: An algebraic characterization of testable Boolean CSPs. In: Proceedings of the 40th International Colloquium Conference on Automata, Languages, and Programming (ICALP), pp. 123–134 (2013)

[82] Bhowmick, A., Lovett, S.: The list decoding radius of Reed-Muller codes over small fields. In: Proceedings of the 47th Annual ACM on Symposium on Theory of Computing (STOC), pp. 277–285 (2015)

[83] Bhowmick, A., Lovett, S.: Nonclassical polynomials as a barrier to polynomial lower bounds. In: Proceedings of the 33rd Conference on Computational Complexity (CCC), pp. 72–87 (2015)

[84] Black, H., Chakrabarty, D., Seshadhri, C.: Domain reduction for monotonicity testing: A $o(d)$ tester for boolean functions in d-dimensions. In: Proceedings of the 2020 ACM-SIAM Symposium on Discrete Algorithms (SODA), pp. 1975–1994 (2020)

[85] Blais, E.: Improved bounds for testing juntas. In: Proceedings of the 12th International Workshop on Randomization and Approximation Techniques in Computer Science (RANDOM), pp. 317–330 (2008)

[86] Blais, E.: Testing juntas nearly optimally. In: Proceedings of the 41st Annual ACM Symposium on Theory of Computing (STOC), pp. 151–158 (2009)

[87] Blais, E., Bommireddi, A.: Testing submodularity and other properties of valuation functions. In: Proceedings of the 8th Innovations in Theoretical Computer Science Conference (ITCS), pp. 33:1–33:17 (2017)

[88] Blais, E., Brody, J., Matulef, K.: Property testing lower bounds via communication complexity. Computational Complexity **21**(2), 311–358 (2012)

[89] Blais, E., O'Donnell, R.: Lower bounds for testing function isomorphism. In: Proceedings of the 25th Annual IEEE Conference on Computational Complexity (CCC), pp. 235–246 (2010)

[90] Blais, E., Raskhodnikova, S., Yaroslavtsev, G.: Lower bounds for testing properties of functions over hypergrid domains. In: Proceedings of the 29th Annual IEEE Conference on Computational Complexity (CCC), pp. 309–320 (2014)

[91] Blais, E., Weinstein, A., Yoshida, Y.: Partially symmetric functions are efficiently isomorphism testable. SIAM Journal on Computing **44**(2), 411–432 (2015)

[92] Blais, E., Yoshida, Y.: A characterization of constant-sample testable properties. Random Structures & Algorithms (2018)

[93] Blum, A.: Learning Boolean functions in an infinite attribute space. Machine Learning **9**(4), 373–386 (1992)

[94] Blum, M., Luby, M., Rubinfeld, R.: Self-testing/correcting with applications to numerical problems. Journal of Computer and System Sciences **47**(3), 549–595 (1993)

[95] Bodnarchuk, V.G., Kaluzhnin, L.A., Kotov, V.N., Romov, B.A.: Galois theory for post algebras. i. Cybernetics **5**(3), 243–252 (1969)

[96] Bodnarchuk, V.G., Kaluzhnin, L.A., Kotov, V.N., Romov, B.A.: Galois theory for post algebras. ii. Cybernetics **5**(5), 531–539 (1969)

[97] Bogdanov, A., Obata, K., Trevisan, L.: A lower bound for testing 3-colorability in bounded-degree graphs. In: Proceedings of the 43rd Annual IEEE Symposium on Foundations of Computer Science (FOCS), pp. 93–102 (2002)

[98] Bogdanov, A., Trevisan, L.: Lower bounds for testing bipartiteness in dense graphs. In: Proceedings of the 19th IEEE Annual Conference on Computational Complexity (CCC), pp. 75–81 (2004)

[99] Bollobás, B., Erdős, P., Simonovits, M., Szemerédi, E.: Extremal graphs without large forbidden subgraphs. In: Annals of Discrete Mathematics, pp. 29–41. Elsevier (1978)

[100] Borgs, C., Chayes, J., Lovász, L., Sós, V., Vesztergombi, K.: Convergent sequences of dense graphs ii. multiway cuts and statistical physics. Annals of Mathematics **176**(1), 151–219 (2012)

[101] Borgs, C., Chayes, J., Lovász, L., Sós, V.T., Szegedy, B., Vesztergombi, K.: Graph limits and parameter testing. In: Proceedings of the 38th Annual ACM Symposium on Theory of Computing (STOC), pp. 261–270 (2006)

[102] Borgs, C., Chayes, J.T., Lovász, L., Sós, V.T., Vesztergombi, K.: Convergent sequences of dense graphs i: Subgraph frequencies, metric properties and testing. Advances in Mathematics **219**(6), 1801–1851 (2008)

[103] Bourgain, J.: On triples in arithmetic progression. Geometric and Functional Analysis **9**(5), 968–984 (1999)

[104] Brody, J., Hatami, P.: Distance-sensitive property testing lower bounds. arxiv.org (2013)

[105] Brown, D.R.H.: Integer sets containing no arithmetic progressions. Journal of the London Mathematical Society **s2-35**(3), 385–394 (1987)

[106] Bshouty, N.H.: Almost optimal distribution-free junta testing. In: Proceedings of the 34th Computational Complexity Conference (CCC), pp. 2:1–2:13 (2019)

[107] Bulatov, A.: A dichotomy theorem for nonuniform CSPs. In: Proceedings of the 58th Annual IEEE Symposium on Foundations of Computer Science (FOCS), pp. 319–330 (2017)

[108] Bulatov, A., Jeavons, P.: Algebraic structures in combinatorial problems. TU Dresden, Preprint MATH-AL-4-2001, 37 pp. (2001)

[109] Bulatov, A.A.: A dichotomy theorem for constraints on a three-element set. In: Proceedings of the 43rd Annual IEEE Symposium on Foundations of Computer Science (FOCS), pp. 649–658 (2002)

[110] Bulatov, A.A.: Complexity of conservative constraint satisfaction problems. ACM Transactions on Computational Logic (TOCL) **12**(4), 24–66 (2011)

[111] Bulatov, A.A.: On the CSP dichotomy conjecture. In: Computer Science – Theory and Applications, pp. 331–344. Springer, Berlin, Heidelberg, Berlin, Heidelberg (2011)

[112] Bulatov, A.A., Marx, D.: The complexity of global cardinality constraints. In: Proceedings of the 24th Annual IEEE Symposium on Logic in Computer Science (LICS), pp. 419–428 (2009)

[113] Canetti, R., Even, G., Goldreich, O.: Lower bounds for sampling algorithms for estimating the average. Information Processing Letters **53**(1), 17–25 (1995)

[114] Chakrabarty, D., Huang, Z.: Testing coverage functions. In: Proceedings of the 39th International Colloquium Conference on Automata, Languages, and Programming (ICALP), pp. 170–181 (2012)

[115] Chakrabarty, D., Seshadhri, C.: Optimal bounds for monotonicity and lipschitz testing over hypercubes and hypergrids. In: Proceedings of

the 45th Annual ACM Symposium on Theory of Computing (STOC), pp. 419–428 (2013)

[116] Chakrabarty, D., Seshadhri, C.: An $o(n)$ monotonicity tester for boolean functions over the hypercube. SIAM Journal on Computing **45**(2), 461–472 (2016)

[117] Chakraborty, S., Fischer, E., García-Soriano, D., Matsliah, A.: Junto-symmetric functions, hypergraph isomorphism and crunching. In: 2012 IEEE Conference on Computational Complexity (CCC), pp. 148–158 (2012)

[118] Chakraborty, S., Fischer, E., Lachish, O., Matsliah, A., Newman, I.: Testing st-connectivity. In: Proceedings of the 11th International Workshop on Randomization and Approximation Techniques in Computer Science (RANDOM), pp. 380–394 (2007)

[119] Chazelle, B., Rubinfeld, R., Trevisan, L.: Approximating the minimum spanning tree weight in sublinear time. SIAM Journal on Computing **34**(6), 1370–1379 (2005)

[120] Chen, H., Valeriote, M., Yoshida, Y.: Testing assignments to constraint satisfaction problems. In: Proceedings of the 57th Annual IEEE Symposium on Foundations of Computer Science (FOCS), pp. 525–534 (2016)

[121] Chen, H., Yoshida, Y.: Testability of homomorphism inadmissibility. In: Proceedings of the 38th ACM SIGMOD-SIGACT-SIGAI Symposium on Principles of Database Systems (PODS), pp. 365–382 (2019)

[122] Chen, X., De, A., Servedio, R.A.: Testing noisy linear functions for sparsity. In: Proceedings of the 52nd Annual ACM SIGACT Symposium on Theory of Computing (STOC), pp. 610–623 (2020)

[123] Chen, X., De, A., Servedio, R.A., Tan, L.Y.: Boolean function monotonicity testing requires (almost) $n^{1/2}$ non-adaptive queries. In: Proceedings of the 47th Annual ACM on Symposium on Theory of Computing (STOC), pp. 519–528 (2015)

[124] Chen, X., Randolph, T., Servedio, R.A., Sun, T.: A lower bound on cycle-finding in sparse digraphs. In: Proceedings of the 31st Annual ACM-SIAM Symposium on Discrete Algorithms (SODA), pp. 2936–2952 (2020)

[125] Chen, X., Servedio, R.A., Tan, L.Y.: New algorithms and lower bounds for monotonicity testing. In: Proceedings of the 24th Annual IEEE Symposium on Logic in Computer Science (LICS), pp. 286–295 (2014)

[126] Chen, X., Servedio, R.A., Tan, L.Y., Waingarten, E., Xie, J.: Settling the query complexity of non-adaptive junta testing. In: Proceedings of the 32nd Conference on Computational Complexity (CCC), pp. 26:1–26:19 (2017)

[127] Chen, X., Waingarten, E.: Testing unateness nearly optimally. In: Proceedings of the 51st Annual ACM SIGACT Symposium on Theory of Computing (STOC), pp. 547–558 (2019)

[128] Chen, X., Waingarten, E., Xie, J.: Beyond Talagrand functions: new lower bounds for testing monotonicity and unateness. In: Proceedings

of the 49th Annual ACM Symposium on Theory of Computing (STOC), pp. 523–536 (2017)

[129] Chen, X., Waingarten, E., Xie, J.: Boolean unateness testing with $\widetilde{O}(n^{3/4})$ adaptive queries. In: Proceedings of the 58th Annual IEEE Symposium on Foundations of Computer Science (FOCS), pp. 868–879 (2017)

[130] Chiesa, A., Manohar, P., Shinkar, I.: On axis-parallel tests for tensor product codes. In: Approximation, Randomization, and Combinatorial Optimization. Algorithms and Techniques (APPROX/RANDOM), pp. 39:1–39:22 (2017)

[131] Chiplunkar, A., Kapralov, M., Khanna, S., Mousavifar, A., Peres, Y.: Testing graph clusterability: Algorithms and lower bounds. In: Proceedings of the IEEE 59th Annual Symposium on Foundations of Computer Science (FOCS), pp. 497–508 (2018)

[132] Chockler, H., Gutfreund, D.: A lower bound for testing juntas. Information Processing Letters **90**(6), 301–305 (2004)

[133] Chomsky, N.: Three models for the description of language. IEEE Transactions on Information Theory **2**(3), 113–124 (1956)

[134] Cohen-Steiner, D., Kong, W., Sohler, C., Valiant, G.: Approximating the spectrum of a graph. In: Proceedings of the 24th ACM SIGKDD International Conference on Knowledge Discovery and Data Mining (KDD), pp. 1263–1271 (2018)

[135] Conlon, D., Fox, J.: Bounds for graph regularity and removal lemmas. Geometric and Functional Analysis **22**(5), 1191–1256 (2012)

[136] Conlon, D., Fox, J., Sudakov, B.: Recent developments in graph ramsey theory. In: A. Czumaj, A. Georgakopoulos, D. Král, V. Lozin, O. Pikhurko (eds.) Surveys in Combinatorics 2015, pp. 49–118. Cambridge University Press, Cambridge (2015)

[137] Coppersmith, D., Rudra, A.: On the robust testability of product of codes. Electronic Colloquium on Computational Complexity (ECCC) **104** (2005)

[138] Cygan, M., Kowalik, Ł., Lokshtanov, D., Marx, D., Pilipczuk, M., Pilipczuk, M., Saurabh, S.: Parameterized Algorithms. Springer International Publishing, Cham (2015)

[139] Czumaj, A., Goldreich, O., Ron, D., Seshadhri, C., Shapira, A., Sohler, C.: Finding cycles and trees in sublinear time. Random Structures & Algorithms **45**(2), 139–184 (2014)

[140] Czumaj, A., Monemizadeh, M., Onak, K., Sohler, C.: Planar graphs: Random walks and bipartiteness testing. In: Proceedings of the 52nd Annual IEEE Symposium on Foundations of Computer Science (FOCS), pp. 423–432 (2011)

[141] Czumaj, A., Peng, P., Sohler, C.: Testing cluster structure of graphs. In: Proceedings of the 47th Annual ACM on Symposium on Theory of Computing (STOC), pp. 723–732 (2015)

[142] Czumaj, A., Peng, P., Sohler, C.: Relating two property testing models for bounded degree directed graphs. In: Proceedings of the 48th Annual ACM SIGACT Symposium on Theory of Computing (STOC), pp. 1033–1045 (2016)

[143] Czumaj, A., Shapira, A., Sohler, C.: Testing hereditary properties of nonexpanding bounded-degree graphs. SIAM Journal on Computing 38(6), 2499–2510 (2009)

[144] Czumaj, A., Sohler, C.: Testing expansion in bounded-degree graphs. Combinatorics, Probability and Computing 19(5-6), 693–709 (2010)

[145] Czumaj, A., Sohler, C.: A characterization of graph properties testable for general planar graphs with one-sided error (it's all about forbidden subgraphs). In: Proceedings of the IEEE 60th Annual Symposium on Foundations of Computer Science (FOCS), pp. 1513–1536 (2019)

[146] Dachman-Soled, D., Servedio, R.A.: A canonical form for testing Boolean function properties. In: Proceedings of the 15th International Workshop on Randomization and Computation (RANDOM), pp. 460–471 (2011)

[147] David, R., Dinur, I., Goldenberg, E., Kindler, G., Shinkar, I.: Direct sum testing. SIAM Journal on Computing 46(4), 1336–1369 (2017)

[148] Diestel, R.: Graph Theory, vol. 173, 4 edn. Springer-Verlag Berlin Heidelberg (2012)

[149] Dikstein, Y., Dinur, I.: Agreement testing theorems on layered set systems. In: Proceedings of the 2019 IEEE 60th Annual Symposium on Foundations of Computer Science (FOCS), pp. 1495–1524 (2019)

[150] Dikstein, Y., Dinur, I., Harsha, P., Ron-Zewi, N.: Locally testable codes via high-dimensional expanders. arXiv.org (2020)

[151] Dinur, I.: The PCP theorem by gap amplification. Journal of the ACM 54(3), 12–es (2007)

[152] Dinur, I., Fischer, E., Kindler, G., Raz, R., Safra, S.: PCP characterizations of NP: toward a polynomially-small error-probability. Computational Complexity 20(3), 413–504 (2011)

[153] Dinur, I., Goldenberg, E.: Locally testing direct product in the low error range. In: 2008 49th Annual IEEE Symposium on Foundations of Computer Science, pp. 613–622. IEEE (2008)

[154] Dinur, I., Harsha, P., Kaufman, T., Ron-Zewi, N.: From local to robust testing via agreement testing. In: Proceedings of the 10th Innovations in Theoretical Computer Science Conference (ITCS), pp. 29:1–29:18 (2018)

[155] Dinur, I., Kaufman, T.: High dimensional expanders imply agreement expanders. In: Proceedings of the 2017 IEEE 58th Annual Symposium on Foundations of Computer Science (FOCS), pp. 974–985 (2017)

[156] Dinur, I., Livni Navon, I.: Exponentially small soundness for the direct product z-test. In: Proceedings of the 32nd Computational Complexity Conference (CCC) (2017)

[157] Dinur, I., Steurer, D.: Direct product testing. In: 2014 IEEE 29th Conference on Computational Complexity (CCC), pp. 188–196 (2014)

[158] Dinur, I., Sudan, M., Wigderson, A.: Robust local testability of tensor products of LDPC codes. In: Approximation, Randomization, and Combinatorial Optimization. Algorithms and Techniques (APPROX/RANDOM), pp. 304–315 (2006)

[159] Dodis, Y., Goldreich, O., Lehman, E., Raskhodnikova, S., Ron, D., Samorodnitsky, A.: Improved testing algorithms for monotonicity. In: Algorithmic Game Theory, pp. 97–108 (1999)

[160] Dolev, E., Ron, D.: Distribution-free testing for monomials with a sublinear number of queries. Theory of Computing **7**(1), 155–176 (2011)

[161] Dumitrescu, B., Irofti, P.: Dictionary Learning Algorithms and Applications. Springer (2018)

[162] Dyer, M., Frieze, A.: Randomized greedy matching. Random Structures & Algorithms **2**(1), 29–45 (1991)

[163] Edelman, A., Hassidim, A., Nguyen, H.N., Onak, K.: An efficient partitioning oracle for bounded-treewidth graphs. In: Proceedings of the 15th International Workshop on Randomization and Computation (RANDOM), pp. 530–541 (2011)

[164] Eden, T., Jain, S., Pinar, A., Ron, D., Seshadhri, C.: Provable and practical approximations for the degree distribution using sublinear graph samples. In: Proceedings of the 2018 World Wide Web Conference (WWW), pp. 449–458 (2018)

[165] Eden, T., Levi, A., Ron, D., Seshadhri, C.: Approximately counting triangles in sublinear time. In: Proceedings of the 56th Annual IEEE Symposium on Foundations of Computer Science (FOCS), pp. 614–633 (2015)

[166] Eden, T., Ron, D., Seshadhri, C.: On approximating the number of k-cliques in sublinear time. In: Proceedings of the 50th Annual ACM SIGACT Symposium on Theory of Computing (STOC), pp. 722–734 (2018)

[167] Edmonds, J.: Edge-disjoint branchings. Academic Press, New York (1973)

[168] Elek, G.: L2-spectral invariants and convergent sequences of finite graphs. Journal of Functional Analysis **254**(10), 2667–2689 (2008)

[169] Elek, G.: Parameter testing in bounded degree graphs of subexponential growth. Random Structures & Algorithms **37**(2), 248–270 (2010)

[170] Elek, G., Lippner, G.: An analogue of the szemeredi regularity lemma for bounded degree graphs. arXiv.org (2008)

[171] Ergün, F., Kannan, S., Kumar, S.R., Rubinfeld, R., Viswanathan, M.: Spot-checkers. Journal of Computer and System Sciences **60**(3), 717–751 (2000)

[172] Ergun, F., Kumar, S.R., Rubinfeld, R.: Approximate checking of polynomials and functional equations. In: Proceedings of 37th Conference on Foundations of Computer Science (FOCS), pp. 592–601 (1996)

[173] Feder, T., Vardi, M.Y.: The computational structure of monotone monadic SNP and constraint satisfaction: A study through datalog and group theory. SIAM Journal on Computing **28**(1), 57–104 (1998)

[174] Feige, U., Goldwasser, S., Lovász, L., Safra, S., Szegedy, M.: Interactive proofs and the hardness of approximating cliques. Journal of the ACM **43**(2), 268–292 (1996)

[175] Feige, U., Kilian, J.: Two prover protocols: low error at affordable rates. In: Proceedings of the 26th Annual ACM symposium on Theory of Computing (STOC), pp. 172–183 (1994)

[176] Fichtenberger, H., Levi, R., Vasudev, Y., Wötzel, M.: A sublinear tester for outerplanarity (and other forbidden minors) with one-sided error. In: Proceedings of the 45th International Colloquium on Automata, Languages, and Programming (ICALP), pp. 52:1–52:14 (2018)

[177] Fichtenberger, H., Peng, P., Sohler, C.: Every testable (infinite) property of bounded-degree graphs contains an infinite hyperfinite subproperty. In: Proceedings of the 30th Annual ACM-SIAM Symposium on Discrete Algorithms (SODA) (2019)

[178] Fischer, E.: On the strength of comparisons in property testing. Information and Computation **189**(1), 107–116 (2004)

[179] Fischer, E., Kindler, G., Ron, D., Safra, S., Samorodnitsky, A.: Testing juntas. Journal of Computer and System Sciences **68**(4), 753–787 (2004)

[180] Fischer, E., Lachish, O., Matsliah, A., Newman, I., Yahalom, O.: On the query complexity of testing orientations for being eulerian. ACM Transactions on Algorithms **8**(2), 15–41 (2012)

[181] Fischer, E., Lachish, O., Vasudev, Y.: Trading query complexity for sample-based testing and multi-testing scalability. In: Proceedings of the 56th Annual IEEE Symposium on Foundations of Computer Science (FOCS), pp. 1163–1182 (2015)

[182] Fischer, E., Lehman, E., Newman, I., Raskhodnikova, S., Rubinfeld, R., Samorodnitsky, A.: Monotonicity testing over general poset domains. In: Proceedings of the 34th Annual ACM Symposium on Theory of Computing (STOC), pp. 474–483 (2002)

[183] Fischer, E., Magniez, F., Starikovskaya, T.: Improved bounds for testing Dyck languages. In: Proceedings of the 29th Annual ACM-SIAM Symposium on Discrete Algorithms (SODA), pp. 1529–1544 (2018)

[184] Fischer, E., Matsliah, A.: Testing graph isomorphism. SIAM Journal on Computing **38**(1), 207–225 (2008)

[185] Fischer, E., Newman, I.: Testing versus estimation of graph properties. SIAM Journal on Computing **37**(2), 482–501 (2007)

[186] Fischer, E., Newman, I., Sgall, J.: Functions that have read-twice constant width branching programs are not necessarily testable. Random Structures & Algorithms **24**(2), 175–193 (2004)

[187] Fleming, N., Yoshida, Y.: Distribution-free testing of linear functions on $\mathbb{R}^n$. In: Proceedings of the 11th Innovations in Theoretical Computer Science Conference (ITCS), pp. 22:1–22:19 (2020)

[188] Forster, S., Nanongkai, D., Saranurak, T., Yang, L., Yingchareontha-wornchai, S.: Computing and testing small connectivity in near-linear time and queries via fast local cut algorithms. In: Proceedings of the 31st Annual ACM-SIAM Symposium on Discrete Algorithms (SODA), pp. 2046–2065 (2020)

[189] Foucart, S., Rauhut, H.: A Mathematical Introduction to Compressive Sensing. Springer (2013)

[190] Fox, J.: A new proof of the graph removal lemma. Annals of Mathematics **174**(1), 561–579 (2011)

[191] Fox, J., Lovász, L.: A tight bound for green's arithmetic triangle removal lemma in vector spaces. In: Proceedings of the 28th Annual ACM-SIAM Symposium on Discrete Algorithms (SODA), pp. 1612–1617 (2017)

[192] Fox, J., Lovász, L.M., Sauermann, L.: A polynomial bound for the arithmetic k-cycle removal lemma in vector spaces. Journal of Combinatorial Theory, Series A **160**, 186–201 (2018)

[193] Fox, J., Wei, F.: Fast property testing and metrics for permutations. Combinatorics, Probability and Computing **27**(4), 539–579 (2018)

[194] Frankl, P., Rödl, V.: The uniformity lemma for hypergraphs. Graphs and Combinatorics **8**(4), 309–312 (1992)

[195] Friedl, K., Sudan, M.: Some improvements to total degree tests. In: Proceedings 3rd Israel Symposium on the Theory of Computing and Systems (ISTCS), pp. 190–198 (1995)

[196] Frieze, A., Kannan, R.: Quick approximation to matrices and applications. Combinatorica **19**(2), 175–220 (1999)

[197] Fujishige, S.: Structures of polyhedra determined by submodular functions on crossing families. Mathematical Programming **29**(2), 125–141 (1984)

[198] Gemmell, P., Lipton, R., Rubinfeld, R., Sudan, M., Wigderson, A.: Self-testing/correcting for polynomials and for approximate functions. In: Proceedings of the 23rd Annual ACM Symposium on Theory of Computing (STOC), pp. 33–42 (1991)

[199] Gishboliner, L., Shapira, A.: Deterministic vs non-deterministic graph property testing. Israel Journal of Mathematics **204**(1), 397–416 (2014)

[200] Gishboliner, L., Shapira, A.: Removal lemmas with polynomial bounds. In: Proceedings of the 49th Annual ACM Symposium on Theory of Computing (STOC), pp. 510–522 (2017)

[201] Gishboliner, L., Shapira, A.: Efficient testing without efficient regularity. In: Proceedings of the 9th Innovations in Theoretical Computer Science Conference (ITCS), pp. 54:1–54:14 (2018)

[202] Gishboliner, L., Shapira, A.: A generalized Turán problem and its applications. In: Proceedings of the 50th Annual ACM SIGACT Symposium on Theory of Computing (STOC), pp. 760–772 (2018)

[203] Gishboliner, L., Shapira, A.: Testing graphs against an unknown distribution. In: Proceedings of the 51st Annual ACM SIGACT Symposium on Theory of Computing (STOC), pp. 535–546 (2019)

[204] Glasner, D., Servedio, R.A.: Distribution-free testing lower bound for basic boolean functions. Theory of Computing 5(1), 191–216 (2009)

[205] Goldreich, O.: Testing graphs in vertex-distribution-free models. In: Proceedings of the 51st Annual ACM SIGACT Symposium on Theory of Computing (STOC), pp. 527–534 (2019)

[206] Goldreich, O.: On the communication complexity methodology for proving lower bounds on the query complexity of property testing. In: Computational Complexity and Property Testing, pp. 87–118. Springer (2020)

[207] Goldreich, O.: Open problems in property testing of graphs. Electronic Colloquium on Computational Complexity (ECCC) 88 (2021)

[208] Goldreich, O., Goldwasser, S., Lehman, E., Ron, D., Samorodnitsky, A.: Testing monotonicity. Combinatorica 20(3), 301–337 (2000)

[209] Goldreich, O., Goldwasser, S., Ron, D.: Property testing and its connection to learning and approximation. Journal of the ACM 45(4), 653–750 (1998)

[210] Goldreich, O., Krivelevich, M., Newman, I., Rozenberg, E.: Hierarchy theorems for property testing. Computational Complexity 21(1), 129–192 (2011)

[211] Goldreich, O., Meir, O.: The tensor product of two good codes is not necessarily robustly testable. Information Processing Letters 112(8), 351 – 355 (2012)

[212] Goldreich, O., Ron, D.: A sublinear bipartiteness tester for bounded degree graphs. Combinatorica 19(3), 335–373 (1999)

[213] Goldreich, O., Ron, D.: Property testing in bounded degree graphs. Algorithmica 32(2), 302–343 (2002)

[214] Goldreich, O., Ron, D.: Approximating average parameters of graphs. Random Structures & Algorithms 32(4), 473–493 (2008)

[215] Goldreich, O., Ron, D.: Algorithmic aspects of property testing in the dense graphs model. SIAM Journal on Computing 40(2), 376–445 (2011)

[216] Goldreich, O., Ron, D.: On proximity-oblivious testing. SIAM Journal on Computing 40(2), 534–566 (2011)

[217] Goldreich, O., Ron, D.: On testing expansion in bounded-degree graphs. In: Studies in Complexity and Cryptography. Miscellanea on the Interplay between Randomness and Computation, pp. 68–75. Springer, Berlin, Heidelberg, Berlin, Heidelberg (2011)

[218] Goldreich, O., Ron, D.: On sample-based testers. In: Proceedings of the 2015 Conference on Innovations in Theoretical Computer Science (ITCS), pp. 337–345 (2015)

[219] Goldreich, O., Ron, D.: The subgraph testing model. ACM Transactions on Computation Theory **12**(4), 1–32 (2020)

[220] Goldreich, O., Safra, S.: A combinatorial consistency lemma with application to proving the pcp theorem. SIAM Journal on Computing **29**(4), 1132–1154 (2000)

[221] Goldreich, O., Sudan, M.: Locally testable codes and PCPs of almost-linear length. Journal of the ACM **53**(4), 558–655 (2006)

[222] Goldreich, O., Trevisan, L.: Three theorems regarding testing graph properties. Random Structures & Algorithms **23**(1), 23–57 (2003)

[223] Gonen, M., Ron, D., Shavitt, Y.: Counting stars and other small subgraphs in sublinear-time. SIAM Journal on Discrete Mathematics **25**(3), 1365–1411 (2011)

[224] Gonen, M., Ron, D., Weinsberg, U., Wool, A.: Finding a dense-core in jellyfish graphs. Computer Networks **52**(15), 2831–2841 (2008)

[225] Gopalan, P., O'Donnell, R., Servedio, R.A., Shpilka, A., Wimmer, K.: Testing Fourier dimensionality and sparsity. SIAM Journal on Computing **40**(4), 1075–1100 (2011)

[226] Gopi, S., Kopparty, S., Oliveira, R., Ron-Zewi, N., Saraf, S.: Locally testable and locally correctable codes approaching the gilbert-varshamov bound. IEEE Transactions on Information Theory **64**(8), 5813–5831 (2018)

[227] Gowers, W.T.: Lower bounds of tower type for Szemerédi's uniformity lemma. Geometric and Functional Analysis **7**(2), 322–337 (1997)

[228] Gowers, W.T.: A new proof of Szemerédi's theorem. Geometric and Functional Analysis **11**(3), 465–588 (2001)

[229] Gowers, W.T.: Quasirandomness, counting and regularity for 3-uniform hypergraphs. Combinatorics, Probability and Computing **15**(1-2), 143–184 (2006)

[230] Gowers, W.T.: Hypergraph regularity and the multidimensional Szemerédi theorem. Annals of Mathematics **166**(3), 897–946 (2007)

[231] Green, B., Tao, T.: The distribution of polynomials over finite fields, with applications to the Gowers norms. Contributions to Discrete Mathematics **4**(2) (2009)

[232] Grigorescu, E., Kaufman, T., Sudan, M.: Succinct representation of codes with applications to testing. SIAM Journal on Discrete Mathematics **26**(4), 1618–1634 (2012)

[233] Guo, A., Haramaty, E., Sudan, M.: Robust testing of lifted codes with applications to low-degree testing. In: Proceedings of the 2015 IEEE 56th Annual Symposium on Foundations of Computer Science (FOCS), pp. 825–844 (2015)

[234] Guo, A., Kopparty, S., Sudan, M.: New affine-invariant codes from lifting. In: Proceedings of the 4th Conference on Innovations in Theoretical Computer Science (ITCS), pp. 529–540 (2013)

[235] Guo, A., Sudan, M.: Some closure features of locally testable affine-invariant properties. In: Electronic Colloquium on Computational Complexity (ECCC), vol. 19, p. 48 (2012)

[236] Gur, T., Rothblum, R.D.: Non-interactive proofs of proximity. Computational Complexity 27(1), 99–207 (2016)

[237] Guruswami, V., Lewin, D., Sudan, M., Trevisan, L.: A tight characterization of np with 3 query pcps. In: Proceedings 39th Annual Symposium on Foundations of Computer Science (FOCS), pp. 8–17 (1998)

[238] Haas, R.: Characterizations of arboricity of graphs. Ars Combinatoria 63, 129–138 (2002)

[239] Hajnal, P.: An $\Omega(n^4/3)$ lower bound on the randomized complexity of graph properties. Combinatorica 11(2), 131–143 (1991)

[240] Halevy, S., Kushilevitz, E.: Testing monotonicity over graph products. In: Proceedings of the 31st International Colloquim Conference on Automata, Languages and Programming (ICALP), pp. 721–732 (2004)

[241] Halevy, S., Kushilevitz, E.: Distribution-free property-testing. SIAM Journal on Computing 37(4), 1107–1138 (2007)

[242] Halevy, S., Kushilevitz, E.: Distribution-free connectivity testing for sparse graphs. Algorithmica 51(1), 24–48 (2008)

[243] Halevy, S., Lachish, O., Newman, I., Tsur, D.: Testing orientation properties. In: Electronic Colloquium on Computational Complexity (ECCC (2005)

[244] Haramaty, E., Ron-Zewi, N., Sudan, M.: Absolutely sound testing of lifted codes. In: Approximation, Randomization, and Combinatorial Optimization. Algorithms and Techniques (APPROX/RANDOM), pp. 671–682 (2013)

[245] Haramaty, E., Shpilka, A., Sudan, M.: Optimal testing of multivariate polynomials over small prime fields. SIAM Journal on Computing 42(2), 536–562 (2013)

[246] Harsha, P.: Lecture notes for "limits of approximation algorithms : PCPs and unique games" (2010). https://www.tifr.res.in/~prahladh/teaching/2009-10/limits/

[247] Hartmanis, J., Stearns, R.E.: On the computational complexity of algorithms. Transactions of the American Mathematical Society 117, 285–306 (1965)

[248] Hassidim, A., Kelner, J.A., Nguyen, H.N., Onak, K.: Local graph partitions for approximation and testing. In: Proceedings of the 50th Annual IEEE Symposium on Foundations of Computer Science (FOCS), pp. 22–31 (2009)

[249] Hatami, H., Lovett, S.: Estimating the distance from testable affine-invariant properties. In: Proceedings of the IEEE 54th Annual Symposium on Foundations of Computer Science (FOCS), pp. 237–242 (2013)

[250] Hatami, P., Tulsiani, M.: Approximate local decoding of cubic Reed-Muller codes beyond the list decoding radius. In: Proceedings of the 29th Annual ACM-SIAM Symposium on Discrete Algorithms (SODA), pp. 663–679 (2018)

[251] Hayashi, K., Yoshida, Y.: Minimizing quadratic functions in constant time. In: Proceedings of the 30th Advances in Neural Information Processing Systems (NIPS), pp. 2217–2225 (2016)

[252] Hayashi, K., Yoshida, Y.: Fitting low-rank tensors in constant time. In: Proceedings of the 31st Annual Conference on Neural Information Processing Systems (NIPS), pp. 2473–2481 (2017)

[253] Hayashi, K., Yoshida, Y.: Testing proximity to subspaces: Approximate ℓ_∞ minimization in constant time. Algorithmica (2019)

[254] Hell, P., Nešetřil, J.: On the complexity of H-coloring. Journal of Combinatorial Theory, Series B **48**(1), 92–110 (1990)

[255] Hellweg, F., Sohler, C.: Property testing in sparse directed graphs: Strong connectivity and subgraph-freeness. In: Proceedings of the 20th European Conference on Algorithms (ESA), pp. 599–610 (2012)

[256] Hitchcock, F.L.: The expression of a tensor or a polyadic as a sum of products. Journal of Mathematics and Physics **6**(1-4), 164–189 (1927)

[257] Hoory, S., Linial, N., Wigderson, A.: Expander graphs and their applications. Bulletin of the American Mathematical Society **43**(4), 439–561 (2006)

[258] Hoppen, C., Kohayakawa, Y., de A Moreira, C.G.T., Sampaio, R.M.: Testing permutation properties through subpermutations. Theoretical Computer Science **412**(29), 3555–3567 (2011)

[259] Imaizumi, M., Maehara, T., Yoshida, Y.: Statistically efficient estimation for non-smooth probability densities. In: Proceedings of the 21st International Conference on Artificial Intelligence and Statistics (AISTATS), pp. 978–987 (2018)

[260] Impagliazzo, R., Kabanets, V., Wigderson, A.: New direct-product testers and 2-query pcps. SIAM Journal on Computing **41**(6), 1722–1768 (2012)

[261] Ito, H.: Every property is testable on a natural class of scale-free multigraphs. In: Proceedings of the 24th Annual European Symposium on Algorithms (ESA), pp. 51:1–51:12 (2016)

[262] Ito, H., Tanigawa, S., Yoshida, Y.: Constant-time algorithms for sparsity matroids. In: Proceedings of the 39th International Colloquium Conference on Automata, Languages, and Programming (ICALP), pp. 498–509 (2012)

[263] Iwama, K., Yoshida, Y.: Parameterized testability. In: Proceedings of the 5th Conference on Innovations in Theoretical Computer Science (ITCS), pp. 507–516 (2014)

[264] Jackson, B., Jordán, T.: Independence free graphs and vertex connectivity augmentation. Journal of Combinatorial Theory, Series B **94**(1), 31–77 (2005)

[265] Jain, V., Koehler, F., Mossel, E.: The vertex sample complexity of free energy is polynomial. In: Proceedings of the 31th Conference on Learning Theory (COLT), pp. 1395–1419 (2018)

[266] Janzer, O.: Polynomial bound for the partition rank vs the analytic rank of tensors. Discrete Analysis **7**, 18 pages (2020)

[267] Jeavons, P.: On the algebraic structure of combinatorial problems. Theoretical Computer Science **200**(1-2), 185–204 (1998)

[268] Jeavons, P., Cohen, D., Cooper, M.C.: Constraints, consistency and closure. Artificial Intelligence **101**(1-2), 251–265 (1998)

[269] Jha, M., Raskhodnikova, S.: Testing and reconstruction of lipschitz functions with applications to data privacy. SIAM Journal on Computing **42**(2), 700–731 (2013)

[270] Joos, F., Kim, J., Kühn, D.: A characterization of testable hypergraph properties. In: Proceedings of the 58th Annual IEEE Symposium on Foundations of Computer Science (FOCS), pp. 859–867 (2017)

[271] Jordan, C., Zeugmann, T.: Testable and untestable classes of first-order formulae. Journal of Computer and System Sciences **78**(5), 1557–1578 (2012)

[272] Jutla, C.S., Patthak, A.C., Rudra, A., Zuckerman, D.: Testing low-degree polynomials over prime fields. Random Structures & Algorithms **35**(2), 163–193 (2009)

[273] Kale, S., Seshadhri, C.: An expansion tester for bounded degree graphs. In: Proceedings of 35th International Colloquium on the Automata, Languages, and Programming (ICALP), pp. 527–538 (2008)

[274] Karger, D.R.: Global min-cuts in RNC, and other ramifications of a simple min-out algorithm. In: Proceedings of the 4th Annual ACM-SIAM Symposium on Discrete Algorithms (SODA), pp. 21–30 (1993)

[275] Katoh, N., Tanigawa, S.: A proof of the molecular conjecture. Discrete & Computational Geometry **45**(4), 647–700 (2011)

[276] Kaufman, T., Krivelevich, M., Ron, D.: Tight bounds for testing bi-partiteness in general graphs. SIAM Journal on Computing **33**(6), 1441–1483 (2004)

[277] Kaufman, T., Lovett, S.: New extension of the Weil bound for character sums with applications to coding. In: Proceedings of the 2011 IEEE 52nd Annual Symposium on Foundations of Computer Science (FOCS), pp. 788–796 (2011)

[278] Kaufman, T., Sudan, M.: Algebraic property testing: the role of invariance. In: Proceedings of the 40th Annual ACM Symposium on Theory of Computing (STOC), pp. 403–412 (2008)

[279] Kawarabayashi, K., Yoshida, Y.: Testing subdivision-freeness: property testing meets structural graph theory. In: Proceedings of the 45th Annual ACM symposium on Theory of Computing (STOC), pp. 437–446 (2013)

[280] Khot, S., Minzer, D., Safra, M.: On monotonicity testing and Boolean isoperimetric type theorems. In: Proceedings of the 56th Annual IEEE

Symposium on Foundations of Computer Science (FOCS), pp. 52–58 (2015)

[281] Khot, S., Shinkar, I.: An $\widetilde{O}(n)$ queries adaptive tester for unateness. In: Proceedings of the 20th International Workshop on Randomization and Computation (RANDOM), pp. 37:7–37:7 (2016)

[282] Kiwi, M., Magniez, F., Santha, M.: Exact and Approximate Testing/Correcting of Algebraic Functions: A Survey, pp. 30–83. Springer Berlin Heidelberg (2002)

[283] Klimošová, T., Král, D.: Hereditary properties of permutations are strongly testable. In: Proceedings of the 25th Annual ACM-SIAM Symposium on Discrete Algorithms (SODA), pp. 1164–1173 (2014)

[284] Kohayakawa, Y., Nagle, B., Rödl, V.: Efficient testing of hypergraphs. In: Proceedings of 29th International Colloquium on the Automata, Languages, and Programming (ICALP), pp. 1017–1028 (2002)

[285] Komlós, J., Shokoufandeh, A., Simonovits, M., Szemerédi, E.: The regularity lemma and its applications in graph theory. In: Proceedings of the 17th Annual Symposium on Theoretical Aspects of Computer Science (STACS), pp. 84–112 (2000)

[286] Kopparty, S., Meir, O., Ron-Zewi, N., Saraf, S.: High-rate locally correctable and locally testable codes with sub-polynomial query complexity. Journal of the ACM **64**(2), 1–42 (2017)

[287] Krauthgamer, R., Sasson, O.: Property testing of data dimensionality. In: Proceedings of the 14th Annual ACM-SIAM Symposium on Discrete Algorithms (SODA), pp. 18–27 (2003)

[288] Kumar, A., Seshadhri, C., Stolman, A.: Finding forbidden minors in sublinear time: an $n^{1/2+o(1)}$-query one-sided tester for minor closed properties. In: Proceedings of the IEEE 59th Annual Symposium on Foundations of Computer Science (FOCS), pp. 509–520 (2018)

[289] Kumar, A., Seshadhri, C., Stolman, A.: Random walks and forbidden minors II: a poly($d\epsilon^{-1}$)-query tester for minor-closed properties of bounded degree graphs. In: Proceedings of the 51st Annual ACM SIGACT Symposium on Theory of Computing (STOC), pp. 559–567 (2019)

[290] Kun, G., O'Donnell, R., Tamaki, S., Yoshida, Y., Zhou, Y.: Linear programming, width-1 CSPs, and robust satisfaction. In: Proceedings of the 3rd Innovations in Theoretical Computer Science Conference (ITCS), pp. 484–495 (2012)

[291] Kuratowski, C.: Sur le problème des courbes gauches en topologie. Fundamenta Mathematicae **15**(1), 271–283 (1930)

[292] Kushilevitz, E., Nisan, N.: Communication Complexity. Cambridge University Press, Cambridge (1996)

[293] Kusumoto, M., Yoshida, Y.: Testing forest-isomorphism in the adjacency list model. In: Proceedings of 41st International Colloquium on the Automata, Languages, and Programming (ICALP), pp. 763–774 (2014)

[294] Kusumoto, M., Yoshida, Y., Ito, H.: Constant-time approximation algorithms for the optimum branching problem on sparse graphs. International Journal of Networking and Computing **3**(2), 205–216 (2014)

[295] Lachish, O., Newman, I.: Testing periodicity. Algorithmica **60**(2), 401–420 (2009)

[296] Lachish, O., Newman, I., Shapira, A.: Space complexity vs. query complexity. Computational Complexity **17**(1), 70–93 (2008)

[297] Ladner, R.E.: On the structure of polynomial time reducibility. Journal of the ACM **22**(1), 155–171 (1975)

[298] Laman, G.: On graphs and rigidity of plane skeletal structures. Journal of Engineering mathematics **4**(4), 331–340 (1970)

[299] Levi, A., Yoshida, Y.: Sublinear-time quadratic minimization via spectral decomposition of matrices. In: Proceedings of the 21st International Conference on Approximation Algorithms for Combinatorial Optimization Problems (APPROX), pp. 17:1–17:19 (2018)

[300] Levi, R., Ron, D.: A quasi-polynomial time partition oracle for graphs with an excluded minor. ACM Transactions on Algorithms **11**(3), 24–13 (2015)

[301] Li, Y., Wang, Z., Woodruff, D.P.: Improved testing of low rank matrices. In: Proceedings of the 20th ACM SIGKDD international conference on Knowledge discovery and data mining (KDD), pp. 691–700 (2014)

[302] Lipton, R.: New directions in testing. In: Distributed Computing and Cryptography, DIMACS Series in Discrete Mathematics and Theoretical Computer Science, pp. 191–202. AMS (1991)

[303] Liu, Z., Chen, X., Servedio, R.A., Sheng, Y., Xie, J.: Distribution-free junta testing. ACM Transactions on Algorithms **15**(1), 1–23 (2018)

[304] Lorea, M.: On matroidal families. Discrete Mathematics **28**(1), 103–106 (1979)

[305] Lovász, L.: Large Networks and Graph Limits. American Mathematical Society (2012)

[306] Lovász, L., Szegedy, B.: Limits of dense graph sequences. Journal of Combinatorial Theory, Series B **96**(6), 933–957 (2006)

[307] Lovász, L., Vesztergombi, K.: Non-deterministic graph property testing. Combinatorics, Probability and Computing **22**(05), 749–762 (2013)

[308] Lovász, L., Young, N.E.: Lecture notes on evasiveness of graph properties (1991). https://www.cs.princeton.edu/research/techreps/TR-317-91

[309] Lovett, S., Meshulam, R., Samorodnitsky, A.: Inverse conjecture for the Gowers norm is false. Theory of Computing **7**(1), 131–145 (2011)

[310] Mader, W.: Homomorphieeigenschaften und mittlere kantendichte von graphen. Mathematische Annalen **174**(4), 265–268 (1967)

[311] Marko, S., Ron, D.: Distance approximation in bounded-degree and general sparse graphs. In: Proceedings of the 9th International Workshop on Randomization and Computation (RANDOM), pp. 475–486 (2006)

[312] Marko, S., Ron, D.: Approximating the distance to properties in bounded-degree and general sparse graphs. ACM Transactions on Algorithms **5**(2), 22–28 (2009)

[313] Meir, O.: Combinatorial construction of locally testable codes. SIAM Journal on Computing **39**(2), 491–544 (2009)

[314] Meir, O.: On the rectangle method in proofs of robustness of tensor products. Information Processing Letters **112**(6), 257 – 260 (2012)

[315] Menger, K.: Zur allgemeinen kurventhoerie. Fundamenta Mathematicae **10**, 96–115 (1927)

[316] Milićević, L.: Polynomial bound for partition rank in terms of analytic rank. Geometric and Functional Analysis **29**, 1503–1530 (2019)

[317] Mitzenmacher, M., Upfal, E.: Probability and Computing: Randomized Algorithms and Probabilistic Analysis. Cambridge University Press (2005)

[318] Monemizadeh, M., Muthukrishnan, S., Peng, P., Sohler, C.: Testable bounded degree graph properties are random order streamable. In: Proceedings of the 44th International Colloquium on Automata, Languages, and Programming (ICALP), pp. 131:1–131:14 (2017)

[319] Moshkovitz, D.: Lecture notes for "6.875: PCPs and hardness of approximation" (2010). https://www.cs.utexas.edu/~danama/courses/pcp-mit/

[320] Moshkovitz, D., Raz, R.: Sub-constant error low degree test of almost-linear size. SIAM Journal on Computing **38**(1), 140–180 (2008)

[321] Moshkovitz, D., Raz, R.: Two-query pcp with subconstant error. Journal of the ACM **57**(5), 1–29 (2008)

[322] Moshkovitz, D., Raz, R.: Sub-constant error probabilistically checkable proof of almost-linear size. Computational Complexity **19**(3), 367–422 (2010)

[323] Moshkovitz, G., Shapira, A.: A short proof of Gowers' lower bound for the regularity lemma. Combinatorica **36**(2), 187–194 (2014)

[324] Motwani, R., Raghavan, P.: Randomized Algorithms, 1 edn. Cambridge University Press (1995)

[325] Nachmias, A., Shapira, A.: Testing the expansion of a graph. Information and Computation **208**(4), 309–314 (2010)

[326] Nagle, B., Rödl, V., Schacht, M.: The counting lemma for regular k-uniform hypergraphs. Random Structures & Algorithms **28**(2), 113–179 (2006)

[327] Nakar, Y., Ron, D.: On the testability of graph partition properties. In: Approximation, Randomization, and Combinatorial Optimization. Algorithms and Techniques (APPROX/RANDOM), pp. 53:1–53:13 (2018)

[328] Nash-Williams, C.S.J.A.: On orientations, connectivity and odd vertex pairings in finite graphs. Canad J Math **12**, 555–567 (1960)

[329] Nash-Williams, C.S.J.A.: Decomposition of finite graphs into forests. Journal of the London Mathematical Society **s1-39**(1), 12 (1964)

[330] Newman, I.: Property testing of massively parametrized problems - a survey. Property Testing **6390**(Chapter 8), 142–157 (2010)

[331] Newman, I.: Testing membership in languages that have small width branching programs. SIAM Journal on Computing **31**(5), 1557–1570 (2012)

[332] Newman, I., Rabinovich, Y., Rajendraprasad, D., Sohler, C.: Testing for forbidden order patterns in an array. In: Proceedings of the 28th Annual ACM-SIAM Symposium on Discrete Algorithms (SODA), pp. 1582–1597 (2017)

[333] Newman, I., Sohler, C.: Every property of hyperfinite graphs is testable. SIAM Journal on Computing **42**(3), 1095–1112 (2013)

[334] Nguyen, H.N., Onak, K.: Constant-time approximation algorithms via local improvements. In: Proceedings of the 49th Annual IEEE Symposium on Foundations of Computer Science (FOCS), pp. 327–336 (2008)

[335] O'Donnell, R.: Analysis of Boolean Functions. Cambridge University Press (2014)

[336] Onak, K.: On the complexity of learning and testing hyperfinite graphs. Available from the author's website (2012)

[337] Onak, K., Ron, D., Rosen, M., Rubinfeld, R.: A near-optimal sublinear-time algorithm for approximating the minimum vertex cover size. In: Proceedings of the 23rd Annual ACM-SIAM Symposium on Discrete Algorithms (SODA) (2012)

[338] Onak, K., Sun, X.: The query complexity of graph isomorphism: bypassing distribution testing lower bounds. In: Proceedings of the 50th Annual ACM SIGACT Symposium on Theory of Computing (STOC), pp. 165–171 (2018)

[339] Oono, K., Yoshida, Y.: Testing properties of functions on finite groups. Random Structures & Algorithms **49**(3), 579–598 (2016)

[340] Orenstein, Y.: Property testing in directed graphs. Ph.D. thesis, Tel Aviv University, TEL AVIV UNIVERSITY (2009)

[341] Orenstein, Y., Ron, D.: Testing eulerianity and connectivity in directed sparse graphs. Theoretical Computer Science **412**(45), 6390–6408 (2011)

[342] Ostrowski, A.M.: Sur l'Approximation du déterminant de Fredholm par les déterminants des systèmes d'équations linéaires. Almqvist & Wiksells (1938)

[343] Oxley, J.G.: Matroid Theory. Oxford graduate texts in mathematics. Oxford University Press (2006)

[344] Parnas, M., Ron, D.: Testing the diameter of graphs. Random Structures & Algorithms **20**(2), 165–183 (2002)

[345] Parnas, M., Ron, D.: Approximating the minimum vertex cover in sublinear time and a connection to distributed algorithms. Theoretical Computer Science **381**(1-3), 183–196 (2007)

[346] Parnas, M., Ron, D., Rubinfeld, R.: Testing membership in parenthesis languages. Random Structures & Algorithms **22**(1), 98–138 (2003)

[347] Parnas, M., Ron, D., Rubinfeld, R.: Tolerant property testing and distance approximation. Journal of Computer and System Sciences **72**(6), 1012–1042 (2006)

[348] Peng, P., Sohler, C.: Estimating graph parameters from random order streams. In: Proceedings of the 29th Annual ACM-SIAM Symposium on Discrete Algorithms (SODA), pp. 2449–2466 (2018)

[349] Polishchuk, A., Spielman, D.A.: Nearly-linear size holographic proofs. In: Proceedings of the 26th Annual ACM symposium on Theory of Computing (STOC), pp. 194–203 (1994)

[350] Poschel, R.: Concrete representation of algebraic structures and a general galois theory. Contributions to General Algebra **1**, 249–272 (1979)

[351] Post, E.L.: The Two-Valued Iterative Systems of Mathematical Logic. Princeton University Press (1942)

[352] Raskhodnikova, S., Smith, A.D.: A note on adaptivity in testing properties of bounded degree graphs. Electronic Colloquium on Computational Complexity (ECCC) **13** (2006)

[353] Raskhodnikova, S., Yaroslavtsev, G.: Learning pseudo-boolean k-dnf and submodular functions. In: Proceedings of the 24th Annual ACM-SIAM Symposium on Discrete Algorithms, pp. 1356–1368. Society for Industrial and Applied Mathematics, Philadelphia, PA (2013)

[354] Raz, R., Safra, S.: A sub-constant error-probability low-degree test, and a sub-constant error-probability PCP characterization of NP. In: Proceedings of the 29th Annual ACM Symposium on the Theory of Computing (STOC), pp. 475–484 (1997)

[355] Rivest, R.L., Vuillemin, J.: On recognizing graph properties from adjacency matrices. Theoretical Computer Science **3**(3), 371–384 (1976)

[356] Robertson, N., Seymour, P.D.: Graph minors. xiii. the disjoint paths problem. Journal of Combinatorial Theory, Series B **63**(1), 65–110 (1995)

[357] Rödl, V., Duke, R.A.: On graphs with small subgraphs of large chromatic number. Graphs and Combinatorics **1**(1), 91–96 (1985)

[358] Rödl, V., Schacht, M.: Property testing in hypergraphs and the removal lemma. In: Proceedings of the 39th Annual ACM Symposium on Theory of Computing (STOC), pp. 488–495 (2007)

[359] Rödl, V., Schacht, M.: Regular partitions of hypergraphs: Regularity lemmas. Combinatorics, Probability and Computing **16**(6), 833–885 (2007)

[360] Rödl, V., Schacht, M.: Generalizations of the removal lemma. Combinatorica **29**(4), 467–501 (2010)

[361] Rödl, V., Skokan, J.: Regularity lemma for k-uniform hypergraphs. Random Structures & Algorithms **25**(1), 1–42 (2004)

[362] Ron, D., Tsur, G.: On approximating the number of relevant variables in a function. ACM Transactions on Computation Theory (TOCT) **5**(2), 7–19 (2013)

[363] Ron-Zewi, N., Sudan, M.: A new upper bound on the query complexity of testing generalized Reed-Muller codes. Theory of Computing 9(25), 783–807 (2013)

[364] Rosenberg, A.L.: On the time required to recognize properties of graphs: a problem. ACM SIGACT News 5(4), 15–16 (1973)

[365] Roth, K.F.: On certain sets of integers. Journal of the London Mathematical Society 1(1), 104–109 (1953)

[366] Rubinfeld, R.: On the robustness of functional equations. SIAM Journal on Computing 28(6), 1972–1997 (2006)

[367] Rubinfeld, R., Sudan, M.: Self-testing polynomial functions efficiently and over rational domains. In: Proceedings of the 3rd Annual ACM-SIAM Symposium on Discrete Algorithms (SODA), pp. 23–32 (1992)

[368] Rubinfeld, R., Sudan, M.: Robust characterizations of polynomials with applications to program testing. SIAM Journal on Computing 25(2), 252–271 (1996)

[369] Samorodnitsky, A., Trevisan, L.: Gowers uniformity, influence of variables, and PCPs. SIAM Journal on Computing 39(1), 323–360 (2009)

[370] Sağlam, M.: Near log-convexity of measured heat in (discrete) time and consequences. In: Proceedings of the IEEE 59th Annual Symposium on Foundations of Computer Science (FOCS), pp. 967–978 (2018)

[371] Schaefer, T.J.: The complexity of satisfiability problems. In: Proceedings of the 10th Annual ACM Symposium on Theory of Computing (STOC), pp. 216–226 (1978)

[372] Seshadhri, C., Vondrák, J.: Is submodularity testable? Algorithmica 69(1), 1–25 (2012)

[373] Shpilka, A., Wigderson, A.: Derandomizing homomorphism testing in general groups. SIAM Journal on Computing 36(4), 1215–1230 (2006)

[374] Sohler, C.: Almost optimal canonical property testers for satisfiability. In: Proceedings of the IEEE 53rd Annual Symposium on Foundations of Computer Science (FOCS), pp. 541–550 (2012)

[375] Spielman, D.A.: Computationally efficient error-correcting codes and holographic proofs. Ph.D. thesis, Massachusetts Institute of Technology (1995)

[376] Szegedy, B.: On higher order Fourier analysis (2012)

[377] Szemerédi, E.: Regular partitions of graphs. Problèmes combinatoires et théorie des graphes 260, 399–401 (1976)

[378] Szemerédi, E.: Integer sets containing no arithmetic progressions. Acta Mathematica Hungarica 56, 155–158 (1990)

[379] Tanigawa, S., Yoshida, Y.: Testing the supermodular-cut condition. Algorithmica 71(4), 1065–1075 (2013)

[380] Tao, T.: Higher order Fourier analysis, Graduate Studies in Mathematics, vol. 142. American Mathematical Society (2012)

[381] Tay, T.S.: Rigidity of multi-graphs. i. linking rigid bodies in n-space. Journal of Combinatorial Theory, Series B 36(1), 95–112 (1984)

[382] Tenner, B.E.: Database of permutation pattern avoidance. `http://math.depaul.edu/bridget/patterns.html`

[383] Tidor, J., Zhao, Y.: Testing linear-invariant properties. In: Proceedings of the 2020 IEEE 61st Annual Symposium on Foundations of Computer Science (FOCS), pp. 1180–1190 (2020)

[384] Tucker, L.R.: Some mathematical notes on three-mode factor analysis. Psychometrika **31**(3), 279–311 (1966)

[385] Tulsiani, M., Wolf, J.: Quadratic Goldreich-Levin theorems. In: Proceedings of the 52nd Annual IEEE Symposium on Foundations of Computer Science (FOCS), pp. 619–628 (2011)

[386] Valiant, L.G.: A theory of the learnable. Communications of the ACM **27**(11), 1134–1142 (1984)

[387] Valiant, P.: The tensor product of two codes is not necessarily robustly testable. In: Approximation, Randomization and Combinatorial Optimization. Algorithms and Techniques (APPROX/RANDOM), pp. 472–481. Springer (2005)

[388] Viderman, M.: Strong LTCs with inverse poly-log rate and constant soundness. In: Proceedings of the 2013 IEEE 54th Annual Symposium on Foundations of Computer Science (FOCS), pp. 330–339 (2013)

[389] Viderman, M.: Strong LTCs with inverse polylogarithmic rate and soundness. In: Proceedings of the 2013 IEEE Conference on Computational Complexity (CCC), pp. 255–265 (2013)

[390] Viderman, M.: A combination of testability and decodability by tensor products. Random Structures & Algorithms **46**(3), 572–598 (2015)

[391] Viderman, M.: Explicit strong LTCs with inverse poly-log rate and constant soundness. In: Approximation, Randomization, and Combinatorial Optimization. Algorithms and Techniques (APPROX/RANDOM), pp. 58:1–58:14 (2018)

[392] Watanabe, T., Nakamura, A.: Edge-connectivity augmentation problems. Journal of Computer and System Sciences **35**(1), 96–144 (1987)

[393] Whiteley, W.: Some matroids from discrete applied geometry. Contemporary Mathematics **197**, 171–312 (1996)

[394] Whiteley, W.: The union of matroids and the rigidity of frameworks. SIAM Journal on Discrete Mathematics **1**(2), 237–255 (2006)

[395] Wimmer, K., Yoshida, Y.: Testing linear-invariant function isomorphism. In: Proceedings of the 40th International Colloquium Conference on Automata, Languages, and Programming (ICALP), pp. 840–850 (2013)

[396] Yao, A.C.: Some complexity questions related to distributive computing. In: Proceedings of the 11th Annual ACM Symposium on Theory of Computing (STOC), pp. 209–213 (1979)

[397] Yao, A.C.: Lower bounds by probabilistic arguments. In: Proceedings of the 28th Annual IEEE Symposium on Foundations of Computer Science (SFCS), pp. 420–428 (1983)

[398] Yao, A.C.: Lower bounds to randomized algorithms for graph properties. In: Proceedings of the 28th Annual IEEE Symposium on Foundations of Computer Science (SFCS), pp. 393–400 (1987)

[399] Yoshida, Y.: Optimal constant-time approximation algorithms and (unconditional) inapproximability results for every bounded-degree CSP. In: Proceedings of the 43rd Annual ACM Symposium on Theory of Computing (STOC), pp. 665–674 (2011)

[400] Yoshida, Y.: A characterization of locally testable affine-invariant properties via decomposition theorems. In: Proceedings of the 46th Annual ACM Symposium on Theory of Computing (STOC), pp. 154–163 (2014)

[401] Yoshida, Y.: Testing list H-homomorphisms. Computional Complexity **25**(4), 737–773 (2016)

[402] Yoshida, Y., Ito, H.: Property testing on k-vertex-connectivity of graphs. Algorithmica **62**(3-4), 701–712 (2010)

[403] Yoshida, Y., Ito, H.: Query-number preserving reductions and linear lower bounds for testing. IEICE Transactions on Information and Systems **E93.D**(2), 233–240 (2010)

[404] Yoshida, Y., Ito, H.: Testing k-edge-connectivity of digraphs. Journal of Systems Science and Complexity **23**(1), 91–101 (2010)

[405] Yoshida, Y., Ito, H.: Testing outerplanarity of bounded degree graphs. Algorithmica **73**(1), 1–20 (2014)

[406] Yoshida, Y., Kobayashi, Y.: Testing the (s, t)-disconnectivity of graphs and digraphs. Theoretical Computer Science **434**, 98–113 (2012)

[407] Yoshida, Y., Yamamoto, M., Ito, H.: Improved constant-time approximation algorithms for maximum matchings and other optimization problems. SIAM Journal on Computing **41**(4), 1074–1093 (2012)

[408] Zhuk, D.: A proof of CSP dichotomy conjecture. In: Proceedings of the 58th Annual IEEE Symposium on Foundations of Computer Science (FOCS), pp. 331–342 (2017)

Printed in the United States
by Baker & Taylor Publisher Services